Historic Events
for Students

The Great Depression

Historic Events
for Students

The Great Depression
Volume 3: Pr-Z

Richard C. Hanes, Editor
Sharon M. Hanes, Associate Editor

GALE®

Detroit • New York • San Diego • San Francisco • Cleveland • New Haven, Conn. • Waterville, Maine • London • Munich

Historic Events for Students: The Great Depression
Richard C. Hanes and Sharon M. Hanes

Project Editor
Nancy Matuszak

Editorial
Jason M. Everett, Rachel J. Kain

Permissions
Debra J. Freitas, Lori Hines

Imaging and Multimedia
Dean Dauphinais, Christine O'Bryan

Product Design
Pamela A. E. Galbreath

Composition and Electronic Capture
Evi Seoud

Manufacturing
Rita Wimberley

This publication is a creative work fully protected by all applicable copyright laws, as well as by misappropriation, trade secret, unfair competition, and other applicable laws. The authors and editors of this work have added value to the underlying factual material herein through one or more of the following: unique and original selection, coordination, expression, arrangement, and classification of the information.

While every effort has been made to ensure the reliability of the information presented in this publication, The Gale Group, Inc. does not guarantee the accuracy of the data contained herein. The Gale Group, Inc. accepts no payment for listing; and inclusion in the publication of any organization, agency, institution, publication, service, or individual does not imply endorsement of the editors or publisher. Errors brought to the attention of the publisher and verified to the satisfaction of the publisher will be corrected in future editions.

LIBRARY OF CONGRESS CATALOGING-IN-PUBLICATION DATA

The Great Depression / Richard C. Hanes, editor; Sharon Hanes, associate editor.
    p. cm. — (Historic events for students)
    Includes bibliographical references and index.
    ISBN 0-7876-5701-8 (set)—ISBN 0-7876-5702-6 (v. 1)—ISBN
0-7876-5703-4 (v. 2)—ISBN 0-7876-5704-2 (v. 3)
    1. United States—History—1933-1945. 2. United States—History—1919-1933.
3. Depressions—1929—United States. 4. New Deal, 1933-1939.
5. United States—History—1933-1945—Sources.
6. United States—History—1919-1933—Sources.
7. Depressions—1929—United States—Sources.
8. New Deal, 1933-1939—Sources. I. Hanes, Richard Clay, 1946- II. Series.

E806 .G827 2002
973.917—dc21
2001007712

Printed in the United States of America
10 9 8 7 6 5 4 3 2 1

Table of Contents

Chronological Table of Contents

Advisory Board

A seven-member board consisting of teachers, librarians, and other experts was consulted to help determine the contents of Historic Events for Students: The Great Depression.

The members of the board for this set include:

Glen Bessemer: Department of History, Wayne State University, Detroit, Michigan

Monica Cornille: Reference Librarian, Adlai E. Stevenson High School, Lincolnshire, Illinois

Professor Charles K. Hyde: Department of History, Wayne State University, Detroit, Michigan

Joel L. Jones, M.L.S.: Kansas City Public Library, Kansas City, Missouri

Ann Marie LaPrise: Junior High/Elementary Media Specialist, Huron School District, New Boston, Michigan.

Margaret Lincoln: Library Media Specialist, Lakeview High School, Battle Creek, Michigan

Scott Durham: Lakeview High School, Battle Creek, Michigan

Credits

Copywrited excerpts in *Historic Events for Students: The Great Depression,* were reproduced from the following books:

A., G. From **Recipes & Remembrances of the Great Depression** by Emily Thacker. Tresco Publishers, 1993. Copyright 1993 Tresco Publishers. All rights reserved. Reproduced by permission.

Adamic, Louis. From **My America: 1928–1938.** Harper & Brothers Publishers, 1938. Copyright, 1938, by Louis Adamic. All rights reserved. Reproduced by permission.

Agee, James and Walker Evans. From **Let Us Now Praise Famous Men.** Ballantine Books, 1960. © 1941 by James Agee and Walker Evans. © renewed 1969 by Mia Fritsch Agee and Walker Evans. All rights reserved. Reprinted by permission of Houghton Mifflin Company.

Asbury, Herbert. From **The Great Illusion: An Informal History of Prohibition.** Doubleday & Company, Inc., 1950. Copyright, 1950, by Herbert Asbury. All rights reserved. Reproduced by permission.

B., Mildred. From **Recipes & Remembrances of the Great Depression** by Emily Thacker. Tresco Publishers, 1993. Copyright 1993 Tresco Publishers. All rights reserved. Reproduced by permission.

Balderrama, Francisco E. and Raymond Rodriguez. From *Decade of Betrayal: Mexican Repatriation in the 1930s.* University of New Mexico Press, 1995. © 1995 by the University of New Mexico Press. All rights reserved. Reproduced by permission.

Baldwin, C. B. (Beanie). From "Concerning the New Deal," in **Hard Times: An Oral History of the Great Depression** by Studs Terkel. Pantheon Books, 1986. © 1970, 1986 by Studs Terkel. All rights reserved. Reproduced by permission.

Bolino, August C. From **From Depression to War: American Society in Transition—1939.** Praeger Publishers, 1998. © 1998 by August C. Bolino. All rights reserved.

Bonnifield, Paul. From **The Dust Bowl: Men, Dirt, and Depression.** University of New Mexico Press, 1979. © 1979 by the University of New Mexico Press. All rights reserved. Reproduced by permission.

Brown, D. Clayton. From **Electricity for Rural America: The Fight for REA.** Greenwood Press, 1980. All rights reserved.

Brown, Josephine Chapin. From **Public Relief 1929–1939. Henry Holt and Company, 1940.** Copyright, 1940, by Henry Holt and Company, Inc.

Burke, Clifford. From "Man and Boy," in **Hard Times: An Oral History of the Great Depression** by Studs Terkel. Pantheon Books, 1986. © 1970, 1986 by Studs Terkel. All rights reserved. Reproduced by permission.

Burns, Helen M. From **The American Banking Community and New Deal Banking Reforms, 1933–1935.** Greenwood Press, 1974. © 1974 by Helen M. Burns. All rights reserved.

Colbert, David. From "Crash," in **We Saw It Happen.** Simon and Schuster, 1938. Reproduced by permission.

Daniels, Roger. From **Asian America: Chinese and Japanese in the United States since 1850.** University of Washington Press, 1988. © 1988 by the University of Washington Press. All rights reserved. Reproduced by permission.

Deutsch, Sarah Jane. From "From Ballots to Breadlines, 1920–1940," in **No Small Courage: A History of Women in the United States.** Edited by Nancy F. Cott. Oxford University Press, 2000.

Deutsch, Sarah Jane. From "From Ballots to Breadlines: Taking Matters into Their Own Hands," in **No Small Courage: A History of Women in the United States.** Edited by Nancy F. Cott. Oxford University Press, 2000.

Edsforth, Ronald. From **The New Deal: America's Response to the Great Depression.** Blackwell Publishers, 2000.

Farrell, James T. From "Introduction," in **Studs Lonigan: A Trilogy.** The Modern Library, 1938.

Meltzer, Milton. From **Violins & Shovels: The WPA Arts Projects.** Delacorte Press, 1976. © 1976 by Milton Meltzer. All rights reserved.

Montella, Frank. From **Memories of a CCC Boy,** in an interview with Kim Stewart. Cal State Fullerton and Utah State Historical Society Oral History Project, July 9, 1971.

Oettinger, Hank. From "Bonnie Laboring Boy," in **Hard Times: An Oral History of the Great Depression** by Studs Terkel. Pantheon Books, 1986. © 1970, 1986 by Studs Terkel. All rights reserved. Reproduced by permission.

Parran, Thomas. From "Shadow on the Land," in **Tuskegee's Truths: Rethinking the Tuskegee Syphilis Study.** Edited by Susan M. Reverby. University of North Carolina Press, 2000. © 2000 by The University of North Carolina Press. All rights reserved. Used by permission of the publisher.

Perkins, Frances. From **The Roosevelt I Knew.** The Viking Press, 1946. Copyright 1946 by Frances Perkins. Reproduced by permission.

Phillips, Cabell. From **From the Crash to the Blitz 1929–1939.** The Macmillan Company, 1969. © The New York Times Company 1969. All rights reserved. Reproduced by permission.

Plotke, David. From **Building A Democratic Political Order.** Cambridge University Press, 1996. © Cambridge University Press 1996. Reproduced by permission of the publisher and author.

Rauch, Basil. From **The History of the New Deal, 1933-1938.** Creative Age Press, Inc., 1944. Copyright 1944 by Basil Rauch. All rights reserved. Reproduced by permission.

Reid, Robert L. From "Introduction," in **Back Home Again: Indiana in the Farm Security Administration Photographs, 1935–1943.** Edited by Robert L. Reid. Indiana University Press, 1987. © 1987 by Robert L. Reid. All rights reserved. Reproduced by permission.

Roosevelt, Eleanor. From "Women in Politics," in **What I Hope to Leave Behind.** Edited by Allida M. Black. Carlson Publishing, Inc., 1995. Reproduced by permission.

Roosevelt, Franklin D. From "Hopkins Before 1941," in **Roosevelt and Hopkins: An Intimate History** by Robert E. Sherwood. Harper & Brothers Publishers, 1950. © 1948, 1950 by Robert E. Sherwood; copyright renewed © 1976, 1978 by Madeline H. Sherwood. All rights reserved. Reprinted by permission of Brandt & Hochman Literary Agents, Inc.

Rothstein, Arthur. From **Just Before the War** by Thomas H. Garver and Arthur Rothstein. October House Inc., 1968. Copyright 1968, Newport Harbor Art Museum, Balboa, California. Reproduced by permission.

Russo, Anthony. From "Prologue," in **Capone: The Man and the Era** by Laurence Bergreen. Simon & Schuster, 1994. © 1994 by Laurence Bergreen. All rights reserved. Reproduced by permission.

S., K. From **Recipes & Remembrances of the Great Depression** by Emily Thacker. Tresco Publishers, 1993. Copyright 1993 Tresco Publishers. All rights reserved. Reproduced by permission.

Schieber, Sylvester J. and John B. Brown. From **The Real Deal: The History and Future of Social Security.** Yale University Press, 1999. © 1999 by Yale University. All rights reserved.

Schlesinger, Jr., Arthur M. From **The Age of Roosevelt: The Coming of the New Deal.** Houghton Mifflin Company, 1988. © 1958, renewed 1986 by Arthur M. Schlesinger, Jr. All rights reserved. Reprinted by permission of Houghton Mifflin Company.

Steichen, Edward. From "Introduction," in **The Bitter Years: 1935–1941.** Edited by Edward Steichen. The Museum of Modern Art, 1962. © 1962, The Museum of Modern Art, New York.

Steinbeck, John. From **I Remember the Thirties.** Copyright 1960 by John Steinbeck.

Steinbeck, John. From **The Grapes of Wrath.** The Viking Press, 1939. Copyright, 1939, John Steinbeck. All rights reserved.

Stockard, George. From **Stories and Recipes of the Great Depression of the 1930's, Volume II.** Edited by Rita Van Amber. Van Amber Publishers, 1999. © Library of Congress. All rights reserved. Reproduced by permission of the author.

Stryker, R. E. From a letter in **Portrait of a Decade: Roy Stryker and the Development of Documentary Photography in the Thirties** by F. Jack Hurley. Louisiana State University Press, 1972. Copyright 1972 by Louisiana State University Press. All rights reserved.

Sueur, Meridel Le. From **Women on the Breadlines.** West End Press, 1984. © 1977, 1984 by West End Press. Reproduced by permission.

Sundquist, James. From **Dynamics of the Party System: Alignment and Realignment of Political Parties in the United States.** Brookings Institution, 1983.

Svobida, Lawrence. From **Farming the Dust Bowl: A First-Hand Account from Kansas.** University Press of Kansas, 1986. Copyright 1940 by The Caxton Printers, Ltd.; 1968 by Lawrence Svobida. All rights reserved. Reproduced by permission.

Swados, Harvey. From "Introduction," in **The American Writer and the Great Depression.** Edited by Harvey Swados. The Bobbs-Merrill Company, Inc., 1966. © 1966 by The Bobbs-Merrill Company, Inc.

Terkel, Studs. From "Concerning the New Deal," in **Hard Times: An Oral History of the Great Depression.** Pantheon Books, 1986. © 1970, 1986 by Studs Terkel. All rights reserved. Reproduced by permission.

Terkel, Studs. From "Three Strikes: Mike Widman," in **Hard Times: An Oral History of the Great Depression.** Pantheon Books, 1986. © 1970, 1986 by Studs Terkel. All rights reserved. Reproduced by permission.

Terrell, Harry. From "The Farmer is the Man," in **Hard Times: An Oral History of the Great Depression** by Studs Terkel. Pantheon Books, 1986. © 1970, 1986 by Studs Terkel. All rights reserved. Reproduced by permission.

Tugwell, Rexford Guy. From **The Bitter Years: 1935–1941.** Edited by Edward Steichen. The Museum of Modern Art, 1962. © 1962, The Museum of Modern Art, New York. Reproduced by permission.

Tully, Grace. From "Pearl Harbor News Reaches FDR," in **We Saw It Happen.** Simon and Schuster, 1938. Reproduced by permission.

Tyack, David, Robert Lowe, and Elisabeth Hansot. From "A Black School in East Texas," in **Public Schools in Hard Times: The Great Depression and Recent Years.** Harvard University Press, 1984. © 1984 by the President and Fellows of Harvard College. All rights reserved. Reproduced by permission.

Tyack, David, Robert Lowe, and Elisabeth Hansot. From **Public Schools in Hard Times: The Great Depression and Recent Years.** Harvard University Press, 1984. © 1984 by the President and Fellows of Harvard College. All rights reserved. Reproduced by permission.

Uys, Errol Lincoln. From **Riding the Rails: Teenagers on the Move During the Great Depression.** TV Books, 2000. © 1999, 2000 Errol Lincoln Uys. All rights reserved. Reproduced by permission of the author.

Van Amber, Rita. From **Stories and Recipes During the Great Depression of the 1930's.** Van Amber Publishers, 1999. © Library of Congress. All rights reserved. Reproduced by permission.

Wasserman, Dale. From "Troubles and Triumphs," in **Free, Adult, Uncensored: The Living History of the Federal Theatre Project.** Edited by John O'Connor and Lorraine Brown. New Republic Books, 1978. Reproduced by permission.

Watkins, T. H. From **The Hungry Years: A Narrative History of the Great Depression in America.** Henry Holt and Company, 1999. © 1999 by T. H. Watkins. All rights reserved. Reprinted by permission of Henry Holt and Company, LLC.

Weinberg, Sidney J. From "The Big Money," in **Hard Times: An Oral History of the Great Depression** by Studs Terkel. Pantheon Books, 1986. © 1970, 1986 by Studs Terkel. All rights reserved. Reproduced by permission.

Winslow, Susan. From **Brother, Can You Spare A Dime?: America from the Wall Street Crash to Pearl Harbor.** Paddington Press Ltd., 1976. © 1976 by Susan Winslow.

Wright, Richard. From "How 'Bigger' Was Born," in **Native Son.** Harper & Row, Publishers, 1940. Copyright 1940 by Richard Wright. Renewed in 1967 by Ellen Wright.

Wright, Richard. From **Uncle Tom's Children: Five Long Stories.** Harper & Brothers, 1938. Copyright 1936, 1937, 1938 by Richard Wright. All rights reserved.

Song lyrics appearing in *Historic Events for Students: The Great Depression,* were received from the following sources:

Guthrie, Woody. From "Talking Dust Bowl." © Copyright 1961 and 1963 Ludlow Music, Inc., New York, N. Y.

Warren, Harry and Al Dubin, lyrics from "We're In the Money." Music and lyrics by Harry Warren and Al Dubin. Copyright 1933, Remick Music, Inc. Reproduced by permission.

About the Series

Historic Events for Students (HES) is a new addition to the Gale Group's *for Students* line, presenting users with the complete picture of an important event in world history. With standardized rubrics throughout each entry, for which the *for Students* line is well-known, and a variety of complementary elements including illustrations, sidebars, and suggestions for further research, *HES* will examine all of the components that contributed to or sprung from a significant period of time, from ideologies and politics to contemporary opinions and popular culture.

A new one- to three-volume set of forty-five to sixty entries will appear each year. The topics are evaluated by an advisory board of teachers and librarians familiar with the information needed by students in today's classrooms. Essays contain consistent rubrics for easy reference as well as comparison across entries and volumes, and each volume contains a complete glossary, general bibliography, and subject index. Additionally, approximately one hundred images are included per volume, including photos, maps, and statistics to enhance the text and add visual depictions of the event.

The standardized headings found throughout *HES* let users choose to what depth they want to explore the subject matter. Take a quick glance at the topic via the Introduction, Chronology, and Issue Summary rubrics, or delve deeper and get a more inclusive view through the Contributing Forces, Perspectives, and Impact sections. A who's who for a particular issue can be found under the heading of Notable People, while excerpts of speeches, personal accounts, and news clippings can be located under Primary Sources. Ideas for further study can be found with Suggested Research Topics and the Bibliography, while numerous sidebars provide additional information on material associated with the issue being discussed.

Historic Events for Students is different from other history texts in that it doesn't just narrate the facts of an event from the past. It traces the social, cultural, political, religious, and ideological threads that combined to create an historic event. *HES* follows these threads to the end of the event and beyond it to discern how it shaped the history that followed it. The result is a comprehensive examination of the causes of and effects from a significant event in history and a greater understanding of how it influenced where we are today.

Introduction

Technologies and accepted behavioral norms comprising the human experience are constantly changing. Such change in society, however, does not occur at a consistent pace. Sometimes change may be slow and barely perceptible to the average person. At other times, extraordinary events spur change much more quickly. While such events most often involve times of war (the American Civil War, World War I, World War II, and the Vietnam War all resulted in fundamental changes to American society), other watershed events may be no less dramatic. The Great Depression was one such event.

Historical Overview—The Great Depression

Though signs of pending economic problems were surfacing in the United States throughout the 1920s, hardly anyone took notice as most people in the country enjoyed prosperity like never before. The dramatic stock market crash in October 1929, however, captured the attention of the American public. Many feared for the first time that the economic health of the United States might not be as good as it had seemed just a year or two previously. The period that followed, known as the Great Depression, may not have actually resulted from the stock market crash, but it is frequently linked to it in the public's mind.

The Great Depression was an extended period of severe economic hard times, first for the United States and then for many of the world's nations. Though the depression was rooted in earlier economic undercurrents, a cascade of economic events followed the stock market crash and exacerbated the problem. Many investors, including banks, lost their fortunes in the Wall Street crash as the value of stocks tumbled. This loss meant less money was available to invest in businesses, which led companies, now short on cash, to layoff workers. The rise in unemployment meant that the public had less money to buy consumer goods and pay back the bank loans it had accumulated in the liberal spending times of the 1920s. As a result, thousands of banks closed and more layoffs resulted from decreased purchases by consumers as inventories of goods mounted. By 1933 almost 25 percent of the U.S. workforce was unemployed, amounting to more than twelve million people. Those who kept their jobs saw their incomes decrease significantly.

The arrival of Franklin Delano Roosevelt to the White House as the thirty-second president of the United States in March 1933 significantly changed the relationship between Americans and their government. Through Congress, Roosevelt orchestrated numerous and diverse pieces of legislation designed to bring economic relief and recovery, and later reform, to the desperate nation. These laws and the resulting government programs are collectively known as the New Deal.

Though the New Deal would not lead to significant recovery, it did end the dramatic economic plunge Americans experienced through the early 1930s. It gave those most affected by the Great Depression food and shelter. For many more it reestablished hope for the future and faith in the U.S. economic system. Historically the federal government had largely been detached from the public's everyday life. The severity of the depression, however, made many Americans consider the possibility—and even to expect—that the government would take action to assure the wellbeing of the people it governed. Significant differences of opinion emerged over how far government should go in regulating business and guaranteeing the financial security of its citizens.

All of this took place at a time when American popular culture was gaining its own distinct character, unique from its predominant European roots. It also occurred in the midst of new mass production technologies in business, mass media, and mass consumerism. The United States would emerge as a profoundly different nation in 1940 than it had been in 1930.

Content

These volumes specifically address the actual event of the Great Depression rather than presenting a general treatment of the 1930s. They describe the events and issues surrounding the economic depression and the New Deal. The authors, editors, and advisors selected forty-five issues that take an inclusive look at the Great Depression as it affected such diverse elements of American society as economics, the arts, literature, mass media, ethnic and gender relations, the functioning of government, international relations, religion, politics, crime, public health, education, and everyday life.

The writers of these volumes, well-versed in the relevant historical issues, sought to provide a comprehensive treatment of each issue, yet in a concise, readily digestible format. They strove to provide an objective overview of each issue, helping the reader to experience and evaluate the diverse perspectives of often-controversial events. The reader is provided with sufficient background information to encourage the formation of his or her own opinions of the complex events and the contemporary reactions to them. In addition to in-depth text, this premier set of *Historic Events for Students* includes maps, statistics, photographs, sidebars, bibliographic sources, and suggestions for further research, designed to meet the curriculum needs of high school students, undergraduate college students, and their teachers.

How Each Entry is Organized

Each of the forty-five issue entries are divided into multiple headings for easy and complete reference:

- **Introduction:** briefly introduces the reader to the topic. Its connection to the Great Depression is established and some of the key concepts and events that will be addressed are presented.

- **Chronology:** a brief timeline is provided for each topic to place the various key events related to it into an easy-to-understand time-frame for the reader.

- **Issue Summary:** the primary source of information describing the topic, firmly set in the context of the Great Depression. The topic is thoroughly discussed, including governmental efforts made to resolve economic and social problems associated with it. The student will gain a keen sense of just how dynamic the topic was and the major consequences of the individual issues at the time. This summary is divided into subheadings that are unique to each issue.

- **Contributing Forces:** identifies the key social, economic, and political currents in U.S. history leading up to the topic. The section explores how the events and prevailing attitudes contributed to the particular issue and how they influenced the New Deal's response to the issue.

- **Perspectives:** prevailing and competing notions and opinions of the day are detailed and, where feasible, the varying viewpoints are distinguished at the local community level or among the general public; at the national level, including the country's political leaders; and internationally as the Great Depression became an increasingly global event. The discussion includes the perspectives of what should be done, if anything, by the federal government and what the implications were of government action or inaction.

- **Impact:** the long-term consequences of the issue and resulting government action are discussed. The New Deal's response to the Great Depression posed dramatic changes to American society. The events of the depression shaped the evolution of the social, economic, and political foundation of the nation after the 1930s and into the twenty-first century. This section highlights the lasting effects for that particular issue.

- **Notable People:** describes the lives and accomplishments of some of key individuals in the context of the specific issue. Each issue commonly has several key people associated with it, including people who advocated for or against government action and those who administered the New Deal programs.

- **Primary Sources:** provide first-hand accounts from the common citizen and notable people such as Franklin Roosevelt and Herbert Hoover. The Great Depression was a traumatic time. As a result emotions were openly displayed and opinions and solutions hotly debated. There is no better way to experience the depression days than through the words of those caught in the turmoil.

- **Suggested Research Topics:** guide students to explore matters further. Many suggested topics ask the student to examine his or her own communities more closely and how New Deal programs might still influence their lives today.

- **Bibliography:** lists key sources used by the writer in researching the topic and also includes suggestions for further reading. The list of further readings is predominantly aimed at the reading level of the high school and undergraduate student and targets sources most likely found in public libraries and book stores.

Additionally, each entry is also accompanied by several sidebars presenting insights into various facets of the issue. The sidebars focus on different kinds of topics related to the particular issue, including descriptions of concepts, extensive biographies of the most important figures to play a role, or more thorough descriptions of particular agencies or other organizations involved in the issue.

Additional Features

In an attempt to create a comprehensive reference tool for the study of the Great Depression, this set also includes:

- A general chronology covers the Great Depression from its start to its finish to place the various issues and events into a historical context, including some key national and international events to underscore what the citizens and leaders of other countries were experiencing at the same time.

- A general bibliography consolidates the numerous and significant research on the Great Depression and offers an easy reference for users, with material divided into books, periodicals, novels, and websites.

- A glossary presents a number of terms and phrases introduced in the entries that may be unfamiliar to readers.

- A subject index provides easy reference to topics, people, and places.

Acknowledgments

A number of writers contributed to these volumes in addition to the lead authors, including Michael Vergamini, Dr. Richard Pettigrew, Dr. Doug Blandy, Dr. Stephen Dow Beckham, Linda Irvin, and Meghan O'Meara. Catherine Filip typed much of the manuscript. Much gratitude also goes to the advisors who guided the project throughout its course.

Comments on these volumes and suggestions for future sets are welcome. Please direct all correspondence to:

Editor, *Historic Events for Students*
Gale Group
27500 Drake Rd.
Farmington Hills, MI 48331-3535
(800) 877-4253

Chronology

1914 Industrialist Henry Ford introduces the moving assembly line to manufacture automobiles; the production technique will revolutionize U.S. industry over the next decade.

1914 World War I begins in Europe, placing a high demand of U.S. goods, though the United States does not itself enter the war for another three years; high wartime production levels will continue following the war, leading to a long term agricultural economic downturn.

1919 The peace treaty of Versailles ends World War I and leads to excessive economic demands on Germany.

1919 The General Motors automobile company introduces a consumer credit program that makes loans available to purchase cars; this program begins the popular installment plan for many other industries producing consumer goods.

1920 The Nineteenth Amendment to the U.S. Constitution is ratified, granting women the right to vote; women voters will become an important element of the Democratic Coalition 15 years later.

January 16, 1920 The Eighteenth Amendment, or the Prohibition Amendment, goes into effect nationwide, prohibiting the sale, transport, and consumption of alcoholic beverages in the United States.

1920s Continued expansion of farming production leads to soil exhaustion in some areas of the United States and expansion into marginal agricultural areas, setting the stage for future topsoil problems; record production causes continued decline in farm prices.

1922 Benito Mussolini takes over Italy, which becomes a fascist nation under his leadership.

1923 The U.S. stock market begins a six-year expansion as the value of stocks begins to climb.

1924 Congress passes the National Origins Act, reducing the number of immigrants allowed to enter the country to only 150,000 per year, and sets quotas favoring northwestern and southeastern Europeans.

October 6, 1927 The first talking motion picture is released, *The Jazz Singer,* starring Al Jolson.

November 7, 1928 Republican Herbert Hoover, an engineer with a reputation as a humanitarian, is elected to the U.S. presidency over Democrat Al Smith, the first Catholic to run for the U.S. presidency.

October 24, 1929 Known as "Black Thursday," the value of stocks plummets on Wall Street, costing many investors vast sums of money, and raises public concern over the health of the U.S. economy.

1930 As economic conditions in the United States continue to worsen following the stock market crash, Congress passes the Smoot-Hawley Tariff Act, which greatly raises taxes on foreign goods to boost sales of domestic goods. In application, however, the act instead causes foreign trade to greatly decline, decreasing the demand for U.S. goods.

1931 The U.S. economic crisis spreads to Europe as American investments decline and trade decreases; the United States pulls back from international affairs and looks increasingly inward.

May 1, 1931 The Empire State Building in New York City, the world's tallest building, is opened.

July 14, 1931 The German banking system fails as all banks in Germany close.

September 18, 1931 Japan begins a military expansion in the Pacific by invading Manchuria and seizing the Manchurian railroad.

1932 With the farm economy in desperate condition, the Farmers' Holiday Association is formed in Iowa, which leads to farmer protests seeking government assistance.

January 22, 1932 To help an economy in crisis President Herbert Hoover creates the Reconstruction Finance Corporation, a federal agency designed to provide loans to struggling banks and businesses.

July 28 1932 Thousands of unemployed and financially strapped World War I veterans and their families, known as the Bonus Army, march on Washington, DC, seeking early payment of previously promised bonus pay. They are denied by Congress and routed violently by U.S. army troops.

October 24, 1932 Gangster Al Capone is sentenced to 11 years in prison for tax evasion.

November 8, 1932 Pledging a "New Deal" for Americans, Democratic candidate Franklin Delano Roosevelt is overwhelmingly elected president over the highly unpopular Hoover; Roosevelt will not be inaugurated until the following March.

February 1933 The U.S. banking crisis deepens as almost five thousand banks have closed and panic spreads among depositors; faith in the U.S. banking system hits an all-time low.

January 30, 1933 Adolf Hitler becomes Chancellor of Germany.

March 4, 1933 Roosevelt is inaugurated as president promising hope to American citizens, claiming the "only thing to fear is fear itself" and beginning a dramatic surge of legislation during his first one hundred days in office forming the New Deal.

March 6, 1933 President Roosevelt closes all U.S. banks, declaring a Banking Holiday, and Congress passes the Emergency Banking Act three days later in a successful effort to restore public confidence in the banking system; most banks reopen on March 13.

March 23, 1933 The legislature is dismissed in Germany and Hitler assumes dictatorial powers of the country.

March 31, 1933 The U.S. Congress passes the Civilian Conservation Corps Reforestation Act, creating the Civilian Conservation Corps (CCC) to provide jobs for young males.

May 12, 1933 Congress passes the Agricultural Adjustment Act and Emergency Farm Mortgage Act to bring economic relief to farmers, and the Federal Emergency Relief Act to provide relief for the needy.

May 17, 1933 The Tennessee Valley Authority (TVA) is created to establish a massive program of regional economic development for a broad region of the American Southeast.

June 16, 1933 Congress passes the Banking Act, reforming the U.S. banking system. The Federal Deposit Insurance Corporation (FDIC) is established to insure depositors' money; the National Industrial Recovery Act (NIRA) is created to regulate industry; and the Public Works Administration begins to provide funding for large public projects.

December 5, 1933 Prohibition ends in the United States after a nearly 14-year ban on the sale of all alcoholic beverages.

1934 Great dust storms sweep across the Plains of the United States; the hardest hit region of the southern Plains becomes known as the Dust Bowl. The drought persists for several years.

June 6, 1934 Congress passes the Securities Exchange Act to regulate the stock market and protect investors.

June 28, 1934 Congress passes the National Housing Act, creating the Federal Housing Administration to provide loans to home buyers and setting national standards for house construction; this marks the end of the First New Deal under the Roosevelt administration.

April 8, 1935 Kicking off the Second New Deal, Congress passes the Emergency Relief Appropriation Act, authorizing the creation of the Resettlement Administration and the Works Progress Administration.

May 11, 1935 Roosevelt creates the Rural Electrification Administration to provide electricity to rural areas through federal partnership with private farming cooperatives.

May 27, 1935 The U.S. Supreme Court issues several rulings against New Deal programs, including *Schechter Poultry Corporation v. United States,* striking down the National Industrial Recovery Act; the day becomes known as "Black Monday."

July 5, 1935 In reaction to the Schechter decision, Congress passes the National Labor Relations Act, recognizing the right of workers to organize in unions and conduct collective bargaining with employers.

August 2, 1935 Roosevelt establishes the Federal Art Project, Federal Music Project, Federal Theatre Project, and Federal Writers' Project to provide work relief for people involved in the arts.

August 14, 1935 Congress passes the Social Security Act, providing old age and unemployment benefits to American workers.

August 28, 1935 The Public Utility Holding Company Act is enacted by Congress, prohibiting the use of multiple layers of holding companies in the utility industry.

October 1935 Italy sends 35,000 troops and volunteers to Ethiopia, seeking to expand its rule into Africa.

November 9, 1935 In organizing unions for semi-skilled workers of mass production industries, John L. Lewis begins to break with the craft-oriented American Federation of Labor (AFL) and creates the Committee of Industrial Organizations (CIO), which later becomes known as the Congress of Industrial Organizations.

January 6, 1936 The Supreme Court rules the Agricultural Adjustment Act unconstitutional in *United States v. Butler.*

March 7, 1936 German troops retake the Rhineland region of Europe without conflict, beginning the German expansion through Europe.

August 1936 Athlete Jesse Owens, a black American, wins four gold medals at the Berlin Summer Olympics, conflicting with Adolf Hitler's white supremacy beliefs.

November 1936 Franklin Roosevelt wins reelection to the U.S. presidency by a landslide, winning a record 61 percent of the vote.

December 30, 1936 Seven General Motors plants in Flint, Michigan, are shut down by sit-down strikes; the company gives in to worker demands on February 11, 1937.

February 5, 1937 Roosevelt introduces a plan to reorganize the U.S. judiciary system. It becomes known as the "court packing" plan and attracts substantial opposition in Congress and the public.

June 22, 1937 Black American Joe Louis defeats Briton James Braddock to become the new world heavyweight boxing champion.

July 30, 1937 Japan invades China and begins a major offensive toward other countries in the Far East.

April 12, 1937 The Supreme Court begins making decisions supportive of New Deal programs by ruling in favor of the National Labor Relations Act in *National Labor Relations Board v. Jones & Laughlin Steel Corporation.*

May 1937 A steelworkers' strike at Republic Steel leads to a violent confrontation between striking workers and Chicago police, leaving ten people dead and 90 injured.

June 25, 1938 Marking the end of the Second New Deal, Congress passes the Fair Labor Standards Act, setting minimum wage and maximum hour regulations.

April 30, 1939 The New York World's Fair opens.

September 30, 1939 Germany invades Poland, starting World War II as France and Great Britain declare war on Germany.

May 1940 Germany invades Western Europe; France surrenders in June.

December 29, 1940 In a "fireside chat" over the radio, Franklin Roosevelt describes the United States as the "arsenal of democracy" to provide war supplies to those nations fighting German expansion. The country's war mobilization efforts help the economy and spur recovery from the Great Depression.

1941 A. Philip Randolph threatens to lead a march of black Americans on Washington, DC, protesting racial discrimination in the war industry; Roosevelt establishes the Fair Employment Practices Commission in response to the pressure.

December 7, 1941 Japan bombs U.S. military facilities in Pearl Harbor, Hawaii; the United States declares war on Japan and later Germany, entering World War II.

April 12, 1945 Franklin Roosevelt dies suddenly from a cerebral hemorrhage at 63 years of age.

April 30, 1945 With defeat imminent, Adolf Hitler commits suicide in Germany.

Prohibition Repealed

National Prohibition, a result of a century of moral and religious crusades, lasted but 13 years, from 1920 to 1933. The newly inaugurated President Franklin Delano Roosevelt (served 1933–1945) commented to an aide in March 1933 that it was surely a good time for a beer. The sentiment Roosevelt expressed had been echoed in America since its birth.

The earliest colonists considered liquor a good gift of nature, a necessity of life. Rum was the beverage of choice for weddings, funerals, and generally all community gatherings. Parents spoon-fed it to crying babies, however, it was a sin to overindulge. Nevertheless, gradually as more and more people misused rum, movements began to curtail its use. Temperance campaigns to promote the use of alcoholic beverages in moderation or to abstain completely began as early as 1808. Maine was the first state to pass Prohibition legislation that prohibited manufacture and sale of liquor. In 1862 the United States government, strapped for cash due to the Civil War (1861–1865), began collecting revenue from a federal liquor tax. Ironically between 1870 and 1915 one half to the two-thirds of the revenue of the United States government came from the liquor tax as no income tax existed.

In the early 1870s women's groups began an assault on the "demon rum." The Women's Christian Temperance Union crusaded against liquor and supported Prohibition. By 1893 the Anti-Saloon League had joined in. Ultimately on January 17, 1920, the

Chronology:

1873–1874: The Woman's Crusade with bands of singing and praying women sweep into saloons to protest the "demon rum."

November 1874: Women's National Christian Temperance Union organizes in Chautauqua, New York, and soon becomes known as the Women's Christian Temperance Union, or the WCTU

1893: Anti-Saloon League (ASL) organizes.

1899–1902: Carry A. Nation wields her hatchet destroying saloons.

January 16, 1919: A full 36 states ratify the Eighteenth Amendment.

May 1919: Congress passes the Volstead Act.

January 16, 1920: The Eighteenth Amendment, or the Prohibition Amendment, goes into effect nationwide.

1920–1932: With every passing year Prohibition is ignored more and more. Organized crime becomes immensely wealthy from "bootlegging" illegal alcohol.

1926: The Association Against the Prohibition Amendment (AAPA), originally founded in 1918, gains support of many influential Americans.

1927: An anti-Prohibition group of lawyers, the Voluntary Committee of Lawyers, incorporates.

1927: Attorney Wayne B. Wheeler of the Anti-Saloon League dies suddenly.

1929–1931: The Wickersham Commission studies problems of Prohibition enforcement and issues inconclusive report.

May 1929: Pauline Sabin forms the Women's Organization for National Prohibition reform (WOWPR).

October 1929: The Great Depression begins.

1932: U.S. citizens elect New York governor Franklin D. Roosevelt president.

February 1933: Congress passes a resolution to submit the Twenty-First Amendment, repealing the Eighteenth Amendment, to the states for ratification.

March 1933: President Roosevelt sends a special message to Congress asking them to pass a bill legalizing 3.2 percent beer; Congress quickly does.

December 5, 1933: The thirtieth state ratifies the Twenty First Amendment.

June 24, 1935: American Can Company and Krueger Brewing Co. of Newark, New Jersey, introduce canned beer.

Eighteenth Amendment, or otherwise known as the "Prohibition Amendment," took effect nationwide. Americans expected Prohibition to make America a wholesome, perfect place, but as Herbert Asbury in his book *Great Illusion* explains:

> They had expected to be greeted, when the great day came, by a covey of angels bearing gifts of peace, happiness, prosperity, and salvation, which they had been assured would be theirs when the rum demon had been scotched. Instead they were met by a horde of bootleggers, moonshiners, rumrunners, hijackers, gangsters, racketeers, trigger men, venal judges, corrupt police, crooked politicians, and speakeasy operators, all bearing the twin symbols of the Eighteenth Amendment–the tommy gun and the poisoned cup (Asbury, p. 137).

From the start Prohibition had been heavily promoted as a reform to protect community and home, yet it appeared by the mid-1920s to have unleashed a crime wave. Gangsters had organized and were becoming wealthy. The boom of "bootleggers," or people who smuggle liquor, in the United States overwhelmed the number of Prohibition agents, respect for law became less every day as reports of bribery and corruption continuously surfaced, and courts were inundated with Prohibition cases. It seemed evading the ban on liquor became a national sport, while speakeasies thrived, otherwise law-abiding citizens made home brews and looked at the activity as only slightly illegal, and even women who seldom drank alcohol began to drink. Thousands of lives were lost in futile attempts to enforce Prohibition, and the federal government lost millions in revenue taxes while enforcement costs reached toward a billion dollars.

Ultimately two factors brought an end to Prohibition. First, American women under the banner of the Women's Organization for National Prohibition Reform (WONPR) pushed for repeal of the Eighteenth Amendment, the Prohibition amendment, and secondly the Great Depression began. In October 1929 the stock market crashed as over valued stocks plummeted in price causing investors to lose millions of dollars. Soon the economic crisis spread to the rest of the economy. Financiers could no longer pour investment money into businesses and factories using new assembly line technology were turning out products faster than the public could purchase them. As a result companies needed to cut payrolls. Banks began going out of business having lost investments in the stock market and citizens not able to keep their loan payments on houses and other property they purchased on credit. The downward economic spiral continued until finally hitting bottom by early 1933 when at least 12 million workers representing 25 percent of the workforce were unemployed.

Americans, confused and dismayed by the economic crisis, listened as "wets," those in favor of repeal, laid partial blame for the Depression on Prohibition. Legalizing alcohol, they claimed, would bring back desperately needed jobs in breweries and distilleries, generate tax revenue for the government's coffers, and stop expensive attempts to enforce Prohibition. By December 5, 1933, the necessary number of states had ratified the Twenty-First Amendment that repealed Prohibition. The Great Depression of course did not come to an end, but what had come to an end was the most extensive social experiment ever undertaken in the United States.

Issue Summary

Results of the Noble Experiment

As the 1920s came to a close illegal manufacture and sales of liquor continued in the United States on a large scale. In geographic areas where the population was sympathetic to Prohibition it was enforced more vigilantly than where the majority of citizens opposed it. Enforcement generally was stronger in small towns and rural areas and considerably weaker in large cities especially those in the North and East. Mid-decade surveys revealed that Idaho, Oregon, Washington, and areas from Texas to California appeared to have somewhat accepted Prohibition. The cities of Seattle, San Francisco, and Los Angeles, however, all had strong wet components. In the Southern states Prohibition seemed to be enforced for black Americans but much less than it was for whites. Throughout the Midwest rural areas generally observed Prohibition, but city residents largely ignored it. Scandinavians of St. Paul and Minneapolis, Minnesota continued drinking as did the large ethic communities in Chicago, Detroit, New York, Boston, Philadelphia, Pittsburgh and Cleveland.

Overall less drinking was taking place largely because illegally obtained liquor was very expensive. The more prosperous middle and upper classes routinely violated Prohibition as did young adults who regarded drinking as a sign of sophistication. The working class, at least those not making their own beverages at home, reportedly reduced drinking the most because of the expense. A quart of beer cost 80 cents during Prohibition, which was six times more expensive than it was in 1916. Likewise the cost of whisky and gin drastically increased after Prohibition commenced. The anger of many Americans was barely repressed. Throughout the nation Prohibition took on an image not of a respected law that reduced alcohol consumption but the image of a law to be widely disregarded. Many Americans realized for the first time that the law of the land could be misguided or, in their eyes, completely wrong and therefore could be ignored.

By the end of the decade the results of the great social experiment were clear. From the start Prohibition had been heavily promoted as a reform to protect community and home. Yet it appeared to be unleashing a crime wave. Prohibition had created a widespread disrespect for the law. Organized crime had become wealthy beyond imagination and would henceforth be a part of the American landscape. Politicians, Prohibition agents, local police, the courts, and prison system were overwhelmed and often corrupted with bribery and payoffs. Citizens lost respect for the legal system and for politicians. Many Prohibition agents, police, and innocent citizens lost their lives in shootouts over the illegal trafficking of alcohol. Physical harm, blindness, and the deaths of over ten thousand people resulted from drinking bootlegged alcohol containing poisonous chemicals. Thousands of honest people employed in the brewery, distillery, and wine industries lost their jobs, and if they chose not to become criminals, they took far lower paying jobs outside their area of expertise.

The drinking habits of America changed dramatically during Prohibition. In pre-Prohibition days little drinking took place at home except for the wealthy, who had wine or beer with dinner and brandy or port wine afterwards. For most of the public, alcohol at home was for medicinal purposes only. During Prohibition, however, drinking at speakeasies was very expensive. As a result liquor was stored at home or made at home and therefore could be drunk more often. Also the cocktail made with liquor became popular. Eight ounces of gin mixed with soda or juice became eight drinks whereas eight ounces of beer was one drink. Those who had disliked the taste of beer, wine, or hard liquor found cocktails irresistible.

Prohibition agents pour liquor down a sewer. Whenever agents found illegal stores of liquor, it was immediately disposed of. (Corbis Corporation. Reproduced by permission.)

Before Prohibition women drank very little, and prohibitionists considered the fact that immigrant women drank beer or wine an outrage. Prohibition was intended to help keep womanhood pure but it had the opposite effect. As soon as drinking became illegal women began to drink. For example, younger women passed the flask with men, and speakeasies invited women in and they came. For those that stayed at home alcohol stored at home allowed women to privately find out what all the uproar was about.

Finally and probably one of the most important reasons leading to repeal was the cost of Prohibition. Enforcement costs by some estimates topped a billion dollars between passage and repeal. Additionally the government lost millions in revenue taxes that would have been collected if alcohol was legal. Also honest brewmasters, wine makers, and distillers were denied the income to pay workers and to turn a profit. Instead liquor revenues went by and large into the deep pockets of organized crime.

Enforcement of Prohibition

From the start of Prohibition agencies charged with enforcement had insufficient funds and manpower. Drys had insisted enforcement would be easy with most Americans voluntarily obeying the law, while wets hoped they were wrong. Congress counted

on enforcement being cheap. Responsibility for enforcement under the Volstead Act was with the Bureau of Internal Revenue, a division of the Treasury Department. The first Prohibition Commissioner appointed was John F. Kramer, a dedicated Prohibitionist and lawyer from Ohio. Kramer formed the Prohibition Unit whose name changed much later, in 1927, to the Prohibition Bureau. The Unit, as organized, had a total of 1,520 enforcement agents operating in the United States or one to every 70,000 Americans. Most were paid approximately $1,680 a year, hardly a decent livable wage for men with families in a city. Kramer predicted that "this law will be obeyed in cities large and small without need of much intervention."

After six months the disillusioned Kramer left his job. Roy Haynes, another Ohioan and ardent supporter of the Anti-Saloon League, was handpicked by the League's lawyer, Wayne Wheeler, to be the new Prohibition commissioner. Within two years Haynes claimed moonshining, or making illegal liquor at home, and bootlegging were all but conquered, yet the facts told a radically different story. His Prohibition Unit had been filled with men owed favors by politicians and was hardly competent to handle the wildfire spread of bootlegging. Bootlegging was becoming, more and more, a highly profitable, gang-controlled business. In

1925 President Coolidge (served 1923–1929) put military man General Lincoln C. Andrews in charge of enforcement. Andrews better organized the bureaus then dealing with liquor control—the Prohibition Unit, the Coast Guard, and Customs Service. He intended to terminate all unqualified men from the Prohibition Unit and replace them with qualified individuals. Politicians, however, scuttled most of his plans, and corruption associated with Prohibition went on as usual. States passed plenty of enforcement laws to keep drys happy but in reality appropriated almost no money to carry out the statutes. Raids on speakeasies were rarely more than an annoyance, and even padlocking doors rarely kept speaks closed more than a day. Courts were overwhelmed with Prohibition cases, and the juries generally sided with the accused. As a result courts began to set aside certain days for bootleggers, moonshiners, smugglers, and speakeasy managers to come, plead guilty, pay a five or ten dollar fine, and go back to what they had been doing.

Federal enforcement agents whose salaries were meager were highly susceptible to bribery and payoffs. In order to operate their speakeasies without trouble, the bootleg crime gangs put police, sheriffs and any other officials likely to get in their way on their payroll. Hundreds of city officials, police officers, state legislators, judges, and prosecuting attorneys were indicted through the 1920s for working with gangs. Often Prohibition Unit agents worked just long enough to learn about contacts then quit to work as bootleggers or speakeasy proprietors themselves.

The Customs Service's Border patrol was charged with stopping liquor from entering the United States over land routes and rivers and lakes. During Prohibition's first years not more than 35 agents were assigned to the Mexican border and one hundred to the Canadian border. Cars and trucks loaded with cases of whiskey had some four hundred roads to enter from Canada and speedboats raced across the Great Lakes and the Detroit and St. Lawrence Rivers. There were probably two hundred routes from Mexico as well has many shallow spots for crossing the Rio Grande. Federal agents admitted two years into Prohibition they seized only one case in twenty crossing the border. Customs Service Agents were also highly susceptible to bribery and corruption.

In 1927 the Customs Service decided on a major effort aimed at the so-called Detroit-Windsor Tunnel where millions of gallons of liquor were smuggled yearly into Detroit from Canada. The Service hand picked one hundred of its best agents with the Border Patrol and committed one half of its patrol boats to the area. The Prohibition Bureau doubled its number of agents at its Detroit headquarters. Yet in 12 months time

More About...
The Eighteenth Amendment

Section 1. Prohibition

After one year from the ratification of this article the manufacture, sale, or transportation of intoxicating liquors within the importation thereof into or the exportation thereof from the United States and all territory subject to the jurisdiction thereof for beverage purposes is hereby prohibited.

Section 2. Enforcement

The Congress and the several States shall have concurrent power to enforce this article by appropriate legislation.

Section 3. Ratification

This article shall be inoperative unless it shall have been ratified as an amendment to the Constitution, within seven years from the date of the submission hereof to the States by the Congress.

Explanations

Section 1: This amendment made it illegal to make or sell alcoholic beverages within the United States. This Amendment was commonly spoken of as Prohibition.

Section 2: Congress and the states could both pass laws to enforce this Amendment. Congress passed the Volstead Act and the states passed numerous enforcement laws.

Section 3: For the first time an amendment included a time limit for ratification. For the amendment to go into effect it had to be ratified or approved by three-fourths of the states within seven years. The Amendment was submitted to the states in the summer of 1917. Nebraska became the thirty-sixth state to ratify on January 14, 1919. The Secretary of State announced on January 16, 1919, that the Amendment had been ratified and would go into effect in exactly one year.

ending March 31, 1928, the Service seized only 148,211 gallons of the 3,388,016 gallons of liquor that left Windsor for Detroit. The project was considered a total failure, illustrating the difficulty in controlling borders.

When the Eighteenth Amendment passed it became the Coast Guard's duty to keep smugglers away from American shores. At the time the Coast Guard was a small branch of the Department of the Treasury. Its duties were to protect government revenues, save lives and property at sea, and prevent ordinary smuggling. It had several thousand men, about 30 cutters and a few small harbor boats. Undermanned and underequipped the Coast Guard was almost helpless against Rum Row.

In 1924 the United States and Great Britain agreed to allow the Coast Guard to greatly expand the water it could patrol—allowing it to search British vessels as far out as one hour's run from the American coast by the Guards fastest cutter. Because of Prohibition the Coast Guard expanded during 1920s into a full military service of the United States. By 1928, not counting small lifesaving boats, the Guard had 560 vessels including 33 cruisers, 25 destroyers, and 243 large offshore patrol boats. The Coast Guard, over the fourteen years of Prohibition, captured hundreds of bootlegging boats and was successful in dispersing Rum Row. Nevertheless the gangsters who bootlegged by sea greatly outnumbered the Guard and by operating with a great deal more care continued smuggling enormous amounts of liquor into the United States until repeal of the amendment.

Presidents William G. Harding (served 1921–1923) and Calvin Coolidge neither pressured Congress nor made any suggestions relating to enforcement. They confined their speeches to complaining about the states' lack of help on enforcement issues and reminding Americans it was their duty to obey the law.

The Build Up to the End of Prohibition

During the ratification process of the Eighteenth Amendment and the passage of the Volstead Act the opponents of Prohibition were weakly organized. They included the brewery, distillery, and wine industries, hotelkeepers associations, real estate men, cigar makers, and the American Federation of Labor (AFL). The AFL called for a modification of the act to allow the manufacture and sale of beer. Millions of everyday Americans were opposed to Prohibition but also lacked organization and spokesmen. Many of their leaders which emerged in the middle and late 1920's actually originally supported the Eighteenth Amendment. One emerging leader was Captain William H. Stayton.

Stayton, who never supported the Eighteenth Amendment, instead watched in horror, as it became part of the U.S. Constitution. A lawyer, businessman, and former naval officer, Stayton had no financial interest in the liquor industry nor did he seek political office. Stayton simply believed deeply in the rights of states and local communities to make independent decisions. To him the Eighteenth Amendment was one more move to the concentration of power in the hands of the federal government. His strongly held convictions led him to establish, along with friends of similar persuasion, the Association Against the Prohibition Amendment (AAPA) in 1918. The political tactics and arguments AAPA developed through the early years of Prohibition allowed it to eventually become one of the most influential groups in the fight to repeal the Eighteenth Amendment.

Although widely thought of as a front for the liquor industry, the opposite was true. The AAPA refused to accept industry money and grew slowly in the first half of the 1920s. A few donations along with Stayton's support at the rate of $1,000 a month kept it going. When AAPA members thought their numbers had grown large enough in a state, a division was created by absorbing various local anti-Prohibition organizations such as the Moderation Leagues of Minnesota and Ohio and the Constitutional Liberty League of Massachusetts. By 1920 nearly every state outside the south that was not thought of as hopelessly dry had a division—twenty-five divisions in all.

An almost entirely male organization, the AAPA did create a women's organization known as the Molly Pitcher Club in some states including New York and Pennsylvania. Led by Louise Gross, the clubs stated their purpose was to prevent the federal government from interfering with the personal habits of people unless they had criminal intent. The clubs unfortunately were never particularly influential, and many women were discouraged from joining because the clubs operated through the male AAPA. Additionally Gross noted that in the early to mid-1920s there was tremendous resistance to women working against Prohibition. By 1924 the clubs died out but Gross, with a small group of women, continued under a series of names including Women's Committee for the Modification of the Volstead Act, and, in 1928, the Women's Committee for Repeal of the Eighteenth Amendment. Nevertheless a powerful independent anti-Prohibition women's group would not develop until the end of the decade.

During the first six dry years the anti-Prohibition groups advocated modification of the Volstead Act not repeal of the Eighteenth Amendment. However, by 1926 newspaper polls consistently showed more and more Americans were beginning to favor not only modification of the Volstead Act but outright repeal of the Eighteenth Amendment. While the AAPA loudly touted the various poll results, the ASL charged the polls were rigged. Nevertheless a shift in public sentiment was beginning—a shift away from support of Prohibition.

Prominent Americans Take Up The Anti-Prohibition Banner

By 1926 William Stayton's AAPA was undergoing a rebirth with its newest members. Many of the same individuals had strongly supported the Eighteenth Amendment during its passage and ratification. By the mid to later 1920s they had come to the conclusion that Prohibition was demoralizing, expensive, and simply unworkable. It had created a total disrespect for the law, an overburdened Court system, and corruption in government. Believing states should govern themselves wherever possible, many saw the Amendment and Volstead Act as infringements on states' rights. Taking it yet a notch higher many now felt the personal liberties of Americans were being violated. Also enforcement of Prohibition cost millions in liquor tax revenues—taxes levied by the government on the sale of liquor when it was legal. Businessmen believed taxes were being levied on their companies to make up the revenue loss.

An amazing group of prominent businessmen, lawyers, bankers, industrialists, railroad presidents, educators, and authors signed on to the rolls of AAPA. They did not stop at merely joining AAPA but quickly took outspoken and active roles. They included Henry Bourne Joy, retired Packard Motor Company President; two prominent financiers, Grayson Mallet-Provost Murphy and Robert K. Cassalt; James W. Wadsworth, Jr. from a family prominent in American affairs for generations; and the three du Pont brothers of Wilmington, Delaware, Piérre, Lammot, and Irénée, the fourth American generation of the du Pont family and keeper of the family business and the family fortune. By 1929 the AAPA listed 227 members on its Board of Directors, all rich and powerful figures in the United States. Among them were General W.W. Atterbury, President of the Pennsylvania Railroad; John J. Raskob, a du Pont and General Motors executive and Chairman of the Democratic National Committee; Arthur Curtiss James, Director of a dozen corporations; Newcomb Carlton, President of Western Union; Haley Fiske, President of Metropolitan Life Insurance Company; Edward S. Harkness, railroad tycoon; Elihu Root, prominent lawyer and former Secretary of State; Percy S. Straus, president of Macy and Company; and, Charles H. Sabin of the Guaranty Trust Company. As would be expected these men freely donated funds to AAPA's cause.

Another anti-Prohibition group incorporated in New York in 1927 was the Voluntary Committee of Lawyers. This group opposed the Eighteenth Amendment on the grounds that it was not consistent with the spirit and purpose of the Constitution and that it violated the Bill of Rights. Professional organizations of lawyers, or bar associations, in New York, New Jersey, Detroit, St. Louis, San Francisco, and Portland passed resolutions in 1928 calling for repeal of the Amendment. Then in 1930 the American Bar Association adopted a repeal resolution by a vote of 13,779 to 6,340.

On the other side, the Prohibition leadership was limping and a lack of unity among leaders was evident. An irreparable loss to the drys occurred in 1927 when Wayne B. Wheeler died suddenly. Wheeler's persuasive leadership style and expertise as an attorney had guided the ASL for years. Methodist Bishop James Cannon, Jr., chairman of the ASL's political activities, replaced Wheeler as the recognized leader of the drys. Cannon attempted to bully Congress in an abusive, violent manner, calling anyone who disagreed with him a hopeless sinner. He lost credibility by the end of the decade with revelations of his own misdeeds such as gambling on the stock market, marrying his secretary shortly after his wife's death, and charges of misspent campaign money. In addition to ineffective leadership the drys also suffered large declines in donations whereas the wets had plenty of donated money. For example, the du Ponts, who had donated to the drys early in the 1920s, now gave freely to the wets. The drys also had a practical philosophical problem. Since they refused to admit any problems with the Eighteenth Amendment or the Volstead Act, by default they were supporting the bootlegger, the speakeasy, and any other problems inflicted on the United States population by Prohibition.

Backed by almost unlimited funds, wet propaganda moved into full swing. Prohibition was a topic of arguments and discussions throughout the United States. Public opinion polls continued to reveal support for the full repeal of the Eighteenth Amendment or at least major modification to the Volstead Act. The Presidential election of 1928 brought the question of Prohibition to a head.

The 1928 Presidential Election

Governor of New York Alfred E. Smith was nominated as the 1928 Democratic Presidential candidate. Although Bishop Cannon, a Democrat, used his influence to get a dry Democratic plank in the party's platform, saying the party would make "an honest effort" to enforce the Eighteenth Amendment, candidate

Smith was clearly a foe of Prohibition and the ASL. Publicly Smith asked for a modification of the Volstead Act, but privately he considered Prohibition unconstitutional, in violation of both states rights and individual rights. Smith was a cigar smoking, gravel-voiced son of an Irish immigrant, a union man, and a Roman Catholic. He had grown up in the city slums and drew much of his support from foreign-born Americans. Many Democratic, Protestant, rural Americans could not buy into Smith's candidacy. Cannon denounced Smith and led a group of Southern Democrats out of the convention.

The Republican candidate Herbert Hoover, before his nomination, had said Prohibition was a great social and economic experiment. He stated that it was certainly noble in motive and also far reaching in purpose. From this speech came the often-used phrase, "the noble experiment." Hoover, a humanitarian and idol of millions, had served as secretary of commerce under two presidents. Many Americans credited him with the ever-rising prosperity of the 1920s. Probably no Democratic candidate could have beaten Hoover in the booming year of 1928. Hoover took 444 electoral votes to Smith's 87. The drys won majorities in most state legislatures and the U.S. Senate and House. The bitter campaign, however, had brought the Eighteenth Amendment into question and the first rumblings for full repeal were heard in Washington, D.C.

President Herbert Hoover (served 1929–1933) became the first president during Prohibition to commit to stricter enforcement of Prohibition. Just before he took office Congress raised the maximum punishment for first time offenders of the Volstead Act to a $10,000 fine and five years in prison. This change in policy, however, did not improve Prohibition effectiveness rather it only served to strengthen its reputation as harsh and unreasonable. In 1929 Hoover authorized construction of six new federal prisons to relieve the existing overcrowded ones. Alcatraz in San Francisco Bay was one of the new prisons to be built, and by 1930 more than one-third of the 12,332 federal prisoners were Volstead Act violators.

Wickersham Commission

One of President Hoover's first acts in office was to appoint the National Commission on Law Observance and Enforcement with former Attorney General George W. Wickersham as Chairman. This body, known as the Wickersham Commission, studied the problems of Prohibition enforcement for almost two years, producing its final report in January 1931. The five-volume well-documented report ended with highly contradictory conclusions. In a brief summary, signed by all members, the Commission declared they were against repeal of the Eighteenth Amendment, against modification of the Volstead Act, and against the return of the saloon. Yet each member also made a separate statement, two of which clearly favored repeal, seven desired major or minor revisions, and two wrote as though they were satisfied with the status quo. One of those favoring repeal thought liquor control should be returned to the states. Another stated that in practicality the people did not support the government in enforcing Prohibition, and he saw no other route but repeal. Whatever one chose to focus on in the Wickersham report it was soon clear that the Eighteenth Amendment had never been and probably never would be properly enforced and was headed for an attempt at repeal. Two pivotal occurrences in 1929 ultimately set the Eighteenth Amendment on the road to oblivion; the establishment of the Women's Organization for National Prohibition Reform (WONPR) and the beginning of the Great Depression.

Women and Repeal

By the late 1920s the Women's Christian Temperance Union seemed stuck in a 19th century mold. Rather than expanding the role and influence following their success at helping to install national Prohibition in 1920, the WCTU constantly looked backward not forward. It continued to see immigrants as a threat to America, and it clung to Prohibition as an evangelical mission, condemning new ideas of young adult dress, use of tobacco, and courtship as demoralizing. The WCTU had long claimed women naturally supported Prohibition to protect family, especially children, home, and community. However, a new women's repeal group would soon meet the WCTU on its own philosophical turf—that of children and family protection—and demand a goal directly opposite to that of the WCTU

Louise Gross, who had headed the AAPA's women's arm, the Molly Pitcher Club, led the Women's Committee for Repeal of the Eighteenth Amendment in 1928. This was the first organized group to call for outright repeal of the Eighteenth Amendment. That same year Gross became president of another women's repeal group, the Women's Moderation Union (WMU). Gross put out a call for women to organize a strong and militant national women's anti-Prohibition organization. The organization would offset the activities of the WCTU headed by Ella Boole since 1925. Boole responded in horror that women would "demean themselves" (Rose, p. 73), to work for repeal. Gross's rhetoric and ideas, which even extended to legalizing moderate use of opium, strayed too far from the center for most American women, as a result the WMU never gained a large following. At this point the socially prominent Mrs. Charles H. Sabin entered the scene.

Pauline Sabin

Pauline Sabin, wife of Charles H. Sabin, New York banker with Guaranty Trust Company and member of the AAPA, declined to have anything to do with Gross' WMU and set about to form, in May 1929, the Women's Organization for National Prohibition Reform (WONPR). Sabin's lofty social standing was an asset in attracting publicity and members. In April 1929 Sabin had announced both her resignation from the Republican National Committee and her determination to work for a change in Prohibition laws.

Sabin crafted an appeal that a large number of women could accept. The appeal was largely based on protection of family and children just as the WCTU's was. In order to protect the family, however, WONPR believed real temperance—real choices by people to drink moderately or not at all—had to be individual decisions not legislated by the federal government. WONPR believed the crime, lawlessness, and corruption spawned by Prohibition was destroying communities. Furthermore it was rendering impossible the ability of parents to instill respect for the law in youth. To WONPR members, repeal meant protection of youth from the hypocrisy of Prohibition.

Within three years, by 1932, the WONPR had over a million members. These women were far removed from the hymn-singing women of the old dry crusades and of the WCTU. They were prominent and active in their community, had social standing, were able to raise funds and attract newspaper publicity. The WONPR stayed staunchly independent and apart from the AAPA and any other men's organization.

The Repeal Coalition

In 1929 the organizations who banned together to form the Prohibition repeal movement seemed a strange group of allies: the AAPA, predominantly businessmen; the WONPR, a large contingent of well-heeled women; intellectuals, writers, critics and journalists who sustained a nearly universal hatred of Prohibition; and, organized labor. Organized labor had long been dismayed by the unfair burden placed on the workingman. While even beer was not legally available anywhere and was too expensive in local speakeasies for laborers, those with more monetary means went right securing and enjoying alcoholic beverages.

Despite rapidly growing support the coalition's goal of repeal of the Eighteenth Amendment was unprecedented in American politics. A constitutional

A woman displays a "Repeal the 18th Amendment" tire cover. The amendment outlawed the sale and production of alcoholic beverages. (The Library of Congress.)

amendment for repeal would have to be crafted and passed through Congress to the states for ratification. The question that loomed was if 36 states would ratify. There was still strong sentiment in the western and southern states for Prohibition. It would take only 13 states to block the repeal effort. Just as many anti-Prohibitionists feared outright repeal might simply not be possible, the Great Depression began.

The Great Depression and the Eighteenth Amendment

Millions of Americans in 1928 had contently voted for Herbert Hoover and what they thought would be four more years of prosperity. In September 1929 the U.S. stock market had reached an all-time high. Beginning in October shock after shock hit the American economy. The stock market plummeted. Businesses closed their doors leaving thousands unemployed. Americans became unable to make payments on home loans and frequently lost their homes. Banks failed leaving some penniless. Individuals and whole families began to go hungry. The happy boom days were over and a somber nation was in no mood for what now seemed the trivial sport of either trying to beat Prohibition or demanding its enforcement.

The Great Depression, historians recognized, was what finally killed Prohibition. Although the nation already appeared to be on a tract to attempt repeal, the Depression pushed the process to a much quicker end than there might otherwise have been. The drys appealed to patriotism in 1919 to help pass and ratify the Eighteenth Amendment. They had asked Americans to create a healthy environment for young soldiers to come home to at the end of World War I (1914–1918).

Now the wets employed the same tactics to bring repeal of that Amendment, exploiting the Depression to the fullest. Every conceivable medium of speech and print was used to lay blame for the Depression at the feet of Prohibition. The wets' trained economists shouted that the stock market crash, business failures, and unemployment had been due to Prohibition. Americans, confused and bewildered by the economic crisis, believed the propaganda. Wets argued the government's budget had been severely stretched by the expensive attempts at enforcement of Prohibition, and that the government could no longer afford to spend any money on enforcement. Legalizing liquor would return much-needed jobs in the breweries, distilleries, and wineries; legal liquor would again generate tax revenue money for a needy government; profits would be taken from the criminals and returned to honest men. A sense of national emergency surrounded the repeal issue, and Americans were desperate for any suggestions that might stop the economic slide. As the Depression deepened demand for repeal got louder and louder.

The 1932 Presidential Convention

President Hoover would again be the Republican Party's nominee in 1932 and although he was ready to eliminate Prohibition he called for a platform that would not directly commit him or his party to outright repeal. The plank as written was considered noncommittal, straddling the fence rather than providing clear direction. It stressed preserving gains made in dealing with liquor traffic but at the same time called for state conventions to consider a new amendment to modify the Eighteenth Amendment. The delegates on the floor called the plank "bunk" and demanded an outright repeal platform. In the end the plank stood as written.

The outcome would be quite different at the Democratic Convention in Chicago. Wet crusader and former Democratic Presidential nominee, Al Smith and John J. Raskob of the AAPA had urged the Democrats to come out against Prohibition in 1931. They were battled by Franklin Roosevelt who thought it was too early for such a pronouncement. In the interest of party unity, Roosevelt, who would be the party's presiden-

tial nominee, had remained quiet on the subject in the months before the 1932 convention. At the convention, however, the completed platform stated the Party's position clearly. To wild cheers and demonstrations on the convention floor, the plank was read. Roosevelt called for repeal of the Eighteenth Amendment.

The Big Parade

All across America in the largest cities and smallest towns it was parade day. Saturday, May 14, 1932, was neither a national holiday nor a day for honoring heroes. It was a day for Americans to turn out in support of a cool refreshing beverage long denied them—beer.

Far from just being a day of fun the goal of the big, or beer, parades was to point out how beer could help America climb out of the Depression. Taxes derived from the legal sale of beer could help fill empty government coffers that in turn could help put Americans to work building roads, schools, and hospitals. Signs in the parades read, "We Want Beer and We Will Pay the Tax." Legalizing beer would also help ease unemployment by starting up legal breweries. Other signs read, "We Want Beer but We Also Want Jobs."

In villages and towns bands marched, citizens followed holding signs high, cars covered with streaming crepe paper held all sorts of politicians and officials tipping their hats to the crowds on the streets. Detroit's parade was some 15,000 marchers strong with floats covered in anti-dry messages. A Baptist church in Syracuse, New York chimed, "Onward, Christian Soldiers," as marchers went by. In Daytona Beach, Florida beer from barrels was served to marchers. The parade in New York City went right up Fifth Avenue. Police estimated crowds of onlookers plus the marchers numbered from several hundred thousand to several million. If the number of gathered people was in question the sentiment was not. Huge posters at the reviewing stand on the corner of Seventy-second and Central Park illustrated how a tax on legalized beer would battle the Depression.

The End of Prohibition

Roosevelt was swept into the Presidency along with a Congress sure to do away with Prohibition. Without waiting for the new president or the new Congress to take office, the old Congress acted in February 1933 on a resolution to submit the Twenty-First Amendment to the states to repeal the Eighteenth Amendment. The plan called for ratification by a simple majority vote of special conventions called in each state to which delegates were to be elected.

People demonstrate against Prohibition in Newark, NJ with the cry "We want beer!" (AP/Wide World Photos. Reproduced by permission.)

President Roosevelt, as soon as he took office on March 4, 1933, issued an executive order reducing the appropriation funds of the Prohibition Bureau from $8,440,000 to $3,600,000. Knowing ratification by the states could take the rest of the year, Roosevelt next legalized beer as suggested in the Democratic platform. He sent a "special message" to Congress urging swift action on a bill legalizing 3.2 percent alcoholic content for beer. The message suggested a five-dollar tax on each barrel to go to government coffers and would

require brewers to take out a $1,000 federal license. The bill, which in effect amended the Volstead Act, became effective April 7, 1933. Over two hundred breweries producing near beer announced they were ready to roll out the "real thing" immediately. Beer trucks began rumbling through the streets delivering to speakeasies that were suddenly legal beer houses.

The need for gangster involvement in alcohol production and distribution evaporated. Brewmaster schools opened and breweries were swamped with employment applicants. Cases of beer arrived at the White House, and parades, sirens, cowbells marked the first day of legalized beer in cities across the country.

The WCTU mustered a comment to the effect that nations cannot drink themselves out of depressions. President Roosevelt predicted ratification of the Twenty-First Amendment would come by Christmas and would bring with it hundreds of thousands of jobs and tax revenue dollars for the government. Texas, home to the author of the Eighteenth Amendment, ratified as did Virginia, home of Bishop Cannon. Maine, dry since 1846, and Vermont, dry since 1852, both ratified, and Utah was the 36th state to formally ratify the Twenty-First Amendment. On December 5, 1933, at 5:32 PM Eastern Standard Time, the greatest social experiment in American history came to an end. By 7:30 PM EST, Roosevelt had issued a proclamation that ratification was complete and that not only beer but liquor was legal again.

Repeal did not end the Depression but it did create an estimated 250,000 jobs in the distillery and brewing industries. Even more jobs were created in the trades serving those industries as machinery, bottling, and transportation, as well as a much-needed flow of tax money came into national, state, and local governments.

Contributing Forces

The first ships to reach the New World in the early 1600s carried alcoholic beverages as part of their vital provisions. The colonists themselves, including the stern Puritans, approved of drinking in moderation and even considered it one of the necessities of life. Those who drank too much, however, were social outcasts. Colonists considered liquor a good gift of nature and to misuse it was a sin to be punished severely.

The first Prohibition attempt in the colonies targeted Indians who were inflamed by the "strong waters" that the settlers themselves had brought to the new world. Massachusetts and other colonies passed stiff laws prohibiting the sale of liquor to Indians. Nevertheless traders "bootlegged" liquor, that is carried bottles in their boots, to Indians to trade for furs. Land hungry settlers used liquor to lessen Indians resistance to giving up choice tracts of property. The Prohibition laws, largely ignored, gradually were lifted.

In the late 1600s New England established a bustling trade with the British West Indies. Colonists developed a taste for the West Indian beverage called rum, and before long New Englanders were importing molasses from the West Indies, which they dis-

tilled into rum. The first large rum-distilling center was in Rhode Island. By 1723 merchants used rum in the notorious slave trade, exchanging an estimated 600,000 gallons of rum a year for slaves.

People drank rum at town meetings, weddings, christening, funerals, and most any other community event. Families considered it a tonic for good health and a cure for all ailments. Parents spoon-fed it to crying babies, clergy drank rum liberally, and rich and poor alike enjoyed its benefits; rare was the abstainer.

The first real attempt to enforce Prohibition in America came in the colony of Georgia. Georgia's founding father, James Oglethorpe, known as the Father of Prohibition, was determined to establish a sober colony. As soon as new colonists settled in Georgia it became clear most did not share Oglethorpe's vision. Instead, they began making rum for their pleasure and entertainment. Oglethorpe and the English trustees in London fashioned an act flatly prohibiting the import or sale of rum in Georgia. Many of the conditions that later surrounded Prohibition in the 1920s developed in Georgia in 1735. Stills in the back country continued to pump out rum, boats smuggled rum into secluded docking points, bar rooms flourished in back rooms of stores and homes, and the average citizen ridiculed Prohibition and made heroes of the bootleggers. Finally in 1742 the London trustees gave up any attempts to enforce Prohibition in Georgia.

The American Revolutionary War (1775–1783) cut off trade with the West Indies halting both imports of good rum and molasses. Whiskey, distilled from rye grains and corn, became a popular substitute for rum. After the war's close in 1789 the new federal government, strapped for money, attempted to tax liquor for revenue. The government put a tax on all imported alcoholic beverages, on molasses for making rum and, two years later, on American made whiskey. Men quickly organized and loaded their guns to fight off the tax collectors and the uproar resulted in the Whiskey Rebellion. President Washington called up the militia (local armies) of three states to move into the Pennsylvania countryside and put down the rebellion. Frontiersmen eventually gave in and agreed to pay the tax. The federal government gained new authority, demonstrating it could enforce the laws of Congress.

Meanwhile Americans downed whiskey at an ever-increasing rate. Employers provided their employees with whiskey as farmers did their laborers. Grocers kept whiskey barrels on tap for customers. Whiskey was used for every ailment. Those who drank to excess often reduced themselves and their families to poverty. More and more responsible citizens called for moderation.

Out of concern for those who couldn't control their drinking and their disgraced families the first temperance movements began to arise. The term temperance refers to the use of alcoholic beverages in moderation or abstinence from their use. The most influential early spokesman for temperance was a medical doctor, Benjamin Rush. Dr. Rush, a signer of the Declaration of Independence, was named physician-general of the Continental (or Revolutionary) Army. In 1778 he warned his troops against excessive use of hard liquor. In 1784 he published a pamphlet that changed the thinking of thousands of Americans. The forty-page, *Inquiry into the Effects of Spirituous Liquors on the Human Body and Mind* argued that instead of improving health liquor damaged the human body. He gained many converts, including merchants who halted the sale of whiskey and rum, farmers and factory owners who quit supplying their workers, and church leaders who reformed and called for informed temperance. Before Rush's death in 1813, he predicted someday soon Americans would turn their backs completely on rum and whiskey and become a healthy, happier people.

The first organized temperance society had been formed in upstate New York in 1808 by approximately forty of the areas most influential men. The Union Temperance Society of Moreau and Northumberland adopted the first written temperance constitution pledging abstinence from drinking distilled spirits for one year as an experiment. Gradually more temperance groups formed often under the direction of local Protestant churches. The clergy of Presbyterian, Methodist, Congregational, Baptist and other Protestant churches preached emotional sermons on the evils of alcohol resulting in thousands pledging to abstain and groups forming in all states by the early 1830s.

The focus of the early temperance movement was to encourage drinkers to decide for themselves to give up liquor. Moral persuasion was used to portray makers and sellers of liquor as sinful and evil. As a result Americans developed a lasting and far different attitude toward even moderate drinking than in most other countries in the world. The term Prohibition came into wide usage.

On June 2, 1851, Maine became the first state to pass legislation forbidding all manufacture and sale of intoxicating liquors in the state. To induce tight enforcement of the law, local law officials were allowed to keep any fines collected by the Courts. In the next four years twelve states passed Prohibition legislation. Within a short time, however, voters rebelled and every state except Maine, that had voted for Prohibition either repealed or drastically cut back its restrictions.

More About...

The Twenty-First Amendment

Section 1: Repeal of Eighteenth Amendment

The eighteenth article of amendment to the Constitution of the United States is hereby repealed.

Section 2: State Laws

The transportation or importation into any state territory, or possession of the United States for delivery or use therein of intoxicating liquors, in violation of the laws thereof, is hereby prohibited.

Section 3: Ratification

This article shall be inoperative unless it shall have been ratified as an amendment to the Constitution by conventions in the several States, as provided in the Constitution within seven years from the date of submission hereof to the States by the Congress.

Explanations

Section 1: This amendment repealed or ended the Eighteenth Amendment. It allowed for alcoholic beverages to be legal again.

Section 2: States could control, regulate or even stop the sale of alcohol within their own borders as they each saw fit.

Section 3: The Amendment had to be ratified by three-fourths or 36 states within seven years to take effect. The Amendment was submitted to the states in February 1933. Utah, the 36th state ratified it on November 7, 1933. The entire process took only ten months.

Engulfed by the devastating Civil war it would be twenty-five years before Prohibition again came to the forefront. Interestingly, President Lincoln (served 1861–1865) in desperate need of money to finance the war, signed the Internal Revenue Act in 1862. The act imposed a federal liquor tax on every retail liquor establishment in the Union and on every gallon of liquor, beer, and ale manufactured. Ironically, in light of the Prohibition activities that began with renewed fervor in the 1870s, the liquor tax provided between one-half and two-thirds of the revenue of the United

States from 1870 to 1915, a time when direct income taxes did not exist.

The Woman's Crusade and Women's Christian Temperance Union

By the early 1870s a new force for the temperance movement—womanhood—began a determined assault on the "demon rum." First in Ohio, then across the nation women began joining "praying bands." The highly charged bands of women swarmed around and into saloons singing and praying. Soon tens of thousands of women from New York and Pennsylvania, through the Midwest to California and Oregon swept into saloons. The uproar had more success in small towns and rural areas than in large cities. At first saloonkeepers treated the demonstrations as a joke, men hooted at the ladies as they knelt on barroom floors to pray. But soon the saloonkeepers hurried to lock doors when they saw the ladies approaching. Undaunted they remained kneeling outside. Known as the Woman's Crusade, the demonstrations lasted from the winter of 1873 until summer of 1874. Although the Crusade had only closed saloons temporarily and changed no laws, the temperance movement gained worldwide publicity. Americans became temperance-minded, while stay-at-home sheltered women dared to break old barriers and speak out.

Leaders of state and local temperance unions met in Chautauqua, New York in November 1874, and organized the Women's National Christian Temperance Union, adopting a position to preserve the mission of the Woman's Crusade. Soon known as the WCTU, the organization stated that Prohibition was essential to a healthy America, a position it never abandoned.

A highly intelligent witty reformer, Frances Willard, gradually rose to the leadership in the WCTU Elected its national president in 1879 she oversaw the growth of WCTU from a few thousand women to a cohesive national force with branches in almost every town and city. Willard energetically oversaw some 50 departments of WCTU. dedicated to improvement in a variety of women's interests including nutrition, family health, cooking, gardening, physical exercise, and welfare work. WTCU promoted political action groups on economic issues, labor, and education in alcoholism. WCTU greatest success came in educating young people, the future voters, about the effects of drinking alcohol. In some states the WCTU's influence was so powerful that school authorities made sure selected textbooks conformed to WCTU policy. Willard held firm control until her death in 1898, knowing that WCTU had become the first great national organization of women. With Willard's death

WCTU dropped most of its causes and reforms to focus almost entirely on the crusade against liquor and in support of Prohibition.

Concurrently with the growth of the WCTU was the organization of the Prohibition Party. Formed in 1869 the party went on for more than 50 years nominating candidates for local, state, and national positions. Never more than a minor party it exerted influence out of proportion to its membership numbers and kept Prohibition alive as a political issue.

Meanwhile during the 1890s waves of Germans and other European immigrants arrived on American shores and largely settled in the cities where the jobs were. Many immigrants were Catholic rather than Protestant, long the dominant religion in America. These new Americans had traditionally accepted moderate drinking; for example the Germans loved beer, the Italians loved wine, and the Irish loved whiskey.

The city population also swelled with workers moving off the farms to jobs in the factories. The male only (except for dance hall girls) saloons were places of irresistible temptations for the otherwise respectable men. Drinking, smoking, gambling, prostitution, dancing, card playing, and all sorts of corruption were tied to saloons.

Residents of rural areas looked upon cities and their saloons as evil places. Prohibition grew into a battle between native-born Americans and immigrants, of rural residents versus city people, and of Protestants versus Catholics. Prohibitionists believed if they could just get the beer stein, or wine glass or bottle out of the hands of immigrants, those individuals would have a spiritual wakening, become good citizens, and most likely convert to the Protestant churches.

The Anti-Saloon League

A major force of the growing Prohibition movement was the Anti-Saloon League (ASL). Founded in 1893 by Dr. Howard Russell, a Protestant clergyman in Ohio, ASL grew quickly into a nationwide organization. It continuously stressed its religious character and its ability to attract members from all political backgrounds. With intensified religious and emotional appeals its avowed goal was to close saloons. ASL constantly spewed forth propaganda to build public sentiment. Its original and basic plan was to dry up the United States in steps—first villages and towns, then counties, states and finally the entire nation. Calling itself the Church in Action against the Saloon it raised and spent millions on propaganda and lobbying. ASL developed its own printing plants that produced a gigantic volume of literature each month, and tried to enlist every churchgoer in the country into political action against saloons. Organizations and individuals favoring temperance or full Prohibition became known as the "drys."

The propaganda battle was never one-sided, and those against Prohibition and favoring liquor availability were known as the "wets." The leading wets, brewers and distillers with their billion-dollar industry at stake, waged war against the drys. The wets chose to make fun of the drys rather than clean up the worst of the saloon conditions that might have satisfied most people. They were poorly organized and chose to bribe political leaders and big city newspaper editors into supporting the liquor industry. The ASL managed to make the liquor organizations seem horribly scandalous and succeeded in shocking and disgusting many respectable Americans. Even those who had never strongly supported temperance believed the saloons must be closed.

Colorful Crusaders

The battle for saloon closure, and ultimately national Prohibition, was carried to the public by a colorful cast of crusaders. Their dramatically captivating speaking skills and outrageous activities held the evils of drinking foremost in the minds and hearts of righteous Americans. Some of the most zealous individuals included politician William Jennings Bryan, Billy Sunday, Carry A. Nation, and Pussyfoot Johnson.

William Jennings Bryan grew up in an Illinois home where liquor was forbidden. As a young man and college student in the late 1870s and early 1880s he praised temperance and tried to convert all around him to give up drinking. He cooled his fever somewhat when he ran as the Democratic candidate for President in 1896, 1900, and 1908 but still quietly denounced saloons. Defeated in all three attempts he again became an all out advocate of Prohibition. He served as President Woodrow Wilson's (1913–1921) Secretary of State in 1913 and banned all drinks but water and grape juice at diplomatic functions. His personal example provided a strong role model for the drys.

Of all the orators that railed against liquor, Billy Sunday drew the largest audiences. Shaping and directing public opinion to despise the dirty, rotten, stinking liquor industry, he worked religious revival meetings of thousands into hysteria. Born in Iowa in 1862 Sunday was turned over to an orphanage after his father died in the Civil War. As a young man his outstanding sandlot baseball skills earned him a job in the major leagues with the Chicago White Sox. One Sunday afternoon he got drunk with his buddies at a Chicago saloon after a baseball game. Across the street was an outdoor preacher with his band playing hymns. One of the band members, thinking Sunday was a drunkard, invited him to a mission meeting. On a lark Sunday went, but it ended up changing his life forever. Sunday left his buddies, went to the mission and quit drinking. By 1896 Sunday began conducting revival meetings in large eastern cities where he denounced drunkards and all businesses that make men drunkards. Drenched with sweat Sunday would pound his feet, stride back and forth on the podium, and roar with outrage. Quickly gaining national prominence, he traveled with up to 50 advance men, a choir director Homer A. Rodeheaver, an army of musicians, and even carpenters to build the giant, temporary wooden "tabernacles" in which the revivals were held. In 1903 he was ordained a Presbyterian minister and continued his ministry. Sunday conducted at least 300 revivals reaching hundreds of thousands.

Almost six feet tall, Carry Amelia Moore Nation was the best known and most radically daunting figure of the temperance movement. She probably did more than any other single individual to keep the nation focused on the evils of saloons. Nation's family had a history of mental instability; for example, her mother became convinced she was the Queen of England. Carry blamed all her personal troubles on liquor including the mental illness of her grandmother, mother, and cousins. From childhood Carry was subject to wild dreams and hallucinations.

Carry's first husband died a helpless drunkard, and until her mid-fifties Carry lived in Medicine Lodge, Kansas, with her second husband, David Nation, who did not drink. Kansas, Maine, and North Dakota were the only states where statewide Prohibition was in effect in 1899. Carry again had wild dreams of fighting hand to hand with the devil and speaking directly with God who instructed her to destroy saloons. Since all of the drinking places in Kansas were illegal she believed she and other citizens had a perfect right to destroy them. In 1899 she started a prayer Crusade patterned after the Woman's Crusade of the 1870s. With the help of other members of her local WCTU she closed down the saloons in Medicine Lodge. Within the year Carry's tactics turned more drastic. Carry and friends marched toward the chosen saloon or "joint" of the day singing "Onward, Christian Soldiers," as they concealed clubs, iron scraps, bricks, and stones under their long cloaks. A towering figure in black, Carry burst through saloon doors, stood in the middle of the floor and challenged anyone to stop what she and her companions were about to do. Raising her shining hatchet she would proceed to destroy row after row of liquor bottles. Her

Patrons of Sloppy Joe's bar in Chicago, Illinois, gather to celebrate on the day Prohibition was officially repealed, December 5, 1933. (© Hulton Archive/Getty Images. Reproduced by permission.)

companions wreaked similar havoc destroying every object that could be smashed in the saloon. Nation spent approximately three years between 1899 and 1902 carrying out her fiery anti-saloon crusade. She was widely admired but at the same time publicly criticized for her unusual tactics. Nevertheless replicas of her hatchet, inscribed "Carry Nation, Joint Smasher," sold by the thousands. Nation even suggested divine guidance for her mission was apparent from her name, Carry (misspelled with a "y" instead of "ie" by her father at her birth) A. Nation.

William Eugene Johnson, "Pussyfoot" Johnson, was appointed by the Commissioner of Indian Affairs in 1906 to clean up the lawlessness in the Indian territories and Oklahoma, which was rampant with shootings, lynching, gambling and illegal liquor trade. In Wild West fashion with cowboy hat, long coat, and toting a rifle, Johnson in town after town cleaned out bootleggers peddling whiskey to Indian reservations. He was Uncle Sam's "Booze Buster." Promoted to Chief Special Officer of the Commission of Indian Affairs, Johnson with his men swept into Indian lands in New Mexico, Idaho, California, and Montana. By 1911 they accounted for six thousand arrests and had won Court convictions in most of the cases. When Johnson left government service his next venture was heading up the Anti-Saloon League's publishing plant. As the real battle for national Prohibition drew closer Johnson had a hand in fund raising, economic studies, organization of states, and publishing volumes of literature.

States Become Dry

The Anti-Saloon League carefully organized and built its political power base step by step. The base included voters and lawmakers from both parties, and as a result of these efforts a new wave of state Prohibition began with Georgia and Oklahoma in 1907. Mississippi and North Carolina followed in 1908 as did Tennessee in 1909 and West Virginia in 1912. Virginia, Oregon, Washington, Colorado, and Arizona all were dry by the end of 1914. The Prohibition wave continued in the states with four to five states becoming dry in 1915, 1916, 1917, and 1918. By 1919 a grand total of 34 states were dry.

Those wets in dry states did not complain too much at first for liquor could still be freely obtained through the mail. Post wagons increasingly clinked, jangled, and sloshed as they made appointed rounds. The drys were infuriated by this, and in 1913 the ASL drew up a proposed law as a solution. Senator William Kenyon of Iowa and Representative Edwin Webb of North Carolina introduced the legislation in Congress. The Webb-Kenyon bill passed by a large margin but President William Howard Taft (served 1909–1913) vetoed it. Congress stood with the ASL and overrode the veto. The Act became known as the Interstate Liquor Act prohibiting the shipment of alcohol into dry states. In December 1913 five thousand men and women of the ASL and WCTU paraded up Pennsylvania Avenue in Washington, DC, demanding a saloon free nation by 1920.

The marchers asked Congress to pass a Constitution Prohibition amendment for submission to the states for ratification. Senator Morris Sheppard of Texas and Representative Richmond P. Hobson of Alabama introduced the ASL's resolution to Congress where it stayed in committee for a year. Passage of an amendment resolution requires two-thirds majority in both the Senate and House of Representatives. Meanwhile in 1914 the ASL sent approximately 50,000 trained speakers, volunteers, and regular members into every village, town, and city to attack the wets and influence Congressional elections of 1914. The November 1914 election returns revealed a major gain

in seats for the drys. Although fully aware they did not have the two-thirds majority, the dry legislators took the Hobson/Prohibition Resolution out of the Judiciary Committee. The first full debate in the U.S. House of Representatives over whether Prohibition should be part of the Constitution commenced. When a vote was taken 197 voted in favor of Prohibition and 190 voted against it. The ASL had demonstrated its power and would not try again until it was positive it had the votes to carry an amendment. The increasingly powerful ASL appeared to control the outcome of the 1916 Congressional elections. Candidates were afraid to challenge the ASL for it meant sure political suicide. Enough dry votes appeared to be within the incoming 1917 Congress to pass a resolution to add a Prohibition amendment to the Constitution.

Entry Into World War I

As the United States prepared to enter World War I in 1917 the ASL attempted to make the public view Prohibition as an act of patriotism. For example many brewers were German Americans, and after America entered into the war in 1917, hatred of everything German became a national frenzy. The drys began an unrelenting campaign of propaganda to paint beer as un-American. Saloons were cast as harboring enemy agents and it was rumored that beer for American consumption might be poisoned. ASL members claimed that large brewing industries were anti-American and promoted German culture in the United States. Another dry argument claimed the brewery and distillery industry employed thousands of men that could instead be helping in jobs related to the war effort. Also trucks and trains used to distribute liquor should be used for the transportation of war materials. Drys put forth yet another patriotic argument claiming grain used to make alcohol could provide millions of loaves of bread to feed the troops.

At the end of July 1917 after thirteen hours of debate over three days the Senate passed the Eighteenth Amendment by a vote of 65 to 20. By the time the Amendment reached the House of Representatives, the Congressmen, consumed with war issues, were tired of the pressure of the ASL and voters back home. After only six hours of debate the House voted 282 to 128 to submit the Eighteenth Amendment to the states for ratification. The Eighteenth Amendment would need a majority vote in both houses of the 36 state legislatures to be ratified and added to the U.S. Constitution. The state ratification process turned out to be no battle at all. The ASL had been working and influencing lawmakers in every state capital for years.

On January 16, 1919, the Secretary of State announced that the required number of states, 36, had ratified the Amendment and it would become part of the U.S. Constitution on January 16, 1920. Within the next three years twelve more states ratified. Eighty percent of the members of all state legislatures in the country had voted in favor of Prohibition. Only two states failed to ratify, Connecticut and Rhode Island.

A flaw of the Eighteenth Amendment was that it included no clause against the purchase of alcohol. Without breaking the law Americans were still perfectly free to buy liquor and keep it at home. The seller, if caught, could be thrown in jail, a fact that meant nothing to the purchaser. To ensure Prohibition could be adequately enforced a law would have to be created that did not violate other parts of the Constitution concerning search and seizure of homes and personal belongings but that prevented the purchase of alcohol. Realizing this deficiency, Attorney Wayne Wheeler of the ASL had been working for months before ratification to draw a draft of enforcement laws acceptable to Prohibitionists. He, along with input from a special ASL committee and those already experienced with matters in the dry states, produced the National Prohibition Act. The Act was given to ultra-dry House Judiciary Chairman Andrew J. Volstead of Minnesota who introduced it into the House in May 1919. The act became known as the Volstead Act. The ASL anticipated and prepared for a hard fight in both the House and Senate but wets were so disorganized and disillusioned that they offered little resistance. With only a few changes and little debate the Act sailed through both the House and Senate in October 1919. The Volstead Act prohibited the manufacture, sale, barter, transport, import, export, delivery, or illegal possession of any intoxicating beverage. It would not take effect for one year allowing the liquor industry to wind up business. The term "intoxicating" was defined as one-half of one percent of alcohol by volume. For example one hundred ounces of a beverage could contain no more than one-half ounce of alcohol or it would be considered intoxicating. Beer normally contained three to seven percent, alcohol and wine, up to 15 percent; therefore both fell under Prohibition. Special permits were allowed for the manufacture of industrial alcohol and alcohol for medicinal and religious use.

The Noble Experiment: National Prohibition Begins

Americans viewed January 17, 1920, the day the Eighteenth Amendment would take effect throughout America, with either great anticipation or great resig-

nation. Drys believed the start of Prohibition promised a cure to poverty, crime, and corruption. They expected it would be the fulfillment of a dream for a more perfect, healthy, happy, and prosperous nation. America would forever be free from the "demon rum." Since Prohibition had become part of the U.S. Constitution, drys were convinced it would remain the law of the land. Prohibition, the noble experiment, had begun.

Most every town in America had a chapter of the Women's Christian Temperance Union (WCTU) and they held night watch services in churches to ring in the victory. Prominent Prohibitionists attended a service in Washington, DC, and cheered along to a rousing speech by William Jennings Bryan, politician and inspirational orator for the cause. The Anti-Saloon League of New York wished everyone, everywhere a "Happy Dry Year." In San Francisco amid festive ceremonies, a WCTU official described Prohibition as "God's present to the nation" (Asbury, p. 143). In Chicago the WCTU glorified in the victory, announced it would now proceed to dry up the rest of the world. Billy Sunday, fiery evangelist, entertained a crowd of ten thousand in Norfolk Virginia, with a mock funeral service for John Barleycorn, fictional model of the drinking man.

The wets greeted Prohibition with resignation. Since the ratification of the Eighteenth Amendment in January 1919 anyone who could afford it had been feverishly buying and storing whiskey and other liquor. No one ever knew just how much had been squirreled away but large cities like New York, Chicago, and San Francisco reported that trucks, automobiles, and vans transported liquor all over the cities throughout 1919.

As the fateful hour of 12:01 AM January 17, 1920, neared officials in most cities braced for what they thought would be a last night fling—a drunken orgy of sorts. But the binge in saloons, restaurants, and hotels failed to occur. Police were stationed in all the well-known drinking places to seize all liquor on tables at midnight. Yet the night proved very tame, even in the wettest cities of New York, Chicago, San Francisco, Boston, Detroit, Baltimore, Philadelphia, and Louisville. In New York City's Delta Robbia Room of the Hotel Vanderbilt cases of fine champagne were served free to guests at midnight. In Washington, DC, bars between the Capitol and White House on Pennsylvania Avenue stayed crowded all day and evening. When midnight struck customers made final toasts and went home. Of course in New Orleans, Prohibition was simply ignored that night and every night thereafter. Nevertheless for 99.9 percent of the United

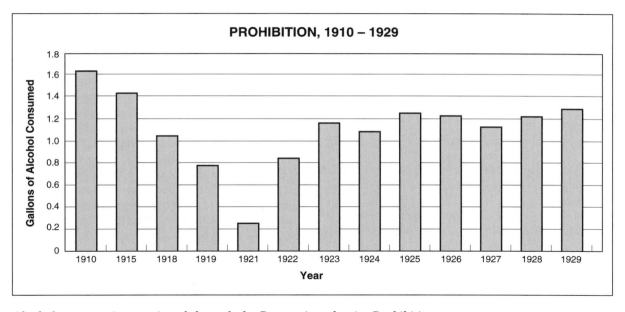

PROHIBITION, 1910 – 1929

Alcohol consumption continued through the Depression, despite Prohibition. (*The Gale Group.*)

States the forces of righteousness were completely convinced that a new age of clean living and clean thinking had begun.

No One Will Violate Prohibition

Prohibitionists believed the enforcement laws of the Volstead Act would be easily instituted and that wets, obeying the law, would gracefully accept the inevitability of Prohibition. A revenue agent, Colonel Daniel Porter of New York, observed the penalties provided by the Volstead Act were so severe, a fine up to one thousand dollars and imprisonment up to six months for the first offense, that no one would attempt to break the law. Prohibitionists assured the American people that all remained to be done was a simple mop up operation. All were quite wrong.

Nevertheless Americans had been indoctrinated with the idea that the destruction of liquor traffic was the will of God and would cure all the problems of mankind. They were bound to try it.

There were some, however, that doubted Prohibition would work, and during debate in Congress a few senators and representatives feared in practicality it could not work. Former President William Howard Taft prophetically stated that the business of manufacturing liquor would fall out of the hands of law abiding citizens into the criminal element. He believed there were large numbers of communities where a majority of residents would refuse to go along.

Foretelling the challenge of what was to come, less than an hour after Prohibition begun a gang of six masked men bound and gagged the yardmaster and watchman in a Chicago rail yard. They proceeded to round up other trainmen then hijacked $100,000 worth of medicinal liquor from freight cars. Within the week over one hundred other large thefts were reported including from government warehouses where liquor was stored.

During the first year of Prohibition problems with enforcement multiplied rapidly. Within months raids on stills had increased one thousand percent. Saloons and barrooms simply went on behind closed doors, became known as speakeasies, and went right on serving liquor, obtained illegally. In Chicago as in the rest of the country doctors issues thousands of fake prescriptions for whiskey. Courts became clogged with thousands of Volstead Act violations. People of wealth and influence frequently failed to set examples of compliance with Prohibition. Liquor stashes were found with delegations to the Republican National Convention in Chicago and the Democratic National Convention in San Francisco.

Drys generally ignored the trend and continued making optimistic statements and enforcement officials hoped things would get better. Congress hesitated to appropriate more money having been told few dollars would be needed to force compliance with Prohibition. No one really believed the "noble experiment" would fail.

More About...

Izzy Einstein and Moe Smith

The most publicized, colorful federal agents to attempt enforcement of Prohibition were the New York based team of Izzy Einstein and Moe Smith. Between them in four years they made over four thousand arrests and hauled in more than fifteen million dollars worth of liquor. Newspapers and magazines kept running accounts of their exploits.

Izzy and Moe were masters of disguise—musicians, pushcart vendors, streetcar conductors, opera singers or German Beer Garden singers—whatever it took to get the information they needed or set a trap for an unsuspecting speakeasy manager. They posed as deliverymen or even offered Thanksgiving turkeys. When thanked with a refreshing alcoholic beverage, they arrested their server. Izzy and Moe shut down an average of twenty places a week. Their sport was chasing bootleggers. Although the public laughed, some Prohibition Bureau officials became disgruntled at Izzy and Moe's clowning with serious law enforcement. When Izzy and Moe left their government jobs they both became successful life insurance salesmen.

Within the first year it became apparent that many Americans did not feel obligated to stop drinking the moment Prohibition became part of the U.S. Constitution. Although the precise degree of compliance with the law was difficult to access, polls indicated that at least one third of the adult population abstained, but Prohibition did not stop anyone who wanted to drink. As soon as saloons were outlawed and liquor made illegal and comparatively more difficult to get, it seemed everyone who wanted it was determined to have it. The forbidden beverages became irresistible for many. Judging from the demand the supplies stored away before Prohibition began must have dwindled rapidly. In response to consumer demand a variety of sources provided at first a small amount then later a flowing torrent of alcoholic beverages.

Where Did the Liquor Come From?

The great majority of alcohol came from illegal stills. The stills, large and small, spread by the hundreds of thousands across the country. During the first five years of Prohibition federal agents seized approximately 697,000 stills but admitted there were nine more operating for every one they shut down. Stills were in remote areas, in villages, towns, and cities. Hill country moonshiners got their names from working mainly at night by the light of the moon. Many stills were family operations set in basements, in tenement buildings, behind stores, and in old warehouses. After only a few years organized gangs began taking over alcohol makers' operations. Many were too small for gangs to bother with but others became part of the gang networks. Many still owners had to pay off the gangsters to protect their deliveries of alcohol to customers. Organized gangs also operated their own large distilleries and paid off enforcement agents, police, and politicians to look the other way. Prohibition defined the future of organized crime, which, overseen by the likes of Al Capone, was established and immensely wealthy by the late 1920s.

Pre-Prohibition real whiskey was made from mashes of various grains, mostly barley. The grains were allowed to ferment naturally, and no actual sugar was ever used. Real whiskey came out of the still pure white and took on its color and flavor only after aging in oak barrels for four to eight years. The illegal stills of the 1920s turned out cheap raw alcohol, not whiskey, made from a blend of sugar, water, yeast and any fermentable food scraps available, often from garbage scraps.

The second largest source of illegal alcohol for making false whiskey and gin came from the industrial chemical industry. Tremendous industrial growth after World War I led to the expansion of factories that required alcohol for manufacture of their products as medicines; candy, spices, extracts, cosmetics, insecticides, soap, and photography supplies. The Volstead Act allowed industrial alcohol to be manufactured by licensed distilleries. Industrial alcohol was "denatured" or made unfit for human consumption by adding any of some 76 substances, some of them strong poisons. To get a permit to buy the industrial alcohol, applicants simply had to show they had a use for it. Thousands of new chemical companies, many backed by bootleggers and gangs, sprang up but they never manufactured anything at all. They withdrew all the industrial alcohol their permits would allow and stored it until it was sent to "cleaning plants" where attempts were made to clean it and convert it back to pure alcohol fit for human consumption. The danger of course was in all the additives that could not be removed, leaving substances that made consumers very ill or that were deadly.

A third source of liquor was smuggled liquor, which was brought in to the country from boats anchored just beyond the U.S. jurisdiction, 12 miles out from the U.S. Eastern Shore. The rows of anchored boats became known as Rum Row. The boats brought liquor that had been imported from Britain, or from two tiny French islands, St. Pierre and Miquelon, off the coast of Newfoundland that imported 118,600 gallons of British liquor in 1922. Considering the islands only had 6,000 residents, this was a sizeable amount of liquor. Boats laden with spirits obtained predominantly from Canada were likewise anchored off the Pacific coasts. On both coasts some of the boats catered only to the professional bootlegger affiliated with organized crime, while others sold by the case to anyone who motored out. Not surprisingly the rental of motorboats greatly increased during Prohibition.

Smugglers bringing liquor into the United States by way of land from Canada or Mexico had some advantages over smuggling on the high seas. Rum ships had to approach the United States from a limited number of routes, while the routes by land were numerous. An estimated 650 roads and trails led from Canada into the United States and one fourth as many led from Mexico into the U.S. American organized crime units operating out of Canada could draw from the legal production of Canadian distilleries and breweries which increased production dramatically. Smugglers ran boats into the United States by way of the Great Lakes, St. Lawrence and Detroit rivers, and Lake Champlain. Mescal and Tequila rather than American type liquor came from Mexico. In both Canada and Mexico liquor was a legal commodity and did not become illegal until it crossed the U.S. border. Although it took approximately two years for Rum Row to be fully operational smuggling at the borders began immediately. It was impossible for Customs Service agents on land and the Coast Guard on waterways to maintain watches at more than a few places. With almost nothing to stop them fast boats raced across lakes and rivers, cars and trucks sped over border roads, horses and mules lumbered across trails, all carrying loads of liquor. By far the greatest quantity of liquor from Canada came aboard fast boats— some could carry one thousand cases at a crossing. In the mid-1920s officials estimated eight hundred to 1,500 rum boats traveled the Great Lakes. In winter boats were put on skis and pulled by cars across the frozen lakes. Only very old cars were used in case they broke through the ice and sank. More liquor landed at Detroit docks than in any other border city. The *Detroit News* in 1928 reported $35,000,000 worth of liquor came in to the United States through Detroit. Gangs made estimated payments of over two million dollars in pay-off money to Detroit officials alone.

In October 1921 the first airplane loaded with liquor left Winnipeg, Canada, for the United States. By 1930 sixty planes a month headed for landings in the U.S. Midwest. Rail cars were also employed in the liquor smuggling, and a common route ran from Buffalo, New York through Canada to Detroit. Even American tourists and Canadians visiting the United States wore coats and suits with many pockets to fill with pint bottles. Even congressmen were persistent smugglers from their overseas trips.

Amusing stories developed of smugglers bringing cartons of eggs, with blown-out eggs filled with whiskey. Life preservers filled with liquor containers if used to save a life would instead cause the person to sink. Wild stories developed such as the unsubstantiated tale that torpedoes filled with liquor roared through the Detroit River between Windsor, Ontario and Detroit each night.

Yet another source of liquor originated from government storehouses intended for medicinal use only. By 1926 one half to two thirds of the original supply had been removed by various means. The plan was for liquor to be released to wholesalers who in turn sold it to drugstores. Physicians could write a prescription for one quart of whiskey per patient per month. Almost anyone could get a prescription for a two-dollar office call fee. There were also thousands of false prescriptions with doctors' names forged. All involved wholesalers, physicians, and druggists had to be licensed. The Prohibition Bureau gave permits to an average of 63,891 doctors annually, and by 1929 over one hundred thousand permits were in force. The physicians wrote over 11 million prescriptions per year.

Some of the big bootleg gangs used more direct methods to take liquor from warehouses. George Remus, a Chicago lawyer became one of the most successful liquor dealers in the country. He bought distilleries in Kentucky, Ohio, and Missouri and thus became the legal owner of whatever whiskey was stored away in warehouses. After bribing any official that might conceivably get in his way he removed liquor at night with trucks and then transported it by railroad.

Whether the basic alcohol was moonshine alcohol, industrial alcohol, or real liquor smuggled into the United States or out of warehouses, all went to "cutting plants." There the cheap alcohol or real whiskey was diluted with water, then colored and flavored. To give it punch, or "bead," various chemicals were added such as glycerin, iodine, or even embalming fluid. Customers always looked for the fiery "bead" which they assumed was a sure sign of fine aged whiskey.

At the cutting plants, one case of alcohol or whiskey became three to five cases each bringing $50 to $70. Some bootleggers did their own cutting but most work was carried on in large plants in building basements or country hideaways. Thousands of cutting plants existed across the country. The *Detroit News* reported at least 150 in the city in 1928, most running full blast on three shifts each. Cleveland, Buffalo, St. Louis, New Orleans, San Francisco, and Los Angeles, all had at least as many operating as Detroit. An estimated five hundred to one thousand operated in New York, Philadelphia, and Chicago. Large cutting plants were well protected by payoffs to officials and politicians.

The Real McCoy and Rum Row

At the onset of Prohibition in 1920 Bill McCoy was a boat builder in Jacksonville, Florida. One spring day a fellow in a fancy car drove up to the boatyard and offered McCoy $100 a day to sail from Nassau in the British Bahamas Islands to Atlantic City with a cargo of whiskey. McCoy turned him down but an idea had been planted in his mind. He immediately sold his boatyard business, and with the proceeds he bought a boat that could hold three thousand cases of liquor and began making trips from the Bahamas into remote southern locations. Carrying only genuine Scotch whiskey bought cheap in Nassau, McCoy soon learned that more money could be made selling the alcohol further up the coast in New York. After all, he was selling "the real McCoy!" Anchoring off the Long Island Coast beyond what was then the three-mile limit, McCoy sold to dozens of bootleggers who met him in small boats, and within hours of his arrival his entire cargo would be sold. McCoy made one voyage a month evading the Coast Guard for three years eventually delivering an estimated three million dollars of real liquor. He set a pattern that was mimicked by others, and soon a flotilla of hundreds of boats calling themselves Rum Row, lined up off the New England coast all supplying liquor to bootleggers who took it to shore for distribution. The term "rum" was a romantic holdover from rum smuggling in the 1700s and from the Prohibitionists' habit of referring to all liquor as the "demon rum." Actually, most rumrunners carried whiskey not rum. Keeping Rum Row well supplied, British exports of liquor to the Bahamas increased dramatically. For example Britain exported 944 gallons to the islands in 1918 but 386,000 gallons in 1922. Likewise the British exported 118,600 gallons of liquor to the tiny French islands off the coast of

Newfoundland in 1922, which was quite a supply of liquor for an island population of six thousand.

After long negotiations the United States won an agreement with Britain and other foreign countries to push Rum Row to twelve miles from shore. All this accomplished in the government's fruitless war on rum running was to drive the individual bootleggers in their small boats out of business. It strengthened gangster control of bootlegging since the gangster syndicates had the large fast boats.

The quality of goods actually reaching customers began to fall precipitously because bootleggers took the real imported whiskey and greatly diluted it so that one case of liquor became five cases. Out at sea most rum running boats now had holds full of cheap alcohol instead of real imported whiskey. They had full bottling and labeling operations on board and filled "custom" orders from the bootleggers. Bootleggers could order just what type of liquor they needed. To fill an order the on-board crew added appropriate coloring to the alcohol, bottled it with a label of a real brand, then dipped the bottles in saltwater to give them that "just off the boat" appearance. Thirsty Americans paid millions for the bootlegged whiskey but rarely was it ever again the "real McCoy."

Near Beer

Beer freely flowed through the biggest hole in the Volstead Act. Although all breweries were suppose to close down they could reopen with permits as "cereal beverage" plants which meant they could produce beer that contained not more than one-half of one percent alcohol or a beverage called "near-beer." The catch was the only way to make near-beer was to first make real beer in the usual way then draw off alcohol until the beer reached the legal percentage of alcohol. Not surprisingly that second step was often left out. Prohibition agents could do nothing as long as it remained in the brewery since breweries could say it was awaiting the final step. Then when no agents were aground, trucks rolled out carrying the real beer. Agents were frequently paid protection money to be sure all officials looked the other way as trucks left to deliver the beer.

Made at Home

Although some wineries were allowed to go right on producing wines for sacramental religious use, the Volstead Act also allowed making fruit juices and cider at home. The maker was supposed to stop the process before fermentation took place. Pamphlets were published instructing makers to be careful and told them what not to do, otherwise they would have wine in 60

Beer was one of the first types of alcohol allowed to be manufactured and sold by the end of Prohibition.
(AP/Wide World Photos. Reproduced by permission.)

days. Not surprisingly juice-makers often made just the mistakes warned against and ended up with wine.

Americans could learn everything they needed to know at any library where books and magazines described methods of distilling alcohol in ordinary kitchen utensils such as coffee percolators or teakettles. Almost immediately after Prohibition began stores sprang up selling hops (from grain which beer is made), yeast, corn, meal, grains, and all the apparatus for home brewing or home distilling. Ready to use stills, of one to five gallon capacity, were available for sale. Different flavorings such as imitation rye, bourbon, or scotch were sold. At times the family bathtub would be filled with water and alcohol purchased from a bootlegger, and by adding a few drops of juniper oil "bathtub gin" was ready. Drunk with juices or ginger ale the concoctions were quite passable. Once the knowledge of making liquor, beer, or wine was widespread little could be done to halt the process. Millions of Americans were breaking the law

At a Glance

Prohibition Might Have Worked If....

Some historians believe Prohibition, making America a clean, healthy, more perfect nation might have worked if the Anti-Saloon League had not gotten so greedy. Perhaps generation after generation of abstainers and moderate drinkers might have been created if people had been allowed to continue to obtain mail order liquor as they could before the 1913 Interstate Liquor Act. Or perhaps Prohibition might have been accepted if the term "intoxicating liquors" was left to mean whiskey, rum, and other distilled spirits that were between 40 and 90 percent alcohol. Many who supported the Eighteenth Amendment had done so with this definition in mind. They assumed beer and wine, with some restrictions, would be permitted. When the Volstead Act, banning beer and wine also, passed many Americans felt betrayed. If Americans had still been able to have their beer and wine they might have given up the hard liquor.

and no force could reach into all homes to stop them. Before Prohibition nearly all heavy drinking was done in saloons, restaurants, cafes, and cabarets, however, during Prohibition drinking became commonplace mainly in homes. The lemonade pitcher, formerly holding the beverage of choice for guests, might now be filled with gin. Home liquor cabinets were often elaborately concealed in case they should be raided.

Speakeasies

The major watering holes outside the home were the speakeasies. Saloons had merely gone behind closed doors and resurfaced as speakeasies. The name was derived from the fact many "speaks" required an entering individual to speak an easy code word or phrase such as, "Joe sent me," and some issued official looking cards to patrons. According to various estimates New York City's 16,000 saloons grew to at least 33,000 speakeasies. Across the nation several hundred thousand speakeasies gaily served drink after drink. If agents raided a speak and arrested its bartender another bartender quickly took over and the speak was generally reopened the very same night.

To almost everyone's horror except the women, speaks catered to men as well as women. Many American women began drinking as soon as liquor became illegal. Before the Eighteenth Amendment a nice girl would never think of taking a drink and the boy that did owed his hostess an apology.

A National Pastime

In 1920 alcohol became a symbol of independence, sophistication, romance and adventure. Young people began to carry flasks and if a boy took a girl out on a date without offering her alcohol he was considered a "drip." Getting "plastered" seemed to be a national goal, and rarely was a college fraternity party planned without alcohol. Upper middle class Americans dealt with their favorite bootlegger who delivered liquor directly to their homes.

Breaking the law seemed to have become a national pastime, perhaps surpassing baseball as Americans' favorite game. Otherwise law-abiding citizens had great fun devising ways to break the law. Undermanned and poorly equipped, government agencies had the impossible task of trying to dry up America and also keep it dry.

Impact

After repeal of the Eighteenth Amendment, liquor regulation once again became the responsibility of local and state government. A flurry of experimenting with controls led to a few outrageous debates such as: should people stand or be required to sit while they drank and could establishments allow their patrons to be seen through the windows? Before long most areas settled down to well-enforced controls and regulations. The obsessive discussions during Prohibition concerning public and private drinking ceased. The basic forms of liquor control were government control of liquor sales through systems of licenses, taxes, and regulations such as location, hours of operation, and advertising. Some states decided on sales of liquor only through state liquor stores while a few continued Prohibition. Eight states prohibited the sale of hard liquor in 1936 but by the end of the 1930s most lifted Prohibition. Kansas kept Prohibition in place until 1948, Oklahoma until 1957, and Mississippi until 1966. Most states allowed a local option to ban liquor if a certain community so desired. In those states certain localities were "wet" and others were "dry" depending on what the voters of the area wished. As of 2000 wet and dry sections within a single metropolitan area still existed in a few locations such as Dallas, Texas.

During World War II (1939–1945) the brewing trade was viewed as a vital war industry for both civilian and military morale. Brewery workers were even given draft deferments. This point of view contrasted dramatically with the hostility directed at the brewing industry in World War I. During World War II, however, fifteen percent of beer produced was reserved for the military.

By 1940 all states had laws barring the old style saloon, and with the introduction of electric refrigeration and canned beer in the 1930s, a central drinking place lost some of its importance. Both men and women drank together at private parties, restaurants, bars, and at nightclubs that became symbols of ultimate sophistication. By the mid-twentieth century public drinking was only another form of entertainment, with alcohol once more becoming acceptable in the mainstream of American life.

From a legislative standpoint reformers and legislators recognized that laws must be voluntarily accepted by a vast majority of those affected in order to succeed. Enforcing a widely unpopular law upon an uncooperative populace proved to be a disaster. Lawmakers became resistant to try and reshape moral behavior with legislation. The New Deal set a pattern of dealing with improving economic, social and political opportunities but did not attempt to alter Americans' wants or desires. The failure of national Prohibition closed the door on future national attempts to legislate abstinence, moreover legislators accepted that ordinary legislation should not be placed in the Constitution.

One lasting legacy of Prohibition was highly powerful and immensely wealthy organized crime syndicates. Drug trafficking proved to be a natural extension of bootlegging. Again it supplied a demand of an illegal substance desired by the public. During Prohibition government enforcers seized only five percent of liquor illegally entering the United States. Drug enforcement agencies reportedly seize no more than ten percent of illegal drugs coming into the United States. Over half of America's prison population at the close of the twentieth century was jailed on drug charges. By 2000 trafficking in illegal drugs and dealing with its enormous monetary proceeds were organized crime's biggest businesses.

With the end of Prohibition all individuals did not immediately drink only in moderation. Excessive drinking or alcoholism began to be viewed as a disease. Most people drank alcohol responsibly, but a minority was unable to control their drinking. Groups such as Alcoholics Anonymous formed and their members, all alcoholics, sought to help one another

through to abstinence. Statistics show that alcohol consumption in America in 1990s was 2.8 gallons yearly of pure alcohol per person in the drinking age population. This was above consumption in the 1911 to 1915 pre-Prohibition level of 2.56 gallons. The youthful culture was given to underage drinking and binge drinking, which is characterized by consumption of a large quantity of alcohol (usually six or more drinks) in a few hours, a few times a week. In 1996 there were 17,126 highway deaths from alcohol related accidents. Mothers Against Drunk Driving (MADD) since 1980 has pushed for stronger penalties against drunk drivers. "Designated driver" programs, where one partygoer pledges not to drink and be the driver for the group, have been emphasized throughout the nation. The concern for health and safety of young people echoes back to the underlying reasons for America's Prohibition years.

Perspectives

Early to Mid-1920s

Advocates of Prohibition in the early 1920s did not want to just reduce alcohol consumption but wanted to eliminate it completely as part of the American lifestyle. They envisioned Prohibition as the centerpiece of a healthy, wealthy, law abiding and unified nation. The values of the Women's Christian Temperance Union (WCTU) and the Anti-Saloon League (ASL) were formed in the late nineteenth century. Those values were based on faith in God, duty, self-denial, a strict social code, and protection of family. Prohibition seemed a necessary reform, and few doubted that, after a few years of trial enforcement of Prohibition, alcohol would cease to be a problem. The drys tended to ignore the growing lawless pattern, while federal officials presumed things would get better, and Congress was reluctant to appropriate more money for enforcement so as not to annoy voters.

In contrast a growing worldly consumer culture of the 1920s focused on youth, entertainment, and self-fulfillment. Where the saloons of the late nineteenth century and early twentieth century had greatly offended the values of the middle class, the Prohibition speakeasies supplied a hint of mischievous adventure and enjoyment to the modern sophisticated 1920s middle class. More and more of these citizens began to view the Eighteenth Amendment as a social mistake and violation of personal liberties.

Both wets and drys at the turn of the century had expected women, once they had the right to vote, to form a powerful bloc of dry voters. This proved not

At a Glance
The Alcoholic Blues

Broadway Music Corporation, 1919

The beginning of Prohibition was put to words in this popular song. Its chorus:

> I've got the blues, I've got the blues
> I've got the alcoholic blues.
> No more beer my heart to cheer.
> Goodbye whiskey, you used to make me frisky
> So long high ball, so long gin.
> Oh, tell me when you're comin' back again.

Source: www.mainehistory.org

to be the case. Women, just as men, demonstrated a wide variety of opinions on Prohibition. Unlike saloons, speakeasies welcomed women and women indeed came. Men and women drinking together became a popular social gathering.

College students, both male and female, also rather enjoyed the adventure of procuring alcohol, whether it was the less expensive domestic liquor or a more expensive "imported" liquor, and it was a social must to show up at parties with a flask. Of course there was always the chance a policeman might show up also but it was all part of the game. Plenty of bootleggers near college campuses kept the pocket flasks in raccoon coats and the garter-held flasks, well supplied. Drinking forbidden liquor was an act of bravado and evading the Volstead Act became a national sport among young adults.

At home, brews became family pastimes. Considerable time was spent discussing what brands of malt and yeast to buy for the home brew and how much sugar to add. Most of the otherwise law-abiding citizens looked on their home brews as only slightly illegal. The upper middle class, businessmen, and professionals could afford the expensive liquor at speakeasies or dealt with personal bootleggers who made home deliveries. More and more individuals routinely ignored Prohibition as the decade moved on.

Immigrants from European countries regarded drinking of alcoholic beverages as a normal part of everyday life. Alcohol was not regarded as a means

to drunkenness rather it was drunk for enjoyment with most meals.

Despite growing disgruntlement with Prohibition, wets and drys alike believed any talk of repeal was a waste of time. Having Prohibition a part of the Constitution appeared to assure its continuance. Instead wets pushed for modification of the Volstead Act, particularly to allow the manufacture and sale of 2.75 percent beer.

Strong Anti-Prohibition Sentiments Develop

From its start, Prohibition had been strongly promoted as a reform that protected home and community from the influences of liquor. As the years went by, however, many Americans began to form the opinion that quite the opposite was occurring. Bootleggers became famous and organized crime groups became wealthier and more powerful by the day. Neighborhoods once considered respectable experienced shootouts. The public became outraged as increasing numbers of people died or became seriously ill or harmed from drinking bad bootlegged liquor. Moreover hundreds lost their lives or were injured in the violent gunplay of enforcement and gangster wars. Many viewed the U.S. government as responsible for creating the circumstances that caused injury and death to its own citizens. Daily news accounts of bribery and payoffs of enforcement officials, local police, politicians, mayors, governors, all dismayed the public. Americans who had supported Prohibition in 1919 began to view it as a failure. By 1926 many of those early Prohibitionists had shifted to supporting repeal.

The most strident opponents of Prohibition all along were writers, journalists, and intellectuals, who believed the government was trying to enforce a law that invaded millions of individuals' personal lives. While some newspapers came out by the late 1920s as wet proponents, many others remained timid to do so. In 1929 newspaper tycoon William Randolph Hearst stated his opposition to Prohibition. Hearst viewed it just as corrupting to women and children as it was to men and as the creator of a powerful criminal class. Once Hearst made his pronouncement the floodgates opened for paper after paper to endorse their approval of a repeal.

Many wealthy businessmen began to back repeal not only because they feared growing lawlessness but because they wanted to cut their taxes. Prohibition was costing the federal government an estimate loss of one half billion dollars a year in liquor tax revenues that would have been collected if liquor was legal, therefore business taxes were up to cover the loss. By 1926 more businessmen became active members of the

Association Against the Prohibition Amendment (AAPA). Likewise lawyers, realizing Prohibition had put an impossible burden on the Courts, formed the Voluntary Committee of Lawyers to work for repeal.

Other opponents charged that Prohibition violated states' rights. They believed liquor should be regulated by the states not the federal government. Still others claimed the dry movement had long been a front for racial and religious bigotry. In the south Prohibition was largely enforced against black Americans but not against whites. Many Protestants looked upon Roman Catholics, who tended to be more recent immigrants and drank as part of their European heritage, as useless drunkards. Labor leaders saw little of the changes promised by Prohibitionists, and slums and poverty still dominated many of the lives of laborers.

Women Make the Decisive Stand

Although by the late 1920s, repeal of the Eighteenth Amendment was supported by a number of groups for several different reasons, it was the women's influence on repeal that was decisive. Due to the fact that women had long been associated with Prohibition, support of its repeal by large numbers of women was surprising and carried considerable influence. Some of the nation's most prominent women devoted themselves to the repeal movement and formed the Women's Organization for National Prohibition Reform (WONPR) in 1929. Women exposed the moral problems that Prohibition had caused and linked repeal with protection of home, family and community. Women called on other women to battle the foe that threatened their ability to instill in their children a respect of the laws of the land. William H. Stayton, founder of the AAPA, observed that the women of WONPR had done more in only two years to bring about repeal than all the work done by men in the last decade.

Presidential Election of 1932

As Republicans gathered for the 1932 Presidential Convention considerable number of Republicans believed endorsing repeal of the Eighteenth Amendment was their only hope of victory, while others thought endorsement would bring disaster to the party. Republicans ended up with a confusing platform, it did not support appeal but spoke of retaining federal government gains in liquor control nevertheless allowing some sort of revision for states to gain more control. Whatever the issue, most found it to be unintelligible.

In contrast the Democratic Party's platform clearly stated they advocated repeal of the Eighteenth Amendment. Democratic presidential candidate Franklin D. Roosevelt, despite his wavering earlier in the decade, clearly threw his support behind repeal in 1932. In the American public's perspective the parties were in opposite camps. The Republican Party became identified as dry and the Democrats as wet.

Prohibition Internationally

Many countries had experimented with Prohibition through history. Ancient China, Japan, India, the Scandinavian countries, and Canada are all examples. Finland adopted then repealed Prohibition in roughly the same time period as the United States. Finland had tried to steer its population to beer that had a lower alcoholic content than liquor. Sweden tried to stem alcohol use by issuing liquor ration books to its citizens. These attempts, just as in the United States, have been short lived. Only a few Muslim countries maintain national Prohibition.

Notable People

Ella Boole (1858–1952). Ella Boole grew up in Ohio, was educated in public schools and graduated from the College of Wooster. Ella married William Hilliker Boole, a Methodist minister and in 1883 settled into a spartan home at a pastorate in Brooklyn, New York. She immediately became active in the New York Women's Christian Temperance Union (WCTU). In 1925 Boole was elected national president of WCTU. Running as a Prohibition party candidate she made three unsuccessful bids for the U.S. Senate in 1920, 1922, and 1926. During a 1928 Congressional Hearing on Prohibition Boole proclaimed, "I represent the women of America." Apparently disagreement with this comment led Pauline Sabin to form the Women's Organization or National Prohibition Reform (WONPR). Boole served as President of WCTU until 1933 and was head of the World WCTU from 1931 to 1946.

The du Pont brothers. The three du Pont brothers, Pierre (1870–1954), Irénée (1864–1935) and Lammot (1880–1952), belonged to the fourth American generation of du Ponts. The du Pont family had moved to Delaware in 1800 to escape the unrest in France. The brothers' ancestors founded a gunpowder manufacturing business that prospered. The brothers, however, greatly expanded the family business by diversifying their manufacturing to include many chemical products. The oldest, Pierre, a shrewd businessman, built their wealth into a vast fortune. Irénée often served as the spokesman for his quieter two brothers. Lammot, the youngest, would actively run the family business after Pierre and Irénée stepped down.

By the mid-1920s the du Pont brothers became increasingly concerned about national Prohibition. Irénée, firmly believing in temperance, expressed alarm that Prohibition had made drinking fashionable and that all liquor money flowed to corrupt officials and bootleggers. He felt legitimate businesses were being heavily taxed to make up for lost liquor tax revenues. Irénée and Lammot joined the Association Against the Prohibition Amendment (AAPA) and Pierre followed in 1925. Pierre was concerned with the lawlessness, threats to property rights, loss of local government, decision-making power, and the fact that Prohibition had not stopped excessive drinking. Having stepped down from the active leadership in Du Pont Company and General Motors by 1925 Pierre had plenty of time to devote to AAPA. Lammot, although still actively running the business, contributed generously to AAPA. The du Pont brothers, along with their business associate and close friend John J. Raskob, became so involved with the repeal movement that many Americans instantly thought of these men when they thought of repeal.

John J. Raskob (1879–1950). Born to poor immigrant parents in Lockport, New York, John Raskob was forced to support his mother, three brothers and a sister when his father died. Full of ambition, Raskob studied bookkeeping and stenography (writing in shorthand) and obtained a position as secretary to Pierre du Pont in 1902. The capable Raskob quickly rose to treasurer, then director and finally to vice-president of the du Pont Company. At the same time Raskob had invested in the struggling General Motors (GM) firm, while urging the du Ponts to do the same. Raskob and Pierre du Pont played a key role in restructuring GM. Raskob founded the General Motors Acceptance Corporation to allow Americans with modest incomes to buy cars with installment purchase (down payment, plus regular payments). As a loyal Democrat he served as the head of the Democratic National Committee from 1928 through Roosevelt's landslide victory in 1932.

Early in the 1920s Raskob became concerned with the developing lawlessness around the sale of illegal liquor. He joined the AAPA in 1922 and each year increased his monetary contributions. A Roman Catholic, Raskob worried about the country's disrespect for law officials and the effect it had on raising American children with proper values. He was also deeply disturbed at what he considered the federal government's intrusion into social affairs of his family and friends. Along with the du Pont brothers,

Raskob became an outspoken member of the AAPA and greatly influenced the repeal of the Eighteenth Amendment.

Just prior to repeal Raskob had headed a consortium that built the Empire State Building in New York. It opened in 1931 as a mighty symbol of optimism for Depression-fearful Americans.

Pauline Sabin (Mrs. Charles H. Sabin) (1887–1955). Born Pauline Morton of the famous salt company, Pauline was raised in a prosperous and highly political family. Her early life followed the path of fashionable education, marriage to a wealthy New York sportsman, J. Hopkins Smith, J., two sons, divorce, and owner of a profitable interior decorating shop. In 1916 she married Charles Hamilton Sabin, chairman of Guaranty Trust Company. The new Mrs. Sabin soon became involved in politics and helped found the women's National Republican Committee. When women were added to the Republican National Committee she became New York's first female representative.

Sabin's concern over Prohibition developed gradually. At first she supported the Eighteenth Amendment explaining she thought the world without alcohol would be a "beautiful world," however, the lawlessness and ineffectiveness of Prohibition soon began to change her mind. She also disdained the hypocrisy of politicians whom she observed voting for enforcement of Prohibition one hour and enjoying cocktails the next. But it appeared the "mother" in Sabin mainly put her on the road to fighting for repeal. In 1929, along with several other socially prominent friends, she founded the Women's Organization for National Prohibition Reform (WONPR). In less than a year 100,000 members were enrolled and 13 state branches were formed. The WONPR remained entirely apart from the AAPA of which Sabin's husband was a member. WONPR's appeal centered ironically on home protection just as the WCTU had in 1919 when the Eighteenth Amendment was first passed. Sabin explained that young women were working for repeal because they did not want their babies to grow up in the hipflask, speakeasy atmosphere that had polluted their own youth. By the 1932 presidential election the WONPR reportedly had 1.1 million members and when repeal was achieved in December 1933 over 1.5 million women were members. Among supporters for appeal, it was widely held that the women's movement for repeal was decisive in doing away with Prohibition.

Alfred E. Smith (1873–1944). Born in New York City, Al Smith grew up in the immigrant Irish-Catholic world—hardworking, Democratic and devoutly

The headline of the New York Daily Mirror on December 6, 1933 announced the end of Prohibition after Utah was the last state to ratify the 21st Amendment. (AP/Wide World Photos. Reproduced by permission.)

Catholic. An excellent politician, Smith was elected governor of New York in 1918, 1922, 1924, and 1926. Smith was a candidate for the Democratic presidential nomination in 1924, a nomination he eventually won in 1928. Smith was an outspoken foe of Prohibition and of the Anti-Saloon League. In the 1928 presidential election Smith asked only for modification of the Volstead Act instead of outright repeal of the Eighteenth Amendment. Nevertheless, he made it clear he considered Prohibition unconstitutional, an intrusion into individual liberties, and a violation of state's rights. His opposition to Prohibition, his Roman Catholicism, and support of immigrants was too much for many American voters, and he lost the presidential election to Republican Herbert Hoover.

William H. Stayton (1861–1940). Born on a farm in Delaware, Stayton, of Swedish dissent, greatly valued his education. As a child he walked several miles to the nearest school in Smyrna. An appointment to the U.S. Naval Academy at Annapolis provided his escape from the farm. He later earned his law degree from Colombia (now George Washington) University Law School in 1891. By 1918 the white haired successful lawyer, businessman, and former Naval officer watched with alarm the progress of Prohibition. Having no financial interest in liquor, Stayton's objection to the Eighteenth Amendment was

based on his sincere belief in state's rights. The loss of local decision-making power to a centralized federal government also deeply distressed him. The Eighteenth Amendment, according to Stayton, would be one more intrusion of the federal government into matters that should belong to the states. He and his friends formed the Association Against the Prohibition Amendment (AAPA) in November 1918 to oppose the Eighteenth Amendment. As a result of Stayton's commitment, he became the guiding spirit behind the AAPA. At the core of AAPA philosophy was the belief that the Prohibition amendment and laws represented an intrusion of national government into local and private affairs. The AAPA attracted the support of prominent business leaders by the mid-1920s and grew into a significant force behind the repeal movement in the late 1920s and early 1930s.

James W. Wadsworth, Jr. (1877–1952). James Wadsworth, elected as U.S. Senator from New York in 1914, opposed Prohibition throughout his political career. He voted against the Eighteenth Amendment when it came before Congress and publicly endorsed the AAPA. He believed the Constitution should not deal with matters properly left to the state as Prohibition. He predicted the unhappiness with Prohibition would result in disrespect for the law and the constitution itself. Wadsworth did not take an active role in the AAPA until after his defeat for reelection to the Senate in 1926. During the next seven years, Wadsworth worked tirelessly for AAPA's campaign against national Prohibition. By his own estimate he delivered 131 speeches throughout the country on behalf of the AAPA.

Wayne Bidwell Wheeler (1869–1927). Born in Brookfield, Ohio, Wayne Wheeler graduated from Western Reserve law school in 1898. Wheeler joined and went on to become a prominent member of the Ohio Anti-Saloon League (ASL). The League helped defeat an anti-Prohibition governor of Ohio, Myron T. Herrick in 1906. Wheeler, as an attorney for the national ASL pressed for passage of the Eighteenth Amendment. During the dry years of the 1920s Wheeler remained in Washington, DC, as ASL's representative and attorney. He continued to push for ASL policies to reflect a strict law and order approach with big prison sentences for violators as opposed to an alcohol education focus. Wheeler died suddenly of a heart attack in 1927, leaving a major void in ASL leadership that Bishop James A. Cannon, Jr. unsuccessfully tried to fill.

Primary Sources

Rumrunning

C.H. Gervais in his book *The Rumrunners: A Prohibition Scrapbook* (p. 45), describes how he would smuggle liquor over the border from Canada into the United States during Prohibition.

> I used to do it all the time—smuggle booze that is—I'd take my daughter over (to the States) in her pram. But underneath her, there was a false floor and I'd put the bottles in there. Then I'd give her a sucker, and off we'd go. And just as we got to Customs, I'd pull the sucker out of her mouth, and she'd howl. The Customs man, not wanting to put up with a screaming baby would just look at me and say, 'Get out of here.' And off we'd go. And of course, as soon as we were through, I'd give her another sucker.

Thoughts and Comments

John J. Raskob, General Motors executive and member of AAPA, shared in 1928 his concerns about the disrespect for the law and he wondered how he could teach his children temperance (quoted in Kyvig, *Repealing National Prohibition,* 1979, p. 84).

> I am not a drinking man (this does not mean I never take a drink), am a director in corporations employing over three hundred thousand workmen and have a family of twelve children ranging in ages from five to twenty-one years. `The thing that is giving me the greatest concern in connection with the rearing of these children and the

future of our country is the fact that our citizens seem to be developing a thorough lack of respect for our laws and life except getting caught ... What impressions are registering on the minds of my sons and daughters...when they see thoroughly reputable and successful men and women drinking, talking about their bootleggers, the good "stuff" they get, expressing contempt for the Volstead Law, etc.? ... what ideas are forming in their young and fertile brains with respect to law and order?'.

In Herbert Hoover's speech accepting the nomination to be the Republican Party's presidential candidate in 1928 he reveals his belief on Prohibition (from *What Herbert Hoover Stands For,* 1928, p. 15). Taken from this comment is the often used phrase, "noble experiment," referring to the Eighteenth Amendment and Prohibition.

> I recently stated my position upon the 18th amendment which I again repeat:
>
> I do not favor the repeal of the 18th Amendment. I stand for the efficient enforcement of the laws enacted thereunder. Whoever is chosen President has under his oath the solemn duty to pursue this course.
>
> Our country has deliberately undertaken a great social and economic experiment, noble in motive and far-reaching in purpose. It must be worked out constructively.
>
> Common sense compels us to realize that grave abuses have occurred—abuses which must be remedied. An organized searching investigation of fact and causes can alone determine the wise method of correcting them. Crime and disobedience of law cannot be permitted to break down the Constitution and laws of the United States.
>
> Modification of the enforcement laws which would permit that which the Constitution forbids is nullification. This the American people will not countenance. Change in the Constitution can and must be brought about only by the straightforward methods provided in the Constitution itself. There are those who do not believe in the purposes of several provisions of the Constitution. No one denies their right to seek to amend it. They are not subject to criticism for asserting that right. But the Republican Party does deny the right of anyone to seek to destroy the purposes of the Constitution by indirection.
>
> Whoever is elected President takes an oath not only to faithfully execute the office of the President, but that oath provides still further that he will, to the best of his ability, preserve, protect and defend the Constitution of the United States. I should be untrue to these great traditions, untrue to my oath of office, were I to declare otherwise.

Financier John D. Rockefeller Jr. announced his disappointment in the results of the Eighteenth Amendment before the Republican Convention in 1932. Rockefeller explained in the June 7, 1932, issue of the *New York Times,* (reprinted in Kyvig, p. 152):

> When the Eighteenth Amendment was passed I earnestly hoped—with a host of advocates of temperance—that it would be generally supported by public opinion and thus

the day be hastened when the value to society of men with minds and bodies free from the undermining effects of alcohol would be generally realized. That this had not been the result, but rather that drinking has generally increased; that the speakeasy has replaced the saloon, not only unit for unit, but probably two-fold if not three-fold; that a vast array of lawbreakers has been recruited and financed on a colossal scale; that many of our best citizens, piqued at what they regarded as an infringement of their private rights, have openly and unabashedly disregarded the Eighteenth Amendment; that as an inevitable result respect for all law has been greatly lessened; that crime has increased to an unprecedented degree—I have slowly and reluctantly come to believe [that repeal is necessary].

Groups for Repeal

Association Against the Prohibition Amendment (AAPA)
The leaders and supporters of the AAPA agreed to a resolution drawn up by the new Board of Directors in 1928 (reprinted in Kyvig, p. 97).

> RESOLVED, That we shall work, first and foremost, for the entire repeal of the Eighteenth Amendment to the Constitution of the United States ... the intrusion of which into constitutional realms has so severely hurt our country ... a task which is an affair for the policy power of each of our forty-eight separate and sovereign states, and never should be the business of the Federal Government.

Wickersham Commission

The final Wickersham Commission reports, put out in 1931, sent contradictory messages concerning Prohibition. Franklin P. Adams, writer for the *New York World* made fun of the Commission's report (reprinted in Kyvig, p. 114):

> Prohibition is an awful flop.
> We like it.
> It can't stop what it's meant to stop.
> We like it.
> It's left a trail of graft and slime
> It don't prohibit worth a dime
> It's filled our land with vice and crime,
> Nevertheless, we're for it.

End of Prohibition

The *New York Daily Mirror* rejoices with the city's citizens in its final edition, Wednesday, December 6, 1933, that Prohibition was over. Utah was the 36th state to ratify the Twenty-First Amendment. The headline and story was reprinted in Cabell Phillips' *From the Crash to the Blitz: 1929–1939,* 1969, p. 174, 175:

> PROHIBITION ENDS AT LAST!
>
> New York got the breaks from Utah . . . The lid is off! . . . The 36th and most necessary State to ratify repeal of the Prohibition Amendment had dillied and dallied

yesterday while New York fumed and then "out of consideration for the rest of the nation" . . . New York in particular . . . the long-dry Mormons opened their hearts and cast their ballots for repeal hours ahead of the time expected . . . Then the fun began!

Suggested Research Topics

- Should drugs be legalized in the United States? Are current anti-drug laws hindering or helping the fight against crime? List pros and cons of legalizing drugs.
- Research organized crime in the United States at the start of the twenty-first century. What is its main revenue source?
- Explore the relationship between drinking and automobile accidents. What attempts are being made to discourage drinking and driving?
- Compare and contrast the goals and beliefs of the Women's Christian Temperance Union (WCTU) and the Women's Organization for National Prohibition Reform (WONPR). Did they have any common ground or common goal?
- Consider your cultural background. Do you think your ancestors supported or ignored Prohibition? Explain.

Bibliography

Sources

Asbury, Herbert. *The Great Illusion: An Informal History of Prohibition.* Garden City, NY: Doubleday & Company, Inc., 1950.

Franklin, Fabian. *The ABC of Prohibition.* New York: Harcourt, Brace and Company, 1927.

———. *What Prohibition Has Done to America.* New York: Harcourt, Brace and Company, 1922.

Hoover, Herbert. *What Herbert Hoover Stands For: The Republican Candidate's Speech of Acceptance,* Washington DC: Republican National Committee, 1928.

Kyvig, David E. *Repealing National Prohibition.* Chicago: The University of Chicago Press, 1979.

McWilliams, Peter. *Ain't Nobody's Business If You Do: The Absurdity of Consensual Crimes in a Free Society.* Los Angeles: Prelude Press, 1993.

Merz, Charles. *The Dry Decade.* Garden City, NY: Doubleday, Doran & Company, Inc., 1931.

Pegram, Thomas R. *Battling Demon Rum: The Struggle for a Dry America, 1800–1933.* Chicago: Ivan R. Dee, 1998.

Phillips, Cabell. *From the Crash to the Blitz: 1929–1939.* New York: The Macmillan Company, 1969.

Rose, Kenneth D. *American Women and the Repeal of Prohibition.* New York: New York University Press, 1996.

Further Reading

Behr, Edward. *Prohibition: Thirteen Years That Changed America.* New York: Arcade Publishing, 1996.

Bergreen, Laurence. *Capone: The Man and the Era.* New York: Simon & Schuster, 1994.

"The Center for Maine History. Rum, Riot, and Reform," available from the World Wide Web at http://www.mainehistory.org.

Farrell, James T. *Studs Lonigan: A Trilogy.* New York: The Modern Library, 1938.

Fisher, Irving. *The "Noble Experiment."* New York: Alcohol Information Committee, 1930.

Gervais, C.H. *The Rumrunners: A Prohibition Scrapbook.* Thornhill, Ontario, Canada: Firefly Books, 1980.

McDonnell, Janet. *America in the 20th Century, 1920–1929.* New York: Marshall Cavendish, 1995.

"Ohio State University Department of History. Temperance and Prohibition," available from the World Wide Web at http://www.cohums.ohio-state.edu/history/projects/prohibition

Parker, Marion, and Robert Tyrrell. *Rumrunner: The Life and Times of Johnny Schnarr.* Victoria, BC, Canada: Orca Book Publishers, 1988.

Perrett, Geoffrey. *America in the Twenties: A History.* New York: Simon & Schuster, 1982.

Rogers, Agnes. *I Remember Distinctly: A Family Album of the American People, 1918–1941.* New York: Harper & Brothers Publishers,

See Also

Crime; Everyday Life

Public Health

Introduction

The October 1929 stock market crash and following Great Depression brought massive unemployment over the next decade, particularly the next several years. By 1933 25 percent of the U.S. workforce was out of work, amounting to over 12 million people. In reaction President Franklin Delano Roosevelt (served 1933–1945) introduced the New Deal in early 1933 when he took office. The New Deal consisted of a range of federal social and economic relief and recovery programs addressing a broad span of issues including work relief for the unemployed. The rise in poverty contributed to a decline in sanitation and hygiene in the rural areas and inner cities of the nation. The suicide rate was also on the increase.

During the Great Depression the public health movement of the United States had many successes and some spectacular failures. The New Deal programs played a key role in promoting health, particularly among the most impoverished. Leading up to the Great Depression the leading causes of death in the United States had become degenerative conditions. Heart disease and cancer killed twice as many people as influenza, pneumonia, and tuberculosis. Rates of infectious childhood diseases including measles, scarlet fever, whooping cough, and diphtheria had dropped significantly, and deaths from enteritis, typhoid, and paratyphoid fevers had been drastically reduced. These reductions were due in large part to medical advances and public health successes from the previous decades. Knowledge of how disease spread led to

Chronology:

1927: The Committee on the Costs of Medical Care begins its five-year study of the state of public health in the United States. A joint effort of private philanthropic foundations and government agencies, it examines the economic costs of disease and poor health.

1930: The Ransdell Act changes the name of the Hygienic Laboratory to the National Institute of Health and gives it authority to provide public funds for medical research.

1932: The United States Public Health Service begins the Tuskegee Syphilis Study, which withholds medical treatment for syphilis from black American males. The experiment finally ends in 1972.

1935: Polio vaccine trials are conducted using live polio virus. After nine deaths are reported out of 20,000 inoculations, the vaccine is withdrawn.

August 14, 1935: President Roosevelt signs the Social Security Act that provides federal funds for state and local health programs.

1937: In response to the increase of deaths from cancer in the United States, the National Cancer Institute is established with unanimous support from every Senator in Congress.

June 25, 1938: Roosevelt signs the Federal Food, Drug, and Cosmetic Act replacing the basically ineffectual 1906 Food and Drugs Act.

July 1938: The National Health Conference gathers public health officials, health care providers, and representatives from labor unions in Washington to discuss the medical needs of the nation.

1938: The Venereal Disease Act is passed seeking to eradicate venereal disease through education and medical treatment.

1939: The Wagner Bill, which proposes federal grants to establish state insurance systems, is introduced into the Senate. The bill dies in committee as attention shifts to an increasingly unstable Europe.

public health efforts to clean up water supplies, suppress epidemics through quarantines, and vaccinate populations threatened with infectious diseases. Research demonstrating that poor diet caused pellagra and scurvy and that unpasteurized milk could carry bovine tuberculosis resulted in education on how to prepare and store healthy foods and legislation that monitored the quality and content of food products. After 1932 public health officials in New Deal programs could point to these successes to prove the need for more health care spending as part of providing relief to those most affected by the economic crisis of the Great Depression.

During the period of the government social and economic recovery programs of the New Deal, the 1930s saw the second great push for national health insurance and the second great fight to defeat it. The battle illustrated the struggle between those who worried that health insurance would inevitably lead to government control of the American medical profession. That fear was already felt by many because of the rapidly growing role of the government under Roosevelt in combating Great Depression economic woes. It also highlighted the fear that public health professionals were overstepping their boundaries and treading on territory best left to private physicians. Public health after all was historically an issue of sanitation and water safety, not medicine. Even though medical economists and health insurance supporters such as Isidore Falk could prove how much money illness cost society, that did not mean that society should pay for its prevention. There was also the belief that the federal government could not adequately respond to local needs as they varied, depending on where you lived. Counties in the rural South were in desperate need of doctors, nurses, and hospitals. Cities in the urban North had better access to medical care but continued to suffer from the effects of overcrowding and poor sanitation. Finally there was the belief that additional funding for public health simply was not necessary. Statistics from the Metropolitan Insurance Company showed that despite slashed health department budgets, widespread unemployment, and the general lack of medical care, the death rate continued to decline. Between 1900 and 1930 the average life expectancy of a Caucasian male had increased by 11 years.

Despite such opposition nearly every piece of New Deal legislation provided funds for public health initiatives. The New Deal was President Roosevelt's plan for new reform and relief policies in the United States. Even the Federal Art Project of the Works Progress Administration (WPA), a New Deal agency, designed posters warning against cancer, and the Federal Writers Project created educational brochures describing syphilis and tuberculosis. The Social Security Act provided grants to states for the development of public health and the WPA and the Public Works Administration (PWA) built health centers, hospitals, and laboratories, as well as water and sewer systems. Public health functions were scattered among many government agencies. The Public Health Service, the largest agency devoted to health, was part of the Treasury Department. The Children's Bureau, which handled both maternal and child health, was in the Department of Labor, and the Food and Drug Administration was part of the Department of Agriculture. Unfortunately, because there were so many departments providing public health services during the Depression, some efforts inevitably became bogged down in bureaucratic bickering. Even the Interdepartmental Committee to Coordinate Health and Welfare Activities, a committee formed by President Roosevelt in 1936 to organize health efforts nationwide, fell victim to political influence when Martha Eliot, the assistant chief of the Children's bureau, suggested they all work separately on the sections of the program that would affect their particular agencies.

Failures such as these, however, did not detract from the successes of New Deal legislation. By the start of World War II (1939–1945) the Public Health Service had expanded its traditional role of monitoring and preventing infectious disease, protecting water supplies, and insuring the provision of clean milk, to actively providing both emergency and preventative health care. The public health movement was able to provide a safety net for those too indigent to provide one of their own.

Issue Summary

U.S. Public Health Service

At the start of the Great Depression the primary functions of the U.S. Public Health Service were sanitation, investigation, and education. Public health officers had considerable experience tracking down sources of disease and concentrated significant portions of their time on improving sanitary conditions. Since 1912 the Service had been providing health information to the public and by the end of the 1920s, it had worked closely with private philanthropic, or charitable, organizations, local health boards, and other government agencies in campaigns against hookworm, pellagra, and venereal disease. Venereal diseases include syphilis and gonorrhea, two types of disease that attack reproductive organs. Unlike other agencies with strong federal direction, the Public Health Service

had to balance the need for federal action with the prevailing opinion that health matters were largely local concerns and best handled by local health boards and by privately-funded agencies. County health departments existed but they were newly created and were not funded by the federal government but rather by the Rockefeller Foundation, that provided nearly three million dollars between 1914 and 1933 to support county health departments. By 1931 there were 599 county health departments providing health services to one fifth of the U.S. population.

An even bigger obstacle for the U.S. Public Health Service was the widely held belief, by both public health non-professionals and medical professionals, that public health was not improved by community action, but instead by personal effort and individual responsibility. In short, the idea of being a good citizen meant learning and practicing good personal hygiene. In 1932 the assistant Surgeon General R.C. Williams called this sense of personal responsibility toward public health, "one of the qualities of individual citizenship that should be fostered by every means at our command." It was "one of the basic elements of greatness of the American nation...which will make possible the development in this country of the most effective system possible of public-health protection" (quoted in R.C. Williams, "The Research Work of the United States Public Health Service"). Yet by the end of the Depression individual responsibility had been replaced by governmental oversight, private funds had been increasingly replaced by public, and the government's role in health had been broadened at local, state, and federal levels. The Social Security Act of 1935 expanded public health spending dramatically by authorizing health grants to states. Additional legislation was passed to battle venereal disease and to establish standards for food and drug products. The decade of the Depression changed the focus, the funding, and the future prospects of federal public health services.

The New Deal programs of President Roosevelt's administration focused on the plight of Americans hurt most by the economic crisis. Beginning with his presidential campaign swing through Tupelo, Mississippi, in the summer of 1932, where he was struck by the pronounced poverty of the population, Roosevelt targeted many programs, such as the Tennessee Valley Authority (TVA), which provided electricity to rural areas of the South, to give people electricity, indoor plumbing, food, and shelter. Only with these basics established did Roosevelt believe the health of the needy could be improved for the long-term. Improved sanitation and hygiene were crucial. Electricity would help keep food fresher and decrease spoiling and would also preserve fruit and vegetables longer for family consumption. Other programs such as the Civilian Conservation Corps (CCC) and the National Youth Administration (NYA) taught youth basic skills to improve hygiene. Of course other programs such as the Works Progress Administration (WPA) provided jobs so people could afford more nutritious diets and maintain better shelters in the first place.

Private Money for Health Care

While government spending on health care was increased with every piece of New Deal legislation, many health care dollars still came from private or corporate sources. A public health care problem was often first brought to the attention of private philanthropic foundations. The Rockefeller Foundation, one of the biggest philanthropic foundations working on health care projects, established the Rockefeller Institute for Medical Research in 1902 and by 1928 had been endowed with 65 million dollars for medical research.

One of their programs, the Rockefeller Sanitary Commission, was established to eliminate hookworm in the south through surveys, education, and treatment. Its efforts inspired interest in public health throughout southern states. Many of the major public health initiatives of the 1930s had the support of these private foundations and organizations. The Red Cross provided funds for many of the early food demonstration projects. The projects demonstrated how various foods could best be prepared and stored to ensure that vitamins were retained and to minimize spoilage while stored. Christmas Seals, the American Red Cross, and the National Tuberculosis Association supported the anti-tuberculosis campaigns. Research on syphilis was funded by the Rockefeller Foundation, the Milbank Memorial Fund, the Rosenwald Foundation, and the Reynolds Foundation.

Corporate philanthropy was also active in health care. Pharmaceutical companies were long-time supporters of medical research. In addition to sponsoring public health research, The Metropolitan Life Insurance Company had provided visiting nurses to their clients since 1909 when it was demonstrated that by providing health care services, the company could reduce the number of death benefit payments. By 1912 the Metropolitan Life Insurance Company was spending half a million annually on their visiting nurse program. By 1939 critics of the program argued the visiting nurses were actually visiting salespeople. Although it would take until 1953 before the program actually stopped, the critical comments highlighted the potential conflict for both privately funded and corporate programs in health care. Unlike the Metropol-

itan Life Insurance Company or the Rockefeller Institute for Medical Research, the federal government was accountable to all of its citizens and could not appear to be motivated by profit or by private interest.

The Beginning of Legislative Reform: The Committee on the Costs of Medical Care

During the 1920s and 1930s maintaining personal health was portrayed as a civic duty. Illness, however, was recognized as a financial burden that had consequences for society as well as for the individual. The first of three committees during the Depression to study the effects of illness on the economy was actually formed in May 1927, well before the economic crash. Composed of seventeen doctors and dentists, 10 institutional representatives, six public health workers, six social scientists, and nine representatives of the general public, it was funded by philanthropic foundations. The committee was charged with surveying the costs and the quality of medical care. Five years and 28 volumes of reports later, the Committee on the Costs of Medical Care (CCMC) finished its work and published its recommendations. It found that even though, on average, the American people paid about 30 dollars per capita (for each person) annually on health care, the majority of money was spent on recovering from a sudden illness rather than on maintenance of good health or illness prevention.

By 1929 the burden of medical costs fell on those hospitalized and accounted for 50 percent of all medical bills. The Committee also reported that access to medical care depended on where you lived and the difference between rural and urban areas was considerable. In 1929 in South Carolina there was one physician for every 1,431 persons, but in California there was one physician for every 571 patients. If general practitioners were available in rural areas, they typically lacked access to hospital and laboratory facilities. And while there were plenty of physicians in the cities, more than forty five percent of them were specialists who ignored general medical cases. Money was not efficiently spent as evidenced by the fact that physicians used 40 percent of their own income on general expenses of having an office. Patients also spent unwisely, according to the committee, when they bypassed traditional medical care and spent more than $125 million on the services of "cultists and irregular practitioners" and 360 million dollars on special "patent medicines." Health care professionals were inadequately compensated and there was a "shockingly large amount of illness" that went untreated. Most importantly little if any money was spent on preventive services, a situation that C.E.A. Winslow, the public health professor at the Yale School of Medicine and the committee's executive chair, described in "A Program of Medical Care for the United States (1933) as "a grave lack of the applications of modern medical science to the prevention of disease."

The majority of the committee members recommended that rather than working independently, physicians, dentists, nurses, pharmacists, and other medical professionals should be organized into groups, preferably centered around a hospital, and provide complete home, office, and hospital care. Medical costs were to be paid through the use of voluntary health insurance plans that were seen as a necessary first step to equalize the costs of medical care across the population. Local governments were expected to pay for individuals too poor to contribute. The resulting prepaid group practice plans, meaning the cost of healthcare was paid to some extent before illness occurred were not liberal enough for more progressive committee members including Walton Hamilton and Edgar Sydenstricker who feared that voluntary insurance would prevent the establishment of required health insurance plans. The idea was too radical for some healthcare professionals who feared that group practice would apply the principles of mass production to health care and establish a medical monopoly dictating who could practice in any given community. They also viewed voluntary insurance plans as one very quick step away from compulsory medical insurance.

Isidore Falk, the medical economist who led the committee's research staff, vigorously supported many of the recommendations that angered conservative members of the medical establishment. He pointed out that medical costs were fundamentally different from other costs of living. Whereas money for food, clothing, and housing could be budgeted and planned, medical costs were too variable to be budgeted by an individual or a family and needed to be borne over a larger group of people. He suggested the costs might be borne more easily if they were spread over a large group of people, both healthy and unhealthy people. The American Medical Association (AMA) called the committee's recommendations an "incitement to revolution." Declaring that what was at stake was "Americanism versus Sovietism [strong government control] for the American people," the AMA condemned the CCMC's report as a thinly veiled attempt to institute compulsory health insurance and remove control of medical care from medical professionals. Inevitably more attention was paid to the dissenters and to the conflict between the majority and minority reports than to the very real problems of the U.S. health care system that were diagnosed by the CCMC. Unable to generate a consensus within its own

group, the CCMC was a political failure at generating health care reform.

Medical Relief

The AMA's zealous condemnation of the CCMC's health care proposals was not lost on Franklin Roosevelt or on members of his staff looking at the health care needs of the nation. While medical relief was a large part of the Federal Emergency Relief Act (FERA) of 1933, it was carefully orchestrated and presented within the context of emergency unemployment relief. Broad guidelines were written but the execution of medical relief was left largely in the hands of state and local relief agencies that administered the federal grants. Medical care was available for acute conditions, not chronic. Emergency illnesses were treated but preventative care, which in many cases would have eliminated the need for emergency care, was not authorized. FERA did not provide funds for long-term hospital stays or convalescent care, which is care provided to those gradually recovering from an illness. Treatable conditions were those that "cause acute suffering, interfere with earning capacity, endanger life, or threaten some permanent new handicap that is preventable" (quoted in Brown, Josephine Chapin, *Public Relief 1929–1939,* 1940, p. 258). More importantly federal rules required that at all times the traditional relationship between physician and patient be respected and protected. Once an individual was approved to receive medical care by the relief administration, the type of care was left in the hands of the physician and not overseen by any government official. The results of this emergency relief were mixed and depended on how well or how poorly the funds were administered at the state and local levels.

FERA succeeded, however, where the CCMC failed. It made the general public and federal, state, and local governments aware of the wide inequality of medical care across the nation. Due to its "Health Inventory," a study of 850,000 families across the country, the lack of medical care in rural areas was again brought to public attention and in 1934, one million dollars of FERA's budget was specifically slated for public health services in rural areas. Nursing programs were also established and run through FERA and through the WPA and PWA. These programs were part health care and part health education with public health nurses making home visits to those too sick to travel or simply unaware of available medical care. Most of the problems associated with FERA related to its structure as an emergency relief organization. It was not designed to handle ongoing health care services and the fluctuations in funding and the limits placed on monies received impacted its ability to provide

A nurse cares for the children of migrant farm workers at a camp in Arvin, California on January 18, 1937. Lack of medical care in rural areas was of grave concern during the Great Depression. (AP/Wide World Photos. Reproduced by permission.)

long-term assistance. It did however establish a very important precedent for federally funded health care.

The Great Depression following the October 1929 stock market crash steadily worsened through 1932. By 1933 25 percent of the U.S. workforce was out of work, amounting to over 12 million people. The resulting economic suffering and need quickly overwhelmed private charities and local government relief agencies. President Herbert Hoover (served 1929–1933), believing in the rule that people are responsible for their own plights and also insisting the Depression would be short-lived, refused to establish an expansive federal response. The poverty found in the United States in 1933 was startling to Americans. The poverty spawned by the Depression further highlighted to the public the poverty that had already existed in many areas of the nation previously, even during the economic boom years of the 1920s. Among those who were concerned was newly elected President Roosevelt.

A Tactical Retreat: Social Security and Health Care

Roosevelt called the Social Security Act of 1935 the beginning of a broader social program and he approached its provisions for health care services with some caution. When Roosevelt formed the Committee on Economic Security in June of 1934 to investigate and define a social security program, three of its five members—Secretary of Labor, Frances Perkins, federal emergency relief administrator, Harry Hopkins, and staff director, Edwin Witte—felt that health insurance would have to wait because of AMA opposition. In his message to Congress on the Social Security Act in January of 1935 Roosevelt stressed the need for governmental unemployment compensation and old-age benefits. He called for federal aid to dependent children and their mothers and asked for additional services for the care of those left homeless by the Depression. And while he asked to strengthen the Federal Public Health Service and increase federal grants to state and local public health agencies, he carefully backed away from the topic of "so-called 'health insurance.'" He did admit, however, that "groups representing the medical profession are cooperating with the Federal Government in the further study of the subject and definite progress is being made" (quoted in B.D. Zevin, ed. *Nothing to Fear: The Selected Addresses of Franklin Delano Roosevelt 1932–1945,* 1946, p. 43).

This careful sidestepping of the issue of national health insurance recognized the political clout of the AMA and reflected how priorities were changing with the deepening economic crisis. Unemployment insurance was the first priority because millions were unemployed. A safety net for the elderly came next because of Francis Townsend. An advocate for the elderly, Townsend suggested his own unique form of old-age pensions that would provide two hundred dollars a month to anyone over 65 who would retire and boost the economy by spending the money. Although Roosevelt's advisors recognized the need for increased health spending they were leery of inciting the AMA. The AMA, however, went on the offensive as soon as they heard that Walton Hamilton was chairing the Committee on Economic Security's subcommittee on medical care and Edgar Sydenstricker was conducting its technical study. Hamilton and Sydenstricker were the two progressives who dissented from the CCMC's report because it had not recommended compulsory (required) health insurance. The AMA bombarded the White House with protest telegrams

and published an editorial in their journal declaring that Roosevelt was using Social Security to force Congress to pass mandatory health insurance. Throughout the rest of 1934 and until the act was signed in August of 1935 the AMA was quick to react and denounce any mention of health insurance. Even when health insurance was left in the Social Security Act as a future subject for study, it was attacked by the AMA, which condemned any insurance plan that would give control of medical benefits to lay people. Roosevelt's reaction to the attacks was to shelve plans for any type of health insurance program within the Social Security Act.

Even though the Social Security Act did not contain provisions for health insurance, it provided millions of dollars for public health services and its impact on state health programs was immediate and significant. Eight million dollars was appropriated for maternal and child welfare and an additional eight million was given to the U.S. Public Health Service to dispense to state and local governments. Additional funds were channeled through other government agencies for the construction of health facilities. In addition to the great infusion of cash, the Social Security Act established federal health standards. In order to qualify for the federal grants, many state and local agencies reorganized resulting in more consistent health care services from state to state. Social Security funds were used for a variety of programs from tuberculosis prevention in Wisconsin to venereal disease control in Missouri. Nearly every state board reported an expansion of services through the use of Social Security funds.

The Final Push for Health Insurance

The last push for health insurance in the 1930s came in an indirect way. By 1935 nearly every New Deal agency was providing federal funds for health care. Due to the variety of agencies dispersing federal monies for health care, Roosevelt created the Interdepartmental Committee to Coordinate Health and Welfare Activities. Chaired by Josephine Roche, the assistant secretary of the Treasury, the committee's mandate, as its name suggests, was to reorganize and consolidate federal health, education, and welfare services. Initially it did concentrate on coordinating programs. By 1937, however, it had created the Technical Committee on Medical Care (TCMC) and gave it the task again (for the third time) of creating a health program to meet the medical needs of the nation. Using the recently completed National Health Survey—conducted with WPA Funds by the U.S. Public Health Service and involving 776,000 families in 22 states—the TCMC endorsed many of the same measures as the previous two committees. In addition to recommending compulsory health insurance in the form of state grants, the TCMC wanted to expand the public health and maternal and child health services of Social Security, build more hospitals, increase medical relief, establish a general medical care program supported by taxes and insurance, and create a workman's compensation program for illness or disability that occurred on the job. Isidore Falk, a committee member for the third time, was again a chief supporter for health insurance. When Roosevelt received the report he did not immediately publish its recommendations. Instead he convened with the National Health Conference in July of 1938 to discuss the results of the National Health Survey and the TCMC's analysis of health care needs.

Held in Washington, DC, the National Health Conference brought together a diverse group of over 170 individuals from the medical profession, public health service, and labor organizations. All of the participants strongly supported the suggested program of the TCMC. The AMA became worried about the positive public response to the National Health Conference and the renewed interest of labor unions in federal health benefits that would "complete the Social Security Act." As a result it tried to back down from its hard-line approach and now offered to support the recommendations of the TCMC with the exception of compulsory health insurance. After the TCMC refused to drop health insurance from its recommendations, the AMA endorsed the expansion of public health services, agreeing that voluntary insurance plans might be acceptable, and hinted that federal funds might be necessary to guarantee care for some. Just when the standoff between the AMA and health insurance supporters seemed to be edging against the AMA, the mid-term congressional elections of 1938 changed the make-up of Congress and made it far more difficult to pass any type of social legislation.

Despite the results of the 1938 election which gave more power to conservatives, Senator Robert Wagner of New York introduced the National Health Bill of 1939. Incorporating most of the TCMC's recommendations, the bill expanded the health provisions of the Social Security Act but left the matter of health insurance to the states. This concession, however, was not enough for the AMA who backed away from their more friendly gestures made before the 1938 election. They campaigned against the entire act with renewed vigor declaring in an editorial that Americans were not interested in "any form of totalitarianism." With attention shifting towards foreign policy due to the rising tensions in Europe and with no firm support from Roosevelt, the Wagner Bill died in Congress.

The Changing Focus of Public Health

While the events of the Depression caused major changes in how public health services were funded, it also resulted in major shifts in the types of services provided. Long-time crusaders against infectious disease, the U.S. Public Health Service had achieved many successes against typhoid, cholera, and tuberculosis. Through the development of municipal water and sewage systems and through the pasteurization of milk supplies, the rates of contagious diseases had been drastically reduced. Due to these successes health was now more likely to be impacted by chronic conditions. Heart disease became the number one killer and identified cancer rates were on the rise. It was only by the late nineteenth century that medical researchers were beginning to understand how cancer develops in the body and this research would carry on during the Depression. The government responses brought on by the Great Depression, mixed with the advances in modern medicine brought this shift in number one killers.

With the introduction of research, which proved the impact of diet on health, more attention was paid to the content and quality of food products. Before the end of the decade, major legislation had been passed that monitored the manufacturing process of both food and drugs. The U.S. Public Health Service expanded their educational efforts with major campaigns against tuberculosis and venereal disease and explaining personal hygiene and prenatal care. Increased federal funding meant increased dollars for vaccination programs, with a special emphasis placed on the development of a polio vaccine. Early use of the vaccine, however, was met with mixed results. Some field trials of these vaccines actually resulted in polio infection of healthy patients that received vaccines. The changing face of public health during the Depression reflected both the medical advances of the previous generation and the new challenges that faced the population. It also reflected the strong personalities and interests of the officials in charge. Public health is a portrait of prevailing medical opinions and the evolution of its service during the Depression mirrored the developments in research and science.

The National Institute of Health

The Public Health Service always had a branch conducting research. Its original research facility, the Hygienic Laboratory, was established in 1887 and was most celebrated for its campaign against cholera and its vaccines and antitoxin serums that had been instrumental in bringing smallpox and diphtheria under control. By 1930 as the rates of infectious disease dropped a new research policy began to pervade

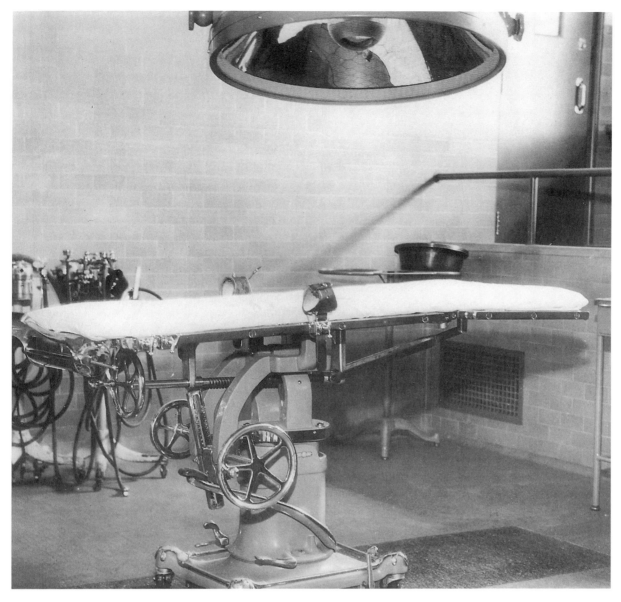

A 1930s operating room outfitted with the most modern equipment of the day. (AP/Wide World Photos. Reproduced by permission.)

the U.S. Public Health Service. The biggest symbol of this change was the creation of the National Institute of Health (NIH).

The newly created NIH was more than a token name change of the Hygienic Laboratory, of which it took the place. It symbolized a shift in the type of research being conducted by the Public Health Service and its sponsorship. For the first time federal grants were offered to scientists conducting basic studies designed to obtain "fundamental knowledge."

While still tracking down infectious agents and the sources of parasitic diseases caused by organisms living in a patient, NIH scientists under the direction of Surgeon General Hugh Cumming expanded their efforts and began to research chronic illness. This dual focus was evident in 1931 when the Public Health Service established a laboratory in Montana where it researched and produced a vaccine preventing Rocky Mountain spotted fever and expanded its research efforts into tuberculosis, venereal disease,

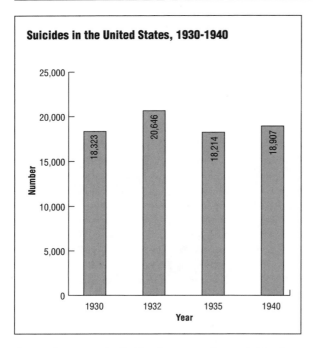

Suicides in the United States, 1930-1940

Some desperate individuals resorted to suicide during the Depression, with the highest rate being in 1932. (The Gale Group.)

and infectious childhood diseases. At the same time Cumming and the NIH developed new studies on cancer, including the chemical conditions controlling the growth of normal and abnormal cells, and they began a pilot study of rheumatic heart disease. One of Cumming's more dubious achievements, the initiation of the Tuskegee Syphilis Study in 1932, also reflected greater interest in chronic illness.

Under the direction of Cumming the Macon County Public Health Department began a joint federal and local study of the effects of untreated syphilis in black American males. The U.S. Public Health Service thought they had a rare opportunity to perform a "study in nature." Macon County was selected as the site of the study after an earlier research project, funded by the Rosenwald Foundation showed that one of the highest per capita rates of syphilis in the country was in Macon County, Alabama. The men believed they were patients being offered medical care by the government for their "bad blood," a local way of referring to both the syphilis and anemia that afflicted so many in the county.

Six hundred men, 399 men in the late stage of the disease and 201 control subjects, were offered exams, diagnostic spinal taps, placebos, tonics, aspirins, free lunches, and eventually burial services. Researchers

were particularly interested in conducting autopsies on the men so they could study the ravages of syphilis on internal organs. In 1958 survivors received a certificate recognizing their voluntary service and one dollar for every year of service.

At the start of the study, syphilis was being treated with varying degrees of success with arsenic and mercury. By the end of the Depression syphilis was being healed with sulfa drugs, and by the 1950s syphilis was effectively cured by penicillin. The subjects of the Tuskegee Syphilis Study received yearly exams and some treatment for the symptoms caused by syphilis, but never received the standard cures available for their venereal disease. Not only was treatment withheld from the study's participants, the PHS went to great lengths to insure that they were not treated by anyone. Local black American doctors were asked in 1934 to refrain from treating the test subjects for syphilis. In 1941 after a number of the subjects were drafted and sent immediately for treatment, the PHS intervened and requested that 256 participants be excluded from treatment.

While the participants gave their spinal fluid, their blood, their urine, and their bodies, they never gave their permission. Involuntary participants in a government sponsored study, they were written about in 13 reports of the study that were published in medical science journals. The first report was published in 1936, and the final papers were published in the 1960s. The articles were largely ignored by medical ethicists who had long insisted that informed consent of participants was a necessary and ethical requirement of any responsible medical experiment regardless of the potential scientific advances. Supporters of the study claimed it would be a waste to not take advantage of the opportunity to research untreated syphilis. They viewed it as a study in nature that required simple and passive observation. Critics disagreed. They pointed to the deceptions of the PHS doctor and the beliefs of the participants that they were being treated. They also pointed out that at the moment of diagnosis, it was no longer a passive study but an experiment. Diagnosis after all was an action performed on the study's subjects.

Another key national health issue was the rise in the incidence of suicide. Some lasting lore of the stock market crash of 1929 was investors and brokers jumping out of building windows to their death after losing a fortune for themselves or their clients. Though such incidences did occur, the key issue was the prolonged effect of the Great Depression on the mental health of the population. As economic conditions worsened through the early years of the Depression, desperation also grew for many. They saw their options for escape narrowed with suicide remaining one of them. Parents saw their utilities shut off as they could no longer afford the monthly payments leaving their children in declining sanitary conditions. Though many contemplated suicide, relatively few actually did. The suicide rate rose from almost 14 per 100,000 population in 1929 before the Depression to over 17 per 100,000 by 1933 when economic conditions were at their worst. The rate declined from that point.

The greater number of research studies meant, of course, that the NIH needed more research dollars. They were able to achieve these additional funds through the Social Security Act. The Science Advisory Board, established by Roosevelt in 1934 and headed by future Surgeon General Thomas Parran, went to bat for the NIH and recommended that an additional two and a half million dollars be given to the research facility for studies in cancer, heart disease, tuberculosis, malaria, venereal disease, and dental problems. When the Social Security Act was approved, it authorized up to two million dollars for the investigation of disease and problems of sanitation. While Congress never gave the NIH the full two million, they were given increasingly larger sums of money. This made medical research one of the main functions of the U.S. Public Health Service. It also spawned the establishment of the National Cancer Institute in 1937, which was organized as a division of the NIH and became a prototype for many national research institutes established since the 1930s. Illustrating the growing public concern over the rise in cancer, the NCI awarded grants and fellowships to scientists working both within and outside the Institute and demonstrated the benefits of disease-oriented research agencies.

The Impact of the Surgeon General: Thomas Parran and the National Venereal Disease Act

One of the most successful public health campaigns against venereal disease was brought about through the efforts of Roosevelt's Surgeon General, Thomas Parran. Parran, a career public health officer, had been crusading against venereal disease even before he reached the national stage. As the state health commissioner of New York, Parran began a public information campaign aimed at removing the stigma of sexually transmitted disease. Parran approached syphilis and gonorrhea as treatable, infectious diseases, as solvable health problems, not shameful secrets. His educational campaign reflected this straightforward approach. When radio executives at the Columbia Broadcasting System censored his use

A public health poster promotes the fight against syphilis. Nearly all New Deal legislation provided funds for public health initiatives. (The Library of Congress.)

of the word syphilis, he cancelled his appearance and received far more public attention when newspapers reprinted his censored speech. Parran brought the same direct attitude to his job as Surgeon General where he insisted public health workers use the appropriate medical term rather than vague local expressions that avoided the more formal terms.

Capitalizing on the Social Security grants to states to control venereal disease, Parran stepped up his education campaign and convened a National Conference on Venereal Work in 1936 that was attended by one thousand medical professionals and public health workers. Parran ignored critics who believed syphilis and gonorrhea were moral punishments of immoral behavior and publicized the tremendous costs of venereal disease. Before the advent of sulfa drugs in the mid-1930s and penicillin in the 1940s, treatments could range from three hundred to over a thousand dollars per family member. Yet, left untreated, the costs were even higher. Public health researcher Harry H. Moore attributed 14 percent of mental illness to syphilis, and it could also lead to cardiovascular disease, stillbirth, blindness, and premature death.

In his 1937 best-selling book, *Shadow on the Land,* Parran called for a "New Deal" for the innocent victims of sexually transmitted diseases, and in 1938

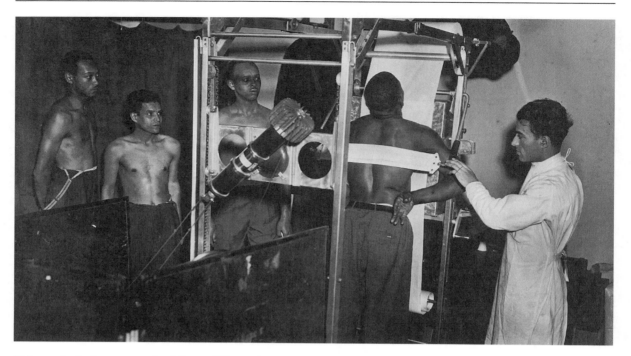

Tuberculosis, known as the "Great White Plague," was controlled in part by screening programs that included chest x-rays that allowed doctors to catch the disease in its early, treatable stages. (Corbis-Bettmann. Reproduced by permission.)

he succeeded when Congress enacted the National Venereal Disease Control Act. The act provided three million in matching grants to states for the first year, with additional funds promised the following two years and even more money slated for research. Despite Parran's success in increasing funding for public education, treatment, and research, venereal diseases remained a significant public health problem until the advent of the widespread use of sulfur drugs, 90 percent effective in curing gonorrhea, and penicillin, 90 percent effective against syphilis in the 1940s.

The Public Fight Against Tuberculosis and Polio

Parran's campaign against venereal disease modeled a process of publicity, education, funding, and research that was used to combat other public health problems of the 1930s. While tuberculosis rates had dropped to 71.1 per one hundred thousand by 1930 (down from two hundred per one hundred thousand in 1900), health departments still considered it the Great White Plague.

Renewed efforts to eradicate the lingering disease again centered on the milk supply and consisted of testing cows for tuberculosis and showing dairy farms how to safely dispose of infected cattle. Health departments also began large-scale screening drives of schoolchildren using recently developed X-ray machines that could take four X-rays a minute. Hoping to catch the disease as early as possible when it was most treatable, health officials combined the screening drives with educational programs on treatment and prevention. By 1940 early screening and treatment and improved living conditions had contributed to an additional drop in the death rate by tuberculosis to 45.9 per 100,000.

The Polio Vaccine Trials

The battle against polio was just starting. With significant outbreaks occurring in 1931, 1932, 1934, and 1939, it spawned a massive research effort that had Roosevelt, as a victim of polio, becoming its most prominent spokesman. Though many pondered whether poorer living conditions in rural areas and inner cities due to poverty caused by the Great Depression might have been driving this increase, researchers even decades later still had little knowledge what caused polio epidemics or even how the virus spread. Beginning in 1934 the President sponsored "Birthday Balls" on his birthday to raise funds and awareness for the Warm Springs Foundation in Georgia where he and many other polio victims received treatment.

Franklin D. Roosevelt in a pool at Warm Springs, Georgia in 1930. After Roosevelt contracted polio, which left him disabled, he traveled to Warm Springs to reap the benefits of its therapeutic waters. (Corbis. *Reproduced by permission.)*

The Warm Springs Foundation became the National Foundation for Infantile Paralysis in 1938 and Roosevelt's "Birthday Balls" evolved into the annual March of Dimes Campaign during which radio listeners were encouraged to send their dimes to the White House. This campaign marked one of the first large-scale nationwide fundraising efforts and it was a remarkably successful volunteer effort. The March of Dimes Campaign was to provide a much-needed booster for polio research that had suffered a crucial setback during the 1930s.

Research and development of a polio vaccine began early in the 1930s and followed the normal course of vaccine research. Vaccines provoke a response from the immune system. This immune response results in protection from a certain disease and can be achieved through injecting an individual with a vaccine containing a live virus or a vaccine containing a virus that has been deactivated or in effect, is dead. Vaccines had been used by the U.S. Public Health Service to combat a number of infectious diseases including smallpox, diphtheria, and typhoid. Two vaccines were developed against polio in the early 1930s, the Kolmer and Brodie vaccines.

The Kolmer vaccine created by pathologist John Kolmer used a minute amount of live poliovirus, as he believed that it was necessary to create a permanent immune response. After testing the live polio vaccine on a number of monkeys without any noticeable side effects, Kolmer used the vaccine on himself, his wife and children, and 323 other children. Maurice Brodie, a Canadian physician, simultaneously developed a killed-virus polio vaccine. He tested this vaccine on himself and six adult volunteers from the New York Board of Health along with twelve children. From April to September 1935 nearly 11,000 children received Kolmer's live vaccine and nine thousand had received Brodie's killed-virus vaccine. Nine participants apparently died from polio caused by the live virus vaccine, after which Kolmer withdrew his vaccine. His belief that a virus too weak to infect monkeys would be too weak to infect humans was wrong. Brodie's vaccine also proved to be ineffective. Even though members of the American Public Health Association denounced the vaccine trials, both scientists maintained they used proper research methods. The questions raised by the polio vaccine trials were questions of timing. Exactly when does an experimental medicine become safe for clinical trial and, who, or what organization gets to decide it is safe for consumption—the scientist or the government?

The Federal Food, Drug, and Cosmetic Act of 1938

In 1936 Franklin Roosevelt Jr. had a throat infection that quickly turned serious. When Eleanor Roosevelt sought the help of researchers at John Hopkins University, where recent trials using sulfanilamide—a sulfur-containing drug—had shown tremendous success in treating infections, they treated him with sulfanilamide and saved his life. The sudden onslaught of publicity for this "new wonder drug" resulted in its quick adoption by the nation's doctors and health care professionals. Children especially benefited from sulfanilamide, which was very effective against many childhood infections. It also proved to be a remarkably potent remedy for gonorrhea, a fact publicized by Surgeon General Parran in his campaign against venereal disease. It was not a very pleasant drug to take, however, as it came in the form of a large and bitter pill. Therefore when Harold Cole Watkins of the S.E. Massengill Company of Bristol, Tennessee, was able to create a liquid form of the drug in July 1937 using the chemical diethylene glycol, the company excitedly began production and distribution.

Watkins did not conduct any tests on the product since, according to his knowledge, the actions of both ingredients were known to be safe. By September of that same year the product was on the market and it was advertised as particularly "suitable" for children. By October, however, six people who had taken Elixir-Sulfanilamide-Massengill had died. After hearing of the deaths the AMA conducted tests on the elixir and, discovering its toxicity, or the degree to which it was poisonous, quickly notified the press and the Food and Drug Administration (FDA). When the FDA visited Massengill, company president Samuel Massengill informed the FDA representative that he had already telegraphed the salesmen and the wholesalers who had purchased the drug. Unfortunately his telegrams did not contain the reason for the recall as Massengill did not want to admit fault, and more than 240 gallons remained on the market.

The FDA was powerless. They had no legal ground to stand on, as there were no laws preventing the release of a dangerous drug. They were, however, able to claim that the elixir had been mislabeled. Elixirs typically contain alcohol and this one contained the toxic glycol instead. Using the "misbranding," the FDA unleashed their entire force of 239 inspectors and chemists to hunt for the medicine. All but 11 gallons and six pints were retrieved. Tragically 107 people, many of them children, died an agonizing death as a result. The FDA filed criminal charges against Massengill and his firm although the case was never brought to trial. Watkins later committed suicide.

The Elixir-Sulfanilamide deaths revived interest in revising the 1906 Pure Food and Drug Act. A proposed bill was already in Congress whose main objective was to toughen the regulations governing the food, drug, and cosmetic industries. But the bill had been going nowhere for years because of harsh industry opposition. FDA officials, senators, and "consumer-minded" congressmen began the arduous task of creating a bill acceptable to industry yet still protecting consumers. Their legislative effort was spurred on by Ruth de Forest Lamb, the FDA's chief educational officer who authored a book on their fight, and a growing consumer movement nicknamed the "guinea pig muckrakers." The consumers were called this because of their desire to publicly expose misconduct in the food, drug, and cosmetic industries and specifically because of a book called *100,000,000 Million Guinea Pigs,* which accused companies of using American consumers as experimental subjects (guinea pigs) for their advertised products.

FDA inspector George Larrick assembled a "Chambers of Horrors" exhibit for Senate hearings on the proposed Food Drug and Cosmetic Act. Eleanor Roosevelt was so impressed by Larrick's Chamber of Horrors that she borrowed the exhibit and put it on display at the White House for Congressional wives to view. Among its "horrors" were food products such as "Bred-Spread," which consisted of food dye, pectin, and grass seeds, and Doe Brand Vanilla Extract, whose one-ounce bottle was actually bigger than its two-ounce bottle.

After a five-year public relations and legislative battle, Roosevelt signed the Federal Food, Drug, and Cosmetic Act on June 25,1938. It gave the FDA oversight of cosmetics and therapeutic devices, authorized packaging and labeling standards for food products, called for factory inspections and safe tolerance levels for "unavoidable poisonous substances" contained in food products. Most importantly it required the manufacturers of new drugs to prove to the FDA with scientifically conducted studies that their products were safe for human consumption.

The Federal Security Agency

Shortly after the Federal Food, Drug, and Cosmetic Act was passed, the FDA was moved from the Department of Agriculture to the newly formed Federal Security Agency. Its move was part of a broad reorganization of federal agencies that Roosevelt undertook in the final years of the Depression. He initially wanted to consolidate the welfare, educational, and health activities of all federal agencies under one Federal Department of Public Welfare which would

More About...
Public Health Soldiers

The Public Health Service had their fair share of "martyrs" to the cause of researching infectious disease. Research-related deaths were reported during the 1930s in the medical literature and in the popular press along with the most common causes of death occurring from typhus, tularemia, Rocky Mountain fever, psittacosis, and polio. By 1941, 17 PHS workers had died from infections including one bacteriologist, Anna Pabst, who died on Christmas Day in 1936 from meningitis contracted from a laboratory animal. So infectious was the disease psittacosis, which is derived from birds, that investigators at the public health service laboratories developed the disease repeatedly. Several investigators developed more than one illness with one NIH researcher reporting that he had tularemia in 1913, undulant fever in 1928, and parrot fever in 1930. While the number of illness and deaths were small in comparison to the number of workers researching infectious disease, the way they were reported in the press began to change. In the 1920s the *Journal of the American Medical Association* and the *New York*

Times began indexing research-related deaths under the terms heroes and martyrs. This new attitude towards these medical researchers was indicative of the growing esteem for medical research in the 1920s and 1930s in the popular press.

This same admiration could be seen in several fictional accounts of medical research into infectious disease. The 1934 Broadway play *Yellow Jack,* which told the story of Walter Reed's yellow fever experiments at the turn of the century, was praised by critics for depicting "what spiritual force it takes to ask such sacrifices." Later turned into a film in 1938, it was one of a number of 1930s films that celebrated the nobility of the medical profession. MGM produced popular feature films such as *The White Parade, Women in White,* and *Men in White* (starring highly popular actor Clark Gable), and short films on Pasteur's discovery of a rabies vaccine and on insulin. To the popular press and to Hollywood filmmakers, doctors, researchers, and public health workers were soldiers and heroes in the fight against infectious disease.

---

become a major department of the government with a secretary who would be a member of Cabinet.

Congress, which had become decidedly more conservative in the recent election, did not approve this plan. So instead Roosevelt proposed a new reorganization plan that would establish three general agencies, two of which involved federal relief and assistance efforts. The resulting Federal Security Agency resembled his proposed Public Welfare Department, but was not made a major department of the government and lacked the power of a cabinet-level secretary. It gathered under its umbrella many of the welfare agencies created by New Deal Legislation. The Social Security Board was made part of the Federal Security Agency as well as the United States Employment Service, the Office of Education, the NYA, and the CCC. The Public Health Service was also transferred to the Federal Security Agency. The newly formed agency administered health and welfare and was the forerunner of today's U.S. Department of Health and Human Services.

Contributing Forces

The First Campaign for Health Insurance

During the decades preceding the Depression many of the pieces of legislation that were passed during Roosevelt's New Deal had their first airing before Congress and before the American public. The first movement to pass a national health insurance plan happened at the peak of the Progressive Era and was coordinated by the American Association for Labor Legislation (AALL). This group of "social progressives" was founded in 1906 and its mission was to give a more humane and a more socially progressive face to American capitalism. Comprised of academics, social scientists, and labor leaders, it initially focused on eliminating hazardous working conditions. Its first successful campaign was against the occupational disease of phossy jaw, which afflicted workers exposed to phosphorous in match factories. It fought against child labor and its influence was pivotal to the passage of the first federal child labor law in 1916. They also campaigned for unemployment insurance and for a system of workmen's compensation.

In 1912 they turned their attention to health insurance. Inspired by the British National Insurance Act of 1911, the AALL formed a social insurance committee that quickly narrowed their focus to health insurance. After studying the British system of health insurance and comparing it to the liberal insurance benefits available in Germany, the AALL drafted a compulsory health insurance bill that was to cover medical, surgical, and obstetric (pregnancy and childbirth) care for laborers and their families who earned less than twelve hundred dollars annually. The cost of the program was to be split with employers and workers each paying two fifths and state governments contributing the final one fifth.

Initially the proposed system had the support of many. The AMA, who supported the AALL health insurance proposal in editorials published in their journal, thought at the time that a health insurance law was necessary and inevitable and formed its own Committee on Social Insurance in order to smooth "the new sociologic relations between physicians and laymen." Surgeon General Rupert Blue and national leaders in medicine and in national health organizations all spoke in favor of a compulsory health insurance law which Blue called "the next great step in social legislation." Encouraged by the positive preliminary reviews the AALL helped introduce compulsory health insurance bills in New York, Wisconsin, and several other states.

Right about the time the AALL started proposing health insurance, however, the medical profession was beginning to change its mind. While the AMA leadership still supported the proposals for health insurance at the time, their members were revising their opinions. Before World War I (1914–1918) health insurance was seen as a way of insuring their income. By the start of World War I in 1917 many physicians' incomes were on the rise. The higher their earnings, the less likely they were to support a compulsory insurance plan. Many physicians also viewed progressive proposals such as compulsory health insurance as a not-so-subtle attempt to put private physicians under the control of the Public Health Service and force them into group practices where they would be paid a flat rate per patient per year. While they agreed that there needed to be better access to medical care, they felt both their income and their independence were threatened. Working through state medical societies, they began lobbying the state legislatures that were discussing proposed bills. Private

insurance companies also foresaw a drop in profits if health insurance bills were passed so they too began lobbying and were joined by labor organizations who thought their priorities should be improving compensation and shortening the work day rather than achieving health coverage. Their combined pressure, coupled with the increasing conservatism of the U.S. voters, resulted in the defeat of every proposed state insurance plan.

The First Campaign Against Syphilis

During World War I the U.S. Public Health Service increased the reach and exposure of its health care duties. They were initially put in charge of maintaining sanitary conditions in army camps. Mostly this meant anti-mosquito campaigns to reduce the threat of malaria and education and training on sanitation and proper camp hygiene.

Once those programs were organized and underway, however, the U.S. Public Health Service established a venereal disease division in order to provide prevention services and medical care for sexually transmitted diseases. Called simply an army appropriation measure, the division was given two hundred thousand dollars for organizational purposes and two million dollars to be given as grants to states. After the end of World War I funding for venereal disease control was gradually reduced until it was finally eliminated in 1923.

The First Maternal and Child Health Bill

During the decade preceding the Depression, the political climate was increasingly conservative and primarily focused on bolstering a weakening economy. It was a difficult environment to discuss the lack of health care needs of anyone. Women and children were the exception. In 1921 the Sheppard Towner Act was signed. This five-year act authorized an annual appropriation of one and a quarter million for the "Advancement of Maternity and Infant Welfare." Although it was considered by some as a demonstration of the type of emotional social legislation favored by women who had recently been given the vote, results of the act could actually be seen in the increasing attention paid to the welfare of children by governmental and philanthropic organizations. The year 1918 had been declared "Child Health Year" by the Department of Labor's Children's Bureau. The Child Health Organization was founded and five years later it was merged with the American Child Hygiene Association to become the American Child Health Association. This Association under the direction of future U.S. President Herbert Hoover (served 1929–1933) conducted a survey of child health in 86 cities and the results were dismal. Half of the 86 cities did not keep accurate birth and death records. Nearly twenty made no provisions for school medical exams. Forty-four percent of the children surveyed had received no vaccinations.

Despite the relatively low amount of money appropriated by the Sheppard Towner Act, especially given the relatively high level of need demonstrated by both private and public agencies, the Act was attacked by the AMA. While critics agreed that every mother and child should receive adequate medical care, they didn't think the federal government should pay for it. Although there was much grousing by the AMA and several state medical societies, forty states immediately applied for the federal grants made available by the act. They were used to increase the number of public health nurses and implement health education programs in schools. By 1924 all but three states were taking advantage of the money. Unfortunately, opposition by the AMA grew louder and the act, which was renewed for two years in 1926, was allowed to expire in 1929. It did however, serve as a preliminary model for federally matched grants to states, meaning states must provide funding to match federal funds, a particularly popular feature of New Deal legislation, and it paved the way for the grants to mothers of dependent children in the Social Security Act of 1935.

Margaret Sanger, a nurse and founder of Planned Parenthood, appears before a Senate committee for birth control legislation. (AP/Wide World Photos. Reproduced by permission.)

The First Food and Drug Act

When the Federal Food, Drug, and Cosmetic Act of 1938 was passed, it replaced a law that most public health service employees thought was ineffectual and useless. The 1906 Pure Food and Drug Act had started out with some muscle however. Brought about through the efforts of Dr. Harvey Wiley who headed up the Division of Chemistry, the "Wiley" law prohibited the manufacture and interstate shipment of "adulterated" or "misbranded" foods and drugs. Members of the food manufacturing industry originally inspired it seeking to decrease competition from highly processed foods, such as oleomargarine. Trade representatives also wanted federal standards that would eliminate the manufacturers' need to "manufacture differently for every state." A grassroots consumer movement similar to the one that would spur passage of the 1938 Act soon joined business interests and the General Federation of Women's Clubs and the National Consumers League lobbied hard for the "Wiley Act."

Wiley's motivation came from his own research. In 1902 he began the "Poison Squad," a group of male volunteers who agreed to eat foods treated with measured amounts of chemical preservatives in order to demonstrate their ill effect on health. The Poison Squad experiments, which went on for five years, fed the male volunteers foods laced with borax salicylic acid, sulphurous acid, benzoic acid, and formaldehyde. Wiley's research demonstrated that preservatives should be used only when necessary and that they should be proven safe by the producer before eaten by the consumer. Both of these provisions were part of the 1906 Act.

The weaknesses in the Pure Food and Drug Act were quickly apparent. While the law allowed the government to go to court against mislabeled products, there was no explanation of what a properly labeled product looked like. This was somewhat remedied by the 1913 Gould Amendment which required contents to be declared. Food adulteration continued unchecked, however, because no standards had been set for what constituted a true product. Who decided what jam consisted of, and why couldn't it be made without fruit? Patent medicines went largely unsupervised as well because the government had to prove that the false claim of the product was done intentionally. The manufacturer need only show that he personally believed in the product's effectiveness in order to escape prosecution.

Despite the weaknesses of legislation such as the Pure Food and Drug Act of 1906 and the Sheppard Towner Act of 1921, they were important and vital steps towards the more revolutionary legislation of the 1930s. It would take the mis-steps of the progressive era, the failure of the state health insurance proposals, and the death of the first federal program aimed at mothers and their children to provide the necessary lessons on who stood on what side—who believed social legislation was not only just but inevitable and who believed it was just plain socialism.

Perspectives

The expansion of federally funded health care services during the Depression provoked a wide variety of reactions. Even though Presidents Hoover and Roosevelt shared a common interest in improving the health care of their citizens, their approaches were radically different. The same disparities were also evident at the organizational level with the AMA violently opposing every attempt to remove medical care from their control while several other organizations silently and not so quietly cheered for the government expansion. Even at the individual level, opinions of health care and funding for services varied widely and depended on income level and on personal superstitions and beliefs of how disease spread.

The Presidents

When Herbert Hoover was elected president of the United States, he brought a long history of child health advocacy to his new job. The first president of the American Child Health Association (CHA) in the 1920s, Hoover was instrumental in the fundraising successes of the organization. During his tenure as CHA president, the group raised several million dollars for health education and child health demonstration projects. Hoover believed that public health services had the power to radically change human life and that the elimination of disease was merely a matter of "administration and moderate expenditure." Proclaiming public health as essential as public education, he declared that society would be rewarded "a thousand fold in economic benefits and infinitely more in reduction of suffering and promotion of human happiness" (quoted in R.C. Williams. "The Research Work of the United States Public Health Service," p. 82). Unfortunately Hoover's public health efforts as president of the United States were not as glowing as his successes in the private sector. Although he was a strong supporter of federal aid for county health work and convened a White House Conference on Child Health and Protection in both 1929 and in 1930, he was hampered by his economic policies that restricted the use of federal money for relief efforts. During his administration, funding for health care was slashed in an effort to slow the decline of the U.S. economy.

Although Roosevelt was elected in 1932 on the basis of campaign promises to eliminate national debt and reduce federal spending even further, by the time he took office the state of the economy required drastic and emergency measures. This had an immediate impact on health care. Roosevelt ordered the Health Inventory, a study conducted by the Federal Emergency Relief Administration that surveyed 850,000 families across the nation. The study results were used to campaign for increases in rural health spending and the expansion of public health nursing. Although he did not take the same personal interest in children's health that Hoover did, Roosevelt was actually far more successful in providing funding for public health programs that targeted the needs of children including the Social Security Act's provisions for aid to families with dependent children. Ultimately, Roosevelt approached health care needs pragmatically and politically. While it is true that all of the major acts of the New Deal did contain funding for health care, he was quick to abandon initiatives that would not serve him politically.

The Social Security Act was to have contained provisions for health insurance until AMA opposition became so strong that Roosevelt told his Secretary of Labor Frances Perkins to file separate recommendations on health insurance that he later declined to make public. After the National Health Conference of 1938, Roosevelt was initially so enthusiastic about a national health program that he wanted to make it a campaign issue for the 1938 elections. He later backed off that plan and decided the 1940 presidential election would be a better forum. In the end, it was not a campaign issue in either election. The 1939 bill died a much quicker death in Congress because it lacked Roosevelt's support, and when later asked about health insurance in 1943, Roosevelt told a Senate committee chairman that, "We can't go up against the State Medical Societies; we just can't do it." Critics of the Roosevelt administrations claim that his support of any initiative, be it health care or social security, depended entirely on who lobbied the most. Ironically, even though health care programs were supported erratically during the twelve years of his presidency, health care spending vastly increased.

The American Medical Association

Although initially the American Medical Association, (AMA) supported compulsory health insurance plans—even going so far as to establish their own committee in 1916 to investigate what they then believed was an inevitable reorganization of the medical system—by the advent of the Roosevelt administrations, they were decidedly anti-insurance of any kind. By the Depression, the AMA viewed federal emergency relief as an invasion, a violation of the patient/physician relationship. It was a decidedly single-minded stance supported vigorously by an "active minority" of primarily urban specialists that held most of the influential positions within the organization during the 1920s and 1930s.

Opposing any change in how physicians were compensated, the AMA publicly lobbied and actively boycotted any individual or organization advocating government intervention in health care. Instead of viewing health insurance as a means to guarantee payment, the AMA viewed it as a way of putting medical service in control of non-medical personnel. The AMA response was to try and limit the number of doctors by encouraging medical schools to restrict their admissions. They also adopted more stringent requirements for foreign doctors seeking U.S. licenses. Despite being run by a vocal minority, the AMA continued to gather new members. A doctor had to belong to a local medical society in order to have access to hospital privileges and malpractice insurance. In order to be in a local medical society, a doctor had to join the national organization. In this way the AMA was able to sustain membership even though the membership was not being well represented by the organization.

The AMA was striking a difficult balance. Physicians' incomes had dwindled, as people were far more likely to spend their money on food and housing than on medical care. In fact people were likely to spend their money on just about anything except medical care. By 1933 physicians had seen their average income drop 47 percent nationwide. The rate of default (failure to pay) on medical bills was more than twice as high as the default rate for rent and mortgages. Even though their income was dropping the AMA still believed everyone should have access to medical care "whether able to pay or not." It was far more difficult, however, to convince poorer doctors to provide free medical service. These less-privileged professionals were also the most likely dissenters from the AMA position opposed to insurance.

Despite the AMA opposition to any form of health insurance, voluntary or compulsory, there were several forms of health insurance plans that were available during the Depression. Some of them were even federally funded. Medical cooperative societies had been around since 1929. They were organized around the principles of group practice, prepayment for services, preventive care, and patient participation in designing medical services available. Cooperatives were found commonly in rural communities. During the New Deal they served as good models for the medical plans created by the Resettlement Administration (RA) that took over many functions of the Federal Emergency Relief Administration (FERA) for rural areas. FERA was a New Deal program established in 1933 that provided funds to states to assist in relief efforts for those affected citizens by the Great Depression.

Part of the RA's broad relief plan for rural communities were several medical prepayment plans that operated throughout the Dakotas in the late 1930s. There was also private insurance that started with prepaid insurance plans for hospital stays. Under the guidance of the American Hospital Association these plans offered coverage for hospital costs only, not physicians' fees. Later additional plans of voluntary prepaid coverage for physicians' services were started in several states. The AMA viewed these voluntary plans, eventually renamed Blue Cross and Blue Shield, with reservations. They appeared less threatening, however, if controlled by county medical societies and were carefully endorsed following the National Health Conference of 1938.

The British and German Systems of Healthcare

Many of these alternative medical societies and voluntary insurance plans were based on European models. European countries tended to be far more liberal in social legislation. Great Britain had been guaranteeing healthcare for their citizens since 1911, when the British National Insurance Act established compulsory unemployment and health insurance through approved societies. Local committees administered benefits that included doctor visits, drugs, appliances, and sanatorium care for patients with tuberculosis. Germany had a national health care system as early as 1883 that provided medical benefits through a network of locally run independent funds. Sick-funds grouped workers where they lived on the basis of their occupation or industry. Medical benefits included physician visits, surgery, drugs, and eyeglasses, while maternity benefits lasted generally six weeks. Employees contributed two-thirds of the cost and employers paid one-third.

Supporters of compulsory insurance in the U.S. pointed to the wide access to healthcare in Great

Britain and Germany. Detractors pointed to the lack of efficiency and to the control exercised by the local organizations that would surely try and limit medical expenditures in order to remain economically healthy.

Anti-Vaccine and Anti-Vivisection Societies: "Your Dog and Your Baby"

With the increase in medical research in the first three decades of the twentieth century, there was an accompanying backlash against the use of animals in medical experiments and the testing of new vaccines and medicines on vulnerable populations. For the anti-vaccine and anti-vivisection societies it was not a question of "your dog *or* your baby," as medical researchers would say, but rather "your dog *and* your baby." It was only a matter of time before ambitious researchers would turn their attention to human beings.

The anti-vaccination movement had been around as long as vaccines were developed against infectious disease. Long a pillar of public health care programs, vaccinations were viewed with great suspicion by many that received them. During a smallpox epidemic in Milwaukee in 1894, riots broke out in the city's German and Polish neighborhoods where parents refused to comply with the city's vaccination program. So effective were their demonstrations that the city council dismissed the health commissioner and reduced the powers of the local health department.

While membership and interest in these societies peaked during the 1880s and 1890s, there was a brief surge during the 1930s in response to stories of the polio vaccine trials and reports in the popular press of the use of orphans, soldiers, and prisoners in research trials. In 1933 the New England Anti-Vivisection Society had 534 members. By 1944 that number had increased to five thousand. Experiments on infants and children received special attention by anti-vivisection societies and they raised questions about the consent of so-called volunteers who were being used with their parents' permission. Because children lacked the cognitive ability to consent with full knowledge to medical experiments, critics commented that the use of the term volunteer was inaccurate. Castigating these "unnatural parents" for exposing their children to dangerous infections, they used their stories to demonstrate the need for government oversight of medical research.

The American Public

There did seem to be some detachment between physicians and their patients. In the American Institute of Public Opinion Survey conducted from 1938 to 1939, 42 percent of respondents said they had put off going to a doctor because of the cost. Sixty-three percent of physicians believed that the people of their communities were receiving adequate medical care and that included those who could not pay for it. The physicians that were polled overwhelmingly approved of voluntary insurance plans and believed that voluntary plans would increase their income. Eighty-one percent of all the respondents thought the government should be responsible for providing medical care for people unable to pay. More than half of them were willing to pay taxes to fund such a system.

The public as it was becoming more educated about disease and health was becoming more concerned about health issues, particularly with the increased incidence of polio and greater awareness of cancer. The unknowns about polio regarding how it spreads and what causes it generated a good deal of fear in the population. As a result the public was largely supportive of the new governmental efforts to tackle some of these health issues. As with New Deal programs, in general, support was less critical at first and the call for universal health care was strongest in the early part of the Great Depression. Fears of the rapidly growing government, particularly among congressional members, by the later 1930s tempered their enthusiasm for health care proposals. In addition Congress and the public were continually bombarded by the medical profession that fought hard in opposition to any government role in the health care field. Swayed to a large degree by the arguments in opposition to national health care programs, patients feared losing control over their freedom of choice of doctor and type of care received. Such public sentiments would carry forward for the rest of the twentieth century.

Impact

Many of the public health achievements of the 1930s had far reaching consequences. Public health historians point to Thomas Parran's anti-venereal disease campaign as the first time a Surgeon General used science to advance a politically unpopular position. Luther Terry used the same tactics in 1964 to warn about the hazards of smoking and hepatitis, and C. Everett Koop approached HIV/AIDS in the same manner in the 1980s. Historians also point to the 1938 Federal Food, Drug, and Cosmetic Act as one of the most significant achievements of the Food and Drug Administration. Amended in 1962 to more stringently regulate prescription drugs, the act has been used repeatedly to safeguard consumers against food additives, pesticides, and harmful agents. The

Social Security Act created a permanent vehicle for distributing funds to the public for welfare needs. Even though the Depression ended with World War II Social Security did not and it was amended in 1939 to extend coverage and raise benefits and in 1956 to include disability insurance. Health insurance would have to wait though until 1965 when Lyndon Johnson's War on Poverty created Medicare and Medicaid, health programs that made comprehensive health care available to millions of poor Americans.

The U.S. Public Health Service celebrated its bicentennial anniversary in 1998. Now part of the U.S. Department of Health and Human Services, a cabinet-level department since 1953, the U.S. Public Health Service today faces new versions of many historic challenges. Instead of yellow fever, polio, or cholera, the Public Health Service fights against HIV/AIDS, hepatitis C, and the Hunter Virus. While the last case of smallpox occurred more than three decades ago and polio could be stamped out worldwide in the next decade, there are renewed concerns about more virulent strains of malaria and tuberculosis and the even more unsettling threats of bioterrorism. The Public Health Service is still carrying out many programs initiated during the 1930s including vaccination programs, sanitation efforts, prenatal care, and screening programs for cancer. Working through eight divisions—including the Food and Drug Administration, the Centers for Disease Control and Prevention, the Agency for Health Care Policy, and the National Institutes of Health—the Public Health Service's mission remains the same, to use the advancements of science to improve human health.

Notable People

Grace Abbott (1878–1939). Social activist and author of the 1938 book *The Child and the State,* Grace Abbott was Chief of the Department of Labor's Children's Bureau. Initially trained as a teacher Abbott worked for immigrants' rights before joining the Children's Bureau in 1917 where she was made director of the child labor division and put in charge of enforcing the first child labor law. Abbott was one of the authors of the provisions for Aid to Dependent Children in the Social Security Act of 1935.

Walter G. Campbell (1877–1963). Campbell started his career with the Food and Drug Administration in 1907 when he was appointed one of the first 28 food and drug inspectors. Later promoted to chief inspector by Harvey Wiley, the author of the 1906 Pure Food and Drugs Act, Campbell devised the legal process for the first seizure of a product in violation, wrote the first Inspector's Manual in 1908, and set up the FDA's first project system to ensure uniform enforcement. During the 1930s Campbell directed the five-year campaign for the passage of the 1938 Food, Drug, and Cosmetic Act. Campbell remained in charge of enforcement for nearly forty years and became the first "Commissioner of Food and Drugs" in 1940, retiring in 1944.

Hugh Smith Cumming, M.D. (1869–1948). Surgeon General of the U.S. Public Health Service from 1920 to 1936. Hugh Smith Cumming joined the Marine Hospital Service in 1894 and was involved with immigration and quarantine duty in 1912 when the Marine Hospital Service became Public Health Service. He was also active in controlling water pollution through the Hygienic Laboratory and was a sanitary advisor for the Navy during World War I. Cumming was appointed Surgeon General in 1920. Initially he was concerned with the care of veterans that was the responsibility of the Public Health Service until Congress created the Veterans Bureau in 1922. He also revised immigration policies so that immigrants received medical exams in their country of origins eliminating the number of immigrants who were turned back after making the trip to the United States. Cummings expanded the work of the Hygienic Laboratory and supervised its transformation into the National Institute of Health. Cummings also expanded PHS work in the areas of mental health and drug addiction and oversaw the first expansion of the PHS corps to admit dentists, pharmacists, and sanitary engineers. Hugh Cumming retired as Surgeon General and from active duty in the PHS in 1936.

Ruth de Forest Lamb (1896–1978). Ruth de Forest Lamb was the Food and Drug Administration's chief educational officer during their five year campaign to pass the 1938 Federal Food, Drug, and Cosmetic Act. Author of *The American Chamber of Horrors,* which exposed manufacturers who violated the 1906 Pure Food and Drug Act, she organized consumer support for the 1938 law. Her career before the FDA included degrees in economics, history, and biochemistry and stints as a writer with New York newspapers and advertising firms.

Isidore Falk (1889–1984). One of the first "medical economists," Isidore Falk was originally trained as a bacteriologist and later developed a model for social research on medical care that was to be used until the end of World War II. Author of numerous publications on the economics of medical care including *Security Against Sickness: A Study of Health Insurance,* Falk served on the Committee on the Costs of Medical Care, the Committee on Economic Security, and on the Technical Committee on Medical Care.

Harry H. Moore (1881–1960). Author of *American Medicine and the People's Health,* Moore was a public health economist with the U.S. Public Health Service until he left to serve as staff director of the Committee on the Costs of Medical Care. In 1927 Moore argued that medical services in the United States were poorly distributed and badly organized when he said, "What exists is not so much a system as a lack of system."

Thomas Parran, M.D. (1892–1968). Surgeon General of the U.S. Public Health Service from 1936 to 1948. Thomas Parran began his career in the Public Health Service in the field of rural sanitation. He later took on assignments in rural health services administration and the control of communicable diseases. After completing a six-month course of study in public health at the Hygienic Laboratory, he became Chief of PHS's Division of Venereal Disease. Parran viewed venereal disease as a medical condition and a solvable public health problem and he campaigned accordingly to change public opinion away from moral condemnation of venereal diseases. Parran served as the health commissioner of New York under then-Governor Franklin Roosevelt and he worked primarily on revamping the state's county health departments to accommodate the needs of the Depression.

Roosevelt appointed Parran to the Committee on Economic Security, which drafted the Social Security Act of 1935. Following the retirement of Surgeon General Hugh Cumming, President Roosevelt appointed Parran as Surgeon General. Parran used the office of Surgeon General to launch a national campaign against syphilis with funds from the Social Security Act that supported efforts to identify and treat syphilis. In 1937 Parran published *Shadow on the Land* in which he stated that "Studies show that syphilis cuts in half the ability to do a full day's work, doubles the load of the unemployables. Yet the cost of finding and treating a case of syphilis among rural Negroes is less than one week's relief wages. If the Government were to take one fifty-second of the annual average wage, one week's pay, and spend it in finding and treating syphilis, the results would more than pay for the cost in better labor efficiency" (quoted in Susan M. Reverby, ed. *Tuskegee's Truths: Rethinking the Tuskegee Syphilis Study.* Chapel Hill: University of North Carolina Press, 2000, p. 66). In 1938, largely due to Parran's long campaign, the National Venereal Disease Control Act was signed.

In addition to his campaign against syphilis Parran also successfully reorganized the Public Health Service into four bureaus, a structure that would last until 1967, and expanded NIH research. Parran later chaired the International Health Conference during which the World Health Organization (WHO) was organized.

Parran also supported national health insurance and focused on creating a regionally organized health services infrastructure. The AMA attacked Parran for his views, and President Truman's decision not to reappoint him in 1948 may have been the result. Parran retired from the PHS in 1948 but remained active in international health organizations until his death.

Primary Sources

The U.S. Public Health Service added a nursing division early in the 1930s and worked closely with other government agencies such as the Children's Bureau and their Child Health Nursing Project and with private organizations such as the National Organization for Public Health Nursing. By 1936 more than six thousand graduate nurses were employed by the Works Projects Administration who ran over 75 projects in 16 different states.

The following two excerpts are from the Federal Writers Project on American Life Histories. Two nurses, one working in a rural county and the other employed by a city hospital, describe a day in their work life. Their language and attitudes, although typical for the decade, do contain some racially insensitive material.

South Carolina Writers' Project

Mrs. Martin, Public Health Nurse

Date of First Writing February 10, 1939

Name of Person Interviewed Mrs. Walter W. Herbert (White)

When my husband was in the hospital and the situation was so desperate, I knew that I had to do something quickly. Fortunately I had nursing to turn to. It was in 1933, in the day of the FERA, before it was changed to the WPA, I applied for, and succeeded in getting, a place with the public health department, and went to work. I worked very hard, and when a change was made in the administration and all the other nurses were let out, I was kept on and put in charge of the newly organized department.

Then in 1936 I heard that there was a vacancy in the City and County Health Department I know that if I should get it that it would be a permanent position and would take me off the WPA. So I applied, and to my surprise, got it. I really hated to give up my work on the WPA, and shall feel eternally grateful for the chance given to me through the New Deal. But I had to think of the future.

[L]et me show you a letter which I received a few days ago. It will give you an idea of some of my experiences. Here it is, written in pencil: "Dear Mrs. Martin: today is two weeks Ive been confined to bed very ill now little Helen has had feaver since Saturday very high feaver all night if the nurse comes there today tell her to please be sure come here to see about her for me. Thanks, Helen's Mother.

I went to this house which consisted of one large room—nothing more. It was almost bare. In a corner some sacking had been nailed to the rafters in order to give a slight amount of privacy to the bed and its occupants, for mother and daughter were in the same bed. I found that the neighbors had become so concerned about the condition of the family that they had taken up a collection to pay for the services of a doctor. So, of course, I could do little for them. I did, however, bathe and freshen them up as much as possible under the circumstances, and left a note for the doctor telling him what I had done. I had given temperature readings. The little girl's temperature was 103 degrees. If he had not been called I would have telephoned an ambulance and taken them to the hospital immediately, but public health nurses never interfere when a regular doctor has been called. The child has double pneumonia. It is a pathetic case, though only one of many.

At nine o'clock every morning I am at my office. I spend an hour checking over reports and letters, and taking telephone calls. Then the doctor and I attend to these calls before visiting at least one, and often two or three, schools before lunch time, where we examine and test the children for various symptoms of disease, including eye-trouble; teeth, heart and lungs affections. Every child is weighed, and a card index is carefully kept of each case. After lunch I go to the hospital and work in the wards doing dressings until five o'clock. Often at night I attend classes, either teachers classes or first aid.

South Carolina Writers' Project

The County Health Nurse

Date of First Writing January 31, 1939

Name of Person Interviewed Miss Mattie Ingram

"Want to come with me for a trip into the country? I'm making the rounds of my colored pre-natals this afternoon." Miss Brunson, the plump little blue-uniformed county health nurse smiled and held open the door of her car invitingly, while she transferred her familiar black bag to the back seat beside a stack of newspapers.

"What's in that?" she repeated my question as she stepped on the starter. "Nothing more exciting than a stethoscope, a fluid for testing urine, and some first aid articles. And the newspapers are for those nearing confinement. We have so little to work with among the Negroes, you know. They seldom enough sheets and those they have are usually so dirty that there's danger of infection. We have found that newspapers solve the problem satisfactorily.

"How did I come to be a nurse?" She laughed and pushed back a curl which the brisk spring breeze had whipped across her face. "Well, I really wanted to go to college, but I happened to have been born one of a family of twelve children on a farm in South Georgia. A farmer with a dozen children to feed and clothe doesn't save much toward college educations for them, so I had to be content with high school. When I graduated, I decided to be a nurse and entered training in Macon. I finished my course in 1920, did private and institutional work for nine years, had one year of public health work and came here about nine years ago."

Miss Brunson slowed down and turned off the highway onto a country road. "You want to know something about my work? Well, I conduct three venereal and three pre-natal and well-baby clinics each month, instruct a weekly class of mid-wives, examine and vaccinate school children and, in between times, do home visiting. I can tell you, it keeps me pretty busy."

. . . The nurse gestured in the direction of the cabin. "The woman who lives there—Sara Roberts—won't have her baby for sometime yet, but she hasn't been coming in to the clinics lately and she needs to take the shots for syphilis. In spite of the fact that twice as many Negroes in this county took treatment for venereal diseases this year as last, it is still hard to persuade them to keep up the treatments. No matter how carefully we explain, they become alarmed when they begin to feel the effects of the shots."

. . . The nurse's eyes were thoughtful. "It's a vicious circle. When they don't take treatment for venereal disease, the babies die and that makes the mortality rate for South Carolina appallingly high. And when they do take the treatment, the birthrate shoots up just as appallingly. Although that makes the vital statistics records look pretty, it clutters up this part of the earth with thousands of ragged, half-fed children . . . ."

"Do I find it depressing? Well, yes, in a way. But I try not to let myself think about it when I am off the job. I do other things in order not to think about it . . . .

We have to keep remembering not to be impatient about it, and to hold on to our sense of humor. There's a lot to appeal to the sense of humor in this work, if you don't get too serious to see it.

Suggested Research Topics

- Trace how the office of Surgeon General has changed depending on the needs of society and depending on the interests of individual surgeon generals.

- Analyze the FDA recall of Elixir-Sulfanilamide in 1937 and compare it with more recent FDA recalls.

- Compare the daily lives and working experiences of public health nurses working in rural counties and in urban areas.

Bibliography

Sources

American Institute of Public Opinion. "Surveys, 1938–1939," *Public Opinion Quarterly,* 3 (4): 581–607 (1939).

"American Life Histories Manuscripts from the Federal Writers Project 1936–1940," [cited March 4, 2002] available from the World Wide Web at http://memory.loc.gov/ammem/wpaintro/wpahome.html.

Bilkey, Warren J. "Government and the Consumer Interest," *American Economic Review,* 47 (2): 556–568 (1957).

Brown, Josephine Chapin. *Public Relief 1929–1939.* New York: Henry Holt and Company, 1940.

Derickson, Alan. "Health Security for All? Social Unionism and Universal Health Insurance, 1935–1958," *Journal of American History,* 80 (4): 1333–1356 (1994).

Duffy, John. *The Sanitarians: A History of American Public Health.* Urbana: University of Illinois Press, 1990.

Epidemiology Program Office. "Changes in the Public Health System," *Morbidity and Mortality Weekly Report,* 48 (50): 1141 (1999).

Falk, I.S. *Security Against Sickness: A Study of Health Insurance.* New York: Da Capo Press, 1972.

Galdston, Iago. "Health Education and the Public Health of the Future," *Journal of Educational Sociology,* 2 (6) : 341–348 (1929).

Horwood, Murray P. "An Evaluation of the Factors Responsible for Public Health Progress in the United States," *Science,* New Series 89 (2319): 517–526 (1939).

Lederer, Susan E. *Subjected to Science: Human Experimentation in America before the Second World War.* Baltimore: Johns Hopkins University Press, 1995.

Lubove, Roy. *The Struggle for Social Security, 1900–1935.* Cambridge: Harvard University Press, 1968.

Meier, Paul. "Safety Testing of Poliomyelitis Vaccine," *Science,* New Series 125 (3257): 1067–1071(1957).

"Overview and History of FDA and the Center for Food Safety and Applied Nutrition," [cited March 4, 2002] available from the World Wide Web at http://www.cfsan.fda.gov/~lrd/fdahist.html

Reverby, Susan M. ed. *Tuskegee's Truths: Rethinking the Tuskegee Syphilis Study.* Chapel Hill: University of North Carolina Press, 2000.

Roemer, Milton I. and Ray H. Elling. "Sociological Research on Medical Care," *Journal of Health and Human Behavior,* 4 (1): 49–68 (1963).

Stapleton, Stephanie. "PHS at 200 Lots Done, Lot to Do," *American Medical News,* 41 (34): (1998).

Starr, Paul. *The Social Transformation of American Medicine.* New York: Basic Books, Inc., 1982.

Swain, Donald C. "The Rise of a Research Empire: NIH, 1930 to 1950," *Science,* New Series 138 (3546) : 1233–1237 (1962).

Williams, R.C. "The Research Work of the United States Public Health Service," *Scientific Monthly* 35 (1): 82–85 (1932).

Winslow, C.E.A. "A Program of Medical Care for the United States," *Science,* New Series 77 (1987): 102–107 (1933).

Young, James Harvey. "Three Southern Food and Drug Cases," *Journal of Southern History,* 49 (1): 3–36 (1983).

Zevin, B.D. ed. *Nothing to Fear: The Selected Addresses of Franklin Delano Roosevelt 1932–1945.* Cambridge: Houghton Mifflin Company, 1946.

Further Reading

Bondi, Victor ed. *American Decades: 1930–1939.* Detroit: Gale Research Inc., 1995.

"Food and Drug Administration," available from the World Wide Web at http://www.fda.gov/.

"March of Dimes," available from the World Wide Web at http://www.modimes.org/home.htm.

"Office of the Public Health Service (PHS) Historian," available from the World Wide Web at http://www.lhncbc.nlm.nih.gov/apdb/phsHistory/History.html.

Starr, Paul. *The Social Transformation of American Medicine.* New York: Basic Books, Inc., 1982.

"U.S. Department of Health and Human Services," available from the World Wide Web at http://www.hhs.gov/.

"Virtual Office of the Surgeon General." available from the World Wide Web at http://phs.os.dhhs.gov/sgoffice.htm.

See Also

Social Security

Radio

Introduction

The stock market crash and following Great Depression brought economic hard times to many Americans. By 1933, 25 percent of the workforce, or over 12 million people, were out of work. Millions of others saw their paychecks reduced or lived in constant fear that they, too, would finally be hit with economic hardship. Many had more leisure time on their hands, but less money to spend. As the Great Depression deepened in the United States and around the world in the early 1930s, reliance on radio increased. More people owned radios, were listening to radio in increasing numbers, and were listening to radios for an increasing amount of time each day. Radio was an inexpensive way to keep up with news events of the Great Depression and farming news, and provided a ready means for escape from the economic hard times through sports broadcasts and entertainment programs.

President Franklin Delano Roosevelt (served 1933–1945) immediately seized on the popularity of radio with his series of Fireside Chats that he conducted beginning in the second week of his presidency. Roosevelt would use radio to not only lobby for public support of his programs, but also to inform the public of important events and perhaps most importantly reassure the public through his unique personal character that faith in the future was warranted. Though only relatively wealthy Americans owned radios a decade earlier, in the 1930s radios became a common appliance owned by the majority of Ameri-

Chronology:

1895: Guglielmo Marconi first sends radio communication through the air.

1922: William S. Paley buys several small radio stations, which he eventually grows into the Colombia Broadcasting System (CBS).

1926: The Radio Corporation of America (RCA), founded in 1919, establishes the National Broadcasting Company (NBC).

1928: "Amos 'n' Andy," a program that played on racism in America, which increased during the Great Depression, premieres and becomes the most popular radio show of the 1930s.

1930: As the Great Depression sets in, Lowell Thomas begins a nightly radio news program on NBC.

1932: "The Jack Benny Show," a radio comedy featuring a character who is tight with his money, premiers on NBC. His stingy behavior was something everyone affected by the Depression could easily relate to.

1932: "Buck Rogers in the Twenty-Fifth Century" premieres on CBS adding to the growing list of programs that provide escape for Americans from the troubles of the Great Depression.

1933: President Roosevelt delivers his first of many radio addresses, known as Fireside Chats.

1934: Congress passes the Communications Act of 1934 and creates the Federal Communications Commission (FCC) to oversee the nation's mass-communications industry.

1938: Orson Welles' Mercury Theatre of the Air broadcasts a radio adaptation of H.G. Wells's 1898 novel *The War of the Worlds,* causing widespread panic.

1939: Edward R. Murrow broadcasts from London during the Nazi bombing raids on the city shifting public concerns away from domestic economic issues to foreign issues.

1939: The National Association of Broadcasters adopts a code that promotes objectivity in news broadcasts.

cans and by a large number of people in other areas of the Western world. Radio was fast becoming a way of life.

Radio became the primary media for entertainment and, increasingly, for information. The number of programs and types of programming for radio grew astonishingly quickly. Old genres of entertainment, such as vaudeville, which was a form of live entertainment consisting of various short acts including songs and comedy routines, were adapted for radio, and new genres were developed for the emerging media. Stars of the stage, including theater stars and musical groups, became the stars of radio, with performers such as Edgar Bergen, Jack Benny, Bob Hope, Kate Smith, Guy Lombardo, Orson Welles, Barbara Stanwyck, Cary Grant, and Humphrey Bogart gracing the airwaves. New stars were also created, as performers discovered the medium and created unique shows. As radio became more sophisticated, new areas of skill and talent emerged, such as sound effects. It was a time of rapid, exciting growth for radio, much like the 1990s were for the growth of the Internet.

Beyond the proliferation of entertainment, radio addressed some more serious issues. The 1930s were a time of profound and lasting changes at home and abroad. Major shifts in the United States' political and policy priorities were happening under President Roosevelt as he sought to lead the nation out of the Depression, and the radio played a key role in reporting these changes. The radio also became a forum for discussion—and promotion—of all aspects of the policy changes. Politicians and critics used the media to comment as well as to convince.

Outside of the United States, the world was in a state of flux. Germany was mobilizing to occupy a large portion of Europe and much of the world was moving towards what would come to be known as World War II (1939–1945). As the world faced changes and challenges, radio was an integral part not only in reporting and commenting on the changes, but in some cases, in instigating them.

Radio of the 1930s provided a blueprint for the understanding and expectations of media for the rest of the century. The genres and stars of the 1930s became the genres and stars of television in the 1950s. Approaches to news, commentary, and political persuasion were established during the early days of radio and were adapted to later media.

1930s radio created an environment for new expressions of cultural identity and cultural criticism. Not only news shows, but also entertainment shows, frequently provided perspective and gentle criticism, helping to break down barriers between communities.

Comedies took on issues of race relations, poverty, and cultural misunderstandings, providing a framework to help people make sense of their rapidly changing country and world. Many radio shows were broadcast all over the country, and served to create a community of shared experience for a diverse and widespread world.

Issue Summary

The Golden Age of Radio

Following the stock market crash in 1929 life in America changed dramatically. The deepening Depression impacted every aspect of American life and Americans looked for new avenues to escape the dreariness of unemployment, homelessness, and hunger. Besides escape, the radio also brought the news and President Roosevelt's Fireside Chats. With the growth of broadcast news organizations at this time, the public could be informed as never before. Regional differences further melted as national programs brought the same information and advice to everyone with a radio. One bright spot was the exciting explosion of radio programming. Radio itself was not brand new in the 1930s, but it is during this time that it became an integral part of the lives of Americans.

As increasing poverty made many other forms of entertainment prohibitively expensive, America's reliance on radio grew. In the early 1930s the phonographic record player was a standard appliance in many middle class American households, but as the Depression continued fewer people could afford the steep price of $.75 per record, resulting in the decline of record sales. Attendance at the movie theaters remained strong through the first few years of the Depression, but that also would eventually decline substantially. About $75 could by a Marconi console, a common reference to a popular type of radio in a wooden cabinet and named after the inventor of radio, Guglielmo Marconi of Italy, who remained active until his death in 1937. The price was a steep, but often worthwhile, investment for families that were foregoing most other forms of paid entertainment. In 1933 alone 3.6 million radio sets were sold.

By the mid-1930s two-thirds of American homes had radio sets, and by 1939 about 80 percent of Americans—about 25 million people—owned radios. Radios were in almost every house and some Americans even had radios in their cars. Americans were buying radios at a rate of 28 per minute. They were a good investment—after the initial expense, the family

was able to enjoy drama, comedy, quiz shows, the news, and more for free in the comfort of their homes.

Studies showed that Americans were listening to radio for an average of five hours a day. Americans were spending so much time listening to radio that some child development specialists worried that children would be harmed from the activity. They warned that children should be running and playing outside, not sitting inside being entertained by a box. Radio use was not confined to economic class. In fact lower income families were most likely to listen to it on a daily basis. Radio became the central communication vehicle of the Depression especially including Roosevelt's Fireside Chats. Radio was how America got its news and how it was entertained. Radio was how America escaped the harsh world outside—as four national and 20 regional networks and hundreds of smaller stations piped programming directly to the listening public.

Programming was innovative and daring, with pioneers exploring new ways of making the medium of radio captivating. Daily soap operas, mysteries, science fiction, and fantasy programs were performed alongside radio productions of classic plays and live musical performances. The public found these programs a welcomed escape from worries of the Depression and the demand grew for more. News shows and commentary kept everyone informed of the dire situation at home and the deteriorating situation in Europe. Radio provided a shared national experience of entertainment and information. It was "The Golden Age of Radio."

The Rise of the Networks

The economic situation during the Depression directly impacted radio. Radio stations consolidated during the Depression, as smaller stations went out of business. In the mid- to late-1920s, networks were formed as companies bought stations all over the country, forming a "network" of radio stations. In 1926 NBC (National Broadcasting Company) went on the air nationally, using telephone lines to carry the signal to nineteen stations and ten million listeners. The formation of NBC was followed by the formation of CBS (Columbia Broadcasting System). In 1934 four powerful stations—WOR New York, WGN Chicago, WLW Cincinnati, and WXYZ Detroit—banded together to form "The Quality Group," which later became the Mutual Broadcasting System. The networks encouraged the companies to develop programming to attract more and more listeners. Advertisement, now nationwide with the networks, brought in much more money to support program development, improve production facilities,

A family listens to the radio during an evening in 1933. Radios proliferated throughout the United States in the 1930s, helping to connect communities across the nation. (AP/Wide World Photos. Reproduced by permission.)

afford more talented writers and performers, and develop more compelling stories and programs.

Even during the Depression, major radio stations turned a profit. In 1932 NBC posted a profit of $1 million and CBS posted a profit of $1.6 million. As at the start of the twenty-first century advertising paid for most radio programming. In the 1930s advertising agencies shifted their advertising dollars from newspapers to radio as public trust and interest in radio increased. Singing commercials became popular. Programs during the Golden Age of Radio frequently took the name of their sponsors. The A&P Gypsies, an orchestra conducted by Harry Horlick, was sponsored by A&P grocery stores. Live musical groups that played on the radio during the late 1920s and early 1930s included The Sylvania (light bulbs) Foresters, The Champion (spark plugs) Sparkers, and The Planters (peanuts) Pickers. "The Fleischmann's Yeast Hour" became the first radio variety show. Variety shows included a range of entertainment including music, singing, dancing, and comedy. "The Maxwell House Show Boat" was a variety show that evoked nostalgia for the old-time South, making listeners forget the griminess of Depression-wracked urban America. "The Chevrolet Chronicles" were one of many "transcription shows"—shows produced for the distribution simply of scripts to stations around the country

to be performed locally—and an example of how radio programming was inseparable from its advertisers.

With the consolidation of radios into networks, the configuration of the radio industry began to look like the major television networks of the late twentieth century. In addition newspapers owned many early radio stations including WGN (named after the "World's Greatest Newspaper," the Chicago Tribune). The U.S. Congress became concerned that one company would control too much of the media in any one town. They felt that if a single company owned all of the radio stations and newspapers in one town, they would not express a variety of views. They feared that the exchange of ideas and clash of opinions essential to democracy would be compromised. Congress soon passed legislation that required diversity of ownership.

As radio blossomed during the 1930s, network censorship did too. The Great Depression had established a fertile bed for radical politics as many were disillusioned with the capitalist economic system of the United States. In addition the rise of communism and fascism (dictatorships) in Europe was increasingly causing alarm in the United States. As a result there was vigilance to keep off the air anything that might be interpreted as supportive of these politics or in opposition to government efforts to bring about economic recovery. Censorship involved a radio network

More About...

A Day from the Golden Age of Radio

Nearly 60 years ago, WJSV, a radio station located in Washington, DC, recorded their entire broadcast day. Here is their schedule for September 21, 1939 (from *Old-Time Radio*. Available from the World Wide Web at: http://www.old-time.com/otrlogs/390921.html).

6:00 Sunrise—including technical problems

6:30 Sunrise With Arthur Godfrey

8:30 Certified Magic Carpet

8:45 Bachelor's Children

9:00 Pretty Kitty Kelly

9:15 Story Of Myrt and Marge

9:30 Hilltop House

9:45 Stepmother

10:00 Mary Lee Taylor

10:15 Brenda Curtis

10:30 Big Sister

10:45 Aunt Jenny's True Life Stories

11:00 Jean Abbey

11:15 When A Girl Marries

11:30 The Romance Of Helen Trent

11:45 Our Gal Sunday

12:00 The Goldbergs

12:15 Life Can Be Beautiful

12:30 Road Of Life

12:45 This Day Is Ours

1:00 Sunshine Report

1:15 The Life And Love Of Dr. Susan

1:30 Your Family and Mine

1:45 News

1:50 Albert Warner

2:00 President Roosevelt's Address To Congress

2:40 Premier Daladier

3:00 Address Commentary

3:15 The Career Of Alice Blair

3:30 News

3:42 Rhythm and Romance

3:45 Scattergood Baines

4:00 Baseball: Cleveland Indians at Washington Senators

5:15 The World Dances

5:30 News

5:45 Sports News

6:00 Amos 'n' Andy

6:15 The Parker Family

6:30 Joe E. Brown

7:00 Ask-It-Basket

7:30 Strange As It Seems

8:00 Major Bowes Original Amateur Hour

9:00 The Columbia Workshop

9:30 Americans At Work

10:00 News

10:15 Music

10:30 Albert Warner

10:45 Repeat of President Roosevelt's Address to Congress

11:00 Livingston's Orchestra (joined in progress at 11:20)

11:30 Teddy Powell Band

12:00 Louis Prima Band

12:30 Bob Chester Orchestra

---

official reviewing the program material and determining what might be morally or politically objectionable to the public. Some comedians liked to tell what at the time were considered risqué jokes, meaning the jokes were on the edge of being considered indecent. For example Fred Allen sometimes told jokes about the "Full Moon Nudist Colony." As censorship became stricter toward the end of the 1930s, the networks ruled that there could be no more jokes about nudity.

Regulating Radio

Early efforts to regulate the radio industry were not very effective. The Radio Act of 1927 created a confusing array of federal agencies to oversee the growing industry. President Roosevelt in early 1934

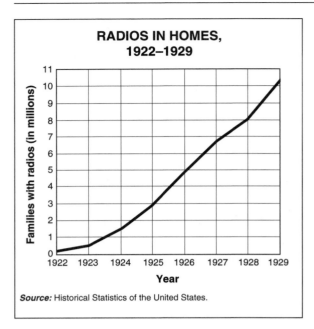

**RADIOS IN HOMES,
1922–1929**

Families with radios (in millions)

11
10
9
8
7
6
5
4
3
2
1
0

1922 1923 1924 1925 1926 1927 1928 1929

Year

Source: Historical Statistics of the United States.

Radio listeners grew markedly over the course of the 1920s. (The Gale Group.)

was concerned about service to rural areas, competition in the communications industry, and recent technological advances. In response the Communications Act of 1934, one of the regulatory foundations of Roosevelt's New Deal, which was a group of policies focused on relief and reform, provided for the establishment of the Federal Communications Commission (FCC). The FCC took the place of the Federal Radio Commission and oversaw the telecommunications industry as well as broadcasting. The FCC was created to regulate communication services and rates and license radio stations. Part of its responsibilities was to assign specific radio frequencies and call letters to radio stations. The FCC consisted of seven members appointed by the president and confirmed by the senate.

Some of the key provisions established by the Communications Act of 1934 are still familiar at the first of the twenty-first century. For example candidates for public office must be treated equally and sponsors must be identified. The "public interest" will determine whether the FCC should provide a license to broadcast. The New Deal's Communications Act of 1934 survives largely intact.

There were moves towards self-regulation in the 1930s also. The National Association of Broadcasters created standards of performance and objectivity that spawned discussion and that evolved throughout the

rest of the twentieth century. Broadcasting had become a profession in the 1930s and was experiencing the growing pains of becoming an established and accepted part of society.

A World of Listeners

Radio offered Americans a shared common entertainment experience, right in their living rooms. Regional differences in the United States began to diminish as radio, hand-in-hand with mass production and mass consumerism, grew through the decade. Not only would Americans share in the hardship caused by the Depression and in the solutions offered by the New Deal, but also in fads which themselves provided further escape from the Depression. Music led the way onto radio, with the broadcasting of swing and big band music in the 1920s. Music programming was the most prevalent throughout the decade, and despite the growth in news, dramas, and comedies, by 1940 music still provided 50 percent of radio programming. Music was performed live during the early days of radio, so studios were built large enough to accommodate full orchestras. Later recorded music was regularly broadcast, and radio stations had a series of continuing battles with ASCAP (American Society of Composers, Authors, and Publishers) over how to charge fees for playing recorded music that had copyrights.

In the 1930s music was the foundation of radio and America's favorite escape from the Depression. Audiences were able to hear performances by entertainers that they would never be able to see in person. Networks competed to hire famous conductors, orchestras, and soloists. While classical music was important to the success of early radio, not everyone liked the side effects. Composer Irving Berlin complained that Americans were becoming listeners rather than singers.

The orchestra of Guy Lombardo and His Royal Canadians were made famous by radio, as was jazz musician Count Basie. Radio provided a huge and attentive audience, but it also provided unique demands. Songwriters were under incredible pressure to produce new material, and many collapsed as a result. The explosion of radio was both exhilarating and exhausting. Music publishing companies hired song pluggers to "place" their songs with singers and musicians. The plugger would sell songs, to which the publisher held the recording rights, to popular musicians who would hopefully make the songs famous, which would increase a song's sales and the publisher's profit. Pluggers were named for "plugging" or aggressively selling the idea of recording a publisher's music.

Given the impacts of the Great Depression on the average citizen's entertainment budget, it seemed that everyone in America turned to radio for entertainment in the 1930s. Radio was the best buy for escape and information during hard times. Jack Benny was one of the foremost radio stars of The Golden Age of Radio. The former vaudevillian actor mastered the unique art of radio and created a variety show of immense popularity. The character he created was complex and his characterization was well known and funny. For example he was tight with money, which many in the Depression could relate to. Everyone in America knew Jack Benny and his foibles. At the time it was said that so many households listened to Jack Benny that you could walk the streets of small towns and not miss a word, as the sound of the program drifted through the open windows of each house.

Vaudeville performers had a challenge in translating their talent to radio. The performers would have a set of gags—jokes—that they could perform night after night in venues all over the world. As they moved to radio and their show was broadcast all over the world they had the awesome task of creating new material for each show. Jokes could not be reused as they could in live stage acts. Some radio performers had teams of writers preparing jokes for them.

Many of the premier entertainers of the twentieth century got their start first on stage and later in radio. Comedian Bob Hope was an exceptional radio performer who went on to an extraordinary career in television and film. The husband and wife comedy team of George Burns and Gracie Allen became representatives of the desired everyday world in American culture. Singer Bing Crosby provided audiences with decades of entertainment. Bandleader Ozzie Nelson, who later married his vocalist Harriet Hilliard, became a radio phenomenon in the 1930s and went on to become a television phenomenon in "Ozzie and Harriet."

Radio Drama

Soap operas were another area of significant growth in radio programming during the Depression. Eighty-five percent of network daytime programming was soap operas—serial dramas portraying the lives of a varied cast of characters. The dramas were called soap operas because manufacturers of the major brands of soap, including Proctor and Gamble and Lever Brothers, sponsored them. Women were the key listeners during the daytime, so household products such as soap were eager advertisers for those time slots. Since most radio soap operas were only fifteen minutes long, many could run in one day. There were

A poster advertises the Federal Art Project's weekly presentation of artists on KUTA in Salt Lake City, Utah. (The Library of Congress.)

61 soap operas on the radio in 1939 alone, and some of the soap operas on television today got their start on radio.

Many people—especially women—looked to soap operas for advice on how to deal with the situations life presented to them. The Great Depression especially brought new and troubling problems. Men were often out of work, stressed by their situation, and maybe even on the road for long periods looking for job opportunities. American women considered how their favorite characters dealt with the challenges of life. Popular soap operas received thousands of letters from women asking for help with real-life problems. Many of the production companies employed correspondents who wrote back with suggestions. This constituted yet another form of escape from the daily problems of the Great Depression by becoming temporarily absorbed in the problems of others, and maybe in even gaining some comfort that others besides themselves were facing difficult times.

"One Man's Family" was a typical radio drama—the story of a multigenerational family, with ongoing stories that weren't too complicated for listeners just joining the show to understand. "Against the Storm," "Brighter Day," "City Hospital," "Tale of Today," and "We Love and Learn" were all popular soap operas.

"Guiding Light" first aired on radio in 1937 and continued on television into the twenty-first century. Women followed the various sagas as if the characters were their neighbors.

Comic strips had long provided a shared form of entertainment in America. Children and adults followed the adventures of their favorite characters and waited for the next installment. Comic strips were transformed into popular radio programs with the debut of shows based on "Little Orphan Annie," "Buck Rogers in the Twenty-Fifth Century," "Flash Gordon," and "Dick Tracy." While some programs were more adult, some programs were specifically designed to appeal to children, such as "Jack Armstrong, All American Boy." Similarly crime dramas were also popular, with shows like "Sherlock Holmes" and "The Green Hornet."

Many advertisers formed long-term bonds with these shows, especially as they tried to reach the young audience. The hot drink Ovaltine and "Little Orphan Annie" were partners for many years. Advertisers were creative in positioning products. For example they created the character of Dick Tracy, Jr. who encouraged listeners to become Dick Tracy Junior Detectives by sending in box tops from certain cereals.

There was so much competition for listeners that children's shows offered premiums such as decoder rings and badges to lure their young audience. Decoder rings enabled listeners to decipher messages given in code language during episodes of the program. Mail-in premium offers were very successful on youth shows, and one of the most successful was the decoder ring offered by "Little Orphan Annie." Children would mail in a label and a modest amount of money for the ring. In the 1983 movie *A Christmas Story,* the advertising partnership with "Little Orphan Annie" was lampooned as the message in the long-awaited decoder ring turns out to be "Be sure to drink your Ovaltine." Such fads were a good buy for entertainment during the Depression when budgets were tight.

Many of the comic-strip-based programs that became popular radio shows during the Golden Age of Radio are still part of American culture at the start of the twenty-first century. "Blondie," "Gasoline Alley," and "Li'l Abner" were closely followed by both children and adults. The "Adventures of Superman" went on to both television and film success. The amount of listening leisure time during the Depression and popularity of radios in this pre-television period provided a golden opportunity for many programs to capture America's imagination.

Theater on the Air

Theater emerged as a popular genre on radio. On-air performances of works by playwrights William Shakespeare and Henrik Ibsen, and author Leo Tolstoy were produced, as well as radio adaptations of some of Hollywood's best films. Many of Hollywood's most glamorous stars appeared on radio. William Powell and Myrna Loy performed "The Thin Man" and Clark Gable and Claudette Colbert performed "It Happened One Night." Barbara Stanwyck, Lucille Ball, and Bette Davis were just some of the stars that appeared on radio during the Depression. Radio and film star George Burns claimed that radio was an easier medium than others since the performers could read their lines rather than having to memorize them.

There were several great radio theater companies during the 1930s including Orson Welles's Mercury Theatre on the Air, the Lux Radio Theatre, Screen Guide Theatre, and Studio One, later known as the Ford Theater. These well-funded productions were high quality with a great deal of planning, classic scripts, and major stars and they attracted large audiences. Productions were often broadcast during "prime time" evening hours so families could enjoy the shows together.

One of Hollywood's greatest celebrities was columnist Louella Parsons. In 1934 Parsons launched a variety hour, "Hollywood Hotel" that included interviews with actors and celebrity news. Actors would appear on the show to plug their movies, and sometimes would appear in brief versions of their movies on "Hollywood Hotel." This program provided a key opportunity during the Depression when many could not afford to go to movie theaters. Movie attendance was down in the Depression and this was a popular way for the family to be entertained. Eventually, the Radio Guild protested the actors appearing on "Hollywood Hotel" without pay and in 1938 the show was cancelled.

Orson Welles would prove to be one of the more influential performers of theatrical works on the radio. On October 30, 1938 a radio musical performance was interrupted by a reporter. As the reporter broke into the performance several times over the next few minutes, he described strange flying vehicles landing in various parts of the United States and strange creatures emerging from them. Soon the reports made clear that the entire world had been invaded by Martians who planned on taking over the planet.

Millions of radio listeners believed the report of the invasion, which was actually an adaptation of H.G. Wells's novel *The War of the Worlds* by Orson

Welles's Mercury Theatre on the Air. Though an explanation had preceded the performance, many listeners didn't hear it, and thousands panicked. Hysterical people hid in basements, and listeners called the police to volunteer in the fight against evil invaders.

The performance of "The War of the Worlds" became one of the most notorious radio performances ever. The radio had become such an integral part of the lives of Americans that it instigated panic throughout the country. In 1983 a television movie, "Special Bulletin" used the broadcast format to tell the fictional story of a nuclear explosion in South Carolina, and, despite regular disclaimers, caused some concern and panic.

With the plays and movies represented on the radio many engaged with U.S. developments in the arts through the Great Depression. Alienation from American traditions was minimized and a foundation for a later boon in such interests following World War II was established.

"Good Evening Mr. and Mrs. America"

Radio was a primary vehicle for the exchange of information and news during the Depression. President Roosevelt used the radio for regular "fireside chats" with the American people, explaining the major events of the time and his response to them in a calm and reassuring voice. Having delivered such addresses to the citizens of New York as governor, he delivered 28 fireside chats to the nation during his presidency. The first, delivered on March 12, 1933, only eight days after Roosevelt took office, attracted more 17 million families. All other chats were similarly big draws among the public. A 1939 poll indicated almost one-fourth of the population usually listened to the chats while almost 40 percent sometimes listened, adding up to almost 65 percent of the population. The fireside chats allowed Americans to feel an intimacy with their president that few had felt before—President Roosevelt was in their living room, expressing his concerns, empathizing with their situation. The fireside chats were crucial to unifying the country during a difficult time and set a standard for communications by future presidents.

With his comfortable style, Roosevelt had the uncanny knack of speaking to the people through the radio as if he was sitting in their living room. The chats were highly popular and pioneered a means for future presidents to communicate directly with the public outside the normal news channels. Even in the 1990s and early twenty-first century presidents Bill Clinton (served 1993–2001) and George W. Bush (served 2001–) used weekly radio broadcasts to

Orson Welles broadcasts "The War of the Worlds," which led listeners to believe that the United States was being invaded by aliens.

(Bettmann/Corbis. Reproduced by permission.)

remain connected to the public. Other politicians and political pundits, regardless of their agreement or disagreement with what Roosevelt had to say, were generally in awe of his natural ability to make great use of the mass media. The open discussions with the public had a major impact on Roosevelt's presidency, building a high level of trust. Roosevelt believed he needed to keep close contact with the American people given the severe hardships many were suffering through the Great Depression and ensuring as much support as possible for his New Deal programs.

Radio emerged as an important method of disseminating news during the 1930s. Many of the major newscasters of the century got their start in radio during the Depression—including H.V. Kaltenborn, Edward R. Murrow, William L. Shirer, and Eric Severeid. Radio producers experimented with different ways to deliver the news. Sometimes the days' news events were dramatized over the radio, with actors playing the roles of major participants. Radios provided an avenue for information that supplemented local newspaper. National stories including those of the Depression and progress of New Deal programs let people see the problems and success stories

Ed Thorgersen, radio announcer and sportscaster, relays the news of the kidnapping of Charles Lindbergh's infant son on March 1, 1932. (AP/Wide World Photos. Reproduced by permission.)

unfolding elsewhere by communities experiencing the same Depression-spawned problems as theirs.

Radio not only widened the scope of Americans past their own communities, it brought the events of the world into their homes. The Spanish Civil War (1936–1939) is considered the first radio war. In February of 1936 the Popular Front, a left wing group, opposed by the military, had been elected. In response to the election, the Spanish military formed a military government, exiled the leaders of the group, and

attempted to isolate the various local groups that supported the Popular Front. In the past this approach had been successful—the military had been able to convince the people that the rebellion was local and that it was futile to fight against the military, thereby discouraging action.

In 1936, however, radio transmitters reached most of the population of Spain. There were eight major transmitters and as many as sixty smaller transmitters. The military tried to convince the people of Spain that the insurgency was under control, but was soon countered by broadcasts calling for a general strike. Radio stations in nearby Morocco and the Canary Islands broadcasted in support of the rebels, and rebel resistance grew. The military government tried to capture the main radio stations with little success. The failure of the government to suppress the rebel broadcasts appeared to signal the collapse of the military government. Throughout the war, broadcasts in many languages and sponsored by many groups rallied support and impacted the outcome of the war.

By the end of the Depression events in Europe as a whole were deteriorating. Germany was invading its neighbors. As the world moved closer to world war, Kaltenborn reported on the invasion of Austria and Czechoslovakia. Murrow provided regular reports on the bombing of London in his "London After Dark" series broadcast by shortwave radio. Shirer reported on the dramatic surrender of France to Germany at Compaigne. Americans listened to the radio and heard bombs exploding in background as a reporter explained that London was being attacked. The world was suddenly smaller and as a result, more frightening for many Americans.

Other news events also came into the homes of many Americans. By the time the infant son of national hero Charles Lindbergh was kidnapped and murdered, the role of communication in radio had become so important that the 1935 verdict in the Lindbergh kidnapping trial was broadcast over radio. In 1937 a reporter captured his reaction to the crash of the Hindenburg. On site to report on the Hindenburg's voyage, instead the reporter's response to the tragedy was recorded and later broadcast, bringing the horror into thousands of living rooms. Later when the Japanese attacked Pearl Harbor on December 7, 1941, the tragedy of the attack and the President's response to it was quickly broadcast to Americans around the country. Radio news had reached its maturity.

Another example of the growth of radio news was the presence of tabloid reporting, which emphasized sensationalized topics. Walter Winchell specialized in publishing gossip and other information that some critics deemed inappropriate. He hosted a celebrity gossip show during much of the Depression that became both very popular and highly criticized.

Sports commentary was popular on radio and play-by-play commentary on baseball and other games was popular, though not always what it seemed. The future president Ronald Reagan, a sports announcer at WHO in Des Moines, Iowa during much of the Depression, called play-by-play for the Chicago Cubs. The studio, however, was three hundred miles from the actual game. Skillful sports commentators were able to imagine the details of a game and pass them along to listeners using play-by-play provided in type across the wires. Sports played a major role in the escapism from the Great Depression. Prominent sports figures became larger than life. This also represented the golden age of sportscasters who eloquently described the sporting events and created colorful images of the sports stars. The Depression listening public followed the exploits of "Babe" Ruth, Lou Gehrig ("The Iron Horse"), the Four Horsemen of Notre Dame football players, female track star Mildred "Babe" Didrikson Zaharias, the boxer Joe Louis ("The Brown Bomber"), and others.

Radio in the 1930s often contrived events to encourage people to listen. Given the hard times of the Depression they had an eager listening public. Stunt broadcasts were a regular part of programming. KSTP in St. Paul Minnesota covered a wedding in a hot air balloon for its listeners. Radio was a burgeoning and competitive field. Listeners couldn't get enough of it, and innovation flourished. Many of the 1930s programs would set the standard for programming in all media for the rest of the century.

"Liberty at the Crossroads"

Radio played an important role in politics during the Depression. Radio was used to communicate political positions, and to show support of, and against, politicians. In the November 1936 election President Roosevelt used the radio much more effectively than opponent Alf Landon, which partially contributed to Roosevelt's victory. In 1940 President Roosevelt's radio skill helped him defeat Wendell Willkie and win an unprecedented third term as President.

Political parties made great use of radio during the 1930s, much as they did television later in the century. In 1936 the Republican Party's radio dramatization, "Liberty at the Crossroads," played an important role in the campaign. Critics complained that the use of radio deterred thoughtful analysis of political issues. They also complained that political conventions were organized for the benefit of radio, rather than to facilitate substantive political discussion.

The power of radio was being exploited in the international arena, also. German Minister of Propaganda Joseph Goebbels was reportedly very sensitive to the enormous impact that radio could have. Two types of music were banned when Adolph Hitler came to power in Germany in 1933: swing and jazz. Swing represented decadent America, and jazz was seen as antithetical to the purity of the Aryan race, which was a term for the non-Jewish white population. Jazz was largely derived by black American musicians and frequently played by Jewish musicians. Such creativity by non-whites and non-Protestants did not mesh well with the racist doctrines of the Nazis who preached the dominance of white society. Later in the 1930s as Spain descended into civil war, radio became pivotal in rallying the forces opposing the military government. As in the United States with Roosevelt's Fireside Chats, other governments in the 1930s clearly recognized the power and potential of radio. Goebbels and other German leaders knew it was the most effective way available to reach the greatest number of people with propaganda and other information.

One master of the use of radio was Father Charles Edward Coughlin. The Roman Catholic priest from the Detroit, Michigan area was broadcast throughout much of the 1930s. Coughlin was highly popular in the early 1930s with his radio program attracting an estimated 30 to 45 million listeners each week. At first his program was primarily inspirational and welcomed by the Depression-weary public but became increasingly political. Initially a supporter of President Roosevelt and his New Deal programs, Coughlin became disillusioned and turned into a fierce critic. Coughlin was extraordinarily popular, with millions of listeners each Sunday. As his comments became increasingly political, his anti-Semitic (Jewish), pro-Hitler views became clear, and CBS dropped his program when his comments became too inflammatory. As Germany's aggression in Europe became increasingly evident, Coughlin lost some of his popularity, however, for much of the Depression he was a significant voice in American radio.

The growing war in Europe produced some of the most creative and thoughtful programming on radio. When German planes bombed the Basque town of Guernica in Spain in 1937, it solidified writer and director Norman Corwin's hatred of fascism. In 1939 he wrote "They Fly through the Air with the Greatest of Ease" for his "Words Without Music" radio series. The program lamented the German military planes flying at will over his native country and wreaking havoc with their bombs. Its premiere was lauded as exceptional, bold radio. Isolationist beliefs, opposition to the United States entering the war, made even the mention of the possibility of war controversial, but the airing of the program resulted in a thousand favorable letters being sent to CBS.

Writer Archibald MacLeish produced "The Fall of the City," which symbolically represented the growing threat of war in 1937. Arch Oboler produced "Lights Out" on NBC, and "Air Raid" by Archibald MacLeish and "War of the Worlds" by writer and performer Orson Welles, which depicted the growing fear of war. Radio had given a voice to Americans' fears about the coming world war.

Contributing Forces

In 1895 Guglielmo Marconi became the first person to communicate by sending radio signals through the air. Radio was born. Radio, however, had a rocky start in America. During World War I, most private U.S. radio stations were either shut down or taken over by the government under order of President Woodrow Wilson, and it was illegal for U.S. citizens to possess an operational transmitter or receiver.

It wasn't until 1920 that radio stations were regularly making commercial broadcasts, beginning with KDKA of Pittsburgh and WWJ of Detroit. Programming began to grow despite the fact that radios were still too pricey for most Americans.

In 1922, David Sarnoff introduced the Radiola console, which sold for $75—not an insignificant amount but still within the reach of middle class citizens in the 1920s. His plan was to make radios affordable and to bring music into the home by way of wireless technology. His company, RCA—the Radio Corporation of America—grew from $11 million in sales the first year to $60 million three years later. The less expensive radio model made radios a household item.

The 1920s saw a steady growth in radio ownership and programming, and radios were becoming increasingly popular. The stock market crash of 1929 and the Depression that followed, however, really spurred the growth of radio. Despite an initial decline in radio ownership in the early part of the Depression, children and others started becoming avid radio listeners. Other forms of paid entertainment had become prohibitively expensive in the lean times, and so Americans turned to radio. Eventually, as social workers reported, families would rather part with their icebox or other necessary appliances than with their radio.

Radio technology was still evolving as the country entered the Depression. The conventional, amplitude modulation (AM) form of radio signal proved limiting in broadcasting, producing much static at times. Frequency modulation (FM) was introduced in which static interference was much less. In 1933 Edwin Howard Armstrong produced the first FM transmitter and receiver, although it was six years before an FM station would air. FM was clearly superior in the quality of the broadcast.

Perspectives

Public Perspectives

The public found radio to be the most accessible form of entertainment and information available. After the initial expense of purchasing a radio, it was rather cheap to enjoy the programs. Also radio programming could be enjoyed by the entire family who gathered in front of the radio in the comfort of their own home. Radio entertainment played on the imagination of the listeners by creating visions of the action and characters portrayed. In this way radio was an excellent form of escapism during the particularly tough period when the public was greatly affected by the Great Depression. The effects of the Depression—poverty, joblessness, homelessness, and hunger—took a mental toll on Americans. Radio, with its thrillers and mysteries, classical theater and musical performances, and slapstick and silliness, provided a means of escaping the dreariness of life. Not everyone approved of the escapism of radio. Some critics called it "bread and circuses," a narcotic for the masses to keep them from fully comprehending the situation in which they found themselves.

Radio became so popular during the Depression that some psychologists grew concerned over the increasing amount of time and attention spent listening to radio. Child development specialists expressed concern that children were foregoing more wholesome activities, such as studying, reading, playing sports, and outdoor activities in favor of sitting passively inside, next to the radio, listening. These concerns were later mirrored by similar concerns expressed over the effects television and personal computers posed on child development. Some became concerned that America was becoming a land of spectators, rather than a land of participants.

For artists radio opened up a whole new medium to pursue their craft. Rather than performing on stage in vaudeville or nightclubs requiring steady travel, they could reach the entire nation from a small studio, week after week. They could also employ elaborate sound effects and various other techniques that would play on the listeners' imaginations. Very quickly programs became fairly sophisticated in these techniques. Advertisers also found a new medium for promoting their goods nationwide. Nationally distributed magazines had been the key medium before the rise of radio and national broadcasting networks. Now the mass produced goods could be promoted through the mass media for mass consumption. The fabric of American life would be changed forever. In the age of the Depression with limited expense budgets, radio provided an economical way of reaching millions of people.

National Perspectives

It was during the Great Depression that America became a more unified nation and regional differences significantly declined. People in the cities, farms, and suburbs listened to the same programs at the same time. Certainly one factor was the loss of jobs and search for new employment opportunities that led to a great deal of population shifts and movement. The expansion of radio also played a key role in this change of national character. Radio offered a unique communal experience not so readily available in America before. No other media of the time was as pervasive. For example, newspapers were still more a local and regional form of information sharing. Individuals all over America laughed together at Jack Benny and worried together over alien invasion orchestrated in a studio by Orson Welles. There was a new profound sense of community, both in the homes, in which families and friends grouped around the radio, and in the discussion of the programs at work and school. At a time when many could feel isolated in their struggle against the effects of the Depression, radio provided a community of experience.

There were also concerns during the 1930s, and later, that radio—and indeed all mass media—would be misused. The wide dissemination of incorrect or selectively chosen information could invite or reinforce opinions. President Roosevelt used the radio to communicate his views and interpretations of the events of the day. His critics charged that he was able to use his unique position and access to mass media to support his views. His Fireside Chats have been considered some of the first forms of managed news. Similarly Father Coughlin promoted anti-Semitic and pro-Hitler positions on the radio. As the country came increasingly close to war, his diocese, in Detroit, chose to review his statements prior to broadcast.

International Perspectives

Throughout the 1930s, as the world careened toward war, America debated the appropriate response to the emerging conflict. In the beginning of the 1930s most Americans—including President Roosevelt— shared the view that the conflict was someone else's. They believed that America should not get involved. As the 1930s progressed, and as reporters such as Edward R. Murrow, H.V. Kaltenborn, and William Shirer broadcast reports of the bombing of London and the German occupation of continental Europe, the view of many Americans began to change. The world seemed to be a smaller place. Czechoslovakia didn't seem so far away, and the invasion of Poland didn't seem so insignificant to the United States. Isolationism seemed less tenable.

More About...

Sound Effects

Sound effects are an important part of communicating drama and comedy over the radio. In the 1930s specialists in radio sound effects emerged to provide that critical element of escapism for those many listeners hoping to escape from the daily problems of coping with the Depression. The specialists had to be very creative to discover ways to communicate and support the action—the sound of walking, breaking glass, a door closing, a train whistling. Sound effects were created in the most innovative ways. The sound of the rocket ship in "Buck Rogers in the Twenty-Fifth Century" was created by placing paper over the air-conditioning vents and placing a microphone in a small spot in the middle.

Radio writers often wrote their sound requirements into the script, as did Irving Reis in his radio play "Meridian 7-1212." The play takes its name from the phone number that New Yorkers could dial in the 1930s to get the accurate time. Below, a lawyer has beaten up a witness who lied, thereby convicting a man who is scheduled to die at midnight. The witness has just confessed, clearing the condemned man. The condemned man's sister is a telephone operator (from Leonard Maltin. *The Great American Broadcast: A Celebration of Radio's Golden Age.* New York: Penguin Putnam, Inc., 1997, pp. 33–34).

NEIL: All right, rat. (*Sock. Body crumples*) There; now he'll be quiet for a minute.

HYLAND: My God, we've got it! We've got it!

NEIL: We'll have to move fast. What time is it?

HYLAND: Quarter to twelve.

NEIL: But you said it what quarter to twelve the last time I asked.

HYLAND: Good lord! My watch stopped . . . I'll get it. (*Picks up phone. Dials ME 7-1212.*)

OPERATOR: (*On filter*) When you hear the signal the time will be eleven fifty-nine. (*Tone: Phone drops to floor*)

HYLAND: An innocent boy is going to die in one minute.

OPERATOR: (*Distant at first, as if coming though receiver on floor*) When you hear the signal the time will be eleven fifty-nine and one quarter. (*Tone. Dissolve next speech from filter to clear*) When you hear the signal the time will be eleven fifty-nine and one half. (*Tone*) (*Her voice starts to break*) When you hear the tone the time will be eleven fifty-nine and three-quarters. (*Tone*) (*The sob is audible now*) When you hear the signal the time will be . . . (*Pause*) twelve o'clock. (*Tone*) (*A high-pitched oscillator whine starts low behind the last call, then is brought up as the full resonance of the Hammond organ and low-frequency oscillator are added. It builds to a crescendo as she screams: 'Tommie! Tommie!' then cuts suddenly into a body fall. Music full, then down and out*)

All over the world the potential of radio was quickly realized. Adolf Hitler in Germany used radio to further his goals. In reaction some countries occupied by German forces in the late 1930s surreptitiously broadcast opposing viewpoints. Radio had become a powerful and influential media for the expression of opinion on an international basis. As more world leaders and their opposition realized that, they were able, increasingly, to take advantage of it to reach millions of prospective supporters for their programs and causes.

Impact

The Golden Age of Radio created a new media environment. At the beginning of the explosion of radio in the 1930s, radio advertising increased while newspaper advertising decreased, though newspapers eventually bounced back. The amazing growth of radio programming during the Depression established all of the major genres in television: dramas, comedies, variety shows, soap operas, talk shows, news commentary, and more. Radio in the 1930s established the framework for broadcasting for the rest of the twentieth century.

The exceptional use of radio news broadcasting in the 1930s created the future expectation of immediacy of information. Americans expected to learn about events quickly, and as television gained momentum later in the century, this expectation was carried into television broadcasting: viewers expected to see events virtually as they happened. The immediacy of information had the added impact of making the entire world feel like one's neighborhood. Nothing seemed too far away, and other cultures that once seemed exotic and strange were more familiar.

The growth in radio provided a large audience for various voices in cultural and political criticism. News programs and commentary provided direct challenges to long-held views, likewise many "entertainment" programs provided cultural criticism. Variety shows lampooned racial preconceptions, theater on the air challenged ideas of war and peace, and comedies provided a humorous critique of Middle American values. While not all radio programs reflected the values in tension during the Great Depression, radio was a forum for exploring the many aspects of America that were being challenged by poverty and decay.

The 1930s were also the genesis of some of the major broadcasting industry conflicts that would continue to be played out throughout the remainder of the twentieth century. Radio companies fought with ASCAP over blanket recording agreements—basically they wanted to be able to play a recording whenever they wanted for a set price. The radio industry wrestled with the government over issues of diversifying ownership and over licensing of AM and FM frequencies. As radio came into its own, it discovered the major issues that would continue to challenge it into the future.

Roosevelt's Fireside Chats set the standard for future presidents to not only use radio to communicate with the public, but the growing mass media of television in the future as well. His successor Harry Truman suffered from his abrupt Midwest behavior before the microphone, which contrasted sharply with Roosevelt's warm wit and charm. The era of television influence came forward in the 1960 presidential campaign between future presidents John F. Kennedy (served 1961–1963) and Richard Nixon (served 1969–1974). Kennedy's good looks and calm demeanor won over many supporters following a live televised debate. Ronald Reagan (served 1981–1989) became another president skilled at using mass media to charm the public and press while seeking to gain support for his programs.

Use of the radio for political purposes by presidents continued into the twenty-first century as President George W. Bush conducted weekly Saturday radio addresses, both in English and Spanish. The shift to television in the 1950s, however, had a major impact on radio. Radio programming shifted away from drama, comedy, and variety shows to other formats including music, talk shows, and news. With these changes radio remained a highly popular medium of entertainment and information for the American public.

Notable People

Jack Benny (1894–1974). Born Benjamin Kubelsky, comedian and musician Jack Benny became an American phenomenon. His career started in vaudeville, and he debuted in 1931 on radio on the Ed Sullivan show, getting his own radio show in 1932. Among the many running jokes on his show were his stinginess, his "feud" with Fred Allen, his ancient Maxwell automobile, and the vault in his basement where he kept his money. His character was particularly appealing to the Great Depression audience that was coping with economic hard times. His special comedic style allowed the joke to be at his expense, instead of at the expense of others. His last radio show was in 1955.

George Burns (1896–1996). Born Nathan Birnbaum, comedian George Burns and his wife and comedic partner Gracie Allen, starred in the Burns and Allen Show on radio beginning in 1933. An outstanding comedic duo, the show was a huge success providing many laughs to the American audiences during the Great Depression and later made the transition to television. Though they married in 1926, Burns and Allen did not tell their radio audience for many years. Later a film and television star, Burns contributed greatly to the development of the early sitcom.

Jean Colbert (?–1995). Colbert was one of radio's earliest and most prolific soap opera performers, appearing in "Stella Dallas," "Life Can be Beautiful," "Young Dr. Malone," "Portia Faces Life," and "Aunt Jenny," among others. Colbert provided an escape for the women of the nation toiling under difficult economic conditions. She also appeared in prime-time programs including the "Lux Radio Theater."

Father Charles Edward Coughlin (1891–1979). Called the "Radio Priest," Father Coughlin began broadcasting weekly sermons in 1926. By the early 1930s Coughlin's broadcasts shifted to economic and political commentary. He began as a supporter of President Roosevelt and the New Deal social and economic programs, but he eventually changed into a harsh critic. Father Coughlin exerted enormous influence on America during the Great Depression. Millions of Americans listened to his weekly radio broadcast. One study showed that more than 15 million Americans listened to Coughlin each month, and more than half of them approved of what he said. While much of his message regarded a type of economic populism, which emphasized the common person, he regularly attacked prominent Jewish people. These attacks that were so strong that he was sometimes called the father of hate speech.

President Roosevelt gives a fireside chat on November 2, 1936, just prior to the 1936 election. (AP/Wide World
Photos. Reproduced by permission.)

Freeman Gosden and Charles Corell (1899–1982). (1890–1972). Freeman Fisher Gosden and Charles James Corell created and starred in the popular radio show "Amos 'n' Andy." Originally broadcast as "Sam 'n' Henry" in 1926, the show was renamed when it changed networks. Gosden and Correll—both white men—appeared in black face and portrayed two Southern men forced to move to a Northern city. The program played on the increased racism related to the hard times of the Great Depres-

sion. The show has subsequently been criticized as racially insensitive and insulting, but some critics contend that it humanized black people.

Have von (H.V.) Kaltenborn (1878–1965). A pioneer in radio, Kaltenborn was first on the air in 1921 and by the 1930s he was a regular newscaster reporting on the Spanish Civil War in 1936. Kaltenborn was close enough to the conflict that listeners could hear gunfire in the background. Kaltenborn also covered the Munich appeasement talks in 1938, reporting—correctly—that Munich was a "complete victory for Hitler." His broadcasts helped lead a shift in public concern away from Great Depression economic problems to foreign policy issues.

Edward R. Murrow (1908–1965). Murrow set the standard for American journalism providing descriptive reports of many of the 1930s and 1940s important events. Murrow reported from Vienna, Austria, in 1938 as the Nazis entered the Austrian capital.

CBS sent Murrow to London in the 1930s and it was from there that he began a series of memorable broadcasts. When war between Germany and the United Kingdom was declared, Murrow reported first-hand. Murrow's broadcasts during the Battle of Britain were often accompanied by air raid sirens or bomb explosions. While in London Murrow brought together several exceptionally talented newsmen, known as "Murrow's Boys."

William S. Paley (1901–1990). Paley developed and ran the CBS radio and television networks. He bought CBS in 1929, building it from a failing network of 22 radio stations into a broadcast empire. Paley and his network worked with many of the major stars of the decade, including Jack Benny, Al Jolson, Kate Smith and Bing Crosby. Paley was responsible for bringing substantial entertainment to the Great Depression audience who could little afford to pursue other forms of entertainment.

David Sarnoff (1891–1971). Former wireless operator Sarnoff rose to president of the Radio Corporation of America. As early as 1916, Sarnoff envisioned a radio that would be as standard in homes as a piano or a phonograph. In 1922 he introduced the Radiola, for $75, and made radio a household appliance. These developments proved timely as the radio provided much entertainment and a source of information for the Depression public.

Orson Welles (1915–1985). Between 1936 and 1941 Orson Welles participated in over one hundred radio drama productions as writer, actor, and director. Welles's Mercury Theatre produced Shakespeare and other classic literature, as well as more popular fare such as "The League of Terror" and "Dracula." In 1937 Welles became the voice of "The Shadow." Welles's work with radio is best remembered for the show on October 30, 1938, when he aired "The War of the Worlds," a story depicting an alien invasion, which caused widespread panic around the United States. Actor John Houseman said of Welles and "The War of the Worlds:" "The reason that show worked as well as it did was . . . nerve . . . the slowness of the show in the beginning." The show, which began

slowly and calmly at first, steadily built to a frantic pace, giving the impression of hours passing in minutes. Welles went on to a legendary career in film; in his film directing debut, the classic *Citizen Kane,* he used many of the techniques—and people—he knew from radio. Welles also took part in the New Deal's Federal Theater Project that provided work for many unemployed actors and stagehands.

Walter Winchell (1897–1972). Winchell is sometimes considered the father of tabloid reporting. After tackling various pursuits in his young life, including time as a vaudevillian dancer, Winchell became a famous news commentator and gossipmonger, drawing millions of listeners during the Great Depression. Winchell had many critics of his approach of publicizing activities that many considered inappropriate for public comment.

Primary Sources

"Amos 'n' Andy"

Hardships of the Great Depression increased hatred toward racial minorities by society in general. This was particularly true of the white unemployed who believed jobs, including those created by New Deal work relief programs, should first go to whites before black Americans. Radio programs capitalized on these emotions that were heightened by the Depression. "Amos 'n' Andy" creators Freeman Gosden and Charles Corell developed a complex world for their characters—two black, Southern men newly transplanted to a Northern city. This reflected the migration of black Americans from Southern rural areas to Northern industrial centers. Listeners waited impatiently for each new episode to discover what troubles would befall the mishap-prone twosome. The complex drama was both criticized for its racial insensitivity and lauded for showing a humanistic portrait of a particular subset of society (from Charles J. Correll and Freeman F. Gosden. *Here They Are—Amos 'n' Andy*. New York: Richard R. Smith, Inc., 1931).

Amos: I wuz sittin' yere dreamin' 'bout Chicago an' 'stead o' puttin' de milk in de bucket, I put half of it on de ground.

Andy: Dat's whut you git fur not tendin' to yore bizness. If I'd been milin' dat cow, son, I wouldn't of wasted a drop o' milk.

Amos: When I tell Mister Hopkins dat I lost half de milk, he goin' git mad wid me.

Andy: Let him git mad wid you. You ain't got no bizness shootin' de milk on de ground.

Amos: I got tell him though 'cause he known I ought to have mo' milk dan dis.

Andy: Instead o' payin' 'tention to whut you was doin', you was sittin' here dreamin'.

Amos: Yeah—if I hadn't been thinkin' 'bout goin' to Chicago den, I'd of got de mil in de buck a' right.

Andy: Well, it's yore own fault—dat's all I got say.

Amos: You know, YOU wuz de one he tol' to milk de COW.

Andy: Dat IS right, ain't it?

Amos: He tol' you to milk de cow—he didn't tell me to do it. You is de one dat's got take de milk in to him.

Andy: On second thought, yere, we better not tell him nothin' 'bout losin' part o' de milk 'cause I don' want him jumpin' all over me.

Amos: Well, whut you goin' do 'bout it? We ought to tell him. Dat's de right thing to do.

Andy: Wait a minute, yere, son. I got a idea.

Amos: Whut you goin' to do now?

Andy: Come on over yere wid me. Han' me dat bucket.

Amos: Where you goin'? Whut you goin' do wid it?

Andy: Yere's de well right yere. We'll fill dat up wid water.

Amos:: Wait a minute—you can't do dat wid de stuff. Dat's goin' make Mister Hopkins mad if he ever find dat out.

Andy: How he goin' find it out?

Amos: He's li'ble to find it out though. We ain't for no bizness puttin' water in de milk.

Andy: Now, lissen yere, Amos—don't never try to tell me whut to do or whut not to do. I know whut I'se doin'.

Amos: I know, but if Mister Hopkins ever see you goin' dat, he's li'ble to fire both of us.

Andy: Hol' dat bucket o' milk dere while I pour some water in it.

Amos: I don' wants to git mixed up in dis. I ain't goin' do it. De man don' want no water in his milk."

Fireside Chats

On March 9, 1937, President Franklin Roosevelt gave his ninth "fireside chat" over the airwaves to the public. Though his topic on this occasion was his proposed reorganization of the Supreme Court, the speech was notable in that he began by reviewing his first fireside chat he made four years earlier. The chat demonstrates Roosevelt's friendly style that many found comforting. Almost one-fourth of the nation normally listened to his fireside chats. They set a new standard for communications between the president and the public (from Franklin Roosevelt. *The Public Papers and Addresses of Franklin D. Roosevelt: 1937 Volume.* New York: The Macmillan Company, 1941, pp. 122–123).

Tonight, sitting at my desk in the White House, I make my first radio report to the people in my second term of office.

I am reminded of that evening in March, four years ago, when I made my first radio report to you. We were then in the midst of the great banking crisis.

Soon after, with the authority of the Congress, we asked the Nation to turn over all of its privately held gold, dollar for dollar, to the Government of the United States.

Today's recovery proves how right that policy was.

But when, almost two years later, it came before the Supreme Court its constitutionality was upheld only by a five-to-four vote. The change of one vote would have thrown all the affairs of this great Nation back into hopeless chaos. In effect, four Justices ruled that the right under a private contract to exact a pound of flesh was more sacred than the main objectives of the Constitution to establish an enduring Nation.

In 1933 you and I knew that we must never let our economic system get completely out of joint again—that we could not afford to take the risk of another great depression.

We also became convinced that the only way to avoid a repetition of those dark days was to have a government with power to prevent and to cure the abuses and the inequalities which had thrown that system out of joint.

We then began a program of remedying those abuses and inequalities—to give balance and stability to our economic system—to make it bomb-proof against the causes of 1929.

Today we are only part-way through that program—and recovery is speeding up to a point where the dangers of 1929 are gain becoming possible, not this week or month perhaps, but within a year or two.

National laws are needed to complete that program. Individual or local or state effort alone cannot protect us in 1937 any better than ten years ago.

It will take time—and plenty of time—to work out our remedies administratively even after legislation is passed. To complete our program of protection in time, therefore, we cannot delay one moment in making certain that our National Government has power to carry through.

Four yeas ago action did not come until the eleventh hour. It was almost too late . . .

I want to talk with you very simply about the need for present action in this crisis—the need to meet the unanswered challenge of one-third of a Nation ill-nourished, ill clad, ill-housed.

Suggested Research Topics

- Compare the growth in and uses of radio during the 1930s with the growth and use of the Internet during the 1990s.

- Discuss how radio changed America's response to the war in Europe—the war that would eventually become World War II. How did radio change American's understanding of the people "over there?" How was radio used to try to change Americans view of the conflict?

- Listen to the radio news, watch television news, and read a newspaper all on the same day. Compare coverage of news events in the three media.

Bibliography

Sources

Barnouw, Erik. *The Golden Web: A History of Broadcasting in the United States, Volume II, 1933 to 1953.* New York: Oxford University Press, 1968.

———. *A Tower of Babel: A History of Broadcasting in the United States, Volume I, to 1933.* New York: Oxford University Press, 1966.

Best, Gary Dean. *The Nickel and Dime Decade: American Popular Culture During the 1930s.* Westport, CT and London: Praeger, 1993.

Bolino, August C. *From Depression to War: American Society in Transition—1939.* Westport, CT and London: Praeger, 1998.

Brown, Robert J. *Manipulating the Ether: The Power of Broadcast Radio in Thirties America.* Jefferson, NC: McFarland & Co., 1998.

Bruccoli, Mathew J. and Richard Layman. *American Decades: 1930–1939.* Detroit, MI: Gale Research, Inc. 1995.

Davies, Alan. "The First Radio War: Broadcasting in the Spanish Civil War, 1936–1939." In *Historical Journal of Film, Radio, and Television.* October 1999.

Douglas, Susan Jeanne. *Inventing American Broadcasting 1899–1922.* Baltimore, MD: Johns Hopkins University Press, 1994.

Garner, Joe. *We Interrupt This Broadcast.* Naperville, IL: Sourcebooks, 1998.

Hillard, Robert L and Michael C. Keith. *The Broadcast Century and Beyond: A Biography of American Broadcasting.* Woburn, MA: Butterworth-Heinemann, 2001.

Hilmes, Michele. *Radio Voices: American Broadcasting, 1922–1952.* Minneapolis, MN: University of Minnesota Press, 1997.

Hilmes, Michele and Jason Loviglio. eds. *Radio Reader: Essays in the Cultural History of Radio.* New York: Routledge, 2001.

Lackmann, Ronald. *This was Radio.* New York: Great American Audio Corporation, 2000.

Watkins, T.H. *The Great Depression.* Boston, MA: Little, Brown & Co., 1993.

Further Reading

Bergmeier, Horst J. *Hitler's Airwaves: The Inside Story of Nazi Radio Broadcasting and Propaganda Swing.* New Haven, CT: Yale University Press, 1997.

Carpenter, Ronald H. *Father Charles E. Coughlin: Surrogate Spokesman for the Disaffected.* Westport, CT: Greenwood, 1998.

Douglas, Susan J. *Listening in: Radio and the American Imagination: From Amos 'n' Andy and Edward R. Murrow to Wolfman Jack and Howard Stern.* New York: Crown Publishing Croup, 2000.

Ely, Melvin Patrick. *The Adventures of Amos 'n Andy: A Social History of an American Phenomenon.* New York: The Free Press, 1991.

Kendrick, Alexander. *Prime-Time: The Life of Edward R. Murrow.* Boston: Little, Brown, 1969.

Nachmann, Gerald. *Raised on Radio.* New York: Pantheon Books, 1998.

Russo, Alexander. *Broadcasting Freedom: Radio, War and the Politics of Race, 1938–1948.* London and Chapel Hill, NC: University of North Carolina Press, 1999.

Warren, Donald. *Radio Priest: Charles Coughlin, the Father of Hate Radio.* New York: Free Press, 1996.

Riding the Rails

1929-1941

Introduction

The crash of the stock market in October 1929 followed by the Great Depression brought considerable economic suffering to millions of Americans. Many lost their jobs or saw their incomes reduced. Schools reduced the length of school years in many areas or closed altogether. By early 1933 over 12 million workers were unemployed amounting to almost 25 percent of the U.S. workforce and hundreds of thousands of children were out of school. Three million of those jobless were also young, between 16 and 25 years of age. Seeing no hope for employment where they lived, many of all ages decided to take to the rails jumping on freight and passenger trains without paying and riding them to various parts of the nation. Most were in search of better job opportunities elsewhere so they could send money back home, while others were looking for adventure. No longer a world of middle aged men, the rails brigade now included thousands of youths, some as young as 13 years of age, and increasing numbers of women and minorities. Along the way they met adventure, hunger, hardship, hostile security guards and law authorities, danger, boredom, and despair, as well as many other people doing the same.

Between 1933 and 1938 President Franklin Delano Roosevelt (served 1933–1945) introduced the New Deal, a large array of social and economic programs designed to combat the Great Depression and provide relief to those most affected. The New Deal made special efforts to provide support for the sudden

growth in the nation's wandering or transient population. New Deal programs that addressed the transient included the Federal Transient Service, the Civil Works Administration (CWA), the Civilian Conservation Corps (CCC), the Works Progress Administration (WPA), and the National Youth Administration (NYA) within the WPA. Each of these programs offered various forms of relief and care services, including jobs on public projects, a network of transient shelters, and education programs. But given the size of the transient population—estimated at two to three million in early 1933, including 250,000 riding the rails—most any effort would ultimately only reach a small percentage. Therefore that assistance would only last temporarily before they were once again out looking for work in private business. Just as the Great Depression lingered through the 1930s, so did the large number of individuals riding the rails across America.

Issue Summary

A Flood of Transients

As the Great Depression worsened through 1930 and 1931, private charities and local relief agencies that had assisted transients in the past several decades were overwhelmed. By 1933 12 million people were out of work as the unemployment rate hit 25 percent. The Great Depression brought not only high unemployment rates but closed many schools as well. Millions of children were affected by shortened school years in the 1933–34 school year. Approximately five thousand schools had closed altogether, affecting 175,000 children. By 1934 there were 25,000 fewer teachers than in 1930, and by 1935, 40 percent of the 10 million high school aged youth in America were out of school. In rural school districts it was up to 60 percent. Success in finding a job for youth both out of school and in school was highly elusive. In New York State in 1934 almost 80 percent of the 16 year olds seeking jobs were unsuccessful. The New York Committee on Unemployed Youth published a handbook on the problem of jobs and schools titled "Youth Never Comes Again."

The Great Depression caused major changes in the nation's homeless and transient population in various ways. The most obvious change was in the increasing number of people roaming the nation's rails and roads. In January 1933 the National Committee on Care of Transient and Homeless conducted a survey of public and private agencies in 809 cities to determine how many were being cared for during a

Chronology:

1932: With a rise in homelessness and transience brought on by the Great Depression, a group of citizens and social workers establish the National Committee on Care for Transients and Homeless (NCCTH) to provide solutions to the problem and lobby Congress.

January 1933: Estimates provided to Congress by various organizations including the NCCTH reveal that well over one million Americans are now homeless and almost one-fourth are riding the rails. Youth comprising 40 percent of that number.

April 1933: President Franklin Roosevelt tackles the problem of jobless male youth by creating the Civilian Conservation Corps (CCC), which will provide jobs for young adults over the next 12 years.

September 1933: The Federal Transient Service is established and creates almost six hundred relief centers for transients including those living on the rails.

November 1933: Roosevelt creates the Civil Works Administration to provide temporary work for transients and other jobless individuals through the winter months.

September 1935: The Federal Transient Service is terminated, transferring those capable of working to work relief on Work Progress Administration (WPA) projects.

1935: As part of the WPA, the National Youth Administration (NYA) is established to help youth stay in school and provide work for those who are not.

specific three-day period. Their count came to over 370,000 homeless population. Based on this figure it was estimated that the total homeless population, including those not receiving shelter or care during the three-day period, was 1,225,000. Some thought that there could be as many as two or three million homeless. It was further estimated that half of the homeless were transients with many of those riding the rails. In February 1935 federal facilities were providing care

A twenty-year-old "hobo" riding in a freight car who had been hopping freight trains for two years. People of all ages were "hopping freights" during the Depression. (National Archives and Records Administration. Reproduced by permission.)

people were looking toward going to another place with better job opportunities and starting a new life as productive members of society. Instead of trying to escape the American Dream that consists of financial security with a house, family, and community attachment, they were searching for it. These new transients mingled with the veteran transients making for a much more diverse transient population.

Hopping a train was clearly a new experience for many in the Great Depression, especially the youth. In 1927 over 50 percent of transients thrown off railroad property were men in their forties or older. By 1932, 75 percent of those accused of trespassing were under 25 years of age. In that year it was estimated 250,000 youth between the ages of 15 and 25 were riding the rails, and one in 20 American youth had left home.

The numbers of transients arriving daily in communities stretched available food supplies and shelters. By 1931 Deming, New Mexico, was seeing 125 transients arrive each day. Tucson, Arizona, had approximately 250 arrivals each day, most less than 21 years of age. In 1932 five thousand transients a month were traveling through New Orleans, most of them youth, a figure also reported in Houston. Kansas City reported seven hundred youths on freight trains a day, and three hundred hitchhiking by car. Los Angeles counted 11,000 transients arriving each month, and city relief agencies did not want to spend local tax revenues on non-residents. State assistance to the communities was very limited. President Herbert Hoover's (served 1929–1933) administration offered little relief and almost no support for transients and youth.

California was the destination for many where they sought migrant farm work. In response the state setup work camps to provide workers for local businesses and farmers. But before long, with state revenues falling due to the economic crisis of the Depression, California was going broke and urged the federal government to deal with the transients. The communities were having a difficult time caring for their own residents affected by the Depression and did not wish to assist those arriving from elsewhere. Towns began setting limits on how long a transient could stay and the practice grew of "passing on" transients to the next community. In "passing on," transients, hopping off trains, would be told to get back on and leave town, or if already in town were sometimes given a meal and a night's shelter then told to leave by the police. Some towns sought to discourage transients jumping off trains in their town by arresting them and sentencing them to 20 days in jail. They were often released, however, after only two days and told to leave town.

for over 300,000 homeless including over 36,000 families. With the transient population changing daily and being highly mobile no accurate estimates were ever available.

The reasons for transience also changed with the Depression. A primary reason for transience before the Depression was to escape from society's norms. Now

Many transients favored riding the rails over hitchhiking along the country's roads. Getting to the next town was slower by car particularly given the condition of many roads in this early period of automobile use. Also rides usually gained by hitchhiking were only for short distances, which required a lot more effort because a hitchhiker would have to catch a series of multiple rides toward a destination. There was always the uncertainty of actually finding a ride whereas trains ran on schedules. In addition rides through the night were rare compared to the routine availability of all-night rides on trains. Hitchhiking would also leave a person away from the series of transient camps along rail lines or shelters in town centers. Perhaps most importantly, a hitchhiker was largely on his own, susceptible to the dangers of meeting up with the wrong people. Riding on trains made a transient part of an army with sometimes several hundred transients on a single train.

Thousands of those riding the rails would follow the agricultural harvest cycle across the country for six or seven months out of the year. Such a cycle could include: the early spring vegetable and citrus crops in California; then hay harvest in interior California and the Mountain states in early summer; corn next ripened in the Midwest in summer; berries, hops, and fruits in the Northwest in the fall; and, during winter, the cotton fields of the Southeast. Transients found the work hard and wages at poverty levels. They would try to save enough money to make it through winter. As the Depression deepened, however, many crops became worthless because there were few means to transport them to markets and few customers with cash to pay for them, therefore harvest work declined. Some transients also found work at big public events such as the 1932 Los Angeles Summer Olympics, the 1933 World's Fair, and the 1939 San Francisco World's Fair.

In addition to the Depression, another factor contributing to the growing number of transients in the later 1930s was the drought that was particularly bad on the Southern Plains of the United States. The region from the Dakotas south to the panhandle of Texas literally dried up. The southern part of the region that was hit worst became known as the Dust Bowl. It was estimated that the drought itself forced four million on the road seeking a better life elsewhere. Most of the Dust Bowl refugees, however, would head west to California.

Riding the Rails

Transients riding the rails formed a society in itself. This society, however, was far different from any kind of society to which a new rider was accustomed. They had much to learn. Common places to ride were inside or on top of boxcars on freight trains or in blinds, which are locations between cars on passenger trains. Some would practice riding the rails at first, catching a freight train on a Saturday and riding to a nearby town and then coming back. This would build up experience and courage to leave for a long-term trip. Hundreds of transients could hop a single train, and it was reported that up to six hundred rode on some trains.

Finding places to briefly stay while not on a train was a daily concern. In towns the Salvation Army, missions, and city shelters provided meals and beds. At the Salvation Army transients were required to attend a brief prayer service before being served food, usually in a small dining room. To discourage youth from living on the road, relief centers would offer only two meals and one night of lodging to teenagers while adults could receive six meals and two nights of lodging.

On the outskirts of towns and in rural areas, camps, commonly called "jungles," could be found in brush or trees. Garbage piles of cans, glass, and other debris, and sometimes the scatter of flimsy shacks marked the camp locations. Often broken mirrors were left hanging from tree limbs for the use of the next transient while shaving or brushing their teeth. Hunting for wood, often twigs, to keep campfires burning during cold weather was a constant task through the night. When camps were unavailable or not desired some transients would sleep under bridges or other locations.

Dangers on the Rails

The hazards of riding the rails were many. Of course, hopping on trains without paying was illegal. Those hopping trains faced the possibility of arrest if caught by railroad security guards, commonly referred to as "bulls," or local police. Railroad companies reported considerable damage to trains and their cargo from stealing and the opening of vents to boxcars ruining cargoes of vegetables and fruits. Young or old, transients could be arrested for just hanging around train yards on charges of trespassing or vagrancy. Sometimes boys caught in the freight yards were beaten by the railroad bulls. Trespass and vagrancy was commonly punishable by time in jail and hard labor. A transient is a person traveling around, usually in search of work. A vagrant is a person wandering about with no permanent address and no visible means of financial support. A trespasser is a person who unlawfully enters the land of another person.

Twelve "hoboes" riding on a typical flat car somewhere between Bakersfield and Fresno, CA.
(National Archives)

In some areas local farms relied on the arrested transients in local communities for field labor. Other communities would impose 30-day jail sentences or work on chain gangs. Riders found better success catching trains at the edge of train yards where tracks converge to the mainline than in the rail yards that were more closely patrolled. Of course bulls could be hiding on trains, or even disguised as a transient ready to catch the trespassers. Sometimes railroad company bulls and town police were at odds over what to do about transients. Railroad guards would be pulling transients off trains and town police wanted them to stay on the trains and move on through to the next town. The Southern Pacific railroad reported that its guards had removed over 683,000 transients from its trains and yards during 1932, up from over 170,000 in 1930 and only 78,000 in 1927 prior to the Great Depression.

Other common hazards of the rails included train wrecks and getting thrown from trains by sudden turns.

In addition train tunnels would fill with black coal smoke leading to near suffocation for those caught unaware while riding on the outside of a train. Another danger came from other transients due to the fact that assaults were commonplace. Riders were advised to travel with partners as danger was always just around the corner. Thousands of transients were killed or injured each year as a result of train wrecks or assaults. The federal Interstate Commerce Commission reported that about 25,000 trespassers were killed and 27,000 injured on trains or in railroad yards during the Great Depression between 1929 and 1939. During a 10-month period in 1932 it was estimated that approximately six thousand transients were killed or injured.

Another difficulty was lack of food with hunger spells sometimes lasting up to several days. Various strategies were learned for surviving. For instance some reported better success at receiving food from homes by going down alleys and knocking at backdoors of houses rather than knocking at the front door. Often the transient would offer to work for some food or money. Many were futilely trying to earn money to send back home. Inexperienced youth, however, faced tough competition and were frequently paid less for doing the same work as an adult.

Aside from the physical hazards was the psychological toll. Fellow train riders or camp residents were often found in quiet, gloomy moods. There were few feelings of fellowship or close-knit ties among the transients. With tempers quick and arguments frequent, camps were particularly dangerous for younger transients.

Other hazards abounded such as problems of sanitation, which were everywhere. With restrooms not often available people had to relieve themselves wherever they could. As a result sanitation was a particular problem around well-used areas such as camps. The camp trash heaps would attract rats that were common sights around camps. Finding good drinking water was also a problem. Creeks and ponds were often available but contamination was always a possibility. In towns public toilets were soon overused by the growth of the homeless population during the Depression. As the Depression deepened they became broken or unkempt. Other options included sneaking into service station restrooms or using the facilities at railroad passenger stations. Socks and other clothes were washed in streams using bars of soap and hung in trees to dry. Many communities refused to provide medical care to transients not wanting to attract more transients to their town.

In 1933 Warner Brothers produced a movie *Wild Boys of the Road* that warned youth of the dangers of riding freight trains. The movie, however, actually served to entice many to the adventure of travel, the exact opposite of its aim.

Racial minorities and women were particularly vulnerable to dangers on the rails. Young women rode the rails in far fewer numbers than young men and often traveled disguised as males for safety reasons. Others traveled with one or two males, or with a group of boys. It was estimated in January 1933 that of the 256,000 transients riding the rails, 11,323 were women with 35 to 40 percent of the women under the age of 21. Before the Depression no more than a thousand would have been women under the age of 21.

A study in Buffalo, New York, in 1935 indicated that of the 20,000 transients identified, only 660 were black. Though racism was prominent throughout the nation, black Americans riding the rails were especially in great danger in the South where lynchings were on the rise during the early years of the Depression. Lynchings were illegal hangings of a person, usually a black man, by a mob without state or local authorization.

Transients and the New Deal

By 1933 the number of transients in America had skyrocketed. No longer were transients middle-aged men, they were increasingly the youth of America. This marked trend caused by the Great Depression alarmed much of the public including then-President-elect Franklin Roosevelt.

Upon taking office on March 4, Roosevelt took action. One of the first acts passed by Congress as part of Roosevelt's New Deal program was the Federal Emergency Relief Act (FERA) in April 1933, which provided funds to states to help those in need, including transients and homeless. FERA also funded a college work-study program to help youth stay in school. For students still in school, FERA also offered a Student Aid Program, which provided part-time work for students. In 1934 and 1935, 100,000 students received funds. The normal amount was only $13 a month, but in the 1930s this was just enough to enable many young people to stay in school.

Roosevelt and the New Dealers consulted with a number of leading experts and organizations concerning social work for the poor. Included in Roosevelt's consultations were: Edith Abbott, dean of the University of Chicago's School of Social Administration; Nels Anderson, professor at Columbia University in New York City and head of the National Committee on Care for Transients and Homeless (NCCTH); and, Bertha McCall, executive director of the National Association for Travelers Aid.

Two policemen wait for "hoboes" on a Saturday night in Millburg, Michigan, in 1940. Hopping trains meant possible arrest if caught by police. (The Library of Congress.)

In September 1933 the Federal Transient Relief Service was established under the authority of FERA. Elizabeth Wickenden was appointed Assistant Director of Transient Activities for the Federal Emergency Relief Administration. The Service set up treatment centers for transients of all ages in 250 cities and towns and established 350 work camps in rural areas. These centers and camps provided a place for a meal and a bed. The work camps provided work for those who were going to stay for a while. Various temporary jobs were provided such as road maintenance work, mosquito control, and improving city parks. These camps also provided recreation and study facilities. Camp residents received room and board and from 1 to 3 dollars a week for spending money. By 1935 the Transient Service was serving 200,000 homeless and one third of these were under 25 years of age. The Transient Service also sent men from its treatment centers to vocational classes often held in unused school buildings where a wide variety of subjects were offered. Some claimed the camps were too nice and contributed to transience by providing such good food and shelter. Many also thought the Service should be aggressive in sending transients back to wherever they had come originally from. The policy of the Transient

Service, however, was to provide care to the transients wherever they happened to be, not to enforce resettlement in other locations against their will.

Like many New Deal programs, the Transient Service was the first federal program of its kind. As a result it had to construct facilities, train staff, and establish standards for transient care. Many felt its closure in September 1935, after only two years of operation, terminated the program just as it was becoming fully effective. Social workers had hailed the program as the most important advance in social work in years. Upon its sudden closure those served by the Service were scattered about. The employable were enrolled to work on projects for the Works Progress Administration (WPA). People just arriving to the federal camps were directed to state and local relief agencies. The small percentage of the unemployable, approximately seven percent, were sent back to committees. The Transient Service continued serving some already settled in camps for the next couple of years before closing the doors completely. Federal transient care between January 1933 and March 1937 cost the federal government over $106 million, averaging $5 million a month during its peak period in early 1935. Unfortunately closure of the Transient Service corresponded with the increased migration of refugees out of the Dust Bowl region of the Southern Plains that had been suffering from years of drought and massive dust storms. Other New Deal agencies such as the Resettlement Administration, primarily created to help poor farmers find a new start, would establish migrant camps in California and the Southwest to accommodate these new transients.

Some New Deal programs also attempted to keep people from riding the rails or entice those who already had begun riding the rails back into a more hopeful situation. A favorite of President Roosevelt's, the Civilian Conservation Corps (CCC), was created in 1933 and recruited young men between the ages of 16 and 25 to work on conservation projects around the nation. The projects included soil erosion control, fighting forest fires, planting trees, building flood control facilities, and fighting insect infestations. Within only a few months 240,000 youth had been settled in 1,200 camps. The enrollees were paid $30 a month of which $25 had to be sent home to their families. Over two thousand camps were established by mid-1935 providing free room and board in addition to the pay. Many youth riding the rails who had home addresses and a family to send money to rushed to join.

Seeing many, including the transients, out of work in late 1933 with winter approaching, Roosevelt launched another work relief program. The Civil Works Administration (CWA) was established to provide work to help people through the tough winter months. It was only a temporary measure, however, and it ended in the spring of 1934.

Roosevelt established the Works Progress Administration (WPA) in 1935 as a massive work relief program, creating jobs in construction of public facilities. With the ending of the Transient Service in September 1935, many of those able to work were enrolled in the WPA. As part of the WPA in June 1935 President Roosevelt established the National Youth Administration (NYA) with Aubrey Williams as its director. The NYA extended the Student Aid Program of FERA by providing financial aid to secondary, college, and graduate students between the ages of 16 and 25. Like the Federal Transient Relief Service under FERA, it was an effort to keep youth in school and off the rails. They provided $6 a month for needy high school students, $20 a month for college students, and $40 a month for college graduate students.

For those not still in school, the NYA also had its own work relief programs building community and recreation centers. The NYA served young women as well as young men and set up 50 camps that served five thousand young women. They stayed at the camps from three to four months and received training for technical and professional jobs. Other work projects of the NYA were predominantly in schools and hospitals.

Through its programs, in 1936 the NYA gave cash aid to over 581,000 youth. Some 45 percent of recipients were female. Also included were 19,000 black American youth through the Negro Branch. Though one of the most responsive New Deal agencies toward minorities, it still was far short of the demand as 400,000 black Americans between the ages of 14 and 16 were estimated to be on relief rolls at the time.

In support of the New Deal programs that assisted transient youth, private organizations also sought new solutions to the problem. The American Council on Education created the American Youth Commission in the mid-1930s to seek ideas in solving problems in education. The goal was to entice youth back into the classroom. At the time one out of seven youths were on relief rolls, or about six million young people. Advocates for helping the youth lobbied Congress for another bill, the American Youth Act in 1936. The act would guarantee a free public education for the needy as well as assistance for living expenses. A pro-youth march on Washington, DC, was held in February 1937. It was during this time that a federation of youth and student organizations around the nation, known as the American Youth Congress, issued a declaration of rights for youth focused on education needs, the right to a safe and warm home, and opportunity to work.

Despite the CCC, the NYA, and other New Deal programs, tens of thousands of youth still rode the rails. They were either ineligible for whatever reason, exhausted their relief availability, or simply were out of reach from New Deal programs.

Private Organizations Influencing the New Deal

Since the end of the nineteenth century increasing numbers of private organizations were formed to assist transients and the homeless as the problem persisted in the newly industrialized nation. A key organization that was active through the Great Depression was the Travelers Aid. First organized in New York City in 1905 the organization provided relief services to transients. The organization provided food, clothing, and transportation. It would also refer transients to the Salvation Army or other places for temporary shelter when needed. Travelers Aid also published pamphlets on the transient problem in the United States and advised the federal government on the issue, at times testifying before Congress.

The National Committee on Care of Transient and Homeless (NCCTH) was formed in 1932 to address the rising transient issue of the Great Depression. The NCCTH was composed of a group of concerned individuals—professional social workers, academic staff, and knowledgeable citizens. It became the primary national group to campaign for solutions to transient problems. The NCCTH collected new data, held public hearings, conducted surveys and research, and lobbied Congress. While the Federal Transient Service was at the height of its operation between 1933 and 1935, the NCCTH served as a watchdog over the agency. It regularly assessed the performance of the agency's camps and evaluated the standards kept. In 1938 the NCCTH changed its name to the Council on Interstate Migration recognizing that homeless issues had broadened away from solely focusing on transient homeless. A year later Travelers Aid absorbed it.

In reaction to the federal government's elimination of the Transient Service, several large regional conferences were held on the subject in the late 1930s. For example the Trenton Conference on Transient and Settlement Laws was held March 1936 and twenty-two eastern states sent representatives. Similar conferences were held in the Midwest and New York. A common purpose of all of them was to call for greater federal action on behalf of transients. No further specific action, however, was adopted by the New Deal.

More About...
Language of the Rails

Those who rode the rails developed their own subculture, important for survival. A key part of this mobile society was communication through language. In addition to a spoken language, a written language of signs also aided communication. Many transients would carry a piece of chalk in their pocket. Through a use of common symbols they would mark locations where food could be found, safe campsites, dangerous dogs, dangerous towns, and clean drinking water.

- Bindle: cloth folded over filled with traveling necessities such as a razor, bar of soap, small towel, socks, drinking cup, and jack knife.

- Blinds: spaces between cars of a passenger train where a person could stand without being easily seen; it is a short walkway surrounded by an accordion-like structure around it.

- Brakie: the train brakeman.

- Bum: someone who did not travel or work.

- Catch out: hop on your first freight train.

- Dingbat: an experienced hobo.

- Dumped: physically attacked or assaulted.

- Gaycat: someone new to hoboing.

- Grab iron: the vertical railing on a train car to catch hold of.

- Hobo: someone who traveled and worked when jobs could be found.

- Hobo tobacco: dried leaves crushed and rolled into a cigarette.

- Hoosiers: people who are not transients; the general public.

- Hoover tourists: homeless catching rides on trains.

- Jungle: transient camps in woods near the train tracks where hoboes could stop overnight or for the short term to wash, cook, rest, and sleep.

- Jungle buzzards: hoboes who lived at camps for weeks or months at a time.

- Knee shaker: receiving a plate of food while sitting on a back porch.

- Lump: a handout consisting of a sack of food.

- Mulligan stew: a soup composed of whatever food scraps may be obtained, boiled over a campfire.

- On the fly: catching a train while it is rolling.

- Railroad bull: security guards employed by a railroad company, hired to get transients off railroad property.

- Sally: Salvation Army facility where temporary food and shelter could be found.

- Sit down: being invited to come inside a house and eat with a family.

- Solid reefers: loaded refrigerator cars filled with ice; they were a source of drinking water from the dripping below the car.

- Tramp: someone who traveled but did not work.

- Yeggs: tramps with a criminal nature.

Contributing Forces

Industrialization and Homelessness

During colonial times the homeless and transients were known as the wandering poor. They included itinerant workers, poor widows with their children, and the disabled. The occurrence of transients led to vagrancy laws based on earlier English law. These laws often dictated removal of the strangers from the community. During the early years of the United States the federal government had no responsibility for addressing transient issues. They were left strictly to the state and local governments resulting in much variation in how transients were dealt with.

As industrialization of America gained momentum through the nineteenth century in the United States, the American populace shifted from predominately rural agricultural communities to an urban society concentrated around industrial centers. No longer did the average American worker have the economic safety net of family and a small rural community when times got hard. The worker was in a much less personal high-density living environment.

With the pace of industrialization rapidly increasing after the Civil War, the economic recession of 1873 and 1874 hit workers hard. Workers found themselves out of a job as factories cut back production. Three million people became unemployed and no unemployment insurance systems existed. The number of transients increased significantly for the first time in U.S. history. Unaccustomed to such widespread homelessness the public became alarmed. In response Rhode Island passed a Tramps Act in 1880 that became a model for other states. In an effort to control transience in their state the law allowed the arrest and conviction of transients and sentenced to time in workhouses. This would be the first of various anti-transient acts around the country. When the economy improved in the 1880s the issue of transience decreased in urgency.

A greater number of immigrants entered the country in the late nineteenth century and, looking for work in U.S. industrial centers, increased competition over jobs. With the arrival of another economic recession in 1893 transients became a permanent segment of the U.S. capitalist economic system. Though not many transients were actually immigrants the increased competition for jobs took its toll. The newly formed permanent transient population actually became a functioning part of the U.S. economy providing seasonal unskilled labor to Midwest farms, mining and logging camps, working on railroad construction crews, and contributing to other projects. They generally rode the rails from job to job. The size of this segment of society would regularly increase and shrink based on the general health of the U.S. economy. There was a steady turnover in its membership through time as well. Besides including those without a job, it also consisted of those who could not adapt to the new industrial society and had a compulsion to wander, resisting integration into an established community. These people sought detachment from society.

In response to this rise of a transient segment of society hundreds of public and private relief agencies were established. For transient youths railroad companies even offered charity rates for their return home. Arrival of the Depression soon overwhelmed these organizations and help was no longer readily available.

During the 1920s those riding the rails were permanent transients and seasonal workers. The Great Depression brought a third category, the unemployed. By the early 1930s, 70 percent of those riding the rails were from this category.

Children in the Depression

Though the Great Depression affected millions of people in a multitude of ways, many claimed it was perhaps the children who suffered the affects the longest, sometimes lasting the rest of their lives. Years of poverty, hunger, and lack of hope for the future left a lasting mark. Often the lights and water service were cut off to a family out of work and unable to pay the bills. The house and car payments fell behind eventually leading to repossession by the bank that held the loan or mortgage. Meals consisting of mainly potatoes were supplemented by leftover meat bones obtained from a butcher.

Life at school might not be much better. With people losing their jobs or receiving pay cuts, tax revenues for public school systems were declining. Plans for new buildings were put on hold and cutbacks were made in textbooks, teacher salaries, and supplies. Classrooms became more crowded as teachers were reduced in number and school years were shortened. By late 1930 in the first full year of the Depression over three million children between ages seven and 17 were out of school. One-third of these had found work in factories or on farms as families sought additional sources of income. Child labor laws were weakly enforced given the dire need of struggling families. By the following year 2,600 schools across the nation had been closed and this number grew further to four thousand by 1933. By then nearly four million students had been affected either by shortened school years or closed schools.

In some circumstances youths found themselves a burden on a family that did not have enough resources to feed every mouth. They felt they had to leave, and then hoped that on the road they could find work. Others left abusive family situations, while some simply were looking for adventure. Often a combination of factors provided the stimulus to leave home, and one of the only options was to take to the rails.

Perspectives

Local Perspectives

The public had varying perspectives of the youth on rails. By 1932 the national press found the story of hundreds of thousands of youthful transients captivating to their readers. To some they represented the adventurous American spirit, the same spirit that pushed earlier Americans further and further onto the frontier as America expanded westward in the nineteenth century. To these individuals the youth displayed an amazing amount of resourcefulness in adapting to life on the rails. In fact they believed the more ambitious youth took to the rails, unwilling to accept the lack of work and opportunity in their hometown.

Two youths search the trainyard for an empty freight car so they can catch a ride. Many young people sought better job opportunities by starting a new life in another part of the country during the Great Depression. (National Archives and Records Administration. Reproduced by permission.)

Others feared the youth would become hardened by experiences on the rails, living off of others, begging for money and handouts, and playing on the sympathies of others. The new transients of the Great Depression were taught petty crimes and stealing by veteran transients, and some eventually turned into criminals.

Public attitudes toward transients and the homeless became more negative at first as the Great Depres-

sion progressed. Rights to public relief or social services were tied to local residence laws, which varied greatly among the states. A common response to the increased occurrence of transients was to make state residency requirements tougher to qualify for. In some states a person could lose rights to relief if they were away from an area for only six months. Other states asserted a person could not qualify for relief until they had resided in the state for at least five years. As a result many transients riding the rails had no relief rights in any state. Their only access to help was the minimal assistance provided by charities.

Before the New Deal programs were established, and given the extent of the problem of the Depression, the public called for a nationwide federal program to solve the transient problem. With President Herbert Hoover firmly believing in self-help, the federal government provided little relief prior to 1933.

Riding the rails was a hardening experience. For many there was the thrill of adventure and freedom at first, however, after several months the thrill was gone with breadlines, begging, trashy camps, and torn and dirty clothes. After a while of riding the rails people would become stoic and fatigued, which some compared to the battle fatigue of war. They had largely given up on life. Months or years of little food and sleep and watching out for tough characters changed a person. After being a transient for so long, some people would lose direction in life and just aimlessly drift in a perpetual state of loneliness. As many later noted in memoirs, after a while you looked and smelled like a bum and people treated you like a bum. Life on the rails also provided a dramatic education of conditions of Americans during the Great Depression. Seeing entire families living on the road seemed particularly difficult to witness for the younger transients.

To combat the public stigma of transients and the homeless, national advocacy groups had studies conducted in the early 1930s to show that the make-up of the transient population had become similar in character to the general population. There were now women, youth, and most strikingly whole families. The local and national press, however, often fed the public negative images of transients by highlighting any violent confrontations with law authorities. Harry Hopkins, head of the WPA, and others tried to underscore that these were not professional bums, but workers and farmers, displaced by economic hard times and looking for a new start. Photographs by federally sponsored photographers such as Dorothea Lange put a human face on transients for much of the public when the photographs began to appear in national magazines and exhibits. To provide further positive images of transients, Warner Brothers movie production company released a film titled *Stranded* that showed transients and the Federal Transient Service in a favorable light.

The more positive and sympathetic messages began to have an effect, and public attitudes toward transients became less hostile through the later 1930s. Many of the transients performed work beneficial to the communities through New Deal programs and assisted in times of need such as seasonal floods.

When in September 1935 Aubrey Williams announced termination of the Transient Service, much of the public objected to the closing of the camps.

Some observed that each part of the country had a different perspective on transients. This variation probably reflected unique economic histories and specific needs of each region during the Depression. One person described the Midwest as empathetic, they were shunned in the Atlantic states, the Southeast was perhaps least helpful, the Mountain states frequently offered work, and Los Angeles had actually declared war by forming police blockades to keep transients out.

National Perspectives

Though some notions of political radicalism, including talk of revolution, lingered around campfires and boxcars there was never much momentum. Most transients were more concerned with day-to-day survival while riding the rails. Even given the younger population riding the rails few would be considered political radicals. The transient population was unorganized and largely politically conservative. Those who still held hope for the future were primarily looking for job opportunities and success in the existing economic system of the United States.

Many found fresh hope with the newly created Civilian Conservation Corps (CCC) in the summer of 1933. They quickly abandoned the rails and enrolled in CCC camps. The CCC was one national answer to providing hope to the youth of the nation, particularly the male youth. Under Roosevelt's leadership the CCC was a unique organization. The Department of Labor recruited the enrollees; the Department of War built the camps, supplied them, and provided transportation to work sites; and the Departments of Interior and Agriculture selected the projects. The projects were both private farmlands and on public lands including national forests and National Parks. Despite the learning of new skills, still 75 percent of the enrollees could not find employment after their first six-month tour with CCC ended. Sixty percent could not find work after their second tour.

The federal government began looking at the "youth problem" attempting to identify the factors driving so many away from home and school. Many feared a "lost generation" would result from the period. Representing the transient youth before Congress and other places was an organization called "Untouched Youth of America." What became clear was that before the Depression it was adventure and rebellion that led youth to the rails. The Depression introduced another key dimension, a search for hope in the future through elusive job opportunities in the next town.

Closure of the Federal Transient Service in September 1935 ended special attention by the federal government to the transient. Many had criticized the program for providing such good food and shelter, holding the belief that the agency was actually enticing transience. Another criticism was that the transient program was actually doing a disservice to the transients who were looking for work. The Service camps were isolated from the general public, reinforcing a transient detachment from job opportunities and mainstream society. There was a growing desire among social workers to include transients in the general New Deal relief programs.

International Perspectives

The dramatic rise in youth in America riding the rails was not in itself unique in the world. Perhaps most notably, a rise of transient youths had begun in Germany by 1900. Youths had begun rebelling against the materialism of Germany's new industrialization period. A key aspect of the rebellion was to take to the road and chase a more romantic notion of freedom. Hiking clubs appeared throughout the nation and many lived in transient camps. By 1919 many buildings were being converted to shelters for the transient youth, and by 1929, 2,200 youth shelters existed across Germany.

With the arrival of the Great Depression in Germany unemployment rates hit 20 percent of the workforce. Few job opportunities existed for youth. Given the severe economic strife of the country the youth movement became more political in nature. Hiking and camping activities took on more of a militaristic focus as many youth joined either the communist party or the Nazi party. This trend concerned those in the United States, including President Roosevelt, who feared that idle youth in the United States including the transients might take a similar path if the opportunity arose.

Similar trends among youth were happening elsewhere in Europe. In the 1917 Bolshevik revolution in Russia, the communist takeover of the government, led to social turmoil and famine. Some 750,000 children became homeless. Many turned to a pack mentality, stealing food and surviving together.

Impact

The combination of military service and employment in the war-related industries lowered the unem-

ployment rate to less than two percent of the workforce by 1944. Homelessness and transience returned to some degree as war-related employment decreased, but in much smaller numbers than during the Great Depression. Most associated the homeless with "skidrows" in larger cities, and once again transience was associated with middle-aged men over 40.

The social upheaval of the late 1960s introduced a new era of youth on the road. Many were seeking adventure and detachment from society's norms. The Juvenile Justice and Delinquency Prevention Act of 1974 established a Runaway Youth Program to provide temporary shelters and other services to youth between the ages of 12 and 18. Attitudes toward teenage runaways changed by 1976 as the arrest rate of juveniles exceeded adults for crimes by transients.

Another surge of homelessness arrived in the early 1980s. The character of homelessness during this period changed once again. It was spurred by high unemployment rates combined with cuts in government social services under President Ronald Reagan's (served 1981–1989) administration, particularly the sharp decline in low-income housing. Like President Hoover in the early years of the Great Depression, Reagan and other conservatives claimed the assistance programs destroyed personal initiative and encouraged idleness. Reagan sharply reduced federal domestic spending while cutting taxes for the wealthy.

The number of homeless increased from two million in 1982 to 2.5 million in 1983. One-fourth of these were estimated to be women, many single mothers with children. In 1988 it was estimated over 577,000 youth were runaways or homeless. In the 1990s whole families continued to be part of the homeless and transient population, and the rate of homeless minorities also increased. Combinations of nonprofit organizations, social service departments of local governments, and charitable efforts by businesses and churches attempted to provide shelter and food. Alcoholism and drug use also became more strongly associated with transient life.

Through the 1980s and 1990s homelessness became one of the more controversial and complex issues of federal domestic policy. A backlash against homelessness led to passage of welfare reform legislation in 1996 signed by President Bill Clinton (served 1993–2001). The Personal Responsibility and Work Opportunity Reconciliation Act ended cash assistance to poor families previous provided through the 1970 Aid to Families with Dependent Children (AFDC) program and replaced it with another federal program offering substantially reduced benefits. Social workers struggled once again, as in the 1930s, with the growing numbers of extremely poor in America.

It was estimated that a higher proportion of American youth lived in poverty in 1990 than in 1960 and the family median income had decreased by six percent between 1989 and 1993. Despite the economic boom years of the 1990s, the wealth gap between the rich and poor increased once again, reminiscent of the 1920s. Significant numbers of families were on the road and living in shelters. Federal programs addressed problems of low-income housing. The problem of transient youths that rose during the Great Depression of the 1930s had risen again in the late 1960s and grew to crisis proportions through the 1990s. The National Network of Runaway an Youth Services in the late 1990s estimated that over one million youth were runaways with half being homeless.

Notable People

Edith Abbott (1876–1957). Abbott was born in Grand Island, Nebraska, to an active, politically progressive family. Her father was the fist lieutenant governor of Nebraska and her mother a women's suffrage (women's voting rights) advocate. Abbott earned an undergraduate degree from the University of Nebraska 1901 and a doctorate degree in political economics from the University of Chicago, graduating with honors in 1905. She worked as a researcher for the Carnegie Institution in Washington, DC, and New York City before traveling to England to study at the London School Economics. While in England she met key social reformers who influenced her future direction in life. She returned to the United States in 1907 and moved into the Hull House in Chicago, a settlement house providing social services to the surrounding community. She also served as director of the Chicago School of Civics and Philanthropy focusing on problems of youth. With Abbott as dean, in 1920 it became the School of Social Service Administration affiliated with the University of Chicago. She also published over one hundred articles and books, the most noted being the book, *Women in Industry* in 1910. The study focused on the affect of industrialization on working women in terms of low wages and poor working conditions.

During the Great Depression Abbott and her influential School of Social Service Administration trained social workers in applying social reform to aid the poor. Abbott advised both President Herbert Hoover and President Franklin Roosevelt and strongly supported New Deal programs. She advised and trained workers

for the Federal Transient Service from 1933 to 1935 and was elected president of the National Conference of Social Work in 1936. Abbott continued to advocate national programs for the poor into the 1950s.

Elizabeth Wickenden (1909–2001). Wickenden was greatly involved in issues involving transients throughout the New Deal. She was first appointed Assistant Director of Transient Activities for the Federal Emergency Relief Administration in 1933. There she helped establish the Federal Transient Service. Later when the Transient Service was terminated in 1935 she became Assistant Deputy Administrator of the Works Progress Administration. Wickenden had observed the various debates surrounding the Transient Service and became an advocate for trying different approaches in addressing the transient problem. In 1937 she authored an article titled " Transiency—Mobility in Trouble" which was published in the journal *The Survey*. Wickenden argued that transients should be included in more general New Deal relief programs rather than singled out for special treatment. She claimed the Service had reinforced public opinion that transients were different and needed rehabilitation rather than just a job and home like everyone else. As she contended, transience was not the problem, it was the lack of work that was the key issue.

Aubrey Williams (1890–1965). Williams was born in Springville, Alabama, to a family of modest means. He was greatly disturbed by the racial discrimination that surrounded him during his youth. During World War I (1914–1918) he joined the French Foreign Legion. Afterwards he became executive secretary of the Wisconsin Conference of Social Work, an organization concerned with finding solutions to poverty and delinquency. With onset of the Great Depression Williams worked with the Reconstruction Finance Corporation in trying to bring relief to people of Texas and Mississippi. He was recruited as an assistant to Harry Hopkins at the Federal Emergency Relief Administration. Williams brought a dedication to the New Deal in seeking equal treatment for black Americans in New Deal work relief programs. In 1935 Williams became deputy director of the Works Progress Administration (WPA) and executive director of the National Youth Administration (NYA) that strove to help transient youth riding the rails. Williams remained lead of the NYA until it was disbanded in 1943.

Primary Sources

Youth on the Rails

Kingsley Davis explored the world of American youth riding the rails during the Great Depression. His

A young man hitchhikes by catching a ride on a freight train. (National Archives and Records Administration. Reproduced by permission.)

observations were published in 1935 by The University of Chicago Press in a educational pamphlet titled *Youth in the Depression* (pp. 1–7).

> "Wheezing and groaning to a slow halt, the long freight train of the Southern Pacific line pulled into the yards of El Paso, Texas. It was a bright April day back in 1932, and the long string of box cars gleamed warmly red in the afternoon sun.
>
> Even before the train stopped, a small army of men and boys began hopping off. In rough clothes, many of them carrying small bundles, these "knights of the road" appeared as if by magic from every part of the train. All told, there were forty-four . . .
>
> The travelers looked around to get their bearings. Then most of them scattered into the city to begin their long, weary search for a meals . . . .
>
> Most of those on the road nowadays are young men. There used to be just two kinds, regular hoboes and seasonal workers; and most of them were older. Now there is a third kind, the unemployed. They make up 70 per cent of the men on the road today, and the majority of them are young fellows . . .
>
> Most of them want to work, but they can't find it. No town, except the cities, will let them stop for long. The life is hard on them. Bad food, dirt, no sleep. Lots of them get hurt. Hundreds are killed or injured every year."
>
> But the worst thing is that the boys may turn into bums. This year, already, they are tougher than they were last

year. If hard times last much longer and nothing is done for these boys, things will be pretty bad for them. They won't get an education. They'll form the habit of getting by without working. . . and they'll learn stealing and vice from the old bums that are always on the road . . .

John Fawcett's Ride to Texas

In June 1936 John Fawcett, sixteen years of age, decided to have an adventure. He hopped a train and traveled from Wheeling, West Virginia, to Dallas, Texas, to attend the Texas Centennial Exposition. He wrote of his experience in a memoir that was later published in the December 1994 issue of *Indiana Magazine of History.* The journey highlighted the dangers and excitement of riding the rails. It took three weeks of hard travel getting to Texas and only five days of travel upon return.

> I was born and raised in Wheeling, W. Va. where I lived until my graduation from high school in June 1937...
>
> I had always been about an average student or maybe a little better, but in February 1936 I was full of anxiety and discontent.... So on the evening of February 7th, 1936, with the temperature down below zero, and the ground covered with snow, I ran away form home! . . . .
>
> We were at the west end of the railroad yard in Cincinnati munching on stale rolls when we heard the unmistakable sound of a big locomotive getting a long freight train under way. Within minutes my friend, Mick, and I were on a gondola car full of sand and reclining in the sunshine. It was a train of over a hundred cars carrying other freeloading "passengers". We. . . came to a rattling stop in the town of North Vernon where we got off. A rather meager hobo jungle was located on the north side of the tracks just a few blocks from the residential part of town. We'd been sitting there in the shade for a while when we got talking to a man named Shorty Frazier.
>
> He was a professional hobo, having been on the road for years . . . . Soon the three of us agreed to "make our presence known" in the community by knocking on doors. We learned that day, the universal transient's rule that, when possible, always enter from the alley and knock on the back door rather than the front. This way there was a much better chance of success. . . .
>
> Another fascinating bit of hobo-ology that our friend, Shorty, showed us that day was the habit of some old Knights of the Road of carrying a piece of chalk in their pockets. When one of those worthies received a handout, or especially a "sit down" (a plate of food brought out while sitting on the porch or back stairs), he would, when returning to the alley, write carefully with his chalk on the fence or garage door, the number eighteen. This was a secret code to others of the brotherhood that here is a house where "I ate" . . .
>
> An hour after rolling out in the morning, we were sitting on a grassy knoll beside the tracks having just herd the wail of steam whistles coming from down in the yards. There she came and what a sight to see! It was a

long double headed freight train pulled by two huge steam locomotives spouting smoke and steam as they came roaring through the switches onto the main line. Nothing compares to that sight and sound and it raises my pulse and blood pressure to this day. No . . . wonder kids run away from home! . . .

Leaving Home

Leaving home to ride the rails wasn't always an adventure. Sometimes it was a choice made when there were few options available. Errol Lincoln Uys relays such a departure scene in his book *Riding the Rails: Teenagers on the Move During the Great Depression* (2000, p. 53).

It was the Depression and I could find no work. I was a burden on Mother and Gus, my stepfather. I knew then what I must do. . . . Mother didn't fight it, but she was sad. She owned no suitcase or tote; she gave me a black satin bag, the size of a pillowcase, to carry my things. I jammed my 'sleeping bag' inside, three or four pairs of socks, shorts, an old sweater. Mother handed me all the money in her purse: seventy-two cents. I gave her a big kiss and a long, tight hug. The tears were streaming down her face. I left with the black satin bag over my shoulder. Had I been brave enough to turn around, I would have been coward enough to go back.

Suggested Research Topics

- Write diary entries from the perspective of a teenager in the 1930s who has left home and is riding the rails. Why did you leave home? What are your hopes, dreams, and fears? Describe your experiences crossing the country.

- What are some of the reasons for homelessness today? Why were people homeless in the 1930s? Do teenagers, both past and present, have different reasons than adults for being homeless?

- Explore the life of late twentieth century hoboes by studying Ted Conover's book *Rolling Nowhere: A Young Man's Adventure Riding the Rails with America's Hoboes* (New York: Penguin, 1987) or *Journey to Nowhere* by Dale Maharidge (Dial Press, 1985).

Bibliography

Sources

Anderson, Nels. *On Hobos and Homelessness.* Chicago: The University of Chicago Press, 1998.

Crouse, Joan M. *The Homeless Transient in the Great Depression: New York State, 1929–1941.* Albany: State University of New York Press, 1986.

Davis, Kingsley. *Youth in the Depression.* Chicago: The University of Chicago Press, 1935.

Fawcett, John E. "A Hobo Memoir, 1936." *Indiana Magazine of History,* December 1994.

Tyack, David, Robert Lowe, and Elisabeth Hansot. *Public Schools in Hard Times: The Great Depression and Recent Years.* Cambridge, MA: Harvard University Press, 1984.

Uys, Errol L. *Riding the Rails: Teenagers on the Move During the Great Depression.* New York: TV Books, 2000.

Further Reading

Cohen, Norm. *Long Steel Rail: The Railroad in American Folksong.* Urbana: University of Illinois Press, 2000.

Davis, Maxine. *The Lost Generation: A Portrait of American Youth Today.* New York: The Macmillan Company, 1936.

Douglas, George H. *All Aboard! The Railroad in American Life.* New York: Paragon House, 1992.

Guthrie, Woody. *Bound For Glory.* New York: E.P. Dutton & Co., Inc., 1943.

Kerouac, Jack. *Lonesome Traveler.* New York: Grove Press, 1988.

Maharidge, Dale. *Journey to Nowhere: The Saga of the New Underclass.* Garden City, NY: The Dial Press, 1985.

Meltzer, Milton. *Brother, Can You Spare a Dime? The Great Depression, 1929–1933.* New York: Alfred A. Knopf, 1969.

Reitman, Ben L. *Sister of the Road: The Autobiography of Box-Car Bertha.* New York: Sheridan House, 1937.

"Riding the Rails," available from the World Wide Web at http://www.pbs.org/wgbh/amex/rails.html.

See Also

Civilian Conservation Corps; New Deal (First, and Its Critics); New Deal (Second); Works Progress Administration

Reconstruction Finance Corporation

1932-1941

A common misconception about the Great Depression was that it was immediately caused by the stock market crash on "Black Thursday," October 24, 1929, followed by a sudden collapse of the economy. Signs of weakness in the banking system, however, had been evident throughout the 1920s and by the crash there had already been a decade-long economic depression in agriculture. Although the historical moment of the great crash was firmly fixed in the collective memory of most Americans of that generation, it became undeniably evident that something more extensive was seriously wrong with the economy. The market had given ominous signs before that date, but investors easily dismissed grim warnings. They spoke of the natural adjustment of prices after a decade of inflated stock prices that would ultimately strengthen the economy. Despite the positive outlook, used to instill confidence in the market before "black Thursday," such cheerful exhortations had little meaning afterwards. The date marked an interval of bewilderment and economic disorder that would continue for several weeks and then months.

The crash of the stock market did not initiate a sudden collapse of the American economy, rather the economy looked relatively unchanged for several weeks. Ongoing speculation built as to what impact such a large fall in stock prices would have on related markets, industry, and employment. Nobody really knew what was happening to the nation economically, but mounting apprehension led quickly to fear

and uncertainty. The confusion was compounded by the fact that very few sources of economic data were available. The Federal Reserve, a system of federal banks that hold money reserves for other banks in their region, produced a monthly bulletin on the state of finance, as did several private banks. But piecing together available information was difficult and would have been incomplete. The little information that was readily available showed declines occurring in production in key industries such as steel, automobiles, and rubber. By spring of 1930 there was still no evidence of improvement in these industries. It soon became clear to state relief agencies that unemployment continued to rise while wages and prices kept falling. To make matters worse, the stock market closed out April 1930 with another series of losses. To many observers, it appeared deeper economic forces were at work than simply a crash on the stock exchange, however enormous that might have been.

On May 1, 1930, newly elected President Herbert Hoover (served 1929–1933) addressed the delegates of the annual meeting of the U.S. Chamber of Commerce in Washington. Hoover asserted that U.S. history had shown that such economic downturns happened periodically, but he was sure the worst was over and recovery would be rapid. Hoover was overly optimistic because the crash of October 1929 was less obviously being followed by a more gradual but much larger fall in stock values and the economy.

With the Great Depression lingering on, Hoover began taking more aggressive action in October 1931. Pushing his reliance on voluntary action by industry, he created the National Credit Corporation (NCC). This private corporation made up of leading banks would increase the availability of loans to other corporations so that they could continue to operate without dismissing more employees. The NCC quickly proved ineffective, however, partly because of stiff requirements imposed on corporations seeking to qualify for loans. It was then that Hoover took what at the time was bold action, creating a new federal organization, the Reconstruction Finance Corporation where government assumed a more active role in spurring the economy. Though the RFC would also prove ineffective at first in the face of massive economic problems brought by the Depression, the organization would see new life under President Franklin Delano Roosevelt (served 1933–1945) as part of the New Deal, a vast array of federal social and economic programs designed to combat the effects of the Depression.

Chronology:

October 24, 1929: Known as "Black Thursday," a record-breaking crash on the New York Stock Exchange begins several weeks of market panics and decline in stock values. The nation's economy steadily erodes into the Great Depression.

October 4, 1931: To help with economic recovery, President Hoover calls on leading banks to organize into a voluntary credit association later called the National Credit Corporation (NCC) and pledges federal support to stem the growing banking crisis.

December 7, 1931: Following the failure of the NCC, President Hoover submits a comprehensive recovery program to Congress that includes establishment of the Reconstruction Finance Corporation (RFC) to provide federal financial support to the banking system.

January 22, 1932: Congress establishes the Reconstruction Finance Corporation.

June 27, 1932: The RFC loans $90 million to the Central Republic Bank of Chicago in an effort to avoid a collapse of the banking system.

March 4, 1933: With banks closed in New York City and Chicago, Franklin D. Roosevelt takes the oath of office as 32nd President of the United States and in two days declares a national bank holiday.

March 9, 1933: The Emergency Banking Act expands the authority of the RFC.

May 12, 1933: Federal Emergency Relief Act establishes the Federal Emergency Relief Administration to provide direct cash grants to state and municipal work relief projects financed by the RFC.

July 1, 1935: Federal Deposit Insurance Corporation goes into effect taking the place of RFC in providing financial stability to the bank system by insuring bank deposits.

June 25, 1940: Congress grants greater authority to the Reconstruction Finance Corporation to transition from economic recovery programs to national defense as the nation begins mobilizing for World War II.

Issue Summary

A Volunteer Approach to Recovery

As the nation's economy continued to struggle for several months after the stock market crash, President Hoover took vigorous action by employing a method that had been effective while he was Secretary of Commerce. He organized a conference of business and government officials in early 1930 to address ways of preventing the economy from backsliding further. Before the conference delegates he pledged to spend $2 billion in construction in 1930, to speed up approval of public works projects, and to consider a proposed tax cut. It was a plan intended to restore public confidence in the business community. In the State of the Union Address in December 1930, Hoover informed the joint sessions of Congress that there would be enough of a tax surplus that year to offset tax cuts. On December 5, 1930, Congress passed the tax cut bill and nearly $2.5 billion was earmarked for public works that would create 600,000 jobs. Several additional conferences of particular industries secured agreements to maintain wages and avoid strikes or lockouts. The Federal Farm Board moved to support the prices of cotton and wheat, commodities that had sharply declined. Hoover had seized the spotlight and appeared to be an active chief executive attempting to bring the full authority of the federal government to combat the depression.

The difficulty was that nearly everyone underestimated the depth of the economic decline. By June 1930 the depression did not look much worse than the recession of 1921. Hoover believed the economy would bounce back quickly as it had then. In fact the depression in 1930 may have been comparable to other downturns in the late nineteenth and early twentieth centuries, but it was also rapidly getting worse. The estimates of unemployment by the Department of Labor, just under 2.3 million in 1930, contrasted sharply with that of state estimates that were much higher. The National Unemployment League concluded the figure was actually closer to 6.6 million by mid-year. The president's efforts to assure business of certain recovery did instill enough pressure to maintain wage, price, and employment levels in 1930, but corporations maintained wage levels only at the expense of laying more people off. Finally in September 1931 U.S. Steel was compelled to cut wages by 10 percent. Within days other industries followed suit.

Spending on public works did increase, but the small number of workers employed on projects and the construction generated did not come close to offsetting the construction losses in the private sector. In the meantime unemployment was increasing every month, and state and municipal relief rolls were growing. Even the cities with the most generous public assistance for the unemployed, Detroit and Boston, could not help more than a third of unemployed families. Breadlines became a common sight in cities across the country.

Hoover's political philosophy upheld the traditional virtue of individualism but also recognized that economic realities of the market and the modern industrial state could easily erode individual liberty. He envisioned an economic system that would be a blend of individual entrepreneurs and a shared technological approach. This could be accomplished, he believed, through the promotion of private associations that represented various trade, labor, and manufacturing interests. Examples of associations, such as the United States Chamber of Commerce, the National Association of Manufacturers, and the American Farm Bureau, had already grown in response to U.S. industrialization. Hoover believed that industrial associations, through voluntary action, were the most able representatives of industrial interests. They could exert pressure on their members and they shared a common, national goal with their competitors, that of increasing productivity and reducing the effects of wasteful competition. A network of associations held out the promise of a self-regulating business commonwealth. Industries would promulgate ethical codes of conduct and professional standards and engage in cooperative problem solving.

The role of the federal government in such a system would be to set objectives for national planning, encourage the creation of trade associations, farm cooperatives, labor unions and professional organizations, assist in research and development, and provide business with reliable economic data. Hoover's faith in the benefits of coordinating voluntary action in the private sector, based on his political philosophy and his pre-presidential experience, led him to develop his first significant program to combat the depression. It would prove a discouraging failure.

Throughout 1930 Hoover did his best to persuade business not to decrease wages or prices. If more money was needed to offset losses in a firm, Hoover reasoned, then credit must be readily available. One of the problems with this approach was that the financial crisis worsened in 1931 when Britain changed the value of its currency to solve its own problems created by the Depression. The change immediately put great pressure on Wall Street and the U.S. dollar. The public, alarmed by possible changes in U.S. currency, was demanding their bank deposits in cash. Many

"Hoovervilles" sprang up around the country after the beginning of the Great Depression during Hoover's presidency. Many people living in these shantytowns called them "Hoovervilles" because they blamed Hoover for the economic downturn and unemployment. (Archive Photos, Inc./American Stock. Reproduced by permission.)

regional banks did not have enough liquid assets, or money on hand, to give clients their deposits and to lend credit at low interest rates as Hoover was encouraging. Banks were increasingly addressing their own problems by calling in loans and refusing to lend money for fear of facing collapse. As a result there was a significant decrease in the availability of credit for business, as opposed to an increase.

To meet the emergency, President Hoover summoned Eugene Meyer, chairman of the Federal

Reserve Board to the White House on September 8, 1931. The president presented a plan in which a voluntary, cooperative effort among bankers, heavily encouraged by the federal government, would establish a private credit corporation to assist troubled banks. He believed the public would then be calmed and would stop demanding their deposits. At a meeting of the Federal Reserve Advisory Council seven days later, the president called on bankers to create a $500 million credit pool. The money lent to weak banks would prevent their collapse until public confidence was restored. Privately Meyer was skeptical that this would be enough, but both the president and the Federal Reserve chairman shared the assumption that economic growth would not resume until commercial banks started making more loans to business and industry. Both believed that through discipline, banks could increase their commercial loans. Meyer, however, did not share the president's faith in the willingness of the financial community to contribute the necessary $500 million. Instead Meyer thought it would be better to revive the model of the War Finance Corporation (WFC), which had undertaken a similar endeavor during World War I. The federal government would underwrite private banking. Hoover, however, was not supportive of such drastic federal intervention in the peacetime economy. It would require a special session of Congress, would probably frighten the public into thinking the situation was more serious and, in the opinion of the president, it would not in the end be necessary. Since it was in the long-term best interest of the financial community to cooperate with the plan, Hoover believed the bankers would surely respond to the proposal.

Both Hoover and the Federal Reserve placed much of the blame for the Depression on the decline in commercial credit at a time when the business cycle was in a downturn and needed the credit. Statistical data showed a definite lack of commercial credit and the administration believed it was because banks were unwilling to lend. There were, however, deeper reasons for the decline in credit that were not fully understood by the administration. An erroneous assumption was that business and consumers desperately wanted and needed commercial credit. In actual fact it was not so much that banks were unwilling to make commercial loans, but a decline in demand for commercial credit was occurring.

Several factors explain the decline. First, most businesses were frightened of borrowing at this time. What if they could not afford to repay it? With the economy in decline, the financial prospects of a corporation often did not present adequate security to ensure repayment of a loan. Overall the administration was doing little to actually stimulate demand. Second, throughout the 1920s, the larger corporations had tended to finance expansion with new securities issues (by issuing and selling more stock) or simply by surplus profits. In the boom economy of the 1920s, the larger corporations often did not have to acquire commercial loans for expansion. The administration was unaware of these developments because they had assumed that bank lending was more involved in the economic boom of the 1920s.

The Ill-Fated NCC

On October 4, 1931, in Secretary of the Treasury Andrew Mellon's Washington apartment, Hoover presented his proposals to the bankers. The president offered both the carrot and the stick. In exchange for forming an association, Hoover promised to push a bill through Congress to relax eligibility requirements for the Federal Reserve System. Banks could enjoy benefits more easily, and if they did not cooperate, the president threatened the creation of a federal credit agency. Ironically, several prominent New York bankers had met the week before and concluded that only a revival of the WFC would end the crisis. At the meeting the bankers praised the president's initiative but then requested he pledge to revive the WFC if the private association failed to stabilize the economy. Somewhat surprised at the willingness of the bankers to embrace federal intervention, Hoover agreed. Two days later the plan was warmly received at a bipartisan meeting of several Congressmen. Most state and local banks welcomed the proposal and the financial community responded favorably. Privately, however, some of the larger banks expressed their misgivings.

The banking community began immediately to organize. The governor of the Federal Reserve Bank of New York, George Harrison, brought together a committee of leading New York bankers to formulate plans for the credit corporation. Under the leadership of Mortimer Buckner, chairman of the New York Trust Company, the committee soon received a pledge of $150 million from the member banks of the New York Clearing House Association. On October 13 Buckner announced the formal organization of the National Credit Corporation (NCC). Its by-laws authorized up to $1 billion in government bonds of which the membership banks would provide $500 million. Any bank subscribing a certain amount to the association could join. Mortimer Buckner was named president and George M. Reynolds, chairman of the Continental Illinois Bank and Trust Company, was named chairman of the board. The NCC divided the member banks into a series of smaller associations. Any member bank could apply for a loan to the local association and once the loan was approved, the national office would forward the money after review.

The newly formed organization was off at a snail's pace. From the beginning the NCC officers were not eager to make loans, and during the last week of October, Hoover and Undersecretary of the Treasury Ogden Mills demanded the leaders of the NCC to quit procrastinating. Despite early delays, however, the NCC seemed initially to have a positive effect.

Bank failures in October and the first half of November dropped following the announcement of the NCC's establishment, and there was reason to believe the association would be a success. But the slight economic upturn only led the NCC leadership to hope the agency could be dissolved without making any loans.

Severe collateral requirements of borrowing banks were put in place if loans should become necessary. The NCC did not accept real estate or agricultural deeds as collateral at all, and U.S. government securities were appraised at only 75 percent of their value. When bank failures increased dramatically at the end of November, the regulations of the NCC discontinued its assistance to many banks. Banks verging on failure were often unable to qualify for a loan, and the more solid banks wanted to avoid involvement in the scheme if it became involved with failing banks. Ironically because of the strict collateral requirements, only banks in good condition could get loans. By December 1931 the NCC had only loaned $10 million. Yet even if the $500 million had been distributed freely, it probably was not enough to end the bank failures.

A Stronger Federal Role Proposed

Late in November many small banks throughout the country began demanding replacement of the NCC with a government agency. President Hoover, realizing that most banks would not act beyond their own self-interest, had no choice but to abandon the program. On December 7, 1931, the president submitted to Congress a proposal for the revival of the War Finance Corporation. It was not a step he wanted to take, but he fulfilled his promise to enact a federal program in the event that the private association failed. For the rest of his life an embittered Hoover would criticize the bankers for being self-serving during the time of a national crisis.

President Hoover now asked Congress for comprehensive legislation aimed at stimulating economic recovery. It was a plan very much in line with his belief that the expansion of commercial credit would end the depression. The president called for an appropriation of $125 million to strengthen the Federal banks to enable them to make loans to farmers and rural banks in the hope of assisting the agricultural economy. He also asked for the establishment of a new system of federal home loan banks to grant loans to building and loan associations. This would encourage mortgage lenders to increase home loans and stimulate the construction industry. Believing that the release of funds tied up in closed banks would stimulate consumer purchasing power, Hoover also formulated a plan for the early distribution of personal

savings deposits that were tied up in closed banks. The president again urged Congress to reduce the eligibility requirements for banks to join the Federal Reserve System. As the most important part of his legislative agenda, the president requested funding for a program that would reestablish the old WFC by creating the Reconstruction Finance Corporation (RFC). The RFC would take over where the NCC had failed. It would offer government credit at low interest to financial institutions in trouble. Hoover explained that the RFC would be able to supply the necessary funds to inject fresh capital into the money markets and increase the number of commercial loans. Privately he hoped that once the fear afflicting so many bankers was somewhat lessened, then banks would increase their lending and the RFC could be dismantled.

The approach expressed the prevailing view of many economists of the day who considered the availability of bank credit to be the essential ingredient to national economic recovery. The theory was that by ending bank closures, the RFC would relieve the fear of banks to grant commercial loans. Business would then be able to acquire capital and increase their investment in equipment, inventory, and payrolls. Unemployment would decline, wages would increase, and consumers would have considerable purchasing power. This purchasing power would then stimulate a national recovery.

Hoover implored Congress to act quickly. The Bank of America chain in California was on the verge of collapse and others would undoubtedly follow. Debate over the bill raised several concerns in the largely Democratic Congress. For example it looked like a huge bailout for irresponsible bank lenders. The bill, however, was finally passed on January 22, 1932. Many progressive Republicans and liberal Democrats were skeptical of the economic theory behind the RFC. Senator Robert F. Wagner of New York, for example, urged that federal money be spent directly on unemployment relief and public works. He supported the bill, however, despite his objections to its approach. There simply were no other alternatives being introduced in Congress.

There were a few minor amendments added by Congress prior to passage of the RFC bill. Senator Carter Glass of Virginia insisted on increasing the five directors of the RFC to seven with only four coming from the same party. Both Senator Glass and Senator Robert La Follette of Wisconsin opposed a clause in the bill permitting the RFC to loan to "bona fide institutions" on the basis that it was too vague. This is exactly what the administration wanted, but Carter and La Follette insisted that it gave the administration too much power. They preferred limiting the RFC's lending authority to a specific list of financial institutions. They also wanted to make sure that the RFC did not assist the NCC. This, the two Senators believed, was an issue that could be handled by the private bankers. Hoover relented, knowing that both amendments would not substantially change his proposal.

There was also substantial support for an amendment introduced by Senator Royal Copeland of New York to allow the RFC to issue loans to municipalities (city governments). This was a radical departure from the administration's recovery plans. Pouring money into relief loans to cities, Hoover believed, would merely postpone the revitalization of banks and corporations. The president was not dogmatically opposed to unemployment relief and public works programs but he did think they would not be needed once the credit machinery of the country was reestablished. The Copeland amendment would, in Hoover's opinion, only detract from the assets of the RFC.

The president was not willing to compromise on this issue and was successfully able to organize a coalition of Republicans and southern Democrats to defeat the amendment in the Senate. The Reconstruction Finance Corporation bill then moved quickly through Congress. The House passed it with 335 to 55 in favor and the Senate with 63 to 8 in favor. Generally, there was broad support for the bill across party lines. The statute required that the RFC would be discontinued on January 1, 1933 unless by executive order it was extended until January 1, 1934.

The RFC Begins Operation

The Reconstruction Finance Corporation Act provided for direct federal assistance to the entire money market in the United States by underwriting loans to commercial banks, savings banks, insurance companies, trust companies, building and loan associations, mortgage banks, credit unions, Federal land banks, joint stock land banks, agricultural credit corporations, livestock credit companies, and receivers of closed banks and railroads. Its scope was unprecedented and, in addition to the $500 million initially subscribed by the federal government, the RFC was authorized to sell bonds to obtain an additional $1.5 billion. Of the original funding from Congress, the RFC allotted $200 million to crop loans to help the agricultural industry.

The men Hoover selected to chair the RFC board were prominent bankers and businessmen. As chairman Hoover appointed Eugene Meyer, a loyal Republican originally from California who served as chairman of the Federal Reserve under Hoover. He was a

cautious banker, politically conservative, and well connected to the New York banking community. Two additional ex-officio positions on the Board were reserved. Ogden Mills became an ex-officio member of the RFC board of directors due to his position as the new secretary of the Treasury. H. Paul Bestor served as the other ex-officio member, having previously presided over the Federal Farm Loan Board. Former Vice-President of the United States Charles G. Dawes was appointed president of the agency. Meyer, Mills, Bestor, and Dawes, all Republicans, completed the number eligible to serve on the board from the Republican Party. Hoover next appointed three Democrats. At the recommendation of Senator Joseph Robinson, Hoover named Harvey C. Couch, a southern Democrat from Arkansas who had become a prominent leader in the Southeast and served on the boards of several banks and railroads. Jesse H. Jones, a banker from Texas, was the second Democratic appointee and finally, to provide regional balance Hoover settled on westerner Wilson McCarthy. McCarthy was a conservative banker and lawyer from Salt Lake City who was an expert on agricultural finance. The eminent qualifications of all seven nominees ensured a quick confirmation by the Senate in the first week of February.

The headquarters of the RFC were moved to the old Department of Commerce Building on the corner of Nineteenth Street and Pennsylvania Avenue in Washington, DC. Hoover and Meyer quickly staffed the new agency. An organizational framework was adopted that nearly duplicated the old WFC. In fact many of the personnel had once worked for the wartime agency. By the end of February Meyer had hired over six hundred people to staff both the Washington headquarters and 33 regional offices.

The RFC began making dozens of loans a day. Perhaps most extraordinary was the unprecedented independence of the agency from both Congress and the U.S. director of the budget. Although the RFC had to issue monthly and quarterly reports to Congress, it did not have to provide the names of borrowers or the amounts of loans. Nor would the agency need to subject itself to congressional scrutiny for additional funding. In theory the RFC could operate indefinitely on the original allocation of Congress.

Without question the creation of the RFC brought temporary confidence to the economy. Many of the problems and assumptions that beset the National Credit Association came to the fore, however, as the operation of the RFC was underway. In large part due to the background of the directors, each wanted to end the crisis with a minimum of expense to the govern-

More About...

Herbert Hoover and the American Relief Administration

Few American presidents have come to the office with the unique experience and qualifications of Herbert Clark Hoover. Born in West Branch, Iowa in 1874, Hoover was orphaned as a child and spent his adolescence in Oregon with the family of his mother's uncle. He never graduated high school but was admitted to Stanford University, then a free university, where he earned a degree in engineering. Hoover embarked upon a remarkable career as an engineer. By 1914 he had distinguished himself as a mining engineer and business manager on projects all over the world. Hoover lived and worked in England, Australia, and China for extended periods and undertook projects in Burma, Germany, Poland, Russia, France, Korea, Japan, Belgium, Italy, and Holland. During the course of his career he also made himself a small fortune.

In 1914 Hoover was called to public service by President Woodrow Wilson to head the Commission for Relief in Belgium during the years of American neutrality in World War I. When the United States entered the war in 1917, President Wilson appointed Hoover the United States Food Administrator. After the armistice, he was then sent with the American delegation to the Paris Peace Conference. He played an instrumental role as a specialist on American loans and terms of credit to the Allies and in the economic analysis of the peace treaty. The young Herbert Hoover privately arrived at the conclusion that the Peace Treaty would sow the seeds of its own destruction.

Following World War I many parts of war-torn Europe, especially the former Austro-Hungarian Empire and Russia, were facing famine. Hoover spearheaded relief efforts of food to countries devastated by the war under the guise of the American Relief Administration (ARA), which had received $100,000,000 through a congressional appropriation. The ARA provided relief to millions of European orphans and undernourished children. Unfortunately the legal life of the ARA was brief and it expired on June 30, 1919, well before its task was finished. Hoover wasted no time in finding alternative sources of revenue. On July 7, 1919, he organized the principal officers of the ARA into a private organization under a board of directors. Committees were established in each state and President Wilson turned over the government food stockpiles to the private ARA. It was agreed that any profits made by Food Administration agencies assisting foreign governments through the ARA would be used for children's relief. A "food draft" program, which generated a significant income, was established at banks. Drafts for specific food items could be purchased, sent to relatives in Europe, and exchanged at one of the ARA warehouses in Europe. Banks agreed to issue the drafts at no charge. The profits, in 1919 totaling $8 million, were turned over to the children's relief fund.

In May 1920 the ARA concluded that the work would have to be continued another harvest year. Further sources of income would therefore have to be found. Hoover embarked on the organization of the European Relief Council, bringing together relief organizations from all over the United States and the world. Fund-raising drives were launched by the state committees and the ARA and European Relief Council. They raised well over the estimated $33 million needed to continue relief efforts another year. Between 1919 and the autumn of 1921 millions of children were fed and clothed. An additional effort was organized to sell surplus grain on credit to Armenia, Austria, Czechoslovakia, Hungary, and Poland through congressional approval. The most serious emergency, however, was in Russia. At one point the ARA was supplying food to 18 million Russian children. Hundreds of thousands still died in the famine but the efforts of the ARA saved millions more. Seed wheat from America, which had been shipped and planted, finally ended the Russian famine with the harvest of 1922. Direct food relief continued until the winter of 1923.

---

ment, and as a result the agency proceeded cautiously. The directors insisted that all loans be repaid promptly and strict collateral requirements approximating those of the NCC were implemented. Only 80 percent of the market value of securities (stocks) was accepted and only 50 percent of the market value of other bank assets. Increased collateral could also be demanded if there were future declines in the value of the collateral such as securities. Thus a bank accepting an RFC loan usually had to deposit its most liquid assets at a fraction of their value. In addition there was a six-month maturation date (waiting period) for the initial batch of loans. This meant that in practice many banks could not be helped before they collapsed. Another obstacle was the interest rate of the loans themselves. To prevent unfair competition with private institutions, the RFC set the interest rates higher than the prevailing private levels. This made the loans expensive and eventually limited the agency's effectiveness.

Hoover believed that the very existence of the RFC, by assuring the public that the federal government was prepared to make loans to sound banks, would be enough to restore confidence. But the administration underestimated the skepticism of the public in the face of numerous bank failures. A fundamental structural problem was that the RFC could only make secured loans to banks. This meant that banks could only borrow what they could match in their assets. But the value of many assets was declining during the Depression, and the value of securities, land values, and mortgages were generally in decline or, in the case of outstanding loans, simply frozen and not being paid. Banks either needed more capital or longer-term loans of three to five years, neither of which were provided by the RFC. By law all loans had to be strictly secured with collateral below market level, and since the agency was only to be in existence for another year, long-term loans were not possible. The short-term maturity dates of the loans often forced many banks to repay the loans well before they had become solvent (in good financial condition), thus imposing additional hardship.

Despite these problems the first month of the RFC was the high point of the Hoover administration, with the arrival of thousands of applications from banks. For a brief period the well-publicized loans that appeared to save banks from imminent collapse inspired confidence in the financial community. In fact the administration did avert some serious crises. Fifteen million dollars was immediately loaned to the Transamerica Corporation in San Francisco to save the Bank of America. Seven million dollars was loaned to the East Tennessee National Bank of Knoxville to the relief of depositors throughout the state. In February alone the RFC authorized more than $45 million to banks and trust companies, while another $25 million went to several railroads. Special funds that had been set aside for crop loans were also issued. By the end of March Secretary of Agriculture Arthur Hyde had loaned nearly $40 million to over 200,000 farmers and the RFC had issued 974 loans totaling

over $238 million. These loans went predominantly to banks and railroads in addition to $18 million to savings and loans associations.

The RFC Runs Into Problems

Bank closings in March 1932 began to decrease. Only 45 banks failed in March as compared to 334 in January and 125 in February. Morale improved in the administration and it looked as if the increase in commercial lending would revive industrial production and employment. But the first signs of political trouble had already appeared as a controversy developed over the dispensing of a railroad loan. Early in March the RFC agreed to lend the Missouri-Pacific Railroad $12,800,000. One of the objectives of the RFC was to end the wave of railroad bankruptcies that had begun the previous year. Railroad bonds during the 1920s formed a substantial part of stock holdings of many commercial lenders including savings and life insurance banks. Strengthening railroad bonds would strengthen thousands of commercial banks but it would also require a substantial amount of loan money.

The Interstate Commerce Commission (ICC), which had approval authority over loans to interstate railroads, was reluctant to authorize the Missouri-Pacific loan. This was because nearly $6 million of it would be turned over to J.P. Morgan and Company, Kuhn, Loeb and Company, and the Guaranty Trust Company of New York as payment on earlier loans. Joseph B. Eastman, head of the ICC, insisted that prior obligations on private loans had to be settled before the RFC would lend to railroads. Meyer resented the interference. To him the ICC did not understand that although much of the loan money would return to investment banks on Wall Street, the underlying purpose of the loan was to strengthen railroad bonds. Therefore Meyer went ahead with the loan but it was not without political fallout.

The Missouri-Pacific loan became an explosive issue in the Senate. Progressive Republicans, particularly Senators James Couzens of Michigan, William Borah of Idaho, and Robert La Follette of Wisconsin, all of whom were increasingly outspoken critics of the administration, attacked the RFC's policies. They charged that the RFC railroad loans were to assist the railroads with their long-term credit obligations. There was nothing in the law creating RFC that allowed for the wholesale assumption of debts by the railroads. Politically, the controversy was a turning point for many progressive Republicans already on the verge of defecting from Hoover's support and support of Republican Party candidates in general. Several, most notably Senator George Norris of Nebraska, committed themselves to Franklin Roosevelt in the next general election.

The Missouri-Pacific loan controversy provided an ideal opportunity for the progressive left of the Republican Party to disassociate themselves from Hoover. The growing criticism in Congress also widened differences on the RFC board. Meyer, Mill, and Bestor favored a policy of loaning to banks to revive the bond market and restore strength to the assets of banks. Dawes, Jones, Couch, and McCarthy struck middle ground between the progressives in the Senate and the more conservative board members. They accepted the Meyer's approach to recovery but felt that before railroad loans were made, banks that held their loans must show good faith by extending the time that railroads had to pay back their borrowed money. Personal relationships on the board also began deteriorating. While Dawes, a Republican appointee, was relatively independent, he joined Jones, Couch, and McCarthy in resenting the dominance of Meyer. He also resented the perceived favoritism that Mills, Meyer, and Bestor had for the eastern banking community at the expense of farmers and rural and Western banks. Since Meyer retained the ear of the president, however, Dawes and the Democratic appointees on the board often felt left out.

Banks, joined by the Federal Reserve, began to criticize the RFC as well. By the end of May 1932 the RFC had purchased over $500 million in government securities, also known as bonds, yet commercial loans remained depressed. In general banks were fearful of another crisis looming and were reluctant to issue more loans. It was clear to them that the RFC had not stimulated recovery. Hoover assumed that bankers did not yet feel secure enough to use their excess reserves for loans, but he was growing increasingly impatient with the banking community. He was also growing impatient with Meyer who continued to promise to Hoover that bankers would respond to RFC loans by increasing their business loans. It simply was not happening. Hoover did believe that the RFC had succeeded in stabilizing the financial system even if it had not brought about recovery. Nevertheless, he began looking for an alternative. He concluded that Eugene Meyer had to be replaced as chairman of the RFC and he once again entertained voluntary schemes. One such project, undertaken by the Federal Reserve Bank of New York, had established a committee to coordinate private credit supplies with business demands. The president urged the Federal Reserve to establish similar programs in each of its twelve districts. It was an indirect admission that the RFC was failing.

On June 6, 1932, Charles Dawes resigned as president of the RFC. At the same time, word spread of a new financial crisis. A series of small banks began failing in Chicago and northern Illinois, undermining depositor confidence in the Midwest. The Central Republic Bank and Trust Company of Chicago, one of the city's largest financial institutions, was also in a precarious situation. If the Central Republic Bank closed, it was conceivable that nearly every bank in Chicago would also have to close. This in turn would suspend the commodities market. If this happened, there would be a chain reaction of bank collapses all over the country. Given that bank failures had increased to 151 in June, the highest since January, Hoover was alarmed. If Central Republic bank was not saved, it was conceivable the entire U.S. banking system might fall with it. On June 27 the RFC loaned $90 million to Central Republic Bank. The loan averted at least temporarily a national banking collapse, at least for the time being, but like the Missouri-Pacific loan, it was not without a political backlash. Early in June the city of Chicago had sent a delegation to Washington to request a loan of $70 million to pay teachers and municipal employees. The RFC was not empowered to make such loans to municipalities and was forced to turn the delegation down. Almost simultaneously with the denial came news of the Central Republic Bank bailout.

The Hoover administration was accused of refusing to assist in paying the salaries of thousands of impoverished workers in Chicago while willing to give one bank $90 million. The loan also brought renewed criticism by small banks that argued that the RFC channeled its resources to the largest financial institutions. Critics neglected to recognize that in 1932, one percent of the banks controlled 40 percent of the deposits. As a result, loans to these larger banks, even though smaller in number, accounted for a larger amount of total funds loaned. The RFC defended the practice of strategically assessing where loans were most in need in order to shore up the money markets and increase the volume of commercial lending. Consistent with this theory was the suggestion that direct loans for relief would be futile or counterproductive, a point which the RFC leadership and the administration continued to make.

By late 1932 this "trickle-down" theory of recovery had few adherents among the liberal Democrats and progressive Republicans, a great deal of skepticism toward it in the banking community, and increasing distrust of it among the public who began to question the assumptions upon which the RFC was founded. The administration and the RFC board continued to insist that direct payments for employment

The aftermath of the battle between the "Bonus Army" and regular Army troops in 1932. The shacks, which housed over 25,000 World War I veterans and their families were destroyed when the Army was called in to diffuse the protesting. (National Archives and Records Administration.)

relief or public works to stimulate economic recovery would only be counterproductive or even damaging. But to the general public, it was a policy increasingly viewed as a hard-hearted refusal to recognize the plight of the unemployed.

The reluctance of the administration to assist the "Forgotten Man" at the expense of banks, railroads, and corporations, as New York's Governor Franklin Roosevelt depicted the administration's priorities in a speech given on April 8 after the Missouri-Pacific controversy surfaced, was a view increasingly accepted by popular opinion. This perception became dramatically magnified in the summer of 1932. President Hoover mishandled a grass-roots movement of World War I veterans who sought approval of a plan to provide direct relief to war veterans. In an administration that had confronted one crisis after another, the resulting Bonus Army controversy would become one of the most alarming political events to beset the struggling presidency.

The Bonus Army Disaster

In the summer of 1932 a ragged multitude of veterans of World War I and their families appeared at the nation's capital to request a service bonus promised to be dispersed by 1945. The veterans, the

majority of whom were unemployed and homeless, had arrived with the intention of petitioning Congress to award them the bonus 13 years ahead of its scheduled date. They became known as the "Bonus Army." Earlier in 1924 Congress passed legislation authorizing the payment of "bonuses" to veterans of the war, $1 a day for each day of service in the United States, $1.25 for each day overseas. The money was to be placed in an endowment fund until 1945 and after interest each veteran would receive an average of a thousand dollars. But in 1929 legislation was introduced to provide for immediate payment to the veterans. President Hoover was opposed to the idea and the bill got nowhere in Congress. With many veterans out of work due to the Depression a compromise bill was introduced in Congress in February 1931, but Hoover vetoed it.

In May 1932 the veterans began to organize a march across the country that would descend on Washington, DC, by the summer to lobby Congress to pass a new bonus bill. The resulting "Bonus Expeditionary Force," as the veterans called themselves, marched into Washington. At the march's peak, there were as many as 20,000 men, women, and children, with some estimates as high as 25,000, living in 27 camps in and around the District of Columbia. All had arrived expecting that their presence would persuade Congress firsthand to pass the bonus bill.

Their reception was initially friendly with the city providing the army with food, donated tents, and help to set up barracks. On June 15 the House passed the resurrected bonus bill by a vote of 209 to 176 but two days later the Senate defeated the bill 62 to 18. In defiance some of the Bonus Army stayed in Washington although the number of men gradually declined to somewhere between eight and ten thousand by late July. Small demonstrations began to erupt, and when police efforts to remove the remaining veterans led to violent street battles Hoover decided to send in U.S. army troops. General Douglas MacArthur, chief of staff of the Army, proceeded to the scene of the disorder with troops, cavalry, and six tanks proceeding along Pennsylvania Avenue. As the troops advanced the cavalry drew their sabers and the crowd scattered. Bonus marchers in the abandoned buildings were routed with tear gas and bayonets and the marchers retreated. Hoover was aghast as MacArthur sent his troops into the camps. Tear gas was fired scattering veterans, spectators, and passers-by alike. In a move that served only to heighten the panic, MacArthur gave the order to set the tents and shacks on fire. The blaze spread quickly and as marchers moved hurried and confused to gather what little belongings they had, it was possible to look up to see the dome of the Capitol outlined against the flames.

The "Battle of Washington," as the event was soon labeled in the sensational press, was splashed across newspaper headlines. The country saw photographs of the marchers, disheveled and weary, fleeing before soldiers with bayonets. They saw troops stamping through the smoking debris of the former camps and resisters, still weeping from tear gas, hauled to police wagons. The photographs of U.S. soldiers attacking veterans were, to many Americans, incredulous images.

A Wounded Administration Watches as the Banking System Crumbles

The day after the attack on the Bonus Army, Hoover informed the press that a challenge to the government of the United States had been met swiftly and firmly. The country was dumbfounded. At Hyde Park the next day, Governor Roosevelt privately confided to his advisor Rexford Tugwell that any chance Hoover had of being reelected was gone. Writer Sherwood Anderson, in an open letter to the president, wrote that the Bonus Marchers had in essence demanded so little from their government. Why, he asked, could Hoover not have gone and talked to the men?

For the man who had entered the White House with such extraordinary personal achievements, a politician billed as the modern technocratic statesman who would bring business efficiency to the art of government, Hoover was now pictured as helpless and inept. Not only did he fail to deal with the economic catastrophe, the administration's perceived inability in the face of the Depression was firmly and symbolically affirmed by the way the Bonus Army was mishandled. The political debacle somehow seemed a key reflection of the Hoover presidency. Events seemed to slip out of the administration's grasp, and the complacency and dominance that characterized the Republican Party during the 1920s was clearly at an end.

In the fall of 1932 the administration's popularity had plummeted to perhaps the lowest any sitting president has endured. The Bonus Army fiasco and the dire state of economic affairs left Republicans with little to campaign on in the general election in November. Democrats focused mostly on the banking system and targeted the RFC to a devastating effect. To the surprise of no one, the Democratic candidate Franklin D. Roosevelt won by a landslide, taking with him enough Democrats to form a House and Senate majority, however, Hoover still had five more months in office. The new administration would not enter the White House until March (this delay was subsequently changed by Constitutional Amendment so that a president now begins his or her term in January). During that time Hoover sought to secure commitments from Roosevelt to maintain the administration's policies on a balanced budget, but Roosevelt remained noncommittal.

Hoover also arrived at the bitter conclusion that banks were using RFC loans to turn their own assets into cash rather than loosen credit for loans to businesses. In November 1932 the president threatened the banking community by proposing to give direct loans to business, but by the end of the year there was evidence of extremely serious financial instability of the banking system. As a state of crisis increased the RFC reverted to its original goal of preventing bank collapses. The first wave of bank closures occurred in Iowa in the last weeks of December. Several important Iowa banks closed and the governor of Iowa was forced to declare a moratorium, meaning a temporary halt, on banking on January 20, 1933. At the same time banks in Tennessee were on the verge of failure. The RFC was considering a $13 million loan to the Bank of America and Trust Company of Memphis to save it. Grave situations also developed in Kansas and Missouri, and late in February the Hibernia Bank and Trust Company of New Orleans, a key financial institution in the South, was on the brink of collapsing.

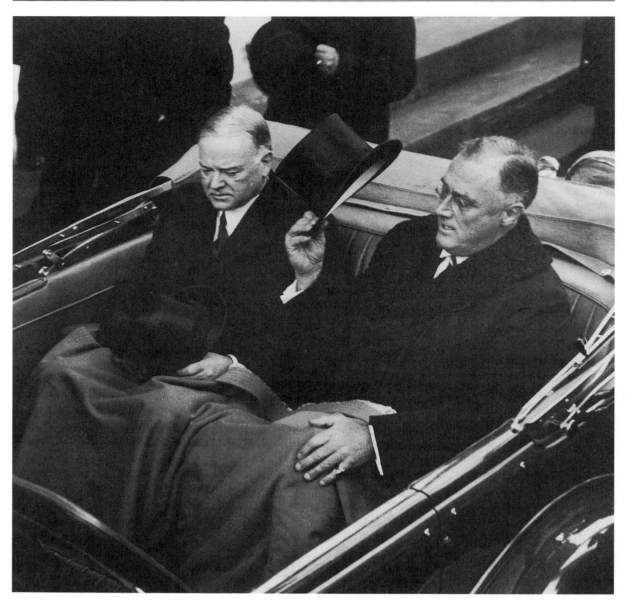

President Herbert Hoover and President-elect Franklin D. Roosevelt on their way to the Capitol for Roosevelt's inauguration on March 4, 1933. Hoover's RFC was greatly expanded by the New Deal. (© Hulton Archive/Getty Images. Reproduced by permission.)

Senator Huey Long appealed directly to the RFC board for a $20 million loan. In January alone the number of bank suspensions across the country climbed to 242, the highest yet.

Panic by depositors now became widespread in many parts of the country. In mid-February, the two largest banks in Detroit closed due to depositor withdrawal. Both banks, the Guardian Detroit Union Group (known as the Union Guardian Trust) and the Detroit Banker's Company, controlled dozens of banks throughout Michigan. The administration was convinced that if both banks failed, a chain reaction would occur throughout the state and then the country. The RFC concluded that $50 million was needed to save the Union Guardian Trust but that it could only loan $36 million. The RFC board therefore expected Union Guardian to raise the rest. The Ford Motor Company agreed to a $7.5 million deposit and

Chrysler and General Motors each pledged $1 million. Hoover personally appealed to executives of Chrysler and General Motors to raise more but they were reluctant to do so. The Ford Motor Company, their rival, was a major stockholder in Union Guardian Trust. They did not want to bail out their competitor.

Hoover then asked Edsel Ford to commit more money but he refused to do so. The elder Henry Ford was disgusted with his rivals and felt they were forcing him to save the entire financial system of the state. Foreseeing collapse, he then threatened to withdraw $25 million from the Detroit Banker's Company and the First National Bank of Detroit. The RFC was unwilling to save these latter two banks since they were considered a hopeless cause. On February 13, 1933, the Union Guardian Trust and the First National Bank of Detroit closed. They were immediately followed by closures all over the state and on the same day Governor Comstock of Michigan declared an eight-day moratorium on all banking activities. Panicked depositors withdrew funds from thousands of banks across the country, and the RFC was unable to cope with such massive drains. State after state restricted withdrawals or declared a banking holiday. On the first and second day of March banking holidays were declared in Arizona, California, Georgia, Idaho, Kentucky, Minnesota, Mississippi, Nevada, New Mexico, Oklahoma, Oregon, Tennessee, Texas, Utah, Washington, and Wisconsin. On inauguration morning, March 4, 1933, the governors of New York and Illinois closed the banks of New York City and Chicago. The day Franklin Roosevelt took the oath of office, the entire banking system of the United States had collapsed.

Roosevelt Continues the RFC

The RFC had completely failed to bring about economic recovery in 1932 but the new administration would attempt to breathe new life into the moribund agency. At first Roosevelt wanted a fresh start on the board membership but decided to appoint Jesse Jones, the dominant Democrat on the existing board, to be chairman. Unlike Hoover and Meyer, Jones did not envision the RFC as only a temporary agency. He had a much broader conception of the RFC's potential and was prepared to provide the banking system with massive amounts of funds. Jones thought big and had the energy and the domineering will to back up his plans.

The Emergency Banking Act of 1933 gave the RFC expanded authority, and Title III of the act authorized the RFC to purchase stock of banks and trust companies. This would provide them with long-term

Jesse Jones was appointed Chairman of the Reconstruction Finance Corporation, and later, as administrator of the Federal Loan Agency.

(© Bettmann/Corbis. Reproduced by permission.)

investment funds and relieve them of their short-term debts to the RFC. It allowed the RFC to make loans that were for a longer term and less expensive. Franklin W. Fort, head of the Federal Home Loan Bank during the Hoover administration originally introduced the proposal. Hoover initially found the idea too extreme, but by February 1933 he conceded it would be necessary. Hoover had Fort, Ogden Mills, and Undersecretary of the Treasury Arthur Ballentine draft a plan to be given to Roosevelt's economic advisors. The bill went to Congress on March 9 and President Roosevelt signed it the same day.

In early 1934 Congress appropriated an additional $850 million to the RFC. As a result the Jones was able to make an immense number of loans. By 1936 for example the RFC issued over $8 billion in loans. It had already received payments totaling $3.2 billion of which $294 million was in interest, with loans in every congressional district. Jones' leadership also broadened the scope of the RFC. Already under the authority of the Emergency Relief and Construction Act of 1932, the RFC had authority to provide $300 million in loans to state agencies for relief payments. In 1933 Roosevelt established the Federal Emergency Relief Administration (FERA) and appointed Harry

An ex-farmer lives with his wife and children in a "Hooverville." Unable to make ends meet on his farm, the ex-farmer found a job with the WPA. (The Library of Congress.)

Hopkins to head it. Hopkins drew from the personnel of the RFC Emergency Relief Division to staff the FERA. Instead of working with only $300 million, however, the RFC provided $1.5 billion to finance relief grants between 1933 and 1935. Under Hoover the RFC had set aside $1.5 billion to finance large-scale public works but the division had only loaned $20 million by the time Hoover left office in March 1933. Roosevelt had the new Public Works Administration (PWA) take over the RFC's construction projects. The RFC then assisted the PWA by purchasing construction bonds that the PWA accepted from counties and municipalities. By 1936 the RFC had purchased over $700 million in PWA bonds, thereby underwriting a host of public works projects undertaken by the agency.

It was an ingenious administrative maneuver. Not only did the agency have a revolving credit fund from which it could issue credit to a greater number of financial institutions at a lower interest for longer maturation periods on the loans, it was also financing New Deal agencies. In essence the RFC was transformed into the bank of the New Deal. Moreover, the independence of the agency and its huge reserves gave Roosevelt the power to appropriate enormous funds without congressional authorization. For almost every New Deal program, there was some RFC funding

behind it. For example a total of $200 million was supplied to the Home Owner's Loan Corporation (HOLC); $40 million to the Farm Credit Administration; $44 million to the Regional Agricultural Credit Corporation; $55 million to the Federal Farm Mortgage Corporation; $83 million to the Federal Housing Administration (FHA); $246 million to the Rural Electrification Administration (REA), and $175 million to the Resettlement Administration (RA).

When the Works Projects Administration (WPA) was established in 1935, it immediately received $1 billion from the RFC. Largely due to the able leadership of Jesse Jones the RFC expanded in size and operated with enormous flexibility. When local business leaders from Los Angeles requested assistance after a 1933 earthquake, the RFC devised short-term loans for rebuilding. Similarly farmers were issued short-term loans for immediate short-term needs. Perhaps most revealing of the contrast with the Hoover administration, Roosevelt had the RFC extend a loan of $22.3 million to the Chicago Board of Education shortly after he took office. It was exactly the type of loan Hoover had denied on the grounds that it was beyond the authority of the agency.

But Roosevelt shared a common objective of his predecessor. Of paramount importance to the administration was restoring public confidence in the

More About...

The Export-Import Bank

The Roosevelt administration, interested in stimulating foreign trade and American exports, tried to increase the volume of international bank credit. The theory was in keeping with the strengthening of private credit in the domestic market through the other federal loan agencies of the New Deal. As part of the decision in February 1934 to diplomatically recognize the Soviet Union, President Roosevelt established the Export-Import Bank of Washington to finance trade with them. The Bank operated as one of the many subsidiaries of the Reconstruction Finance Corporation.

A few weeks later Cuba requested a loan to purchase and mint silver coins. In response Roosevelt created the second Export-Import Bank to handle the loan with Cuba. The second Export-Import Bank soon expanded to finance trade with other nations. Negotiations with the Soviet Union over its World War I debts owed to the United States for assistance it had received during the war disintegrated in 1936. Roosevelt decided to close the second Export-Import Bank and transfer its activities to the other Export-Import Bank.

Roosevelt first appointed George N. Peek, former head of the Agricultural Adjustment Agency, to be the first Export-Import Bank's president eventually replacing him with Warren Lee Pierson in 1936, who had served as the bank's general counsel. Pierson became an able administrator of the Bank and remained with the institution until 1944 when he resigned. Pierson became president of the American Cable & Radio Corporation and later Trans World Airlines.

At first the Export-Import Bank sought to issue loans to private lenders that would in turn stimulate

lending in the international market. It soon became clear that most private commercial banks were reluctant to make export loans. So the Export-Import Bank stepped in and granted huge loans on commodities, mostly tobacco and cotton, being sold overseas. The Bank also granted credit to exporters of railway and heavy equipment. Occasionally it would advance long-term credit to exporters who owed obligations to foreign governments in settlement of claims.

Initially the Export-Import Bank did not do much to stimulate foreign trade. Only $35 million had been extended by the beginning of 1937. Over the next several years, however, the Bank's activities would increase dramatically. China was given a $37 million loan in 1937 secured by a promise to supply oil to the United States. The bank also made loans to Spain and Chile in 1939 and 1940. Conservative isolationists in Congress including Senator Robert Taft of Ohio accused the Roosevelt administration of using the Export-Import Bank to extend American influence abroad. In 1939 Taft succeeded in placing a $100 million limit on the bank's outstanding obligations. In March 1940, however, Roosevelt was able to convince Congress to allow another $100 million. There was a stipulation that no more than $20 million could be extended to any one country. The German invasion of France in the spring of 1940 enabled Roosevelt to persuade Congress to lift the loan ceiling to $700 million. After that the number of loans increased rapidly. By the end of 1945 the bank had issued loans totaling over $1.2 billion. The Export-Import Bank continued operation into the twenty-first century.

---

banking system as quickly as possible. The bank holiday Roosevelt declared on March 6 and then extended as part of the Emergency Banking Act on March 9 closed all banks between March 4 and March 13. The Roosevelt administration shared the belief that bank reconstruction required commercial credit but it was clear that short-term loans to banks and railroads would not be adequate. The new plan was simple. Federal inspectors would guarantee the financial integrity of each individual bank. The president would then assure the public that no bank would be reopened unless it was sound. The key to the operation was speed. If the public grew skeptical as a

result of delay then the plan would fail. Teams of examiners from the RFC, the Federal Reserve Banks, and the Treasury Department went to work right away. National banks whose financial condition was relatively sound received a license to reopen by the president. Those banks that could not fully return deposits or credit were handed over to others who could then reorganize them with the assistance of RFC loans under Title II of the Act. Although the federal government had no authority to regulate state-chartered banks, state banking authorities generally complied with the same licensing process. On the evening of March 12, Roosevelt addressed the country in a fireside chat. He explained the nature of the banking crisis, how it had occurred, and what the federal government was doing to fix it. He then assured the public that all reopened banks would be sound, and the next day the first openings began. To the astonishment of Wall Street there was no panic. By March 15 nearly 70 percent of the banks had reopened. Depositors began returning money and by the end of the month over $1 billion had flowed back into the banks. In one of the greatest public relations campaigns of all time, Roosevelt restored the banking system.

The bank holiday gave the RFC, which was instrumental in the examination process, a firsthand look at the state of the nation's financial system. For the new board it was also an opportunity to evaluate the money markets and reconsider policy. The RFC under the Hoover administration had kept interest rates on loans at 6 to 7 percent, generally above prevailing rates. Jesse Jones decided that he would lower interest rates, beginning by a half percent, and relax the collateral requirements. Later, he reduced the interest rates to three to four percent. The RFC also had to manage the 4,215 unlicensed banks being temporarily held by others. About 1,100 were simply liquidated in 1933 because their assets were so badly eroded that nothing could save them. The remaining 3,100 banks were handled by the RFC through several strategies. Sometimes the RFC would liquidate the bank and merge all of its assets with another bank. At the urging of President Roosevelt, Jones later directed the RFC to loan directly to closed banks. This was handled under the Deposit Liquidation Board, a division created especially for this procedure and continued until early 1936.

The RFC continued to assist banks until Congress passed the Federal Deposit Insurance Corporation (FDIC) on June 1, 1934. Banks that joined the FDIC would have their deposits insured by the federal government up to a certain amount. In the meantime the RFC assisted closed banks in meeting the requirements of the FDIC. Jones created a Non-Member Preferred Stock Board to purchase the stock and capital of banks in order to make them financially solvent. The program was enormous and by September 1934 the RFC actually owned stock in half the nation's banks. But the RFC program was also a phenomenal success, and banks poured into the FDIC and by the end of the year over 14,000 banks had joined. In 1935 bank failures dropped to only 32. Never again would the United States experience the wave of bank failures that the country endured in 1932.

The RFC Continues Through the Depression

The RFC under the New Deal had returned stability to the banking system and ended the cycles of panic and bank collapse. One old problem still remained though. Repairing the banking system had not led to the increase in commercial lending that the early New Dealers, like the Hoover administration before them, believed would be necessary for economic recovery. For some unknown reason banks were not making commercial loans. Instead they were investing their funds in safer government securities. The relationship between industrial production and availability of credit was little understood. The prevailing view, at least in 1933 and 1934, was that more commercial credit had to be made available to stimulate recovery. The success of the New Deal agricultural program and the National Recovery Act depended on it. Business would need working capital loans, mortgage money would have to be made available to finance construction, farmers needed loans for paying mortgages on their land, and cities needed help in meeting their expenses. Any attempt to coerce the private sector had already proven nearly impossible for banks to supply more credit. It seemed there was little choice but for the government to make the loans directly. The New Deal did exactly this and embarked on a series of programs that would bring about a credit revolution.

Roosevelt approached the credit crisis by expanding the role of the RFC to make even lower-interest loans (three to four percent) to insurance companies, joint stock and land banks, livestock credit corporations, and agricultural credit corporations. An extension of the RFC's authority passed on January 31, 1935, allowed the agency to purchase railroad securities directly. The RFC was thus able to underwrite millions of dollars in bonds to railroad companies. The RFC could also purchase municipal bonds to help cities refinance their debt. As part of the overall plan to loosen credit, bankruptcy laws were also drafted to allow municipalities greater latitude in refinancing and reorganizing before filing for bankruptcy. Through the Frazier-Lemke Act of 1934 farmers were allowed to repurchase their land at an interest rate of one percent over six years or to retain possession of the land for five years without foreclosure. Finally with the capital support of the RFC a number of agencies were created to issue credit directly to farmers, businesses, and homeowners.

The farm credit programs were consolidated in the Farm Credit Administration (FCA), which made loans exceeding $500,000 to national farm cooperatives. It also created the Production Credit Association that loaned to 10 or more farmers or to loan associations that could loan to individual farmers. The RFC supplied the FCA with $1.16 billion. In eighteen months more than 20 percent of all farm mortgages in the United States were directly refinanced by the administration. Roosevelt also created the Commodity Credit Corporation by executive order on October 16, 1933. It allowed farmers to hold their crops off the market until seasonal surpluses disappeared thereby driving prices down. The New Deal also revived real estate markets and the construction industry through the Home Owner's Loan Corporation (HOLC), capitalized with over $200 million from the RFC and the right to issue up to $2 billion in bonds. The bonds would then be exchanged for a single first mortgage. By 1940 the Farm Credit Administration loaned $6.87 billion and refinanced nearly a third of all farm mortgages in the United States. The Commodity Credit Corporation loaned hundreds of millions to farmers and the Home Owner's Loan Corporation refinanced more than 20 percent of mortgaged homes in the country, making home ownership more affordable. Lastly to supervise the vast government credit machinery, President Roosevelt created the Federal Loan Agency and appointed Jesse Jones to direct its efforts.

Contributing Forces

War Finance Corporation

The model of the Reconstruction Finance Corporation (RFC) was borrowed directly from the War Finance Corporation (WFC) of World War I, the most successful of the wartime economic coordination agencies. Created by an act of Congress on April 5, 1917, the WFC followed the establishment of several other wartime federal agencies including the War Industries Board, the Food Administration, the Fuel Administration, the U.S. Shipping Board, and the U.S. Railroad Administration. William Gibbs McAdoo headed the WFC. By the end of 1919 the WFC had made direct loans totaling $306.5 million to public utilities, banks, building and loan associations, and railroads. After the war Congress was concerned about boosting domestic production of goods to avoid a severe post-war recession. It authorized the WFC to make export loans. The agency was found to be very useful and Congress did not want it discontinued. In 1921 the role of the WFC was further expanded with the passage of the Agricultural Credits Act. The act provided the agency with an additional $300 million and authorized the WFC to make

loans to farmers needing intermediate credit. The agency finally came to an end in 1924 when the creation of the Federal Intermediate Bank System began to assume the responsibilities of the WFC. Over the next six years the government began liquidating the assets of the WFC.

When Hoover created the RFC in January 1932, he not only had the wartime agency in mind as a model, he nearly replicated the WFC. Eugene Meyer, member of the WFC board, was appointed chair of the RFC board. Both agencies had eight divisions, including auditing, legal, treasury, secretarial, agency, examining, statistical, and railroad) and both had 33 regional offices. The legal and examining divisions of the RFC were almost entirely made up of former WFC staff. Yet although both agencies were essentially designed to undertake the same purpose, the economic problems they confronted were actually quite different. The wartime agencies established by President Woodrow Wilson's (served 1913–1921) administration were in response to pressure to supply the Allies with unlimited war materials. Direct government intervention in the economy through regulations and subsidies during the war occurred at a time when there was urgency to increase industrial production without the hazards competition. In 1917 there were not the same underlying weaknesses in the nation's financial structure as there were in 1932.

Department of Commerce

With his popularity rising, already in 1920 there were calls for Herbert Hoover to run for president. Hoover however was more interested in applying the new scientific business practices to American industry in a different capacity. For the next eight years, as secretary of commerce under the Harding and Coolidge administrations, Hoover would bring his international business experience to transform the Department. It became a modern organization able to confront what Hoover deemed the most pressing economic problem of American industry: the elimination of waste and the increase of productivity. This, he believed after studying the economic slumps of the nineteenth century, was the only practical way to reduce the burdens of debt left by World War I.

Hoover perceived his role as secretary of commerce as one of organizing and directing business, industry, engineers and workers in new methods of scientific management and economics. In this he thoroughly succeeded and the accomplishments of the Department of Commerce during these years was unprecedented. The most immediate improvement came with the development of superior equipment and methods of railway transportation and the establishment of uniform methods of packing and storage. These actions reduced damage claims by millions of dollars a year. Committees were set up between shippers and railway operators to better handle traffic. A mediation board, subsequently formally recognized in the Railway Mediation Act, reduced railroad strikes. The Department made many regional studies of technical problems involved in the expansion and conversion of factories to electrical power. A move to standardize manufactured products was undertaken. The measurements of nuts, bolts, pipes and other construction materials, for example, previously unique to each manufacturer were given uniform specifications. This was a great leap forward.

By standardizing sizes and measurements, manufacturers could now engage more fully in mass production. Inventories carried by consumers were reduced and competition was enhanced. The Department also set up commercial arbitration boards to reduce the expense of litigation. Commissions were organized to study the problems of the oil and coal industries. Studies were undertaken of business cycles and improvements were made in traffic safety regulations. Hoover also worked to eliminate the 12-hour day in the steel industry and embraced various schemes of worker representation. He even turned his attention to agriculture after the Mississippi River flood of 1927. He advocated strategies to enable sharecroppers and tenant farmers to own their own land. By the time Hoover became President of the United States in 1929, his reputation as an international businessman, humanitarian, and successful government administrator was undisputed. He appeared on the American political stage as a new type of character, that of the great statesman-engineer who could bring modern, scientific methods to improve government and industry. It was widely believed that if anyone could apply modern economic knowledge and methods to reversing the economic decline, it was Hoover.

Growth of the U.S. Banking System

After World War I over 50,000 financial institutions existed across the country. Most were commercial banks and the rest were savings banks, building and loan associations, industrial banks, credit unions, and finance companies. State bank authorities granted charters liberally and most had little cash on hand. Rural and small town banks failed throughout the 1920s as a result of the ongoing agricultural depression during the decade. In addition the growth of large chain stores and mail order houses like Sears Roebuck closed many smaller businesses that had been the clientele of rural banks. Between 1921 and 1929 one

quarter of all rural and small town banks failed. With the boom in the stock market, banks tended to put their assets into securities instead of government bonds. There were simply higher returns on stocks, corporate bonds, and mortgages. In fact investment by banks in stocks and bonds was encouraged by several policies of the Federal Reserve Board during the 1920s—a practice that Hoover, as Secretary of Commerce, criticized. Additionally as corporate profits increased during the decade the need for commercial loans declined. It was more economical for businesses to sell stocks and bonds than to secure bank loans. Thus the volume of loans declined putting commercial banks in a precarious position since most were undercapitalized anyway. In 1918 short-term commercial loans comprised the bulk of a bank's assets. In 1929 those assets were either speculative investments or loans such as real estate whose worth was based on ever changing market values. Many banks also had railroad bonds, which were blue chip investments for banks in 1917. During the 1920s, however, their value declined due to competition from trucking carriers to the point of becoming unmarketable by 1932.

In a period of economic growth like the 1920s, stocks, bonds, and real estate were the assets to own for they could be easily sold on the booming stock exchanges. But if for some reason the market declined, the value of those assets would deflate rapidly and banks would lose their capital very quickly. It seemed an impossible scenario in the 1920s, but there were warnings. So many stocks were overrated and railroad bond values steadily declined. When the market crashed, there were even steeper declines in the prices of commodities, land, and securities. Banks could not convert their investments to cash to pay off panicking depositors demanding their money back. With thousands of banks trying to convert securities into cash, the stock market declined further into a vicious cycle. Business activity then declined, followed by bankruptcies, which reduced the ability of businesses to make loan payments. The collapse of thousands of rural banks led to a chain reaction of closures throughout the country. The failure of several key European banks in 1931 only made matters worse. By the time Hoover instituted the RFC in January 1932 the economy looked very different than it had in 1917.

Impact

By the late 1930s, as the administration began preparing for the possibility of war, the recovery effort of the RFC gave way to defense. It was estimated that the increase in government spending and the enormous defense contracts necessary in time of war would require more credit than private capital could provide. On June 25, 1940, Congress passed legislation allowing the RFC to negotiate its own flexible interest rates, collateral security, and payment considerations. Jones began changing the focus of the RFC from recovery to defense. In June 1940 he formed a Rubber Reserve Company to stockpile rubber and end dependency on Japanese controlled supplies in Southeast Asia. He also established a Metals Reserve Company and the Defense Plant Corporation to finance new plant construction for war industries. In August the Defense Supplies Corporation was set up to acquire critical industrial materials. In October 1940 Jones established the Defense Homes Corporation to loan money for the construction of new homes for workers in defense plants. A week after the attack on Pearl Harbor on December 7, 1941, Jones established the War Damage Corporation to assist insurance companies in underwriting business losses due to war. Later in 1943 the Petroleum Reserve Company was created to stockpile oil and gasoline.

It was World War II that would bring the RFC full circle to its origins as a wartime agency. Between 1941 and 1945 the RFC and its subsidiaries advanced $37 billion dollars. Many of the reserves and plants built and managed by the RFC would be turned over to private industry after the war. It was the most massive government investment in the economy up to that time and it ended the Depression. Eventually, the agency was discontinued in 1953 when President Dwight D. Eisenhower (served 1953–1961) reorganized it into the Small Business Administration.

Perhaps the largest impact of all stemming from the RFC was the influence on the U.S. loan system. By the end of World War II, the federal credit system was permanently underwriting money markets, mortgages, construction, crops, and utilities and continued doing so into the twenty-first century. There is little doubt that the RFC laid the groundwork for the state-sponsored capitalism of the post New Deal era.

Perspectives

Government

Establishment of the Reconstruction Finance Corporation was undoubtedly a departure from the policies of former administrations. Never before in peacetime had the federal government became so directly involved in private sector economics. Gone forever were the days when a group of Wall Street bankers would rescue the financial markets during a crash by underwriting massive loans or purchasing stock. The federal government now assumed this responsibility. President Hoover was uncomfortable with this new alliance between the financial community and government but he always viewed the agency as temporary. Comparing the severe economic crisis to war offered at least some psychological comfort to both him and others believing in limited government roles that both events required extraordinary measures that were temporary. Indeed Hoover believed that the Depression was in fact an outgrowth of World War I, perhaps the final phase of the drain on national resources that the war had demanded. A return to prosperity would end the need for such enormous federal involvement in the economy.

Although Hoover may have been committed to government intervention as a last resort, he was also keenly ambivalent about its potential danger. Local committees of the RFC regional offices consisted of local bankers empowered with the enormous authority of the federal government. This power had potential for abuse. For a believer in voluntarism and limited government, the RFC was contrary to Hoover's political philosophy. He was profoundly uneasy about the presence of the federal government in the local economies of cities and counties across the nation.

Public

Surprisingly the RFC also demonstrated that beliefs about the traditional opposition of government and business to federal action were not necessarily accurate. In times of national crisis at least, cooperation was essential between private business and the federal government. It was in a relatively short period of time following the 1929 stock market crash that the financial community generally came to accept the need of federal assistance in the private sector.

The support for RFC activity grew much more by 1933. The expansion of the power of the RFC during the Roosevelt administration was the direct result of the knowledge and experience gained during the Hoover years. The New Deal credit revolution grew out of the inability of either the Hoover or Roosevelt administrations to bring commercial lending by banks back to 1920s levels. Economists did not fully understand the relationship between credit and industrial development until the late 1930s and World War II when early economic ideas of the supply of credit functioning as a stimulant for growth were abandoned in favor of Keynesian models favoring large government spending directly into the economy. Nevertheless the RFC not only rebuilt the banking system but also prevented its total collapse. It also made possible numerous New Deal credit programs.

At a Glance

Hoover's Criticism of the New Deal

Throughout his life President Hoover refused to acknowledge that the Great Depression was the result of weaknesses in the American economic system. Most of the blame, he argued, should be directed at Europe. The war, the economic consequences of the Treaty of Versailles, revolutions, inflation of European currencies, and overproduction of many commodities, Hoover argued, were the reasons so many European economies faced ruin by 1931.

Late in 1935 the former president also went public with his misgivings about the New Deal. Hoover became one of the most outspoken opponents of the Roosevelt administration. He was never quite able to shake his losing image, however. Democrats were able to win congressional seats by campaigning against Hoover well into the 1930s and much of the public viewed him as an embittered failure.

One of the ongoing historical debates about the Hoover administration centers on the question of whether the Hoover presidency marked the end of the old order or the beginning of the new. It is a debate that has provided much material over the years to political commentators and politicians to advance views on both the left and the right and has been applied as a basis of appraisal for subsequent administrations throughout the twentieth century. On the one hand Hoover's policies to fight the Great Depression, particularly the RFC, were unprecedented innovations. Past presidents tended to deal with economic downturns by waiting them out. Hoover, however, was the first president to offer federal leadership in mobilizing resources to meet the problem of the depression. Unlike his predecessors, Hoover responded immediately by holding a series of meetings with business and labor leaders to win support for his program. He eased tight credit by having the Federal Reserve lower interest rates and encouraged private charity to assist the unemployed. As the depression worsened, Hoover created the Reconstruction Finance Corporation and together with the Emergency Relief Construction Act in July 1932, these measures constituted a comprehensive anti-depression program.

Conservative commentators have argued that Hoover actually checked the forces of the Great Depression several times but that events continued to intervene that made the Depression worse. The election of Roosevelt, with his campaign talk of monetary experimentation, only served to undermine the confidence of business in the winter 1932. But most important, Hoover devised a recovery program without compromising the integrity of the American individualist tradition. The drastic innovations of the Roosevelt administration, according to this view, destroyed a venerable American system that remained intact during the Hoover years.

Liberals, on the other hand, welcomed Roosevelt's broad conception of presidential powers and his willingness to experiment. To the left Hoover has been portrayed as a pitiful or tragic figure, inept in politics, stuck in nineteenth century economic theory, and incapable of understanding the defects of the modern economic system. Hoover proclaimed his administration's success in the face of overwhelming evidence of the economic Depression. He resisted instituting programs on the scale necessary to combat the depression and was unwilling to enlarge the power of the federal government to meet the crisis. Both groups have generally conceived of Hoover and Roosevelt as polar opposites in both political philosophy and temperament and ability. The role of RFC was in the center of these debates.

Of course the truth probably lies somewhere in the middle. Historians generally acknowledged that Hoover's policies for dealing with the Great Depression not only drew from past precedent, such as the Home Loan Banks and the Federal Farm Board, but he also introduced innovations like the Reconstruction Finance Corporation. Yet, fundamentally Hoover believed that the federal government's proper role was to coordinate voluntary action. He was uncomfortable with federal power expanding beyond this role. As a result, the scope and effectiveness of his anti-depression policies were limited. By insisting on public works projects that were self-liquidating, balanced budgets, higher RFC loan rates than the prevailing market value, and a fundamental belief that primary responsibility for reviving the economy must come from the private sector, Hoover put many limitations on federal intervention. Hoover, it seems, had a very different view of the American system, emphasizing voluntary organizations and state and local government, than the federal behemoth that later emerged. The question that later perplexed many students of the modern United States political and economic system was whether this development was inevitable. Undoubtedly Hoover contributed to government policies for dealing with economic downturns but his program seemed modest in comparison to the New Deal.

Notable People

Charles Gates Dawes (1865–1951). Dawes was born in Marietta, Ohio on August 27, 1865, the son of Civil War General Rufus R. Dawes and Mary Beman Gates. After graduating from the Cincinnati Law School in 1886 Dawes practiced in Lincoln, Nebraska, until 1894. He won much local acclaim for attacking the unfair rate prices of railroads. While practicing law he also worked as a bank director in Lincoln and wrote a book on banking. He acquired stock in gaslight and coke companies in Wisconsin and Illinois and soon made a small fortune. In 1895 he moved to Chicago and became involved in the Republican Party.

After managing William McKinley's (served 1897–1901) presidential campaign of 1896 in Illinois and was rewarded with an appointment as comptroller of the currency. In 1902 he organized the Central Trust Company of Illinois and became its president. He became a recognized expert on the relation of currency to banks and municipal bonds. When the United States entered World War I Dawes became the general purchasing agent of the American Expeditionary Forces. His job was to procure supplies, eliminate waste, and keep prices low. When the war ended Dawes had earned the rank of brigadier general.

In 1921 President William Harding (served 1921–1923) appointed Dawes the first director of the budget. In 1924 Dawes was sent to Paris where he joined European representatives to attempt to solve the problem of collecting German war reparations (payments to victorious European nations for their damages). Under the plan that would bear his name, the German currency was stabilized by a loan of $800 million gold marks from abroad. The Dawes Plan temporarily saved Germany from the burden of the terrible war debt. It was a phenomenal diplomatic accomplishment and for it Charles Dawes became a co-winner of the Nobel Peace Prize in 1925.

In 1924 Dawes was elected Vice President on the Republican ticket with Calvin Coolidge. After serving as ambassador to Britain since 1929, in 1932 Hoover appointed Dawes to be chairman of the Reconstruction Finance Corporation. Throughout his tenure on the board Dawes never permitted the RFC to make loans to his own bank until after he left government service. He was also reluctant to underwrite completely the bank debts that railroads had accumulated with Wall Street banks and often sided with his Democratic colleagues on the board. In fact he tended to remain politically independent and often mediated between factions in the RFC. Nevertheless when the Central Republic Bank of Chicago looked as if it were on the brink of collapse, Dawes devised a plan to save it though it involved underwriting much of the bank's debts. The "Dawes Loan," as it came to be called, generated a great deal of controversy. The Hoover administration was seen as only assisting large financial institutions, while Dawes felt that if Central Republic collapsed, it would cause a chain reaction. The loan was issued and it did save the bank for two months, long enough to shore up smaller banks under its control. After many difficulties with managing the RFC board and concerned about managing his own bank, Dawes resigned as president of the RFC on June 6, 1932. For the rest of his life he remained active in business.

Eugene Isaac Meyer (1875–1959). Meyer was born on October 31, 1875, in Los Angeles where he grew up before his family moved to New York. His father accepted a partnership in the prestigious banking firm of Lazard Freres, which specialized in international trade. After graduating from Meyer following his father's footsteps into the world of high finance. From investments in the stock market Meyer became a millionaire almost overnight. In the stock market crisis of 1901, he bought cheap stock as panicked sellers dumped their declining securities. The crash was short-lived, prices rebounded and Meyers made a fortune. By the time he was 40 Meyer's net worth was about $60 million. He was one of the major organizers of the Allied Chemical Company and as a financier he developed expertise on the copper mining and automobile industry. He married in 1910 and had five children including one of whom was Katherine Meyer Graham, who later managed his communications empire including the Washington *Post* and *Newsweek*.

In 1918 President Woodrow Wilson appointed Meyer to be director of the War Finance Corporation. Meyer continued in this position after the war assisting farmers dealing with the post-war recession in agriculture. Largely because of this experience, President Calvin Coolidge (served 1923–1929) appointed Meyer to be director of the Farm Loan Board in 1927. In 1929 President Hoover then appointed Meyer governor of the Federal Reserve.

Meyer was regarded as a cautious banker, politically conservative and someone with strong links to the New York banking community. Because of his

President Herbert Hoover established the RFC in an attempt to bolster the failing economy by providing loans to industry. (The Library of Congress.)

political philosophy and experience, Hoover wanted Meyer to be chairman of the board of the newly formed Reconstruction Finance Corporation, which Meyer accepted. He continued to function as chairman of the board until the very end of the Hoover administration. Throughout this time, Meyer remained conservative in his approach to the lending practices of the RFC while Hoover gradually moved toward supporting a more flexible arrangement. By the end of the Hoover presidency, Meyer had taken much of the blame for the RFC's failure to stimulate recovery and Hoover asked for his resignation in July 1932.

After leaving public service Meyer began a new career in publishing. In 1933 he bought the struggling Washington *Post* and turned the paper into a highly regarded institution. In 1946 at the urging of President Harry Truman (served 1945–1953), Meyer was appointed the first president of the World Bank. It was a job he did not particularly enjoy, however, and once the bank was formed, Meyer resigned and returned to his communications group, becoming chairman of the Washington *Post*.

Ogden Livingston Mills (1884–1937). Mills was born into a socially prominent New York family in Newport Rhode Island. After attending Harvard Law

School he began a law practice in New York City. Mills first became active in the Republican Party in 1911 and was elected to the New York State Senate in 1914. When war broke out, Mills secured a commission as a captain in the American Expeditionary Forces in France. Upon returning, Mills successfully won a seat to the U.S. House of Representatives in 1921 where he served three terms until 1927.

After an unsuccessful run in the 1926 New York gubernatorial race, President Coolidge appointed Mills undersecretary of the Treasury in 1927 upon the recommendation of Treasury Secretary Andrew W. Mellon. To Mills fell much of the responsibility of representing the Treasury Department before Congress. When Hoover came into office, Mills continued as undersecretary of the Treasury and became actively involved in the early dominant issue of the Hoover Treasury Department, post-World War I reconstruction in Europe. Hoover promoted Mills to secretary of the Treasury on February 13, 1932. Mills continued the conservative economic policies of his predecessor, Mellon, and recommended a drastic reduction in government spending and a tax increase that would balance the budget by 1934. Mills was a staunch economic conservative who believed in a strictly balanced budget. His proposals in the final months of the Hoover administration fell on deaf ears in Congress and he was able to accomplish little. Nevertheless Mills did exert influence on President Hoover's economic views and as secretary of the Treasury was an ex-officio member of the Reconstruction Finance Corporation board.

Mills left the Treasury Department and government service when Roosevelt came into office on March 4, 1933. He continued to be active in business and politics and criticized the New Deal's "easy money" policies. His views were published in two books, *What of Tomorrow* (1935) and *The Seventeen Million* (1937), in which he attacked New Deal politics and defended Hoover.

Jesse Holman Jones (1874–1956). Jesse H. Jones, facetiously referred to as the "Czar" of the Reconstruction Finance Corporation, was born in Robertson County, Tennessee. His family moved to Dallas when he was young and he graduated from Hill's Business College in 1891. Jones went to work in his uncle's timber company and within a short time had risen to general management and purchased his own firm. In 1903 he entered real estate and construction, then he went into banking two years later and finally newspaper publishing in 1908. He became one of the largest real estate developers in the Houston area. Known as "Mr. Houston," Jones owned over

50 major buildings in the city alone. In 1912, he became president and later chairman of the Texas Commerce Bank. Jones also invested wisely in a small oil and refining company known as Humble Oil and Refining, which later became Exxon Corporation. He was the sole owner of the *Houston Chronicle* and briefly owned the *Houston Post* before selling it. By 1929 Jones was a self-made multi-millionaire.

In addition to the many business interests, Jesse Jones became involved in the Democratic Party. He served as chairman of the Houston Harbor Board between 1913 and 1917, which developed a canal in 1914 that turned the city into a major seaport. In 1917, President Wilson appointed Jones to be director general of Military Relief in the American Red Cross. When the war ended, Jones was instrumental in forming the international League of Red Cross Societies. He also developed a close friendship with President Woodrow Wilson whom he greatly admired. Much later in life Jones would establish the Woodrow Wilson school of Foreign Affairs at the University of Virginia and he would also serve as the president and treasurer of the Woodrow Wilson Foundation.

Hoover appointed Jones as one of the Democratic members of the Reconstruction Finance Corporation board. When Roosevelt came to office, he appointed Jones chairman of the RFC. During his chairmanship from 1933 to 1945, Jones made over $50 billion in loans, the vast majority of which were repaid to the government with interest. As an administrator Jones was a true businessman and gave little consideration to political philosophy. Nevertheless Jones despised the Wall Street establishment for what he viewed as its conservatism and narrow-minded policies that stifled business development in the South and West. Everyone in Washington recognized the tremendous power he exerted over the Reconstruction Finance Corporation. In part this was due to the force of is own domineering personality. He was physically large and tall and always wore double-breasted suits. Jones knew how to move in the world of politics. He was always friendly with the Congressman that would appear at his office to discuss pending loan applications in their district. When he was not in his office, he was paying social visits to congressional offices on the hill. Jones had an uncanny ability to form close relationships with powerful figures in the New Deal including Harry Hopkins and Harold Ickes.

Believing there was nobody else with the experience and knowledge to handle the job, Roosevelt appointed Jones head of the newly created Federal Loan Agency in 1939 in addition to his responsibilities with the RFC. From 1940–1945, he also served

as secretary of commerce. He devoted much of his later life to philanthropic work and founded the Houston Endowment, Inc., which built many community facilities, endowed academic chairs, and provided thousands of scholarships. In his honor the graduate school of Administration at Rice University was named after him.

Primary Sources

President Hoover Proposes the RFC

On December 8, 1931, President Herbert Hoover delivered the State of the Union address to a joint session of Congress, including members of both the Senate and House of Representatives. In the address the president covered a range of topics important to the nation at the time. Prominent among them was the lingering Great Depression which would not seem to go away as some, including Hoover, had thought it would do on its own. The address greatly reflects Hoover's ideas about the proper role of government in the nation. Hoover proposes the Reconstruction Finance Corporation as a primary avenue for federal action to combat the Depression (Hoover, 1976, pp. 580–597).

"It is my duty under the Constitution to transmit to the Congress information on the state of the Union and to recommend for its consideration necessary and expedient measures . . .

Our national concern has been to meet the emergencies it has created for us and to lay the foundations for recovery.

If we lift our vision beyond these immediate emergencies we find fundamental national gains even amid depression. In meeting the problems of this difficult period, we have witnessed a remarkable development of the sense of cooperation in the community. For the first time in the history of our major economic depressions there has been a notable absence of public disorders and industrial conflict. Above all there is an enlargement of social and spiritual responsibility among the people. The strains and stresses upon business have resulted in close application ...

Business depressions have been recurrent in the life of our country and are but transitory (temporary). The Nation has emerged from each of them with increased strength and virility because of the enlightenment they have brought, the readjustments and the larger understanding of the realities and obligations of life and work which come from them . . .

In order that the public may be absolutely assured and that the Government may be in position to meet any public necessity, I recommend that an emergency Reconstruction Corporation of the nature of the former War Finance Corporation should be established. It may not be necessary to use such an instrumentality very extensively. The very existence of such a bulwark will strengthen confidence. The Treasury should be authorized to subscribe a reasonable capital to it, and it should be given authority to issue its own debentures. It should be placed in liquidation at the end of two years. Its purpose is that by strengthening the weak spots to thus liberate the full strength of the Nation's resources. It should be in position to facilitate exports by American agencies; make advances to agricultural credit agencies where necessary to protect and aid the agricultural industry; to make temporary advances upon proper securities to established industries, railways, and financial institutions which can not otherwise secure credit, and where such advances will protect the credit structure and stimulate employment ...

It is inevitable that in these times much of the legislation proposed to the Congress and many of the recommendations of the Executive must be designed to meet emergencies. In reaching solutions we must not jeopardize those principles which we have found to be the basis of the growth of the Nation ...

It is the duty of the National Government to insist that both the local governments and the individual shall assume and bear these responsibilities as a fundamental of preserving the very basis of our freedom.

Many vital changes and movements of vast proportions are taking place in the economic world. The effect of these changes upon the future can not be seen clearly as yet. Of his, however, we are sure: Our system, based upon the ideals of individual initiative and of equality of opportunity, is not an artificial thin. Rather it is the outgrowth of the experience of America, and expresses the faith and spirit of our people. It has carried us in a century and a half to leadership of the economic world. If our economic system does not match our highest expectations at all times, it does not require revolutionary action to bring it into accord with any necessity that experience may prove. It has successfully adjusted itself to changing conditions in the past. It has successfully adjusted itself to changing conditions in the past. It will do so again. The mobility of our institutions, the richness of resources, and the abilities of our people enable us to meet them unafraid.

The RFC Begins

On January 22, 1932, President Herbert Hoover signed the Reconstruction Finance Corporation Act. The act was in response to Hoover's request for federal action to provide financial support for the nation's businesses struggling to survive the economic hardships of the Great Depression (Hoover, 1977, pp. 29–30).

"I have signed the Reconstruction Finance Corporation Act.

It brings into being a powerful organization with adequate resources, able to strengthen weaknesses that may develop in our credit, banking, and railway structure, in order to permit business and industry to carry on normal activities free from the fear of unexpected shocks and retarding influences.

Its purpose is to stop deflation in agriculture and industry and thus to increase employment by the restoration of men to their normal jobs. It is not created for the aid of big industries or big banks. Such institutions are amply able to take care of themselves. It is created for the support of the smaller banks and financial institutions, and through rendering their resources liquid to give renewed support to business, industry, and agriculture. It should give opportunity to mobilize the gigantic strength of our country for recovery.

Suggested Research Topics

- What was the Hoover administration's "trickle-down" theory of economic recovery? Was it fundamentally sound? Under what circumstances might it have been more effective? If commercial lending had recovered, do you think the rest of economy have recovered as well?

- How much were the Hoover administration's policies limited by a lack of understanding of the economic forces affecting the country?

- "A civilized nation is one in which there exists an orderly transfer of power." Was there an orderly transfer of power between the Hoover administration and the Roosevelt administration? If the peaceful transfer of power through an election was not available to Americans in the fall of 1932, might there have been greater appeal for a revolution?

- Was the level of spending by the RFC during World War II simply inconceivable during the 1930s or did it take until the late 1930s to understand spending was necessary to bring the country out of depression?

- In what ways was the RFC a radical departure from previous public policy? Could a RFC exist today? Would it be necessary? Would it be a dangerous concentration of power? What about international repercussions?

Bibliography

Sources

Fausold, Martin L., and Mazuzan, George T., ed. *The Hoover Presidency: A Reappraisal.* New York: Albany, 1974.

Hoover, Herbert C. *Herbert Hoover: Containing the Public Messages, Speeches, and Statements of the President, January*

1 to December 31, 1931. Washington, DC: U.S. Government Printing Office, 1976.

———. *Herbert Hoover: Containing the Public Messages, Speeches, and Statements of the President, January 1, 1932 to March 4, 1933.* Washington, DC: U.S. Government Printing Office, 1977.

Jones, Jesse H. *Fifty Billion Dollars: My Thirteen Years with the Reconstruction Finance Corporation.* New York: Da Capo Press, 1975.

Klein, Maury. *Rainbow's End, The Crash of 1929.* New York: Oxford University Press, 2001.

Olson, James S. *Herbert Hoover and the Reconstruction Finance Corporation.* Ames: Iowa State University Press, 1977.

———. *Saving Capitalism, The Reconstruction Finance Corporation and the New Deal, 1933–1940.* Princeton: Princeton University Press, 1988.

Rosen, Elliot A. *Hoover, Roosevelt and the Brains Trust: From Depression to New Deal.* New York: Columbia University Press, 1977.

Further Reading

Best, Gary Dean. *The Politics of American Individualism: Herbert Hoover in Transition, 1918–1921.* Westport, CN: Greenwood Press, 1975.

Galbraith, John Kenneth. *The Great Crash, 1929.* Boston: Houghton Mifflin, 1972.

Smith, Page. *Redeeming the Time: A People's History of the 1920s and the New Deal, vol 8.* New York: Penguin, 1988.

Warren, Harris G. *Herbert Hoover and the Great Depression.* New York: Oxford University Press, 1959.

Watkins, T.H. *The Great Depression: America in the 1930s.* New York: Little Brown, 1993.

See Also

Farm Relief

Religion

Introduction

American religious institutions on the whole have historically held deep concern about the structure and activities of society. Knowing that a perfect society cannot be achieved, churches have long sought to shape social order in an ongoing process consistent—as they saw it—with the will of God. Churches, whether wisely or misguided, have attempted to confront what they considered the evils in American life. The will of God, however, is often difficult to read. A vocal minority of Protestant leaders blamed the misery of the Great Depression on a cruel and competitive society. In resolution after resolution they called for a change in the social order of the United States. Conversely conservative church members believed the churches needed to concentrate on preaching God's commandments and preparing for the afterlife.

American Catholics formed their ideas of social justice from papal encyclicals (letters from the Pope). In 1931 Pope Pius XI issued the encyclical *Quadragesimo Anno* that outlined a program of massive social reform. Although no unanimous opinion of American Catholics existed, President Franklin Delano Roosevelt's (served 1933–1945) New Deal reform legislation was highly similar to the Catholic Church's teaching on social and economic issues.

American Jewry in the 1930s not only faced the social and economic difficulties wrought by the Great Depression, but were deeply involved with their fellow Jews abroad, particularly in Germany and its

surrounding countries. Although many Americans sympathized with the plight of the European Jews under growing Nazi oppression, they also feared bringing more immigrants needing jobs to America, which could further worsen economic conditions.

For black Americans in the Depression, churches remained the center of community life. For many in the large industrial northern cities, however, life became desperately poverty ridden. Independent, so-called storefront churches, appeared promising to lead impoverished black Americans to a better way of life.

Whatever road the different faiths took, churches certainly displayed great concern for the major issues confronting society during the Depression. This chapter will look at the social and political relationship of churches to American society as affected by the Depression. It will not attempt to explore the theological controversies of the decade.

Issue Summary

The stock market crash of October 1929 followed by the Great Depression brought severe economic hardship to many Americans. By 1933, 25 percent of the workforce was jobless amounting to over 12 million people. As President Herbert Hoover (served 1929–1933) proclaimed the Depression would be short-lived and believed government should not get directly involved in economic affairs of private business, he called on private charities and local relief agencies to assist the most needy. The amount of assistance needed by the jobless and poor soon overwhelmed these organizations. As desperation mounted Hoover's popularity greatly declined and Democratic candidate Franklin Roosevelt handily won the 1932 presidential election. Upon entering office in March 1933 Roosevelt introduced a vast array of social and economic programs for the next few years collectively known as the New Deal. The programs addressed almost every aspect of American life and greatly expanded the government role in people's daily lives. As social issues of caring for the needy rose to historic levels, the various religious denominations responded to varying degrees to the cries for help.

Political Labels Prevalent in the 1930s

To understand discussions about the stands of various religious denominations on social issues certain political labels used extensively in the 1930s, such as liberal, left, socialism, communism, radical, conservative, right, and capitalism must be understood. These terms are not to be confused with the labels of liberal

Chronology:

1931: Pope Pius XI issues the papal encyclical *Quadragesimo Anno* calling for governments to pass laws that benefit the general public good, that use of private property should take into account the overall good of the people.

March 1932: Roman Catholics, Jews, and Protestants meet in Washington, DC, to discuss ways to promote social justice by providing social services for the needy and better wages for workers.

1932: Dorothy Day distributes the first issue of the *Catholic Worker* designed to address social problems including poverty, labor, and racial discrimination issues.

1932: The bishops of the Methodist Episcopal Church meeting in a General Conference express the need for a revised social order.

December 7, 1932: The Federal Council of Churches in Christ in America, an organization of Protestant churches, issues its Social Ideals of the Churches that 16 statements on how society and capitalism should operate for the common good of all.

March 1933: Rabbi Stephen S. Wise organizes a gathering at Madison Square Garden to protest the treatment of German Jews by the Nazi government.

1934: The Catholic-led Legion of Decency is formed to rate movies.

November 1938: Germany carries out *Kristallnacht,* the Night of the Broken Glass, in which German Jews' businesses, synagogues, and cemeteries are destroyed.

and conservative as applied to theological (religious) thinking.

On the whole people who called themselves liberals generally supported Roosevelt and New Deal programs. They favored reform legislation as social insurance programs for aiding the unemployed, social security, and unemployment insurance. They supported minimum wage and maximum work hours, aid to organized labor, increased regulation of business,

A preacher speaks to a crowd in a Campton, Kentucky courtyard. Whatever roads different faiths took during the Great Depression, all of them displayed a greater concern for the major issues confronting society during those difficult times. (The Library of Congress.)

extension of government into the power generation field, taxation based on income levels, and support for farm prices. Socialists generally advocated collective or actual government ownership of business or of the production and distribution of goods so as to more fairly spread wealth among the people. Communism was an economic and political system where all property was in theory collectively owned by all and controlled by a one party government. Radical was a term

used to describe an individual who tended to favor extreme political views or practices such as communism. Liberals are "left" of center, with center referring to political moderates, while leftists are all those who "lean" only slightly left of center or embrace an ideology as far left as communism.

At the other end of the political spectrum, conservatives generally opposed government regulation of business, labor unions, the entry of government into social insurance programs, and believed individuals should take care of themselves without government help. Most conservatives did not support Roosevelt's New Deal programs. Those individuals who are spoken of as being "right" of center or "right wing" are conservatives.

Capitalism is the economic system of the United States where goods and businesses are privately owned. Prices, production, and distribution of goods are determined mainly by competition. One of the theories on which capitalism operates is the concept of supply and demand. This economic concept describes the relationship between the amount of commodities a company produces and the amount of that commodity consumers are willing to purchase. This relationship influences the price of the commodity. Therefore the greater the demand and more limited the supply of an item the higher the price goes up.

Protestantism in the Depression

Protestantism is a Christian religion, that is, its members believe in Jesus Christ. The largest Protestant groups or denominations in the 1930s were Baptist, Methodist, Lutherans, Presbyterians, Disciples, Episcopalians, Holiness Movement, and Congregationalists. Catholicism is also a Christian religion but is not part of the Protestant denominations.

The economic depression of the 1930s was a catastrophe that upset the values of, and in many cases, the very existence of Americans. Within only a few years of its onset in fall 1929, Protestantism felt the full weight of the Depression. Budgets were slashed, membership decreased, ministers were dismissed, and churches were closed. The bitterly difficult time also included the end of Prohibition. Prohibition, called "noble in motive" by President Herbert Hoover (served 1929–1933), had been stridently supported by many Protestants.

Depression Effects on Church Administration

Under the pressure of the Depression churches faced declining income, building debts, loss of staff, and the need for enlarged social services. Church finances began to feel the effects of the Depression in late 1932 and heavily in 1933 and the following years. Large numbers of churches were heavily in debt at the beginning of the Depression due to new construction. As a result congregations had to make focused efforts to meet interest and principal payments and church leadership had to promote special drives to meet financial obligations. As reported by the Federal Council of Churches of Christ in America, in March 1936, total

gifts to its Protestant churches fell dramatically in 1933, 1934, and 1935, paralleling the drop in national income.

The economically forced lay-offs of directors of religious education and other support personnel in churches greatly increased duties of the pastor for watching over his congregation and also carrying the burden of church administration alone. The pastor increasingly relied on and directed a body of volunteers. The presence of crisis in the homes of church members created new demands of counseling to which ministers responded. Some ministers reported becoming more in touch with their members' lives during the Depression. Although being brought closer to their people, some regretted the resulting reduction of time for reading and study.

Social Services

The Depression years brought the church many problems in the field of social services or philanthropy as it was most often called in the 1930s. To local churches philanthropy meant aid to its members, to its community, and cooperative undertakings with community and, later, federal government agencies. Such services could include operating soup kitchens, providing temporary shelter, helping with job searches, and providing more personal aid to its members. The economic crisis pushed social services during 1932 to the limit. Relief activities greatly increased while churches and individual families wrestled with problems of how to meet increasing demands with reduced incomes. Everywhere churches had been making a significant contribution to their communities at large and often referred to their relief work as "caring for their own."

As greater amounts of help were required to meet the needs of the Depression's unemployed, churches began to question the ability to be effective. Protestantism divided over the central issue: should churches maintain and increase their own social charities or should they look to government community agencies? Some groups as the Lutherans favored church organizations to providing social services while other groups wanted to use resources to support governmental agencies. Churches involved themselves more with relief and aid to the poor in the earlier days of the Depression, than in the later days. As the Depression had wore on, some clergymen stated they had fewer calls not because people needed less but because the need was so great and continuous that the needy themselves were aware that only the government could provide adequate aid. Church members, especially ministers, aided in collecting and distributing information on the

The interior of a Southern church in 1936. Many churches faced later financial hardships due to new construction during the first years of the Depression. (The Library of Congress.)

conditions of people in their areas and also organized local hearings which stimulated public opinion to demand action of government to bring relief.

The best known form of social work carried on by Protestant churches was carried out through institutions. In the United States Protestant churches supported approximately 340 hospitals, 310 homes for the aged, and four hundred institutions for children or child-placing organizations—largely through donations by its members. Although funding for these institutions declined by about 26 percent in the early 1930s, as members had less money to contribute, they were still able to maintain operation. In contrast there was an even greater decline in funding support for actual church expenses. For the Methodist Episcopal, Congregational and Presbyterian, U.S.A., the decrease for church expenses in 1930–1935 was much more at 38 percent. The decline was mostly through the drop in donations from members, many of whom had lost jobs or seen their incomes go down.

Local Church Efforts

Communities did their best to give relief to families in need. Few churches actually threw open their doors to the homeless, as health authorities frowned on this practice. Gifts to charitable groups, however,

such as the Salvation Army, Goodwill Industries, the Young Men's Christian Association (YMCA), and the Young Women's Christian Association (YWCA), provided support for housing homeless men and women. Local churches undertook various responsibilities such as operating employment bureaus, canvassing for jobs, distributing coal, wood, food and clothing, and running recreational and educational programs.

As the Depression wore on Protestant church groups advocated development of Protestant charities to match long established Catholic and Jewish charities. Protestant church groups had come to feel the inadequacy of their loosely organized philanthropy and relief efforts. Conversely other Protestant groups advocated for the government to fund all relief and philanthropy. They felt the effort was beyond the churches and some reasoned the church should concentrate on advocating social legislation to eliminate the causes and effects of poverty around them. Social legislation could include a range of assistance for those in need such as financial assistance for the aged after retirement, the unemployed, or the ill, and healthcare for those who could not afford it. This attitude was reflected in the many church pronouncements and resolutions on creating a fairer social order. A number of groups also actively supported proposals for

The Methodist Episcopal Church saw the need for social reform as an answer to the problems of the Great Depression, but did not suggest any reforms that would discard capitalism. (The Library of Congress.)

social legislation, including the YWCA, the YMCA, the Council of Women for Home Missions, and the Bureau of Christian Social Relations of the Woman's Missionary Council of the Methodist Episcopal Church, South.

Protestants as well as members of other denominations made strong efforts to provide relief to those most affected by the Great Depression. They opened soup kitchens, offered temporary shelter, and provided assistance in finding jobs. Aid for their own church members would often go beyond these measures as well. The decision to help not only came from a strong religious spirit of helping those less fortunate than themselves, but also because the Depression struck fear in many. With millions out of work in America by 1932 almost everyone had a relative, close friend, or fellow church member who was jobless. Many wondered that it might be themselves soon looking for help, therefore this daily fear led them to help those already affected. Soon the church organizations were overwhelmed with the magnitude of suffering and could no longer satisfy the need for relief. Though unable to cure the nation's suffering, their relief was greatly welcomed and comfort to those who did receive it. A number of denominations reorganized and strengthened their departments of social service

including the Northern Baptists and the Congregationalists with their new National Council for Social Action. Yet, overwhelmed by the need, others felt all the church could hope to do was to return to its business of preparing souls for the afterlife.

Cooperation with the New Deal Alphabet Agencies

An example of church and government cooperation appeared in New York City in the mid-1930s. Officials of the Works Progress Administration (WPA), a New Deal agency formed in 1933, approached the New York City Society of the Methodist Episcopal Church with a suggestion. The WPA hoped to operate their educational, artistic, social, and gymnastic classes in church centers.

Many churches were reluctant at first, fearing they could not pay additional heat and light charges. Some denominations had already decided that they did not desire to cooperate with these education programs developed outside the religious realm. Nevertheless the Methodist Episcopal churches did open their centers to the WPA with varying results. Some were successful in integrating WPA workers and church workers together and encouraged WPA to open more coordinated projects, such as nursery schools.

To the Left

The Protestant church's political and social attitudes in the 1930s reflected the temper of the 1930s. It concerned itself with the nation's economic problems, and restructuring a social order to help relieve the problems. Protestant churches approached Depression politics and issues from many different directions and levels of effort. The churches' positions on how to deliver relief from poverty seemed to break up along geographic lines, as northern church constituents often took a more liberal political and social stance, while the southern wings of the same denominations demonstrated a decidedly more conservative bend. To make their outlooks known, churches issued resolution after resolution. The resolutions provided general guidance for church leaders and members but were not enforceable. After 1929 fractions of many denominations moved to the left. A large number of clergy became extremely critical of unregulated capitalism. A significant minority believed a new social order with a move to socialism was the only way out of Depression miseries.

Although a discernable swing to the political left by 1930 was typical of many Protestant denominations, within each denomination this swing was fairly minor. Left leaning activists and their supporters were relatively few in number but they operated with zeal and an energetic focus. Of the individual denominations the Methodists were most clearly planted to the left of center in American Protestantism. The bishops of the Methodist Episcopal Church, representing the northern Methodist, were horrified at the toll taken on Americans in the first year of the Depression. They declared that fundamental defects existed in a country where unbearable poverty and distress existed amid plenty.

Though not as vocal as the Methodists, the Baptists, particularly Northern Baptists, also urged every effort be made to find a cure for the nation's economic status that bred massive unemployment. They looked to a more Christian social order to replace the profit motive. Southern Baptists, on the other hand, did not speak in such terms. They appeared reasonably content with the established economic order and entertained no thoughts of socialism. Similar differences in philosophical thought prevailed through most other Protestant denominations. Northern Presbyterians made general pronouncements questioning an economic order that produced breadlines and apple vendors, while Southern Presbyterians made mild statements about concern over poverty. The Episcopalian Department of Christian Social Service faced the problems of the Depression from the view of middle-class liberalism. They were critical of abuses of capitalism but were not calling for its discard.

The Federal Council of Churches of Christ in America, a federation made up of 23 Protestant denominations spoke out for reform of American society. Wasting no time, in 1930 the council tackled unemployment by holding a conference on the Permanent Prevention of Unemployment, forming a nationwide Committee on Religion and Welfare Activity, and making April 27, 1930, "Unemployment Sunday." The Council advocated unemployment insurance and public work programs and admonished businesses for not setting aside sufficient funds to aid those who lost their jobs. The Council advocated cooperation and mutual helpfulness over competition and private gain.

Two years later, at the 1932 General Conference, Methodist leaders called upon members to become more active in helping solve the social and economic troubles plaguing the nation. The Kingdom of God, they warned, could not be built where many lived in poverty and a few enjoyed a cruel and absurdly abundant wealth. In addition, believing the New Deal programs embodied the social ideas they had long advocated, the Federal Council of Churches of Christ in America, without ever directly calling for Protestants to vote for Roosevelt in the 1932 elections, warmly supported the Roosevelt's call for reform and recovery agendas.

Support continued after Roosevelt took office in March 1933. Leaders at regional Methodist conferences, most of who were friendly to the New Deal reform, spoke out on the social issues confronting the nation. The New York East Conference took an advanced position on social issues. They suggested that capitalism must be brought under some form of social control, which to some meant socialism. In contrast a separate organization, the Disciples of Christ, generally supported reforms in economic democracy but talked little of the demise of capitalism. The Disciples journal *Christian Evangelist,* however, edited by Willard E. Shelton after 1934, emerged as a champion of New Deal reforms. Most Unitarians remained middle of the road; yet its journal *Christian Register* swung sharply to the left advocating an end to uncontrolled capitalism, even supporting government control and ownership of the nation's resources. The *Christian Register's* stand illustrated how frequently the religious press was to the left of denomination membership in general.

By 1935, 25 months into President Roosevelt's New Deal, the Methodists' New York East Conference called the reform efforts insufficient and demanded that capitalism be discarded and replaced with an economy more regulated by government and founded on Christian principles. Region by region they called for basic changes in American society. New England annual conference deplored greed of private profit. Missouri Methodists held millions were doomed under the present system. Wisconsin and California Methodists called the foundations of capitalism unchristian. The Methodist Episcopal Church, South, saw the need for reformation of the social order but did not suggest any reforms that hinted at socialism. At the conservative end of the spectrum, the journal *Arkansas Methodist* appeared to not support much of the New Deal.

Despite the above trends, in the 1930s most Protestant clergy remained in the center or even to the right of center. Only a significant vocal few came to embrace socialism as the only hope for a better, fairer, more Christian America. Their socialist ideas ranged from a vague sort of Christian socialism based on cooperation, love and sharing to an establishment of a socialistic society with state owned production and distribution, and even to a radical revolutionary socialism akin to communism.

Baptist Harry Emerson Fosdick of the non-denominational Riverside Church in New York City fell into the first category. One of the most respected ministers in the United States, Fosdick was critical of competition and the abuses of capitalism but stopped short of calling for a socialistic system. Methodist Bishop Francis J. McConnell also favored some sort of socialized economy built on the goodness and rational thinking of Americans. Like Fosdick, McConnell stopped short of being a genuine socialist. Further left, Kirby Page, an ordained Christian minister and prolific writer of books and articles interpreted the social teaching of Jesus as non-violent socialism. He looked for a Socialist heaven to be established on earth. Moving into the radical area was Presbyterian Claude Williams, whose work to organize tenant farmers in Arkansas cost him his pastorate. His close alignment with the Communist party, however, caused the southern Tenant Farmers Union to expel him.

Fosdick, McConnell, Page, and Williams illustrated the range of Protestant thinking from a Christian liberalism to socialism to the edges of radicalism. All of these men, witnessing the misery of the Depression, each in their own way displayed their passion for social justice. On the whole they represented the most idealistic thought of American Protestantism, but in reality few Protestant clergy walked down the socialist path.

Standing apart from all others, Reinhold Niebuhr, minister in the Evangelical Synod of North America,

More About...
Roosevelt's Religion

To a question concerning the religious affiliation of his family, President Roosevelt responded: "In the dim distant past they may have been Jews or Catholics or Protestants. What I am more interested in is whether they were good citizens and believers in God. I hope they were both" (quoted in Flynn, p. 3). Roosevelt's answer illustrated his tolerance for religious differences and his hope for cooperation among church groups. Roosevelt's father was an Episcopalian, the religious affiliation that the President also claimed. Yet, according to his Secretary of Interior Harold Ickes, Roosevelt admitted to preferring a Baptist sermon to one of an Episcopalian. Further Roosevelt often referred with pride to his cousin, Catholic Archbishop James Roosevelt Bayley of Baltimore, known to the family as "Rosey" Bayley.

Difficult as it was to assess the exact religious beliefs of so complex a man, Roosevelt apparently accepted the fundamental tenets of Christianity. His lack of theological background, however, left him open and receptive to a wide variety of faiths.

President Roosevelt despised bigotry, the intolerance of beliefs different from one's own. For example, during Alfred Smith's run as the democratic candidate for the Presidency of the United States in 1928, Roosevelt defended Smith's Catholicism saying there was no reason why a Catholic could not be President. Roosevelt, the governor of New York at the time, reminded citizens in a speech in Buffalo that Americans of all faiths fought and died side by side in World War I. He admonished anyone who cast his ballot in the interest of intolerance as a truly "miserable soul."

exercised an incredibly powerful influence on American and European Protestant thought. Niebuhr, a uniquely gifted writer and speaker, spoke of combining religious zeal with reason and an understanding of justice. Niebuhr urged liberals to side with labor movements. By the late 1930s he turned his energies to halting fascists regimes of Hitler and Mussolini. Niebuhr remained a dominant figure in religions and political affairs for decades.

The modest exterior of a church near Blythe, California in 1936.

(The Library of Congress.)

Overall Protestant denominations, at least portions of each of the denominations, by their pronouncements and resolutions expressed considerable concern for the American social order. This movement was revealed in their inter-denominational church organizations.

Conservatism of Churches

Although Protestantism during the Depression flamed with socialistic speech and resolutions, there were always multitudes of politically conservative clergy to keep the fires somewhat contained. The liberal ministers did influence public opinion, but their social and economic resolutions rarely led to much concrete action. Conservatives eagerly pointed out the limited nature of the pronouncements. Many believed that liberal resolutions were often passed simply to quiet a vocal minority with the understanding they would be forgotten as soon as the meeting adjourned.

The great number of liberal and even radical resolutions passed reflected the great gap between the thinking of some clergy leadership and the laity (nonclergy church members). Such laymen were often not well represented in church leadership, and the official pronouncements were more the opinions of ministers than the viewpoints of the general membership of the congregations. In fact few of the great leaders of social

Protestantism had congregations. Instead they were more likely to be seminary professors or church press editors. Denouncing capitalism was easier from behind a desk than in front of a Sunday congregation. The Sunday sermon was the least likely place for radical social pronouncements.

At least in the earliest years of the Depression many ministers chose to ignore the economic breakdown, hoping confidence might soon be restored. In some church journals as late as the fall of 1930 and even into 1931 it was impossible to tell a depression existed. If the Depression was acknowledged, it was blamed on an angry God. From the pulpits came the message that not more legislation but more attention to religion would lead America out of the Depression. The message rang out—return to God, keep His commandments, and all would be well.

The spread of socialist sentiment alarmed many prominent clergymen. Methodist Episcopal Bishop Warren A. Candler criticized the Left swing and turned to the conservative Southern faithful to save American churches from socialism. Distinguished Episcopal leader Bishop William Manning, Methodist Bishop Edwin Holt Hughes, Methodist Dr. Christian F. Reisner of the New York East Conference and Presbyterian Dr. Guthrie Speers all defended capitalism. In addition to individual clergymen official church organizations championed capitalism. In 1938 the Southern Baptist Convention hailed the American economic system as the best in the world. The Methodist Protestant Church in their 1936 Conference retreated from its socialist position. Increasingly the church press questioned those criticizing capitalism. Presbyterian, Lutheran, and Southern Baptist papers reflected the more conservative viewpoints. Likewise most of American Protestantism was unalterably opposed to godless communism. For that matter, most liberals were also strongly opposed to communism. Even as conservatives organized to defend their views and condemn the policies of the New Deal and radicalism in the churches, the most prevalent argument dominating Protestant churches was an old one. Many charged that churches should only be concerned with aiding the salvation of individual souls. Any pronouncements on politics or economics were "meddling" in areas where churches had no business. This debate between socially conscious religion and personal salvation religion continued throughout the decade of the Depression.

Protestants and Labor

The interest of the churches in economic and labor difficulties during 1933–1934 centered around the programs of the New Deal, especially the National Industrial Recovery Act (NIRA). Section 7 of the act guaranteed the right of workers to organize and negotiate as a group the working conditions with employers, which is called collective bargaining. Many church pronouncements by various denominations and by the Federal Council of Churches of Christ in America strongly commended the announced goals of the New Deal. The churches heartily supported the purposes of the New Deal to establish emergency relief programs, to restore employment, to establish minimum wages and maximum hours, to abolish child labor, to distribute wealth and income more fairly, and to guarantee labor the right to organize. These goals were all in line with the social ideals and objectives of the Protestant churches.

The Federal Council consistently supported the American worker. Many other organizations, some with Catholic and Jewish members, frequently aided in mediating between labor and management. The Methodist Federation for Social Service, the Church League for Industrial Democracy, the Congregational Council for Social Action, the Fellowship of Reconciliation, the Fellowship of Southern Churchmen, and the National Religion and Labor Foundation all played roles in strike mediation. The Methodist Federation for Social Service in 1934 sharply challenged the concentration of wealth in the hands of a few. Most Protes-

tant denominations passed resolutions urging the settlement of industrial disputes by means of arbitration.

Churches have long supported the right of workers to organize and to bargain collectively. The rights of labor were even more strongly supported by the National Labor Relations Act of 1935. The great inequality of bargaining power led some ministers to give active assistance to labor organization efforts. In some industrial sections of the country parish houses were made available for union meetings and ministers would speak, stressing how the social ideals of churches were compatible with labor organization.

Most churches supported labor rights while others did not. Some churches had an honest desire to win the friendship of and cooperate with labor. A majority of northern church journals and approximately half of southern church presses acknowledged labor's right to strike. There were some differences of opinion however. Northern ministers were more sympathetic than their southern counterparts. National leaders were more consistently supportive of labor's rights. Overall churchmen of national fame tended to be more sympathetic to labor than local clergymen. Action of clergymen at the local levels was inconsistent. Large city ministers were more outspoken and active than those in small towns but many exceptions existed. Generally clergy sided with labor but some at times sided with management. There was often a gap between national denominational pronouncements and actual applications. Clergy in numerous instances and without public recognition, however, helped to bring about peaceful settlements between labor and employers.

Presidential Elections of 1932 and 1936

In 1932 the Protestant churches were not openly committed to either Democratic candidate Roosevelt or Republican incumbent President Hoover. In 1928, however, they had explicitly opposed Roman Catholic Alfred Smith. Historians look at the church press and its editorials for clues as to candidate preference. Editorials, although not openly attacking Roosevelt, leaned in favor of Hoover, and the chief reason Roosevelt was not favored was because of his opposition to Prohibition. Although the Protestant press also criticized Hoover for his evasive stand on Prohibition, the press reasoned that a "damp" president was better than a "wet" one. Papers published many more editorials on Prohibition than those focused on ending the Depression. Consequently when Roosevelt emerged as a landslide winner in the elections it was clear many Protestants did not lean in the same direction as the Protestant press. It was obvious many Protestants had voted for Roosevelt.

A minister preaches at a Pentecostal church in Cambria, Illinois in 1939. Pentecostal churches experienced rapid growth in attendance during the Depression. (The Library of Congress.)

By the election of 1936 Protestants had witnessed Roosevelt in action for four years. Only one church paper openly supported him for reelection, the *Christian Century,* a Chicago weekly at the forefront of Protestant liberalism. The outspoken liberalism of Protestant church resolutions often did not reflect general Protestant congregations. For example, 78 percent of the Congregationalists, considered a liberal Protestant denomination, voted for Republican candidate Alfred Landon. Many Protestants believed that Roosevelt's New Deal policies were leading to the build-up of a powerful centralized government bureaucracy which squandered the money of taxpayers upon those who were lazy and would not earn their own living. Although no statistics exist indicating what percent of Protestants voted for or against the ultimately successful Roosevelt, it was evident by 1936 that even though he gained almost 61 percent of the popular vote that a large element of American Protestantism, particularly its leaders, were becoming hostile to Roosevelt and his programs.

End of the Protestant Era in America

Some religious leaders had relied on the perception that previous depressions had pushed men toward religion and many hoped people would be reminded that the spiritual must dominate over the materialistic order. This was not the case, however, as church attendance continued to decline. Once the Depression hit its depths by 1932 and 1933 few American urban areas remained in which Protestant forces were significantly influential enough to religiously represent the larger community.

Although strong Protestant Congregations still participated significantly in community life, the domination of Protestants in American history came to an end during the Depression. Many smaller, newer religious movements outside the mainline denominations offered alternatives to those dissatisfied with the long dominant churches. Pentecostal and Adventist groups experienced rapid growth. American Catholics became more prominent figures in the mainstream as some rose to high-level positions in President Roosevelt's administration. Protestant dominance persisted longer in the South and Midwest with more homogenous populations than in the culturally diverse Northeast and large urban areas. Protestant denominations and institutions did carry on through years of war and peace drawing millions into its fold, but the dream of a Protestant-dominated America had faded.

Catholic Social Thought and the Great Depression

By the time Franklin Roosevelt was elected to the presidency in late 1932, Catholics generally believed the American economic system should reflect the values of Christianity by exhibiting compassionate care for all people. Catholics used these values as standards with which to judge the various measures of the New Deal. This concern for social justice was the result of three major factors: the 1919 "Bishops Program for Social Reconstruction," the 1931 *Quadragesimo Anno,* and the work of prominent Catholics including Reverend John A. Ryan and Reverend Haas. Each factor is described below.

The first factor influencing Catholic social thought were two documents issued by church leadership in the early twentieth century. In 1919 the bishops of the United States published the "Bishops' Program for Social Reconstruction." The document outlined a program of massive social reform including minimum-wage laws, social insurance programs such as unemployment and insurance for the elderly, and labor empowerment in the workplace. A second document which Catholics reference throughout the Depression and New Deal era was issued in 1931 by Pope Pius XI, the *Quadragesimo Anno.* Known as a papal encyclical, which is an official letter from the Pope stating the Catholic Church's position on timely social issues and offering guidance for Catholic living, the document played a vital role in Catholic interpretation of Roosevelt's New Deal policies.

American Catholics who took their religion seriously formed their social ideas directly from the encyclicals or indirectly from interpretations by their bishops, priests, or the Catholic press. The church historically strove to make religious faith relevant to social justice. The *Quadragesimo Anno,* the second factor influencing Catholic social thought, reaffirmed the ideas of a previous papal encyclical that Pope Leo XIII had issued 40 years earlier, the *Rerum Novarum.* The *Quadragesimo Anno* called for the government to have in place laws and institutions that benefited the general public and individual well being; it defended private ownership of goods, but such ownership needed to take into account the overall good of the people. The encyclical stated that both individual and social obligations went with the ownership of property and upheld the right of government to interfere for the common good. Pope Pius XI called for a living wage for families, opportunity to work for all able and willing, a distribution of a nation's wealth for the general public's advantage and encouraged labor organization. The document basically condemned *laissez faire* (free from government regulation) capitalism. *Laissez faire* capitalism had concentrated massive power and wealth in the hands of a few resulting in a cruel life for many people. To improve economic conditions for the masses, Pius XI would substitute cooperation and partnership of labor and capitalists leaders through formation of vocational groupings or guilds.

The fact that presidential candidate Roosevelt had actually quoted from the *Quadragesimo Anno* proved to many American Catholics that Catholic social teaching was affecting the country. Many felt Roosevelt's outspokenness endorsing basic Christian social reform principles took a great deal of courage.

The third factor influencing Catholic social thought was the actions of certain Catholic leaders. During the 1932 presidential campaign Roosevelt, impressed with the 1931 encyclical, quoted from it during a speech in Detroit. Roosevelt referred to the encyclical as one of the finest documents of modern times. Reverend John A. Ryan, a professor at Catholic University and, from 1919 to 1944, head of the Social Action Department of the National Catholic Welfare Conference (NCWC), concluded that Roosevelt and Pope Pius XI had similar social doctrines in caring for the common man and those members of society most in need. He became a staunch supporter of candidate Roosevelt. Ryan possessed a sound knowledge of economics and an awareness of what it would take to move a frightened American society in a moral direction.

By 1932 many American Catholics, both laypersons and clergy, were horrified at the economic collapse. Dissatisfied with President Hoover's attempts at solving the Depression, a statement from American Catholic leadership published under the NCWC on November 12, 1931, called for the American government to adopt and apply elements of the *Quadragesimo Anno.* The NCWC, directed by the bishops of the United States, met frequently each year to discuss public affairs. In their November statement the bishops expressed concern for the victims of the Depression and urged federal and state governments to immediately establish direct forms of relief. To further deal with the Depression, they proposed a joint meeting of government, labor, and business. Within months Reverend James Myers of the Federal Council of Churches of Christ in America, the key organization of Protestant churches, and Rabbi Edwards L. Israel of the Central Conference of American Rabbis, a key Jewish organization, joined with NCWC in issuing an additional statement. Deploring the practice by some businesses of cutting wages in the economic crisis, the statement called for a more equal distribution of wealth and income with planning and control of entire industries.

In addition to Ryan, other Catholic leaders called for relief from unemployment, a redistribution of wealth, and more action by the federal government to combat the Depression. Father Charles E. Coughlin, known as the Detroit radio priest, came out early in support of Roosevelt, urging a direct attack on the Depression miseries by the government. Director of the National Catholic Conference of Social Work, Reverend Francis J. Haas, suggested in July 1932 emergency measures involving massive federal spending and increased taxes on high incomes and inheritances. Reverend Edmund A. Walsh, Vice-President of Georgetown University, a Catholic institution in Washington, DC, called for better wages for laborers to combat the advance of communism in the United States. The National Conference of Catholic Charities (NCCC) held their annual convention in September 1932 and attendees echoed economic reform demands. Additionally they pointed out the failure of Hoover's Reconstruction Finance Corporation to provide effective emergency funds. The NCCC urged immediate direct relief funds. In November 1932 Mayor Frank Murphy of Detroit emphasized applying the papal encyclicals to the economic crisis.

When all votes were counted in the November 1932 presidential election Roosevelt was the overwhelming winner. The Depression and desire for a change affected Catholic voting as much as other Americans voting. Roosevelt even did better among Irish Catholic and Italian voters in Boston than the Catholic Democratic presidential candidate Al Smith in 1928. Roosevelt likewise showed impressive strength in large urban areas with big Catholic populations such as Chicago, Detroit, St. Louis, Milwaukee, New Orleans, and New York City. Clearly American Catholics vigorously supported the energetic leadership of Roosevelt and eagerly anticipated what Roosevelt would soon offer the country.

Catholic Support for the Roosevelt Administration

As President Roosevelt's programs of relief, collectively known as the First New Deal, unfolded over the first one hundred days of his administration Catholic response was enthusiastic. The Catholic hierarchy and press represented the legislation of the First New Deal as utilizing Catholic social teachings and the papal encyclicals. President Roosevelt carefully cultivated the friendship of the American Catholic leadership and kept himself available to the church.

Four cardinals—William Cardinal O'Connell of Boston, head of the American Cardinals, Patrick Cardinal Hayes of New York, an old acquaintance who had dined with Roosevelt before his inauguration, George Cardinal Mundelein of Chicago, and William Cardinal Dougherty of Philadelphia—visited the White House in May 1933 to personally thank Roosevelt on behalf of many Catholic institutions and organizations for his early and fine achievements.

The Catholic Press was practically unanimous in its praise for the Roosevelt's Administration first hundred days. The press consistently represented the First New Deal legislation as putting the papal encyclicals into action. Roosevelt addressed the National Conference of Catholic Charities and commented, "With every passing year I become more confident that humanity is moving forward to the practical application of the teachings of Christianity as they affect the individual lives of men and women everywhere" (Flynn, p. 58).

A sharp increase in the number of Catholic individuals appointed to high-level government and judicial posts garnered even more support for Roosevelt. Before Roosevelt few Catholics had been appointed to presidential cabinets or to any level of the judiciary, however, Roosevelt reversed these trends. Catholics James A. Farley and Thomas J. Walsh were appointed to the Cabinet—Farley as the postmaster general and Walsh as attorney general. Several diplomatic positions also went to prominent Catholics. Detroit Mayor Frank Murphy, a devoted Roosevelt supporter, was appointed as governor-general of the largely Catholic Philippines and Robert H. Gore as governor of Puerto Rico. A number of priests were asked to serve in New Deal agencies. Reverend John A. Ryan was seated on the Advisory Council of the U.S. Employment Service and the Advisory Committee of the Subsistence Homestead Division in the National Reconstruction Administration. Roosevelt appointed Reverend Francis J. Haas to the National Labor Board, who would later serve on numerous labor committees and boards.

Catholics on Finance

Catholics, along with non-Catholics, experienced relief when President Roosevelt declared the bank holiday immediately upon his inauguration and followed quickly with the Banking Act of 1933. With people unable to repay loans made for homes and farms because of lost jobs or decreased wages, the nation had been experiencing widespread bank failures. With the loss in funds on hand, some banks could not keep up with the demands for withdrawals as people needed their money to live. The number of banks declined from 25,000 in late 1929 to only 14,000 in early 1933.

Almost 40 percent of the nation's banks had either closed or merged with other banks.

With the public having lost confidence in the national banking system, on March 6, 1933, President Roosevelt declared a "bank holiday." This proclamation closed all banks for eight days to prevent the public from withdrawing more money. Under Roosevelt's direction, Congress then passed the Emergency Banking Relief Act that would restore confidence in the banking system. This action provided some assurance that those banks allowed to reopen were on firm financial footing. Only two months later, still addressing the banking problems, Congress passed the Banking Act, commonly known as the Glass-Steagall Act, on June 16. The act created the Federal Deposit Insurance Corporation (FDIC) which provided federal insurance for individual bank accounts up to $2,500. The FDIC insurance program provided even more confidence in banks by the public. Importantly the Banking Act restructured how banks operated by separating their commercial banking activities from their investment activities.

Most Catholics praised Roosevelt's banking actions as vital to stopping runaway greed in America. According to the *Catholic Herald* these actions were a "New Deal in which the cards are not stacked by greed and power against the people and their government" (Flynn p. 61). The Catholic magazine, *Commonweal* commented on the New Deal's monetary policy stating it was "public control, through the government of money and credit rather than the system of banker's control" (Flynn, p. 63).

The demand for government oversight of the stock market was also a key point of interest in finance. Catholic leadership strongly backed the Senate's investigation of Wall Street carried on vigorously by its Chief Council Ferdinand Pecora of New York. The administrative council of the National Catholic Welfare Conference (NCWC) supported the resulting Securities Act passed in May 1933 giving the government a considerable measure of control over the buying and selling of stock. The *Commonweal* commented that Roosevelt's New Deal monetary measures were in line with Pope Pius XI's call for monetary reform in the *Quadragesimo Anno*.

American Catholics on Agriculture

As important as the finance problems were involving banking and the stock market many other problems facing the New Dealers also captivated American Catholic thought. Although most Catholics lived in large urban areas, the Catholic hierarchy extensively addressed the plight of the farmer. The

Rural Life Bureau of the NCWC put forth their considerations on the current state of agriculture. The Bureau's philosophy on agriculture problems revealed a uniquely Catholic line of thought. In keeping with Thomas Jefferson and President Roosevelt's love of rural life, Catholics promoted rural living for its social stability and the opportunities it afforded to live a "truly Christian life." Catholic thought perceived that the crowded city living conditions led to unstable personal relationships, while rural life promoted large stable families. Catholics eagerly supported back-to-the-land movements that arose in the Roosevelt administration. The bishops stated that the Depression was partly the result of the industrial revolution that had pushed people off the land and into crowded cities and called for a return to independent life of the farm. In 1932 and 1933 the Catholic hierarchy endorsed proposals of domestic land allotment plans, various payments to farmers to help raise agricultural prices, and reduction of farm mortgages.

The Agricultural Adjustment Act (AAA), a major agricultural measure passed on May 12, 1933, had the strong support of the Catholic Church as did Roosevelt's secretary of agriculture Henry Wallace. Reverend Maurice S. Sheehy, a professor at Catholic University and a close friend of Reverend John Ryan, noted that Wallace often quoted the papal encyclicals. Although often confused by the complexity of the agricultural issues, Catholics praised Roosevelt's spirit of experimentation. The Catholic Rural Life Conference held in October 1933 in Milwaukee, Wisconsin endorsed the AAA and subsistence farming (growing what was needed for a family to live on).

As the control policies of the AAA unfolded certain issues arose in the Catholic communities. By October 1934 the National Conference of Catholic Charities made a plea on behalf of the small farmers of the country. The AAA had been geared to helping large farms that the government believed had a chance to survive, but Catholics stressed the need for attention to the small family farm and a subsistence homestead movement. Not only was rural poverty continuing to drive families off their land, but the crop reduction measures of the AAA and the increasing cost of farming equipment had caused more farmers to lose their land and fall into tenancy (renting, not owning land).

The Catholic leadership again urged back-to-the-land movements and return to small farm ownership and subsistence homesteads. Reverend Schmiedeler urged farmers to cooperate and support rural resettlement attempts. The Catholic Rural Life Conference held in Rochester, New York, October 1935, supported Senator John Bankhead of Alabama in formulating legislation to aid tenant farmers and farm laborers in becoming genuine landowners. During 1936 President Roosevelt appointed Reverend Ryan and Schmiedeler to the Special Committee on Farm Tenancy, chaired by Henry Wallace. The Bankhead legislation and work of the Special Committee resulted in the Bankhead Jones Farm Tenancy Act of 1937. The Act created the Farm Security Administration that between 1937 and 1947 made loans of $293 million to aid 47,104 farmers.

As complex as the problems of agriculture were, the Catholic hierarchy realized all through the 1930s that agrarian problems went hand in hand with the nation's industrial problems.

American Catholics, the NRA, and Labor

Passed by Congress on June 16, 1933, the National Industrial Recovery Act was formulated by the Roosevelt Administration and created the National Recovery Administration (NRA). The NRA was commissioned to create a set of codes to regulate the entire spectrum of industrial operation from labor to production to distribution. Across the United States Catholic organizations heartily endorsed the NRA. They urged parishioners to shop at stores and do business where the NRA's "blue eagle" logo was displayed. The NRA was considered a plan of recovery based squarely on Christian principles of the papal encyclicals and in recognition of Catholic social teaching. Both the NRA and the encyclicals defended the idea that government should intervene to relieve the country of economic disaster; both rejected the laissez faire theory of unregulated business and industrial practices and would substitute industrial rules of order; both condemned cutthroat competition to the blatant detriment of the common good; both called for the formation of groups or guilds, as Roosevelt called them, with voluntary memberships; and, both advocated a living or, at least, a minimum wage. The major difference pointed out by Reverend John Ryan, was that the NRA did not provide for as much participation by labor with management as the encyclical had suggested. Reverend Frederic Siedenourg, ex-dean of Detroit University, commented that Roosevelt's NRA was not trying to destroy capitalism, but rather, to humanize it "to meet the needs of the people during the depression" (Flynn, p. 88).

Many Catholics played an active role in the NRA's administration. Reverend Ryan served as one of three members of the Industrial appeals board formed to hear small businessmen's complaints about the NRA. Reverend Francis J. Haas served in several prominent positions in the NRA's labor department.

Numerous Catholics both from the church leadership ranks and the laity served throughout the country on various NRA boards. This considerable Catholic involvement explained the dismayed reaction of Catholics when the Supreme Court declared the NRA invalid in May 1935.

Apparent from the strong Catholic support of the NRA, was the American Catholics' support of labor rights. This support was rooted in the church's membership consisting primarily of lower working classes and immigrants. Catholics backed Secretary of Labor Francis Perkins's progressive ideas to improve working conditions. Many priests played active roles in mediating the labor disputes of 1933 and 1934. Many, however, felt the NRA had not supported effective unionization of workers, and they argued for a wider role for labor rights. Catholic spokesmen vigorously defended labor's right to freely organize and supported labor legislation. The 1935 National Labor Relations Act, also known as the Wagner-Connery act, specifically upheld the union, elected by a majority of workers in free elections, as the sole bargaining agent for all a company's workers. It prohibited employers from engaging in anti-union activities and established the National Labor Relation Board.

Association of Catholic Trade Unionists

To influence the direction in the rise of industrial unions Catholics formed the Association of Catholic Trade Unionists (ACTU) in 1937. The ACTU was formed around a kitchen table in New York City in the winter of that year. The early Actists, as they called themselves, studied the Pope's social encyclicals. Most members were well acquainted with Catholic social doctrine. Some were intellectuals such as John Cort, a Harvard graduate and convert to Catholicism, while most were already involved in union activities. Martin Wersing and Edward Squitieri, both Utility Workers Union (UWU) members were deeply affected after a member, fired for union activity, killed himself when he could find no work. Some Actists labored in unorganized industries and wanted to learn how to organize. Another, George Donahue, wished to help clean up the International Longshoremen's Association which had felt the impact of gangster infiltration. Actists also included members of locals who wanted to rid their unions of communists. Whatever the motives for joining ACTU, they all believed Pius XI encyclical pointed the way to help labor bring a fairer order to American industry.

The Actists evolved quickly from study to action, by creating several workers' schools in New York City. They began a newspaper, formed a speaker's bureau to teach Catholic social doctrine, and won support of the U.S. Catholic leadership. At the end of 1938 the ACTU had chapters, schools, and union structures in New York, Boston, Detroit, Pittsburgh, San Francisco, and the state of New Jersey. During its 13 years of existence the ACTU ultimately established 20 chapters, taught thousands of local union activists, organized extensive union conferences, published several newspapers, established legal defense, and elected members and supporters to local and international union offices. The ACTU was a significant force in the U.S. labor movement.

American Catholics and Social Security

The Social Security Act was signed by President Roosevelt on August 15, 1935. The act established a cooperative federal-state unemployment compensation system, established old age insurance which commonly became known as social security, and allowed for direct relief payments to poverty stricken elderly, the destitute blind, crippled, and dependent children. President Roosevelt, in a letter addressed to all of America's clergy in September 1935, asked for their help in seeing that the Social Security Act was carried out in a way reflecting its high ideas. He requested they communicate with him about conditions in their communities.

Catholic endorsement was swift and widespread. For example, Patrick Cardinal Hayes of New York praised the elements of the act as vital to man's happiness on earth. President Roosevelt wrote to the National Conference of Catholic Charities stressing the need of their cooperation to aid in the goal of national security. Mary L. Gibbons, a director of the New York Catholic Charities Bureau hailed the Act as an important first step in a much-needed national social security system. The 1935 convention of the National Council of Catholic Women backed the Act, and the Catholic press also supported the aims of the measure and felt it was in accord with the spirit of the papal encyclicals.

The 1936 Presidential Election

When all the votes were counted in the 1936 presidential election President Roosevelt achieved an overwhelming victory. Voters cast 27 million votes for Roosevelt compared to 16 million for Republican candidate Alf Landon and 900,000 for third party candidate William Lemke of the Union Party. Fears that Catholics might defect from the Democratic party had proved to be groundless. Two well-known Catholics, 1928 Democratic presidential candidate Alfred E. Smith and Father Charles E. Coughlin, the Detroit "radio priest," had both moved away from supporting

Father Charles E. Coughlin, the "Radio Priest" from Detroit, frequently made broadcasts denouncing the New Deal. His popularity concerned Roosevelt's supporters who feared losing the support of Catholics. (AP/Wide World Photos. Reproduced by permission.)

the Roosevelt administration over the past four years. Many had wondered how many Catholics would follow them.

Smith believed the Democratic party and Roosevelt had violated state rights with the push for ever-growing power of the central government. Smith went even further and charged that the New Deal and Roosevelt were communist-oriented. Smith shifted his support to Republican Alf Landon and appeared to be indirectly attacking the Catholic leaders who had frequently endorsed the New Deal programs. As the election proved, few Catholics ended up following Smith.

The most dangerous Catholic defector from the Democratic Party was Father Charles Coughlin. Father Coughlin charged that the Roosevelt Administration had communist tendencies. He played on the fears of those who greatly feared Communist influence in the U.S. government—communists infiltrating the New Deal was his favorite tirade. Coughlin was also openly anti-Semitic (anti-Jewish). Because Coughlin was a Catholic priest, the church was deeply concerned over his impact on the Catholic image in America. Coughlin presented difficult problems for the Catholic Church, which was deeply embarrassed by his speech.

Many Americans began to equal Coughlin's remarks as the official position of the church. Yet if the church attempted to silence Coughlin, his fanatical followers would desert the church.

As the 1936 election neared Reverend John Ryan took on the task of public defender of the Roosevelt Administration. Ryan denied emphatically the accusation that Roosevelt or his administration was under communist influence. In fact he pointed out, it was the programs of the New Deal that thwarted the growth of communism in the United States. In a national radio address on October 8, 1936, Ryan urged his audience to not vote "against the man [Roosevelt]...who has brought about more fundamental legislation for labor rights and for social justice than any other President in American history" (Flynn, p. 228).

Apparently many Catholics agreed with Ryan, Gallup polls estimated over 70 percent of Catholics voted for Roosevelt (Flynn, p. 233). Arizona, California, Connecticut, Maryland, Massachusetts, New Mexico, and Rhode Island—states with large Catholic populations—all gave Roosevelt a larger majority in 1936 than in 1932. Roosevelt also won with convincing majorities in the 12 largest U.S. cities, where most of the Catholic vote was concentrated. Catholics not only voted for Roosevelt out of gratitude for his New Deal programs but also because of the recognition he extended to Catholics through governmental appointments and his conscientious communication with American Catholic leaders. The relationship between the Catholic Church and Roosevelt was mutually favorable. Roosevelt won the political support of a majority of Catholics and Roosevelt helped Catholics integrate into the mainstream of American national life.

American Jews and the Great Depression

The field of Jewish interests and activities encompassed much more than strictly religious matters for Jews in the United States. American Jews maintained a network of numerous charitable and social organizations and educational institutions. They were also deeply involved with the welfare of their fellow Jews abroad including the efforts to rebuild a national Jewish homeland in Palestine. As the nation's economy collapsed following the stock market crash in October 1929, however, American Jews had to focus on surviving the Depression. The full impacts of the economic crisis struck home in 1930 when the privately owned Bank of the United States in New York City went out of business, becoming bankrupt. Approximately 400,000 Jewish account holders lost their savings. Its failure and subsequent indictment of its officers shook the confidence of Jewish wage earners of New York's Lower East Side.

The Depression had two major effects on Jewish life in America. First the Jewish community had to apply their energies to prevent the dissolution of charities and schools that had been created in previous years. Secondly the Jewish rise into the middle class was undoubtedly set back.

The impact of the Depression was felt in the Jewish charities. Whereas in the previous decade considerable sums were available for the building of synagogues, hospitals, and community centers, now all went to relief efforts for newly poor and unemployed Jews. With demands for services steadily rising while contributions were declining up only the most desperate people in need received aid. During the first nine months of 1931 charities recorded an average 42.8 percent increase in relief recipients nationwide. In Minneapolis and Baltimore the rise in assistance requests was over 15 percent. By 1932 over 50,000 Jews were unemployed in Chicago and requests for welfare from Jewish charities increased two hundred percent.

The effects of the Depression compelled the charities that depended on philanthropic fund-raising efforts to consolidate. The formation of so-called community federations consisting of large combinations of various charities and social service organizations accelerated. Of the 145 Jewish federations established by 1936, 48 began in 1931. In Philadelphia the Jewish federation joined with similar Protestant and non-church groups in a cooperative campaign that formed the basis for the later United Way.

The decline in fund raising also severely impacted the amount of federation funds available for overseas relief and for land purchases for immigrant resettlement in the Middle East. Soon, as with all voluntary charities, the need for economic assistance in America became too heavy a burden and the charities turned to the federal government for help. By 1934 between 70 and 90 percent of Jewish families who had formerly received Jewish charity relief, received government relief.

Jewish educational institutions also felt the economic upheaval. To American Jews education was of the utmost importance and seen as a way to advance in American society. Albert B. Schoolman, President of the National Council for Jewish Education, reported in May 1932 that the Jews of the United States spent over $6,000,000 annually for Jewish education. The Jewish community was shocked only one month later after its eighth annual commencement exercises, when the Hebrew Union College for Teachers in New York City announced that the school was closing because of lack of funds. The school which had been in operation for nine years had graduated 176 students and had a current enrollment of 2,000. Subsequently nearly all Jewish educational institutions slashed their budgets.

Perhaps the most painful adjustment for American Jewry as a result of the Depression was the loss of the American dream of bettering oneself. American Jews in the early twentieth century found it very difficult to get jobs because of discrimination. To help overcome this form of discrimination during the 1920s Jewish families had been investing in formal education and training for their young adults. Many students were compelled to halt their education in support of their families. Merchant fathers, unable to compete with chain stores, joined the unemployed. For those in business many Jewish merchants sold luxury goods such as furs, jewelry, and furniture. Since many Americans could no longer afford such items, Jews were some of the first to feel the economic contraction. The number of Jewish-owned jewelry stores dropped by half between 1929 and 1933, as did fur stores and their suppliers.

Due to the high level of education in Jewish communities many Jewish young adults were doctors and lawyers. Many of them now drove taxicabs at a time when the use of cabs had drastically declined. Jewish lawyers were likely to be the first to be let go from a firm, and had no hope of finding other law positions.

The dream of attaining middle-class status faded away for many Jews. For others, in order to get a good position with a firm, some Jewish men and women resorted to the tactic of "passing" which meant hiding their Jewish background. Those who did not have stereotypically Jewish physical features could "pass" themselves off as something other than Jewish and acquire employment. Not until Roosevelt's 1941 executive order that established the Commission on Fair Labor Employment Practices did discrimination in employment against Jews decline.

Although just as caught up in surviving the Depression as the general public, American Jews watched as dark clouds gathered in Germany. Jews in the United States not only struggled with the economic situation at home, but became profoundly disturbed by Hitler's treatment of Jews in Germany.

Attention Turns to Europe

In 1932 the Jewish community's greatest concerns lay with the economic depression in the United States, but during the following two years that concern shifted to the rise of Hitler in Germany. The Jews of the United States were heartened as many Americans expressed their condemnation of events in Germany. Nevertheless yet another difficulty American Jews had to contend with was growing anti-Semitism in the United States. The German situation and the rising tide of anti-Semitism had a more profound effect upon American Jewry than did the Depression.

As Adolf Hitler took control of the German government in January 1933 Americans were experiencing the depth of the Depression. Their thoughts and energies were focused on the economic collapse of America. Nevertheless the German Nazi regime would soon alarmingly become a major concern of not only America's Jewish population but Protestants and Catholics as well.

Alarmed as the Nazi government began to arrest and imprison German Jews, Rabbi Stephen S. Wise of the Free Synagogue in New York City organized a protest meeting at Madison Square Garden in March 1933. Fifty thousand people attended, including speakers Bishop William Manning of the Episcopal Church and Methodist Bishop Francis J. McConnell. No one had imagined at the time that the Nazi government's goal was to eradicate Jewish people. In 1935 Germany passed the Nuremberg Laws that stripped Jews of German citizenship and of protection under the law. Hitler effectively used propaganda to convince the German people that their failure in World War I and Germany's subsequent economic troubles could be blamed on the Jews. German Jews became the "scapegoat." On November 9, 1938, responding to an assassination of a German diplomat in Paris by a Jewish youth frightened about the fate of his refugee parents, the Nazi government ordered the first major attack, or *pogrom,* on Jews throughout Germany and German-occupied Austria. Violence ensued throughout Germany. Jews were attacked and killed, their businesses were destroyed, synagogues were burned, Jewish cemeteries were desecrated, and the first 30,000 Jews were arrested and transported to concentration camps. The event became known as *Kristallnacht,* or "Night of Broken Glass," in reference to the broken panes of glass in Jewish shop windows. While the *Kristallnacht* was planned by the government, the German people, convinced by Hitler that Jews were the cause of their troubles, energetically participated. Condemnation of the action was widespread throughout America. In addition to the outrage of the American Jewish community prominent Protestant and Catholic organizations denounced the *Kristallnacht.* Although Americans were sympathetic to the plight of Jews in Germany, the United States had consistently failed to take action to relieve the situation throughout the 1930s.

Inaction, Political Worries, Immigration Policies

Between 1933 and 1941 there would be no formal protest by the American government of German policies against the Jewish people. Although President Roosevelt and State Department officials deplored Nazi treatment of the Jews, two considerations weighed heavily. First was the question of the proper official and diplomatic response. If the Roosevelt administration formally condemned Germany, they would be accused of interfering in German internal affairs and damage already strained relations. Furthermore Roosevelt feared that such official protests would increase hostile actions by Germany toward Jews in retaliation.

The second and highly complicated question was how to deal with the thousands of Jews from Germany or German-controlled areas who sought entry into the United States to escape the persecution. During 1933–1941 the basis of U.S. immigration policy rested on the National Origins Act of 1924. The 1924 Act established quotas of immigrants from all nations except for countries in the Western Hemisphere. Only 150,000 immigrants were allowed to enter the United States per year. Those who wished to emigrate had to obtain a visa from American consular officers in their respective countries. To do so applicants had to produce proof that they had sufficient assets of their own or provide guarantee of support from someone in the United States and provide passports, birth certificates, and police certificates. For Jewish refugees, many of the mandatory documents were difficult or impossible to obtain. In addition, with the Depression tightening around America, President Hoover in 1930 instructed American consuls to pass judgment carefully on each applicant to weed out those who were likely to become a public charge (dependent on social services of local governments). "Likely public charge" was referred to as LPC. Roosevelt allowed the Hoover LPC directive to stand for nearly four years until January 1937 when he ordered consuls to *not* operate under the idea of keeping visas to a minimum and to use *probability*, not mere *possibility* when enforcing the LPC clause.

The yearly immigration combined quota for Germany and Austria was 27,370. For the years 1933 through 1942 far fewer actually immigrated, amounting to only five percent of the quota in 1933, then increasing each of the following years to 65 percent of the quota in 1938 and finally one hundred percent in 1939. The percentage declined slightly to 95.3 percent in 1940 then plummeted to 17.4 percent by 1942. Actual immigration numbers varied from 1,450 individuals in 1933 to 27,370 in 1939. The total number of Jews admitted as immigrants from 1933 to 1943 was 168,128. Of these, 97,325 came to the United States from Germany.

During the nine years from 1933 to 1941 the immigration laws were not changed. Those in Congress in favor of liberalizing the laws for humanitarian reasons were thwarted by those who actually argued for more restrictive provisions. Those favoring more restrictive measures argued that with unemployment rampant there was no room for new immigrants. Neither side succeeded in changing existing law.

Roosevelt also declined to alter the immigration quotas for largely political reasons. Public opinion polls indicated that as late as December 1938, despite almost unanimous condemnation of *Kristallnacht*, 83 percent of Americans would oppose a bill allowing for the admission of more immigrants above current quotas.

Americans were opposed to allowing more immigration into the United States for several reasons. First the United States was suffering the worst economic depression in history. Millions were unemployed or on relief, and new immigrants would surely add to the problem. Although 94 percent disapproved of Nazi treatment of Jews, Americans remained steadfast in the belief that new immigrants would pose economic threats in the United States.

Anti-Semitism

Another major reason Americans refused to allow their leaders to open borders to Jews was a long held negative attitude by many Americans. Rumors had long abounded that Jews were greedy, dishonest, rudely aggressive businessmen. These rumors had been fueled by auto industry magnate Henry Ford, who, beginning in 1922, launched an anti-Semitic propaganda campaign in his newspaper the Dearborn, Michigan, *Independent*. The newspaper claimed Jews plotted to take control of everything from the League of Nations to American politics to baseball, music, and movies.

In the late 1920s Ford apologized but the damage had already been done. Meanwhile the racial hate group, the Ku Klux Klan, had revived talk of Jews as "Christ killers," referring to the death of Christ at the hands of Jews. A poll in March 1938 revealed that 19 percent of Americans would support a campaign by an anti-Semitic political candidate for public office. Although in subsequent polls that figure dropped to 12 percent, many believed up to 25 percent of Americans sympathized with a campaign against Jews in the United States. Members of Christian churches also appeared to harbor such attitudes. As many as 121 anti-Semitic organizations existed in the United States and Protestants dominated most of them. Notable outspoken anti-Semitic Christian leaders were the Reverend Gerald B. Winrod of the Protestant group Defenders of the Christian Faith, and Gerald L.K. Smith, who organized several anti-Semitic groups toward the end of the decade. Although an embarrassment to the official Catholic leadership, radio priest Father Charles E. Coughlin and his Christian Front were openly anti-Semitic. All of the anti-Semitic fervor proved detrimental to easing immigration quotas.

Self-Preservation

A combination of economic conditions, political considerations, immigration laws and American attitudes proved disastrous to those Jews trying to flee the Nazis and escape to the United States. Only one-half as many Jews were able to immigrate to the United States in the 1930s as had immigrated in the 1920s. The Nazi persecution and the hopeless status of the Jews convinced many Americans that Palestine was the last chance for European Jews, and it inspired the collection of funds to get Jews to Palestine. Those who looked to Palestine as the Jewish national home were called Zionists. The Joint Distribution Organization, established in World War I, raised ever-increasing sums from the Jews of America to assist thousands of Jews being uprooted as a result of Nazi persecution. Many Jewish Americans, who previously believed the Jews should make their home in the United States, realized Palestine might be their people's best hope.

By 1938–1940 growing hostility against Jews in Europe had caused the Jewish social network to focus primarily on Jewish self-preservation. The Yearbook of Jewish Social Work, published by the Council of Jewish Federations and Welfare Funds had shown that the demand for services provided by homes for the aged, general hospitals, and clinics was at an all time high. Yet both the Council and the National Conference of Jewish Social Welfare turned to the financing of overseas relief and refugee programs. They asked for unprecedented levels of contributions to meet emergency conditions in Europe. In 1939 the United Jewish Appeal for Refugees and Overseas Needs was formed and combined several groups: the Joint Distribution Committee, the United Distribution Committee, the United Palestine Appeal, and the National Refugee Service, Inc. Over $15,000,000 was raised in 1939 and distributed between the organizations. Sums were given also to the Federal Council of the Churches of Christ in America for Protestant refugees that were also fleeing war conditions in Europe and to Pope Pius XII as a memorial to Pope Pius XI for Catholic refugees.

The Black Church

The churches of black Americans, long the center of black community life, continued to play a central role in the Great Depression years. Many had ventured North in the early years of the twentieth century in search of a better life. Black churches had sprung up throughout the North. Most of the larger religious denominations had some black members, almost always gathered in their separate black church congregations. The great majority of black Christians both in the North and South belonged to the Baptist and Methodist denominations. Northern black congregations were stretched to the limit to accommodate the migration to the Northern cities that continued throughout the 1920s and 1930s. Large black denominations became separate members of the Protestant organization the Federal Council of the Churches of Christ in America. The Federal Council created the Commission on Race Relations in 1921. George E. Haynes, educator and sociologist, led the commission for approximately 25 years. He attempted to guide his people through the difficult Depression years and help white churches better understand their fellow black Christians. Within local communities, however, there was almost no meaningful interrelationship between white and black Christians. In 1936 the percentage of church members in the black population was slightly higher than of the white population. Forty-four percent of the black population were members of black churches while 42 percent of the white population were church members.

The fastest growing black denominations during the Depression years were smaller independent, "store-front" churches. In the early years of the Depression black Americans found their jobs had evaporated as they were replaced with white men. Few had skills and many were illiterate, and as a result blacks became trapped in the crowded ghettos of New York City, Detroit, Philadelphia, and Chicago. The tenement buildings in which they lived were racked with disease, poverty, and hopelessness. Faced with such severe conditions many looked for leaders to help solve the problems and provide hope. Although the older major black churches continued to grow in significant numbers and played central roles in black community life, various black religious sects emerged. Major new groupings were Father Divine's Peace Mission, rival group Bishop Charles E. "Sweet Daddy" Grace's United House of Prayer for All People, and W. D. Farad Muhammad's Nation of Islam.

Father Divine's Peace Mission came into prominence about 1930 in New York. Leader George Baker adopted the name Father Divine. Divine preached that heaven was on earth not in the hereafter. He also preached charity to all, sternly opposing racism and racial discrimination. He promised a higher status for blacks, and promised resolution of want and poverty. In 1931 neighbors protested that the large crowds he attracted were disturbing the peace. He was convicted and sentenced to one year in prison. Two days later the presiding judge died and Father Divine supposedly committed, "I hated to do it." His followers believed he was actually God. He purchased hotels and gave his followers, who were required to leave home and family, food and shelter for modest sums. In 1934 he claimed 72 "heavens" had been established, and by 1939, 152 "heavens", mostly around New York, were open. Divine's Peace Movement claimed that it had many millions of adherents, however, in actuality numbers estimated between 3,000 to 25,000.

Another "savior" was waiting in the wings in 1930, a mysterious Mullah (Muslim religious leader) who called himself W. D. Farad Muhammad. He told a handful of black listeners that he had come from Mecca, the holy city of Islam, to teach the truth about white men and to prepare blacks for the final battle between good and evil, black and white. Farad went as quietly as possible from house to house in Detroit listening to the problems of the destitute black people. His electrifying manner soon caught the attention of many. The fame of the Prophet, as he was called, grew, and he established the first temples of Islam in Detroit. Farad taught that Christianity had enslaved black men and taken them away from their native land and religion, Islam. Animosity toward whites was not all that Farad preached. He also taught cleanliness, thrift, and hard work. He established a school where homemaking, Negro history, and Muslim subjects were taught.

Elijah Poole, son of a Baptist minister and originally from Georgia, had been attracted by Fahad. Poole's leadership qualities quickly became apparent to Fahad and he was given the new name Elijah Muhammad. Fahad had first appeared on July 4, 1930, and disappeared approximately June 30, 1934, never to be seen again. Elijah became the new messenger of Islam and the movement spread from the initial temple in Detroit to almost every major city in the country where a large black population lived.

The actual numbers of members of the black religious sects remained small compared with the bulk of membership of more mainstream organized religion. The larger black dominations included the African Methodist Episcopal Church, African Methodist Episcopal Zion Church, Colored Methodist Episcopal Church, Colored Primitive Baptists, and the Colored Cumberland Presbyterian Church. The communal bond was extremely strong for black Protestant groups and they did their best to ease devastating social conditions of members through the 1930s. Church attendance was very high and served as a focal point for the lives of many black Americans.

Holiness Movement

While many major religious denominations struggled with making ends meet in the economic collapse of the Depression and tried to retrench and hold on, several smaller churches began a spectacular growth pattern. Holiness and Pentecostal churches had originated in the second half of the nineteenth century and very early twentieth century. The so-called Holiness movement emerged after the Civil War in response to the belief that large mainstream denominations had become spiritually lax and had given in to worldly affairs. The movement advocated return to old Bible truths. Holiness churches believed in a literal interpretation of the bible, expected Christ's return any day, focused on strict moral values, and had an interest in faith healing and always stressed missionary work. The Pentecostal doctrine in addition emphasized the Holy Spirit among them evidenced by their ability to speak in tongues (different languages). Pentecostals were encouraged to roll in the aisles in emotional response to religious experiences, gaining the nickname "holy rollers."

The Holiness churches had always ministered largely to poorer Americans. Their freedom, informality, excitement, and claims of healings brought joy and assurance to Depression-weary Americans. Their sense of religious certainty, resistance to upper and upper middle class standards, and their warmth drew in many Americans of the lower and lower middle classes. Some churches doubled or tripled in size.

By 1939 the Holiness Movement churches claimed over one million members, a number almost as high as Episcopalian membership and almost half as high as Presbyterian membership. The largest Holiness Movement churches included: Assemblies of God, Church of God, Church of God in Christ, Church of the Nazarene, Four-square Gospel, Salvation Army, Christian and Missionary Alliance, Volunteers of America, and the Pentecostal Churches—Pentecostal Church, Pentecostal Holiness Church, and the black Pentecostal Assemblies of the World.

Contributing Forces

Prior to World War I involvement of religious denominations in social reform in the United States had a brief history. At the beginning of the twentieth century there were only a few social reformers and theology students interested in the "Gospel," or religious teachings as a social reforming force. Among these were Catholic reformers who had been teaching and writing about social issues such as labor injustices since the late-nineteenth century. In 1910 Catholic social workers founded a network, known as Catholic Charities, to organize and coordinate the many Catholic charitable institutions across the nation. In 1907 German Baptist Walter Rauschenbusch wrote his bestseller *Christianity and the Social Crisis* which described his viewpoint on the role of religion in public life. The so called Social Gospel movement gradually began to appear in most leading Protestant, Catholic, and Jewish church organizations.

Post World War I

The 1920s became a decade of economic prosperity. Standards of living were on the rise for most American families. The automobile, radio, and electric refrigerator became increasingly available to many. Employees in the rapidly expanding fields of business, science, and technology were enjoying new levels of prestige and success. Women, having won the right to vote, played larger roles in society outside the home. Possibilities on these numerous fronts seemed unlimited.

Churches shared in the prosperity; they built beautiful new structures with generous donations. Ministers Harry Emerson Fosdick and S. Parkes Cadman brought their messages to not only their own congregations but across the nation via radio. Despite the energetic spirit of the time, the decade also presented problems for the churches. Traditional moral standards and religious values came under attack by intellectuals, such as writers Sinclair Lewis, H. L. Mencken, and university professors such as William P. Montague. Montague referred to the essential elements of Christian religion as "super naturalism." Criticism abounded of America's moral standards, long defined by mostly Protestant denominations, as repressive and old-fashioned. A large segment of American society became indifferent to organized religion and fewer people attended church.

Nevertheless the idea of the Social Gospel of the early-twentieth century years hung on in many denominational bodies. Many made commitments to helping families and various service activities especially activities serving youth. Protestantism, Catholicism, and Judaism all responded to the cultural climate and challenges of the 1920s from their unique viewpoints.

Protestants

In regard to reforming the social order in the 1920s, the Protestant Church appeared to lose part of the zeal it had exhibited previously when aggressively crusading for Prohibition, which went into effect in 1920. Although still earnestly supported by numerous Protestants, many Americans refused to abide by the unpopular law that contributed to growing lawlessness and gangsterism. A growing number of Protestants thought church should confine itself to prayer, hymn singing, and to sermons preparing mankind for "judgment day" rather than focusing on social issues. Secondly, rather than reform the growing social injustices, America's Protestant churches turned their attention to the sins of the individuals. Dancing, profanity, Hollywood movies, skimpy female clothing, card playing, and illegal drinking all shocked church leaders and became the topics of countless sermons.

Third, to most conservative American Protestants, life was prosperous and there was very little in American society that needed reforming. America's industrious, self-reliant, and righteous people were being rewarded by God with riches such as radios, refrigerators, and indoor plumbing. The Protestant church generally supported the business community and even attempted to copy its techniques. Pastors took courses in advertising and dreamed up slogans such as "Business Success and Religion Go Together." Church attendance for some was a way in which to meet the best people that also offered the attainment of peace of mind. Virtually all leaders of industry and politics were Protestants who attended church regularly. Their charity was reflected in the amount spent for new church buildings, which exploded from 60 million dollars in 1921 to 284 million dollars in 1926. John D. Rockefeller contributed greatly to the building of the Riverside Church in New York City. Some large churches had multi-million dollar structures, with operating budgets as high as a quarter million, and possessed valuable real estate. Protestant churches were caught up in and intertwined with the economic prosperity of the 1920s decade.

While typical 1920s materialistic attitudes existed within church congregations, to think that materialism completely overwhelmed American Protestantism is incorrect. A sense of social justice also existed. For example when the YMCA adopted its "Social Creed of the Churches," which included statements calling for justice in the industrial workplace, businessmen

More About...

Churches and Movies

Although the hundreds of movies produced in the 1920s were silent, they "spoke" volumes as they depicted murder, rape, drug use, and sexual misconduct. Churches and politically conservative individuals became very concerned about the movies and their effect on the United States population, particularly on the young. Thousands of people demanded that the government censor the motion picture industry. In response the industry, in 1922, created the Motion Pictures Producers and Distributors of America (MPPDA) that later became the Motion Picture Association of America (MPAA) and was headed by Will Hays.

Once the chairman of the Republican National Committee and President Warren Harding's (served 1921–1923), Postmaster General in 1921 and 1922, Hays was a Presbyterian elder and presumably knew sin when he saw it. Hays was to institute codes to clean up the film industry and therefore block attempts to establish a new government censorship agency. The MPPDA agreed in 1927 to 11 "don'ts" for film production. Ten "don'ts" dealt with sex and nudity and one with illegal drug traffic, and for several years the general public was appeased.

By 1930, however, fearing the economic impact of the Depression and realizing the potent effect of new talking films, the industry began producing films with a great deal of violence and sex. The industry hoped these films would bring in large audiences to stave off reduction in the industry's income. In response the MPPDA or the "Hays' Office" as it was known, created a 1930 Production Code. The Code established more extensive "don'ts" including showing sympathy towards crime, ridiculing law and justice, and showing methods of crime as theft. Vulgarity, obscenity, sex, profanity, dancing, and cruelty to women, children and animals were all confronted. Religion and its ministers were to always be shown in a favorable light. The 1930 codes, however, were widely disregarded.

Protestant churches and publications protested the further decline with more standards but were too disorganized to be effective. Their largest organizations, the National Board of Review of Motion Pictures and the Federal Motion Picture Council in America, Inc. were strictly volunteer groups. The highly organized Catholic Church then entered the controversy, and in 1934 the American Catholic bishops created the Legion of Decency. Members of the Legion pledged ".... to remain away from all motion pictures except those which do not offend decency and Christian morality" (Bondi, p. 443). Joining the Legion became a regular part of Catholic behavior for the next thirty years. The threatened boycott of any movie deemed objectionable was powerful.

The Legion worked out a four-part category system:

- A-I: Morally unobjectionable for general patronage
- A-II: Morally Unobjectionable for adults
- B: Morally Objectionable in part for all
- C: Disapproved

Joseph I. Breen, an assistant to Hays, was able to enforce the MPPDA's Production Code of 1930 with support of the Catholic Church. The Breen Office as it was now called along with the Legion of Decency certification forced the film industry to monitor itself and adhere to the moral codes. The restrictions were so effective that in 1937, of the 1,271 titles reviewed by the Legion only 13 were rated C and all of those were European or independent productions.

In addition in 1936 Pope Pius XI's only encyclical of the year *Vigilante Cura* dealt with motion pictures. The papal encyclical received commendation from prominent individuals within the motion picture industry. The Legion of Decency enjoyed the confidence of Americans in general for years as it promoted the cause of decency in motion pictures.

---

severely criticized it. The business communities circulated a letter saying anyone who contributed to the Y's fundraising was subverting America's economic order. Many Protestant leaders including Harry Fosdick vocally resented the intimidation by businessmen,

and both Methodists and Presbyterians denounced the businessmen's action. Furthermore Fosdick stated that repression of organizations attempting to humanize working conditions inside factories could result in social revolution. Countless leading ministers and religious press editors warned that churches tending to focus on their materialistic wealth and catchy advertising and sermons were in danger of losing their souls.

Further the religious press wrote widely and critically of the problems in American society. Two journals representing the Federal Council of Churches of Christ in America, an organization of 23 Protestant denominations, the *Federal Council Bulletin* and *Information Service* examined social problems. The *Christian Century,* the most influential Protestant journal, scrutinized every aspect of life in America and demanded that society adhere to Christian morality. The publications of each individual denomination ranged from liberal to conservative in their attitudes on society's ills and admonished church members to live out their faith in actions. Some of the more liberal publications came from the Methodists, Unitarians, and Disciples, while the Presbyterian and Lutheran press were generally more contented and conservative. Although much was written of society's problems, Protestant denominations had no network of charitable organizations in the 1920s.

Protestants and the Election of 1928

The presidential election of 1928 was between Republican Herbert Hoover and Democrat "Al" Smith. Both men had "rags to riches" stories, and had lived the American dream of rising from a lowly social status to the heights through hard work. Their backgrounds, however, were very different.

Hoover was born in Iowa of Quaker parents whose ancestry went back to colonial times. Educated at Stanford University, Hoover had served as secretary of commerce in both the Harding and Coolidge administrations. Though not taking a solid stance on Prohibition, Hoover, a conservative, was considered by the voting public as a "dry," a person who supported Prohibition, in the controversy.

Smith was born into a Catholic family of immigrant stock in New York City. Although poorly educated, Smith had been considered a brilliant governor of New York. Perhaps more important Smith was a "wet" and opposed Prohibition. None of Smith's attributes appealed to the average Protestant, especially Protestants in the rural West and South. Historians have debated at length whether or not Smith's Catholicism turned the election against him. The campaign was marred, however, by anti-Catholic bigotry. Vicious and false charges were made against Smith because of this Catholicism. Prohibition was the issue that most likely sealed the Protestant vote for Hoover, however, Smith also advocated protection of civil liberties, not a popular theme at that time when property

rights were held more important. It was the most important issue of the election and Protestants by in large came down on the "dry" side. Ultimately the election reminded Catholics that they still held second-class status in a Protestant America. Hoover had captured 58 percent of the popular votes and 444 electoral votes to Smith's 87. Many Protestants saw Hoover's victory as an indication that the United States was still a Protestant nation.

The Roman Catholic Church in America

The Roman Catholic Church sharply resisted the secular trends of American society. The Catholic Church in the United States had gained an increased sense of unity coming out of the experience of World War I. Self-confidence and growing strength marked American Catholic leadership. Even though already America's largest Christian church, Catholicism still appeared to not feel fully at home on American soil. The perception that the United States continued as a Protestant nation remained strong.

Feeding this perception was the fact the Catholic Church attempted to isolate its faithful from much of America's worldly cultural environment by educating its students in Catholic schools and congregating its people in Catholic societies and unions. The Catholic school system was impressive. The right of parents to educate their children in private schools was upheld in the U.S. Supreme Court decision of 1925, *Pierce v. Society of Sisters.* As Catholic-educated children grew up and began to move up the economic scale, they gave to funds to build new expensive churches and schools. By 1928 there were approximately 2,500,000 students in 10,000 Catholic schools; two thousand of them were high schools.

Illustration of growing Catholic strength and unity in the United States also came as Catholic leaders from around the world met in Chicago in 1926 for the twenty-eighth international Eucharistic Congress— the first such gathering in the United States. Twelve cardinals attended and approximately 400,000 American Catholics attended the conference.

Catholic Charities

From the earliest years even before the United States was founded, Catholic missionaries and religious orders provided charitable care for widowed, sick, and orphaned settlers. For example in 1727 Ursuline nuns cared for orphans; in 1809 Sister Elizabeth Seton opened a free school and orphanage for poor children; and, during the nineteenth century, religious orders established both child care and care of the aging and local parishes provided needed services within their neighborhoods. These were the first Catholic "charities."

By 1900 Catholic charities supported many institutions providing care to needy people, children, elderly, the sick, and disabled, and prisoners. In 1910 feeling an urgent need to bring a sense of solidarity to the various endeavors, Catholic social service workers convened the first National Conference of Catholic Charities. The organization formed took on the name Catholic Charities. A network of Catholic Charities bureaus was established and 35 bureaus were in place across the nation by 1922. The bureaus' goals were to reduce poverty, support families, and build communities. With the onset of Depression of the 1930s the Catholic Charities already had a network in place to assist Americans. Likewise American Jewry would develop mutual aid networks by the 1930s.

American Jewry

By the end of the Civil War (1861–1865) approximately 150,000 Jews lived in the United States, most of whom were of German descent. The trend to reform and liberalize, or somewhat Americanize Judaism, ran strong and became known as the Reform movement. Dietary laws were relaxed, English was increasingly used in sermons, and Sabbath services often were held on Friday.

Although recognizing the need for adjustment to the times, the pace of change of the Reform Jews was occurring too quickly for some Jews. Jewish scholar Isaac Leeser feared important ties with the past were being lost. Under Leeser's guidance Historical or Conservative Judaism evolved. Conservative Judaism was dedicated to preservation of historic knowledge and practices presented in the teachings of the prophet Moses and expanded by wise men of Israel.

By 1880 the American Jewry numbered approximately 250,000. At this time a vast wave of immigration began. The great majority of the Jewish immigrants came from eastern and central Europe—Russian, Poland, Austria, and Romania. Most were poor and many were fleeing the dreaded pogroms in Russia. Having been reared in close-knit Jewish communities they were suspicious of the ways of America's Reform and Conservative Jews. Most spoke Yiddish, a German dialect with Hebrew and Slavic influence and written in Hebrew characters. Not feeling at home in Reform or Conservative synagogues, they formed their own Orthodox institutions. By 1900 approximately 1,000 Orthodox synagogues had been established. In 1896 an Orthodox theological seminary (religious school of higher learning) was formed and it eventually became Yeshiva University of New York.

In the early-twentieth century Conservative Judaism grew stronger and became a mediating force between Reform Jews and Orthodox Jews. As the Zionist movement arose at the turn of the century much discussion and controversy was stimulated. Zionism was the idea that a Jewish homeland should be established where Israel now exists. Reform Jews opposed Zionism, saying America was their Zion, while conservative Jews generally supported Zionism. Orthodox believed only a Messiah (spiritual leader from God) could restore Jews to Israel. Nevertheless all Jews of America did believe in the need for an American Jewish network of support organizations. All three groups banned together for support of mutual aid, philanthropic, defense, and labor organization for American Jewry. The networks, although not large, were akin to Catholic Charities. In World War I Jewish groups worked together in such organizations as the Jewish Welfare Board in support of the war. By the late 1920s over four million Jews lived in the United States.

Anti-Semitism

Long prevalent in other parts of the world, anti-Semitism began to surface in the United States during the last half of the nineteenth century and first part of the twentieth century. Rumors that some international conspiracy by Jews to control the world's finances spread. Some Americans began to speak in racial rather than religious terms. Some church people began to fear Jews were eroding the Christian character of the United States. Even some Christian publications reflected this attitude with articles bordering on anti-Semitism. Certain Christian groups singled out the Jews for attempted conversion to Christianity. Increasing numbers of American Jews were finding themselves targets of hate mongers.

Perspectives

Protestants

Protestants were split into liberal and conservative camps. Geography was a factor in the differences between perspectives. Protestants of congregations of large northern cities tended to be much more liberal than their southern counterparts. Liberal Protestants blamed the industrial practices of the 1920s for the wide gaps in American society. They saw abundant production of food and starving people; banks bulging with money and severe poverty; tons of idle machinery and millions of unemployed; mountains of coal, and freezing people. To correct this picture many liberal Protestants believed that some sort of

reconstruction of the social order was essential. Denominations with large factions of liberal Protestants were the Methodist Episcopal church (the northern branch of the Methodist denomination), the Northern Baptists, Presbyterians, and Congregationalists.

Within all denominations were considerable numbers of political centrists or conservatives. Congregations often had views far to the right of their denominations' leaders. Many failed to even support the formation of church social service bureaus. Likewise by the mid-1930s many refused to support Roosevelt's New Deal policies. Some viewed the unemployed as "dead-beats" upon whom they did not want to waste their money or taxes. Churches with considerable conservative populations were the Southern Baptists, Lutherans, and Presbyterians.

Catholics

In June 1933 in Washington D.C. Cardinal Patrick Hayes endorsed the New Deal and from reaction in the Catholic press it appeared all American Catholicism seconded his remarks. Also Roosevelt's good will toward the Catholic Church seemed to set the church in a better light in the general public's mind. Catholics believed the previous four U.S. presidents had neglected them. Even Reverend Charles E. Coughlin, while he would later turn against Roosevelt, praised the president's accomplishments.

When in the mid-1930s Coughlin began to personally attack the president as communistic the Catholic hierarchy was embarrassed. This embarrassment no doubt caused Catholic leaders such as Reverend John Ryan and other members of the hierarchy to take an even more pro-Roosevelt position. Catholics as a whole viewed the Roosevelt-Catholic relationship as mutually beneficial. Catholics helped Roosevelt to be re-elected in 1936 and Roosevelt helped Catholics move into the mainstream of American political life.

Catholics and Powerful Centralized Government

In 1932 at the depth of the Depression almost all Catholic spokesmen agreed that the overwhelmed private charities and seeming helplessness of state and local authorities to offer aid dramatized the need for federal action. Roosevelt's New Deal was welcomed.

This perspective represented a sharp break for Catholics who had long viewed constitutional limits on government as fortification against potential anti-Catholic persecution by the government. Therefore those Catholics, mindful that for all practical purposes Catholicism still retained a minority status, stressed the temporary nature of a more powerful federal government. They warned those new federal powers must

At a Glance
Inter-Faith Relations—1932

For the first time in history, on March 7, 8, and 9, 1932 Roman Catholics, Jews and Protestants met in Washington, DC, to discuss areas of conflict and to create ways to promote justice, understanding, and cooperation between the groups. Registered attendees, numbering 475, first discussed situations in their individual American communities then attended various sessions on schools, preaching, local community goodwill, religious teachings, and journalism. Follow-up local conferences of Catholics, Jews, and Protestants were held in cities coast to coast. The year 1932 is historically thought of as a time of unprecedented cooperation between the faiths due in part to the harsh economic conditions facing their people and their churches. The National Catholic Welfare Conference, the Central Conference of American Rabbis, and the Federal Council of the Churches of Christ in America united in issuing a statement on the unemployment situation and in support of relief efforts. Communities became accustomed to Catholics, Jews, and Protestants uniting on social service projects through the decade.

---

be rescinded once the crisis passed. By 1938 as the Depression seemed less severe, Catholic leaders almost universally held grave concerns about the further growth of the federal government.

Fear of a Revival of Anti-Catholicism

Some Catholics in the 1930s feared a revival of anti-Catholicism. This fear stemmed from the fact that Catholics in the 1930s were touting and adhering to the Pope's social teaching closer than ever before because they seemed to directly address problems of the Depression. This adherence in the non-Catholic population seemed to challenge American individualism, freedom of thought, and belief in the democratic process. As a result, Catholics invariably sought to justify their position by stressing the respect and love of American traditions. Time and again they pointed out the compatibility of "true Americanism" and orthodox Catholicism. Professions of loyalty to fundamental American values were widespread.

More About...

Dorothy Day, Peter Maurin, and the Catholic Worker Movement

The Catholic Worker Movement arose from the depths of the Great Depression as an unofficial effort to put church doctrine in practice among victims of social injustice and gather them into a force for change. The story of the Catholic Worker in the 1930s is the story of a remarkable journalist and Catholic convert, Dorothy Day, and Peter Maurin, a French immigrant immersed in ideas of Christian social reform.

As a young journalist Dorothy Day spent most of her early adult years traversing the country and world searching for a meaningful way to meet the political, social, and economic needs of everyday people. Always deeply interested by religious concepts, Day actively and passionately searched for a way to not only make sense of her own life but to find a way to advance the livability of all people. Shortly after the Catholic baptism of her illegitimate daughter, Day herself was baptized as a Roman Catholic on December 28, 1927.

For several years after Day's baptism she migrated from job to job, including writing scripts in Hollywood. While living in Mexico City for a time, she recorded the despair and poverty in the city and submitted a series of famous articles for publication in *Commonweal.*

In 1932, as the harsh realities of the Depression became apparent, Day went to Washington, D.C. to report on the hunger marchers on an assignment for *Commonweal.* Day was dismayed that American Christianity was not helping the hungry men, women, and children. Further, that it was the communists, not the Christians, who had organized the marches.

When Day returned to New York where she met Peter Maurin. Born in France in 1877 Maurin was educated by the Catholic order, the Christian Brothers, and took preliminary vows to join the order. After a few years of teaching, however, he became involved in Sillon, a democratic Christian movement that swept through France in the early twentieth century. Growing disillusioned he left France for Canada, then turned up in New York in the late 1920s, preaching Christian poverty and service. He talked ceaselessly of

Christian reform and was beloved by all he came in contact with.

Together Day and Maurin formed a perfectly balanced system. Maurin had a plan he called "utopian Christian communism, " which Day immediately recognized as a bridge to her own commitment to the poor. Maurin's vision balanced Day's practical impulses and merging their energies they established the Catholic Worker movement. First they created the newspaper *The Catholic Worker,* which by the end of 1933 had a circulation of 100,000. The social program put forth was three-fold and included round-table discussions where communists, radicals, and priests talked about issues of the day. Another aspect of the plan focused on Houses of Hospitality where men and women lived cooperatively in voluntary poverty, meeting the needs of the destitute. The third phase of the program proposed self-contained farming communes. In the next five years, the Catholic Worker grew phenomenally. Feeding over a thousand people a day, Houses of Hospitality were started all over the country.

Conflict and controversy were no strangers to the movement. While Maurin tried to avoid the issue of labor unions because he thought they were unchristian, Day endorsed 1930s union activity. Catholic Workers walked picket lines in the days of union organization and strikers and union organizers were housed and fed by Catholic Workers. Day and *The Catholic Worker* not only advocated justice for the American worker but also responded to the international war situation.

Both Day and Maurin found Christian teachings totally incompatible with war and said so. The Catholic Church officially refused to oppose the growing military conflicts and Day continued to encounter resistance as the United States drifted into war. By the mid-1940s *The Catholic Worker* circulation had dropped to 55,000.

Day remained active and outspoken until her death in 1980. After a lifetime of voluntary poverty she left no money for a funeral so the Catholic archdiocese of New York paid for it.

Furthermore American Catholics drew off limits boundaries around certain economic controversies of the day. Unlike the most liberal Protestant leaders, no important Catholic leader challenged the doctrine of private property. Few questioned the acceptability of profits and competition as long as they were limited by a vague idea of the common good. Likewise almost all stressed their opposition to communism.

An Awakened Catholic Laity

The most conservative Catholics still viewed the church and its rigid hierarchical structure as a central influence in their life. Perhaps the most significant change, however, in perspective in Catholic life due to the severe conditions of the 1930s was an awakened laity.

Just as Dorothy Day and the Catholic Worker movement preached, Catholic men and women began to realize that they each were responsible for every man's welfare. Sensitive laymen rebelled at the idea that only Catholic clergy could care for its people. Everyday Catholics took action to help others including fellow parishioners. Many Catholics began to view their church as a place where far more space and freedom to act existed than before the 1930s.

American Jewry

American Jewry was hit doubly in the 1930s. Not only did the Depression confront them with the same serious economic problems as all Americans, but their difficulties were compounded by the ominous events in Germany. The Jewish people, having long put stock in the value of human ability, strongly supported the New Deal policies. The Jewish community held the New Deal in high esteem, and it was widely believed that Jewish journalist Samuel Untermeyer had conceived the name "New Deal." To show their support American Jews gave Roosevelt an ever greater percentage of their vote in each presidential election, 1932 to 1944.

After 1933 American Jewry's perspectives centered on intercession for Jews abroad. Their request for government intercession and refugee admittance for German Jewry appeared like special pleading in light of the severe unemployment in America. Nevertheless they were compelled to continue to plead their case. Likewise they collected large sums of money, which rather than distribute to the needy at home they sent abroad for relief of European Jews. It was interesting that Jewish voters strongly supported Roosevelt into the 1940s even though he failed to energetically move on the refugee issue.

Pacifism

In the 1920s many Americans looked back at World War I with revulsion. Many felt lives and money had been expended for little reason. Waves of antiwar sentiment swept through many Protestant churches, especially during the first half of the 1930s as domestic issues dominated the American scene. Many felt the United States had its hands full trying to deal with internal economic problems. War was not just condemned, it was totally refuted as unacceptable under any circumstances, which was an idea that became part of the social Christianity of the decade.

Pacifism was deepest in the Protestant communities, where clergy vowed America should never again be used in a warlike way. They regretted their support of the war effort during World War I. Presbyterian minister Norman Thomas had actually refused to support World War I and had moved from his antiwar stance to the Socialist Party, an organization that he believed could help prevent wars in the future. Thomas was the first editor of the pacifist magazine *The World Tomorrow,* the voice of the antiwar group the Fellowship of Reconciliation (FOR). The FOR had members from the left wing of Protestantism. Some Protestants joined the left-leaning League Against War and Fascism headed by Methodist minister and professor at Union Theological Seminary, Harry F. Ward.

By 1935 as fascist regimes such as Hitler's began aggressive ventures across Europe, pacifists split. Some believed war could be used as a last resort but others clung to strict pacifism and refused to support any forceful opposition. The FOR and Socialist party split along those lines and both ceased to be forces. The League split also along similar lines, but officially it supported armed force against fascist powers. The staunch pacifist members of the League left, but many others had no problem working with Communists to stop the fascists of Germany, Italy, and Japan.

Prominent theologian Reinhold Niebuhr believed force could be used to bring justice to the world. Many other prominent Protestants, however, held fast to their pacifist commitments. Leaders such as Harry Emerson Fosdick, John Haynes Holmes, and Bishop Francis McConnell all continued to insist that if Christian principles were applied the "other cheek" must be turned. "Peace" churches such as the Mennonites also remained steadfastly opposed to any war.

The Roman Catholic Church members, many with close ties to family and friends in Europe, were more accepting of the use of force. The Catholic Church had long ago accepted that some wars were justified. Yet there were different outlooks within the church. Prominent Catholic Dorothy Day, founder of the Catholic Worker Movement, insisted Christians, especially Catholics, must oppose all killing.

Impact

At the end of the Second World War in 1945, the United States emerged as the most powerful country in the free world, taking on a major role in global leadership. By the late 1950s and 1960s the churches of America focused on the nation's failure to live up to its own ideals, especially racial equality and religious tolerance. Often church organizations, having established social action organizations during the nation's time of need in the 1930s, again attempted to begin to rectify long-prevalent social wrongs.

In the 1950s and 1960s the most important religious and political interaction came in the civil rights movement. African American churches and the Reverend Martin Luther King Jr. provided leadership. As the movement reached crisis proportions in 1963–1965, King called on Catholic clergy, Protestant ministers, and Jewish rabbis to demonstrate and support blacks and civil rights legislation. Another effort of church organizations emerged from mid-1960s to mid-1970s concerning the war in Vietnam (1964–1975). Although some supported the war effort many church groups joined in protest over what they viewed as an illegal and immoral war. Liberal elements of Protestantism, Catholicism, and Judaism, also worked for improved religious tolerance, women's rights, and economic equality.

The liberal civil rights efforts were countered with a growing movement and resurgence of social religious conservatism beginning in the later 1960s and 1970s. Catholics who were dismayed by the liberalism of their church, ultra Orthodox Jews and Zionists who saw interests in Israel as dwarfing issues in the United States, Southern Baptists, Methodists, Presbyterians, and a host of fundamentalist Protestant groups all resisted civil rights movements and demanded a return to basic spiritual rather than political issues. This new religious right became a force to be reckoned with. Religion and political debates raged late in the twentieth century over issues such as prayer in the public schools, abortion, and gay rights. Catholic forces joined Protestants in anti-abortion campaigns. On economic and social policy issues, however, the Catholic Churches leaned more to the left while Protestant churches generally remained to the right of center. But at the beginning of the twenty-first century, a prime concern for churches was genetic engineering and the human race.

Notable People

Charles E. Coughlin (1891–1979). Newly ordained Catholic priest, Father Charles E. Coughlin was appointed in 1926 to a suburban parish, Shrine of the Little Flower, in Royal Oak, Michigan. On Sunday evenings Father Coughlin began a radio program from a Detroit radio station, the *Radio League of the Little Flower*. His effort to engage more people was highly successful as his parish grew rapidly. A gifted speaker, he focused on religious and moral issues. After the Stock Market crash of 1929 and the onset of the Great Depression Coughlin's radio talks ranged into current topics. He established an independent network of stations from which he broadcast his message through much of the United States attracting not only a Catholic audience but a large Protestant audience as well.

Coughlin endorsed the earliest policies of President Roosevelt's New Deal and Roosevelt actually consulted with him a few times. Roosevelt, however, did not follow Coughlin's advice on money matters. Roosevelt refused to return to the silver standard and Coughlin was embarrassed when it was revealed that the Little Flower was one of the largest silver holders. Apparently Coughlin was playing the market in silver.

In November 1934 Coughlin organized the National Union for Social Justice. Estimates suggest that about one million people belonged to the organization at its peak. Coughlin claimed he and his followers blocked the United States from joining the World Court in 1935. Not only was he an ardent isolationist, but he began making anti-Semitic statements. By 1936 Coughlin began an attack on President Roosevelt charging Roosevelt was moving the nation toward communism. *Social Justice,* a newspaper established by Coughlin in 1937 reflected his now openly anti-Semitic and fascist views and he supported Adolf Hitler at the beginning of World War II in Europe in 1939.

Although an embarrassment to the Catholic Church, he was not silenced until 1942 with government pressure. He continued at Little Flower unit until 1966, when he retired.

Harry Emerson Fosdick (1878–1969). Born in Buffalo, New York, Harry Fosdick was raised as a Baptist. At the young age of seven he pledged his life to Christian service. A gifted student he graduated head of his class from high school and from Colgate University, at the time a small Baptist college. Fosdick studied for a year at Hamilton Theological Seminary where a leading liberal Baptist theologian, Professor William Newton Clarke, greatly influenced

Fosdick's thinking. Shortly, Fosdick transferred to Union Theological Seminary in New York City, a seminary on the cutting edge of religious thought. The interdenominational Union had just severed ties with the Presbyterian Church.

In 1915 Fosdick accepted a professorship at Union but interrupted his teaching for a short duty overseas during World War I. Although he had strongly supported America's entrance into the war, he returned to the United States an avowed pacifist. Although a Baptist, Fosdick's preaching career started in 1918 in New York City's historic First Presbyterian Church where his outstanding oratory skills caused the church's sanctuary to regularly overflow. In 1925 he accepted a call to Park Avenue Baptist Church, the home church of John D. Rockefeller, Jr. By 1931, with Rockefeller's monetary support, a grand new interdenominational church, the Riverside Church, was completed in Morningside Heights in New York City. Riverside Church was one of the largest congregations in the country with over two thousand members. Fosdick's message reached the rest of the United States beginning in 1927 by way of radio. His *National Vesper Hour* established him as dean of America's radio preachers.

Fosdick was considered a mainstream religious liberal. While rarely at the forefront of any social crusade, he was never far back, always speaking of economic and racial justice.

Francis Joseph Haas (1889–1953). Francis J. Haas studied at St. Francis Seminary in Milwaukee, Wisconsin, was ordained into the priesthood in 1913, and graduated from the Catholic University of America in 1922 with a Ph.D. in Sociology. Haas became expert in the field of social reform and was appointed director of the National Catholic School of Social Service in Washington, DC. In 1933 with the inauguration of President Roosevelt, Haas moved into government service in the area of labor relations. Haas first served on the National Recovery Administration's Labor Advisory Board and the General Code Authority. He also began in 1933 his work as a labor dispute mediator on the Nation Labor Board. Haas was chief author of the Haas-Dunnigan Plan that ended the Minneapolis trucker's strike in 1934. After a two-year assignment back at Milwaukee's St. Francis Seminary, Haas returned to government work where he served in a variety of capacities involving labor including on the Labor Policies Board of the Workers Progress Administration (WPA), and as White House emissary attempting to halt a split between labor organizations, the American Federation of Labor (AFL) and the Congress of Industrial Organizations (CIO). During World War II, President Roosevelt appointed Haas as chair of the Fair Employment Practices Committee. Throughout his career Haas wrote many articles concerning higher wages, collective bargaining, and improved working conditions.

John Haynes Holmes (1879–1964). Holmes, a minister and civil liberties activist, was ordained in the American Unitarian Association in 1904 and served in the Church of the Messiah in New York City until it was destroyed by fire in 1919. During World War I Holmes had become a staunch pacifist. He rebuilt his church both physically and philosophically based on these pacifist views, renaming it Community Church and splitting it from the Unitarian Association.

Holmes' ministry in New York was committed to liberal social and political causes. He insisted the church must play a central role. He helped found the American Civil Liberties Union (ACLU) in 1920 and served as its chairman from 1939 to 1949, replacing minister and activist Harry F. Ward. Holmes advocated pacifism and civil liberties including racial equality. In the 1930s Holmes continued his fight for civil liberties. He also became even more passionate about keeping the United States out of war. As war came inevitably he assertively condemned all totalitarian states and helped force all communist-leaning individuals from high positions in the ACLU.

Francis John McConnell (1871–1953). Son of a Methodist minister, Francis J. McConnell became one of the most well-known and respected liberal Protestant leaders of his time. After serving as the minister of several Methodist Episcopal Churches (the northern branch of the Methodist denomination) in Massachusetts and New York, McConnell was elected as a bishop in 1912 of the denomination and moved to Denver, Colorado. There he became chairman of the unofficial and often radical Methodist Federation for Social Service. Moving to Pittsburgh, Pennsylvania in 1920, he directed his attention to labor disputes and called attention to the inhumane 12-hour day of steel workers. McConnell became bishop of the New York City area in 1928 and was subsequently elected president of Federal Council of Churches of Christ, the most influential federation of Protestant churches. McConnell supported Socialist Party presidential candidate Norman Thomas in 1928 and 1932. During the Depression of the 1930s, McConnell lectured widely and wrote, continuing his advocacy of what he called a democratic socialism.

Reinhold Niebuhr (1892–1971). Born in Wright City, Missouri, Reinhold Niebuhr grew up in Missouri and in the German-American town of Lincoln, Illinois. He decided to follow his father, a German

Evangelical Synod of North America minister, into the same ministry. Niebuhr attended Yale Divinity School in 1914 and 1915 where he established his theological liberalism.

Niebuhr immersed himself in the study of social and political affairs, and in 1922 he became an editorialist and contributor to the *Christian Century,* a liberal Protestant weekly in Chicago. In the 1920s he urged liberals to take the side of labor in the disputes between labor and the ruling capitalists. Niebuhr believed a social movement could not be built only by a faith in reasonable actions by man. Rather only a social movement sparked by a religious base and an understanding of social justice could hope to succeed.

In 1928 Niebuhr accepted a professorship at Union Theological Seminary in New York City. In 1929 Niebuhr joined the Socialist Party and unsuccessfully ran for the New York State Senate. As the Great Depression deepened he ran for Congress in 1932 but did no better. The message to Niebuhr was clear, the Socialist Party was not an acceptable means to a social movement for most Americans. He remained in the party but did not take an active role after 1932. Instead Niebuhr turned to writing, lecturing, and religious pursuits. He authored *Moral Man and Immoral Society* in 1932, *An Interpretation of Christian Ethics* in 1935, and later the major works of *Beyond Tragedy* (1937) and *The Nature and Destiny of Man* (two volumes, 1941 and 1943). In 1933 German theologian Paul Tillick was ousted from Nazi Germany, which greatly influenced Niebuhr's theological thinking.

By the late 1930s he put aside his efforts for social reform to focus on establishing united fronts to stop Hitler and Mussolini in Europe. Lecturing widely in England at the end of the 1930s, including as a Gifford Lecturer at the University of Edinburgh, Niebuhr cemented his reputation as the most influential Christian thinker of the time. In 1941 he founded and edited the *Christianity and Crisis,* an "interventionist" newspaper as an alternative to the pacifist *Christian Century.* He also founded the Union for Democratic (UDA), an anti-fascist, noncommunist, pro-labor, educational group. Niebuhr was active on many fronts during the war including attempting to facilitate the entry of more European Jews into the United States.

In 1944 Niebuhr published *The Children of Light and the Children of Darkness* which provided the philosophical basis for the new Liberal party of New York. It also provided the basis for the Americans for Democratic Action (ADA), an outgrowth of the UDA. Vice-President Lyndon Johnson presented the Medal of Freedom, the nation's highest civilian honor, to Niebuhr. Niebuhr was one of the last great liberal Protestant orators of the twentieth century.

Father John A. Ryan (1869–1945). Born in Vermillion, Minnesota, to Irish immigrant farmers, John Ryan was thoroughly steeped in a rich culture of Irish Catholicism and American populism (belief in the importance of the common man). As a youth he devoted himself to preparation for the priesthood, and in 1887 he entered St. Tomas Seminary in Minnesota. There he immersed himself in Catholic social teachings, particularly Pope Leo XIII's encyclical *Rerum Novarum.*

Ryan, ordained into the priesthood in 1898, went onto receive his doctorate in sacred theology from the Catholic University of America in Washington, DC, in 1906. Immediately published as a book, his thesis *A Living Wage: Its Ethical and Economic Aspects* was a standard of Catholic social thought in America in the twentieth century. In 1915 Ryan began a lifelong teaching career at Catholic University. Ryan authored the Bishop's Program for Social reconstruction in 1919, another standard in Catholic social thought.

In his work, Ryan, as head of the Social Action Department of the new National Catholic Welfare Conference, encouraged businessmen and labor to cooperate. Having been further influenced by the Pope's *Quadragesimo Anno* in 1931 and elevated to a monsignor by Pope Pius XI in 1933, Ryan became an outspoken defender of President Franklin Roosevelt and the New Deal policies. Roosevelt appointed Ryan to the Industrial Appeals Board of the National Recovery Administration in 1934. Ryan also staunchly defended Roosevelt from attacks by Father Charles I. Coughlin who accused Roosevelt of being pro-communist. Mandatory retirement brought Ryan's academic career at Catholic University to a close in 1939. Ryan was a leading American Catholic presence in the fight for social justice.

Harry F. Ward (1873–1966). Born in England, Harry Ward joined his uncle in Utah in 1891. Already espousing social reform, Ward, along with his uncle tried to convince parishioners to care for and minister to the poor. Educated at the University of Southern California, Northwestern, and Harvard, Ward settled in Chicago as head resident of the Northwestern Settlement House. The settlement house was a neighborhood social welfare organization providing various forms of social assistance including friendship clubs, childcare, counseling, and even job training classes to the surrounding community in that part of the city. Ward became a Methodist minister in 1902 and served at several churches in the Chicago area where he developed both a religious and social response to the inequality he saw all around him.

In connection with the creation of the Methodist Federation of Social Service, Ward authored in 1907 what became known as the Social Creed of the Churches. The creed attempted to articulate social Christian ethics as equal rights for all, improve working conditions and wages for laborers, arbitration of labor disputes, abolition of child labor, and foster a more socially responsible attitude. The Federation of Social Service attempted to put the creed into practice. Ward served as its general secretary from 1911 until 1941. The Federal Council of Churches of Christ adopted the Social Creed in 1908. Roman Catholic and Jewish religious bodies would also echo many of its guidelines in their own pronouncements. Through the next quarter century, historians claim much of the 1930s New Deal legislation was based on the creed and other pronouncements.

Ward joined the faculty of the Union Theological Seminary in New York City as a professor of Christian ethics in the fall of 1918, teaching there until 1941. In 1920 Ward co-founded the American Civil Liberties Union (ACLU) for the defense of civil rights.

Yet another socially active organization of which Ward was a member was the American League against War and Fascism, a mass movement for peace and also served as its president. All major denominations joined and supported the League, however, the Communist Party was also a member and by the mid-1930s the League was widely accused of being communist. The League disbanded in 1940 but Ward became a target of conservative charges that he was a communist. After retiring from the Union Theological Seminary Ward continued to write and lecture until his death.

Stephen Samuel Wise (1874–1949). The descendant of six generations of rabbis, Rabbi Stephen Wise was a prominent figure in both national and international Jewish affairs. At the age of 23 Wise helped found the Federation of American Zionists. Wise was one of the first rabbis of the Reform movement to support Zionism, the return of Jews to Palestine.

In 1907 Wise began the Free Synagogue of New York and became involved with reform of New York City politics. He became close friends with the Reverend John Haynes Holmes. In the 1920s together they fostered interfaith cooperation and also attacked corruption in the city government of New York. In that same decade Wise oversaw the growth of the American Jewish Congress from a temporary wartime grouping to a permanent organization dealing with Jewish issues and humanitarian reforms. He also founded the

Jewish Institute of Religion in New York as a liberal alternative to the Hebrew Union College, the official Reform rabbinate.

Wise recognized the danger that Adolf Hitler posed very early and organized efforts to encourage opposition to the Nazi's regime. In 1933 he organized a rally of over 50,000 people at Madison Square Garden in New York City and also helped to organize a boycott of German products and attempted to halt American participation in the 1936 Olympic Games in Berlin.

As the Nazis increasingly persecuted the German Jews, Wise tried throughout the 1930s to have immigration restrictions eased. Unsuccessful, he then turned to securing Palestine as a homeland. He lived to see the establishment of the State of Israel and American recognition of the new Jewish State in 1948.

Primary Sources

Presidential candidate Franklin Roosevelt gave a speech titled "The Philosophy of Social Justice Through Social Action" on the campaign trail in Detroit, Michigan, on October 2, 1932. In the speech he quotes the 1931 papal encyclical *Quadragesimo Anno* and a statement by Rabbi Edward L. Israel (quoted in Roosevelt, Volume One, pp. 778-780)

It is becoming more and more clear that the principles of our religion and the findings of social sciences point in the same direction. Economists now call attention to the fact that the present distribution of wealth and income, which is so unbrotherly in the light of Christian ethics, is also unscientific in that it does not furnish purchasing power to the masses to balance consumption and production in our machine age.

And now I am going to read you another great declaration and I wonder how many people will call it radical. It is just as radical as I am. It is a declaration from one of the greatest forces of conservatism in the world, the Catholic Church. I quote, my friends, from the scholarly encyclical issued last year by the Pope, one of the greatest documents of modern times:

It is patent in our days that not alone is wealth accumulated, but immense power and despotic economic domination are concentrated in the hands of a few, and that those few are frequently not the owners but only the trustees and directors of invested funds which they administer at their good pleasure....

This accumulation of power, the characteristic note of the modern economic order, is a natural result of limitless free competition, which permits the survival of those only who are the strongest, which often means those who fight most relentlessly, who pay least heed to the dictates of conscience.

This concentration of power has led to a three-fold struggle for domination: First, there is the struggle for dictatorship in the economic sphere itself; then the fierce battle to acquire control of the Government, so that its resources and authority may be abused in the economic struggle, and, finally, the clash between the Governments themselves.

And finally, I would read to you from another great statement, a statement from Rabbi Edward L. Israel, Chairman of the Social Justice Commission of the Central Conference of American Rabbis. H ere is what he says:

We talk of the stabilization of business. What we need is the stabilization of human justice and happiness and the permanent employment of economic policies which will enable us to preserve the essential human values of life amid all the changing aspects of the economic order. We must have a revamping of the entire method of approach to these problems of the economic order. We need a new type of social conscience that will give us courage to act. . . .

We so easily forget. Once the cry of so-called prosperity is heard in the land, we all become so stampeded by the spirit of the god Mammon, that we cannot serve the dictates of social conscience . . . We are here to serve notice that the economic order is the invention of man; and that it cannot dominate certain eternal principles of justice and of God.

And so, my friends, I feel a little as if I had been preaching a sermon. I feel a little as if I had been talking too much of some of the fundamentals, and yet those fundamentals enter into your life and my life every day . . .

And so, in these days of difficulty, we Americans everywhere must and shall choose the path of social justice— the only path that will lead us to a permanent bettering of our civilization, the path that our children must tread and their children must tread, the path of faith, the path of hope and the path of love toward our fellow man.

Social Creed of Protestant Churches

The Council's Commission on the Church and Social Services presented the Social Ideals of the churches to the Federal Council of the Churches of Christ in America. The presentation and adoption of the creed took place at the Quadrennial meeting of the council held in Indianapolis, Indiana on December 6–9, 1932. This creed was originally based on Methodist Minister Dr. Harry F. Ward's Social Creed of the Churches, which he penned in 1907. Ward's creed was first adopted by the Federal Council in 1908 and appropriately revised periodically. Below are selected positions of the 1932 Social Statement (quoted in Weber, *Yearbook of American Churches*, 1933, pp. 319–320):

Adopted at Indianapolis, December 7, 1932

1. Practical application of the Christian principle of social well-being to the acquisition and use of wealth; subordination of speculation and the profit motive to the creative and cooperative spirit.

2. Social planning and control of the credit and monetary systems and the economic processes for the common good.

3. The right of all to the opportunity for self-maintenance; a wider and fairer distribution of wealth; a living wage, as a minimum, and above this a just share for the worker in the product of industry and agriculture.

4. Safeguarding of all workers, urban and rural, against harmful conditions of labor and occupational injury and disease.

5. Social insurance against sickness, accident, want in old age and unemployment.

6. Reduction of hours of labor as the general productivity of industry increases; release from employment at least one day in seven, with a shorter working week in prospect.

7. Such special regulations of the conditions of work of women as shall safeguard their welfare and that of the family and the community.

8. The right of employees and employers alike to organize for collective bargaining and social action; protection of both in the exercise of this right; the obligation of both to work for the public good; encouragement of cooperatives and other organizations among farmers and other groups.

9. Abolition of child labor; adequate provision for the protection, education, spiritual nurture and wholesome recreation of every child.

10. Protection of the family by the single standard of purity; educational preparation for marriage, homemaking and parenthood.

11. Economic justice for the farmer in legislation, financing of agriculture, transportation and the price of farm products as compared with the cost of machinery and other commodities which he must buy.

15. Justice, opportunity and equal rights for all; mutual goodwill and cooperation among racial, economic and religious groups.

16. Repudiation of war, drastic reduction of armaments, participation in international agencies for the peaceable settlement of all controversies; the building of a cooperative world order.

President Roosevelt Reaches Out to Religious Charities

In the following address of October 4, 1933, before the National Conference of Catholic Charities, President Franklin Roosevelt spoke on the need for cooperation between religious charities and the government during the harsh times of the Great Depression (quoted in Roosevelt, Volume Two, pp. 379–381). He spoke, quite simply, on the need for faith.

. . . A democracy, the right kind of democracy, is bound together by the ties of neighborliness.

That tie, my friends, has been the guiding spirit of your work for the sick, for the children in need, and for the aged and friendless. And you who have participated in the actual day-to-day work of practical and useful charity understand well that no program of recovery can suddenly restore all our people to self-support. This is the time when you and I know that though we have proceeded a portion of the way, the longer, harder part still lies ahead; we must redouble our efforts to care for those who must still depend upon relief, to prevent the disintegration of home life, and to stand by the victims of the depression until it is definitely past.

The Federal Government has inaugurated new measures of relief on a vast scale, but the Federal Government cannot, and does not intend to, take over the whole job. Many times we have insisted that every community and every State must first do its share.

Out of this picture we are developing a new science of social treatment and rehabilitation—working in out through an unselfish partnership, a partnership between great church and private social service agencies and the agencies of Government itself.

Suggested Research Topics

- Identify and describe the types of responses the various religious denominations in the United States made to relieve the economic suffering brought on by the Great Depression. What trends were apparent through the 1930s in perspectives of various denominational church leaders toward the New Deal programs of President Roosevelt?

- What denominations are present in your community? Do they offer certain forms of social services to their members and to the community in general?

Bibliography

Sources

Flynn, George Q. *American Catholics & the Roosevelt Presidency, 1932–1936*. Lexington: University of Kentucky Press, 1968.

Handy, Robert T. *A Christian America: Protestant Hopes and Historical Realities*. New York: Oxford University Press, 1984.

————. *A History of the Churches in the United States and Canada*. New York: Oxford University Press, 1977.

Kincheloe, Samuel C. *Research Memorandum on Religion in the Depression*. New York: Social Science Research Council, 1937.

Landis, Benson Y., ed. *Yearbook of American Churches: 1941 Edition*. Jackson Heights, NJ: Yearbook of American Churches Press, 1941.

Levinger, Rabbi Lee J. *A History of the Jews in the United States*. Cincinnati: Commission on Jewish Education, 1949.

Miller, Robert M. *American Protestantism and Social Issues, 1919–1939*. Chapel Hill: The University of North Carolina Press, 1958.

O'Brien, David J. *American Catholics and Social Reform: The New Deal Years*. New York: Oxford University Press, 1968.

Roosevelt, Franklin D. *The Public Papers and Addresses of Franklin D. Roosevelt, Volume One, 1929–1932*. New York: Random House, Inc., 1938.

————. *The Public Papers and Addresses of Franklin D. Roosevelt, Volume Two, 1933*. New York: Random House, Inc., 1938.

Weber, Herman C., ed. *Yearbook of American Churches: A Record of Religious Activities in the United States for the Year 1932*. New York: Round Table Press, Inc., 1933.

————. *Yearbook of American Churches: A Record of Religious Activities in the United States for the Years 1933 and 1934*. New York: Association Press, 1935.

————. *Yearbook of American Churches: A Record of Religious Activities in the United States for the Years 1935 and 1936*. New York: Yearbook of American Churches Press, 1937.

————. *Yearbook of American Churches: A Record of Religious Activities in the United States for the Years 1937 and 1938*. Elmhurst, NY: Yearbook of American Churches Press, 1939.

Further Reading

Blantz, Thomas E. *A Priest in Public Service: Francis J. Haas and the New Deal*. Notre Dame: University of Notre Dame Press, 1982.

"Catholic Charities U.S.A.," available from the World Wide Web at http://www.catholiccharitiesusa.org.

Coles, Robert. *Dorothy Day: A Radical Devotion*. Reading, MA: Addison-Wesley Publishing Company, Inc., 1987.

Feingold, Henry L. *A Time For Searching: Entering the Mainstream, 1920–1945*. Baltimore: The John Hopkins University Press, 1992.

Heineman, Kenneth J. *A Catholic New Deal: Religion and Reform in Depression Pittsburgh*. University Park, PN: The Pennsylvania State University Press, 1999.

"Jewish Defense League," available from the World Wide Web at http://www.jdl.org.

"National Council of the Churches of Christ in the United States of America," available from the World Wide Web at http://www.ncccusa.org.

Nawyn, William E. *American Protestantism's Response to Germany's Jews and Refugees, 1933–1941*. Ann Arbor, MI: UMI Research Press, 1981.

Nelsen, Hart M., Raytha L. Yokley, and Anne K. Nelsen, eds. *The Black Church in America*. New York: Basic Books, Inc., 1971.

O'Grady, John. *Catholic Charities in the United States*. New York: Arno Press, 1971.

Seaton, Douglas P. *Catholics and Radicals: The Association of Catholic Trade Unionists and the American Labor Movement, from Depression to Cold War*. Lewisburg: Bucknell University Press, 1981.

Skinner, James M. *The Cross and the Cinema: The Legion of Decency and the National Catholic Office for Motion Pictures, 1933–1970.* Westport, CN: Praeger, 1993.

Strong, Donald S. *Organized Anti-Semitism in America: The Rise of Group Prejudice During the Decade 1930–40.* Washington, DC: American Council on Public Affairs, 1941.

The League of American Writers. *We Hold These Truths . . .* New York: The League of American Writers, 1939.

Troester, Rosalie R., ed. *Voices From the Catholic Worker.* Philadelphia, PA: Temple University Press, 1993.

See Also

Everyday Life; Prohibition Repealed

Rural Electrification Administration

Introduction

1934-1941

Electrical power began to serve American industry, cities, and homes in the 1880s and for many years was regarded by most as a luxury and a curiosity. By the 1920s, however, largely (but not entirely) through the efforts of private industry, more than half of all urban homes had electric lights and a sizeable minority had a wide range of electrical appliances. Electric power, with its associated conveniences and efficiencies, became regarded as an essential element of modern life. Since bringing power to rural areas was more expensive, however, less than ten percent of farm families had electricity. Increasingly, this disparity between cities and the countryside was seen as unfair and a threat to the American social fabric.

Early efforts by private power companies to encourage rural electrification failed because they did not address the main obstacle, which was the cost of the service. By the 1920s other countries, such as Europe, Canada, and New Zealand had made much better progress in electrifying rural areas through public cooperatives and government assistance, but until the Depression most people in the United States believed that such approaches were un-American and threatened traditional values of self-reliance and private enterprise.

The extreme trauma of the Great Depression finally changed the conservative climate of power supply in America and made it possible for the public to accept a government program that would provide elec-

Chronology:

February 13, 1934: Morris L. Cooke submits a proposal, "National Plan for the Advancement of Rural Electrification Under Federal Leadership and Control with State and Local Cooperation and as a Wholly Public Enterprise," to Secretary of the Interior Harold Ickes. This document proposes a new federal bureaucracy, a Rural Electrification Agency, within the Department of the Interior.

April 8, 1935: President Franklin D. Roosevelt signs the Emergency Relief Appropriation Act of 1935, which lists rural electrification as one of eight categories of projects intended to provide employment for unemployed workers.

May 11, 1935: President Roosevelt issues Executive Order 7037, creating the Rural Electrification Administration.

May 20, 1935: President Roosevelt appoints Morris L. Cooke as the first REA Administrator.

July 22, 1935: Presidential Letters 104 and 105 approve the first four REA loans.

August 6, 1935: President Roosevelt issues Regulation No. 4, establishing REA as a lending agency and giving it wide authority to set lending policy.

May 21, 1936: President Roosevelt signs into law the Rural Electrification Act, making REA a permanent agency with statutory (legal) authorization.

February 23, 1937: John M. Carmody, a believer in "scientific management," succeeds Cooke as REA Administrator.

July 1, 1939: The REA, no longer independent, becomes part of the Department of Agriculture.

September 26, 1939: Harry Slattery succeeds Carmody as REA Administrator.

---

tricity to rural areas. The stock market crash of 1929 and subsequent Great Depression would highlight the increasing poverty of rural America. President Herbert Hoover (served 1929–1933) believed in individuals helping themselves and using private charities—taking a hands-off approach to such problems as rural poverty. President Roosevelt, however, during a campaign swing through the South in the summer of 1932,

was particularly struck by poverty and associated sanitation problems. Roosevelt was convinced that having electricity available to such areas in the nation would be one major step toward modernization and increased productivity. Electricity would make possible running water in homes and power refrigerators to keep food from spoiling, but the power would have to be inexpensive for people to afford it. With the election of Franklin Roosevelt to the presidency in 1932, many Americans, facing dire economic circumstances, were willing to try new ideas to bring about the return of prosperity.

In March 1933 Roosevelt and his advisors began introducing numerous economic relief and recovery programs that would be collectively known as the New Deal. An essential element of the earliest New Deal programs was relief for the agricultural industry and rural America. After establishing the Agricultural Adjustment Administration (AAA) to bring relief to farmers and the Tennessee Valley Authority (TVA) to develop power projects in the Southeast, the Roosevelt administration in 1935 established the Rural Electrification Administration (REA) to create badly needed jobs and to build prosperity in rural areas by bringing electricity, modernization, and efficiency to rural families and American agriculture. Under the guidance of Morris L. Cooke, REA tried at first to partner with private power companies, already well equipped to construct the needed infrastructure and deliver the service. Very quickly, however, when private industry proved unable or unwilling to abide by REA terms, the agency adapted its program to work with rural cooperatives as the recipients of REA loans.

Initial progress of the REA program was slow, but by the end of the 1930s many new cooperatives had formed to take advantage of the agency loans to build electrical distribution systems in rural areas. These cooperatives were generally made up of farmers who owned and operated them. Through a combination of publicity, educational services, and engineering and organizational advances, REA aggressively pursued its goal of full electrification of the countryside. Most of its success was achieved after World War II (1939–1945), when a booming American economy, freed from the constraints of the Depression, made possible large REA budgets for its loan program. This funding, however, simply fueled a program that had been fully developed by the late 1930s.

By the late 1950s the combined efforts of REA and private industry had essentially completed the job of rural electrification. The modernization of rural America profoundly changed the lives of rural people and contributed to the establishment of American agriculture as the envy of the world. The standard of living rose dramatically. Although much of the rural population moved to the cities, farms vastly increased their production. Through the availability of abundant electricity, new industries sprang up in rural areas, further diversifying and decentralizing the American economy. In the end, REA, a product of the Depression, contributed to prosperity in the United States to an extent far beyond the expectations of its founders.

Issue Summary

The Status of Rural Electrification in the Early 1930s

At the beginning of the 1930s electricity, at least for lighting, was an accepted part of American life in cities. Most farmers and others in rural America, especially in the Midwest and South, however, were still living much as they and their ancestors had lived in the nineteenth century. More than 90 percent of rural homes still used kerosene lamps for lighting and had no powered pumping systems to make possible running water and indoor bathrooms. Except for the already widespread use of automobiles and tractors, farmers and their families relied on manual labor and animal power to do their daily work.

Despite general agreement that this was a serious problem, Americans disagreed about how to solve it. President Herbert Hoover (served 1929–1933) was solidly in favor of electrification and wanted to improve the lives and productivity of all Americans, including the farmer. He also believed, however, that private enterprise should, and would, accomplish this objective. This was the view of those who hung onto faith in the marketplace as the primary solution. Very influential among this group were the electric companies and the holding corporations that owned them, for which decisions were driven mostly by the desire to maximize profits. These private companies, whose focus was electric power for industry, did not believe that most farmers could afford to pay what it would cost to deliver power to them at profitable rates. On the other side of the question were those who observed that rural electrification, which they saw as a social and humanitarian issue, was proceeding far too slowly in the hands of the electric companies. This camp was supported by "progressives," who believed that government should assert its authority into the field of electrification to bring about important social changes.

Among the leading proponents of public authority over rural electrification was Morris L. Cooke, who had been involved very directly with public power projects in Pennsylvania since 1923. Franklin D. Roosevelt, a progressive elected as governor of New York in 1928, envisioned a hydroelectric plant on the St. Lawrence River that would supply power for both cities and rural areas. To accomplish this he worked to pass a bill in 1931 to create the New York Power Authority and appointed Cooke, a highly respected expert on public power issues, as a trustee. For Cooke this appointment was well timed. President Hoover, still favoring private electric companies, in that same year had rejected his proposals for a national plan to implement rural electrification for the improvement of farm efficiency and the creation of badly needed jobs across the country.

The most important outcome of Cooke's work with the New York Power Authority was a detailed study of the costs of rural electrical service. Utility companies previously had insisted that electrical lines in rural areas cost about $2,000 per mile, but no systematic and public analysis of distribution costs had ever been done. Cooke had little confidence in what he suspected were figures inflated by the power companies to justify their inattention to rural service. The Cooke study team, after scrutinizing and itemizing all possible expense items, concluded that construction costs should be between $300 and $1,500 per mile. This result, published in 1933, demonstrated the feasibility of rural electric service and encouraged the proponents of rural electrification, which was growing as a social and political issue.

Roosevelt made rural electrification an issue in the 1932 presidential campaign when he declared in a speech given in Portland, Oregon, that electricity "... is no longer a luxury. It is a definite necessity ... It can relieve the drudgery of the housewife and lift the great burden off the shoulders of the hard-working farmer ..." (Brown, *Electricity for Rural America: The Fight for the REA,* p. 34). As a result Cooke, although a Republican, publicly announced his support for Roosevelt, the Democratic candidate. When Roosevelt won the 1932 presidential election, Cooke had an unparalleled opportunity to realize his dream of electrifying rural America.

The Formation of the Rural Electrification Administration (1935)

During the first two years of the New Deal in 1933 and 1934, Cooke worked as a consultant for the Public Works Administration (PWA) and served as an advisor to President Roosevelt on conservation and electrical power. The PWA provided jobs to build roads, tunnels, bridges, dams, public buildings, and hydroelectric power projects. He strongly advised that the government take action to spur rural

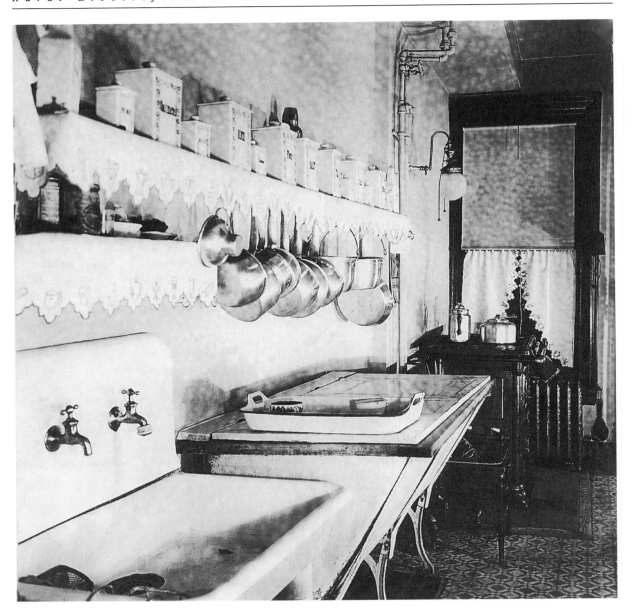

Kitchens like the one pictured here were common in farmhouses around the United States. The Rural Electrification Administration focused on providing electricity to homes in rural areas. (Hirz/ Archive Photos, Inc. Reproduced by permission.)

electrification. Roosevelt supported the cause in principal, but delayed the creation of a federal program because he did not have a plan of action that he believed would work. At the same time, pressure was building for some form of federal action. Representing the farmer, both the American Farm Bureau Federation and the National Grange (a fraternal organization of farmers) in 1934 passed resolutions urging the government to act. In 1934 both North

Carolina and South Carolina had applications pending before the PWA for federal funds to institute state-operated power systems to serve rural areas. Both states lobbied strongly for immediate action.

At the same time, a working example of an effective program for rural electrification had just sprung up. The Tennessee Valley Authority (TVA), a federal agency created in 1933 to develop hydroelectric power on the Tennessee River, had set up an experimental cooperative for publicly developed rural electrification. A cooperative is a private, nonprofit enterprise locally owned and managed by those it serves, and incorporated under state law. The experimental cooperative was the Alcorn County Electric Cooperative in northeastern Mississippi, a very economically depressed region with many tenant farmers. Although only 1.5 percent of Mississippi farmers had electricity and the common wisdom of electric companies was that such people were too poor to make electric service profitable, the success of this cooperative was dramatic. Once power lines had been extended from the town of Corinth, Mississippi, to the surrounding rural area, the cooperative began delivering electricity bought from the TVA at wholesale rates. Rural homeowners, with the help of a new federal loan program, the Electric Home and Farm Authority (EHFA), immediately began buying electrical appliances, which greatly pleased town merchants. Farmers began using even more electricity than city dwellers, helping to pay for the cost of building the rural lines. The success of the Alcorn cooperative and the TVA in promoting rural electrification was the final element that tipped the scales in favor of a New Deal program.

With the encouragement of Secretary of the Interior Harold Ickes, Cooke prepared a public plan that proposed a "Rural Electrification Agency" inside the Department of the Interior. Submitted to Ickes in February 1934, this ambitious plan involved the use of cooperatives that would employ low-interest, long-term federal loans to construct lines in areas not already served by electric companies. This was a huge area, since 90 percent of American farms at that time did not have electric service. The new agency would also provide low-cost federal loans to consumers for home appliances, as the EHFA had, to encourage electricity consumption and bring electric rates down. Although the Roosevelt administration reacted favorably on a verbal level to Cooke's plan, it took no action on it in 1934. As Chairman of the Mississippi Valley Committee (MVC), Cooke directed the preparation of the MVC report filed in October 1934. A multi-faceted study of the natural and human resources of the Mississippi Valley, this report recommended the use of cooperatives supervised and financed by the federal government to implement rural electrification, but in addition recommended a federal appropriation of $100 million for the purpose. Again the administration did not take immediate action.

Cooke, however, had only a few months to wait. The eagerness of national farm organizations and state governments, the recent positive experience of the Alcorn Cooperative, and the 1934 planning documents prepared under Cooke's direction and influence convinced President Roosevelt in early 1935 that the time was right to act. In January of that year, in his annual message to Congress, Roosevelt proposed a massive relief program to create jobs. This idea became the Emergency Relief Appropriation Act of 1935 (ERAA), which was approved by Congress on April 8 and included an allocation of $100 million (the very amount proposed by the MVC report in 1934) for rural electrification. The President, on May 11, 1935, with Executive Order No. 7037, created the Rural Electrification Administration (REA), an independent agency with an Administrator empowered to "initiate, formulate, administer, and supervise a program of approved projects with respect to the generation, transmission, and distribution of electric energy in rural areas." An executive order, which has the force of law, is a directive issued by the President regarding the operations of the Executive Branch of the federal government. He appointed Cooke as the first REA Administrator on May 20, the same day on which Cooke, eager to begin work, met with power company representatives to discuss how to move ahead with the REA program. This meeting, although representing a triumph in the long struggle to institute a federal program, began what was to be a difficult search for a practical means to achieve the long-sought goal of rural electrification.

How To Do It: Cooperatives Emerge as the Solution

Cooke's first challenge as REA Administrator was to find a way to implement the directives of Executive Order 7037. As part of a program to put people to work, REA had to follow the order that "in so far as practicable, the persons employed under the authority of this Executive Order shall be selected from those receiving relief" (Brown, p. 47). More specifically the REA, operating as a relief agency would, was required to spend a quarter of its funds directly on labor, with 90 percent of the workers coming from unemployment rolls. This requirement was applied to all relief agencies, but Roosevelt had not anticipated the difficulty of finding suitable workers for constructing power lines. Such work demanded skilled laborers, most of who were already employed. Another problem was the condition that a large part of REA funds had to go toward equipment and material. As a result the REA had very little flexibility in its budgets for directly tackling specific projects which each have their own unique needs. Cooke very quickly recognized these obstacles and convinced Roosevelt to issue orders setting up REA as a lending agency rather than a relief agency. This freed the REA from the constraints associated with relief spending and made it an exclusive

This farmer's wife uses an electric stove and adjoining wood range. Although many homes were wired for electricity, rates were higher than many farmers could afford. (The Library of Congress.)

source of loans to any organizations building rural power projects.

Despite his proposals to electrify rural America through the use of cooperatives, Cooke still believed that the power companies, already well equipped and experienced in building power transmission lines, could be convinced to participate in the REA program by its low interest rates and an appeal to the companies' ethic of public service. At first this approach seemed to make progress. The May 20, 1935, meeting between Cooke and the industry representatives was friendly and seemed to indicate a spirit of cooperation. The companies agreed to study ways by which they could work with the REA to develop rural electrification. Cooke was ready to make loans to private companies to finance the construction of rural lines. Beneath the surface, however, fundamental differences existed that doomed hopes for practical cooperation. The power companies still did not believe that rural service would be immediately profitable and did not want the federal government to dictate terms and control rates. Cooke and the REA required that the companies accept some sacrifices as well as active government leadership to ensure that all farmers, rich and poor, would receive electric service.

The cooperation bubble burst on July 24, 1935, when the industry committee met with Cooke and sub-

mitted a letter with its conclusions on the use of REA loans. The committee proposed to make use of most of the available REA funds for 1935–1936 to build rural lines at an estimated cost of $1,356 per mile. The response greatly disappointed Cooke, not only because of this relatively high cost estimate, but also because the report reflected the same industry attitudes that had resulted in the existing snail's pace of rural electrification. The letter asserted that reduced electric rates to households would not create increased demand for electricity and a profitable situation for the power companies. Despite the positive experience of the EHFA and the TVA with rural electric service to households, the committee response reflected a continuing industry fixation on serving larger electricity consumers and a lack of faith that service to smaller household users through area coverage could be made profitable.

The July 24 meeting was a turning point for the REA. No longer did it appear that the private power industry was a viable solution to the rural electrification problem. Although Cooke was still willing to make loans to individual electric companies if they agreed to federal terms, few loan applications from that sector arrived at the REA office. Contributing to this situation was a deteriorating relationship in 1935 between the power companies and the federal government due to the government's battle to break up the holding companies that owned and controlled the power industry. Holding companies are simply companies that purchase and gain control of various manufacturing or other kinds of companies, or in this case private utility companies. One holding company may own a number of supposedly competing utilities. In addition one holding company might be owned by another creating multiple layers of ownership. Each of these layers drew money from the profits made by the utility companies they owned to pay for their "management services." This practice kept the costs of power high for consumers and often led to monopolies since competing companies were actually under the same management direction of a holding company. Because of these growing business arrangements, public opinion against private utilities was growing rapidly in the early 1930s and government officials wanted to take legal action to break up the layers of holding companies.

If private companies would not make use of REA funds for rural electrification, who would? The remaining options were municipal utilities, publicly owned by city residents, and rural electrical cooperatives similar to the Alcorn Cooperative in Mississippi. Cooke, always mindful of the need to keep his options open, met with municipal power representatives on May 25, 1935 (only four days after meeting with private power company officials). They agreed to hold a joint meeting on November 7–8, 1935, which was attended by 152 delegates from 17 states. The municipal representatives very quickly demonstrated that they would not be practical partners. The city dwellers did not exhibit a concern for rural problems, worried about possible rate increases if they extended service into the countryside, and expressed concerns that rural expansion would bring adjacent cities into conflicts about jurisdiction over intervening territory. There was even anxiety about possible legal disputes between cities and state legislatures. The final blow to any hope for municipal utilities as the prime mover of rural electrification came when Cooke rejected a loan application from Wisconsin Power and Light, a public utility that had displayed unusual interest in rural electric affairs. In Cooke's view, this application did not adequately address the issues of affordable rates and area coverage. Its rejection discouraged further loan requests from public utilities.

That left the cooperatives as the only remaining solution. As evidenced by the plans put forth by Cooke and his staff in 1934, Cooke looked favorably upon cooperatives. After all, the Alcorn Cooperative had been a huge success. The Alcorn Cooperative involved

At a Glance
What is a Co-op?

A rural electric cooperative is a nonprofit enterprise owned and managed by those it serves, and incorporated according to state law. Each member, regardless of the amount of electricity they use, has one vote in co-op decisions.

Generally, profits are not allowed; income and expenses ultimately should be equal. In many cooperatives, money saved after paying expenses is considered capital that can be given back to individual members. Boards of directors decide how to dispose of this capital.

The bylaws of most cooperatives require one annual meeting of members. At that time, the co-op consumers elect a Board of Directors from the membership. Board members elect officers, and then the officers hire a manager to run the co-op's affairs. The manager supervises employees and in turn must answer to the board. The board in turn must answer to the members, who can vote to remove directors.

Organized in this way, the co-op serves the interests of those who comprise it, primarily the average farmer or rural resident.

---

both urban and rural areas and was supervised by the TVA, so it was not a perfect model for purely rural electric cooperatives that would need to form at the grass-roots level. Furthermore, farmers were well experienced at forming and running cooperatives for marketing their products, but those tasks did not require high levels of technical expertise as electrical cooperatives would. Although others in the REA preferred the cooperatives as the solution, Cooke worried that the average farmer would not have the technical, managerial, and legal skills to handle the complexities of setting up and running a rural electrical cooperative successfully. After all, establishing *successful* local electrification programs was key to the long-term success of the REA.

Despite his reservations, Cooke and his staff, while still negotiating with power companies, met with representatives of agricultural marketing cooperatives on June 6, 1935. In the meetings participants discussed the obstacle of technical expertise and the REA offered to provide services that the farmers could not, including designing appropriate electrical transmission systems to meet their needs. The meeting participants were encouraged by the success of the Alcorn Cooperative and were ready to try their hand at rural electric cooperatives to take advantage of the REA program. Other meetings were held that summer with consumer nonprofit organizations, the American Farm Bureau Federation, the Grange, the national Association of Master Plumbers, and other groups with some interest in rural electrification. Cooke came away from these discussions feeling that cooperatives were a viable option (although power companies were still his first choice) as REA loan recipients. He sent Boyd Fisher, head of the REA Development Section and a strong proponent of cooperatives, into the field to promote co-ops at the local level. He also encouraged farmers to request information about setting up co-ops. These activities prompted many farmers to feel that working with REA would finally satisfy their long yearning for electrical service.

By late 1935 it became evident that applications from private industry and public utilities would not be received in anything approaching sufficient numbers. Cooke and the REA were obliged to depend on cooperatives as the only remaining solution. The REA approved loan applications from 11 proposed co-ops early in November 1935. The terms were very favorable to the applicants: 3 percent loan interest and a payback period of 20 years. Co-op participants could obtain low-interest loans from EHFA for wiring homes and buying electrical appliances. The co-ops would then buy their power from a private power company, a municipal utility, or the Federal Reclamation Service.

This was the beginning, albeit a very small one, of the close relationship between the REA and rural electric cooperatives that ultimately achieved great success. The slow pace of progress in 1935, however, discouraged proponents of rural electrification and prompted a rethinking of the temporary and limited status of the REA. This rethinking in 1936 led to the establishment of REA as a permanent agency with legal authority created by Congress.

REA Becomes a Permanent Agency (1936)

Cooke knew by October 1935 that the REA would need to be a permanent federal agency if it was to be truly effective. As a temporary agency set up by executive order, the REA had to compete with other offices in the Executive Branch for funds allocated by Congress. Although Congress had set aside $100 million in April 1935 for construction of rural power lines, this money was under the control of President Roosevelt, who ultimately dispensed only $14 million to the REA. Cooke had agreed with Roosevelt that the allocated funds should be spent slowly until the REA more clearly specified its policy and procedures. It had taken months to decide that cooperatives should be the main recipients of REA loans. By early 1936, once that decision was made and loan applications began arriving in larger numbers, the Roosevelt funding allotment for the REA proved to be an obstacle to the speedy pursuit of the REA program. There just wasn't enough money to fund all the eager and qualified applicant co-ops.

Cooke had a powerful ally in Senator George Norris of Nebraska, a long-time supporter of rural electrification and a strong force behind the establishment of the TVA. Cooke and Norris had shared an interest in rural electrification for a generation and no doubt closely coordinated their efforts in the push to set REA up as a permanent agency. The effort began when Cooke suggested on October 14, 1935, in a report to the National Emergency Council, that the REA was so important that it should be made permanent. Soon thereafter, on October 24, Senator Norris wrote a letter to Cooke emphasizing the importance of rural electrification to the nation, suggesting that REA be made a twin agency of the TVA and asking what it would take to speed up the rural electrification process. Cooke released the Norris letter to the press and wrote a formal response, approved by President Roosevelt and dated November 14, 1935, indicating that with $1.5 billion of public and private money over 10 years, half of all rural homes could be electrified. The letter also pointed out that the long delay in realizing rural electrification was due to excessive line construction charges to farmers, high electric rates that discouraged electric usage, and the power company policy of extending their monopoly while providing service only where it was judged profitable. All of these issues would be addressed by the REA.

This exchange of letters made the front pages of newspapers and spurred a national campaign for rural electrification. The National Grange at their annual convention in November 1935 and the Farm Bureau at their annual convention in December endorsed this campaign. Farmers wrote letters to Senators and Representatives urging congressional action. Senator Norris introduced the REA bill to the U.S. Senate on January 6, 1936, and Representative Sam Rayburn of Texas agreed to introduce a similar bill in the House of Representatives on the same day. The proposal called for an appropriation of $100 million per year for 10 years, amounting to $1 billion, and loans at an

More About...

"Spite" Lines

In the early years of the REA competition often arose between rural cooperatives and private utility companies over the same customers. Private companies did not like to see co-ops taking over areas that might otherwise prove to be profitable. One strategy frequently followed by these companies involved the use of "spite lines," which were transmission lines built quickly after the formation of a cooperative in some of the paths where the co-op planned to build. Spite lines usually were located to serve the most prosperous customers and siphon away cash that the co-op would need to become self-sufficient. With only the poorest farmers left to serve, co-ops would not be able to organize successfully.

For example a Louisiana power company built line extensions in a spoke-like pattern from a central point, but did not connect the homes between the lines. Because REA policy was to serve only those areas without existing private service, the local cooperative then could not sign up enough customers in its area

to make the effort worthwhile. Sometimes companies ran private lines into uninhabited areas to prevent any future co-op from forming.

Usually spite lines were built only after the companies learned about a group's plans to form a cooperative. REA tried to help by sometimes purchasing a private company's lines. In one case REA Administrator Carmody learned that a company was about to start construction at midnight Sunday to disrupt a Michigan co-op. He sent an REA crew to begin construction at midnight Saturday, in that way serving notice to the company that their tactics would not work.

Observers did not fail to see the irony in companies furiously working to serve rural areas that previously they had ignored. Companies argued that market conditions had changed to make the rural areas profitable, but critics responded that the private companies had only just realized what others had been telling them for years.

---

interest rate of three percent or less and repayable within 40 years. Only public cooperatives and municipalities would be eligible for REA loans. Negotiations reduced the proposed appropriation to a total of $420 million and the payback period to 25 years.

After little opposition the Senate approved the bill on March 5 and sent it on to the House, where it encountered much more opposition. It became necessary during committee hearings on March 12–14 to alter the interest rate provision, making 3 percent the minimum rate allowed, and to include private electric companies among the possible borrowers. Even then, the bill cleared the committee by only one vote and was vigorously debated by the full House of Representatives. Only the skillful diplomacy of Sam Rayburn, a democrat from Texas, made possible its approval by the House. Conservatives argued that the creation of a permanent REA would further bloat the federal bureaucracy and take another step toward socialism (government ownership of business and property). They reasoned that it was wrong to place so much power in the hands of one person, the REA Administrator; that power companies could be ruined by REA intervention in their business; and that farm-

ers were not technically competent to manage electric cooperatives successfully and would not be able to pay back their loans to the government. Rayburn argued that the government was obliged to help farmers who had not been served by the electric companies and that rural people were so motivated to get electricity that they would do whatever necessary to manage their co-ops successfully. He pointed out that other agencies handling large amounts of money had not become socialist and that REA was designed to empower local and regional public groups, not the Washington bureaucracy. In addition he emphasized that the electric companies were also allowed to apply for REA loans.

Progressives objected to the inclusion of the electric companies, who they believed had badly mistreated farmers in the past. Rayburn was not fond of the companies, either, but realized that the bill would not pass the House if they were excluded. He sympathized with the power company opponents, but argued that the job of rural electrification was so huge that it made sense to include all possible partners in the enterprise. Rayburn won the confidence of his colleagues and the House approved the Norris-Rayburn bill. But

The Rural Electrification Administration program not only involved setting up electrical lines to homes and farms, but also loans for wiring buildings, purchasing electrical appliances, and even installing plumbing systems. (The Library of Congress.)

to become law it still had to pass the conference committee, where the two versions of the bill approved by the Senate and the House had to be reconciled.

In the conference committee Senator Norris himself was the greatest objector. He vigorously opposed the House amendments raising the interest rate above 3 percent and allowing private electric companies to participate. For a time it appeared that a decision on the bill would be deadlocked and the bill would die for lack of compromise. Both Rayburn and Cooke went to work soothing feelings and diplomatically suggesting ways around the standoff. Norris felt that in case the average interest rate in the Unites States went up, giving the farmer a break on the interest rate was justified. Cooke suggested tying the interest rate to the rate paid by the United States on its obligations or on U.S. bonds. At the time the interest rate was 3 percent but could fluctuate. He also told Norris that it made little difference if private companies were allowed to submit loan applications, because REA would require area coverage, which the private companies were unlikely to accept. Finally Norris accepted the compromise, which the Senate and House approved on May 11, 1936. President Roosevelt signed the Rural Electrification Act of 1936 into law on May 21 and nominated Morris Cooke to be the first

Administrator of REA as an independent agency established by Congress. Senate confirmation of Cooke in his new post followed quickly on May 26.

As established by the Rural Electrification Act of 1936, REA finally had the funding and the authority to carry out a rural electrification program that could work. Cooperatives across the U.S. were destined to play the major role in bringing electric power to the countryside. Applications from many new co-ops set up for this purpose streamed in from many states and territories. Realizing the dream of widespread rural electrification, however, demanded more than passing laws and setting up programs. It required finding ways to assist rural people in forming and managing co-ops, in actually getting the power lines built, and in other essential tasks. This last but difficult step of implementation was the final element that would assure the success of the REA program.

Developing a Program That Worked

The "new and improved" REA officially began operation at the beginning of the fiscal year on July 1, 1936. The principal challenge from the beginning was to speed up the process of cooperative formation and the submittal and approval of loan applications.

Cooke was acutely aware of this and realized that the job of administrator would be very demanding. As he was already 64 years old, approaching retirement, and preferred innovation to administration anyway, he immediately began a search for someone to replace him as REA administrator. As his successor, he chose John M. Carmody, whom he appointed Deputy Administrator on August 1, 1936. With experience as a coal company manager and magazine editor, Carmody had a reputation as an able administrator with innovative ideas on how to manage organizations. Although he did not become REA Administrator until February 1937 when Cooke finally resigned, he effectively ran the REA from the time when he started with the agency since Cooke had been busy with special tasks for President Roosevelt.

Carmody was faced at the start with a flood of loan applications that were taking too long to be reviewed. Although plenty of money was available for the purpose, few farmers were being connected to the power grid. All participants in the program, including farmers, lawyers, and REA staff, were trying to figure out how to make the system work. Most loan applications were improperly drawn up and could not be funded. When Carmody stepped in, he very quickly informed farmers that it was up to them to organize the co-ops properly, and that people at the local level had to take the initiative.

This was no easy task for rural people who had never done anything of the kind; to them, the process was daunting. To become eligible for an REA loan, farm families had to organize and incorporate according to the laws of their State. They then had to convince the REA that their project would run properly and that they would be able to pay back the loan. They also had the tasks of hiring lawyers, electing officers, and persuading their neighbors to join them. In addition they had to retain engineers to design transmission line systems. Other problems included learning how to pass resolutions as permitted by their own bylaws, arranging to buy electric power at wholesale rates, calculating costs, and maintaining proper records. Record maintenance would help them to determine whether the system they designed would earn enough to pay off the loan, and how to work with commissions and state legislatures. In the beginning few states had laws that specifically permitted electric cooperatives, so in 1937 REA staff drew up a model law that states followed over the subsequent years to specify how co-ops could be legally formed and regulated.

This is only a single example of the many ways the REA worked to assist local groups in getting their areas electrified. Although at first the agency was reluctant to provide active assistance to prospective borrowers, it soon became obvious that without hands-on REA help at the local level, the program would not achieve its goal of rapid rural electrification. The REA hired many lawyers to find answers to legal questions that had not been asked before. REA staff had written over nine hundred legal opinions by the end of 1938, amounting to nearly an entire new body of law. They settled such issues as whether electric transmission lines in Minnesota could be considered property for tax purposes, whether a town in Louisiana could build lines beyond the city limits to serve rural residents, and whether a co-op in Illinois could use highway rights-of-way to string lines. They also defended the interests of rural people against persistent efforts by private electric companies and even state agencies to prevent them from organizing cooperatives or building their construction projects.

The REA hired not only lawyers but also engineers, accountants, and other experienced professionals that could go out into the field and give practical advice to prospective borrowers on all phases of their projects. REA field staff worked directly with individual cooperatives rather than with State or regional organizations. Truly the agency was assisted by the Depression because it was able to hire very skilled and experienced staff at low government salaries. In turn the REA provided much-needed jobs to these skilled and experienced workers. These people were very effective at instructing farmers, eager to receive electricity, in all the many facets of organizing and operating a successful electric co-op. Beyond that, the REA also worked with co-ops to show people how to use electricity. For example home economists worked with wives and daughters while engineers showed farmers how electric motors could help with farm work. The most visible expression of REA involvement at the local level was the Demonstration Farm Equipment Tour, also called the "REA circus." From 1938 until 1942 this traveling show used a tent big enough for one thousand people to exhibit the proper uses for electrical household and farm equipment. Thousands of people in 20 states viewed this exhibition.

Carmody's industrial experience and passion for efficiency produced benefits both in the REA office and in the construction of transmission lines. To clear up the logjam of loan applications that faced his office when he arrived, he hired an expert in automobile assembly lines to design an assembly line for loan applications. He set targets and deadlines for processing applications and held weekly production control meetings. Through standardization, short-cuts and increased volume, the REA reduced the average time

Workers on a transmission line in rural San Joaquin Valley, California in 1938. REA engineers worked to bring down the cost of rural electricity by employing more efficient materials and construction methods. (The Library of Congress.)

between loan approval and construction contract from 36 weeks in 1936 to 12 weeks in 1939.

In the field a serious challenge was the cost of building electric transmission lines. REA engineers worked to bring down this cost by employing more efficient materials and construction methods. This effort involved many innovations such as new, high-strength wires permitting longer spans between poles, lowering the number of poles per mile from 30 to 18.

Cross-arms were eliminated from poles and wires instead were attached one above another on a single pole. The REA standardized poles, hardware, transformers, and electrical wires and used large-scale bidding and mass construction to bring down costs. Construction crews adopted assembly-line principles in building transmission lines. Instead of having one crew perform all tasks, specialized crews followed one another on the line, including crews for staking, hole-

More About...

When the Lights Came On

To rural residents receiving electricity for the first time, it was a miracle that they remembered for the rest of their lives. Families remembered the date as they did births and marriages. In many homes that first night, the lights stayed on all night long to allow people time to admire the insides of their dwellings. Celebration was the order of the day. At one place in Texas ranchers dug a "grave" and cast their kerosene lamps into it. A Missouri woman paid little attention to the lights when they came on. She ran to the kitchen, however, to examine her new refrigerator—when the little light came on, she broke down with tears of joy. A woman more than one hundred years old wrote a letter to REA, thanking the agency for her electric lights. For the first time in her life, she said, she felt she had been born too soon.

To many people, electricity was still a mystery. A storekeeper in Georgia bragged to his customers for a month about his new electric light, until he learned that this was only the cash register night light. When he was shown how to turn on the rest of the lights, he was so amazed he didn't know what to say. A housewife wrote the REA Administrator to ask how to turn off her bedroom light; she had not been told she had a switch. The wife of a co-op director refused to bake with her new electric range, as she had won the blue ribbon at the county fair ten years in a row for her angel food cake, cooked in her wood range using very precise techniques. Her husband convinced her to try an experiment: she baked two cakes at one time, one with the wood range and the other in her new electric oven. She entered both in the county fair and won the blue ribbon with the cake from the electric oven.

Some were fearful. A woman in Kentucky waited weeks before turning on her new electric iron, and her neighbor would not touch the switches without the protection of a potholder. According to another story, one person kept all sockets plugged so as to prevent the electricity from leaking out.

The novelty of electric appliances was a special pleasure. When one farm family got their radio, they placed it in the open kitchen window, aimed it at the fields and turned up the volume. For a full week, the men working in the fields demanded that they hear the radio while they worked.

---

digging, equipment, hardware, pole-guying, wire-stringing, transformer-hanging, and so forth. Contractors were highly motivated to find solutions to problems they met in building the lines. Using these approaches the REA was able to reduce the per-mile construction cost from $1,500 to $2,000 before the REA program to $941 by the end of 1936 and to less than $825 by 1939. This cost reduction greatly encouraged rural electrification by making it more affordable for the co-ops.

The electrification program involved not only building transmission lines to homes and farms, but also loans for wiring buildings, purchasing electrical appliances, and even installing plumbing systems. Co-ops set up group plans to minimize costs for their members. Ways were found for even the poorest people to benefit. For example the "Arkansas Plan," widely adopted in the South where the poorest farmers lived, permitted families living in one- to three-room houses to pay only $1.89 per month for their co-op membership, electrical service, wiring the house, and an iron and radio. Farmers with no money were allowed to work on REA crews in exchange for obtaining electrical service for their homes.

The dedication of the REA and the rural cooperatives combined with the improved efficiencies in all facets of the process greatly accelerated the electrification of rural areas. From 1936 to 1939 the miles of line in operation under the REA program rose from four hundred to 115,230 and the number of consumers served increased from 693 to 268,000. The total amount of loans advanced climbed from $13.9 million in 1935–1936 to $227.2 million in 1939. This was the defining period for the REA, in which its program gained the momentum that in later years carried it to the completion of its appointed task.

Contributing Forces

In the early twentieth century most rural Americans were without electrical power at a time when most city dwellers had already begun to forget what

Electric poles run through a farmer's field in Pulaski County, Arkansas in June 1938. (The Library of Congress.)

life had been without it. Although this inequity was recognized early, many assumed that market forces would naturally lead to rural electrification without any government intervention. It was only when private enterprise clearly had failed to light the countryside that progressive activists succeeded in establishing an effective federal program that ultimately resulted in that accomplishment.

Adoption of Electrical Power in America

Thomas Edison designed and built the first central electrical power plant in the world in New York City in 1882. Early electrical systems were small, low-powered, and served small numbers of preferred customers. Importantly for practical reasons electric power was limited primarily to cities in the first decades. Even so, electrical systems sprang up very early in cities of all sizes across the United States. For example the first electrical power plant built in Eugene, Oregon, appeared in 1887, three thousand miles away from New York City but only five years later. Electric lights, another Edison invention, were the first use for electricity.

The use of electricity spread steadily in American cities, so that by the early 1920s, half of all urban

homes were electrified, and all of those had at least some electric lights. Much of this development was done by private industry, although municipal utilities, publicly owned by city residents, played a major role as well. During the 1920s a large number of American homes, primarily those in the top 20 percent of the income scale, modernized through the adoption of such electrical inventions such as full electric lighting, appliances for heating and cooling, and power tools. By 1929 most electrified homes had electric irons, half had radios, more than a third had vacuum cleaners, and almost a third had clothes washers. By contrast as late as 1935 only 10 percent of U.S. farms were electrified. The benefits of electrical power for industry and homes were accepted facts by the 1920s. Cities had been served first because dense concentrations of many customers made producing and supplying power profitable to them. Unfortunately for those who lived outside of cities, power companies did not believe that there was much money to be made by delivering electricity to the countryside. Prospective customers were widely scattered and generally not well-to-do.

Early Efforts by Private Industry to Power the Countryside

Even before most people in cities had electrical service, private industry gave some thought to rural electrification. In 1911 the National Electric Light Association (NELA), representing the private power industry, discussed the subject at its annual meeting. A committee was appointed to ask the U.S. Department of Agriculture to print a special bulletin about uses of electricity on the farm and to request that the Census Bureau tally the number of farms already using electricity. No other action was taken to promote rural electric service, which was not surprising, because at that time electricity in rural areas was still considered a luxury.

In 1923 the NELA took another look at the matter and formed the Committee on the Relation of Electricity to Agriculture (CREA), a cooperative program with the American Farm Bureau Federation and state agricultural colleges. The strategy of the CREA was to demonstrate the many uses and advantages of electricity and thereby to convince the farmer to order the service. Campus farms financed by private power companies conducted experimental demonstrations of farm uses, including some large-scale experiments involving rural customers, and published the results in farm publications. These experiments were valuable in achieving technological progress and sharing the information with farmers, but they did not tackle the main obstacle confronting rural electrification, which

More About...

Life on the Farm Without Electricity

Until electricity came to the countryside, life on the farm in its basic form had changed little since the Middle Ages. Farmers depended on tools that their ancestors had used for centuries or even for thousands of years, such as the wheel, the lever, the block and tackle, and the plow. Toil and drudgery were accepted as unavoidable companions. Power for most uses came from the muscles of people and their animals. Kerosene lamps and candles supplied illumination at night, so bedtime came not long after dusk.

Women cooked on wood stoves and washed clothes by hand outside on washboards in an outdoor kettle heated over a fire. One report indicated farmers' wives spent 20 days more each year washing clothes than city women who owned electric washers. Ironing clothes was particularly burdensome, requiring use of the "sad iron" heated on a wood stove. Most people had no indoor plumbing or toilets. Water for cooking and washing had to be hauled into the house in buckets from an outside well or a nearby stream. A U.S. Department of Agriculture study in 1919 reported that pumping and carrying water alone took an average of 10 hours per week for a family. Sanitation was

poor as it was much work to clean the house let alone one's body.

Storing food was done in ways unchanged since ancient times. Farm families kept smokehouses, root cellars, and icehouses. Milk, butter, eggs, and fresh fruit were kept in a well or springhouse. Meat was dried, smoked, and salted. Food spoilage and lack of fresh produce caused numerous health problems such as dysentery from bacterial contamination and pellagra, resulting from vitamin deficiency, which caused chronic fatigue, skin lesions, and mental illness. Poor nutrition also caused problems in pregnancy that resulted in stillbirths, deformities, and impaired intelligence.

Gasoline engines became common on the farm after World War I (1914–1918). Gasoline-powered tractors made plowing much more efficient. Gasoline engines could pump water and even power an electrical generator to run a few lights. Automobiles made it much easier to deliver farm produce to market. Gasoline engines, tractors, and automobiles, however, were expensive and needed frequent repair.

---

was the cost of electricity. At that time, rates for electricity were highest for those who used the least amount, so farmers of modest means faced a significant cost hurdle unless they used, and could afford, larger amounts of electricity to bring the per-unit rate down. Not only that, but they would have to pay the cost of building the transmission lines to their farms, wiring their buildings, and buying the lights and electrical equipment, a significant investment. Few rural residents could afford to do that on their own, especially when it was not clear that they would increase their profits as a result.

Critics of the private power industry pointed out that cost was the primary obstacle to rural electrification. They urged more serious efforts to address this issue, including some sacrifice and a long-term perspective on the part of the power companies. They did not accept the private industry estimates of the cost of constructing power lines because they were unreasonably high. The power companies argued that they had to make a profit to stay in business and provide their service.

Successful Rural Electrification Programs in Other Countries

American advocates of public power (electric power provided by public agencies or cooperatives) pointed to other countries as evidence that rural electrification under the right conditions could be accomplished quickly. Rural cooperatives in Europe and Canada had put some countries far ahead of the United States in electrifying rural areas. By 1930, in some countries, 90 percent of farms had electrical service compared to only 10 percent in the United States. A well-known case was Sweden, where rural cooperatives had formed to buy power from the state and distribute it among members. By 1936, 50 percent of Swedish farms were electrified. With large government subsidies to cooperatives, France had reached 71 percent electrification by 1930. The German government offered easy credit terms to cooperatives and reached the 60 percent level by 1927. Other examples were Finland (40 percent), Denmark (50 percent), Czechoslovakia (70 percent), and New Zealand (35 percent). Higher population densities in European rural areas made it less expensive to establish rural electrical systems than in the United States and people in other countries were more willing to accept government subsidy programs to help pay for it.

One of the most visible and successful foreign programs was just across the Canadian border, in Ontario, where the government helped pay the cost of transmission lines in rural areas and made loans to rural people for buying appliances. With this assistance, rural customers could more quickly increase their electrical usage and bring down the rates they had to pay. By the late 1920s, 27 percent of farms in southern Ontario were connected to the power grid, nearly three times the American average. This program encouraged rural electrification advocates in the United States and provided a model alternative to the American reliance on private industry to solve the problem. Private industry saw the Ontario program as a threat to their interests and strongly criticized it. Despite this criticism the Ontario experience influenced the state of Washington, with its plentiful hydroelectric power, to authorize rural Public Utility Districts in 1930. These districts were public agencies organized to distribute power in specific areas.

Opposing Visions: Giant Power Versus Super Power

The slow pace of rural electrification in the 1920s prompted action on the part of some important political leaders who regarded this as an issue of social justice rather than simply a matter of economics. One of these leaders was Pennsylvania Governor Gifford Pinchot, a well-known conservationist, who wanted to use the authority of the state to promote social welfare. He felt that the power companies were irresponsible in their electric rate structures and in their failure to provide service to rural areas. Encouraged by the examples of Ontario and the European countries, Pinchot wanted to establish a Pennsylvania statewide public power system that would rectify these problems. To study the issue and plan for such a system, he set up the Giant Power Board in 1923 and appointed as its director the former director of the Philadelphia Department of Public Works, Morris L. Cooke.

In 1914, in his position with the City of Philadelphia, Cooke filed suit against the Philadelphia Electric Company to lower its electric rates. The Philadelphia Electric Company was the power provider throughout the city and one of the country's largest power companies. At that time, Cooke knew very little about electrical engineering and had a very small staff. Nevertheless in 1916 Cooke won the case, securing a large out-of-court settlement for the city, and in the process developed a reputation as an innovative reformer. He was a natural choice for Pinchot and Giant Power.

The Giant Power concept was to bring electric power to every household in the state, urban as well as rural, at reasonable rates through a public approach rather than through reliance on private industry. Pinchot and Cooke paid special attention to rural residents, who had mostly been denied access to electricity. They also had grander goals: they assumed that what would work for Pennsylvania would also work for the United States as a whole, so they saw this as a critically valuable task. The Giant Power Board studied all aspects of electrical service, including farm service, city gas supply, water power development, mine-mouth electric generating plants (utilizing coal as fuel at the source rather than transporting it), public utility generation, high-voltage transmission, and other related matters. Planning emphasized total system design across the state rather than incremental growth based on increased sales. Cooke visited Wisconsin and Ontario to see examples of rural electrification programs. Projecting electric rates for rural areas, however, was a difficult problem. Cooke felt that rural rates could fall below city rates because farmers had more potential uses for electric power than city homes, but on that point his colleagues disagreed.

In February 1925 the Giant Power Board delivered its report to the Pennsylvania legislature with recommendations for legislation. The Board proposed strong state regulation and planned development of energy resources. It recommended creation of a new Giant Power Board to oversee the program. New generating plants would be located near coalmines and would also be required to recycle mining wastes. All transmission lines would be interconnected to facilitate the procurement and distribution of power across state lines, which would require the approval of Congress. The state Public Service Commission would have power over the activities of electric companies, even to the point of setting a standard valuation of $1.00 for each share of company stock. This was to create a basis for setting standard electricity rates. Power companies would have to justify why they should not serve particular areas. All potential customers in a given area, regardless of their projected usage, would have to be served. The plan recommended legislation permitting farmers to form electrical power cooperatives if companies refused to serve them. The Board assumed that private industry would do most of the line building and service providing.

The private utility industry strongly opposed the Giant Power proposals and developed a plan of its own to accomplish the same ends. Their proposal, called SuperPower, was national in scope and similar in many ways to Giant Power. It also proposed systematic development of energy resources, including even tidal power on the coastlines, and interconnecting distribution systems across the country for greater efficiency and the elimination of local shortages. Super-Power, however, called for no increase in the level of government regulation, leaving the state public utility commissions to oversee the companies as they had been but without exercising strong control. Regulation of share prices and the matter of rates were not mentioned. No plan was put forth to encourage rural electrification, which was considered important, but less so than providing for industry. Pinchot referred to SuperPower as designed to achieve "profit for the companies" and Giant Power as "a plan to bring cheaper and better electric service to all those who have it now, and to bring good and cheap electric service to those who are still without it" (Brown, p. 28).

An intense public debate, focusing on Giant Power and SuperPower, ensued about rural electrification. "Progressives" like Pinchot and Senator George Norris saw a need to establish social justice through government intervention in key areas, not only with regard to electrical power, but also labor, agriculture, conservation, and consumer rights. But the forces behind SuperPower were stronger and included then Secretary of Commerce Herbert Hoover, the banking and mining industries, the U.S. Chamber of Commerce, the private electric industry, and the press. This conservative force staunchly protected the prerogatives of free enterprise against government control. In the end the proposals of Giant Power were too bold to be passed in those times, and the legislature voted them down. The ideas behind SuperPower remained dominant and plans for bringing electrification to rural areas were pushed back.

Although the failure of Giant Power discouraged proponents of public rural electrification at that time, the Giant Power study and proposals were not forgotten. Their work spread recognition of the fact that farmers were potentially even greater users of electricity than city dwellers. It also made clear that areas with low population density might need assistance to receive electrical power because they could not afford to do it themselves. The Giant Power study also established Morris Cooke as the leading proponent of rural electrification, increasingly seen as an essential element in improving the lives of farm families. It would take a decade of time and an economic depression to change the conservative climate and make possible a government program that would achieve rural electrification. Later, when Cooke became Administrator of

the Rural Electrification Administration (REA), Giant Power proposals formed the basis for REA policies. Cooke even brought some of the former Giant Power employees on board as the first REA staff members.

Perspectives

The issues and controversies surrounding the formation and operation of the REA illustrate the variety of viewpoints present in the United States in the twentieth century. Some saw the issue from the standpoint of their ideologies, whether conservative or progressive. Others, including the owners and managers of private utility companies, many dedicated reformers such as Morris L. Cooke, and rural residents who yearned for electricity by any possible means viewed the matter pragmatically and in the context of their individual and group interests.

Left Out

After World War I, when Americans began to view electricity as a necessity of modern living, rural people increasing felt left out and wherever possible voiced their desire to receive electric service. From their ranks came such notable political leaders as Senator George Norris of Nebraska and Representative Sam Rayburn of Texas, who had grown up in impoverished farm families.

Those farmers who could afford to pay for electrical service, ten percent or less than the total number of farmers, with the exception of the West, where large farms and ranches were more common, did so early on. Most, however, lacked the capital to invest in electrical service and thereby increase their productivity and improve their lives. Therefore, they were locked into what appeared to be a hopeless hand-to-mouth existence. They lacked the technical knowledge and economic understanding required to lift themselves out of the situation, and they looked to political leaders to find a solution.

Be Pragmatic and Make a Profit

Viewing things from the other end of the pragmatic spectrum were the private utility companies and their owners, the holding companies. They existed in order to make profits for their owners and stockholders, giving lip service to the notion of public responsibility. From their standpoint, they could not afford to spend money building transmission lines into the country and hooking up scattered farms without seeing how they could assure a return on their investment.

Their reluctance to take such a risk was reasonable in the context of the times, when the economics of electric power were still poorly understood and the dynamics of the power market were still unpredictable. Still their profit-driven attitude provided insufficient incentive to look beyond approaches with which they were comfortable. Their primary interests were their stockholders, not the public, especially not those who were not already their customers.

Reform the Industry

Reformers such as Morris Cooke were driven by the ethic of public service and looked for solutions wherever they could be found, regardless of ideology. The best indicator of this fact is that Cooke looked first to private industry to provide service to rural areas, both in the Giant Power plan and in the first year of searching for an operation plan for the REA. His lawsuit against the Philadelphia Electric Company made him appear to be an enemy of private industry, but in fact he spent years trying to work with industry to achieve rural electrification before finally aligning himself with public cooperatives.

In political battles Cooke sought allies wherever they could be found to achieve his desired ends. For ideological purists this was unethical behavior, but for Cooke it was the most ethical behavior because it resulted in public good.

The Ideological Divide

Ideologies in the first half of the twentieth century were divided between traditionalists, or conservatives, who believed in the American ideal of self-reliance and private enterprise, and progressives, who believed in public solutions to important issues of social justice. Many Americans had always distrusted government and believed that free citizens could achieve anything. Large corporations that arose in the late nineteenth century and later felt they represented this tradition, although in many cases the interests of the corporation differed dramatically from the interests of the public at large. For many representing the private power companies, the struggle to defend their prerogatives in choosing which customers to serve and what prices to charge was part of the battle to protect the American way of life. Political leaders such as Herbert Hoover saw the issue in the same way.

On the other side of the ideological divide were the progressives, whose philosophical descendants later in the century would be labeled "liberals." Prominent names in this camp were George Norris, Gifford Pinchot (Governor of Pennsylvania in the 1920s), and Franklin D. Roosevelt. In their way of thinking the concentration of wealth in corporate hands was a threat to American values of justice and equal opportunity. For them, rural electrification was essential to preserve the agrarian foundation of American moral strength. From the time of Thomas Jefferson (served 1801–1809), rural America had been considered the source of democratic values and of individual leaders of moral character, but rural impoverishment threatened this keystone. Progressives believed that unrestrained free enterprise, especially in the hands of huge and powerful corporations, could have dire consequences for the country and its people. They worked to exert public control over essential industries and services and to achieve important social goals through the actions of government. For them, rural electrification was a mission that fit their definition of social justice.

Impact

The rural electrification program as established by REA in the 1930s continued through the following decades and achieved its goals. Its effects on American life in the 1930s were quite modest, because at the end of the decade most rural people were still not served with electric power, but in later years its benefits were remarkable.

The REA through the 1990s

During World War II the program of the REA, which had been moved into the Department of Agriculture in 1939, continued at a slower pace because money and materials were diverted to the war effort. To a substantial extent, the agency assisted borrowers to provide for military needs such as the production of aluminum. The electrification of farms served also to improve the production of food, a highly valued wartime commodity. A conscious effort was made to assist borrowers who could produce more food by using electricity.

With the end of the war approaching, Congress in 1944 extended indefinitely the REA's loan authority (which would have expired in 1946) by the Department of Agriculture Organic Act, otherwise known as the Pace Act. This legislation also liberalized credit terms by lowering the interest rate to two percent and stretching the payback period to 35 years. By this time the rural electrification program had proven itself beyond doubt and was primed for the post-war push to complete the job of rural electrification.

After the war Congress appropriated large sums of money for REA loan programs. Between 1945 and

A mother and daughter outside of their home in Orange County, North Carolina in 1939. Even by this date, many rural homes were still not equipped with electric power. (The Library of Congress.)

1959 the number of consumers served by REA-financed systems grew from 1,287,347 to 4,653,502. Although 55 percent of American farms lacked electrical service in 1944, less than 5 percent were unconnected only 15 years later. In 1956 the number of active borrowers began to decline as more cooperatives finally paid off their loans and fewer new borrowers were added, fulfilling the REA's original purpose. After several more decades of servicing its loan program, Congress discontinued REA in 1994 and its functions assumed by the Rural Utilities Service.

The Benefits of Electrification

The most obvious effects of rural electrification were on the lives of the people. The electric light brightened homes and eliminated dark corners. Kerosene lanterns were joyfully abandoned. Children no longer had to be reminded countless times a day to be careful around the lanterns. This had an immediate effect on leisure time, which grew by two to four waking hours a day. It became possible to play outdoor sports and read at night. Rural schoolchildren, more interested in homework, greatly improved their grades. Electric lights cut in half the time needed to do farm chores with a lantern.

Even more popular than electric lights was indoor plumbing, made possible by electric pumps. Indoor faucets reduced one-half hour of labor per day that had been spent hauling water. Indoor bathrooms erased the outdoor privy. Electric clothes washers saved 20 days per year that had been spent manually scrubbing laundry outdoors. The electric iron, generally the first electric appliance obtained, needed no hot stove as its heat source, was light, kept an even temperature, and was very cheap to operate. The refrigerator permitted a healthier diet and reduced food poisoning while eliminating the need to haul ice.

Electricity promoted other health benefits as well. By the late 1940s the U.S. Public Health Service concluded that electric lighting was good for eyesight and encouraged cleanliness. It also reduced home accidents, which caused injury to five million people each year. Half of all home accidents were the result of insufficient illumination. Dim light also caused depression, but brightly-lit homes improved people's mood. Indoor plumbing helped prevent disease caused by polluted water and promoted better family hygiene. Comforts in the home promoted health in an intangible but real way.

After the iron, the radio was the most popular electrical device. It had practical benefits in bringing useful information about weather, markets, meetings, and other news. Radio entertainment brought joy to people's lives and helped lessen the cultural differences between city and countryside. Ironically, the radio, by bringing a view of the wider world to young people, encouraged them to leave the farm and find satisfaction in the city. This result was unanticipated by those who thought electricity would keep more young people on the farm by bringing the benefits of the city to them.

A very important benefit of electricity to the farmer was the use of electric motors to power a wide assortment of chores. It was much more efficient and less expensive to operate saws, grinding wheels, drill presses, and other equipment this way than by hand. In fact farmers found that the cost savings more than paid for the new electrical equipment. Electricity became a new hired hand that milked cows, sawed wood, warmed pigs, hatched eggs, bred chicks, sharpened scythes, and drilled holes. Electric motors also began pumping water for irrigation. All of these improvements helped farms become much more productive. Yet another outcome of electrification was the diversification of agriculture, especially in the South, where cotton had been the principal crop. With elec-

trification farmers were more easily able to establish dairies and raise poultry, both of which became important components of Southern agriculture. These changes in turn raised southern living standards more dramatically than elsewhere. An influential agricultural magazine reported in 1956 that living standards since 1940 had more than tripled in the South compared with an increase of a little more than two times the standard of living for the entire country, largely because of electrification. The world-renowned productivity and standard of living of the American farmer that was a fact of life at the start of the twenty-first century could not have been possible without rural electrification.

Electrification of the countryside served more than farmers and farm families, however. It permitted decentralized industrialization of the countryside. Previously, mills and factories had been concentrated near power sources such as waterfalls, coalfields, and municipal electrical systems, but now they could be set up almost anywhere. Packing plants began using electricity for all parts of their production assembly lines, further promoting agricultural output.

Improved productivity, standards of living, education, communication, and economic diversification in rural areas brought about by electrification greatly reduced the economic and cultural differences between city and country people. At the same time improved farm efficiency, which meant that fewer people could produce much more food, made possible the migration of rural dwellers to the cities. The fact that the United States, at the beginning of the twenty-first century, was seen as a largely urban country is an indirect outcome of rural electrification.

Ironically the success of REA programs in promoting the use of electric power resulted in such an increased demand that power shortages began to appear as early as the late 1940s. Producing electricity to meet the booming demand required building hydroelectric dams and coal-fired and nuclear power plants whose environmental consequences began to be widely recognized in the 1960s and 1970s. The benefits of electrification are obvious when the lives of rural Americans before and after the REA are compared. As often occurs with the adoption of new technology, however, these twentieth century benefits have led to unanticipated problems that must be solved by the people of the twenty-first century.

Notable People

John M. Carmody (1881–1963). John Carmody was Administrator of REA in the critical period from

1937 to 1939 when the agency developed the programs and practices that ultimately fulfilled the long-standing goal of complete rural electrification. Born in Towanda, Pennsylvania, Carmody was educated in business and held executive positions in the steel, garment, and coal industries. His first government job was to direct a study for the United States Coal Commission in 1922. For six years he edited *Coal Age* and *Factory and Industrial Management* magazines. He acquired international experience in the period of 1927 to 1931 on a survey of industrial development of the Soviet Union for the McGraw-Hill Publishing Company. In 1933 the Roosevelt Administration brought him to Washington, DC, where he held a variety of positions, including the Chairmanship of the Bituminous Coal Labor Board, memberships with the National Mediation Board and the National Labor Relations Board, and Chief Engineer of the Civil Works Administration.

Morris Cooke selected Carmody to replace him as REA Administrator because of Carmody's reputation as a man who would not give in under pressure and a strong manager who emphasized efficiency. In only three years at the REA Carmody hired numerous specialists, devised a highly efficient system of loan application processing, and developed an aggressive program of assistance for farmers in forming and managing rural cooperatives. Carmody's influence developed an agency pattern that persisted for decades and resulted in essentially complete electrification of rural areas by the late 1950s.

Carmody resigned in 1939 when the REA, an independent agency, was shifted to become a part of the Department of Agriculture. He felt this move marked the end of the REA's autonomy. After this, President Roosevelt put him in charge of all major federal relief agencies. He held other government posts in the 1940s and 1950s and died on November 10, 1963, at the age of 82 after a hip injury and ensuing complications.

Morris L. Cooke (1872–1960). Morris Cooke was a principal leader of the rural electrification movement whose reputation as a tireless and systematic reformer won him the admiration of President Roosevelt and appointment as the first Administrator of the REA. Cooke was born in Philadelphia and educated at Lehigh University. After training as a mechanical engineer, he set up a consulting firm in Philadelphia that did work for electric power utilities. Cooke's career as an advocate of public power began after he was appointed Director of the Philadelphia Department of Public Works in 1911. In 1916 he won an important lawsuit for the city against the formidable Philadelphia Electric Company to reduce that company's electric rates. The reputation gained in that episode earned him the attention of Gifford Pinchot, Governor of Pennsylvania, who in 1923 appointed him to head the Giant Power Board, which thoroughly studied the subject of electrical power generation, transmission, and use. Giant Power in 1925 submitted to the Pennsylvania legislature a detailed plan for a public statewide power distribution system that would provide service to all, including rural residents. Although the plan was voted down, the study elevated Cooke to high regard among those who championed rural electrification.

Cooke's experience caused Franklin Roosevelt, then Governor of New York, to appoint Cooke to the New York Power Authority, where he directed a study of the costs of rural electrical service. This study was a milestone because it demonstrated that a rural power distribution system could be constructed for significantly less than the private power industry had estimated. Subsequently, after Roosevelt became President and initiated the New Deal, he chose Cooke as administrator of the new Rural Electrification Administration, which incorporated the ideals and knowledge Cooke had developed during his career as an advocate for public power and rural electrification. Under Cooke the REA became a lending agency for rural cooperatives and one of the most successful New Deal agencies, ultimately succeeding in the task of electrifying the countryside.

Cooke, an innovator rather than administrator, left the REA in 1937 and served the Roosevelt Administration in other posts. His last government job was as Chairman of the Water Resource Policy Commission, to which President Truman (served 1945–1953) appointed him in 1950. He remained active in public affairs until he died in 1960.

George Norris (1861–1944). George Norris, as Senator from Nebraska, vigorously promoted rural electrification and was instrumental in the establishment of both the REA and the Tennessee Valley Authority (TVA). Born in Sandusky County, Ohio, Norris grew up in a very poor farm family, where he learned first-hand how difficult rural life could be. He taught school and studied law, completing his education at Valparaiso University, in Indiana, and earning admission to the bar in 1883. He moved to Nebraska in 1885 and later became a county prosecuting attorney. He was elected to a district judgeship in 1895 and re-elected in 1899. In 1902 he was elected to the U.S. House of Representatives and served five successive terms. He became Senator from Nebraska in 1912.

During his decades in Congress, Norris championed the causes of ordinary Americans, especially farmers. He particularly espoused public power and pushed for controls on private utility companies. In the 1920s he fought for federal development of the Muscle Shoals hydroelectric project on the Tennessee River. The federal government had built this system of hydroelectric dams and factories during World War I to manufacture munitions for the war effort. While some felt that the project should be turned over to private industry for development, Norris saw an opportunity to provide cheap power to poor Southern farmers as well as city people. He opposed Henry Ford's offer to purchase the project for $5 million and deliver the power to private manufacturers and in 1922 recommended that the federal government distribute the power to states, counties, and municipalities within a three hundred mile radius. This proposal later evolved into the TVA, established as a New Deal program in the 1930s.

Norris was a close associate of Morris L. Cooke and in the 1920s lobbied strongly in favor of the Giant Power proposals in Pennsylvania. Nominally a Republican, he saw his loyalties to the people rather than the Party. He supported New Deal policies that he saw as beneficial to farmers. He was a major supporter of the REA and introduced the bill to the Senate that ultimately passed to create an independent REA financed by congressional authorizations.

After leaving the Senate in 1942 Norris died on September 3, 1944, in his adopted state of Nebraska.

Gifford Pinchot (1865–1946). As governor of Pennsylvania, Gifford Pinchot created the Giant Power Board, which conducted a study of electrical power systems that greatly influenced later decisions regarding ways to achieve rural electrification. Born in Connecticut Pinchot graduated from Yale University in 1889 and then studied in France, Switzerland, Germany, and Austria. He specialized in forestry and in 1896 became a member of the commission that developed a plan for American forests. He moved up in government offices responsible for forests and became the first head of the Forest Service in the Department of Agriculture. In this position, which he held until 1910, he became a principal leader of the conservation movement and subscribed to the progressive ideology. This ideology held that government action was sometimes needed to assure the public good. He teamed up with Theodore Roosevelt to found the independent Bull Moose Party in 1912. After leaving the federal government, Pinchot became state forester of Pennsylvania in 1920. This led to his election as governor of Pennsylvania, an office he held from 1923 to 1927 and from 1931 to 1935.

While serving as governor of Pennsylvania, Pinchot set about asserting state authority in the areas of capital and business and in promoting social welfare. Since he believed that private utility companies were setting unreasonably high rates and by not providing rural service were unresponsive to the needs of the public, he created the Giant Power Board under the direction of Morris Cooke to study the matter and propose solutions. Although the forward-looking (and in the climate of the times, even radical) proposals of the Giant Power Board were not approved by the Pennsylvania legislature, the Giant Power study and proposed plan formed a strong basis for a continuing fight nationwide to bring electric service to rural areas.

Sam Rayburn (1882–1961). As a leader in the U.S. House of Representatives, Democrat Sam Rayburn was instrumental in the passage of the bill that created the REA as an independent agency authorized by Congress. Rayburn was born in Tennessee, but moved to northeastern Texas at that age of five with his family, who bought a cotton farm. One of 11 children, he experienced the privations of a poor Southern farmer. He nevertheless worked his way through East Texas College and studied law at the University of Texas. After practicing law for a time, he was elected as a U.S. Representative in 1912 and remained a member of Congress until he died in 1961. During his long tenure there, he became a powerful leader, well known for his abilities to achieve consensus and compromise. In 1936, when it became clear that the REA could not become an effective agency within the Executive Branch, where it had to compete for funding with other Executive offices, Rayburn agreed to lend his assistance. He saw the REA as a way to help farm families improve their standard of living. While Senator Norris introduced a bill in the Senate to establish an independent REA by statutory authority of Congress, Rayburn introduced a similar bill to the House and guided it through the legislative process. When faced with a dispute between those who wanted to exclude private power companies from REA programs and those who felt that the private companies were essential partners, Rayburn urged that there was a place for both private and public participants in rural electrification. His experience with the personalities involved and his skills as a parliamentarian proved effective in securing enough votes for passage in the House and in finding a compromise between the Senate and House versions of the bill.

Rayburn became Speaker of the House in 1940 and presided over the 1952 and 1956 Democratic Party National Conventions.

Primary Sources

Electricity Can Improve the Lives of Farmers...

Gifford Pinchot, political and conservation leader and governor of Pennsylvania, saw the American farm as a traditional source of American strength and stability. He was concerned that the farm sector of the population was falling behind the urban sector in terms of opportunity. This excerpt is from a speech (Speech of Gifford Pinchot Before National Electric Light Association) he delivered on May 21, 1924. It was printed in the Morris L. Cooke Papers, and reprinted in Clayton Brown's *Electricity for Rural America: The Fight for the REA,* 1980, p. xvi.

Only electric service can put the farmer on an equality with the townsmen and preserve the farm as the nursery of men and leaders of men that it has been in the past.

...And the Lives of All Americans

Herbert Hoover, as Secretary of Commerce, was among those who believed that electrical power was a key to improving the lives of all Americans. He made the following statement to the Super Power Conference on October 13, 1923 (also from Brown, p. 28).

Every time we cheapen power and decentralize its production, we create new uses and we add security to production; we also increase the production; we eliminate waste; we decrease the burden of physical effort upon men. In sum, we increase the standards of living and comfort of all our people.

The Importance of Electricity

The personal significance of electrification on the American farm is poignantly communicated by this poem written by an anonymous housewife and printed in 1938 in "REA Co-op Message," Bulletin [July 1938]; (quoted in Brown, p. 75).

When you and I were seventeen, it was different on
the farm . . .
Sure we had running water, but we had to run out to
the pump with a pail to get it.
Blue Monday got its name from the way the
womenfolk felt at the end of the washday.
We didn't have radio, electricity is required to power
them.
Now things are different—since the high line went in.
There is just as much to do on the farm as ever, but it
is a lot easier to do it.

Need for Helping Cooperatives

John M. Carmody, who succeeded Cooke as REA Administrator, recognized that farm people themselves had to take the initiative in forming cooperatives that could qualify for REA loans. This was not an easy task, as farmers generally were inexperienced

in such forms of organizing. Carmody and the REA encouraged and assisted farmers in this enterprise. His understanding of the problems involved is expressed in this quote from a radio address sponsored by the National Grange in 1937 and reprinted in the Rural Electrification Administration's *Annual Reports, 1935–1956,*(p. 10):

Much as the farmers have wanted electricity—and they have wanted it; they have seized it wherever it has been made available at reasonable terms—they have not seen the way clear to overcome the obstacles presented by the necessity of an organization for financing, promotion, construction, and operation. One doesn't go into a retail store and buy a package of electricity over the counter.

Anticipating Electricity

The anticipation and excitement of farm people who were soon to be connected to the power grid was remarkable. They typically did all they could to prepare for the coming of electricity. The following quote from a letter written to the REA by the superintendent of a Michigan project, from the REA's *Annual Reports, 1935–1956,*(p. 22), describes this phenomenon.

If you were here, I could take you to hundreds of homes completely wired, with fixtures hung and bulbs in place, ready for the 'zero hour' when the lines will first be energized. I could take you to homes where electric ranges, electric refrigerators, radios, and even electric clocks are installed and ready for operation.

The First Day of Electricity

People at the beginning of the twenty-first century find it difficult to imagine the feelings of farm families when their homes were supplied with electrical power for the first time. For those who lived through it, this was one of the most memorable experiences of a lifetime. The following narrative is by a dairy farmer in Kentucky who was a boy when this event took place. It is from the REA's *Annual Reports, 1935–1956,*(p. 23).

We kept a lantern hanging beside the kitchen door . . . Winter mornings I'd take that lantern and head for the barn. It would be so dark out you'd think you were in a box with the lid shut. We always had at least a dozen cows to milk, and just my Dad and me to do it.

I had a lot of other chores to do before I went to school . . . that made me late to school some mornings. I'd fill the wood box beside the kitchen stove and I'd bring in a bucket of water. Sometimes the pump would be frozen solid and I'd have to thaw it out before I could pump the water.

Soon as I'd get home from school I had chores to do, and then an early supper, and after that I'd get at my homework. I'd study by a kerosene lamp in the kitchen, up close to the stove. We all spent most of our time in the kitchen during the winter.

We'd heard that the Government was going to lend us money to get lights, but we didn't believe it until we saw the men putting up the poles. Every day they came closer, and we realized it really was going to happen. So Dad went ahead and had the house wired.

It was almost two months later before they finished the job and turned on the power. I'll never forget that day—it was late on a November afternoon, just before dark. All we had was wires hanging down from the ceiling in every room, with bare bulbs on the end. Dad turned on the one in the kitchen first, and he just stood there, holding onto the pull-chain. He said to me, 'Carl, come here and hang onto this so I can turn on the light in the sitting room.'

I knew he didn't have to do that and I told him to stop holding it, that it would say on. He finally let go, and then looked kind of foolish.

Suggested Research Topics

- As a thought experiment, imagine a typical day in your life without electricity. List all the ways in which your life would be different and what that would mean to you.

- Follow your home's electricity back to its source. Where does your electricity come from, how is it generated, distributed, and transmitted? Who sends your electric bill and how is your electric payment used?

- Explore the history of electric service in your community. When and how did electricity first become available? What were the first uses and who were the first users? Describe the process whereby electricity became an accepted part of everyday life where you live.

Bibliography

Sources

"Biographies: Morris Llewellyn Cooke (1872–1960)," [cited February 28, 2002] available from the World Wide Web at http://newdeal.feri.org/bios/bio10.htm.

Brown, D. Clayton. *Electricity for Rural America: The Fight for the REA.* Westport, CN: Greenwood Press, 1980.

Cooke, Morris L. "The Early Days of the Rural Electrification Idea: 1914–1936," *American Political Science Review,* June 1948.

Rural Electrification Administration. *Rural Lines, USA: The Story of the Rural Electrification Administration's First Twenty-five Years, 1935–1960.* Washington, DC: U.S. Department of Agriculture, Rural Electrification Administration (Miscellaneous Publication No. 811), 1960.

Stone, Norman F. *Bountiful McKenzie: The Story of the Eugene Water & Electric Board.* Eugene, OR: Parkstone Company, 1986.

Tobey, Ronald C. *Technology as Freedom: The New Deal and the Electrical Modernization of the American Home.* Berkeley: University of California Press, 1996.

Further Reading

Cooke, Morris, ed. *What Electricity Costs.* New York: New Republic, 1933.

Garwood, John D. *The Rural Electrification Administration, An Evaluation.* Washington, DC: American Enterprise Institute, 1963.

Muller, Frederick. *Public Rural Electrification.* Washington, DC: American Council Public Affairs, 1944.

Person, H. S. "The Rural Electrification Administration in Perspective," *Agricultural History,* 24 (April 1950): 70-89.

Richardson, L. K. *Wisconsin REA: The Struggle to Extend Electricity to Rural Wisconsin 1935–1955.* Madison: University of Wisconsin Experiment Station, 1961.

Rural Electrification Administration. *Annual Reports, 1935–1956.*

Slattery, Harry. *Rural America Lights Up.* Washington, DC: National Home Library Foundation, 1940.

See Also

Tennessee Valley Authority; Water and Power

Social Security

Introduction

Historians consider the Social Security Act of 1935 one of the most revolutionary pieces of social legislation ever passed by Congress. The Social Security program was one of many pieces of legislation passed as part of President Franklin D. Roosevelt's (served 1933–1945) New Deal. The New Deal was a sweeping series of federal relief and recovery measures passed between 1933 and 1938 designed to bring prosperity back to the United States. The measures greatly increased the role of government in the daily lives of citizens and in the private marketplace of the economy. The Social Security program speaks to a universal human need—the need to face the future with some measure of economic security. All people at one time or another face uncertainties brought on by job loss, illness, disability, or old age.

Prior to the twentieth century, most people in the United States relied on the family farm and their extended family for economic security. The industrial revolution brought fundamental and permanent changes. By the early twentieth century being old, disabled, or jobless too often meant being penniless and helpless. The Great Depression triggered a crisis in the nation's economic life more severe than ever before. Twenty-five percent of workers could not find employment, and poverty among the elderly grew dramatically. By 1934 over half the elderly in America lacked sufficient income to support themselves.

1935-1941

Chronology:

June 8, 1934: President Franklin D. Roosevelt notifies Congress that he will seek federal legislation to promote economic security.

June 29, 1934: President Roosevelt creates the Committee on Economic Security to study problems related to economic security and to make recommendations for legislation.

January 17, 1935: The Committee on Economic Security introduces its recommendations to the 74th Congress.

August 14, 1935: President Roosevelt signs into law the Social Security Act.

August 23, 1935: The Senate confirms the President's nomination of the first members of the Social Security Board: John G. Winant, chairman; Arthur J. Altmeyer, and Vincent M. Miles.

November 24, 1936: The U.S. Post Office distributes applications to the public for Social Security account numbers.

January 1, 1937: Workers begin earning credits toward old-age insurance benefits.

February 19, 1937: Arthur J. Altmeyer is named as new chairman of the Social Security Board.

March 11, 1937: The first old-age insurance benefit is paid (one time payment only).

May 24, 1937: The U.S. Supreme Court upholds the constitutionality of the old-age and unemployment insurance provisions of the Social Security Act.

June 30, 1937: All states approve laws making available unemployment compensation under Title III of the Social Security Act making it a nationwide program.

September 1938: All states, the District of Columbia, and the territories of Alaska and Hawaii begin making old-age assistance payments under Title I of the Social Security Act.

August 3, 1939: Arthur J. Altmeyer is reappointed for a six-year term as the chairman of the Social Security Board.

August 10, 1939: Social Security Act Amendments of 1939 provide old age and survivors' insurance benefits for dependents and survivors.

By 1934 President Roosevelt was convinced the nation needed some sort of long-term social insurance program. Social insurance is a broad term referring to government sponsored social programs such as old age retirement programs, unemployment insurance, support for workers injured on the job, and healthcare programs. Social insurance programs had been prevalent in European countries since the late nineteenth century.

President Roosevelt assembled a team in the summer of 1934 to hammer out details of an American social insurance program, called a "cradle to grave" plan. Thirteen and a half months later President Roosevelt signed the Social Security Act of 1935. Americans eagerly climbed on the bandwagon of Social Security and have proved fiercely protective of the program ever since.

The original Social Security Act of 1935 reached out to Americans under four broad categories: (1) monetary assistance for needy elderly persons, children, and blind individuals; (2) a federal old-age retirement plan; (3) unemployment compensation; and, (4) extension of public health services. For the first time the American public came to expect that the federal government would be involved in its social welfare.

In the years following 1935 the Social Security program broadened to include survivors' benefits when a family's wage earner dies, disability benefits, health care benefits, and automatic cost of living increases. The program has remained flexible and changed over time to meet changing circumstances. The twenty-first century brings new challenges with an aging population and a continuing need to provide security for workers and their families.

Issue Summary

Introduction of Social Insurance

The campaign for a general security program had to be conducted on a broad front involving the viewpoints and experiences of many. Central to this fight would be Frances Perkins. Four years into the Great Depression in 1933, the 53 year-old Perkins came to Washington. Reared in Massachusetts and educated at Mount Holyoke College, Perkins had earlier traded a privileged life for the slums of Chicago. There she lived with Jane Addams, a prominent social worker, at Hull House. She vigorously supported social justice causes in Chicago, then in New York City where she became fast friends with progressive Democrats like Franklin D. Roosevelt and U.S. Senator Robert F. Wagner of New York. Perkins served as director of investigations for the New York State Factory Commission, and as chairman of the State Industrial Board. In 1919 Governor Alfred E. Smith appointed her to the office of Industrial Commission of the State of New York. When Franklin D. Roosevelt became governor of New York in 1928, he appointed her industrial commissioner to head New York state's labor department. The enormously effective Perkins persuaded Governor Roosevelt to aggressively fight the Great Depression in New York by supporting state and regional unemployment insurance and relief projects. In 1930 Governor Roosevelt, highly interested in all aspects of social insurance, signed New York State's old-age pension legislation. Within a few years about 35 states had passed old-age pension plans in various forms.

Following his election as U.S. president in 1932, President-elect Roosevelt chose Perkins to head the Department of Labor, a department she later recalled to be full of large, cigar-smoking men. Prior to accepting the appointment, Perkins laid out extensive goals. These included unemployment and old-age insurance, and setting minimum wage and maximum hours standards. President-elect Roosevelt, the single national political leader to identify himself with the social insurance cause, agreed that he and Perkins would explore unemployment and old-age insurance as soon as he assumed office. Hence in March 1933 Perkins agreed to become the first woman cabinet member in U.S. history. Concerning social legislation, Perkins was to be the most knowledgeable, dominant voice in the ear of President Roosevelt. For Perkins, known as "Madam Secretary" to her subordinates, once the immediate problems of hunger and poverty had been addressed, the foremost goal was to create a permanent system of social insurance to aid the personal security of the people of the United States.

Wagner-Lewis Bill—An Unemployment Insurance Plan

The distress of the country was great at the time of President Roosevelt's 1933 inauguration and the unemployment numbers alarming. In response the president speedily began to investigate unemployment

Biography:
Frances Perkins

1880–1965 Always proud of her New England common sense and generally wearing a felt triangular hat, Perkins became the first woman ever appointed to a cabinet post. Franklin D. Roosevelt appointed her as Secretary of the Department of Labor in 1933.

Perkins left the privileged life of her birthplace, Boston, Massachusetts, to become a vigorous advocate for social justice in Chicago and New York. She became secretary of the New York Consumers' League (1910–1912) and of the Committee on Safety of the City of New York (1912–1915), where she was exposed to the horrors of sweatshops. Perkins was named to the New York State Industrial Board where she handled workmen's compensation cases. She took over the chairmanship in 1926 and Roosevelt reappointed her when he became governor of New York in 1929. Perkins lobbied for stricter factory safety laws, protective labor laws for women and children, and an eight-hour workday.

When Roosevelt was elected president in 1932, he chose the articulate Perkins as his Secretary of Labor where she was known as "Madam Secretary." They shared similar views on the need for social insurance including unemployment and old age pensions. Named chairman of Roosevelt's Committee on Economic Security in 1934, she guided the crafting of the Social Security Act of 1935. At the act's signing, Roosevelt gave much of the credit for its passage to Perkins.

and old-age insurance. Of these two forms of social insurance, unemployment insurance seemed the most urgent. The only plan in existence in the United States was the Wisconsin plan adopted in 1932 with which both the President and Perkins were thoroughly familiar. The plan, originally worked out by Professor John R. Commons of the University of Wisconsin, required corporations to set aside unemployment funds to care for their own employees. The amount of money the Wisconsin plan required each employer to set aside was based on a "merit rating." Each corporation was

Frances Perkins greets President Franklin D. Roosevelt in 1943. Perkins was instrumental in getting the Social Security Act passed in 1935. (© Bettmann/Corbis. Reproduced by permission.)

rated on how successful it was in maintaining employment. Those companies who frequently laid off workers had to put away the most money in an unemployment fund. On the other hand, employers who provided their workers with steady employment had low rates of contributions to their unemployment fund. The plan, therefore, encouraged corporations to keep employment steady.

Another unemployment scheme, proposed in 1932 by the Ohio Commission on Unemployment Insurance but not actually in operation, differed considerably. The Ohio plan proposed that contributions come from both employers and workers. The funds would be pooled in a large single statewide fund rather than having individual corporations maintain their own separate funds. Neither plan envisioned government contributions to the funds.

Some experts believed both plans had serious flaws. One of the most outspoken critics was Abraham Epstein, a key contributor to the creation of early social insurance policies in the states. According to Epstein the Wisconsin plan was doomed because no one business could control overall economic conditions so as to totally control their employment needs. Another criticism of both unemployment plans was that the contributions required of employers would increase the cost of doing business. This would in turn decrease corporate profits and hinder their ability to compete.

In the fall of 1933 a group of liberal businessmen and young New Dealers met in Washington, DC with Paul A. Roushenbush, an early shaper of the Wisconsin plan. His wife, Elizabeth, was the daughter of Supreme Court Justice Louis D. Brandeis. Brandeis had devised a clever plan calling for a payroll tax on employers to be paid into a pooled fund for each state. The amount of the tax could then be deducted from the companies' federal tax bill. With the tax deduction, the plan would cost employers less. This was the plan that the Roushenbushes shared at the meeting.

Thomas H. Eliot, a lawyer in the Department of Labor, attended the Roushenbushes' meeting and relayed the plan to Perkins. Perkins, impressed with the creativity of the plan, instructed Roushenbush and Eliot to draw up a bill using this new idea. They realized the bill was rough but hoped it could provide a sounding board from which more complete legislation would evolve. Enthused, President Roosevelt encouraged immediate introduction of the unemployment insurance bill. So in February 1934 the Wagner-Lewis bill went to Congress. Senator Robert F. Wagner introduced it into the Senate and Representative David J. Lewis of Maryland in the House of Representatives.

Dill-Connery, an Old Age Pension Bill

Meanwhile a bill dealing with old-age pensions was working its way through Congress. The issue of old age pensions actually had a much longer history in the United States than unemployment insurance. The American Association for Labor Legislation (AALL) called for development of old-age pension plans in 1906 and states began to explore the issue. Eight states passed voluntary programs in the 1920s. The Great Depression accentuated the plight of the aged. By the early 1930s, 35 states and many private companies enacted various forms of pension plans. Their payment and coverage varied widely among the states. Epstein, who had founded the Association of Old Age Security, believed a nationwide approach was essential. He proposed a plan where the federal government would give states monetary grants equal to a third of the amount each state spent on pensions. For example, if a state spent $300,000 on pensions, the

At a Glance
Workers' Compensation—Social Security Related Legislation

The first form of social insurance to develop in Western Europe and the United States was Workmen's Compensation. Workers' Compensation, as it came to be called, exists in all fifty states today. Additionally there were two federal programs: the Longshore and Harbor Workers' Compensation Act and the Federal Employees' Compensation Act. Programs provided cash benefits and medical care to workers who sustained a work related illness or injury. Benefits were also paid to surviving dependents of workers who died as a result of illness or injury.

States enact their own workers' compensation laws. The programs are generally financed by employers with the costs higher in more dangerous industries. The length of time benefits may be paid varies among states. Total disability is often 66 percent of the worker's wage at the time of injury.

federal government would give the state $100,000. Senator Clarence C. Dill of Washington and Representative William P. Connery, Jr. introduced a bill to Congress in 1932 incorporating these ideas. By 1934 the House of Representatives had passed the Dill-Connery Bill and the Senate Pensions Committee had given it a favorable report.

Spring 1934—Congressional Hearings; Townsend Stirrings

Hearings before Congress on both bills were in full swing in the spring of 1934. Experts testified as to the effectiveness of the measures. President Roosevelt hoped the congressional committees could fashion acceptable programs.

President Roosevelt urged Frances Perkins to discuss the matter with as many groups as possible. She began with the Cabinet, bringing up the matter frequently until other cabinet members became as interested as she was. Perkins also made hundreds of speeches across the country, always stressing social insurance as a way of assisting the unemployed in

Social Welfare Public Program Expenditures, 1890-1940

Year	Total Dollars in millions	Percent of Government Expenditures
1890	$318	38.0%
1913	1,000	24.0
1929	3,921	36.3
1930	4,085	n/a
1931	4,201	n/a
1932	4,303	n/a
1933	4,462	n/a
1934	5,832	n/a
1935	6,548	48.6
1936	10,184	n/a
1937	7,858	n/a
1938	7,924	n/a
1939	9,213	n/a
1940	8,795	49.0

U.S. government became much more involved in social welfare programs during the 1930s, with expenditures peaking in 1936. (The Gale Group.)

depression times. Further, she suggested it was a means to aid in preventing further economic depression. With social insurance payments people would continue to have a little money to spend on goods, thus helping businesses. Americans nationwide began to talk and write about social insurance topics.

Francis E. Townsend and Huey P. Long

As Congress was debating the insurance bills a medical doctor in California, Francis E. Townsend, and U.S. Senator Huey P. Long of Louisiana suggested their own versions of social insurance plans. Both rapidly gained widespread popular support.

Dr. Townsend's medical practice in Long Beach provided such a meager income he had to supplement it with work as a realtor. Sixty-seven years old in 1933 and nearly destitute, Townsend wrote a letter to the editor of the *Long Beach Telegram.* Townsend described his idea of a two percent national sales tax, the proceeds of which would pay $200 per month to every citizen over 60 years of age who was not employed and not a criminal. Recipients had to spend each monthly payment within thirty days. As a result this expenditure would create jobs for young people. George Murray, editor of the Townsend movement newspaper, recounted that the letter was published in newspapers all over the country. Immediately thousands of letters came to Townsend in support of his plan and Townsend Clubs sprung up all over the

nation. Those eligible for the benefits suddenly saw a way out of economic misery. The $200 proposal in 1934 would be roughly equivalent to $3,900 per month in 1998 dollars.

Popularity of the Townsend Plan pressured President Roosevelt to act on the issue of old-age insurance. As concerned as Roosevelt was over the Townsend plan, however, he was even more alarmed over Senator Long and his "Share-Our-Wealth" societies, which enrolled five million members by 1934. Long proposed programs for old-age pensions for those over 60, which included health care, free college education, unemployment insurance, and public relief. He called for a massive redistribution of wealth in the United States, playing on the widely held public sentiment that the wealthy were to blame for the Great Depression. He proposed levying huge taxes on incomes over $1 million and inheritances over $5 million. Revenue from the taxes would pay for such offerings as a $2,500 base income for every family and a $5,000 homestead allotment. Long's slogans of "every man a king," "soak the rich," and "a chicken in every pot" sparked public imagination. Senator Long intended to run for president in 1936 using his proposals as a springboard. Roosevelt feared Long's strength would steal enough votes from the Democrats to allow the election of a Republican as president in 1936. The pressure of the Townsend Plan and the "Share-Our-Wealth" movement no doubt propelled the formation of Roosevelt's social security plan.

President Roosevelt's Plan for Action

As Congress and the public debated and contemplated the various proposals in the spring of 1934, President Roosevelt began to raise concerns. He stressed that the provisions within the bills before Congress needed more study. Committee agreement had not been reached on the Wagner-Lewis bill. Testimony and recommendations varied widely. Moreover, the president began to believe that a social insurance program for the United States should be a single piece of legislation, a package deal rather than piecemeal laws. Yet with millions of Americans following Townsend and Long, President Roosevelt did not have much time for further study.

As hearings proceeded the weather grew hot in Washington, and by June 1934 Congress was exhausted and grumpy. Rather than continuing to push for immediate action, President Roosevelt decided to follow another course. He told Congress he would happily agree to an adjournment as long as they understood his summer and fall plans to pursue social insurance issues. He would have an in-depth study conducted during the next six months, and then he would present a full proposal for social insurance to Congress when they reconvened on the first of January 1935. Congress readily agreed, and President Roosevelt prepared a message of formal notification of his plans.

On June 8, 1934, President Roosevelt sent to Congress a message addressing broad social insurance issues relating his intention to have a plan formulated by year's end. With the hardships facing many Americans weighing heavy on his mind, Roosevelt stated, "People want some safeguard against misfortunes which cannot be wholly eliminated in this man-made world of ours." He noted that lessons could be taken from the states, from industries as in Wisconsin, and from many nations of the civilized world. He emphasized that the various forms of social insurance are related, therefore they should be addressed together, not "piecemeal," with random pieces of legislation. He expressed his desire to safeguard individuals against "several of the great disturbing facets in life," particularly those associated with "unemployment and old age." (Roosevelt, *The Public Papers and Addresses of Franklin D. Roosevelt,* p. 291) Congress promptly accepted the notification and gratefully adjourned.

Committee on Economic Security

On June 29, 1934, President Roosevelt issued Executive Order No. 6767 creating the Committee on Economic Security. The committee would study social insurance issues raised in his June 8 address. He scheduled December 1, 1934, as the date for the committee to report its recommendations to him. The order also created a Citizen Advisory Council to assist the committee. Frances Perkins had recommended the committee consist of cabinet members, an idea President Roosevelt readily agreed to. He immediately realized a program developed by a committee of cabinet members would be under his control. It would not likely get into political disputes or publicity showmanship. President Roosevelt insisted Perkins be the committee's chairman, saying: "I know you will put your back to it more than anyone else and drive it through." (Perkins, *The Roosevelt I Knew,* p. 281). Thus the committee consisted of Chairman Frances Perkins, secretary of labor; Henry Morgenthau, Jr., secretary of the Treasury; Homer Cummings, U.S. attorney general; Henry A. Wallace, secretary of agriculture; and, Harry L. Hopkins, Federal Emergency Relief Administrator.

This cabinet committee turned out to be a good mix. Consideration of the issues came from people with different lines of responsibility and with different approaches. The treasury department examined both the most conservative as well as advanced views for financing such a program. The attorney general made it possible to have legal and constitutional problems analyzed before viewpoints became fixed. Hopkins, the principle relief officer, presented the most pressing needs of the people caught up in the Depression.

An executive director and staff would analyze how the whole social insurance program would work under the direction of a Technical Board. Dr. Edwin E. Witte, chairman of the Department of Economics at the University of Wisconsin, was offered the executive director position on July 24, 1934. He arrived in Washington on July 26, ready to work. Having just graduated from the University of Wisconsin, 21-year old Wilbur J. Cohen also came to Washington to serve as research assistant to Witte. Arthur J. Altmeyer, also from Wisconsin, became the chairman of the Technical Board. Having all come from Wisconsin, Witte, Cohen, and Altmeyer were heavily schooled in Wisconsin's social insurance ideas. Witte and Altmeyer, along with Perkins, controlled virtually all development of the economic security proposals.

From "Cradle to Grave" As the Committee on Economic Security began its work, President Roosevelt's imaginative mind had begun to establish certain basic principles that he hoped would be at the center of the economic security proposal. The President wanted a simple system that everyone could understand. Also President Roosevelt saw no reason why only industrial workers should get benefits. Instead, he believed that every worker and his entire family should be involved. When he expressed these ideas to Perkins she shook her head in dismay. To Perkins, Roosevelt's suggestion for so broad a system right from the start seemed over ambitious since they had almost no experience in such matters. Roosevelt pressed Perkins, however, saying, "I don't see why not. I don't see why not. Cradle to the grave—from the cradle to the grave they ought to be in a social insurance system." (Perkins, *The Roosevelt I Knew,* p. 283) In the beginning Roosevelt had to compromise many of his ideas; however, 60 years later, at the end of the twentieth century, social insurance programs looked remarkably like the program he first envisioned in 1934.

Debates of the Committee on Economic Security

The Committee on Economic Security began six months of intense work, resolving conflicting positions on both unemployment insurance and old age pensions. Problems of the unemployment compensation plan took more time than anything else. The basic question was: (1) whether to have a state based program employing the methods suggested in the original Wagner-Lewis plan, or (2) a national plan run and financed by the federal government. The arguments swayed back and forth all summer and into the fall. The president was known to favor the state plan for several reasons: (1) it would allow states to experiment; (2) he feared Congress would not approve a national plan; and, (3) he was unsure of the constitutionality of a national plan. Witte and Altmeyer also favored the state-based plan, while Perkins leaned more to a national system. Observers noted the committee steered clear of such experts as Epstein, who was known to advocate a national plan with federal government funding. His exclusion reflected the overall skepticism they had of the federal government funding an entire national program. Although President Roosevelt had set a December 1 deadline, the debate carried on until late December.

At last Perkins issued an ultimatum, the Committee would meet at her house at eight o'clock on a Christmas week evening. The telephone service was disconnected and she declared they would work all night if need be until they resolved the thorny question. At two in the morning with some reservations, all present agreed to the state based system of the Wagner-Lewis bill. That is, states would set up their own unemployment funds. The federal government would tax employers and those taxes would go to the state funds. Employers could deduct the amount of the tax from their federal tax bill.

The old-age pension plan caused less fuss. The Townsend Clubs were in full swing and the public clamored for an old age pension plan. The major question was not whether to have a plan but how to fund such a plan. Should it be funded out of government general revenues? Or should employers and employees make equal contributions with employees gradually accumulating credits to receive monetary payments in their old age? The second approach won, much to the dismay of liberals who saw the first option as a redistribution of wealth. Redistribution of wealth thinking worked like this: Most all citizens, including the wealthy, paid taxes so some of the wealthy people's tax money would go to pay old-age pensions. Few wealthy, however, actually worked at a job where they would have contributions taken from their paychecks. Many viewed the employer-employee contribution plan as the poor and middle class worker paying entirely for their own old-age pension.

President Roosevelt looked at the winning old-age pension plan funding from another angle. With

payroll taxes funding pensions, the cost to the treasury was nothing. More importantly, since workers had paid their own money into the plan they would always have a moral and legal right to collect the money back in the form of pensions. No one could call it charity or a handout. Besides, Roosevelt observed, if Congress funded the plan out of general government revenues, Congress could always cut back or even eliminate the programs when economic times improved. President Roosevelt forcefully stated, "With those [payroll] taxes in there, no damn politician can ever scrap my social security program." (Leuchtenburg, William E. *Franklin D. Roosevelt and the New Deal: 1932–1940*, p. 133) It is notable that a new term, "social security" had now replaced "social insurance."

Another recommendation coming out of the Committee included federal grants to states that came to be known as public assistance. These grants would pay for support of the already aged population who would not be paying into the social security pension system. The committee recommended grants to the states to help pay benefits to the blind and to dependent children. This recommendation led to the creation of the Aid to Dependent Children program, which formerly had been called mother's pensions, widow's pensions, or mother's aid.

The Committee made no recommendation on the question of national health insurance. Overwhelming opposition was coming from the American Medical Association and the business community, who were fearful of government control of medical procedures and payment to doctors. It was the same reaction of any employer to potential government imposed costs on their business. This indicated to the Committee that a national health insurance proposal might severely damage the chances of passing the entire social security package.

To Congress—The Social Security Bill

On January 17, 1935, President Roosevelt submitted to Congress the work of the Committee on Economic Security. Altmeyer drafted the legislation and Senator Wagner introduced the bill in the Senate. Representatives Lewis and Dobert L. Doughton of North Carolina, chairman of the House Ways and Means Committee, introduced the bill in the House. In a rare procedure, hearings in both chambers were to take place at the same time. The Roosevelt administration had requested simultaneous hearings to hasten passage of the bill, which had become known as the "social security bill."

Before 1933 the term "social security" was not used in the United States or in other countries.

President Franklin D. Roosevelt did not use the term on June 8, 1934, when he notified Congress that he would undertake the task of developing a plan to further the security of individuals and their families. Nor did he use the term later that month when he created the Committee on Economic Security to study economic security and make proposals for legislation. "Social insurance" was the commonly used expression at the time.

In early 1935, during the course of Congressional hearings on the social insurance legislation, several witnesses spoke of "social security." William Green, president of the American Federation of Labor and Abraham Epstein, theorist, both used the term. The *Washington Post* referred to the legislation as the "social security bill." According to Arthur J. Altmeyer, however, a key developer of the bill, Mr. Epstein was probably most responsible for conception of the term.

Mr. Epstein founded the American Association for Old Age Security in the 1920s. He had spent all of his monetary resources trying to keep the association alive. Epstein decided to change the name of the association to one that implied a broader scope but he still wanted to use all his old letterhead stationery. He hit upon the name American Association for Social Security. Epstein could simply cross out "Old Age" and substitute "Social" which is just what he did. Epstein made no attempt to actually define "social security" but it quickly replaced the term "social insurance." Members of Congress began to refer to the "social security bill." "Social security" would soon be in everyday usage throughout the United States. Senator Pat Harrison of Mississippi, chairman of the Senate Committee on Finance, shepherded the "social security" bill through the Senate.

So much publicity surrounded the introduction of the bill that Doughton scheduled his House Ways and Means Committee hearings to start a day earlier than Harrison's Senate committee hearings. In addition to Perkins, Witte and Altmeyer, a battalion of economists, labor leaders, and social workers who had advised the Committee on Economic Security during previous months testified before the House and Senate committees. Perhaps the most famous individual to come before the committee was Dr. Francis Townsend. Townsend, facing a semicircle of hostile senators, testified before the Senate Finance Committee. The angry senators knew that Townsend's plan sounded like a fix-all to the public but in reality would cost so much that it would ultimately bankrupt the government.

At an early hearing before the House Ways and Means Committee, Secretary Morgenthau startled his fellow members of the Committee on Economic Secu-

Public Program Expenditures, 1890-1940
as a percentage of Gross National Product

Year	Percent of GNP
1890	2.4%
1913	2.5
1929	3.9
1930	4.2
1931	5.1
1932	6.4
1933	7.9
1934	9.7
1935	9.5
1936	13.2
1937	9.1
1938	9.0
1939	10.5
1940	9.2

Public program expenditures as a percentage of Gross National Product, select years, 1890–1940.
(The Gale Group.)

rity by arguing against coverage for everyone under the bill. Universal coverage had already been agreed to by the Committee on Economic Security members including Morgenthau. Nevertheless, he now testified that it would be very difficult to collect payroll payments from scattered farm and domestic workers and from the many small businesses employing less than ten people. The Ways and Means Committee agreed. President Roosevelt and his administration felt pressure to compromise on this key issue. Much to their consternation they realized that the bill would not cover everyone.

On April 5, the House Ways and Means Committee reported out to the House of Representatives its version of the social security bill. House Republicans faithfully, reflecting the opposition of business to the bill, lashed out at the legislation. But in the end, fearing defeat at the polls, most Republicans who had resisted every step of the way voted in favor of the bill. On April 19 the House passed the social security bill 371 to 33.

The Senate Finance Committee did not report the bill out of committee until May 17. Debate began in the full Senate on June 14. It took five days for Senator Harrison to move the bill through the Senate. Huey P. Long, in his usual cocky manner, gave notice he would lower the pension age from 65 to 60 and enlarge benefits through his "share the wealth, soak the rich" plan. Long was finally silenced and his $5 billion wealth distribution plan fell to defeat. Senator

Left to right, Arthur J. Altmeyer, John G. Winant, and Vincent E. Miles, the new Social Security board, meet in 1935. John G. Winant was appointed as chairman of the group. (AP/Wide World Photos. Reproduced by permission.)

Bennett Clark of Missouri threw up the next obstacle. He wanted to exempt industries from the plan if they already had private pension plans. The Senate adopted Clark's amendment and the entire bill passed by a Senate vote of 76 to 6 on June 19.

The House and Senate versions of the bill were in complete agreement except for the Clark amendment. The House refused to go along with exemption of any private companies from the pension plans. The Senate yielded to the House and struck out the Clark amendment. On August 14, 1935, President Roosevelt, surrounded by more than 30 individuals who had worked for passage of the bill, signed the Social Security Act of 1935 into law. President Roosevelt insisted on singling out Perkins as one of those most responsible for the bill's passage.

The Social Security Act of 1935

President Roosevelt created the Committee on Economic Security on June 29, 1934, and signed the Social Security Act on August 14, 1935. As remarkable and impossible as it seemed, the complex and innovative piece of legislation took only thirteen and a half months to become law.

The explanation for the government's quick action lies in the fact that the United States was in the middle of an extreme economic depression and in a state of massive social disruption. Bankrupt states could not support even the smallest social programs. Radical quick fixes such as the Townsend Plan and Long's Share-Our-Wealth societies had gathered public support and put pressure on the government to act. A determined Committee on Economic Security calmly set about to create a practical social insurance program—one that Congress could actually pass. The plan they formulated had the unfailing support of an extremely popular president who remained involved throughout the development process.

The original act had eleven titles or parts. The eleven could be grouped into four categories: (1) public assistance for the elderly who had already retired, dependent children and needy blind; (2) a federal old-age retirement plan; (3) unemployment compensation; and, (4) extension of public health services.

Title I dealt only with the elderly poor who had already retired when the Social Security Act passed. Since they were already retired they would never pay into the Social Security system. Title I provided to the states grants that paid half the cost of old age assistance (OAA) to the already retired elderly. States would pay the other half and determine the amount each retiree would receive monthly.

Title II was the most controversial provision. The Old-Age Benefits, later called Old-Age Insurance (OAI), established how the system of old-age pensions operated. Title VII actually spelled out the taxation of employers and employees to finance OAI. Holding to the notion people should provide for their own old age, business groups, Republican congressmen, and most conservatives were bitterly opposed to Title II. Although Title II was the beginning of the modern Social Security retirement system, only Roosevelt's shear determination to have the act passed in its entirety kept Title II intact.

Title III, the unemployment compensation plan, was considered the most important provision at the time of passage. Title IX dealt with its financing.

Title IV provided federal grants to states for dependent children. A dependent child was considered any child under the age of sixteen, who had been deprived of parental support or care. Formerly known as mother's or window's pensions, it was now Aid to Dependent Children (ADC).

Title V provided grants to states for promoting health of mothers and children, for care of crippled children, protection and care of neglected children, and small grants for retraining persons disabled in industry. Title V and Title X (aid to needy blind) were the only original programs dealing with the disabled.

Title VI provided grants to be made available by Public Health Services to aid states in establishing and maintaining public health services. It also provided funds to the Public Health Service for investigation of disease and for sanitation problems.

Title VII established a three member Social Security Board (SSB) to run all of the programs. It also contained wording to allow for research and study into "related subjects." It gave the SSB authority to research programs for future needs. This tiny part of the act was invaluable through the years and led to amendments adding Medicare and provisions for the disabled.

Title VIII directed the financing of Title II (OAI). Employers and employees would both pay a one percent tax on wages up to $3,000 yearly. In 1940 the tax was scheduled to increase by half a percentage point until it reached three percent in 1949. So in 1937 a person receiving wages of $3,000 a year would have a total of $30 taken out of their checks for OAI and their employers would match the contribution.

Title IX directed taxation of employers with eight or more employees to finance unemployment compensation. Each state would be responsible for setting up its unemployment system. As unemployment sys-

tems were set up employers could deduct the tax levied on them from their federal tax bill. The tax was 1 percent of payroll in 1936, 2 percent for 1937, and 3 percent for 1938.

Title X required the federal government to pay half the cost of benefits to the needy blind, while states would pay the other half.

Title XI defined terms and dealt with administration details.

The Social Security Board and the U.S. Postal Service

Three members for the Social Security Board needed to be chosen immediately to begin the monumental tasks before it. Perkins recommended John G. Winant, a former governor of New Hampshire, who had worked in industrial relations. President Roosevelt, considering Winant reliable and trustworthy, named him chairman. Perkins also recommended Arthur Altmeyer who had been involved from the very start in developing the social security plan. President Roosevelt cautioned that a Southerner must also be on the board. Vincent Miles, an Arkansas lawyer, became the third member.

The SSB threesome initially had no staff, no facilities, and no budgets. Yet they were to operate as an independent agency. A temporary budget came from Harry Hopkins' Federal Emergency Relief Administration. The SSB had the overwhelmingly complex tasks of providing employers, employees, and the public with information on how to report payroll earnings that would be subject to the Old Age Insurance Tax, what benefits would be available, and how benefits would get to the people.

The first massive undertaking was to register all employers and employees by January 1, 1937. That was when the first payments would be due to begin financing the old-age insurance plan. Certainly, three men could not accomplish this; therefore they contracted with the U.S. Postal Service to distribute applications beginning in November 1936. The post office employees collected all completed applications, assigned Social Security numbers (SSN), created the SSN cards, and then returned these cards with post office efficiency to the applicants. The application forms next arrived at the SSB's procuring center in Baltimore, Maryland. The agency recorded numbers and established employment records. Over 35 million SSN cards were issued in 1936 and 1937 and to many this new card in their wallets signaled a beginning attempt by the U.S. government at long term planning to lessen the suffering caused by

Applications for the first benefits of the Social Security Act are taken at a branch office in New York on December 13, 1939. (Bettmann/CORBIS. Reproduced by permission)

economically difficult times. All this was accomplished in record time well before the age of computers.

Despite staggering obstacles facing the Social Security Board, the challenge of start up had been undertaken with quiet efficiency. The SSB registered and issued millions of SSN cards, plus the programs of OAA gave state governments new funds to deal with their needy elderly. Within two years all 48 states had passed unemployment compensation laws taking advantage of the allowed federal tax offset.

The Early Years—1936, 1937, 1938

Social Security, particularly old-age insurance (OAI), became a major campaign issue in the presidential election of 1936. With paycheck withholdings scheduled to begin in 1937, the Republican candidate, Alfred M. Landon struck out against social security, calling it "a fraud on the workman. The savings it forces on our workers is a cruel hoax" (Schieber and Shoven, *The Real Deal: The History and Future of Social Security,* p. 53). Although few Americans understood the OAI plan they continued to trust President Roosevelt. Roosevelt won re-election overwhelmingly and support for OAI quickly grew. The economy again experienced a downturn later in 1937, which many attributed to the start of the Social Security tax. Employers and employees each were subject to the one percent tax on wages. Overall, approximately $2 billion came out of the pockets of consumers to begin the OAI fund. Although the first lump sum payments were paid to eligible workers, these were very small.

Other provisions of the Social Security Act also became active in 1936 and 1937. The first state unemployment benefit was paid in Wisconsin. The first public assistance payments from federal grants were made to old-age assistance, aid to dependent children, and the blind. States, for the first time, began actively participating under Title V in maternal and child services.

All the Social Security programs, however, during these early years were more of a demonstration of commitment to a principle rather than providing significant help to people. By the end of June 1937 unemployment benefits paid amounted to only $45 million and retirement benefits $20 million. One year later those figures rose to $436 million and $26 million, respectively. Overall Social Security played only a minor role in recovery for the rest of the decade. Yet by 1939 a pattern of revision and expansion of the programs emerged—a pattern that continued into the twenty-first century.

1939 Amendments

Congress' interest in revising the act began when the 1937–38 Advisory Council on Social Security established under Title VII began to study a major flaw in the act.

The act only provided for old-age pensions to workers at age 65 who retired completely from covered employment. No provisions were in existence for pensions of widows or other survivors or for dependents. The Advisory Council recommended the act be amended to include these categories of people.

The House Ways and Means Committee, still under the chairmanship of Robert L. Doughton, took over 2,600 pages of testimony on the proposed amendments. The Amendments that came out of Congress concentrated on the fundamental change of benefits to families.

The Amendments added two new categories of benefits: (1) payments to the spouse and minor children of a retired worker and (2) survivor's benefits paid to the family in the event of the premature death of the worker. This fundamental change transformed

A poster outlines the steps that U.S. citizens had to follow to be eligible to receive old-age benefits through the Social Security Administration.

(Bettmann/CORBIS. Reproduced by permission.)

Social Security from economic security plan, focused primarily on the employee, into a broader family based economic security program. The 1939 Amendments also moved up the start of monthly benefit payments from 1942 to 1940.

Contributing Forces

The establishment of a social security program in the United States was not really a sudden development. Rather it came after decades, roughly from 1883 to 1934, of discussion and debate between individuals in the United States who studied the worldwide social insurance movement. Social insurance programs began appearing in western Europe as early as 1883. The passage of the Social Security Act of 1935 launched the American version of social insurance. Historical forces in the late nineteenth and early twentieth century made 1934 and 1935 the time for action on social security in the United States.

Industrial Revolution and Urbanization

Social insurance movements largely began in response to the industrial revolution and urbanization

At a Glance

Social Security Firsts:

The lowest Social Security number (SSN) ever issued was SSN 001-01-0001 to Grace Dorothy Owen from Concord, New Hampshire, who applied for her number on November 24, 1936.

The first old-age Social Security insurance payment went to Ernest Ackerman of Cleveland, Ohio, in March 1937. Monthly benefits under the 1935 act were scheduled to start in 1942 (later moved up to 1940). Between 1937 and 1940 benefits to retirees were single, lump-sum refund payments. Ernest Ackerman, a Cleveland motorman, retired in January 1937 one day after the Social Security program began. During his one day of participation in the program one nickel was withheld from his pay. His employer also had to pay a matching one nickel. Upon retiring Ackerman applied for his lump-sum refund becoming the very first applicant. Ackerman received 17¢. During the period when only lump sum payments were made the average lump sum payment was $58.06. The smallest Social Security payment ever made was 5¢.

Ida May Fuller of Ludlow, Vermont, a retired legal secretary, received the first ever monthly benefit on January 31, 1940. The amount of her check was $22.54. Miss Fuller lived to be 100 years old, receiving over $22,000 in benefits during her 35 years as a beneficiary.

---

taking place in western European countries and in the United States. The industrial revolution transformed many working people from self-employed farmers into wage earners working for large industries. In an agricultural society a farmer who owned his own land could at least feed his family in hard times and maintain independence. Increasing numbers of the urban working class, however, rented their living spaces, therefore their income and livelihood depended entirely on wages from their job. If they lost their job due to an injury or during a period of economic downturn and could find no other work, they and their families found themselves in desperate situations. Economic downturns are when money is in short supply

and companies lay off workers. These had been occurring in the United States on a relatively regular basis—1857, 1873, 1893, 1914, and 1929. Each downturn or depression was worse than the one before because of the increasing number of individuals who depended solely on wages from jobs. Through the early twentieth century more and more people continued to leave their family farms and small communities to earn their living in the industrial cities. Only 28 percent of the population lived in cities in 1890 but by 1930, 56 percent lived in cities.

Aging presented other unique problems. As people aged, they could not keep up with demands of heavy industrial work and long hours. Elderly persons, no longer supported by extended farm families, would drop into extreme poverty when they left their jobs. With improved healthcare programs and sanitation, however, people began to live longer. Average life spans in America increased by ten years between 1900 and 1930. Therefore the elderly lived longer but often in poverty. In response to the problems created by older, more urban, and industrializing societies, social insurance programs began to appear in various countries.

European Social Insurance Movement

The Social Security program eventually developed in the United States was based on the concept of "social insurance." By the time America adopted social insurance in 1935, at least 34 European nations had already operated some form of a social insurance program. Social insurance emphasized government-sponsored efforts to provide economic security for its citizens. Social insurance coverage provides for several types of conditions, from injury on the job (workman's compensation), to disability, illness, old age, and unemployment.

Models of workmen's compensation and health, old age, and unemployment insurance emerged in Western Europe in the early 1880s. Some of the earliest programs dealt with workmen's compensation. These programs made payments to a worker injured on the job. Germany, Austria, Hungary, Norway, and Luxembourg all adopted workmen's compensation programs. Germany also established a national health insurance system in the 1880s as did Austria (1888), Hungary (1891), Luxembourg (1901), Norway (1909), Great Britain (1911), Russia (1912), and the Netherlands (1913). Other countries including Denmark, Sweden, Belgium, France, and Switzerland paid out "sickness benefits." Old-age insurance then appeared in Germany (1899), Austria (1909), and France (1910). Tax supported old-age pension programs appeared in the 1890s in Denmark, New Zealand,

Australia, and France. Unemployment insurance was the slowest social insurance to start up, however, in 1911 Great Britain applied the first national program of unemployment insurance to specific groups of industries. Despite substantial development of social insurance protection in Europe, the matter largely went unaddressed in the United States.

Charities and Volunteers

Although both the U.S. Commissioner of Labor and the New York State Bureau of Labor Statistics conducted detailed studies during the 1890s of the German social insurance plans, the topic was not a subject of serious debate in the United States, and most Americans knew nothing of the European programs. The whole issue seemed unimportant to them. Why, with the need obviously growing in an industrializing United States, was social insurance such a non-issue?

The answer lay in the uniquely American belief in self-reliance and individualism. People in the United States had long held to the notion that they could completely care for themselves and any help coming from government sources seemed a threat to personal liberty. Help for the truly needy had been left to volunteer programs, charities, and mutual aid societies. This charitable help was more in keeping with the American character than government assistance and was typically carried out locally with no coordinated plan. Furthermore, even among the charitable organizations the prevailing attitude was that relief or handouts damaged the work ethic. The public widely feared recipients would prefer relief to work. Most Americans steadfastly resisted any suggestion that they needed help, least of all government help. Dependence on charitable organizations and volunteerism for social needs delayed any movement on social insurance.

AALL and Its Influential Thinkers

In 1906 a handful of university economists, political scientists, and social scientists, mostly middle-class intellectuals, formed the American Association for Labor Legislation (AALL). The creation of the AALL launched the first organized American social insurance movement. Early leaders of AALL were Henry Farman of Yale University, elected president in 1907 and considered its founder, and John R. Commons of the University of Wisconsin elected secretary. Guidance by Farman and Commons insured the early survival of AALL. Commons was responsible for the appointment in 1908 of John B. Andrews as executive secretary. Andrews had been a student of Commons at the University of Wisconsin and had become a leading social economist of the day. The

AALL became a "think tank" promoting greater public and government awareness of the need for social insurance. They began calling for unemployment and old age insurance as a way to maintain industrial economies. AALL counted membership of only two hundred, mostly intellectuals, in 1908, but those members spearheaded the movement. They served as consultants for voluntary groups and government agencies. They drafted legislation for numerous city and state governments and lectured tirelessly on the progress of social insurance in the United States. AALL concentrated on issues of industrial accident compensation, industry safety, and unemployment and old-age insurance.

Another early influential member of AALL was Isaac Max Rubinow. As a young man in his twenties, Rubinow immigrated to the United States from Russia in 1893. He earned a medical degree in 1898 and practiced among the poor of New York. He was more interested, however, in government insurance systems and became an outspoken advocate of medical, unemployment, old age, and disability insurance. He believed the federal government should fund such programs. Rubinow had encyclopedic knowledge of European legislation and was convinced that social insurance must come to the United States. He severely criticized America's volunteer charities as inefficient and felt people suffered needlessly.

States Pass Social Insurance Legislation

AALL members tended to promote practical programs rather than just ideas. Results of AALL's efforts appeared in 1909 when Wisconsin, Minnesota, and New York passed workmen's compensation legislation. Franklin D. Roosevelt was a state senator in New York at the time and supported his state's measure. Forty-three states had passed such laws by 1920.

By the early 1930s various forms of old-age pension plans had been passed in approximately 35 states. As governor of New York in 1930, Roosevelt signed an old age pension plan into law. Roosevelt commented at the time that the problem of insecurity in old age could not be solved without an old-age insurance plan. These plans, however, generally were inadequate and ineffective and many elderly refused to participate. Only about three percent of the aged actually received benefits under the state plans. The average benefit amount was 65¢ a day. Old age pension plans differed greatly from one state to the next. Payments in Montana ran approximately $7.28 per month while Maryland payments were $30 per month.

Reasons for the low participation in state-run plans varied simply because any elderly refused to

Social Security Beneficiaries and Cash Benefits, 1937-1999

Year	Number of Beneficiaries	Dollars Paid in Cash Benefits
1937	53,236*	$1,278,000
1938	213,670*	10,478,000
1939	174,839*	13,896,000
1940	222,488	35,000,000
1950	3,477,243	961,000,000
1960	14,844,589	11,245,000,000
1970	26,228,629	31,863,000,000
1980	35,584,955	120,511,000,000
1990	39,832,125	247,796,000,000
1995	43,387,259	332,553,000,000
1999	44,585,624	385,768,000,000

* one-time lump sum payments

The government invested more money in public programs during the years of the Great Depression than it had at any time in the past. (The Gale Group.)

apply because they were reluctant "to go on welfare." Very strict eligibility requirements kept many poor seniors from applying. Some states had programs on the books but failed to actually put any program into practice. Furthermore some states allowed counties to opt out of the program.

At a 1931 Conference of State Governors, Governor Roosevelt broke new ground in social insurance matters by speaking favorably about unemployment insurance. By 1932, however, Wisconsin was the first and only state to pass a compulsory or required statewide unemployment insurance program. The Wisconsin plan and its developers strongly influenced the national social security plan in the months and years to follow.

Abraham Epstein Pushes for Nationwide Programs

Another key contributor toward developing social insurance policies in the United States was Abraham Epstein, who was research director of the Pennsylvania Commission on Old Age Pensions from 1918 until 1927. He established the American Association for Old Age Security, which later became the American Association for Social Security in 1933. Epstein wanted to see an old age insurance program established nationwide. Like Rubinow, Epstein believed the federal government should finance the program and strongly supported some form of national health insurance.

Despite increasing passage of social insurance legislation in the states and calls for a national system, only two social programs involving the federal government existed before Roosevelt's election to the presidency in 1932. Those two programs involved job training and help for needy mothers and children.

Onset of the Great Depression

By the onset of the Great Depression in 1929 social insurance programs had been discussed and developed to some extent in the states. Debates had resulted in a considerable body of literature. Certain individuals emerged as experts in the field and political leaders had at least become aware of social insurance issues.

The Great Depression pushed these issues to the forefront. Social changes that started with industrial revolutions had passed a point of no return. Confidence in traditional sources of economic security such as farming, family, charity, and volunteerism had failed to one degree or another. The depression had cut the total wealth of the nation in half in just three years. Some form of national unemployment insurance and old-age insurance suddenly seemed essential to everyday Americans. Social insurance would prove to be an idea whose time had come.

By the 1932 presidential election, the Democratic Platform contained a call for unemployment and old-age insurance, which probably reflected Roosevelt's rising influence. Roosevelt had identified himself with the social insurance cause for sometime. After his presidential election victory, he appointed Frances Perkins as secretary of the Department of Labor. Both Roosevelt and Perkins believed they must create a permanent system of personal security for the people of the United States.

Seven Forces

By 1933 no fewer than seven key forces over the preceding four to five decades had moved the United States toward a national social insurance policy. Those seven forces were: (1) industrial revolution and urbanization in Europe and the United States; (2) the development of European social insurance plans; (3) the realization that volunteerism by itself was not sufficient to aid the unemployed and elderly; (4) the activities of the AALL; (5) the innovative thinking of economists, social scientists, and certain politicians, including Franklin Roosevelt; (6) social insurance legislation passed within the states; and, (7) the onset of the Great Depression.

As the Depression deepened, the traditional American hope was that charity could find a way to help and that the dip in the economic cycle would soon right itself. Bearing all of these economic, social, and political factors in mind, Roosevelt concluded otherwise. He decided that he must actively set in motion the process for developing an unemployment and old-age insurance program in the United States. Roosevelt was aware that the 1936 presidential election was not far off and there was no guarantee that he would be reelected. Therefore, as Frances Perkins in her book *The Roosevelt I Knew* (1946) commented, " . . . this program, which, in his own mind, was *his* program, would never be accomplished, or at least not for many years, if it were not put through immediately."

Hence on June 8, 1934, Roosevelt notified Congress of his intention to develop a social insurance program. On June 29, 1934, he created the Committee on Economic Security to do just that.

Perspectives

Among the general public, three separate groupings had played significant roles during the birth and maturing of social security. Those groupings were the public who benefited from the social security programs, organized business, and organized labor. Among policymakers, the perspectives of advisory councils, academic communities, and politicians all shaped social security.

Beneficiary Population

In the heady times of the 1920s the general public had shown almost no interest in or knowledge of social insurance programs. People believed in taking care of themselves, and the care of the destitute was left up to charities and volunteers. Charitable organizations stressed prevention and education, fearing handouts would destroy the work ethic. These long-held American ideas were challenged by the Great Depression. Volunteerism offered too little to those in desperate economic need, and by 1934 public sentiment for some type of unemployment and old-age insurance was overwhelming. Hundreds of thousands supported the Townsend plan for old-age pensions, and Huey Long's campaign to "soak the rich." Much of the general public blamed the very wealthy for the country's misery. Responding to this groundswell, President Roosevelt's administration managed to develop and Congress passed the highly complex Social Security Act of 1935, in just thirteen and a half months. Followers of Townsend and Long felt the act was stingy in that it did not do enough for the elderly.

As an organized group, beneficiaries of the social security programs remained relatively quiet until the system matured. As benefits, however, began to make real differences in people's lives, organizations would spring up if benefits were threatened. At the end of the twentieth century the American Association of Retired Persons (AARP) was an example of a large organized group supporting social security programs. Today's public is still highly protective of social security.

Organized Business

During the development of social security legislation organized business warned against such notions as unemployment and old age insurance. Business conservatives argued it was un-American and would lead the country to socialism. Manufacturers' associations were convinced that social security legislation would destroy individual initiative and discourage personal savings and responsibility. Opposition was a natural reaction of employers to government-imposed costs on employment.

On the other hand Marion Folsom, a Kodak executive, testified in favor of the social security bill before the Senate Finance Committee hearings in 1935. After observing how employees who retired from Kodak did not get along very well, he set up one of the first funded plans in industrial America. He planned to blend his company's plan with the government plan.

After passage of the act various business groups from time to time would raise philosophical questions about social security but they could never mobilize their members to wage an organized campaign against its programs. Gradually businesses began to appreciate that benefits to business were substantially greater than costs. They realized elderly persons had enough money to continue buying in the marketplace. The U.S. Chamber of Commerce actually began running articles praising the tremendous benefits that were building under the system.

Organized Labor

Labor unions exist to promote economic and social welfare for their members. Initially the Social Security Act seemed a threat to their reason for existence. If the government was going to take over Americans' social welfare needs, the unions feared they would no longer have a role to play. Gradually, however, the labor unions began to see the act as opening doors of tremendous opportunity. Unions handled negotiations between employers and employees to establish private pension plans that supplemented the Social Security programs. According to Martha Derthick of the Brookings Institution in Washington, DC, "In building the social security program, organized labor was by far the most important ally of the Social Security Administration" (Schieber and Shoven, *The Real Deal: The History and Future of Social Security,* p. 129).

Advisory Councils

Starting with the Committee of Economic Security that developed social security in the summer and fall of 1934, numerous advisory councils operated during the development and the maturing phase of the social security programs. Councils have been periodically appointed since 1937. Despite their often differing origins and diverse members they consistently seemed to be dominated by people committed to the program.

Academics

Academics have long taken interest in social security. Social scientists generally conclude the more social security the better. During the 1960s when Presidents John F. Kennedy (served 1961–1963) and Lyndon B. Johnson (served 1963–1969) focused on poverty, social scientists touted social security programs as vital to the elimination of poverty. At the end of the twentieth century, academics, including leading economists, generally agreed that funding of social security must rise. Little consensus, however, existed on where the funding should come from. Historians and political scientists point to the overall effectiveness of Social Security in retirement security, universal coverage, and a public acceptance.

Politicians

As Congress debated the proposals in 1935, conservative politicians of both parties charged that social security violated the traditional American ideas of self-help and individual responsibility. Conservatives believed the Depression was a temporary problem that would go away, eliminating the need for old age pensions in a few years. Therefore they preferred only old-age public assistance to the truly needy. This approach would have restricted government aid to the smallest possible number of people. Many Southern politicians did not like the fact that blacks could receive benefits. Republicans, reflecting the business communities' views, cried charges of socialism, dictatorship, and enslavement of workers. They believed fewer jobs would be available for people because employers would not have enough money left to pay wages. Progressive Democrats supported social security measures, however, apparently fearful of rejection at the polls, most Congressmen voted in favor of Social Security. The act passed in the House of Representatives 372 to 33 and in the Senate 77 to 6.

Democrats have come back to the American public time and time again seeking to expand the social security protections against the insecurities of life. The Republicans, in contrast, immediately opposed the program again in the 1936 presidential election. Their active opposition continued for decades, including opposition to Disability Insurance and Medicare.

Impact

Policymakers basically agreed on the principal causes of "insecurity" for Americans in the 1930s: unemployment, poverty in old age, loss of the wage earner of the family and, sickness. The original Social Security Act of 1935 sought to protect Americans against the threat of these insecurities. Title I made old-age assistance a right that could be legally enforced. Title II reduced the likelihood that the aged would become impoverished. Title III provided a measure of reassurance during times of unemployment. Other than expanded public health services, health insurance was ignored.

Social Security never intended to relieve the individual of primary responsibility for his or her own well being. Neither did it downplay the role of family members' duty to one another. Edwin Witte observed that the social insurance system was only meant to provide a floor below which no individual would fall.

Under the original act very little actual help came to Americans of the 1930s. The act was a commitment to the social insurance principle by the United States government. Several decades would pass before that commitment translated to meaningful help.

From passage of the 1939 Amendments to 1950 no changes were made in Social Security, and retirement benefits were very low because the program was still in its infancy. By 1950 the average benefit was only about $26 a month. In fact, the average welfare benefit received under the Title I old-age assistance was higher than the average retirement benefit under Title II. In 1950 only a quarter of those over 65 received retirement payments and only 50 percent of American workers were even covered under the program. In comparison by 1985, 94 percent of those over 65 received Social Security pensions. The 1950 Amendments that began addressing Social Security weaknesses set the stage for continued reform of the system through the second half of the twentieth century.

1950 Amendments

The 1950 Amendments raised old-age pension benefits for the first time, providing for a gradual raise in the percentage of payroll tax both employers and employees had to pay, and added ten million new workers to its rolls.

Congress passed a 77 percent increase in the old-age pension benefits. Those who retired after the 1950 Amendments took effect received average benefits of between $50 and $55 per month. Future benefit increases could only be enacted by special legislation. Also the first increase in payroll tax, to be levied in 1951, moved the percentage to 1.5 percent and then gradually to 3.25 percent in 1970. The 1950 Amendments also placed the old-age pension program on the road to coverage for all. Ten million more people came under the coverage, including domestic and farm workers, certain self-employed, and various other employees.

Disability Amendments

In 1956 the Social Security Act was amended to provide benefits to disabled workers aged 50–65 and disabled adult children. Previously only disabled workers over 65 were covered. Disabled adult children included any child of a parent who was no longer a minor (under 18 years of age) but was disabled and could not work. The act also provided funding to help pay for their care. Disabilities range from physical disabilities resulting from illness, injury, or birth defects to mental disabilities. Congress continued to broaden disability benefits until disabled workers of any age could qualify.

Medicare

In 1965 President Lyndon B. Johnson (served 1963–1969) signed into law health coverage for Social

Ida M. Fuller, 76, of Ludlow, VT, was the first person to receive Old Age Insurance benefits from the government in 1940. Here she is the first person to receive increased benefits under a 1950 law. (AP/Wide World Photos. Reproduced by permission.)

Security beneficiaries aged 65 or older. This landmark program, known as Medicare, enrolled 20 million beneficiaries in its first three years. Medicare consists of two related insurance plans. One is a hospital plan financed through Social Security taxes that pays for such services as in-patient hospital care, nursing home care, and certain health services provided at homes. The plan covers most hospital expenses for up to 90 days for each illness. The patient only has to pay a modest fee at first (the deductible) and a daily co-payment after 60 days. The second plan is a supplementary plan that provides additional benefits if a person chooses to take it. This plan operates outside the Social Security system and is supported by general taxes and the members' monthly payments.

Supplemental Security Income (SSI)

The original Social Security Act introduced programs for the needy, aged (Title I), and blind (Title X). Disabled individuals were added in 1956. These three programs came to be known as the "adult categories," and were administered by state and local governments. The state programs were complex and inconsistent, for example, payments varied more than 300 percent from state to state. President Richard M. Nixon (served 1969–1974) identified the need to reform and combine these programs. He did this by signing into law the 1972 Amendments creating the Supplemental Security Income (SSI) program. Under SSI the adult categories were federalized and brought under the administration of the Social Security Administration which allowed for more uniform benefits throughout the United States.

COLA

When Ida May Fuller received her first $22.54 benefit check in 1940 she could expect to receive that same amount for the rest of her life. In 1972 President Nixon signed amendments creating the Cost-of-Living Adjustments (COLAs).

COLAs provided for automatic annual cost of living increases for old-age retirement benefits. COLAs were based on increases in consumer prices, which generally matched the rise in inflation. Beneficiaries no longer had to wait for special acts of Congress to receive a benefit increase. No longer did inflation decrease the value of benefits.

Program Changes Since 1980

Legislation in 1983 made numerous changes including taxation of Social Security benefits, coverage of some federal employees, and raising the retirement age eventually to age 67 starting in 2003. Legislation in 1994 created a permanent seven-member Social Security Advisory Board to provide independent advice and legal council for Social Security programs.

In 1999 President Bill Clinton (served 1993–2001) signed work incentive programs to rehabilitate the disabled and assist them in returning to work. President Clinton also signed into law the "Senior Citizens' Freedom to Work Act of 2000." This law allowed approximately 900,000 seniors who collected benefits but also worked to keep all their Social Security benefits. Previously, benefits were cut as income from work increased.

Unemployment Insurance in 2000

Just as originally designed in Title III of the Social Security Act of 1935, unemployment insurance partially replaced the income of regularly employed workers who lost their jobs through no fault of their own. In 2000 states administered their own programs but followed national guidelines. The state collects contributions, maintains wage records, takes claims,

determines eligibility, and pays benefits. Contributions collected under state laws are then deposited in the Unemployment Insurance Trust Fund in the U.S. Treasury.

While unemployed, a worker receives weekly cash payments according to a benefit formula used by each state. It is based on the amount of the worker's past earnings. A worker must be ready and willing to accept work. In 2000 the most common length of benefit payments was 26 weeks but additional payments up to 13 or 20 weeks were possible under an Extended Benefits program.

Importance of Social Security in 2000

The Social Security Act of 1935, the essence of Franklin D. Roosevelt's New Deal programs, endured and evolved through the decades becoming an essential part of modern life. Very few benefits actually went to Americans in the 1930s. Slightly more than 222,000 people received small monthly Social Security benefits in 1940. Perhaps peace of mind that a program was beginning provided the main benefit for Americans in the 1930s. In 2000, however, almost 45 million people received benefits, approximately one in six Americans. Almost one in three of the beneficiaries were not retirees but younger persons who received disability and survivor's benefits. While only 50 percent of American workers were covered by old-age pension insurance under Title II of the Social Security Act in the 1940s, in 2000 about 98 percent (approximately 150 million) of all workers were covered. For nearly two-thirds of the elderly, Social Security was their major source of income; and, for a third of the elderly, Social Security was their only income. Social Security helped the elderly have financial independence. Only 11 percent of those over 65 lived in poverty in 2000, while a staggering fifty percent lived in poverty in the 1930s and 1940s.

The beginning of the twenty-first century found young people asking if social security will be there for them? In 2000 three major issues were debated. First, some people proposed the retirement age for full benefits be raised even older than age 67. Beginning in 2003 the full retirement age will increase gradually from 65 to 67. Proponents said Americans live longer, healthier lives, therefore are able to work longer. Critics said many people will find it difficult to work beyond the retirement age of 65.

Second, some proposed Social Security taxes should be paid on all income. In 2000 earnings over $72,600 were not subject to Social Security taxes. Therefore, wealthier Americans avoided paying Social Security taxes on some of their income. Critics said if the wealthy pay more in Social Security taxes they would have to receive much higher benefits.

Third, it has been proposed that individual savings accounts and investments for all workers replace part of social security benefits, and critics say that is too risky.

In 2000 Social Security took in more money from taxes than it paid out in benefits. The excess went into trust funds. Benefit payments, however, are expected to exceed taxes paid in 2014. Withdrawals from the trust fund would be needed to make up the difference. The trust fund would run out of money in 2034. At that time if no changes are made Social Security would be able to pay only about three-fourths of benefits owed as incoming taxes would not cover all payments.

Despite the concerns about the future of Social Security, no other government program has touched the lives of so many millions of Americans—the aged, the unemployed, the sick, the needy, mothers, children, and the disabled.

Notable People

Arthur Joseph Altmeyer (1891–1972). Altmeyer, born in DePere, Wisconsin, first became interested in social insurance at the age of twenty when he read a pamphlet on the new Wisconsin Worker's Compensation Act. He entered the University of Wisconsin where he studied under John R. Commons.

Altmeyer became the Chief Statistician of the Wisconsin Industrial Commission in 1920, where he began a monthly publication, the first of its kind, called the *Wisconsin Labor Market.* It listed data on employment throughout the state. In 1922 he assumed the position of Secretary of the Wisconsin Industrial Commission. Altmeyer was instrumental in the 1932 passage of the Wisconsin Unemployment Reserves and Compensation Act, which provided financial assistance to workers who lost their jobs. It was the first such act to be passed in the United States. Because of the experience he acquired in a state noted for its progressive social legislation, Altmeyer was chosen to serve in President Roosevelt's Administration. He served in the National Industrial Recovery Administration, the Department of Labor, and on the Committee on Economic Security. The Committee was formed in 1934 to develop a social insurance plan for the United States. Heading up the committee's Technical Board, Altmeyer, along with Edwin Witte and Frances Perkins, directed the creation of the Social Security Act of 1935. With the act's passage he was

The American Population: Age 65 and Older		
Year	Age 65+ in millions	Percent of Total Population
1946	11	8%
1999	35	13
2030 (est.)	70	20

As time goes on, more people are living longer, impacting Social Security and other assistance programs. (The Gale Group.)

appointed one of the three original Social Security Board (SSB) members. Altmeyer served as a SSB member from 1935 to 1937, chairman from 1937 to 1946, and Social Security Commissioner from 1946 to 1953. He has been called the "father" of Social Security because more than any other single person, he shaped the administration of Social Security.

John B. Andrews (1880–1943). Andrews was a student of John R. Commons at the University of Wisconsin. Commons appointed Andrews executive secretary in 1908 of the newly formed American Association of Labor Legislation (AALL). The AALL was a "think tank" promoting social insurance such as unemployment and old-age insurance. Andrews held his position with AALL until 1946 and was highly influential in the creation and passage of social security measures in the United States.

Wilbur J. Cohen (1913–1987). Cohen moved to Washington, DC after graduating from the University of Wisconsin in 1934. He became Research Assistant to Executive Director Witte of President Roosevelt's cabinet-level Committee on Economic Security and helped craft the original Social Security Act of 1935.

John Rogers Commons (1862–1944). Commons was an economics and sociology professor at the University of Wisconsin where he became an expert in business, industrial, and labor economics. He drafted Wisconsin's Unemployment Reserves and Compensation Act, which was enacted in 1932, the first such law in the United States. Commons also strongly influenced the creation of the Social Security Act. John B. Andrews, Edwin Witte, and Arthur Altmeyer, all Commons' students, became leading developers of social security in the United States.

Robert Lee Doughton (1863–1954). Doughton, born in North Carolina, served in the House of Representatives from 1911 until 1953. A conservative Democrat, yet a Franklin D. Roosevelt loyalist, he exerted great power as chairman of the House Ways and Means Committee. He presided over hearings for the Social Security bill in 1935.

Thomas Hopkinson Eliot (1907–1991). Eliot graduated from Harvard Law School in 1932. He served as assistant solicitor in the Legal Division of the Department of Labor under Frances Perkins at the time of the development of the social insurance policies that evolved into the Social Security Act of 1935. Eliot authored the Wagner-Lewis Bill, an unemployment insurance plan, introduced to Congress in February 1934. Later in 1934 Eliot served on the Technical Board of the Committee on Economic Security, which developed the Social Security Act. Eliot was instrumental in crafting the act so that it could withstand constitutional challenges in the Supreme Court. After the act passed, Eliot became counsel to the Social Security Board until 1935.

Abraham Epstein (1877–1942). Born in Russia, Epstein immigrated to the United States in 1910. He graduated from the University of Pittsburgh in 1917 and worked as research director of the Pennsylvania Commission on Old Age Reviews. He established the American Association for Old Age Security and changed its name to the American Association of Social Security in 1933. That name change is widely attributed to turning the term social insurance into the very American term, social security.

Epstein tirelessly labored to develop old-age insurance plans in the United States. He believed the plans should be financed by the federal government, not employer and employee contributions.

Byron Patton Harrison (1881–1941). Pat Harrison served in the Senate from 1918 until 1941. A Democrat, Harrison became chairman of the Senate Committee on Finance in 1933. Under Harrison's leadership the Finance Committee handled many of the New Deal Measures. Harrison is credited with carefully guiding the Social Security Act of 1935 through the Finance Committee and then the full Senate until its passage. Without his effort historians believe Title II of the act would have not made it out of committee.

David J. Lewis (1869–1952). Lewis was a member of the House of Representatives from Maryland. In 1933 he introduced into Congress the Wagner-Lewis Bill, an unemployment compensation bill that died in Congress. He then introduced the Social Security bill in 1935. Lewis, a former coal miner and self-taught lawyer, was a member of the House Ways and Means Committee. His mastery of the provisions of the bill made him the leading expert of social insurance among committee members.

Huey Pierce Long (1893–1935). Long, known as "the Kingfish," was born in Einnfield, Louisiana. Long passed the Louisiana Bar Exam in 1915. Running on the slogan of "Every man a king, but no one wears a crown," he was elected governor of Louisiana in 1928. Elected to the U.S. Senate in 1930, Long supported Franklin D. Roosevelt in his 1932 presidential bid. Long, however, quickly broke with Roosevelt when the president failed to support his wealth redistribution plan.

In 1934 Long organized the Share-Our-Wealth Society guaranteeing everyone a middle class income of $2,500 and a homestead allowance of $5,000. Long gathered millions of supporters by the end of 1934. He used his support as a springboard to announce his candidacy for president in 1936. Although Long's chances for success were slim, President Roosevelt feared the votes Long might gain could pull enough support from the Democrats to allow a Republican to win the presidency. Passage of Roosevelt's Social Security Act was one way to relieve the Long pressure. Long's life ended abruptly when Dr. Carl Weiss, son-in-law of a ruined political opponent of Long's, assassinated him in 1935 in the Louisiana State Capital building.

Henry Morgenthau, Jr. (1891–1967). Morgenthau served as President Franklin D. Roosevelt's Secretary of Treasury. Appointed on New Years Day, 1934, he served in that position until 1945. In the summer of 1934 President Roosevelt and Secretary of Labor Perkins chose Morgenthau to be a part of the Committee on Economic Security to craft the Social Security Act of 1935. When the bill was before the House Ways and Means Committee, Morgenthau's testimony led to the deletion of farm and domestic workers from coverage under Social Security.

Franklin Delano Roosevelt (1882–1945). First as a New York State Senator, then later as governor, Roosevelt was interested in all aspects of social insurance programs. He signed New York's old-age pension law in 1930 and advocated state and regional unemployment insurance to aggressively fight the Great Depression. Even before his presidential inauguration, he discussed with Francis Perkins, who would become his secretary of labor, the need for long term, nationwide old age and unemployment insurance. In 1934 Roosevelt established the Committee on Economic Security charged with developing a social insurance plan for the United States. He signed the Social Security Act into law in 1935.

Isaac Max Rubinow (1875–1936). Born in Russia, Rubinow immigrated to the United States in 1893 and graduated from medical school. He worked for a short time in private practice among the poor in New York City but was more interested in government social insurance systems. He returned to school and obtained a Ph.D. in economics from Columbia University. Rubinow became an early and strong advocate for healthcare and social insurance. His encyclopedic knowledge in the field led to published studies on the European system in 1911 and 1913. The 1913 book, *Social Insurance,* was the most influential early work on the subject. Rubinow advocated government funded social insurance programs in the United States, including unemployment, old age, disability, and medical insurance. His 1934 book, *The Quest for Security,* further established Rubinow as the foremost expert and theorist in social insurance. President Roosevelt owned a copy and had been reading it as the Committee on Economic Security formed. The committee drafted the administration's proposals on social security.

Francis Everett Townsend (1867–1960). Born into a poor farm family in Illinois, Townsend worked various jobs before attending and graduating from the University of Nebraska Medical School. He practiced medicine in Bear Lodge, South Dakota, for approximately twenty years before moving to Long Beach, California in 1920. He worked as a health officer in the Long Beach Health Office for a time but was laid off. Sixty-seven years old with no savings and no prospects, Townsend became outraged at the plight of old people and the public's lack of concern. He became a self-proclaimed champion of the cause of the elderly. In 1933 he suggested all persons sixty and over should receive $200 a month on the condition they spend it within thirty days. The plan would be financed by a 2 percent national sales tax.

Townsend's idea rapidly gained followers and Townsend Clubs sprang up all over the nation. When the Townsend Plan was actually introduced into Congress in January 1935, within three months 20 million supporting signatures were collected.

President Roosevelt and Congress viewed the plan as impractical and felt it could bankrupt the country. Its popularity, however, spurred the passage of the Social Security Act by the summer of 1935. Townsend has been referred to as the "stepfather" of the Social Security Act.

Robert F. Wagner (1877–1953). Elected in 1926 to the U.S. Senate, Wagner was an advocate for all working people and the poor of the United States. When Franklin D. Roosevelt became president in 1933, the Democrat from New York became the Senate's leader on New Deal legislation. At the urging of President Roosevelt, he introduced the Wagner-Lewis bill, an unemployment insurance proposal, into the Senate in 1933. Although the bill died, it influenced the Social Security Act of 1935, which Wagner also had the honor of introducing in the Senate.

John Gilbert Winant (1889–1947). Winant became the first head of the new Social Security Board in 1935. He was instrumental in establishing the organization that would carry out the Social Security Act of 1935.

Edwin E. Witte (1887–1960). Witte was a teacher and expert in the field of economics and social insurance from the University of Wisconsin. In the spirit of the "Wisconsin idea" Witte balanced teaching with public service by holding numerous positions on industrial commissions and research associations for the state of Wisconsin. Witte also served as the Chief of the Wisconsin Legislative Library.

In 1934 Frances Perkins appointed Witte executive director of the Committee on Economic Security. Witte resolved differences between the members of the Committee and the many experts and advisers for over six months. The result was the plan presented to Congress in 1935, which became the Social Security Act of 1935. Following its enactment, Witte served on advisory councils for Social Security.

Primary Sources

Notification to Congress, June 8, 1934

On this date President Franklin D. Roosevelt notified Congress of his desire to develop a national social insurance plan in the United States. This speech was reproduced in *The Public Papers and Addresses of Franklin D. Roosevelt* (Volume Three, p. 291).

> Next winter we may well undertake the great task of furthering the security of the citizen and his family through social insurance. This is not an untried experiment. Lessons of experience are available from States, from industries, and from many nations of the civilized world. The various types of social insurance are interrelated; and I think it is difficult to attempt to solve them piecemeal. Hence, I am looking for a sound means which I can recommend to provide at once security against several of the great disturbing factors in life—especially those which relate to unemployment and old age.

Cradle to Grave

Franklin D. Roosevelt's famous "cradle to grave" statement was made just after the Committee on Economic Security launched its study into the creation of a social insurance program. He made these comments to Frances Perkins when she seemed appalled by the administrative challenges of so large a program. (From Perkins, *The Roosevelt I Knew.* pp. 282–283).

And what's more, there is no reason why everybody in the United States should not be covered. I see no reason why every child, from the day he is born, shouldn't be a member of the social security system. When he begins to grow up, he should know he will have old-age benefits direct from the insurance system to which he will belong all his life. If he is out of work, he gets a benefit, if he is sick or crippled, he gets a benefit.

The system ought to be operated through the post offices. Just simple and natural—nothing elaborate or alarming about it. The rural free delivery carrier ought to bring papers to the door and pick them up after they are filled out. The rural free delivery carrier ought to be the one who picks up the claim of the man who is unemployed, or of the old lady who wants old-age insurance benefits.

And there is no reason why just the industrial workers should get the benefit of this. Everybody ought to be in on it—the farmer and his wife and his family.

I don't see why not, I don't see why not. Cradle to the grave—from the cradle to the grave they ought to be in a social insurance system.

Passage of the Social Security Act of 1935

President Roosevelt commenting on August 14, 1935 at the signing of the Social Security Act. The quote comes from the Social Security Administration's Publication No. 21-059, p. 15.

We can never insure one-hundred percent of the population against one-hundred percent of the hazards and vicissitudes of life. But we have tried to frame a law that will give some measure of protection to the average citizen and to his family against the loss of a job and against poverty-ridden old age. This law, too, represents a cornerstone in a structure, which is being built, but is by no means complete . . . It is . . . a law that will take care of human needs and at the same time provide for the United States in economic structure of vastly greater soundness.

United States' Presidents Speak on Social Security

The following quotes, taken from SSA Publication No. 21-059, represent the attitudes of the Presidents toward the Social Security program.

John F. Kennedy (served 1961–1963):

The Social Security program plays an important part in providing for families, children, and older persons in times of stress. But it cannot remain static. Changes in our population, in our working habits, and in our standard of living require constant revision. (June 30, 1961)

Gerald R. Ford (served 1974–1977):

We must begin by insuring that the Social Security system is beyond challenge. [It is] a vital obligation each generation has to those who have worked hard and contributed to it all their lives. (February 9, 1976)

Jimmy E. Carter (served 1977–1981):

The Social Security program . . . represents our commitment as a society to the belief that workers should not live in dread that a disability, death, or old age could leave them or their families destitute. (December 20, 1977)

George Bush (served 1989–1993):

To every American out there on Social Security, to every American supporting that system today, and to everyone counting on it when they retire, we made a promise to you, and we are going to keep it. (January 31, 1990)

Bill Clinton (served 1993–2001):

Social Security . . . reflects some of our deepest values—the duties we owe to our parents, the duties we owe to each other when we're differently situated in life, the duties we owe to our children and our grandchildren. Indeed, it reflects our determination to move forward across generations and across the income divides in our country, as one America. (February 9, 1998)

Suggested Research Topics

- Explore the life and career of Frances Perkins. Was it unusual for a woman to be a cabinet member at the beginning of the twenty-first century?

- Social Security is an economic compact among generations. Explore the issues surrounding the question, "Will a person in their youth at the turn of the twenty-first century be able to count on Social Security for retirement?"

- In January 1973 the Social Security Administration's main headquarters building in Washington, D.C., was renamed the Arthur J. Altmeyer Building. Who was Altmeyer and what were his accomplishments?

- Figure a modest monthly budget for living expenses for one person. Would a Social Security monthly check of $700 cover expenses? Is Social Security a supplement to income or sufficient to be a person's entire income?

Bibliography

Sources

Altmeyer, Arthur J. *The Formative Years of Social Security.* Madison: The University of Wisconsin Press, 1968.

Eliot, Thomas H. *Recollections of the New Deal: When the People Mattered.* Boston: Northeastern University Press, 1922.

Leuchtenburg, William E. *Franklin D. Roosevelt and the New Deal: 1932–1940.* New York: Harper & Row, 1963.

Lubov, Roy. *The Struggle for Social Security, 1900–1935.* 2d ed. Pittsburgh: University of Pittsburgh Press, 1986.

Martin, George. *Madam Secretary: Frances Perkins.* Boston: Houghton Mifflin, 1976.

McElvaine, Robert S. *The Great Depression: America, 1929–1941.* New York: Times Books, 1993.

Nash, Gerald D., Noel H. Pugach, and Richard F. Tomasson. *Social Security: The First Half-Century.* Albuquerque, NM: University of New Mexico Press, 1988.

Olson, James S., ed. *Historical Dictionary of the New Deal: From Inauguration to Preparation for War.* Westport, CN: Greenwood, 1985.

Patterson, James T. *America's Struggle Against Poverty: 1900–1994.* Cambridge, MA: Harvard University Press, 1994.

Perkins, Frances. *The Roosevelt I Knew.* New York: Viking Press, 1946.

Roosevelt, Franklin D. *The Public Papers and Addresses of Franklin D. Roosevelt.* New York: Random House, 1938.

Schieber, Sylvester J., and John B. Shoven. *The Real Deal: The History and Future of Social Security.* New Haven: Yale University Press, 1999.

Schlesinger, Arthur M., Jr. *The Coming of the New Deal: The Age of Roosevelt.* Boston: Houghton Mifflin Company, 1988.

Swain, Martha H. *Pat Harrison: New Deal Years.* Jackson, MS: University Press of Mississippi, 1978.

Witte, Edwin. *The Development of the Social Security Act.* Madison: University of Wisconsin Press, 1962.

Further Reading

Baker, Dean, and Mark Weisbrot. *Social Security: The Phony Crisis.* Chicago: University of Chicago Press, 1999.

Brinkley, Alan. *Voices of Protest: Huey Long, Father Coughlin, and the Great Depression.* New York: Knopf, 1982.

Burns, James McGregor. *Roosevelt: The Lion and the Fox.* Norwalk, CN: Eaton Press, 1989.

Pasachoff, Naomi E. *Frances Perkins: Champion of the New Deal.* New York: Oxford University Press, 1999.

Perkins, Frances. *The Roosevelt I Knew.* New York: The Viking Press, 1946.

Social Security Administration. *A Brief Description of the U.S. Social Security Program.* SSA Publication No. 61-009, January 1997.

———. *A Brief History of Social Security.* SSA Publication No. 21-059, August 2000.

———. *The Future of Social Security.* SSA Publication No. 05-10055, July 1999.

"Social Security Administration Website," [cited November 20, 2001] available from the World Wide Web at http://www.ssa.gov.

Williams, T. Harry. *Huey Long.* New York: Vantage Books, 1981.

Supreme Court

1934-1938

Introduction

When Franklin Delano Roosevelt (served 1933–1945) took office on March 4, 1933, he faced a formidable task in trying to lead the nation to economic recovery from the Great Depression. Almost 25 percent of the U.S. workforce was jobless, amounting to over 12 million people. He also faced a conservative federal judiciary predominantly appointed by the past three Republican presidents. Particularly at the district court level, judges were hostile to the New Deal, a wide spectrum of federal social and economic programs created by Roosevelt to fight the Depression. Most of the 140 judges of the federal district courts were Republicans; they had been largely drawn from small town practice, and shared a nineteenth century view of law and economics. The typical judge was over 60 and had completed law school by the late 1890s. Judges on the next higher federal court level, the Court of Appeals, were slightly older, somewhat more cosmopolitan, but almost equally as partisan, which is favoring one particular political party over another.

On the highest tribunal seven members of the Supreme Court owed their appointments to Republican presidents and three had been active politicians before sitting on the bench. But the Court, under Chief Justice Charles Evans Hughes was not immovable on all issues. Past decisions often demonstrated that this Court was divided into three voting blocs. On the far right were four justices—Willis Van Devanter, James C. McReynolds, George Sutherland, and the most con-

Chronology:

March 5, 1934: In a close vote, the U.S. Supreme Court rules in *Nebbia v. New York* that states can regulate the prices of products when it is for the public good and it can be shown to be fair and reasonable.

June 8, 1934: In another close vote the Supreme Court rules in *Home Building and Loan Corporation v. Blaisdell* that the governments can regulate business in times of extraordinary national conditions such as the Great Depression; this decision gives the New Dealers hope for future favorable rulings on federal New Deal laws.

January 7, 1935: The Supreme Court rules in *Panama Refining Company v. Ryan* that the federal government cannot regulate petroleum shipments under authority of the National Industrial Recovery Act (NIRA); it is the first adverse Supreme Court ruling for the New Deal.

May 6, 1935: The Supreme Court ruling in *Railroad Retirement Board et al. v. Alton Railroad Company et al.* highlights the Court's narrow interpretation of the federal government's authority to regulate commerce, a bad omen to the New Deal.

May 27, 1935: In a set of three decisions, including *Schechter Poultry Corporation v. United States,* in which the Supreme Court determines that the NIRA is unconstitutional, the New Deal suffers a

severe legal setback; the day becomes known as "Black Monday."

January 6, 1936: The Supreme Court rules in *United States v. Butler* that the Agricultural Adjustment Act is unconstitutional dealing another major blow to New Deal programs.

February 5, 1937: President Roosevelt sends a lengthy message to Congress proposing reorganization of the judicial branch of government, including expanding the size of the Supreme Court.

March 9, 1937: In the face of strong public and congressional criticism of his proposed judicial reorganization plan, President Roosevelt goes on the radio with a "fireside chat" to answer his critics.

March 29, 1937: Giving an indication of a change in direction more favorable to the New Deal, the Supreme Court upholds the right of government to regulate business in *West Coast Hotel v. Parrish.*

April 12, 1937: In a major victory for the New Deal, the Supreme Court rules in *National Labor Relations Board v. Jones & Laughlin Steel Corporation* that the National Labor Relations Act is constitutionally valid and workers have a right to organize into unions.

---

sistently conservative, Pierce Butler, who came to be referred to as the "Four Horsemen of Reaction." The Court's liberal wing was made up of three justices—Louis D. Brandeis, Benjamin Cardozo, and Harlan Fiske Stone. In the center sat Chief Justice Hughes and Justice Owen Roberts, who both represented the swing votes necessary for any majority of justices in making a ruling. Of course their partisan ideas varied to some degree from case to case. McReynolds could be a strong advocate of individual liberties in some situations while Stone showed conservative elements in many of his decisions. Nevertheless, as the New Deal progressed, these alignments on the Supreme Court became more pronounced.

After seeing Supreme Court decisions in 1934 seemingly supportive of state laws regulating business to relieve economic hardships of the Great Depres-

sion, the New Dealers had hopes the Court would also similarly support New Deal laws when they were challenged by business and others. Those hopes, however, were soon dashed as the Court threw out major New Deal programs in 1935 and 1936, including the regulation of industry under the National Industrial Recovery Act and the regulation of agriculture under the Agricultural Adjustment Act. Such decisions infuriated President Roosevelt and the public as well.

Emboldened by the landslide reelection victory in November 1936, Roosevelt unveiled a daring plan in January 1937 to reorganize the Supreme Court in retribution for its rulings against his programs. The attack proved highly unpopular with the public and Congress triggering a substantial decline in the support of New Deal programs. The president's attacks on the Court substantially diminished public support for additional

New Deal programs. The threats of change and the public pressure, however, did lead to more favorable Court rulings concerning other already existing key New Deal programs, such as the National Labor Relations Act and the Social Security Act.

Issue Summary

Some Early Decisions of the 1930s

Response to the Great Depression led to a host of both state and national plans to deal with the economic crisis. The problem for legal draftsmen was determining under what authority a state or the federal government could impose economic regulations. Social and economic theories of the nineteenth century were still very much alive on the bench. Courts were very willing to invalidate laws on theories of *laissez-faire,* which is free market capitalism using the substantive due process clause of the Constitution. Substantive due process means judging a law based on its subject matter rather than simply determining if the government had legal authority in that particular area. The Supreme Court's willingness to decide a major case on substantive due process grounds in order to protect "entrepreneurial liberty" occurred as late as 1932.

In *New State Ice Co. v. Liebmann* (1932) the Court reviewed a 1925 Oklahoma law that declared the manufacture and sale of ice a public business and prohibited the granting of new licenses to sell ice except where a community could show a definite need. The practical effect of the legislation was to shut out new ice businesses and as a result create a monopoly for the existing businesses. But the act was also an attempt to deal with "destructive competition" in an industry that was affected by falling prices. Concluding that the Oklahoma law unreasonably hindered the common right to engage in a lawful business, Justice George Sutherland, in writing for the six to two majority (Justice Cardozo did not participate), concluded that the statute violated the due process clause of the Fourteenth Amendment. Anticipating the division on the Court for the next several years, Justice Brandeis wrote a lengthy dissent in which he argued that this was indeed an appropriate matter for legislatures to regulate. Federal and state governments must have the power, Brandeis argued, to try different economic practices to meet society's changing social and economic needs.

The first nationally significant case that revealed the sharp divisions on the Supreme Court over issues related to the economic Depression involved the review of a critical state law passed during the worst year of the Depression. In *Home Building and Loan Association v. Blaisdell,* (1934), the Supreme Court ruled on the constitutionality of a 1933 Minnesota Mortgage Moratorium Law. The act authorized the Minnesota state courts to consider exempting property from foreclosure during the economic emergency but not beyond May 1, 1935. The case arose when Mr. and Mrs. John H. Blaisdell received a mortgage on a house and lot from the Home Building and Loan Association. Facing financial problems owing to the Depression, the Blaisdells sought to extend their mortgage period and avoid foreclosure through the Minnesota statute. The Loan Association challenged the moratorium (temporary suspension of an action) but a Minnesota district court sided with the Blaisdells and the Minnesota Supreme Court affirmed the ruling. The Loan Association then appealed to the United States Supreme Court. The Association argued that the Minnesota law violated several provisions of the Constitution, including the Contract Clause in Article I, section 10. The Loan Association argued that the language of the clause, "No State shall enter into any...Law impairing the Obligation of Contracts..." prohibited the state from modifying the contractual agreement between the Blaisdells and the Loan Association. In a vote of five to four Chief Justice Charles Evans Hughes and Justice Owen Roberts joined with the three liberals, Justices Cardozo, Stone, and Brandeis, in upholding the Minnesota statute. It turned out to be the most important case interpreting the contract clause in the twentieth century. Government could pass laws affecting existing private contracts.

Hughes acknowledged in the case that the Contract Clause is a safeguard against state restrictions on private contracts but that it was not an absolute ban. The majority's argument was based on two points. First, the state reserved the power under extraordinary conditions to protect the public interest and that may include temporary relief from the enforcement of contracts. Second, the national economic crisis, the Great Depression, constituted just such an emergency.

Writing for the four conservative dissenters, Justice Sutherland refused to acknowledge that emergencies could justify state governments modifying private contracts. He predicted that by the Court allowing the Minnesota law to stand, it would lead to greater invasions against the sanctity of contracts. Although the split on the Court did not bode well for future review of federal legislation, the New Dealers were at least hopeful that they might have a majority who agreed with Chief Justice Hughes' reasoning in favor of the legislation.

A third important case from this early 1930s period involving state economic regulation, *Nebbia v. New York,* was decided on March 5, 1934. As in *Blaisdell* the case involved emergency legislation passed by New York Assembly for the purpose of easing the economic hardship brought on by the Depression. In 1933 New York passed legislation to create a Milk Control Board with power to fix minimum and maximum retail prices of milk. The reason the Milk Board was created was because in 1932 the prices received by farmers for milk was so much below the cost of production that dairy farmers were going out of business. Moreover the decline of prices for milk was much greater than the decline of prices generally. Various remedies were suggested including setting minimum prices for cream and milk and imposing taxes on milk dealers that would equalize the cost of milk and cream to all dealers. The taxes would largely remove the cause of price cutting.

When Leo Nebbia, a grocer in Rochester, New York decided he was going to sell a quart of milk for more than the fixed maximum price, the Milk Board fined him. At his trial Nebbia asserted that the statute violated the equal protection and due process clauses of the Fourteenth Amendment. Equal protection refers to a constitutional guarantee that no one can be denied the same protection of the laws as other people in similar circumstances. When the case finally made its way to the Supreme Court, the five to four split upholding the New York law was exactly the same as what occurred in *Blaisdell.*

In the majority opinion Justice Owen Roberts concluded that a state may regulate business in any of its aspects including the prices to be charged for its products. Roberts maintained that due process did not prohibit government regulation for the public welfare but only demanded that it be accomplished fairly and not unreasonably. The four dissenters relied on half a century of substantive due process jurisprudence (history of case law) in concluding that the Fourteenth Amendment gave the Supreme Court license to strike down economic legislation they believed unreasonable. Again the decision was a close split and New Dealers watched the Court with some ambivalence as they wondered how it would rule on similar efforts by the federal government to regulate and manage the economy.

The two swing votes on the Supreme Court were Chief Justice Hughes and Justice Owen Roberts. They occupied a middle ground, although a largely conservative one, between the reactionary "Four Horsemen" and the three liberals. The New Dealers hoped that Hughes and Roberts might be as receptive to the

expansion of federal power to combat the Great Depression as they seemed to be in cases involving state economic regulation. This hope was soon dashed, however, as the Court struck down one New Deal measure after another. New Deal legislation had been increasingly challenged in the lower federal courts (district courts and courts of appeals) by 1934. The assault from the highest court began in earnest in 1935 as the cases made their way up through the appeals process.

Conflict With Court Develops

The first major Supreme Court decision invalidating (determining unconstitutional) a New Deal program came on January 7, 1935, in *Panama Refining Co. v. Ryan.* The case involved the regulation of petroleum shipments under section 9(c) of the National Industrial Recovery Act (NIRA). The NIRA was a major New Deal economic recovery law passed by Congress in June 1933 creating the National Recovery Administration (NRA). The NRA organized hundreds of boards to regulate individual industries. Section 9(c) gave the president authority to regulate petroleum shipments and Roosevelt through the NRA established the Petroleum Administrative Board to administer the petroleum code. Through the board, executive orders were issued prohibiting the shipment of "hot oil" (oil exceeding previously set production limits) across state lines. The board was trying to control surpluses of oil. During the early 1930s oil prices collapsed as a result of both industry overproduction and consumer underconsumption due to the economic downturn. The oil-producing states, unable to limit production on their own, demanded congressional controls. The result was the "hot oil" provision of the NIRA that attempted to regulate oil production.

An employee of the Panama Refining Company was arrested and jailed for violating the rule set by the board. The company challenged not only the jailing of their employee but also challenged the regulatory authority of the Petroleum Administration Board. They argued that the executive orders made no mention of criminal liability, and the case made its way to the U.S. Supreme Court.

In a complete surprise to the New Dealers, Chief Justice Hughes not only struck down the criminal penalty provisions, but he held that the entire board was unconstitutional on the grounds that Congress, in passing the NIRA, had delegated essentially legislative power to the executive branch. The ruling based on the separation of powers doctrine was unanticipated by the Roosevelt administration. Separation of powers is a fundamental principle of the Constitution in

The Scottsboro Boys, nine black Americans accused of the rapes of two white women, in their cell. The case resulted in a landmark Supreme Court decision in 1932, ruling that the state was responsible for providing adequate defense counsel. (UPI/Corbis-Bettmann. Reproduced by permission.)

which each of the three branches of government—executive, legislative, and judicial—are given specific unique powers that cannot be legally transferred from one to another.

Until the *Panama Refining* case the Supreme Court had never held that Congress had violated this principle by delegating its power to the executive. In previous cases the Court had simply insisted that Congress set standards to guide administrative decisions.

The justices would typically accept general guidelines as meeting the requirement. Eight of the nine justices formed the majority in the *Panama Refining* case making it a decisive ruling. Hughes held that the statute established absolutely no criteria to govern the president's decisions and that Congress had not set a policy regarding the transportation of "hot oil."

Only Justice Cardozo dissented (formally disagreed with the decision) arguing that congressional intention to control the production of "hot oil" was obvious from the statute, and delegations of a similar nature had not encountered a judicial ban in the past. The statute, moreover, according to Cardozo, was designed to meet a "national disaster" in the form of the Great Depression that presented issues only the executive could deal with effectively on a day-to-day basis.

Congress responded to the Court decision by passing the Connally Act in February. The act prohibited the interstate shipment of "hot oil" altogether and authorized the President to lift the ban if prices recovered. The large majority on the Court striking down the provision, however, was a bad omen for the future of the National Recovery Administration (NRA).

The Court ruled again a month later in a series of cases collectively referred to as the "Gold Clause Cases." All four cases had been argued in January and were decided on February 18, 1935, and all essentially dealt with the same issue. As part of the New Deal program to conserve the nation's gold reserves, Congress banned clauses in private and public contracts that required payments must be made in gold. Instead Congress required that they be paid in currency. In all of these cases, parties challenged this action as a breach of their contract obligations and the taking of property without due process under the Constitution. Due process is the right of an accused party to a formal hearing.

In one case for example the petitioner, or suing party, was required to give back $10,000 in gold certificates in exchange for currency. He claimed there was a difference between the value of the gold certificates and the currency he received in exchange because of the struggling economy in the Great Depression. Speaking for the majority, Chief Justice Hughes sustained the authority of Congress to regulate the nation's monetary system. He asserted that the gold clauses in private contracts were merely provisions for payment in certain forms of money. Congress could override such clauses in private contracts that conflicted with its national authority to manage the nation's monetary system. In effect the Supreme Court permitted Congress to restrict existing private contracts. The *Gold Clause Cases,* however, only reaffirmed congressional power over monetary policy not in other business matters. Nevertheless Justice McReynolds led a heated and dramatic dissent joined by Sutherland, Butler, and Van Devanter in which he described the "slippery slope" toward congressional confiscation of private property leading to financial ruin. Any doubt by Roosevelt about how the conservative faction on the Court would review later cases involving New Deal programs had been erased.

On May 6, 1935, the Supreme Court handed down another five to four decision that sent shockwaves through the White House and New Deal agencies. It came on a relatively minor piece of legislation, the Railroad Retirement Act (commonly called the "Pension Act") that Congress passed in June 1934. The law provided a retirement and pension plan for all employers of carriers regulated by the Interstate Commerce Act. Contributions were required of all such carriers and their employees at two percent of their wages to create a retirement fund and pension. The pension would be provided for both current and future employees and also included those who had worked for a railroad a year before the law passed. It was not, however, considered part of the New Deal legislation. Roosevelt, in fact, was initially reluctant to sign the bill into law. The bill was hastily drafted and did not anticipate the costs to the railroads over time. The success of the bill had been the result of the powerful railway unions, or "brotherhoods," and the able piloting of the measure through the Senate by Robert Wagner of New York and through the House by Robert Crosser of Ohio.

Roosevelt was likely not too surprised when 134 railway companies and the Pullman Company filed suit in the District of Columbia in October 1934. The Supreme Court of the District of Columbia invalidated the act and issued an injunction restraining the Railroad Retirement Board from collecting the money for the pensions. The Supreme Court took the case before it could go to the Court of Appeals. What made the administration nervous was the close resemblance the law bore to a pending Social Security bill in Congress in which the White House did have a very large political investment. Most felt that the combination of Hughes, Roberts, Brandeis, Cardozo, and Stone, however, would overturn the ruling of the district court and let the law stand.

The administration miscalculated the votes on the Court, however, with Roberts siding with the "Four Horsemen" in upholding the decision by the District Court, ultimately striking down the law. It was a vote of five to four against the law. Writing for the majority Justice Owen Roberts wrote that the law was both a violation of due process and not the proper exercise of congressional regulatory power over interstate commerce. First, there had been no contractual agreement as to pensions during the period of employment. As a result railway workers had contributed nothing toward the cost of the newly granted pensions. The Court found that requiring the railroads to pay pensions for former employees who had not contributed violated the due process clause of the Fifth Amendment since it was taking the property of the carriers and giving it to the employees. This aspect of the decision was somewhat expected and largely the result of a poorly drafted law. The majority, however, also found that the Retirement Board was not a proper regulation of interstate commerce. In its brief the government argued that the act promoted safety and efficiency by increasing worker morale. This argument relating to the social welfare of the workers was not persuasive and the Court struck down the law.

Although Chief Justice Hughes agreed deficiencies existed in the act, he felt that the majority placed too narrow of an interpretation of the authority of Congress to regulate interstate commerce and he wrote the dissenting opinion. Even though he had not supported the bill initially, Roosevelt understood the peril of the Court's decision. If Justice Roberts continued to think along these lines on national welfare measures, the New Deal would be in serious trouble. As events would soon reveal, *Railroad Retirement Board* was an indicator of decisions to come.

Black Monday for the New Deal

Despite clues coming from the earlier Court decisions of the previous year, nothing could have fully braced the administration for the Supreme Court's announcement on May 27, 1935. The decision would soon acquire the label of "Black Monday." The Court in three unanimous decisions held that the president's removal of an administrator from the Federal Trade Commission was illegal; that the Frazier Lemke Farm Bankruptcy Act of 1934 was invalid; and most significantly, the National Industrial Recovery Act as unconstitutional. It was the most comprehensive judicial assault on the New Deal yet.

When the Court convened the previous Monday, with an overflow audience in its chamber, it became immediately apparent that the day would bring disaster for the New Deal and the Roosevelt administration. Justice Sutherland began by reading a unanimous opinion that the president had exceeded his authority over an independent regulatory agency by removing its director. In deciding *Humphrey's Executor v. United States* Justice Sutherland stated that a president may only remove a commissioner of an independent regulatory agency for cause (a result of inappropriate behavior). Otherwise an arbitrary removal violates the separation of powers doctrine. The case involved the removal of a conservative member of the Federal Trade Commission, William E. Humphrey, by President Roosevelt. A Republican, Humphrey was a mem-

ber of Congress between 1903 and 1917 from Washington State. In 1924 he was campaign manager for Calvin Coolidge's (served 1923–1929) successful presidential bid. Humphrey had long been a bitter opponent of the Federal Trade Commission's investigations of the timber industry in the early 1920s. Coolidge appointed him to a six-year term as commissioner in 1925 with the hope that he would remake the agency into a pro-business organization. Humphrey dominated the Federal Trade Commission, transforming it from a progressive agency working to guarantee free competition into a business-dominated body.

In 1931 President Herbert Hoover (served 1929–1933) appointed him for another six-year term. Roosevelt, however, considered Humphrey to be a hopeless reactionary and fired him in 1933 shortly after taking office. Humphrey brought suit, and although he died in 1934, his estate would carry the case all the way to the Supreme Court. The Court's opinion in the case was clearly viewed by the administration as hampering the New Deal economic program. They claimed that the Court ignored that a commissioner of the Federal Trade Commission is a member of the executive branch. It was a minor ruling compared to the other two that day but Roosevelt was personally angered by the implication of the Court that he had attempted to undermine the U.S. Constitution.

The next decision was read by Justice Brandeis who again spoke for a unanimous Court in *Louisville Joint Stock Bank v. Radford.* This decision invalidated the Frazier-Lemke Act, which was passed by Congress to protect bankrupt farmers from loss of their farms. It provided several alternatives to bankruptcy of the mortgaged property such as allowing a bankrupt farmer to retain his land for five years. During this period of time the farmer could try to satisfy his debt obligations. In 1933 William W. Radford, a farmer in Kentucky who had twice mortgaged his farm with the Louisville Joint Stock Land Bank, defaulted on his payments. Radford failed to negotiate any agreements on his debts and the state court entered a judgment against him to foreclose his farm. Relying on the newly passed Frazier-Lemke Act a federal district court overruled the judgment and ordered the bank to comply. The bank, however, refused to cooperate with a receiver appointed by the district court in accordance with the act. The case was appealed and affirmed in favor of Radford by the Sixth Circuit Court of Appeals in February 1935. When the bank appealed to the Supreme Court Justice Brandeis wrote the opinion striking down the law. The Court concluded that the bank had been deprived of its property without just

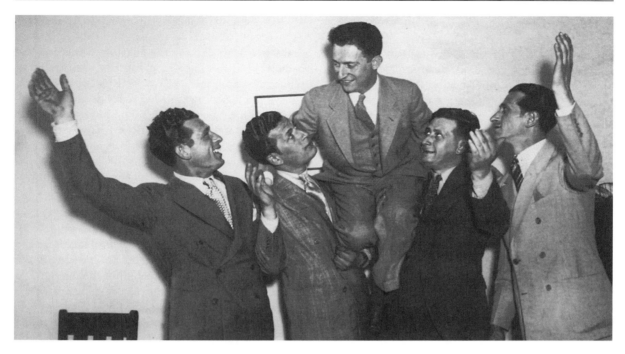

The Schechter brothers with their attorney, Joseph Heller. As a result of the Schechter case, the Supreme Court found that the National Industrial Recovery Act (NIRA) was unconstitutional. (UPI/Corbis-Bettmann. Reproduced by permission.)

compensation. The law was therefore in violation of the Fifth Amendment. Congress later made changes to the law in the Farm Mortgage Moratorium Act of 1935.

For the third opinion of that day Chief Justice Hughes read the decision in *Schechter Poultry Corporation v. United States.* This was the decision the administration was dreading. In it the Supreme Court reviewed the constitutionality of the National Industrial Recovery Act (NIRA) of 1933, the Roosevelt administration's first and most important recovery program. The statute was wide ranging but its principle reliance was upon codes of fair competition approved by the president after development by a trade or industry committee. Violations of the codes were a misdemeanor punishable by a fine.

The "Live Poultry Code," the code at issue in the *Schechter* case, was approved by President Roosevelt on April 13, 1934. It established a 40-hour workweek in the industry, prohibited certain practices of unfair competition, established a 50 cents per hour minimum wage for poultry workers, and required the submission of weekly reports reflecting the volume of sales. The poultry code had been successful in raising wages and banning unfair practices in the industry but there

remained the problem of enforcement. Based on earlier Court decisions, the Justice Department recognized from the outset of the case that the constitutionality of the regulatory scheme administered by the National Recovery Administration (NRA) would be difficult to establish before the Supreme Court.

Considerable effort was made by opponents of the NIRA to find an appropriate "test case" but none was found. Instead a case arose from a relatively minor series of violations by a Brooklyn slaughterhouse, the ALA Schechter Poultry Corporation, and the Schechter Live Poultry Market for violating wage and hour provisions of their industry's code and for selling "unfit chickens." The Schechter brothers who ran the two businesses were indicted and found guilty on eighteen counts of violations in the District Court of New York, while the Circuit Court of Appeals upheld sixteen counts. On the other two counts, those involving the wages and hours provisions, the Court of Appeals reversed the District Court decisions. The Appeals Court ruled that such matters were beyond the regulatory authority of Congress. Both the Schechters and the government appealed the decision to the Supreme Court. The case was argued on May 2 and 3, 1935.

After reviewing the facts of the case in his resounding and dignified voice, Hughes then paused, looked up, and said with a calm voice that the defendants were not involved in interstate commerce. Donald Richberg, the government attorney who argued the case, and who had also been a counsel in the NRA, literally slumped in his chair. Hughes had pronounced the death sentence of the agency.

The Court was unanimous in rejecting the government's case for the regulatory scheme. Writing for the majority, the Chief Justice quickly rebutted the government's argument that the national economic emergency justified the program by succinctly stating that difficult times do not change the Constitution. Hughes called the adoption of the codes by trades and their approval by the president a practice unsupported by law. First the statute had unconstitutionally delegated legislative power to the executive. Secondly the Chief Justice concluded that the poultry code involved regulation of local business transactions, not interstate commerce that is more properly subject of congressional regulation. The Chief Justice relied on the distinction between the "direct" and "indirect" effects on commerce that characterized commerce clause decisions at the time. Hughes asserted that the effects in the *Schechter* case were clearly "indirect" and not enough to warrant congressional regulation. By the end of the day, the NRA lay in ruins.

Roosevelt withheld public comment on the decisions for several days. Finally on Friday, May 31, two hundred reporters crowded into the White House auditorium to hear Roosevelt's statement on the Court decision. The President read excerpts from the letters and telegrams of citizens disgruntled with the Court's ruling. He compared the historical significance of the case to that of the *Dred Scott* decision. He then went on to say that the Court seemed to indicate that the U.S. government had no national economic problems. As to his view of the *Schechter* decision the President warned that the Court had an outdated interpretation of the Constitution's interstate commerce clause. At the time Roosevelt avoided any comment on plans to limit the power of the Supreme Court or to reform the Court through legislation. He was being reserved in his response because the second key component of the New Deal recovery program, the Agricultural Adjustment Administration (AAA), was soon to be reviewed.

The New Deal's AAA Falls

The next several months witnessed further onslaughts on the New Deal recovery program. The most devastating decision after *Schechter* occurred early in 1936. On January 6 in *United States v. But-*

ler the Supreme Court invalidated the Agricultural Adjustment Act by a vote of six to three. Under section 9 and 16 of the act, the federal government was authorized to pay benefits to farmers who agreed to reduce their crop acreage. Funds for the program came from a tax levied on the food processor of the commodity. Butler, a cotton processor, refused to pay the tax and went to federal district court. The court found the government's claim valid and upheld the tax. Butler then appealed to the First Circuit Court of Appeals, which reversed the order. Finally the government appealed and the Supreme Court took the case.

The case was argued in December 1935 and decided only a month later with the Supreme Court voting six to three and completely striking down the Agricultural Adjustment Act. Justice Roberts wrote the somewhat disordered opinion for the majority. In an extraordinary decision the majority invalidated the act on the argument that the regulation and control of agricultural production invaded the powers of the states reserved under the Tenth Amendment. Disagreeing with the decision Stone, joined by Brandeis and Cardozo, launched a scathing attack on the majority's ruling calling it a "tortured" interpretation of the Constitution. As in *Schechter,* the *Butler* decision aroused a storm of controversy from the public.

The final blow from the Court came on May 18, 1936, when they held in *Carter v. Carter Coal Company* that the Guffey-Snyder Bituminous Coal Act was also unconstitutional. The act was designed to bring some economic stability to the soft coal industry after the collapse of the NRA. The Guffey bill had guaranteed collective bargaining in the industry, provided uniform wages, and established a national commission to fix coal prices and control production. In many ways the act amounted to the bituminous coal code of the defunct NRA. Once again the Court's majority was six to three with Brandeis, Stone, and Cardozo in dissent. Sutherland's majority opinion held that the law's labor provisions violated the Tenth Amendment by having Congress intervene in state matters. He completely brushed aside the government's arguments concerning the direct effect of coal mining on the nation's economy. Chief Justice Hughes in a concurring opinion even suggested that if Americans wanted to give such power to Congress to regulate interstate commerce, then they should amend the Constitution. In dissent Cardozo attempted to argue that in a modern, industrial economy labor problems do affect interstate commerce, which was a sentiment that appeared to fall on deaf ears.

By now it appeared to most knowledgeable observers that the conservative bloc of justices were

President Roosevelt addresses the joint session of Congress in 1935, asking for the authority to give jobs to all those receiving relief who were able to work. *(AP/Wide World Photos. Reproduced by permission.)*

freely interjecting their own political views into opinions. When in June the Court overturned a New York minimum wage law for women in *Morehead v. Tipaldo* the Supreme Court appeared even more partisan. Justice Butler read the opinion for the majority asserting that no state legislation could violate the Fourteenth Amendment right of an employee and employer to bargain privately for their terms of employment. Again Justices Stone, Brandeis, and Cardozo were in dissent. Newspapers throughout the country attacked the decision and even the Republican platform of 1936 denounced it. The decision was eclipsed, however, by the landslide reelection victory of Roosevelt in November 1936. Secretly the president began planning his own assault on the Court.

Roosevelt Considers Actions

In November 1936 Roosevelt won the greatest electoral victory to date by capturing the electoral votes in all but 2 of the 48 states. The New Deal had been strongly supported though the ballot box. Roosevelt now felt it a key opportunity to direct his reaffirmed position of strength toward the Supreme Court. Of tremendous concern to New Dealers was the future of wage and hour provisions in the National Labor Relations Act, passed in July 1935, and the constitutionality of the Social Security Act, passed in August

1935. Both were the cornerstones of the Second New Deal. The prospect for these laws, given the recent history of the Court, was grim indeed. It was conceivable that at least one justice, either Hughes or Roberts, would switch allegiance and favor the New Deal legislation. The conservative faction on the Court, however, had become so arrogant by 1936 in its majority opinions that it seemed unlikely. What then, was the administration to do?

Several plans emerged. One was a constitutional amendment to broaden government powers in times of national emergency. The Justice Department had been studying the possibility since early 1935 but there was no agreement on a draft. The president's close advisor Felix Frankfurter opposed the idea and counseled the President not to pursue such a course. In the first place the amendment had to be drafted which had already proved to be difficult. Next it would have to be accepted by two-thirds of the Congress which might be possible given the recent election victories with the Democratic landslide. Finally it would have to run the gauntlet of ratification by the states. Three quarters of state legislatures would have to approve the amendment. This meant that an adverse vote in only 13 states would kill the amendment. Conservative wings of both the Democratic and Republican parties controlled many state legislatures. In addition

Roosevelt did not have much faith in the integrity of several state assemblies.

Money to fight the amendment could be poured into any number of corrupt state legislatures. Both Secretary of the Interior Harold Ickes and counsel for the Reconstruction Finance Corporation Tommy Corcoran thought ratification was impractical. Even if it were possible it would take a long time, something the reformers in the administration believed the New Deal might not have. Besides there was already a child-labor amendment, in its thirteenth year, attempting to win ratification. Finally any amendment, even if passed and ratified, would still be subject to review by the Supreme Court. Eventually Roosevelt and Attorney General Homer Cummings were persuaded that an amendment would indeed be futile. A congressional statute was another possibility but seemed no more promising than an amendment before judicial review of the Court. A majority of justices could invalidate the law.

There was one other idea that had been bouncing around for some time, although in a different context. As early as 1934 judges from several districts, most notably from the Southern District of New York, had lobbied the president for an expansion of the judiciary. Judge William Denman of the Ninth Circuit had also encouraged the Chief Justice to reform and expand the federal court staff to meet the requirements of increasingly large dockets (backlogs of cases). Roosevelt was aware of the problem and discussed it with the Attorney General the night he returned to Washington after his electoral victory in November 1936. It was not until the end of December that an attorney in the Solicitor General's Office drafted a memo in which he outlined a plan to "pack" the Court by increasing the number of Supreme Court Justices. But there were many formidable objections outlined as well. The liberal justices could be antagonized by the assault on the Court to the point where they would retaliate by voting against the constitutionality of the legislation. More likely, however, was the possibility that a significant political backlash would occur. The Court after all was not viewed as a political body that could be staffed by partisan judges. Loading it with new members would appear to undermine its integrity as an autonomous judicial tribunal.

In a sort of test, President Roosevelt in a magazine interview in late 1936 suggested that the number of Justices might be increased by Congress to permit the appointment of men in spirit with the age. Surprisingly there was very little public reaction by the statement; in fact it seemed to go unnoticed. Known to only a handful of advisors in the Justice Depart-

ment, Attorney General Cummings, Solicitor General Stanley Reed, and Donald Richberg had been drafting such a proposal in secret.

The draft of the bill was shown to the president for approval on January 30, 1937. The finishing touches were completed by the afternoon of February 4 and Roosevelt continued to insist on its secrecy. No advanced mention was made about any plan to address the Supreme Court issue in the upcoming State of the Union Address. But the administration did make some convenient leaks. Donald Richberg mentioned the possibility to a reporter at a cocktail party on January 20, and Roosevelt let the leader of the Congress of Industrial Organizations (CIO), John L. Lewis and the American Federation of Labor (AFL) Chair Charlton Ogburn in on the secret. In the meantime the Court was scheduled to hear arguments on the constitutionality of the National Labor Relations Act on Monday, February 8. Roosevelt wanted to submit the bill before then so that it would not be interpreted as a direct threat.

The President's Plan

On Friday, February 5, 1937, Roosevelt sent to Congress his plan for reorganizing the federal judiciary. Among his stated claims in making the proposal was that the federal docket was overcrowded. In one year for example the Supreme Court had denied 87 percent of petitions for hearings on appeal without citing reasons. The provisions included an increase in the membership of the Supreme Court from 9 to 15 justices if justices passed the age of 70 decided not to retire, adding 50 judges at all levels of the federal court system, and assigning more district judges in congested areas to improve the efficiency of the courts.

Despite a strong reaction against the proposal from the public and many in Congress, passage of the bill still looked promising. The forceful Joseph T. Robinson of Arkansas, chairman of the Senate Judiciary Committee, favored the proposal and confided to the president that he could supply the votes. Ardent backing came from Senators Hugo Black of Alabama and Sherman Minton of Indiana. The White House assessed that only 15 Democrats would absolutely not support the bill. In support of the bill Senator Robert J. Buckley of Ohio implored his colleagues to think carefully about the proposal and to realize that the Constitution is an instrument of government to be worked. That it was a document, flexible and responsive to the times. But the bill's opposition became greater than expected. Senators Carter Glass of Virginia and Josiah Bailey of North Carolina effectively defected from the New Deal in response to the court-packing scheme and the loss of Burton K. Wheeler spelled ultimate disaster. Many in Congress also took exception to the emphasis on the age of the Justices. It seemed obvious that Roosevelt wanted to pack the Court with liberal Justices of any age. By far however the dominant opposition came from moderates who feared that only the Court could protect civil liberties in the future and this would weaken their ability to do so. In the minds of most Senators and Congressmen, the Court was the last bulwark of protection against a future Congress or President who might exercise dictatorial power and strip citizens of the freedom of the press or speech. Such developments were occurring in Europe at that time.

Hearings began in the Senate Judiciary Committee in March 1937. At the urging of the Republican minority leader Charles McNary of Oregon, the Republicans kept quiet on the issue as much as possible so as not to give the Democrats cause to reunite. The president, meanwhile, continued to push his proposal at an address to the Democratic Victory Dinner in Washington, DC, and in a fireside chat. By the end of March it looked as if the administration might have a victory.

Labor Problems Capture the Public Attention

In the meantime other events unfolding in the winter of 1936–1937 did much to intensify concern over the Great Depression and the state of the country. On December 30, 1936, a great wave of sit-down strikes at General Motors began. In response to General Motors firing two workers, the entire seven thousand employees at the Fisher Body Plant No. 1 sat down on the job and refused to work. Within minutes Plant No. 2 followed them. Sit-downs soon spread to the other plants and for 40 days two thousand striking workers engaged in outright urban warfare, turning fire hoses on the police who in turn attacked them with tear gas. Eventually the police were driven back, but only after 13 workers were seriously injured. A nervous Governor Frank Murphy of Michigan had to call in the National Guard to quell the siege.

Sit-downs became a widely used tactic in other industries in 1937. In 1936 there were only 48 sit down strikes in various industries across the country. In 1937 after the wave of sit-downs in Flint, there were 10 times as many. Sit-down strikes paralyzed the automobile industry in Flint, Michigan, and the rubber industry in Akron, Ohio. Both were front-page news in every paper across the country. Many of the strikes in 1937 were violent. The most famous incident occurred on Memorial Day 1937 at the Republic Steel Plant in Chicago. Police fired upon a picket line killing 10 of the striking workers. It was a level of civil unrest not seen since the Civil War (1861–1865).

Another labor-related issue was also raising public concern. Beginning in 1936 a subcommittee of the Senate Committee on Education and Labor conducted the most extensive investigation of civil liberties infractions ever undertaken by Congress. It was authorized to investigate violations of the rights of free speech and assembly and undue interference with the right of labor to organize and bargain collectively. The committee focused on the Constitution's Bill of Rights and the National Labor Relation Act's guarantees of the right to organize and bargain, which relate directly to the First Amendment rights to freedom of speech and assembly. During 1936 the Civil Liberties Committee worked closely with the National Labor Relations Board (NLRB). Hearings had begun in April 1936 and though most of the revelations of the committee would come out after 1937, the findings released by late 1936 were shocking. Testimony was given about the extensive and lucrative business of labor espionage and strikebreaking. Revelations of spies in union leadership positions were rife. Corroborated and well-publicized incidents of violence were described such as the assassination of union leaders in the 1934 San Francisco Longshoremen strike by hired sharpshooters. The Committee also made a careful study of munitions sales. Between 1933 and 1937 Republic Steel, United States Steel, Bethlehem Steel, and Youngstown Sheet and Tube each purchased more tear gas, gas guns, and gas canisters than any law enforcement agency in the country. Republic Steel's arsenal included hundreds of revolvers, rifles, shotguns, and gas guns, thousands of gas grenades, and numerous nightsticks and gas revolvers. When newspapers and magazines referred to the prospects of an imminent "industrial war," they meant it quite literally.

The Court's Change in Direction

Of central concern to activists in the labor struggle occurring all over the country was whether workers had the right to bargain collectively as guaranteed in the Labor Relations Act. Only four days after Roosevelt's announcement of the court-packing plan, the Supreme Court began hearing arguments in a case challenging the validity of the act.

The National Labor Relations Board (NLRB) had charged Jones & Laughlin Steel Corporation with unfair labor practices in violation of the National Labor Relations Act. The corporation was accused of discriminating against union members in its hiring and tenure (job security) policies, of using intimidation to discourage union membership, and firing employees who were active in union affairs. Jones & Laughlin insisted that employees were discharged for reasons other than union membership. But counsel for Jones & Laughlin challenged the constitutionality of the NLRB and moved for a dismissal of the case. When the NLRB denied the motion, the counsel for Jones & Laughlin walked out. The NLRB investigated further and sustained the charges. In accordance with its authority granted by the National Labor Relations Act, it ordered the corporation to stop its intimidation of union members, to reinstate the discharged employees, and to post notices for 30 days that the company would not discriminate against union workers. Again Jones & Laughlin refused to comply and the NLRB petitioned the Fifth Circuit Court of Appeals to enforce the order. The Fifth Circuit denied the petition, however, holding that it was beyond the scope of federal power to appeal the case. The United States then appealed to the Supreme Court.

At issue was whether Congress had authority under the Commerce Clause to enforce those provisions of the Labor Relations Act that guaranteed the right to bargain collectively and if it also had authority to compel employers to recognize unions. Solicitor General Stanley Reed presented the government's arguments, providing substantial testimony from labor experts and economists that labor unrest had a significant impact on interstate commerce. The crux of Reed's position was that the act applied only to industry involved in interstate commerce and to businesses in which labor disputes would affect interstate commerce. In addition the NLRB decisions did not undermine the separation of powers doctrine, Reed contended. Though the Board is an administrative agency, any appeal of the NLRB's decisions goes directly to the Court of Appeals, not the lower District Courts. At 4:08 PM on February 11, 1937, the Justices left the Courtroom to convene in their private chambers and the fate of the National Labor Relations Act was entirely in their hands.

On March 29, 1937, the Supreme Court was scheduled to read its decision in the *Jones & Laughlin* case. The Court's ruling would determine not only the future of collective bargaining under the National Labor Relations Act, but also the future of industrial relations in the country. The decision could potentially bring an end to the New Deal but it could also potentially destroy the authority of the Supreme Court by adverse public reaction. There was little doubt that whatever the Court concluded, the decision would be a turning point in history. The Court, however, had a surprise up its sleeve and to the amazement of everyone, Chief Justice Hughes announced to a packed room that he would not be reading the decision in *Jones & Laughlin* that day. He then proceeded to read the opinion of an entirely different case, *West Coast*

Hotel v. Parrish that involved a Washington State minimum wage statute almost identical to that of *New York v. Tipaldo* decided a year before.

The Washington statute set a minimum number of work hours for women and minors. It also established an Industrial Welfare Commission to set standards for wages and work conditions. The case was first brought forth by Elsie Parrish, a hotel maid who lived in Wenatchee, Washington. She decided to sue the Cascadian Hotel, the leading hotel in town, for back pay. She asked for $216.19, the difference between what she had been paid and what she should have been paid under the State's minimum wage mandated for her occupation. The trial court ruled that the law was unconstitutional because it violated the liberty of contract principle read into the Fourteenth Amendment. The Supreme Court of Washington, however, took a different view on appeal and on April 2, 1936, overturned the lower court's opinion. Only eight weeks later, it would be before the Supreme Court of the United States.

In one of the most dramatic reversals of past precedent in the history of the Court, the majority upheld the Washington law. Chief Justice Hughes and Justice Roberts sided with the liberal bloc with the Four Horsemen now in the minority. Chief Justice Hughes concluded that while the Constitution protects liberty of contract, it is subject to reasonable regulation in the interest of the community. State power to restrict freedom of contract was especially relevant in protecting vulnerable workers against abuses of unconscionable employers who paid less than a living wage. Most importantly Hughes acknowledged that though the wisdom of the law was debatable, it was a matter for the legislature not the courts. Despite the predictable dissent by Sutherland, McReynolds, Van Devanter, and Butler, the decision was a watershed. The majority of the Court established a position of support the States and legislature and explicitly overruled the earlier *New York v. Tipaldo*. Justice Roberts provided the fifth and most crucial vote in the decision. There has been much speculation as to whether the switch of Hughes and Roberts was genuine or the result of pressure on the Supreme Court.

On April 12 the Court finally read its decision in *National Labor Relations Board v. Jones & Laughlin Steel Corporation*. Chief Justice Hughes, writing for the majority, immediately announced that the Court had upheld the constitutional validity of the Labor Relations Act. After reviewing the major provisions of the act, Hughes discussed the complex and extensive operations of the Jones & Laughlin Steel Corporation. It left no doubt that the corporation was involved in interstate commerce on a massive scale. He concluded the following things: the act was within congressional

Members of the 1937 Supreme Court. Chief Justice Charles Evans Hughes (front row, center) was one of the most ardent opponents of President Roosevelt's plan to add members to the court. (© *Hulton Archive. Reproduced by permission.*)

authority; that employees had a fundamental right to organize and select representatives for collective bargaining; and, that the effect of labor strife on interstate commerce would be direct and catastrophic. In dissent the Four Horseman called for invalidation of the National Labor Relations Act on grounds that the production enterprises in manufacturing were local in nature and only affected interstate commerce indirectly. Sutherland, Butler, Van Devanter, and McReynolds, however, were no longer in the position they had been only a year before. The Court would no longer veto the federal government's attempts to regulate the economy. *Jones & Laughlin* became one of the most important Supreme Court decisions of the twentieth century.

The Court Battle Ends

It was a decision that heralded a turning point for the Supreme Court and in doing so it also removed the principle reason for Roosevelt's court-packing plan. In addition on May 18 Justice Van Devanter announced that he would resign from the bench. The "conversion" of Roberts had given Roosevelt a five to four majority. Soon it would be six to three with a new appointment to replace Van Devanter. Privately Roosevelt was urged to call off the fight by Senate Democrats. Before

the end of May, Roosevelt's lieutenants in Congress had also concluded that they no longer had enough votes. Five unofficial polls in the Senate came out with the same result—defeat. When the Senate Judiciary Committee announced its conclusion of the bill, the language was less than complimentary. The report described the proposal both as an effort to punish the Justices, whose decisions were resented and a measure that would create a dangerous precedent in undermining the entire system of checks and balances. A new Gallup survey showed that support for judicial reform was only at about 41 percent. It now appeared Roosevelt was facing the largest legislative defeat of his presidency. All was not yet lost, though, nor was Roosevelt about to give up the fight. On June 16 the President announced that all the Democratic Congressmen were invited to spend three days with him picnicking on an Island in Chesapeake Bay. The foes of the President who had painted him as a man consumed with revenge instead found a merry host who radiated geniality and warmth. The Roosevelt charm worked its magic and the president was able to clinch a few votes needed to consider a compromise on the Court plan.

Meanwhile, Senator Joe Robinson, the Senate majority leader, was assembling a coalition that would support the bill and the debate would open in July. Robinson hoped that, although he could not predict how several in his own ranks would vote, he might prevail if he could turn the debate into an endurance contest. But secretly Robinson knew he did not have enough votes. His plan was therefore to browbeat the Democratic Senators into submission by warning of the political price his colleagues would likely pay for defying the popular president. On the opening day of the debate, Robinson charged around the floor and bellowed for two hours about the importance of passing the bill and at times his face would turn purple with anger. When the opposition Senators began peppering him with questions, he grew louder and angrier. Then suddenly, he stopped, took a match out of his pocket and struck it to light a cigar. His colleagues were stunned. One did not smoke in the Senate and for a brief moment Robinson appeared bewildered. Then he told the assembly that there would be no more questions and abruptly left the chamber. For the next several days, lawmakers had a difficult time enduring the July heat and Robinson especially looked exhausted. Then on July 14, a week after the debate had begun, Senator Joe Robinson of Arkansas died.

Robinson's death had a marked effect on the Senate. Whatever momentum the court-packing bill had gathered under his stewardship was now lost. On July 22 Senator Marvel Logan of Kentucky moved that the bill be sent back to committee. The motion passed by a vote of 70 to 20 where the bill died in the Senate Judiciary Committee. A compromise measure was passed on August 26 reforming some lower court procedures. It did not, however, touch upon the appointment of judges in the federal court system. Roosevelt's fight to pack the Supreme Court was at an end.

In many ways the court battle marked the beginning of the end of the New Deal. Although the Supreme Court no longer overturned New Deal legislation, Roosevelt would never again enjoy the political dominance on Capitol Hill that he had at the beginning of 1937. The battle created a rallying point around which his political opposition came together. The court struggle squandered the electoral advantage of the major Democratic election victories of 1936. The court battle also produced divisions in the Democratic Party that ultimately weakened the administration's reform program.

Contributing Forces

State Powers Versus Federal Powers

A predominant judicial philosophy of constitutional interpretation arose out of the nineteenth cen-

tury. Prior to the 1930s the courts consistently sought to preserve certain rights for the states under an interpretation of the Tenth Amendment. The amendment specifies "the powers not delegated to the United States by the Constitution, nor prohibited by it to the States, are reserved to the States respectively, or to the people." Tenth Amendment jurisprudence developed during the nineteenth century in such a way as to limit the influence of the federal government over the states.

In 1875 for example a federal Civil Rights Act was declared unconstitutional on the grounds that it was contrary to the Tenth Amendment. But almost directly in conflict with the Tenth Amendment interpretations that developed during the latter half of the nineteenth century was the interpretation of the Constitution's Commerce Power that developed in the early twentieth century. Article I, section 3 of the Constitution gave Congress power "to regulate Commerce with foreign nations, among the several States, and with Indian Tribes." This power to regulate interstate commerce was not often in conflict with the Tenth Amendment during the nineteenth century. Most of the cases involved railroads and the question as to what point and to what extent states could regulate rates on interstate lines. Courts did their best to apply an interpretation laid out in an 1852 case in which the Supreme Court adopted a rule of "selective exclusiveness" which means that when a commerce issue requires a national uniform rule, only Congress can regulate it. If the commerce is of a local nature, only states can regulate it.

It was inevitable that interpretation of the federal government's power to regulate interstate commerce would change in the late nineteenth century as the economy became more industrialized and complex. In a series of cases between 1887 and 1914 the Court upheld the authority of the Interstate Commerce Commission (ICC) to oversee rates on interstate railroads. In the *Shreveport Rates Cases* (1914), the Supreme Court even upheld the ICC's authority to regulate rates on carriers that were strictly within a state. In 1905 the Supreme Court was finally forced to develop a new doctrine with which to analyze the Commerce Clause. In *Swift & Co. v. United States* (1905), the Court unanimously agreed that a price-fixing arrangement among meatpackers, although done locally, did restrain interstate commerce. Justice Oliver Wendell Holmes formulated the "stream of commerce" theory, specifying that Congress could regulate the local business that affected interstate commerce so long as the business actions had not been simply accidental. Through the first two decades of the twentieth century, the Court increasingly relied on this doctrine to uphold an increasing number of national regulatory measures over business.

Still the courts frequently ruled that federal regulatory programs violated the Tenth Amendment. In 1903 for example the Supreme Court upheld a congressional act forbidding the shipment of interstate lottery tickets in *Champion v. Ames* (1903). The most obvious purpose of the act was to regulate interstate commerce but it secondarily intruded upon an area of regulation, gambling, which had always been within the exclusive domain of the States. In fact the Court upheld a number of regulatory measures during the period based on the commerce power, including the Pure Food and Drug Act (1906), the Meat Inspection Acts (1906 and 1907), and the White Slave Traffic Act (1909). The problem was that the Supreme Court was never entirely consistent in its rulings during this period. Limitations on the commerce power by virtue of the Tenth Amendment were sometimes upheld. In *Keller v. United States* (1909) for example the Court concluded that an act preventing alien women from immoral trafficking, which is crossing state lines for the purpose of prostitution, was an unconstitutional violation of the Tenth Amendment.

Nevertheless there appeared to be a gradual erosion of state powers under the Tenth Amendment until 1918 in *Hammer v. Dagenhart* (1918). In that decision the Court held that a federal law prohibiting the interstate shipment of products from mines or factories that employed children under the age of 14 was unconstitutional. Four years later the Supreme Court struck down a second child labor law. Thus a distinct conflict between the Tenth Amendment promoting state powers and the Commerce Clause promoting federal powers had distinctly emerged by the 1920s.

There were a host of other legal traditions that made conservatives, who dominated the American judiciary of the period, suspicious of regulatory legislation (laws that restrict the certain of selected industries). In theory regulatory agencies could be ruled unconstitutional under separation of powers principles such as the delegation of congressional authority to the executive branch. The U.S. Constitution had assigned distinct responsibilities to each of the three branches of government—executive, legislative, and judicial—that could not be legally transferred from one branch to another. This legal doctrine is referred to as the separation of powers. Regulatory schemes were also often found in violation of substantive due process under the Fourteenth Amendment. The Court could bar a state from enforcing legislation that would limit the freedom of contract or liberty of conducting business. Minimum wages and collective bargaining

guarantees, for example, were generally considered in violation of common law's support for private property interests and the freedom to contract without state interference. Late nineteenth century judges held such measures interfered with the free marketplace and equality of economic opportunity.

A Conservative Court for the 1920s

Following World War I a distinctly conservative tone of the Supreme Court became even more pronounced with the appointment of William Howard Taft as Chief Justice in 1921. The ideology would characterize the 1920s was a steadfast opposition to both state and federal efforts to regulate the economy. The opinions of the Court reflected a classic view of economic theory that arose out of the nineteenth century. It embraced a doctrine committed to: a total free market control of the economy; a hostility to any type of government regulation; the embrace of Social Darwinism, which extolled the virtue of competition in the struggle economic survival of the fittest; and, a rigidly formal approach to court decisions that did not consider relevant social and economic issues. Underlying the hostility toward restraints on competition and the praise of American individualism was a fear of social unrest, immigration, and organized labor. This conservative ideology of the period was often referred to as "*laissez-faire* constitutionalism." It first surfaced in the Supreme Court decisions through the dissents of Justice Stephen J. Field and Joseph B. Bradley in the *Slaughterhouse Cases* (1873).

By the 1890s it commanded a majority on the Court. In 1905 for example the Court held in the landmark case *Lochner v. New York,* that the due process clause in the Fourteenth Amendment included the doctrine of "liberty of contract," a concept used by Field in his dissent in the *Slaughterhouse Cases.* The doctrine held that parties capable of entering into a contract and giving their consent to its terms ought not to be restricted by the government, unless it was to protect the health, welfare, and morals of the community.

Though this ideal looked sensible on the surface, judges from the 1890s until the mid-1930s inserted the freedom of contract doctrine much further into other parts of the Constitution including interpretations of civil liberties to the same extent as employment contracts. For example the Supreme Court held that states could not prevent an employer from dismissing an employee for joining a union (*Adair v. United States,* 1908) and that states or the federal government could not enact minimum wage laws (*Adkins v. Children's Hospital,* 1923). In the cases that followed, "freedom of contract" clearly favored powerful employers. The

More About...

Development of a New Deal Legal Philosophy

In a series of articles published between 1905 and 1923, Roscoe Pound of the Harvard Law School criticized the prevailing assumptions of what he considered "mechanical jurisprudence." Mechanical jurisprudence meant that judges were solely looking at the purely technical aspects of how the law in question was crafted. Pound called for a "sociological jurisprudence," a judicial outlook that would view the law as a part of the political, economic, and social situations in which the law was drafted. Judges, Pound asserted, by seeking enlightenment from disciplines outside of the law, would become more knowledgeable about the impact of legal decisions on society. The "Brandeis Brief," a legal argument submitted by Louis D. Brandeis, then a well-known attorney and social activist, in *Muller v. Oregon* (1908) highlighted this approach in practice. The argument supported the constitutionality of an Oregon law that limited the number of hours per day that women could work in laundries and other industries. The brief devoted only two pages to a discussion of actual legal issues, while the remaining 110 pages were devoted to evidence of the harmful effects of long work hours from medical reports, psychological assessments, statistical compilations, and conclusions of various public studies. Brandeis used the brief to demonstrate that a reasonable basis for the Oregon law existed. He won the case and the Brandeis brief forever changed legal arguments before the Supreme Court. Such evidence became routinely admitted in arguments by New Deal lawyers in arguing the need for government action to spur economic recovery from the Great Depression and thereafter.

In the 1930s another movement led by "legal realists" went even further than proponents of socio-logical jurisprudence. Legal realists viewed law as constantly in a state of change in response to social conditions. Karl Llewellyn, the leading proponent of legal realism, argued that one had to look not at abstract legal rules but at how a law actually came to be made to understand it. One argument of his was that judges and legislatures did not "discover" law as the traditional common law notion held, but they made it up as they went along attempting to solve society's problems. And this process of developing law was the result of any number of psychological, economic, and sociological factors. The fundamental principle of the realist movement was promoting that there must be an examination of what effect a law actually has. The law should not be judged on narrow, abstract principles, such as the fundamental right to enter into a contract without interference, the realists argued. Rather an analysis must include the law's wider impact.

The realists found a couple of allies on the Supreme Court bench in Cardozo and Brandeis, who were sympathetic to their arguments. There were many more adherents of legal realism in the New Deal agencies, however, most notably Jerome Frank who was general counsel to the Agricultural Adjustment Administration. Frank wrote an influential book entitled *Law and the Modern Mind* (1930), in which he argued that it was necessary for lawyers and judges to consider the real life elements at play in assessing the appropriateness and fairness of a law. The realist movement achieved several objectives in the development of American jurisprudence including during he Depression of assessing the actual social and economic need for a measure.

---

doctrine was not without its critics on the Court; Justice Oliver Wendell Holmes strongly contested the majority in *Lochner*. In his 1912 campaign for President, Theodore Roosevelt hammered at the Supreme Court's decision in *Lochner* and *Adair*. He accused them of hiding behind a veil of judicial independence while favoring the powerful and limiting the legal options of organized labor and minorities.

The ideology of *laissez-faire* constitutionalism also embraced a restrictive view of federal regulatory power when it so much as touched on liberty of contract. In *United States v. E.C. Knight Co.* (1895), the Court severely limited the scope of the Sherman Anti-Trust Act to limit business monopolies. The majority held that indirect links to interstate commerce was not a sufficient basis for Congress to pass regulatory laws.

The Court also made a distinction between manufacturing and commerce. Manufacturing did not constitute interstate commerce, the Court reasoned, and therefore could not be regulated by Congress. In *Hammer v. Dagenhart* (1918) the Court struck down a 1916 federal law, the Keating-Owen Child Labor Act, that would abolish child labor.

The law used the constitutional authority of Congress to regulate interstate commerce to bar goods made by children form interstate commerce. The five-justice majority held that it was a matter for the states. Justice Oliver Wendell Holmes fashioned one of the most heated dissenting opinions in the Court's history. He accused the Court majority of being in defiance of the democratic will of the people. Congress responded by enacting a second federal child labor law. This time it used the taxing power to restrict the use of child labor so as to achieve the same regulatory standards contained in the Keating-Owen law. The Court, however, overturned this statute in *Bailey v. Drexel Furniture Co.* (1922). It was not until two decades later, after the constitutional revolution of 1937, when a unanimous bench in *United States v. Darby Lumber Co.* (1941) vindicated Justice Holmes' 1918 dissent and recognized the authority of the federal government to regulate child labor practices.

Perspectives

Public Perspectives

With growing public discontent over previous Supreme Court decisions that were detrimental to New Deal program, the public became enraged by the Court decisions on Black Monday. The public put considerable pressure on President Roosevelt to make a public statement in the wake of the *Schechter* decision striking down the NIRA. Roosevelt avoided doing so, even in a press conference two days later. For the next several days citizens sent telegrams to the White House from all over the country. Many were from small businessmen seeking protection by New Deal programs from big business in these economically difficult times. They urged the president to challenge the Court in some way, perhaps by pursuing a constitutional amendment expanding the presidential powers in times of national crisis or to enacting further legislation.

This strong public support for the president and his programs was further demonstrated that fall in the presidential election. Voters gave Roosevelt a landslide victory in his reelection bid. The president interpreted this overwhelming support as a strong vote of confidence in New Deal programs and continued dissatisfaction with the Supreme Court's obstructionist position.

The judicial reorganization plan Roosevelt unveiled that winter, however, enraged the public even more—this time against him. His persistence in promoting the plan through the early half of 1937 despite strong widespread criticism only made public disenchantment with the president more permanent.

As a result voters would never again support politicians who supported the New Deal. They would never again enjoy the election victories of the magnitude of 1936. Many middle class voters were simply too uneasy with the president's attack on the independence of the judiciary.

National Perspectives

The adverse decisions by the Supreme Court against the New Deal programs brought much scorn at the national level. For example in the media it had become commonplace to refer to the Justices as the "Nine old men." The term had been thrown out in an off-the-cuff remark by brain truster Adolph Berle to a journalist after a press conference. The widely circulated columnists Drew Pearson and Robert S. Allen made it a household expression by the publication of a book titled *Nine Old Men* in October 1936. Both authors suggested that scores of antiquated and senile judges were on the federal bench, and the book quickly climbed the best-seller lists. There was even a call in the Senate to investigate several of the allegations made in the book. Senator Guffey of Pennsylvania called it the most shocking disclosure on public officials he had ever read. Following in the wake of the story's interest, the widely circulated *Collier's* magazine published an article in December discussing the constitutional authority of the Supreme Court to declare acts of the legislature unconstitutional.

The scorn, however, was soon to include the president as well. What began as a fight between the White House and the judiciary quickly turned into a full-scale war between the administration and Congress. The "court-packing" bill introduced by President Roosevelt on February 5, 1937, attracted some of the most intense response of any legislative proposal in the twentieth century. For the next several weeks, newspapers carried headline banners about the Supreme Court issue. Constituents inundated Congressmen with letters and everyone was talking about the plan. The administration hoped to concentrate its lobbying efforts on the Senate, in part to avoid the hostile House Judiciary Committee. A storm of criticism, however, descended upon the president from both chambers.

Many of Roosevelt's faithful supporters in Congress suddenly felt blindsided, having not been alerted or informed by the president before his public announcement. Opponents of the plan labeled the bill nothing more than a superficial plan to pack the Court in order to find Justices who would be more responsive to the president's legislative aims. The charge of court inefficiency, though recognized as a real problem, was considered as nothing more than a disingenuous excuse by Roosevelt to further his aims and many conservative Democrats were outraged. They accused Roosevelt of attempting to wield dictatorial power and tamper with the separation of powers in American government. Several of the conservatives in the Democratic Party who were not strong supporters of New Deal legislation before abandoned the president for good. Bipartisan support for the New Deal from Republican Progressives seeped away. Most Senators, however, opposed the bill on grounds that it would weaken the Supreme Court in the future.

Democratic opposition was led by Senator Burton K. Wheeler of Montana, an early Democratic supporter of the New Deal who had gradually drifted away from Roosevelt's agenda. Wheeler counterattacked the President's proposal in one public statement after another. The Court battle resulted in a break in the close relationship between Senator Burton K. Wheeler of Montana, who had been instrumental in getting New Deal bills through Congress, and the president. It soon became clear that although the Democrats had an overwhelming majority in the Senate, the administration was in for a long battle.

The Court controversy also divided the Democratic Party in the states. In Massachusetts, for example, the Democratic Governor opposed the plan while the rest of his agency heads supported it. For states that had two Democratic senators, including Indiana, Missouri, New Jersey, North Carolina, Ohio, Rhode Island, South Carolina, Tennessee, Texas, Utah, and West Virginia, each senator took opposite positions on the bill from the other in his state.

Impact

The political cost of the Court fight to the New Deal was enormous. For decades many were left puzzled by President Franklin Roosevelt's dramatic actions against the Court. The court-packing fight of 1937 had greatly weakened the New Deal. As a result the proposal has been considered the most important political blunder of the Roosevelt administration. It was a debacle all the more astonishing given that it was

pushed by a president who at all other times showed extraordinary political cunning. Many Democrats in Congress at the time began asking how Roosevelt could not have known that the effort would end in political disaster. Other factors, however, were also leading to a decline of political support for the New Deal in 1937 and 1938. An anti-New Deal coalition had been gaining momentum in Congress as both parties were electing more conservative politicians. Also an economic recession toward the end of 1937 did not help the administration's popularity. The battle over the Supreme Court, however, undoubtedly accelerated the New Deal demise. The Court controversy helped bind a growing bipartisan coalition that opposed the New Deal. Prospects for more far-reaching reform had greatly diminished after the Court fight. Years later former Secretary of Agriculture Henry Wallace reflected that the Court fight had been the end of the New Deal reform program. It would not be until almost three decades later in the 1960s that advocates of social reform would again see success in Congress.

Although Roosevelt may have lost the battle, a battle in changing the Court structure, that undoubtedly took a great toll on the future of his administration, he did win the war with the Court. Roosevelt saved the major programs left in the New Deal from being struck down by the Supreme Court. After 1937 the Supreme Court dramatically expanded the commerce power by its ruling in *Jones & Laughlin.* It also supported the Social Security Act in the *Helvering v. Davis* decision announced on May 24, 1937. It would not again strike down a single piece of federal legislation simply because it constrained business in some way. The Court had clearly discarded the notion of *laissez-faire,* noninterventionist government. A major step was made in adapting the Constitution to the needs of the twentieth century.

This victory in changing the philosophical direction of the Court was accomplished largely through appointments. By the end of 1941 only four years after the Roosevelt's Court battle had been waged, the president had been able to choose seven of the nine Justices on the Court due to deaths and retirements. This is more than any other President since George Washington. Roosevelt's nominee Hugo Black was confirmed on August 12, 1937 after Justice Van Devanter retired. Stanley Reed, who had argued for the government in *Jones & Laughlin,* was placed on the Court when Justice Sutherland retired in 1938. The president's long time friend and advisor Felix Frankfurter replaced Pierce Butler who died suddenly in November 1939. William O. Douglas was appointed on the Court the same year to replace the retiring Louis Brandeis. In 1940 Roosevelt named Frank Murphy, the former Governor of Michigan, and a year later the President named Robert Jackson and James F. Byrnes. The new majority on the Court ruled favorably on every New Deal measure that came before it. This new Court—the "Roosevelt Court" as it was called—ultimately became the most liberal and progressive Supreme Court in American history.

Over the next generation, the Supreme Court would expand the Bill of Rights to reach into the states ending government supported racial segregation. It also further enlarged the federal government's commerce power to the point of allowing Congress to prohibit anti-discriminatory practices in business against minorities because it affected interstate commerce. Some legal scholars refer to this change over in Court history as the "Constitutional Revolution of 1937." In the history of the Supreme Court, no event has had more momentous consequences.

Notable People

Charles Evans Hughes (1862–1948). Hughes became one of the most prominent figures in American politics and government during the first half of the twentieth century. Born in Glen Falls, New York, Hughes' father was an itinerant preacher and he grew up in the strict atmosphere of a Christian household. After graduating from Brown University he entered Columbia Law School in 1882 where he completed his degree and passed the bar in 1884. Accepted to the prominent law firm of Walter S. Carter, Hughes became both a partner and a son-in-law to the senior partner after he married Antoinette Carter in 1888. Hughes developed a busy commercial law practice.

During this time, Hughes developed an interest in Republican reform politics. In 1905 this interest began in earnest when he became a counsel to state legislative committees investigating abuses in the New York gas utilities and insurance trades. Hughes attracted the attention of New York progressives when he exposed the malpractice in these industries. The resulting notoriety enabled Hughes to run and win against William Randolph Hearst for governor of New York in 1906 in an extremely close race. In his first term as governor, Hughes was an able administrator who helped secure passage of important progressive reform legislation in utilities regulation and workmen's compensation. He was however never popular with local party bosses whom he alienated when he maintained the state's ban on racetrack betting. Hughes also managed to offend President Theodore Roosevelt by rejecting an offer

from the president to intervene in a New York insurance controversy. Unfortunately the split between Hughes and Theodore Roosevelt was permanent. In 1908 Hughes was re-elected but he was isolated in his party. When President Taft (served 1909–1913) offered Hughes a seat on the Supreme Court in 1910, governor Hughes accepted without reservation.

For the next six years Hughes wrote 151 opinions, dissented 32 times only, and encountered dissent in only nine of his opinions. He was also regarded as a liberal and an activist for his decisions in the Minnesota Rates Case (1913) and the Shreveport Case (1914) in which Hughes, writing for the majority, asserted the exclusive power of Congress to regulate interstate commerce and areas of state commerce where it intertwined the national economy. In 1916 Hughes was persuaded to leave the Court and run for president against Woodrow Wilson (served 1913–1921). The campaign did not go well, however, since the Theodore Roosevelt wing shifted the party's position on foreign policy in a way that seemed overly aggressive to largely isolationist voters. Additionally Hughes could not challenge Wilson's domestic reform agenda and seemed stuck in campaigning on traditional Republican views on labor and the tariff. He failed to unite Republican progressives from the mid and far West, a move which might have helped considerably, and Hughes lost the election.

Out of politics Hughes returned to the practice of law in New York, though he continued to be outspoken on political issues. The Republicans were back in office when Warren G. Harding (served 1921–1923) won the presidency in 1920 and Hughes was appointed Secretary of State. His greatest accomplishment occurred in 1921 and 1922 when he successfully negotiated a series of treaties limiting the naval arms race and reducing tensions in the Far East.

Hughes resigned as Secretary of State in 1925 and returned to his law practice. It would not be long before he again returned to government service. In 1930 President Hoover nominated Hughes to be Chief Justice of the Supreme Court to replace Taft who retired. He had embraced progressive causes throughout his political life but was now presiding over a conservative Supreme Court in the midst of the Depression. In the early years of the New Deal, the Supreme Court seemed to stand in the way of Roosevelt's programs, striking down legislation that conflicted with the conservative view of the Constitution. Hughes often sided with the "Four Horseman," McReynolds, Sutherland, VanDevanter, and Butler, as a swing vote along with Roberts to strike down New Deal legislation. In many decisions after 1935, he took sides against the conservative faction. Consistent

Hugo LaFayette Black was President Franklin Roosevelt's first appointee to the United States Supreme Court in 1937. (The Library of Congress.)

with his previous government service, Hughes also continued to defend the rights of labor and minorities. On June 2, 1941, at the age of 79, Hughes resigned, citing health reasons.

Harlan Fiske Stone (1872–1946). Stone was born in Chesterfield, New Hampshire. He attended Amherst College, graduated in 1894, and then went to Columbia Law School where he graduated in 1898. Stone allied himself with the Republican Party but always remained flexible and practical when it came to his political views. He opened a law practice in New York City and was invited to become a member of the Columbia law faculty in 1899. In 1910 he was appointed dean of the law school where he remained until 1923. In the wake of political scandals in the Harding administration, President Coolidge appointed Stone, an old Amherst classmate, to be the new attorney general to replace the controversial Harry M. Daugherty in 1924.

Stone hit the ground running and began immediately to reorganize the Justice Department. He initiated a reform of the Federal Bureau of Investigation, then a small and obscure division in the Justice Department, and recommended J. Edgar Hoover as director. Stone also began reforms in the federal prison system. Basically conservative, Stone strongly believed that a

public servant's role carried responsibilities different from a private citizen and he sought to detach the Justice Department of any political influence. In the process, he gained a national reputation for honesty and, within the administration, earned credentials as a loyal Republican. When Justice Joseph McKenna retired from the Supreme Court in 1925, Coolidge nominated his old friend. The Senate confirmed Stone on February 5, 1925.

Stone's judicial philosophy was well known at the time of his appointment. At Columbia University he developed a reputation as a defender of civil liberties and held a belief that the law must adapt to changing social and economic conditions. Stone resented the conservatism of the Justices during the 1920s and viewed the Constitution as a living document subject to interpretation rather than rigid legal formulas. It was during the 1920s that Stone increasingly parted with the conservative members of the Court who aggressively protected private property rights at the expense of Congressional regulatory authority or state legislatures.

In a 1927 case Stone wrote a vigorous dissent against the majority led by Chief Justice Taft. He argued that before the Court tells a state it cannot regulate intrastate commerce, the Court had a responsibility to investigate the impact of the regulations. Stone was upholding a philosophy of judicial restraint, maintaining that the Court should rely on the judgment of the legislature once the Court was satisfied that the national interest was not imperiled. This view surfaced again several years later in Stone's dissenting opinion against the majority's invalidation of the Agricultural Adjustment Act in *United States v. Butler* (1936).

By the end of the 1920s, Stone was clearly identified with Justice Brandeis and Holmes as the "liberal minority" on the Court. Stone also grew impatient with Republican conservatism during the early years of the Depression. Though a close personal friend of Herbert Hoover, he disagreed with the President's *laissez-faire* economic principles in the face of economic disarray. Stone sympathized with the governmental activism of the New Deal even though he disagreed with a few measures. He dissented bitterly when the Court ruled the AAA unconstitutional in *United States v. Butler* (1936). In that case Stone deplored the Court's setting its own view of proper federal economic power above that of Congress, and he sided with Louis Brandeis. When the Court assaulted other New Deal programs, Stone was outraged by the conservative majority's refusal to allow the federal government to deal with the depression. When Roosevelt introduced the Court packing plan, Stone remained neutral. Although he did not like the idea of expanding the Court, he did welcome the switch in loyalty by Justice Owen Roberts and Chief Justice Charles Evans Hughes after 1937 in upholding New Deal legislation.

When Chief Justice Hughes retired in 1941, Roosevelt nominated Stone to be Chief Justice. The Senate confirmed him on June 27, 1941. Toward the late 1930s and early 1940s, Stone became increasingly concerned with civil liberties.

Benjamin Cardozo (1870–1938). Cardozo was born in New York City where he graduated from Columbia College in 1889 at the age of 19 and received a Master's degree a year later. He then attended Columbia Law School for a year before he was admitted to the New York bar. Cardozo's early career was spent working behind the scenes for other attorneys. He quickly gained a reputation for his legal briefs and scholarly publications in the law. He developed expertise in commercial law and soon developed a profitable legal practice. In 1913 he was elected justice of the New York Supreme Court and after only one month, the governor elevated him in February 1914 to a position on the court of appeals, the state's highest court. In 1926 Cardozo won unopposed the election to be chief judge on the Court of Appeals.

Cardozo never married and had few close friends, instead he engaged in intense legal work. By the 1920s, Cardozo was known internationally as an outstanding common law judge. He had an extraordinary capacity to outline the facts of a case and explaining them in a way that dramatized the broader principles of the common law. He also wrote three books, *The Nature of the Judicial Process* (1921), *The Growth of the Law* (1924) and *The Paradoxes of Legal Science* (1928) that established his reputation as a scholarly and brilliant jurist. During Cardozo's tenure, the New York Court of Appeals came to be regarded as the most distinguished court in the nation, rivaling that of the U.S. Supreme Court. It was a surprise to no one that Cardozo would eventually be nominated to serve on the highest court.

In 1932 President Hoover nominated Cardozo to take the place of the retiring Oliver Wendell Holmes, a friend of Cardozo whom he held in great admiration. But there were problems with the nomination. There were already two New Yorkers on the bench (Charles Evans Hughes and Harlan Fiske Stone), and there was already a Jewish member of the Court (Louis Brandeis). With the help of Senator William E. Borah of Idaho, a powerful Senate leader, the objections were overcome and Cardozo won confirmation.

Justice Cardozo came on the Court just as Hoover was leaving office. He quickly emerged, however, as the most persuasive member of the liberal faction. In his many early dissents with the conservative majority, Cardozo would blaze the path of interpretation that the Court would follow in the decades to come. His career on the Court, however, was cut short after serving only six years. He has been regarded as one of the greatest jurists to serve on the Supreme Court in the twentieth century.

Hugo Black (1886–1971). Black was one of the more interesting and controversial of the Roosevelt appointments to the Supreme Court. Beginning with a rather controversial nomination that raised questions about Black's position on civil rights, he ultimately became one of the foremost champions of individual liberties in the history of the Court.

Black was born in Harlan, Alabama, the heart of cotton country. When he was three his family moved to Ashland, a town with a population of 350, where his father ran a general store. Hugo attended Ashland College and then went on to the University of Alabama to pursue a career in medicine. After a year of medical school he switched to law and graduated from the University of Alabama Law School in 1906. Black practiced briefly in Ashland but soon moved to Birmingham where he specialized in labor and contract law. For a brief period between 1910 and 1911 he served as police court judge in Birmingham. In addition to his private clients Black also became legal counsel to the miner's union and the carpenter's union. Then in 1915 he was elected county solicitor (similar to a district attorney) for Jefferson County. When the United States entered World War I, Black resigned his position to join the army and rose to the rank of captain in the 19th Artillery Brigade. When the war ended he returned to Birmingham.

In 1926 Senator Oscar Underwood announced his retirement and Black decided to campaign for his seat and won the election. In the first term Black remained discreetly in the background and studied how the legislative process worked. At the same time, he began a life-long habit of reading in history, philosophy, and economics to make up for deficiencies in his education. He paid particular attention to the accounts of the Federal Constitutional Convention of 1787 and the State ratifying conventions, which gave him an increasing reverence for the text of the Constitution itself.

In time Black plunged into Senate business as a member of the judiciary committee. In 1932 he was reelected with the landslide Democratic Congress. Black emerged as a strong supporter of the New Deal and voted for all the major New Deal measures except for one, the National Industrial Recovery Act, which he felt was doomed to fail. In 1933 Black launched an investigation into the costs, salaries, and corruption of the United States Shipping Board, something that he personally spearheaded. He was also instrumental in passing a key piece of New Deal legislation, the Public Utilities Holding Company Act in 1935.

Black's career in the Senate ended when Franklin Roosevelt nominated him for the Supreme Court on August 12, 1937, to replace the conservative Justice Van Devanter. Soon a series of articles in the Pittsburgh *Post-Gazette* alleged that he had joined the Ku Klux Klan in 1923, and resigned two years later when he began his campaign for the Senate. These revelations set off a round of denunciations in the Senate. He explained that he had joined the Klan but resigned. Black later explained in an interview that many jurors and lawyers belonged to the Klan in Birmingham and he had to join to have an equal advantage.

Any lingering doubt about Black's background in the Klan was soon dispelled as he emerged as a consistent champion of individual liberties and minority rights. He consistently dissented with the Court and attracted the ire of conservatives who thought he was far too liberal. In 1940 Black wrote the majority opinions in two cases, one in which he overturned a conviction four black Americans whose confessions were obtained under duress and the other in which he asserted that a black defendant had not received a fair trial because blacks were excluded from the jury.

Black always sided with the "liberal bloc" and the "judicial activists" of the Supreme Court under Earl Warren in the 1950s and 1960s. Black carried a copy of the Constitution in his pocket wherever he went, and employed the literal text to browbeat his opponents.

Black would later be criticized for his opinion in *Korematsu v. United States* (1944), upholding the authority of the federal government to remove Americans of Japanese descent from along the Pacific coast. Perhaps his greatest accomplishment was to persuade colleagues to extend the guarantees of the Bill of Rights to the states in a series of cases in the early 1960s. On Sunday, September 26, 1971, Justice Hugo Black resigned from the Supreme Court, after 34 years on the Court. He died eight days later. He is generally acknowledged as one of the greatest civil libertarians in the history of the Supreme Court.

Primary Sources

The President Unveils His Court Reorganization Plan

On February 5, 1937, President Franklin Roosevelt sent his plan for reorganizing the judicial branch of government including the Supreme Court to Congress requesting legislation to carry it out. The lengthy message describes in detail his reasons for pursuing such a course (from Roosevelt, pp. 51–66).

I have recently called the attention of the Congress to the clear need for a comprehensive program to reorganize the administrative machinery of the Executive Branch of our Government. I now make a similar recommendation to the Congress in regard to the Judicial Branch of the Government, in order that it also may function in accord with modern necessities . . . .

[T]he Constitution vests in the Congress direct responsibility in the creation of courts and judicial offices and in the formulation of rules of practice and procedure. It is, therefore, one of the definite duties of the Congress constantly to maintain the effective functioning of the Federal Judiciary.

The Judiciary has often found itself handicapped by insufficient personnel with which to meet a growing and more complex business ....

In almost every decade since 1789, changes have been made by the Congress whereby the numbers of judges and the duties of judges in federal courts have been altered in one way or another. The Supreme Court was ... increased to nine in 1869.

The simple fact is that today a new need for legislative action arises because the personnel of the Federal Judiciary is insufficient to meet the business before them ....

A letter from the Attorney General, which I submit herewith, justifies by reasoning and statistics the common impression created by overcrowded federal dockets—and it proves the need for additional judges.

Delay in any court results in injustice.

It makes lawsuits a luxury available only to the few who afford them . . . Only by speeding up the processes of the law and thereby reducing their cost, can we eradicate the growing impression that the courts are chiefly a haven for the well-to-do . . . (I)n the last fiscal year, although 867 petitions for review were presented to the Supreme Court, it declined to hear 717 cases . . .

A part of the problem of obtaining a sufficient number of judges to dispose of cases is the capacity of the judges themselves. This brings forward the question of aged or infirm judges—a subject of delicacy and yet one which requires frank discussion.

In the federal courts there are in all 237 life tenure permanent judgeships. Twenty-five of them are now held by judges over seventy years of age and eligible to leave the bench on full pay . . .

In exceptional cases, of course, judges, like other men, retain to an advanced age full mental and physical vigor. Those not so fortunate are often unable to perceive their own infirmities . . .

With the opening of the twentieth century, and the great increase of population and commerce, and the growth of

This political cartoon by C.K. Berryman lampoons President Roosevelt's "court-packing" plan. Roosevelt wanted to appoint six more justices to the Supreme Court, which would allow him to assert his influence into the judicial branch of government. (The Library of Congress.)

a more complex type of litigation, similar proposals were introduced in the Congress . . .

It is well to remember that the mass of details involved in the average of law cases today is vastly greater and more complicated than even twenty years ago. Records and briefs must be read; statutes, decisions, and extensive material of a technical, scientific and economic nature must be searched and studied; opinions must be formulated and written. The modern tasks of judges call for the use of full energies . . .

A constant and systematic addition of younger blood will vitalize the courts and better equip them to recognize and apply the essential concepts of justice in the light of the needs and the facts of an ever-changing world . . .

I, therefore, earnestly recommend that the necessity of an increase in the number of judges be supplied by legislation providing for the appointment of additional judges in all federal courts, without exception, where there are incumbent judges of retirement age who do not choose to retire or to resign . . .

More About...

The New Deal's "Jones & Laughlin" Defense Team

When Charles Fahy came to the National Labor Relations Board (NLRB) as general counsel in 1935, he was only given 14 lawyers that were already on staff. Fahy had been serving as the assistant solicitor general of the Interior Department and was also chairman of the Petroleum Administration Board until it was struck down by the Supreme Court's decision in *Panama Refining Company v. Ryan* (1935). He welcomed the opportunity to develop a legal strategy for the NLRB, but he also inherited a large case docket and needed to hire more legal staff. The staff Fahy eventually hired was unusual for the time in two respects. First, he showed no reluctance to hire Jewish lawyers, many of whom had excellent records but due to prejudice were not able to get jobs at prestigious New York law firms. Secondly the NLRB under Fahy was the first New Deal agency to make an effort at hiring women lawyers and professional staff members on a basis of equality with men. This approach was well ahead of its time as Harvard Law School did not admit women until 1952 and as late as 1963, women comprised less than three percent of the legal profession.

I attach a carefully considered draft of a proposed bill, which, if enacted, would, I am confident, afford substantial relief.

The President Defends His Court Proposal

After receiving considerable adverse reaction to his plan to reorganize the Supreme Court, President Roosevelt used a fireside chat on March 9, 1937, to discuss with the people why he is pursuing the plan. In the radio address he also attempted to answer his critics (from Roosevelt, pp. 122–133).

The Courts . . . have cast doubts on the ability of the elected Congress to protect us against catastrophe by meeting squarely our modern social and economic conditions . . .

Last Thursday I described the American form of Government as a three horse team provided by the Consti-

tution to the American people so that their field might be plowed. The three horses are, of course, the three branches of government—the Congress, the Executive and the Courts. Two of the horses are pulling in unison today; the third is not . . .

It is the American people themselves who expect the third horse to pull in unison with the other two . . .

But since the rise of the modern movement for social and economic progress through legislation, the Court has more and more often and more and more boldly asserted a power to veto laws passed by the Congress and State Legislatures in complete disregard of this original limitation.

In the last four years the sound rule of giving statutes the benefit of all reasonable doubt has been cast aside. The Court has been acting not as a judicial body, but as a policy-making body.

When the Congress has sought to stabilize national agriculture, to improve the conditions of labor, to safeguard business against unfair competition, to protect our national resources, and in many other ways, to serve our clearly national needs, the majority of the Court has been assuming the power to pass on the wisdom of these Acts of Congress . . .

(T)here is no basis for the claim made by some members of the Court that something in the Constitution has compelled them regretfully to thwart the will of the people . . .

The Court in addition to the proper use of its judicial functions has improperly set itself up as a third House of the Congress—super-legislature, as one of the justices has called it—reading into the Constitution words and implications which are not there, and which were never intended to be there.

We have, therefore, reached the point as a Nation where we must take action to save the Constitution from the Court and the Court from itself . . .

What is my proposal? It is simply this: whenever a Judge or Justice of any Federal Court has reached the age of seventy and does not avail himself of the opportunity to retire on a pension, a new member shall be appointed by the President then in office, with the approval, as required by the Constitution, of the Senate of the United States . . .

The number of Judges to be appointed would depend wholly on the decision of present Judges now over seventy, or those who would subsequently reach the age of seventy.

If, for instance, any one of the six Justices of the Supreme Court now over the age of seventy should retire as provided under the plan, no additional place would be created. Consequently, although there never can be more than fifteen . . .

Those opposing this plan have sought to arouse prejudice and fear by crying that I am seeking to "pack" the Supreme Court . . .

If by that phrase "packing the Court" it is charged that I wish to place on the bench spineless puppets who

More About...

The First Assault on Racial Segregation in Education

Advances in the courts in the late 1930s not only came in the fields of regulating economic activity but in civil liberty cases as well. Roosevelt was personally reluctant to engage in any issues related to civil rights for racial minorities. He feared that supporting such causes would lose critical political support from the South for his economic programs. Some he recruited into the New Deal, however, contributed to lasting change in the recognition and protection of individual rights.

On November 9, 1938, the Supreme Court heard a case launched by the Legal Defense Fund of the National Association for the Advancement of Colored People (NAACP) in 1930 to challenge the "separate but equal" principle that had characterized racial segregation in the American South. The "separate but equal" principle came from a Supreme Court decision in 1897 saying that state laws requiring segregation of public facilities were legal if facilities of equal quality were provided for both races. The case provided an early test in the long campaign to end segregation through the courts that was earlier outlined by Nathan Margold, a young white lawyer, in the 1920s. Margold would later become Roosevelt's Solicitor General in the Department of the Interior during the New Deal. Charles Hamilton Houston, dean of Howard law school, was hired as the first full-time legal staff member of the NAACP's Legal Defense Fund in 1935 and began lawsuits to force Southern universities to admit black Americans to their graduate and professional schools. *Missouri ex rel Gaines v. Canada* was the first of several challenges leading to the striking down of racial segregation in public schools by the Supreme Court in the landmark case of *Brown v. Board of Education* in 1954.

The case involved Lloyd L. Gaines, a black American resident who sought admission to Missouri's all-white law school in the absence of a "separate but equal" facility for blacks. The university denied Gaines' admission on racial grounds and state courts upheld the denial. Gaines' attorney, Charles H. Houston, appealed to the Supreme Court and the Supreme Court took the case. Chief Justice Hughes, writing for the majority (six to two, Hughes for the Court, McReynolds and Butler in dissent, Cardozo had just died) ordered Gaines be admitted to the all-white facility. He dismissed the State's offer to pay Gaines' tuition out of state as inadequate. Nor was Hughes persuaded that Missouri's stated intention to build an all-black law school would meet the "separate but equal" test. The *Gaines* case thus became a pivotal case in the NAACP's campaign to end segregation. After *Gaines,* segregation was outlawed in graduate and professional programs. Unfortunately Lloyd Gaines never enrolled in law school. Perhaps exhausted by the process of litigation or fearful of the ordeal that would await him if he started classes, Gaines disappeared from the pages of history.

---

would disregard the law and would decide specific cases as I wished them to be decided, I make this answer: that no President fit for his office would appoint, and no Senate of honorable men fit for their office would confirm, that kind of appointees to the Supreme Court . . .

Like all lawyers, like all Americans, I regret the necessity of this controversy. But the welfare of the United States, and indeed of the Constitution itself, is what we all must think about first. Our difficulty with the Court today rises not from the Court as an institution but from human beings within it . . .

This plan of mine is no attack on the Court; it seeks to restore the Court to its rightful and historic place in our system of Constitutional Government . . .

Two groups oppose my plan on the ground that they favor a constitutional amendment. The first includes those who fundamentally object to social and economic legislation along modern lines . . .

The other group is composed of those who honestly believe the amendment process is the best and who would be willing to support a reasonable amendment if they could agree on one.

To them I say: we cannot rely on an amendment as the immediate or only answer to our present difficulties . . .

During the past half century the balance of power between the three great branches of the Federal Government, has been tipped out of balance by the Courts in direct contradiction of the high purposes of the framers of the Constitution. It is my purpose to restore that balance.

Suggested Research Topics

- It has been described that the Supreme Court underwent a "constitutional revolution" in the 1930s. What does that mean? How did the Court change in the way it interpreted the Constitution? What role did President Roosevelt and the New Deal play in stimulating this change?

- Select two key Supreme Court cases affecting the New Deal during the 1930s and briefly outline the arguments presented by both parties before the Court. The Court decisions may be found on the Internet at Findlaw (http://www.findlaw.com/casecode/supreme.html).

- Key constitutional issues before the Supreme Court in hearing New Deal cases included states rights under the Tenth Amendment to the Constitution, separation of powers in government, and due process of law. Briefly describe the key aspects of each of these legal doctrines. The U.S. Constitution may be found on the Internet at Findlaw (http://www.findlaw.com/casecode/supreme.html).

Bibliography

Sources

Bloomfield, Maxwell H. *Peaceful Revolution: Constitutional Change and American Culture from Progressivism to the New Deal.* Cambridge, MA: Harvard University Press, 2000.

Cushman, Barry. *Rethinking the New Deal Court: The Structure of a Constitutional Revolution.* New York: Oxford University Press, 1998.

Irons, Peter H. *The New Deal Lawyers.* Princeton, NJ: Princeton University Press, 1982).

Leuchtenburg, William E. *The Supreme Court Reborn: The Constitutional Revolution in the Age of Roosevelt.* New York: Oxford University Press, 1995.

Maidment, Richard A. *The Judicial Response to the New Deal: The U.S. Supreme Court and Economic Regulation, 1934–1936.* New York: Manchester University Press, 1991.

Roosevelt, Franklin D. *The Public Papers and Addresses of Franklin D. Roosevelt: 1937 Volume.* New York: The Macmillan Company, 1941.

Further Reading

Baker, Leonard. *Back to Back: The Duel Between FDR and the Supreme Court.* New York: Macmillan, 1967.

Dunne, Gerald T. *Hugo Black and the Judicial Revolution.* New York: Simon & Schuster, 1977.

Hockett, Jeffrey D. *New Deal Justice: The Constitutional Jurisprudence of Hugo L. Black, Felix Frankfurter, and Robert H. Jackson.* Lanham, MD: Rowman & Littlefield Publishers, 1996.

Irons, Peter H., and Howard Zinn. *A People's History of the Supreme Court.* New York: Viking, 1999.

Kaufman, Andrew L. *Cardozo.* Cambridge, MA: Harvard University Press, 1998.

O'Douglas, William O. *The Court Years, 1939–1975: The Autobiography of William O. Douglas.* New York: Random House, 1988.

Rehnquist, William H. *The Supreme Court.* New York: Knopf, 2001.

Schwartz, Bernard. *The Law in America: A History.* New York: McGraw-Hill, 1974.

"The Supreme Court Historical Society," available from the World Wide Web at http://www.supremecourthistory.org

"The Supreme Court of the United States," available from the World Wide Web at http://www.supremecourtus.gov

Note: One of the best ways to understand the issues involved in the battle between FDR and the Supreme Court is to read the cases themselves.

See Also

Farm Relief; Labor and Industry; National Industrial Recovery Act; New Deal (First, and Its Critics); New Deal (Second); Social Security; Tennessee Valley Authority

Tennessee Valley Authority

Introduction

The Tennessee River, one of the largest rivers in the United States, flows for 652 miles and drains an area of 40,900 square miles that includes parts of seven states: Tennessee, Virginia, North Carolina, Georgia, Alabama, Mississippi, and Kentucky. In the early twentieth century the Tennessee Valley was one of the most impoverished regions of the United States, and yet its rivers held a potential to produce huge amounts of hydroelectric energy. This potential was not yet discovered, of course, until Americans came to realize what electrical power could do to promote industrial development and improve the everyday lives of people. Electrical energy began to serve industry, cities, and homes in the 1880s, but it took several decades before Americans considered it a necessity of modern life rather than a luxury. Until the 1920s, the primary users of electricity, generated mostly by private power companies, were industries rather than homes.

During World War I (1914–1918) the American government sought to develop a domestic source of nitrates. Nitrates are used for explosives but only available from Chile. The industrial process favored for nitrate production at that time required huge amounts of electricity. The government decided to build its production facilities in northern Alabama at Muscle Shoals on the Tennessee River because at that location hydroelectric dams could generate the necessary power. One nitrate plant was completed just as the war ended, leaving the government with an expensive facility with which it did not know what to do.

Chronology:

March 3, 1931: President Herbert Hoover vetoes Senator Norris's latest version of a bill to develop a major power production project at Muscle Shoals on the Tennessee River.

September 21, 1932: Democratic presidential candidate Franklin D. Roosevelt, in a speech in Portland, Oregon, proposes that the federal government build four "yardstick" power developments around the country, including one on the Tennessee River at Muscle Shoals.

April 10, 1933: President Franklin D. Roosevelt asks Congress to establish an agency designed to plan and oversee the development and wise use of the Tennessee Valley.

May 18, 1933: President Roosevelt signs legislation establishing the Tennessee Valley Authority (TVA).

January 4, 1934: The TVA and a leading power company in the region, Commonwealth and Southern Corporation, sign a contract agreement to share the power market in the Tennessee Valley region.

May 18, 1936: President Roosevelt reappoints David Lilienthal to the TVA Board of Directors.

December 14, 1936: Judge John J. Gore issues a temporary injunction temporarily stopping the TVA power program.

March 23, 1938: President Roosevelt removes Arthur Morgan from the TVA Board.

August 15, 1939: TVA takes possession of the Tennessee Electric Power Company for the purchase price of $78 million.

Congress debated throughout the 1920s and into the 1930s about whether to demolish the facilities, lease them to private industry, or operate them as a government program.

The Tennessee Valley was home to millions of poor subsistence farmers who had little opportunity to improve their lives because the economy there had been depressed since at least the end of the Civil War (1861–1865). Economic development was held back in this area partly because the Tennessee River was not well suited to navigation nor agriculture. Industrial products were expensive to transport overland and a century of efforts to develop a practical navigation channel had not yet been successful. The land was damaged by many years of overly intensive and unwise farming and timber harvesting practices. The people could not afford good schools or adequate medical facilities and the region's future looked bleak without massive outside help. Before the 1930s, however, there was no expectation that the government would step in to change the picture.

The Depression created a desire among the American people for new leadership. The overwhelming victory of Franklin Delano Roosevelt (served 1933–1945) and the Democrats in the 1932 presidential election brought sweeping changes. Among the most visible and effective New Deal programs was the Tennessee Valley Authority (TVA). The TVA included the Muscle Shoals facilities but had a much broader vision: the planned development of the entire Tennessee Valley and surrounding areas. Born of the struggle over Muscle Shoals, the TVA in the 1930s endured battles both internally among its directors and externally with the private power companies before finally realizing Roosevelt's dream of a region revitalized through planning and the harnessing of electric power. A new series of hydroelectric dams generated massive amounts of new electricity, driving down electric rates and stimulating the modernization of industries and homes in the cities and countryside. Navigation locks alongside the dams finally established a practical shipping channel into eastern Tennessee, lowering shipping costs and improving the profitability of local businesses. The TVA promoted agricultural and forestry reforms that improved the fertility of the land and put money into the pockets of farmers. The TVA continued to serve the Tennessee Valley into the twenty-first century as a self-sustaining government corporation, producing more electricity than any other utility in the country.

Despite the successes of the TVA and its popularity in the South, it was an experiment that would not be repeated elsewhere in the United States. Its creation in the 1930s was the product of historical currents that converged at that time and place and would never unite again. It represented a triumph of progressive thinking, but only during a time when Americans were in trouble and willing to try something different. Once the crisis of the 1930s passed, the traditional American fondness for free enterprise and distrust of government reasserted themselves, although it was in a new world in which the TVA illustrated the potential benefits of massive government action.

Loyston, Tennessee was part of the area that would be flooded by the construction of the Norris Dam. This school would eventually be completely submerged. (National Archives and Records Administration. Reproduced by permission.)

Issue Summary

As the decade of the 1930s began, several historical threads were converging that would lead to the first massive regional development program carried out by the United States government. The Tennessee Valley in the southeastern United States for decades had been economically depressed and its resources poorly managed. A century of efforts to engineer the Tennessee River and its tributaries as a water highway for commerce and transportation had largely failed because of a lack of long-range, centralized planning, and adequate financing. Government hydroelectric dams and fertilizer production facilities built for the World War I effort at Muscle Shoals, Alabama, on the Tennessee River were embarrassing the nation because twelve years of debate had brought about no final decision about how to manage them after the war. The economic downturn of the early 1930s brought these threads together in a dramatic way that would profoundly affect American life, especially in the Tennessee Valley, for the rest of the century.

The Early 1930s: The Tennessee Valley and Shifting Political Currents

Senator George Norris of Nebraska submitted a new Muscle Shoals bill to the U.S. Senate in 1930. It was in a form identical to a bill that had been approved by Congress in 1928 but stopped by President Calvin Coolidge's (served 1923–1929) veto. Enactment of Norris's new bill, which easily passed the Senate, would have established public operation of the project for power production and fertilizer research and the distribution of surplus power on a preferred basis to public utilities. A competing bill that would lease Muscle Shoals to private interests instead of maintaining government operation passed in the House of Representatives. The two bills differed so much that a House-Senate conference committee set up to reconcile them was deadlocked until 1931.

In the meantime in March 1930 the U.S. Army Corps of Engineers issued the final report of its comprehensive survey of the Tennessee River and its tributaries. This report made clear the huge benefits of cheap electrical power, navigation, flood control, and sanitary and health conditions that could be realized by an integrated and systematic development of the river system. Although the report anticipated that private power companies would carry out the proposed development, it amounted to support for Norris's nearly decade-long arguments for multiple-purpose development of the Tennessee River.

In February 1931 the House-Senate conference on the Muscle Shoals bill finally compromised on a

Senator George W. Norris was considered the "Father of the TVA." Norris Dam, constructed by the TVA, was named in honor of him. (The Library of Congress.)

measure that gave Norris nearly all that he wanted, including government operation of the power facilities. The compromise bill easily passed the House and the Senate and was submitted to President Herbert Hoover (served 1929–1933) for his signature, required by the Constitution before the bill could become law. Most observers expected that Hoover would veto the bill. After an exchange of public comments by Hoover and Norris that were critical of each other, Norris made a dramatic public offer to resign from the Senate if Hoover would sign the bill. This was not to be, for Hoover vetoed the bill on March 3, 1931. His veto message, reprinted in Preston J. Hubbard's *Origins of the TVA: The Muscle Shoals Controversy, 1920–1932*, p. 293, outlined the philosophical reasons underlying his decision:

> This bill raises one of the most important issues confronting our people. That is squarely the issue of Federal Government ownership and operation of power and manufacturing business not as a minor by-product but as a major purpose. Involved in this question is the agitation against the conduct of the power industry. The power problem is not to be solved by the Federal Government going into the power business ... The remedy for abuses in the conduct of that industry lies in regula-

tion ... I hesitate to contemplate the future of our institutions, of our government, and of our country if the preoccupation of its officials is to be no longer the promotion of justice and equal opportunity but is to be devoted to barter in the markets. That is not liberalism, it is degeneration.

Hoover's statement touched on the basic disagreement between liberals and conservatives about the role of government. Muscle Shoals was a very visible battlefield between these two opposing forces.

Norris re-introduced his bill to the Senate in early 1932. Although his committee passed and referred the bill to the full Senate, a vote was not taken before adjournment of Congress. Norris felt that the best place to fight for his proposal was later in the presidential election campaign of 1932. In that campaign, President Hoover, the Republican candidate, differed greatly from the Democratic candidate, Governor Franklin D. Roosevelt of New York, on the public power issue. Roosevelt was promoting public development of waterpower on the St. Lawrence River in New York. While Hoover took no formal stand on the matter during the election, his views had been eloquently expressed by his veto of the Norris bill and public statement.

During the campaign, Roosevelt's views on public power came out most clearly in a speech he gave on September 21, 1932, in Portland, Oregon, where public power was very popular with the region's residents. In that speech he declared that he did not advocate complete government control of utilities. Rather he stated that he believed control of utilities should be mostly in the hands of private enterprise. He contended, however, that utilities should be firmly regulated by the government. Roosevelt contended that the people had a basic right to electrical power at a reasonable rate. In cases where private industry did not act in the public interest by charging reasonable rates the government had the right to generate and transmit power. Therefore the government could judge whether the private companies were providing fair and reasonable service to the public. His proposal, reprinted in Thomas K.McCraw's *TVA and the Power Fight*, pp.33-34, called for the federal government to build four yardstick projects:

> Here you have the clear picture of four great Government power developments in the United States—the St. Lawrence River in the Northeast, Muscle Shoals in the Southeast, the Boulder Dam project in the Southwest, and finally, but by no means the least of them, the Columbia River in the Northwest. Each one of these, in each of the four quarters of the United States, will be forever a national yardstick to prevent extortion against the public and to encourage the wider use of that servant of people—electric power.

Men working at the Norris Dam in 1933. The Norris Dam was one of the most important projects of the Tennessee Valley Authority. (National Archives and Records Administration. Reproduced by permission.)

When Norris heard of Roosevelt's Portland speech, he was jubilant. He strongly supported Roosevelt in the 1932 election, seeing in Roosevelt the final solution to passage of his Muscle Shoals bill. The realization of Norris's long-held dream finally came true when Roosevelt and the Democrats won an overwhelming victory in the presidential election. Norris would be even happier after the election when he learned that Roosevelt's vision for the Tennessee River was even grander than his own.

Muscle Shoals Becomes TVA

Before his inauguration Roosevelt invited Norris on a tour of the Tennessee Valley that must have been one of the happiest events in Norris's long life. Near the end of that tour, as the two stood gazing at Wilson Dam at Muscle Shoals, the President-elect said, "This ought to be a happy day for you, George." Norris reportedly answered, "It is, Mr. President. I see my dreams come true" (Hubbard, p. 314). Later, after he returned to Washington, a reporter asked him if

More About...

Norris, Tennessee: A Planned Community

TVA planned for the town of Norris, Tennessee, to be a showcase for its programs, including rural electrification, decentralized industry, and town planning. TVA head Arthur Morgan, intensely interested in community planning, was strongly behind the concept and its execution. Located near the site of Norris Dam, many thought it should become home to the many poor people of the Norris Basin displaced by the reservoir behind the dam. But TVA decided the town would serve initially to house construction workers and their families who needed a place to live while they built the dam.

Norris was not planned as well as it should have been. For example TVA officials did not allow black families to move there, supposedly because they wanted to follow the local customs and traditions including racial segregation (keeping the races separated). As pointed out by furious black leaders, however, blacks and poor whites had lived and worked together in the local mountains and valleys for a long time before TVA arrived. TVA in the 1930s withstood

three separate investigations by the National Association for the Advancement of Colored People (NAACP) for racial discrimination in hiring, housing, and job training.

Following Morgan's vision, TVA helped set up cooperative businesses in Norris including canneries, poultry raising, and creameries. The public school served as the community center, offering classes for adults as well as children and for townspeople as well as rural residents. Norris, however, was run very much like a company town, with stores owned by TVA, whose ownership extended even to the town's auto repair shop, the cafeteria, and the gas station.

When Norris Dam was completed, construction workers moved away and professional people from TVA and Knoxville moved into Norris. The attractive town became a Knoxville suburb. As the population became wealthier, the cooperatives and community activities faded away. In 1948 the government sold the town to a private corporation which resold the lots to the people who lived on them.

Roosevelt was truly with him. "He is more than with me," he responded, "because he plans to go even farther than I did" (McCraw, p. 35). The two men apparently had discussed Roosevelt's plans for an integrated, government-sponsored development of the Tennessee Valley. The grand dimensions of Roosevelt's idea were suggested in a speech he gave in Montgomery, Alabama, during the tour:

> Muscle Shoals gives us the opportunity to accomplish a great purpose for the people of many States and, indeed, for the whole Union. Because there we have an opportunity of setting an example of planning, not just for ourselves, but for the generations to come, tying in industry and agriculture and forestry and flood prevention, trying them all into a unified whole over a distance of a thousand miles so that we can afford better opportunities and better places for living for millions of yet unborn in the days to come (McCraw, p. 35).

In early February 1933 Roosevelt announced to the press his comprehensive plan for the development of the Tennessee Valley, which was not limited to Muscle Shoals. Having carried out statewide land-use planning in New York, Roosevelt saw a similar need and the opportunity afforded by the Muscle Shoals

project and the Tennessee Valley. He called for a coordinated program for the entire watershed involving flood control, reclamation of land subject to flooding, power development, navigation improvements, and promotion of industry. He saw this project as "the widest experiment ever conducted by a government" (Hubbard, p. 314).

Roosevelt formally proposed the Tennessee Valley Authority Act to Congress on April 10, 1933. The Tennessee Valley Authority (TVA) was to be "a corporation clothed with the power of Government but possessed of the flexibility and initiative of a private enterprise" (Roosevelt, p. 122). Despite the vast scope of the TVA Act, the debate in Congress was remarkably brief, if at times intense. The power companies testified that government generation and distribution of power would put them out of business. The new Congress, however, was ready to enact the Roosevelt program as Roosevelt signed the TVA Act into law on May 18, 1933. For Senator Norris it was the victory of a lifetime. Neither he nor Roosevelt realized, however, that another round of battles was soon to begin.

Plants like the Kingston steam plant, shown here, were built by the TVA to help produce electricity for their rural electrification projects. (UPI/Corbis-Bettmann. Reproduced by permission.)

The Battle Within: The TVA Board of Directors

Roosevelt brought the idea of a "public authority" from New York where he had created such organizations, including the Power Authority of that state. The TVA Act called for a governing board of three directors, one of whom would be called chairman. This was to be a government corporation not connected to other federal departments and answerable only to the President.

A month before he signed the TVA Act into law, Roosevelt selected Arthur E. Morgan as TVA Chairman. Roosevelt put him to work to select the other two directors. Morgan was Roosevelt's choice because he shared Roosevelt's enthusiasm for planning as a way to improve the lives of people. By training and experience, he was a water-control engineer and known for his innovative approach to problem solving. He was also an idealist and philosopher that could inspire great loyalty in some people but cause others to regard him as strange. Morgan founded an engineering company that developed a national reputation for excellent work all over the country. He had become the President of Antioch College in Ohio in 1921, where he instituted a unique program in which students worked on-campus in real industries to apply what they learned in the classroom. When Roosevelt

offered him the TVA directorship he jumped at the chance to design a multi-purpose project. He and Roosevelt both saw TVA as way to develop the economy and society of the Tennessee Valley rather than simply a power production or navigation project. His broad vision eventually clashed with the very different ideas and purposes held by the other directors.

Roosevelt asked Morgan to select two different men for the director positions: one that was familiar with electric power and another with experience in agriculture. That way the Board would encompass the diversity of expertise needed for the broad purposes of TVA. The agriculturalist selection was Harcourt A. Morgan, then president of the University of Tennessee. Originally from Canada, Harcourt Morgan had moved to Louisiana and become an expert on crop pests before taking a job at the University of Tennessee. At the university he rose rapidly through the ranks. Like Arthur Morgan, he had a philosophical approach to his work and a commitment to making a real contribution. He saw TVA as an important agent for much needed agricultural reform through education. Although his job was to set up and guide the TVA farm program, he had definite views on the issue of private versus public power. He believed that private power companies had neglected their duty to farmers by not providing electricity to rural areas.

Selection of the third director was a very sensitive and important matter. Roosevelt and Arthur Morgan seemed to agree that this director, well versed in power issues, should be someone who could avoid explosive confrontations with the private power companies. Morgan felt that Roosevelt's first two suggestions were too hostile to the companies. Behind the scenes, other interested parties including Senator Norris provided input to Roosevelt about who should or should not occupy this position. The final selection was David E. Lilienthal, an ambitious 33-year old lawyer with the Wisconsin Public Service Commission who was highly recommended to both Morgan and Roosevelt.

Despite being so young, Lilienthal had a rather long list of accomplishments. He was highly regarded because of his great energy and intelligence, his published articles on public utility law, and some important legal cases he had been involved with. He was very committed to social causes and had a very low regard for private utility companies. Senator Norris and others committed to public power were very pleased with Lilienthal's appointment. They believed he would be a strong and aggressive force in what they expected would be a bitter fight with the private power companies.

The three TVA directors combined a remarkable variety of knowledge, experience, and skills well suited to the task before them. Their personalities and visions, however, differed in ways that led to serious internal strife. The greatest contrast was between Arthur Morgan and David Lilienthal. Morgan wished to avoid a battle with the power companies. He believed that company executives were reasonable people who could be convinced to work cooperatively with the TVA. Lilienthal did not trust the power companies at all and was eager to defeat them in a struggle for control of power systems in the Tennessee Valley. For five years these two directors of the TVA contested the direction and strategy of the project.

The trouble began early on when Wendell L. Willkie, the young and energetic president of Commonwealth and Southern Corporation, a holding company that owned private power companies in the Tennessee Valley, sent a letter to Chairman Morgan suggesting a meeting to discuss ways to cooperate. Willkie had earlier testified against the TVA Act before Congress, so obviously the TVA was a threat because it might take over territories held by his companies. Morgan was aware of Willkie's thoughts but confident that the TVA's powerful position as an arm of the government would make it safe to deal openly and fairly with Willkie and the other company representatives. To him, the power issue was about technology and economics. Lilienthal, on the other hand, deeply distrusted Willkie and other power company business leaders and sought to find ways to gain advantage for the government in any negotiations. For him, the power issue was basically political. In the beginning, Morgan's moderate viewpoint prevailed and the directors agreed that he should meet with Willkie, but should not make any important agreements.

One of the first issues to be settled with the power companies was which territories the TVA would serve with electrical power. These would be the yardstick areas, where fair rates would be determined. This meant that some areas had to be given up by the power companies, which they naturally were reluctant to do. When Willkie's companies failed to live up to an important agreement on this matter, Morgan still wanted to work cooperatively with him. Lilienthal strongly objected to further cooperation, and the two men grew increasingly antagonistic. Morgan saw Lilienthal as unethical and willing to stop at nothing to undermine the private companies and viewed this perspective as dangerous to the TVA's reputation. Lilienthal, on the other hand, saw Morgan as naive in his dealings with the power companies and unguarded in his grandiose public statements about the social mission of the TVA. Most of the time, Harcourt Morgan agreed with Lilienthal, making Arthur Morgan the minority chairman.

In 1935 Morgan recommended to Roosevelt that Lilienthal, whose term would soon expire, be replaced or he would resign if Lilienthal were reappointed. Roosevelt wavered at first, but reappointed Lilienthal. Morgan backed off on this threat and remained in his position. From that point on, relations within the Board of Directors were very strained and full of intrigue. The ill will within the boardroom soon became public knowledge. By 1937 Morgan was disgusted with President Roosevelt's New Deal social and economic programs designed to bring the United States out of the Great Depression. To him Roosevelt, Lilienthal, and others seemed more interested in punishing the companies than in a fair settlement. Lilienthal in turn was disgusted with Morgan, who he believed was conspiring with the companies. All of this was brought to a head when Morgan decided to take his case to the public. He wrote articles for major magazines and newspapers in which he openly criticized such TVA practices as misleading propaganda against the companies. Without referring to him by name, he also clearly criticized Lilienthal and his personal ambition.

The feud within the Board became an embarrassment and a political liability for President Roosevelt. He called the Board before him and demanded that they provide evidence for their charges or withdraw them. His primary concern was Morgan, who refused to provide details to substantiate his charges against Lilienthal and instead proposed an investigation by Congress. Roosevelt felt he had no choice but to fire Morgan, which he did on March 23, 1938. This action was very bad publicity for the TVA and led to a highly visible investigation of the TVA by a joint committee of Congress later in the year. Although the committee ultimately found little wrongdoing by the TVA, the TVA spent much of its time that year preparing for the investigation. This distraction delayed the resolution of the battle the TVA had been waging, outside the boardroom, with the power companies.

The Battle Without: TVA and the Power Companies

The TVA Act, as written, emphasized government responsibility for navigation improvements and flood control. It also provided for government generation and distribution of electric power. The power issue captured the greatest amount of attention because it had a huge and direct impact on the lives of millions and on the profits of some of the biggest corporations in America. The act authorized the government to distribute publicly generated power throughout the Tennessee Valley and adjacent areas, primarily to public agencies such as municipal utilities and nonprofit cooperatives. It also explicitly stated its intent not to duplicate existing power facilities, which would prevent direct competition with private companies within any given area. Roosevelt's idea was that yardstick areas would be set aside for the TVA as the power supplier. Analysis of the TVA's experience in these areas would establish reasonable rates. Since private companies already were in place, the only practical way such yardstick areas could be set aside was to negotiate agreements with the companies to establish the boundaries between public and private service territories. Otherwise it would be a free-for-all in which the TVA and the companies would compete for customers, a situation frowned upon by the TVA Act and not in the interest of either side.

The champion of the power companies was Wendell L. Willkie, the young President of the Commonwealth and Southern (C & S) Corporation, the holding company that owned a number of power companies in the Tennessee Valley. Trained and experienced as a lawyer, Willkie was a strong proponent of free enterprise and a likeable man with a talent for public speaking. His battle with TVA for control of the region's customers made him a national figure important enough to become the Republican candidate for President in the 1940 election. In 1933 the C & S corporation was huge, with assets of over $1 billion and ownership of 11 major electric utilities that served five million people.

One of the first decisions of the TVA Board was to establish the initial area in which the TVA would provide power. A long corridor was identified along which the TVA planned to build a transmission line between Wilson Dam at Muscle Shoals and the proposed Norris Dam in eastern Tennessee. It also included certain areas adjacent to the corridor and at least one major city. This corridor passed directly through areas already served by Willkie's companies. Another complication was that one of Willkie's companies, the Alabama Power Company, held the contract awarded in 1925 to buy power from Wilson Dam, which would expire on January 1, 1934. The TVA needed to renew that contract or else lose the largest part of its income, making C & S both its customer and adversary.

Willkie and Lilienthal met on October 4, 1933, to discuss ways to resolve the situation. Willkie proposed to buy all of TVA's electricity, but Lilienthal made no commitment. A short time later the TVA signed an agreement with the town of Tupelo, Mississippi, to provide power by February 1934. This agreement served notice that the TVA was moving ahead with its program whether Willkie agreed or not. As a result negotiations with C & S became very tense and high-pressured. Willkie did not want a TVA transmission line through the heart of his electricity market and he even offered to sell the Tennessee Electric Power Company (TEPCO) to the TVA, but for a price the TVA did not want to pay. As time was running out for the Alabama Power Company contract, Lilienthal gave Willkie an ultimatum. If C & S would not sell its transmission lines, in the areas the TVA wanted, at a price the TVA Board thought was reasonable, then the TVA would build its own duplicate transmission facilities in the areas. Willkie decided to sign an agreement on January 4, 1934, to continue to buy Wilson Dam power and to sell electrical systems in certain areas that the TVA wanted. The TVA agreed not to move farther into C & S territories for five years or until Norris Dam began producing power, whichever came first. This contract seemed to mark a truce between the two sides, but peace was short-lived.

The January 4 agreement failed to resolve key issues because the two sides still had fundamentally opposing interests. Therefore they could not agree on details of implementing the agreement. For example,

C & S insisted on cash payments from cities that were to buy municipal power distribution systems. Cities, however, did not have enough cash at this stage of the Great Depression and wanted to pay with bonds instead. The TVA and C & S worked out a deal in which the TVA would purchase the municipal systems and then resell them to the cities. That agreement would later fail when C & S refused to turn over the property because of a legal technicality. Similar legal problems cropped up throughout the contract territory. For a long time the TVA had a very small area in which it could sell electricity while at the same time it was busy building dams that would produce more power.

Negotiations between the two sides soon broke down and it became clear that the battle would have to be resolved in the courts. Private power companies and their stockholders filed many lawsuits against the TVA and other federal agencies. They wanted to stop the takeover of their electrical facilities by the government and the cities. Two cases were most influential in deciding the issue in favor of TVA. In the first of these, filed on September 13, 1934, George Ashwander and thirteen other stockholders of the Alabama Power Company tried to stop their company from following through on the January 4 contract. They argued the contract was illegal because the TVA itself was unconstitutional. The District Court judge in northern Alabama ruled in favor of Ashwander, but an appeals court reversed the lower court's decision and ruled in favor of the TVA. The case was referred to the Supreme Court, which at the time was in the habit of deciding cases against Roosevelt's New Deal programs. In February 1936 to the surprise of many, the Supreme Court ruled 8 to 1 in favor of the TVA, but deliberately avoided the issue of the TVA's constitutionality.

In the second case, known as the "TEPCO case," five of Willkie's companies filed suit against the TVA on May 29, 1936, to force the courts to decide the question of the TVA's constitutionality. As the legal process moved forward, Judge John J. Gore issued a legal order to stop an action, known as an injunction, temporarily freezing the TVA's power program for six months. An appeals court put the TVA back in business again, but sent the case back to the same court presided over by Judge Gore, who would certainly rule against TVA again. TVA lawyers, however, deliberately inserted a clause into the Judiciary Act of 1937 that required a three-judge panel, not a single judge, to hear constitutional cases like TEPCO. This clever tactic worked and in early 1938 the judicial panel voted two to one, with Judge Gore casting the dissenting vote, in favor of the TVA. The companies

appealed this decision to the Supreme Court that ruled five to two in TVA's favor.

In five years of litigation to stop the TVA program, the power companies lost every case. They had, however, prevented the TVA from capturing the biggest electricity markets in the region. In the meantime the TVA sold power, which it was generating in greater amounts as it finished dams, to some small cities and to some private power companies and industrial firms. At the same time it carried out a massive and well-planned publicity campaign to garner public support for its programs. Once the legal issues were resolved, the TVA was able to force the power companies to give up key market territories in its yardstick areas.

A typical example of the TVA's successful tactics was carried out in the city of Knoxville, Tennessee, where the TVA set up its main office in 1933. The people of Knoxville in November 1933 voted overwhelmingly to set up their own public utility system to deliver power in place of the private company already there. The cheaper TVA power was a powerful inducement. The city offered to buy the existing private facilities, but the company refused because that system was central to their whole operation. The city then applied for a loan and a grant from another New Deal agency, the Public Works Administration, to build their own parallel system. Faced with that prospect, the company offered to sell or lease its facilities to the city, but the two sides for some time could not agree on a purchase price. Just when a deal was reached, a lawsuit by company stockholders prevented the agreement from going through. The legal maneuvering continued for years until finally the company accepted an offer made by the TVA and Knoxville together. The city finally took control of the system in September 1938.

A very similar series of events took place in Memphis where the public voted 17 to one in 1934 to establish municipal ownership of the power system. The local private power company fought in court until finally surrendering in 1939. Probably the most important battle of this kind began in Chattanooga. There the public voted in 1935 to adopt a public system, but political and legal wrangling delayed any purchase. This case was an embarrassment to C & S because its own company, TEPCO, was headquartered there. As legal decisions continued to move in favor of TVA, Willkie realized that the best solution for C & S was to sell TEPCO to the TVA. He came under particularly strong pressure because Chattanooga actually began building its own system in 1938. The long and difficult negotiations continued until an agreement

More About...

The Tupelo Experiment

In late 1933 TVA had plenty of power to sell from Wilson Dam, but still had no "yardstick" demonstration area in which to show how its power program would work. Negotiations with Wendell Willkie's huge Commonwealth and Southern Corporation (C & S) to set aside part of its territory for TVA were just getting under way and were bound to be difficult. Willkie had proposed that TVA just sell all its surplus power to C & S, which would mean that the TVA would have no yardstick area at all. To show Willkie that TVA was serious about moving ahead with its program and to strengthen its bargaining position, the TVA worked out an agreement with the small town of Tupelo, Mississippi, which had its own municipal utility, to begin selling power in February 1934. In the following months Tupelo became the theme of a propaganda war between the two sides as well as a testing ground for predictions about how the TVA programs would work.

The people of Tupelo, a town of six thousand, were happy to be in the spotlight and to be the first to receive cheap TVA power. The Chamber of Commerce began receiving inquiries from industries attracted by the low electric rates. A hotel proprietor reported that she was able to operate her 38-room building including lights, fans in all the rooms, two vacuum cleaners, two electric irons, a refrigerator, and a radio with an electric bill of only about $20 per month. Six companies sold electrical appliances and equipment. When TVA provided new inexpensive appliance models, these stores sold 137 refrigerators and 17 ranges in just 17 days. The reduced cost of appliances was substantial: refrigerators reduced from $137 to $80, hot water heaters from $95 to $60, and ranges from $137 to $80.

Working with TVA, the cost of installing an electric stove, which requires a special circuit with higher voltage than regular house current, fell from $60 to $5. Many people in Tupelo and the surrounding countryside began wiring or rewiring their homes and buying appliances to take advantage of the new low rates. TVA publicized their success in Tupelo on a grand scale to promote public support. The private power companies sharply criticized the Tupelo experiment as an example of government subsidy that benefited Tupelo but cost American taxpayers.

---

was reached. TEPCO was turned over to the TVA in a formal ceremony on August 15, 1939. After this sale the TVA held exclusive electricity markets in most of Tennessee and large parts of northern Alabama and northeastern Mississippi. The TVA continued to confine itself to this territory throughout the remainder of the twentieth century.

By the end of the 1930s the TVA was finally at peace both internally and externally and could focus on carrying out its programs. Although the power companies obstructed the TVA in its efforts to serve electrical markets, the other parts of the program had been moving full speed ahead.

TVA Programs in the 1930s

TVA was set up from the beginning as a multipurpose organization to develop the physical and human resources of the Tennessee Valley and pull it out of its decades-long regional depression. The TVA involved itself in a wide range of activities, from building dams for flood control, improved navigation, and generation of electricity, to creating a publicity campaign to inform the public of its activities and gain support. These are the two activities for which the TVA is most widely recognized. The TVA also produced fertilizer and conducted agricultural experiments, including demonstrations and experiments with electrical farm equipment; provided loan assistance to rural citizens for the purchase of electrical appliances and home wiring; promoted improvement in health care and education, including a program to eliminate malaria; and built roads, bridges, model cities, and recreation areas near new reservoirs.

The most visible TVA program was the construction of dams. Wilson Dam at Muscle Shoals had already been completed in 1925, and it was a key point of contention in the Muscle Shoals controversy prior to the establishment of TVA. Once established the TVA very quickly planned dams on the Tennessee River and its tributaries guided by the Corps of Engineers recommendations. The TVA built them in rapid succession. The first of these was Norris Dam, named

A test field showing the difference between a field treated with phosphate produced by the TVA, right, and an untreated field, left. Agricultural development was an important part of the TVA program. (FDR Library. Reproduced by permission.)

after Senator Norris and begun in October 1933, while construction on Wheeler Dam began the following month. In June 1934 the TVA employed 9,173 people, mostly in dam construction and by 1935 that number had risen to 16,000. By 1936 five dams were under construction and Norris Dam, the first to be completed, was finished in 1936. These dams were popular tourist destinations during the Depression and one thousand people visited Wilson, Wheeler, and Norris

dams each day. By the time the system was completed in 1944 the TVA had built 16 dams, rendering the Tennessee River navigable for ships for 650 miles from the Ohio River to Knoxville, controlling floods, and generating huge amounts of hydroelectric power.

Another very visible and successful TVA program was its publicity campaign. Headed by William L. Sturdevant, the TVA Information Office was well funded and employed a dozen staff members. The staff

More About...

Lorena Hickok Reports from the Field

In 1933 Harry Hopkins, the head of the New Deal's Federal Emergency Relief Administration (FERA), asked journalist Lorena Hickok to tour the country and report on its condition at the grass roots level. FERA was responsible for providing financial relief to those suffering from the Depression through grants to states and local governments. Hickok visited the Tennessee Valley in June 1934 and reported her observations about how people were reacting to TVA. Below are some excerpts.

... A Promised Land, bathed in a golden sunlight, is rising out of the grey shadows of want and squalor and wretchedness down here in the Tennessee Valley these days.

... Ten thousand men are at work, building with timber and steel and concrete the New Deal's most magnificent project, creating an empire with potentialities so tremendous and so dazzling that they make one gasp. I knew very little about the Tennessee Valley Authority when I came down here last week. I spent part of my first day, in Knoxville, reading up on it. I was almost as excited as I used to get over adventure stories when I was a child. This IS an adventure!

... "Oh, I haven't heard anybody say anything about the Depression for three months," remarked a taxicab driver in Knoxville the other day. "Business is three times as good as it was a year ago. You ought to see the crowds at the ballgames."

... "I put in an electric hot water heater sometime ago," one man told me, "but I haven't been able to use it because it cost too much. But now, with this new rate, I can. I can run that, with all my other equipment—range, iron, mangle, vacuum cleaner, lights, and radio—for the same cost as I went without it before."

... And all over the state, in the rural areas, the story is the same—an illiterate, wretched people, undernourished, with standards of living so low that, once on relief, they are quite willing to stay there the rest of their lives. It's a mess.

... But then—there's TVA. It's coming along. My guess is that, whatever they do or don't do about rural rehabilitation down in Tennessee, in another decade you wouldn't know this country. And the best part of it is that here the Government will have control. There's a chance to create a new kind of industrial life, with decent wages, decent housing. Gosh, what possibilities! You can't feel very sorry for Tennessee when you see that in the offing (The New Deal Network website).

---

included a motion picture director and writers that specialized in power, agriculture, and engineering. TVA employees published a flood of articles in professional journals. The TVA directors gave scores of speeches, and staff members responded personally to every one of 100,000 letters between 1933 and 1940. The Information Office published 15 major pamphlets with plenty of illustrations, some of which won awards and were adopted as models of writing for school classes. TVA photographers busily documented every aspect of work and their pictures became highly regarded works of art. The TVA installed exhibits at hundreds of conventions, meetings, schools, and colleges around the country. Their exhibit at 1939 World's Fair in New York drew 3.3 million visitors. Trained guides led visitors to the dams where 4.3 million people visited between 1933 and 1940. TVA films, including such titles as *TVA at Work, Norris Dam,* and *Electricity on the Farm,* were used in hundreds of schools and seen by nearly one million people by 1940. More than two thousand magazine articles were written about the TVA by 1940. To keep itself informed, the TVA subscribed to about five hundred periodicals and more than one hundred newspapers. Visiting writers and students were given special treatment and assistance and encouraged to study and write about what the TVA was doing. This massive effort and attention to detail in informing the public paid off: the TVA won immense popular support in the Tennessee Valley and around the country.

TVA in 1939

By the end of the 1930s the TVA had overcome great difficulties and was well established as a successful public organization. No more lawsuits threatened its existence and it was generating and distributing large and growing amounts of electrical power within a secure and integrated territory. Ship traffic was growing as new dams and navigation locks were completed, rural homes were modernizing through the use of electrical power, and new industries were springing up. The huge investment in the region was having an effect on the both economy and on the lives of the people.

The TVA was a model of efficiency and organization and was extremely popular, having employed many thousands of people and bringing electricity to the countryside. By working cooperatively with local people and agencies to accomplish its goals, the TVA became part of the social and economic fabric of life in the Tennessee Valley. As demonstrated even more convincingly in later years, when it was in full operation and its effects clearly measurable, the TVA was one of the crowning achievements of the New Deal.

Contributing Forces

Technological advances in the nineteenth century, particularly those relating to electrical power, communication, and transportation, created expectations in the United States and elsewhere that the way of life of the average citizen would soon change for the better. Many Americans in the early twentieth century electrified their homes and businesses and acquired telephones, automobiles, and radios. For many who could not afford these improvements, especially in rural areas, this promise of a new life led to frustration and disappointment. One of the most visible of the New Deal federal programs designed to address this fundamental problem, the Tennessee Valley Authority (TVA), arose from a series of unique conditions and historical events that might have led to a quite different result without the focused dedication of a few key individuals.

Electrical Power in Early Twentieth Century America

Although the theory of electricity was well established in the early nineteenth century, commercial power production first appeared in the early 1880s. It was then that Thomas Edison installed the world's first central electric power plant in New York City. Ironically these first power systems were built largely to create a market for electrical equipment, beginning with electric lights, made by Edison's company and others like it. They were not to serve an existing demand for power. They also served only those close to the power plants who could afford the high cost of the power. Electric systems soon appeared in cities all across North America. For example electrical generation arrived in Eugene, Oregon, three thousand miles from New York City, in 1887. Even so, it took several decades before everyday use in homes became commonplace.

By the early 1920s half of all urban homes in America were electrified and had at least some elec-

tric lights. In some communities, such as in Seattle and Los Angeles, municipal utilities owned by city residents provided electrical service. In most places private companies owned the power plants and the transmission lines. Many American families in the 1920s, largely limited to the wealthiest 20 percent, modernized their homes by installing full electric lighting and purchasing power tools and appliances for heating and cooling. By the end of that decade electric irons, radios, vacuum cleaners, and clothes washers were seen in many, but far from all, electrified homes, while less than 10 percent of U.S. farms had electricity. It was expensive to install power lines in rural areas where fewer prospective customers existed to help pay for them. As a result power companies did not believe it could be profitable to serve those areas. Cost was an obstacle for rural people as well as many city dwellers who were not well-to-do and could not afford to buy much electricity at the high rates of that time.

Enough Americans began benefiting from the use of electricity in the 1920s that it came to be seen as a necessity rather than a luxury. Many citizens and political leaders began to feel that American progress was being held back by greedy power companies who sought maximum profits rather than to serve the interests of their customers. Examples from other countries and from some American communities demonstrated to many that public programs could deliver universal electric service at much lower rates than the private companies were willing to consider.

Efforts to promote public power projects in the 1920s met largely with failure. At that time the American economy appeared to be very healthy and private enterprise was held in high regard. Most people felt that government should not interfere with private business, which was seen as responsible for the economic success that the United States had achieved. In the biggest public power proposal of that time, Gifford Pinchot, Governor of Pennsylvania and a progressive who believed that government should promote social welfare, set up the Giant Power Board in 1923 to design a statewide public power system. He felt that the power companies had been irresponsible in charging unreasonably high electric rates and in failing to serve rural areas. He and his appointed Director, Morris L. Cooke, had visions of an even grander public power system that would serve the entire country. After an exhaustive study, the Giant Power plan, proposing strong state control over power companies, universal service even in rural areas, and a way to set standard electric rates, was submitted to the Pennsylvania legislature in 1925.

More About...

Power, *a Living Newspaper*

The Federal Theatre Project (FTP) was an agency of the Works Progress Administration (WPA) created to make jobs for unemployed actors and theater workers. "Living Newspapers" were dramatic productions illustrating contemporary issues. In 1937 the FTP produced *Power,* a Living Newspaper about the history of the electric power industry in which Scene Fifteen portrays why many people supported the TVA.

Listed below are some excerpts from Scene Fifteen that illustrate both the feelings of the time and the means by which the New Deal promoted its programs.(Excerpted from The New Deal Network, available from the World Wide Web at http://newdeal.feri.org/tva/tva18.htm)

PROLOGUE

(*Movies of Tennessee Valley come on the screen. They are integrated with the following* **LOUDSPEAKER** *announcements:*) **LOUDSPEAKER:** In the Tennessee Valley . . . . Parts of seven States, 40,000 square miles, two million people. All living in a region blighted by the misuse of the land, and by the wash of small streams carrying away the fertile topsoil. In these cabins, life has changed but little since some pioneer wagon broke down a century ago, and for them this became the promised land. Occupations—when they exist at all—are primitive, a throwback to an earlier America. Here stand the results of poor land, limited diet, insufficient schooling, inadequate medical care, no plumbing, industry, agriculture, or electrification! . . . Meanwhile, the entire country seeks cheap electric power, and the demand for a cost yardstick comes from every section. In the Tennessee Valley, 1933. (*Screen goes up.*)

SCENE FIFTEEN-C
(Farmer and Electric Company Manager)
(Lights come up on desk. MANAGER of Electric Company is seated at desk. FARMER, left of desk, stands.)
FARMER: My God, I've got to have lights, I tell you!
MANAGER: Certainly, Mr. Parker. You can have all the lights you want. All you've got to do is pay for the cost of the poles and wires.
FARMER: But haven't got four hundred dollars! And my farm's mortgaged up to the hilt already. (*Desperately*) Can't you see? If I could only get juice I could get me an electric churn and make enough money to pay for the poles!
MANAGER: I'm sorry, Mr. Parker, but that's the way we operate. I'm afraid I can't do a thing for you.
FARMER: And I got to go on livin' the rest of my life with a kerosene lamp and a hand churn like my grandfather did when he came here?
MANAGER: Until you can raise the cost of the equipment.
FARMER: (desperately): Isn't there anybody else I can talk to?
MANAGER: I'm the manager here. There's nobody else.
FARMER: Isn't there any other company I can go to?
MANAGER: We're the only one in this part of the State.
FARMER: Then when you turn me down I'm finished?
MANAGER: That's right. (*A pause.*)
FARMER: By God, the Government ought to do something about this!

The private power industry opposed this plan and proposed one of their own, called "SuperPower." This plan proposed to interconnect distribution systems but would maintain private company control. It did not provide for universal service or a standard basis for rates. Supporting the power companies against Giant Power were Secretary of Commerce (and later President) Herbert Hoover as well as the U.S. Chamber of Commerce, a variety of private industries, and the press. After an intense public debate, the legislature voted against the Giant Power proposals. The debate, however, succeeded in introducing to many people the possibilities of public control over regional power systems. In the 1930s, when power companies were no longer so highly regarded because of the struggling national economic system, these ideas became much more acceptable.

The Boats Can't Get Through: A Short History of Navigation in the Tennessee Valley

The Tennessee Valley region receives much annual precipitation, but the river flow is about twenty times greater in the winter than in the summer. This variation combined with natural obstructions in the river channel made the Tennessee River system a big challenge for those who wanted to use it as a means of transporting goods and people.

Native peoples of the region used the rivers for thousands of years as transportation routes, but only in canoes that could be carried around the many rapids. European and Euro-American explorers and traders in the seventeenth and eighteenth centuries traveled on the rivers in the same way. Despite the many obstacles, the rivers still were the most efficient way to move from

---

Hiwassee Dam, a TVA project, under construction in 1938. By 1941 the TVA was the largest producer of electrical power in the United States. (National Archives—Southeast Region, Atlanta)

place to place. For example a group of settlers led by John Donelson in 1779 migrated from the Watauga colony in eastern Tennessee down the Tennessee River, through what is now Tennessee, Alabama, Mississippi, and Kentucky, to the Ohio River, up the Ohio to the Cumberland River, and up the Cumberland to settle at what is now Nashville, Tennessee. This journey covered about three or four times the distance that an overland trip might have taken, but it was much less difficult than an overland migration.

Settlement of the Tennessee River drainage in the late eighteenth and early nineteenth centuries created a need for ways to move people and products along the rivers. Local two-way river transport using boats propelled by poles called keelboats was possible, although expensive, along stretches between obstacles. Boat traffic upstream from New Orleans, the major source of goods in the region on the Mississippi River by way of the Mississippi, Ohio, and Tennessee rivers, was not at all practical until the arrival of the steamboat in the 1820s, and even they were limited to use in the high-water season. Neither could overcome the obstacles of Muscle Shoals in northern Alabama, where in 37 miles of rapids the river dropped 134 feet.

Muscle Shoals effectively split Tennessee into two regions: western and central Tennessee with its two major cities of Memphis and Nashville, and east-

ern Tennessee with its principal urban centers of Chattanooga and Knoxville. As a result people in eastern Tennessee were effectively cut off from markets and supplies in the Mississippi River valley and were economically disadvantaged in comparison with people in the central and western part of the state. Eastern Tennessee would remain economically depressed until a way could be found around or over the Muscle Shoals impediment. Similarly, northern Alabama, fertile ground for cotton production that enriched other areas in the South, could not participate in the bounty because shipping products downstream on the Tennessee River was not feasible.

Numerous attempts to improve the rivers for navigation met with little success. As early as 1817 the Tennessee state legislature created a board to look into navigation improvements on the Holston and Tennessee rivers. The people of Knoxville and others put up prize money in the 1820s to induce steamboat owners to find a way to navigate the entire length of the Tennessee River. The prize was won in 1828 by the enterprising captain of the side-wheeler *Atlas.* This feat, however, did not lead to regular steamboat service, and only eight boats succeeded in passing the shoals in the next decade. In the 1830s the federal government conducted a survey of the Tennessee and Holston rivers and recommended channel deepening among other improvements.

Once finished it enabled steamboats to operate for a greater part of the year upstream from the Alabama state line. Similar small improvements made on river tributaries in the 1840s and on the main river in 1852 accomplished very little.

Alabama focused on ways to overcome Muscle Shoals, beginning with federal aid in carrying out a survey of the shoals area in 1827. A 14-mile canal to bypass the obstruction was completed in 1836 but failed to solve the problem because navigation was still obstructed both upstream and downstream from the canal. The canal was abandoned and eventually filled with silt. In 1890 the U.S. Army Corps of Engineers completed two canals, including navigation locks, around major obstacles in the shoals region, but did not completely overcome the Muscle Shoals problem until 1927. At that time the huge Wilson Dam and a smaller companion were completed.

Beginning in 1868 the federal government made more serious attempts to deepen the main river channel. The main strategy was to dredge the channel in some places and narrow the river in others to achieve sufficient depth. This effort and similar ones over the next 50 years served to open the lower 225 miles of the river. They did not succeed in the greater stretch of river above Muscle Shoals. Eventually, open-channel methods were abandoned in favor of much more expensive dams and navigation locks. The first of these, built privately and mostly to produce electrical power, was completed in 1913 at Hales Bar about 33 miles downstream from Chattanooga, overcoming a major obstacle to navigation. The U.S. Army Corps of Engineers completed another dam at Widow's Bar about 23 miles below Hales Bar in 1925.

Despite a century of efforts to improve the Tennessee River as a navigable waterway, in 1930 it still was poorly suited to water transportation. It was especially difficult upstream from Muscle Schoals where the water depth in most of the stream was sufficient only during the high water season. It would take a huge federal commitment and a grand plan to make the river a truly effective artery of commerce.

Living Conditions in the Tennessee Valley

Euro-American immigrants to the Tennessee Valley in the eighteenth and nineteenth centuries were largely subsistence farmers. They grew food primarily for their own use and did not have much cash to buy products from other areas. Slow economic development of much of the region into the early twentieth century brought little fundamental change in the lives of the people, particularly in eastern Tennessee beyond the reach of river navigation. In the late 1920s

most people in the Tennessee Valley were still farmers. Much of the farmland had been misused through intensive cultivation causing soil erosion. Also timber in many areas had been clear-cut for short-term profit without replanting or consideration for the long-term productivity of the land. Hill slopes had been cleared of forest, crops were planted on these slopes, and then badly eroded by the rainfall that washed the soil down into the streams. Because of unwise farming practices, much of the land was no longer very fertile; corn would grow only a third as tall as it would in Iowa. The valley bottoms were favored places for people to live and farm, but floods frequently caused widespread damage to homes and fields.

Because the region was poor, large numbers of its two million people lived in deplorable conditions. Their houses were substandard with no indoor plumbing or electricity. Many people could not read and were undernourished and medical care was inadequate. This lack of education meant that good farming practices were not widely known.. Without some form of outside assistance and investment to boost the economy, there seemed little hope for improvement in living conditions.

The Muscle Shoals Controversy

Although the United States did not enter World War I until 1917, by 1916 national defense had become a major concern. One worry was that the country was too dependent on Chile as a source of nitrates. Nitrogen compounds, such as nitrates, are an important component of explosives. Other great powers in the world were developing synthetic nitrogen facilities so they would not have to depend on sources that could be cut off in wartime. Accordingly, Congress passed the National Defense Act of 1916, which included a provision authorizing the President to design, build, and operate synthetic nitrogen plants. In peacetime the nitrogen was to be used for making fertilizer instead of munitions, which would reduce the cost of fertilizer to American farmers.

President Woodrow Wilson (served 1917–1921) appointed committees to recommend how and where to build the nitrogen plants. Of the two plants that were built, one of them was designed to use a method requiring large amounts of electrical power. For this reason it was located at Muscle Shoals, Alabama, where a hydroelectric dam could be built to provide the needed power. This plant was ready to begin production by October 1918, but was not put into service because the World War had just come to an end. Construction of the dam, named Wilson Dam after the President, was authorized in February 1918. Because the dam would not be completed before the nitrogen plant was ready, a steam power facility was installed to generate the needed power until the dam was finished.

Almost immediately after the end of the war, the Muscle Shoals project came under attack by Republicans who saw it as an issue for the 1920 presidential election. They charged that the project was a costly failure and might lead to government competition with private industry. At the same time, the government attempted to find private buyers for the facility. When no buyers could be found, the Wilson administration in 1919 presented a bill to Congress. The bill proposed to continue government operation of the nitrate plant by an agency run very much like a private corporation. Nitrogen products not needed for national defense would be sold for fertilizer. When Wilson Dam was finished, its surplus power beyond that needed for the nitrate plant would be sold on the open market. Proponents of the bill argued that the dependence of national defense and American agriculture on Chilean nitrates was a bigger concern than the possible competition between the government and private enterprise.

An investigation of the Muscle Shoals project by a Republican-led committee found evidence of some waste and petty graft. The Republican majority of the committee also charged that the project had been built with the hidden motive of turning it over to a particular company, the American Cyanamid Company, after the war. American farmers, however, responding to a shortage of fertilizer supported government control of the Muscle Shoals nitrate plant and immediate completion of Wilson Dam to power it. In the end, in 1921 after a lengthy and heated debate that captured the attention of the nation, the Senate approved the bill but the House rejected it. Funding for completion of Wilson Dam also was turned down, and it appeared that government operation of the Muscle Shoals project was doomed.

The new Republican administration under President Warren Harding (served 1921–1925), however, was reluctant to scrap the project. They felt that the government should receive a fair return on its investment. They proposed that if private industry could make use of the project and pay the government for it, the project—including Wilson Dam—should be completed and then leased to a private operator. Initially no private companies expressed interest in the proposal and it appeared the project would be abandoned. One of those contacted about the project, the prominent industrialist Henry Ford, famous for making automobiles that many Americans could afford to buy, then stepped forward and made an offer for Muscle Shoals.

The Ford offer started another phase of controversy over Muscle Shoals. Differences of opinion arose within the government about whether the offer should be accepted. It also incited heated debate among the public. Many felt that Ford's offer was an opportunity for the government to rid itself of a white elephant, while critics charged that accepting the offer would amount to a government giveaway. During the negotiations between Ford and the government, an important point of dispute over the Wilson Dam was how much it would cost to complete. Ford arranged a high-profile tour of the Muscle Shoals facilities with another famous and highly regarded American, Thomas Edison, to promote public support of his bid. In speeches delivered to the people of the Muscle Shoals area, Ford declared that he intended to develop the Muscle Shoals project to rid the world of war by creating the "energy dollar" to replace the dollar based on gold. He made many enemies when he further declared that the international financial system was under the control of Jews who created wars, including the American Civil War and World War I, for financial profit. The *New York Times* and others took great issue with Ford's interpretation of history and his anti-Semitism, however, at the same time he gained strong popular support in the South for his bid. This support grew still more when he proposed to build a great city, 75 miles long, in the Muscle Shoals area and bring great prosperity to the South through development of waterpower and other natural resources. This created great excitement among people in northern Alabama who had only dreamed that their region could have the economic success of other parts of the country.

The Harding administration submitted the Ford bid to Congress in 1922, but recommended that it be rejected. Among the major problems with the proposal was that it violated terms of the Federal Water Power Act, since it did not provide that the waterpower would be subject to government regulation. The administration also felt that the Ford bid would not pay a fair amount to the government for the project. Once before the Congress, the Ford offer spurred a vigorous public debate. While this debate raged, the Alabama Power Company submitted a competing bid that Congress also began to consider.

In what proved to be a fateful decision, the U.S. Senate referred the Ford bid for consideration by the Senate Agriculture Committee. Senator George W. Norris of Nebraska, a progressive who believed strongly in public power chaired the committee. Norris had his own bill providing for public rather than

The Norris Dam located in Tennessee. The dam helps control floods in the area, provides electricity, and helps to regulate the depth of the Tennessee River. (The Library of Congress.)

private operation of Muscle Shoals. He mobilized opposition to the Ford offer while dragging the hearings out as long as possible. Norris introduced his first Muscle Shoals bill to the Senate in May 1922. In July the Senate Agriculture Committee rejected both the Ford bid and the offer by the Alabama Power Company. Norris's bill called for completion of Wilson Dam and a companion dam on the Tennessee River. It also provided for a government corporation to make fertilizer and sell surplus power, giving preference to

public utilities. The bill called for a survey of the waterpower resources of the Tennessee River and its tributaries and authorized the Secretary of War to build dams where economically feasible. These dams would be designed also to facilitate navigation as well as to provide power.

The Norris bill prompted great interest and started a debate that lasted more than a decade. In the meantime the Ford offer was still under consideration in the House of Representatives. In late 1922 Congress authorized the completion of Wilson Dam, which included both hydroelectric power generation and navigation locks. This work made the Muscle Shoals project even more valuable and a bigger prize to fight over. Congress did not approve Norris's plan for a government corporation to operate the project, leaving that matter for later consideration.

In January 1924 a group of nine southern power companies, including the Alabama Power Company, submitted a bid for Muscle Shoals. In the same month Senator Norris gave a speech in which he proposed a nationwide plan for development of all possible water-power resources by the federal government and a single public power system connecting the entire country. When the Ford offer, however, was finally brought before the House of Representatives in March 1924, it passed by a vote of 227 to 143. Immediately Norris went to work to defeat the proposal when it was transmitted to the Senate and referred to his Agriculture Committee. Again Norris's strategy was to prolong the hearings to allow time for the opposition to gain strength. At the same time he more strongly pushed his own bill for public operation of Muscle Shoals. In May 1924 the Agriculture Committee voted 11 to four to recommend the Norris bill instead of the Ford offer. Many viewed this as just a temporary setback for the Ford plan, and they expected that it would fare better in the next session of Congress. All were surprised in October 1924, however, when Henry Ford withdrew his offer without warning.

Despite the rejection of the Ford bid and other private offers to operate the Muscle Shoals project, the vision of economic benefit connected with it was not diminished. No longer considered a white elephant, Muscle Shoals, as an issue, became even larger when people saw it as a highly valued resource that might be used to benefit the public. The disappointed people of the Tennessee Valley continued to hold out hope that the water power of their region would be developed to help lift them from economic stagnation. Increasingly, as the 1920s progressed, people in the United States felt that electrical power could help improve the lives of ordinary people.

With Henry Ford removed from the Muscle Shoals controversy, the issue boiled down to public versus private control of the hydroelectric power. In the Senate the Norris bill faced opposition from those who still favored leasing the project to private interests. In 1925 the Senate, in a defeat for Norris, voted in favor of leasing the project. When that bill was under consideration by a joint House-Senate conference to resolve differences between the House and Senate versions, Norris successfully filibustered, or

stalled by delivering long speeches, against it. This killed the bill by preventing any vote before Congress adjourned.

Throughout the remainder of the 1920s, the struggle between Norris and those who favored private operation of Muscle Shoals continued. Norris reintroduced his bill during each congressional session and his opponents offered theirs in opposition. Much of the time, Congress was effectively stalemated because neither side could win a clear majority. The lengthy debate raised awareness of the potential value of hydroelectric development, not only of the Muscle Shoals project area, but also of the entire Tennessee Valley. The U.S. Army Corps of Engineers released a study in 1925 that documented the huge hydroelectric power potential of the Tennessee River and its tributaries. Norris advocated this wider development, but never succeeded in gaining strong support for government operation of a project so much bigger than Muscle Shoals where the controversy was focused.

By 1928 it was clear that Muscle Shoals was much more valuable for power production than for fertilizer, which was no longer in short supply. In the same year Norris won his biggest victory during his long fight for public control of the project, when the Senate passed his resolution by an overwhelming vote of 48 to 25. The House of Representatives passed a similar bill and both houses then worked out a compromise measure in conference. It appeared that the Muscle Shoals development finally would be established as an exclusively public project. To the great dismay of Norris and his supporters, President Coolidge (served 1923–1929) decided not to sign it into law within the constitutional time limit, following a tactic called a "pocket veto." Norris accused Coolidge of bending to the interests of the private power companies, which he called the "power trust."

Coolidge's pocket veto of the Norris bill created a national issue for the 1928 presidential election. In that campaign Norris, a Republican, supported Alfred E. Smith, the Democratic candidate, instead of the Republican candidate Herbert Hoover. Smith leaned more toward public control of electrical power systems, while Hoover clearly expressed his distaste for what he thought was government competition against private enterprise. Hoover and the Republicans won an easy victory in that election, but public opinion was beginning to move against the private power companies. An investigation by the Federal Trade Commission (FTC) in 1928 showed that the power companies had used their money improperly to win public support. Additional revelations of that kind by the FTC investigation in 1929 further damaged the image of the power companies. This was much to the delight of the Norris camp that emphasized the wrongdoings of the "power trust" in their public statements. By this time many people felt that the power companies were overcharging their customers. Governor Franklin D. Roosevelt of New York proposed that Muscle Shoals, in addition to a power project on the St. Lawrence River and Boulder Dam on the Colorado River, be publicly operated to serve as "yardsticks" in order to establish reasonable power rates. His idea was that the government, by operating these projects, could find out how much it really cost to produce and distribute electrical power. The government would then require the power companies to lower their rates to a fair level.

When President Herbert Hoover delivered his annual message to Congress on December 3, 1929, he advocated the lease of the Muscle Shoals facilities to private companies. However as shown by the congressional passage of the Norris bill in 1928 and by the FTC investigations of the power companies, the tide was already turning against reliance on private enterprise to manage natural power sources in the public interest. Thus the stage was set for events and circumstances in the 1930s toward a massive federal development of the Tennessee Valley.

Perspectives

Private Tradition vs. Public Tradition

The political and ideological battle associated with the creation of the TVA was a clash between two American traditions with different and opposing visions about the proper control of electrical power resources: the private tradition and the public tradition. Beginning at the turn of the twentieth century this struggle reached its peak during the New Deal. The private tradition, represented by private power companies and their stockholders and supporters, built the first electrical power systems in the 1880s and 1890s and rapidly expanded to become a major force in the American economy by the 1920s. In their view, what was good for private enterprise was good for America. It stimulated innovation and economic activity for the benefit of all. They chafed at government regulation or, even worse, government ownership and operation of competing utilities, which they felt was un-American. The public tradition comprised a group of reformers who defended what they saw as the public interest against the excesses and abuses of the private companies. These people often referred to themselves as "progressives;" to them, private power companies were essentially monopolies because only

one company realistically could supply power to a given area. A lack of competition meant that the government had an obligation to regulate the industry to assure that its rates and services were reasonable and fair. Expecting self-regulation in the absence of competition would be unreasonable. Furthermore in their view, power generated from public resources such as rivers should be considered itself also a public resource to be used first and foremost for the public benefit and not to profit private interests.

Building electric power production and distribution systems required large capital investments. This meant that private power companies were started and run by people who had large amounts of money to begin with and borrowed still more money that had to be repaid. Profits could be substantial because the companies could charge rates that could yield impressive cash flows, but the risks were high as well. Hundreds of small private utilities were bought out by larger companies, called "holding companies," that had sufficient capital (money) to afford the ups and downs of the business. By the 1920s most private companies were owned by holding companies who in turn were often owned by still larger holding companies. Because each layer of ownership had to make a profit, this ownership structure did little to reduce the rates to the electricity consumers or to encourage widespread use of electricity by ordinary people who could not afford the high rates. The situation was ripe for abuse and many abuses did take place. Profits were held in higher regard than the customers who were served, and government regulation was very weak. Especially in the 1920s many holding companies made incredible profits either by enriching themselves at the expense of the companies they owned or by manipulating stock prices in the poorly regulated stock market. The company owners and stockholders felt that they were within their rights to run their companies as they pleased.

The public tradition reacted to power company activities by promoting government regulation and public ownership of utilities. Some cities, such as Seattle and Los Angeles, established their own public utilities very early. By the end of the 1920s most states had commissions to regulate private utilities based on the systems set up in New York and Wisconsin in 1907. Unfortunately these commissions were ineffective against companies that had much larger budgets and armies of lawyers. Political leaders such as Senator George Norris of Nebraska and Governor Gifford Pinchot of Pennsylvania led a charge against private power companies and especially against the holding companies. These two and many others like them saw the private tradition as an enemy of social progress.

Select TVA Dam Projects Estimated and Actual Costs

TVA Dam Project	Estimated Cost in millions	Actual Cost in millions
Norris	$36 million	$31 million
Wheeler	32.1	29.3
Pickwick	32.5	29.7
Hiwassee	15.3	16
Guntersville	29.5	31.1
Chickamauga	31.7	33.7

The Chickamauga Dam project proved to be the costliest TVA project of the New Deal. (The Gale Group.)

By the 1920s electricity was regarded as essential to modern life, but it was largely under the control of a powerful few that had little incentive to spread the benefits to the middle and lower rungs of the economic ladder. The power companies had gained enormous public prestige through the successful development of their industry and their generous investment in public relations. The leaders of the public tradition, believing that they held the banner of the common people, used the political arena to attack the abuses and advantaged position of the power companies. Through proposals, hearings, and publicity at the local, state, and national levels, these leaders undermined public support for the power companies. They eventually succeeded in largely dismantling the holding companies and establishing the largest public utility the country has ever seen, the Tennessee Valley Authority.

Impact

TVA Beyond the 1930s

The Tennessee Valley and the nation experienced the greatest effects of the TVA in the decades following the 1930s. Dam construction was still actively under way in 1940 and did not conclude until 1944. As dams were completed, power generation grew and the navigation and flood control systems began to work as designed. These engineering achievements and the broad-scale developments carried out by the TVA yielded the benefits for the region that President Roosevelt had envisioned. However despite the success of this massive experiment and contrary to Roosevelt's prediction, it was never repeated elsewhere in the country.

TVA developments came just in time to make a significant contribution to the war effort in World War II (1939–1945). Construction was at its peak in 1942 when 28,000 workers were busy on 12 hydroelectric projects and a steam plant. TVA power was critical to wartime industries, particularly aluminum plants essential to the production of airplanes and bombs. By war's end the TVA had completed the 650-mile navigation channel and was the largest electricity supplier in the United States. Demand for electricity grew faster than the TVA's hydroelectric power production. By the 1960s the TVA was generating power from coal-fired plants and began construction on nuclear power plants. As for other utilities around the country, the TVA encountered rising construction costs and political resistance to nuclear power plants. Several plants were canceled before the TVA finally abandoned nuclear plant construction entirely in the 1990s. Beginning in the 1970s and continuing into the 1990s electricity costs rose dramatically. These higher costs severely challenged the TVA to improve efficiency and productivity so it could remain competitive in the industry. As it moved into the twenty-first century, the TVA continued to justify its role in the electric power industry as a yardstick by which private companies could be measured. What many considered an unfair advantage for the TVA was removed in 1959 when Congress made the TVA's power system depend entirely on its own revenues. It became completely independent of government funding or financing. Of course the initial massive investment that funded the construction of hydroelectric facilities in the first place was public money, direct comparisons between the TVA and private systems may not be entirely fair.

Future TVAs

The perception of unfair dealings by the government with private industry in the creation of the TVA led to a kind of backlash against further developments of this kind. In the 1940 presidential election campaign, Republican candidate Willkie, a veteran of the battle against the TVA, severely criticized the Roosevelt administration for sinking so much public money into a single project and in the process allegedly damaging the free enterprise system. The fact that business investment declined in the latter half of the 1930s provided support for Willkie's arguments. These arguments had their effect on public opinion even though Roosevelt won the 1940 election. Even earlier in 1937 when Senator Norris introduced legislation to create TVA-like authorities across the country, he faced opposition not only from private interests but even from within the Roosevelt administration. The Agriculture and War departments felt such authorities would duplicate what the depart-

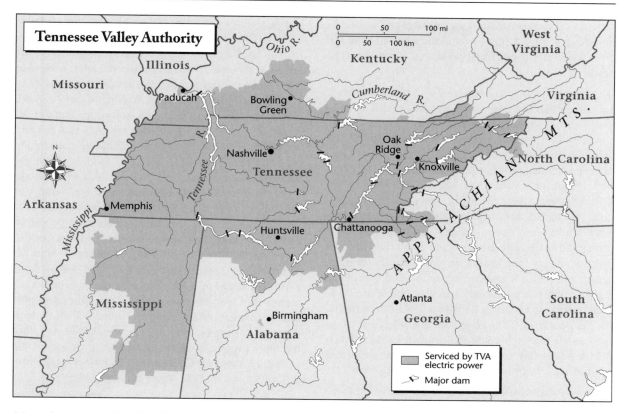

Map of areas serviced by TVA electric power and sites of major dams. (The Gale Group.)

ments already were doing. Political wrangling within the government and opposition from private companies and their supporters effectively prevented the creation of any more public organizations like the TVA.

In fact, analysis of the historical forces that led to the TVA suggests that it was only the convergence of certain unique circumstances that made it possible in the first place. World War I led to Wilson Dam. Abuses by the private power companies lowered their popularity dramatically by the early 1930s, even though later reforms within the industry rectified many of the errors that they had committed. The Depression was a national crisis that made new approaches popular. The persistently depressed economy of the Tennessee Valley made it a popular cause for government assistance. Once the TVA was established, the power needs of World War II made the TVA a highly valued national asset. These circumstances were not repeated elsewhere in the country or at any other time in American history. They also did not change the traditional American ambivalence regarding government competition or interference with private enterprise.

Although the country did not repeat the TVA experiment elsewhere, the TVA did have profound impacts in the Tennessee Valley and elsewhere. As the fulfillment of a unified plan for development of an entire river basin, it probably has no equal in the world. The combination of a massive financial investment, generation of huge amounts of affordable electrical power, and establishment of an uninterrupted navigation channel all the way to Knoxville stimulated the economy and dramatically raised standards of living in the Tennessee Valley and to a large extent the entire American South. Ironically this huge government program, criticized by many as "socialistic," was a fantastic success in promoting private economic activity. Despite the vision of Roosevelt and Arthur Morgan, however, the TVA never achieved similar success as a regional planning agency in the promotion of social, educational, and health programs.

Notable People

David E. Lilienthal (1899–1981). David Lilienthal was one of the original three TVA directors appointed in 1933. He served as the principal TVA strategist and spokesman in the political and legal battle with the private power companies to establish the TVA as principal electrical power utility in the Tennessee Valley.

The son of Jewish immigrants from Czechoslovakia, Lilienthal was born in Illinois and raised in Indiana where he graduated from DePauw University. As a student he spent his summers working in mills and factories where he developed his concern for social justice. He attended Harvard Law School, studying under Felix Frankfurter who later became a Justice of the U.S. Supreme Court. Idealistic, energetic and ambitious, Lilienthal as a law student corresponded with labor leaders and public figures. He began his legal career with a Chicago law firm and then set up his own practice. As a young lawyer he wrote articles for magazines and journals and became associated with some highly visible legal cases. One was before the U.S. Supreme Court in which he won a $20 million refund for the people of Chicago against the telephone company. After that he became an acknowledged expert on public utility law, in 1931 Lilienthal was appointed head of the Wisconsin State Utility Commission.

Lilienthal's brilliance early in his career led to his appointment as a Director of TVA, where he employed his legal and political skills against the private power companies in the Tennessee Valley region. Extremely distrusting of the companies, he employed every possible tactic to undermine their bargaining position. Lilienthal strongly disagreed with TVA head Arthur Morgan who felt that the TVA should strive to work cooperatively with the private companies. Lilienthal worked instead to compete directly with the companies in the power business and fought with them successfully for several years in the courts. Following a major dispute between Lilienthal and Morgan, President Roosevelt fired Morgan in 1938. In 1939 Lilienthal achieved final victory over the companies when TVA bought out the Tennessee Electric Power Company and gained control of its territory in the Tennessee Valley.

Appointed as head of TVA in 1941 and given another nine-year term in that position in 1945, Lilienthal left the TVA in 1946 to become the first head of the Atomic Energy Commission. He moved into private business in 1950 and in his later years spent time writing and publishing his recollections.

Arthur E. Morgan (1878–1974). Arthur Morgan, President Roosevelt's choice to be the first head of TVA, ran the TVA's program to design and build dams as well as a variety of other projects until 1938, when Roosevelt fired Morgan after an internal power struggle between him and David Lilienthal.

Visionary engineer Arthur Morgan was born in 1878 in Cincinnati, Ohio, and grew up in St. Cloud, Minnesota, where he learned engineering through his father, a surveyor. With a formal education limited to three years of high school and six weeks at the University of Colorado, Morgan decided to enter a field, water-control engineering, that was young and did not require a degree. He devoted himself to this pursuit, becoming a nationally regarded field engineer by the time he was 30 years old. By 1910 he had established his own engineering firm in Memphis, Tennessee. Over the next 20 years Morgan supervised scores of projects all over the country. After the Miami River flood of 1913, which killed three hundred people in Ohio, that state hired him to establish a flood-control program. For that project Morgan set up the innovative Miami Conservancy District and adopted an expanded scope of work. The program included organizing dam workers into small communities and providing instruction for them in sound values, which began his reputation as an educator. While directing the Ohio project in 1919, he became a trustee of the struggling Antioch College in Yellow Springs, Ohio, and was hired in 1921 as its president.

Under Morgan's leadership, Antioch College prospered and became known for Morgan's creation of a cooperative plan in which students worked at campus industries associated with their classroom studies. His concept was to create a generation of philosopher-engineers with a cultivated moral philosophy. Many admired him for his utopian vision and non-religious moral philosophy. An influential Antioch College supporter was Eleanor Roosevelt, wife of Franklin Roosevelt, who was to become Governor of New York and then President of the United States. Franklin Roosevelt no doubt learned about Morgan through Eleanor and admired Morgan's vision and his fondness for planning. To Morgan's surprise, Roosevelt invited him to the White House in 1933 and asked him to accept the chairmanship of TVA. Morgan accepted without hesitation, seeing TVA as the opportunity of a lifetime to see his social vision become reality.

Morgan was very successful in designing and building TVA's dams, keeping them on schedule and within budget. He ran into opposition from the other TVA directors, however, in instituting unusual programs such as recreation, a credit exchange for cash-poor areas, development of specialized forest industries, a forest genetics program, a local porcelain industry, bean-growing ventures in mountain valleys, and a commission on race relations. He also wanted to work cooperatively with the private power companies, but TVA Director Lilienthal saw that approach as naive and dangerous. Friction arose between Morgan and the other directors, particularly Lilienthal. Morgan spoke out publicly against the TVA of what he thought were unethical practices and in 1938 was fired by President Roosevelt. Arthur Morgan spent the remaining 37 years of his long life publishing a series of diverse and thoughtful books, and he produced his own account of events at TVA in a book called *The Making of the TVA.*

Harcourt A. Morgan (1867–1950). Harcourt Morgan, one of the three original TVA directors, organized the TVA's agricultural programs and ultimately sided with David Lilienthal in his internal dispute with Arthur Morgan.

Born in Stratroy, Ontario, Canada, Morgan graduated from the University of Ontario in 1889 and attended graduate school at Cornell University where he studied horticulture and agriculture. He moved to Louisiana to teach entomology at Louisiana State University and work with the newly organized agricultural experiment station. Morgan became an expert on plant pests, gaining this reputation by battling boll weevils, armyworms, cattle ticks, and grasshoppers. He became head of the University of Tennessee agricultural experiment station at Knoxville in 1905. His easy-going personality helped him gain the trust of southern farmers and ability to convey his progressive agricultural methods. He became Dean of the College of Agriculture in 1913, then Food Administrator for Tennessee during World War I, President of the University of Tennessee in 1919, and finally President of the Association of Land Grant Colleges and Universities in 1927.

Morgan believed strongly in a balanced approach to land use. He witnessed the damage to Southern agriculture that had been caused by short-term thinking and improper farming methods. Morgan had very firm ideas about what was needed to reform the region's agriculture and restore the land. He was committed to helping the farmers of the region and held a poor opinion of the private power companies who he believed had neglected rural people by not extending electrical service into the countryside. Arthur Morgan selected him in 1933 as the second TVA Director because of his agricultural expertise in the region, his personal connections with the people there, and his commitment to agricultural reform.

Within the TVA Board, Harcourt Morgan gave support to large commercial farmers and in turn was supported by farm interest groups. This disturbed Arthur Morgan who was partial to the small subsistence farmers of the region. This difference of opinion and Harcourt Morgan's inclination to side with David Lilienthal on strategies for dealing with power

companies made Arthur Morgan a minority of one on the Board. After Arthur Morgan was fired in 1938, Harcourt Morgan was made head of TVA, a position he held until 1941. He remained on the TVA Board until 1947, when he retired.

George W. Norris (1861–1944). George Norris, as Senator from Nebraska, vigorously promoted government control of electrical utilities and was instrumental in the establishment of both the New Deal's Rural Electrification Administration (REA) and the Tennessee Valley Authority (TVA). The REA was created to ensure that cheap electricity was available in rural areas across the nation.

Born in Sandusky County, Ohio, Norris grew up in a very poor farm family. He learned first-hand how difficult rural life could be. He taught school and studied law, completing his education at Valparaiso University, in Indiana, and earning admission to the bar in 1883. He moved to Nebraska in 1885 and later became a county prosecuting attorney. Norris was elected to a district judgeship in 1895 and re-elected in 1899. In 1902 he was elected to the U.S. House of Representatives and served five successive terms, and he became U.S. Senator from Nebraska in 1912.

During his decades in Congress, Norris championed the causes of ordinary Americans, especially farmers. He particularly espoused public power and pushed for controls on private utility companies. In the 1920s he fought for federal development of the Muscle Shoals hydroelectric project on the Tennessee River. The federal government had built this system of hydroelectric dams and factories during World War I for the purpose of manufacturing munitions for the war effort. While some felt that the project should be turned over to private industry for development, Norris saw an opportunity to provide cheap power to poor Southern farmers as well as city people. He opposed Henry Ford's offer to purchase the project for $5 million and deliver the power to private manufacturers. In 1922 Norris recommended that the federal government distribute power to states, counties, and municipalities within a three hundred-mile radius. He repeatedly introduced legislation to establish permanent federal control of the Muscle Shoals project. His resolution passed both houses of Congress in 1928, but was stymied by President Calvin Coolidge's veto. His bill again passed in 1931, but was vetoed this time by President Herbert Hoover. After the sweeping Democratic election victory of 1932, President Franklin Roosevelt in 1933 expanded Norris's Muscle Shoals concept into the even more ambitious TVA, which became one of the most visible and successful of New Deal programs. After leaving the Senate in 1942, Norris died on September 3, 1944, in his adopted state of Nebraska.

Wendell L. Willkie (1892–1944). Wendell Willkie was President and Chief Executive Officer of Commonwealth and Southern Corporation, a holding company that owned many private utilities in the Southeast. He fought to protect his company's holdings from virtual takeover by TVA. Willkie eventually lost a series of decisive lawsuits and sold the Tennessee Electric Power Company to the TVA.

Raised in Elwood, Indiana, and the grandson of four German immigrants, Willkie was the son of an unusual couple who both practiced law and taught school. Although not especially bright in school, he displayed a remarkable gift for debate and public speaking. He attended Indiana University where he admired Woodrow Wilson (then Governor of New Jersey) and became active in the student Democratic Club. He taught high school in an effort to earn money to attend law school. He also worked briefly in a Puerto Rican sugar plant where he witnessed brutality that kept him mindful of the plight of powerless people. Upon entering law school at Indiana University, he focused on his studies and rose to the top of his class. Willkie enlisted for World War I but arrived in France just before Armistice Day, which ended the war.

In 1921 Willkie joined a private law firm in Akron, Ohio, one of whose clients was Northern Ohio Traction and Light. This company would become part of Commonwealth and Southern Corporation (C & S). Willkie developed a reputation as a trial lawyer, often defending Northern Ohio Traction and Light against lawsuits. He attended the 1924 Democratic National Convention as a delegate. In October 1929 he moved to New York as a legal adviser to the new C & S and three years later rose to the top as the C & S President. The creation of TVA by President Roosevelt immediately put him into conflict with the federal government even though he had voted for Roosevelt for president. He did not believe the government had the right to use its power and authority to take territory away from his corporation. Therefore he fought TVA in the courts charging that the TVA was unconstitutional. After losing the legal fight, he sold one of the companies, the Tennessee Electric Power Company, to TVA for $78 million, yielding to TVA the Tennessee Valley and some adjacent areas.

Partly as a reaction to this experience, Willkie sought and won the Republican nomination for president in 1940, but lost the election to Roosevelt. Roosevelt nevertheless admired Willkie for his international perspective and in 1942 recruited Willkie to tour Asia to promote the creation of an international body of law. In 1944 Willkie again entered the race for the Republican presidential nomination, but dropped out. He died later that year.

Primary Sources

Just prior to the 1931 presidential veto of the Norris Muscle Shoals bill, President Herbert Hoover and Senator George Norris of Nebraska engaged in a war of words. Their debate demonstrated the attitudes of the two sides on the issue of public power and toward each other. Preston Hubbard quotes Hoover and Norris in his book, *Origins of the TVA: The Muscle Shoals Controversy, 1920–1932,* 1961, p. 291. Speaking to the press on February 28, 1931, Hoover said:

> To be against Senator Norris's bill appears to be cause for denunciation as being in league with the power companies. It appears also to be emerging as the test of views upon government operation and distribution of power and government manufacture of commodities. In other words, its adaptation to the use of the people of the Tennessee Valley and to the farmers generally is now enmeshed in an endeavor to create a national political issue . . .

> This happens to be an engineering project and so far as its business merits and demerits are concerned is subject to the cold examination of engineering facts. I am having these facts exhaustively determined by the different departments of the government and will then be able to state my views upon the problem.

On March 1 the next day, Norris, obviously expecting the veto, heaped ridicule on Hoover for his reference to the issue as primarily an issue about engineering:

> The President, being an engineer, it would seem he would have no difficulty in solving the problem and, therefore, it is rather surprising to learn from his statements that he is referring the matter to the heads of his departments, none of whom is an engineer.

> The great engineer is asking advice on an "engineering project" from those who are not engineers, and when those who are not engineers tell the engineer what to do with "an engineering project" the engineer will know whether to sign or veto the bill.

> It reminds me of the New England country justice who, at the close of a law suit, said he would take it under advisement for three days, at which time he would render judgment for the plaintiff.

The vision of President Roosevelt as he proposed the Tennessee Valley Authority extended far beyond the provision of electrical power. It included sweeping improvements in the lives of the people of the Tennessee Valley. This vision is well described in Roosevelt's formal proposal to Congress on April 10, 1933 (*The Public Papers and Addresses of Franklin D. Roosevelt; Volume 2: The Year of Crisis, 1933,* 1938, pp. 122–123):

> The continued idleness of a great national investment in the Tennessee Valley leads me to ask the Congress for legislation necessary to enlist this project in the service of the people.

It is clear to me that the Muscle Shoals development is but a small part of the potential public usefulness of the entire Tennessee River. Such use, if envisioned in its entirety, transcends mere power development; it enters the wide fields of flood control, soil erosion, afforestation, elimination from agricultural use of marginal lands, and distribution and diversification of industry. In short, this power development of war days leads logically to national planning for a complete river watershed involving many States and the future lives and welfare of millions. It touches and gives life to all forms of human concerns.

I, therefore, suggest to the Congress legislation to create a Tennessee Valley Authority, a corporation clothed with the power of Government but possessed of the flexibility and initiative of a private enterprise. It should be charged with the broadest duty of planning for the proper use, conservation and development of the natural resources of the Tennessee River drainage basin and its adjoining territory for the general social and economic welfare of the Nation. This Authority should also be clothed with the necessary power to carry these plans into effect. Its duty should be the rehabilitation of the Muscle Shoals development and the coordination of it with the wider plan.

Many hard lessons have taught us the human waste that results from lack of planning. Here and there a few wise cities and counties have looked ahead and planned. But our Nation has "just grown." It is time to extend planning to a wider field, in this instance comprehending in one great project many States directly concerned with the basin of one of our greatest rivers.

This in a true sense is a return to the spirit and vision of the pioneer. If we are successful here we can march on, step by step, in a like development of other great natural territorial units within our borders.

David Lilienthal, one of the three original TVA directors, championed the TVA cause whenever possible. He contrasted the public goals of the TVA with the private motives of the power companies. The following is from a speech (cited in his *TVA Years,* pp. 79–81; referenced by McCraw, *TVA and the Power Fight* pp. 123–124) given in Memphis and broadcast by radio on October 20, 1934:

We are proud to count among our leading enemies the whole Tory crowd concentrated in New York and Chicago that always fights every move toward giving the average man and woman a better chance. The interests of this crew of reactionaries and your interests are diametrically opposed. There is a conflict here that can not be reconciled. Either TVA has to be for you or it has to be for this other crowd. When that crowd begins to sing the praises of TVA, it is time for you to throw us out.

The power companies, after a long struggle, eventually found that they could not win a competition with the government for the power market and in the end sold out. Wendell Willkie, the head of Commonwealth and Southern Corporation and later the opponent of

President Roosevelt in the presidential election of 1940, put it this way:

When it got at the point where the cities were actually going up the city streets, building duplicate distribution lines, and the Supreme Court had said that they would not pass on the constitutionality of the question, then I became a realist."

The creation and survival of the TVA was the product of a long struggle between opposing forces and resulted from a combination of unique circumstances. A chief participant in this struggle from the beginning was Senator George Norris of Nebraska. In 1941 when he was more than 80 years of age, Norris reflected with wonder on the achievement:

When I think of the work which has been done and the difficulties which have beset those in charge of this project, and the malicious attempts made to destroy it by the power trust, I can hardly believe the development which has taken place ... It seems, when I think it over, that it is too good to be true. It seems almost like a dream."

Suggested Research Topics

• The national debate about TVA pitted the proponents of the free enterprise system against those who believed that the public would benefit most from government control of electrical power. What current issues today resemble this dispute? Do the opposing sides in the TVA issue have ideological descendants today?

• Make a census of the dams in your state or a nearby state. Describe them. Why and when were they built and by whom? What benefits and problems have resulted from their construction? Should more dams be built or should some dams be dismantled?

• Pick a public or a private utility near you. When and why was it established? How is it run? How does it relate to its community? What services does it provide? How is the public assured that its electric rates are fair and reasonable?

Bibliography

Sources

Brown, D. Clayton. *Electricity for Rural America: The Fight for the REA.* Westport, CN: Greenwood Press, 1980.

Clapp, Gordon Rufus. *The TVA; An Approach to the Development of a Region.* Chicago: University of Chicago Press, 1955.

Droze, Wilmon H. *High Dams and Slack Waters: TVA Rebuilds a River.* Baton Rouge, Louisiana: Louisiana State University Press, 1965.

Hubbard, Preston J. *Origins of the TVA: The Muscle Shoals Controversy, 1920–1932.* New York: W. W. Norton & Co., 1961.

McCraw, Thomas K. *TVA and the Power Fight.* Philadelphia: J. B. Lippincott Co., 1971.

Morgan, Arthur E. *The Making of the TVA.* Buffalo, NY: Prometheus Books, 1974.

" 'The State is the University's Campus:' Harcourt A. Morgan, Thirteenth President of UT," [cited February 28, 2002] available from the World Wide Web at http://web.utk.edu/~mklein/morgan.htm.

Tobey, Ronald C. *Technology as Freedom: The New Deal and the Electrical Modernization of the American Home.* Berkeley: University of California Press, 1996.

"TVA: Electricity for All," [cited February 28, 2002] available from the World Wide Web at http://newdeal.feri.org/tva/index.htm.

"The Visionary," [cited February 28, 2002] available from the World Wide Web at http://www.tva.gov/heritage/visionary/index.htm.

Further Reading

Chandler, William. *The Myth of TVA: Conservation and Development in the Tennessee Valley, 1933–1983.* Cambridge, Massachusetts: Ballinger, 1984.

Lilienthal, David E. *The Journals of David Lilienthal: The TVA Years, 1939–1945.* New York: Harper & Row, 1964.

Roosevelt, Franklin D. *The Public Papers and Addresses of Franklin D. Roosevelt; Volume 2: The Year of Crisis, 1933.* New York: Random House, 1938.

See Also

New Deal (First, and Its Critics); Rural Electrification Administration; Water and Power

Water and Power

1928-1941

Introduction

The stock market crash of 1929 and the following Great Depression left millions of workers unemployed. By 1933 when President Franklin Roosevelt (served 1933–1945) took office the unemployment rate had climbed to 25 percent of the workforce, or over 12 million people. Roosevelt responded to the Depression with the New Deal, a vast array of federal programs addressing a broad spectrum of social and economic issues. A key element of those programs was work relief, putting the unemployed back to work on public projects that would benefit society. A major element of New Deal work relief was massive construction projects. Among these was the construction of major dams that provided thousands of long-term jobs, developed untapped natural resources, and provided a boost to industry and local economies through inexpensive electric power. Dams played a central role in making America what Roosevelt thought it should be in the twentieth century, a society characterized by individual ownership of electrified homes and a developed rural economy. To achieve this goal, Roosevelt promoted development of multipurpose dams that would produce hydroelectric power, provide irrigation water for farmers, flood control downstream, and promote recreation around the shores of the reservoirs.

As head of the New Deal's Public Works Administration (PWA), in addition to being Roosevelt's Secretary of Interior, Harold Ickes wielded considerable influence in economic development of the nation. Though nationwide in scope, the water and power

Chronology:

1928: Congress authorizes construction of Hoover Dam, known as Boulder Dam during the New Deal, on the Colorado River; construction begins in 1930 and is completed in 1936.

June 16, 1933: Under authority of the National Industrial Recovery Act (NIRA), President Roosevelt creates the Public Works Administration (PWA) to provide substantial federal funds for constructing public facilities including hydroelectric projects.

July 27, 1934: Congress passes the Tennessee Valley Authority Act launching a model region planning project for water and power in the Southeast.

1933: Congress passes the National Housing Act creating the Federal Housing Administration (FHA) which sets new standards for electrical wiring in houses.

July 5, 1934: President Roosevelt creates the National Power Policy Committee under leadership of Secretary of Interior Harold Ickes to coordinate the public power activities of numerous federal agencies and programs.

1935: Congress passes the Rivers and Harbors Act authorizing final construction of the Bonneville and Grand Coulee dams on the Columbia River in the Pacific Northwest.

1937: Bonneville Power Act establishes the Bonneville Power Administration to market public power in the Pacific Northwest.

---

projects of the New Deal would exert profound influence on future economic development of the Western United States. Some of the largest dams in the world were constructed during the Great Depression including Hoover Dam, a rare carryover from the President Herbert Hoover (served 1929–1933) administration, and one of Roosevelt's favorite water and power projects, Grand Coulee Dam in northern Washington State. Besides the key roles of the PWA, the U.S. Bureau of Reclamation, the U.S. Corps of Engineers (COE), and the Tennessee Valley Authority (TVA) in constructing the water and power facilities, the New Deal created

the Rural Electrification Administration (REA) to get electricity to rural America, the Bonneville Power Administration (BPA) to distribute electricity in the Pacific Northwest, and the Federal Housing Administration (FHA) to establish modern housing construction standards making homes ready for electrical consumption. Through Roosevelt's vision, a modernized America emerged from the Great Depression.

With the goal of a steady and abundant supply of water and power, New Deal projects would construct dams, canals, tunnels, reservoirs, power plants, pumping stations, transmission lines, electrical substations, new towns for workers, and pipelines. The projects would spawn camp communities that provided residence for workers and their families. With the high unemployment rates of the Depression, workers would come from all parts of the country and a broad spectrum of backgrounds. The projects would contribute to increased pasture and forage for livestock, extensive crops of vegetables, fruits, and grains, and construction of food processing plants, especially throughout the American West.

Issue Summary

Modernizing America Through Electrification

President Roosevelt fully believed in electrical modernization of America on a broad basis. He was convinced that only through the fullest possible use of inexpensive electricity could the quality of life for American families improve. To achieve this goal Roosevelt also believed that broad governmental planning at the national level was needed and should be applied to various regions of the nation.

Electrification was also tied to another basic belief of Roosevelt's, that a society focused mostly on rural life made for a much healthier nation than a predominately urban society. As a result Roosevelt sought to reverse population trends of movement from the farm and small town to the city. This trend had rapidly progressed through the industrialization of America following the Civil War (1861–1865). For the first time in U.S. history most Americans lived in the city rather than in rural areas by the 1920s. Roosevelt wanted to see a shift of the population back to rural areas. Roosevelt believed he could reverse this trend by locating industries away from city centers. This "ruralization" could be achieved by providing local cheap electrical power in the rural areas, power generated by either public utilities or by private industry under government regulation.

Undaunted by such grand schemes Roosevelt believed in adopting social policy designed to improve the lives of the majority of Americans. This belief in government activism was a dramatic departure from perceptions of the role of government held by presidents before him and counter to prevailing U.S. traditions. The vast majority of the public and nation's leaders had believed that government should be quite limited, dealing with defense and international and interstate trade, and not involved in the daily lives of its citizens.

Roosevelt's idea of electrical power priorities sharply contrasted with the private utility industry. In 1933 private utilities were primarily focused on better serving the 20 percent of Americans who were already consumers of electricity, Roosevelt focused on the 80 percent of households not electrically modernized. For example by the early 1930s very few farmers had electricity. They were also suffering poverty due to low prices for crops and as a result were deeply in debt. They could not afford to pay high electrical rates, if any at all. Only government intervention could save them.

To Roosevelt the key was modernization. Modernization to Roosevelt meant social justice and a moral improvement of life in addition to the material improvement. This vision of government was well expressed in a September 1932 campaign speech in San Francisco. In the speech Roosevelt described what he thought was a right of all U.S. citizens. That right was that anyone willing to work should have the opportunity to own an electrically modernized home. As he often did, Roosevelt also looked to the needs of children, that they should enjoy food and shelter. The cornerstone of social modernization was the modernization of homes that would provide for public health and greater financial security. Modernized homes would at least meet minimum standards of shelter and hygiene.

This perspective represented a major new national vision. The traditional Jeffersonian belief was that the right to hold private property leads to limited powers of government. Roosevelt's more progressive philosophy was that the right of property ownership justified larger government to guarantee that the common person could enjoy the right of property ownership. During his 1932 campaign, Roosevelt promoted large water and power projects in every region of the country. America needed a much larger supply of cheap electricity than was currently available. He pointed to opportunities on the St. Lawrence River in the Northeast, on the Tennessee River in the Southeast, on the Columbia River in the Northwest, and continued development of the Colorado River in the Southwest

with the ongoing construction on Hoover Dam begun in 1930.

Projects on these rivers could provide cheap electricity, store water for domestic and irrigation use, control floods, and improve navigation for increased commerce. The voting public, desperate for a new approach to solving the economic problems of the Great Depression, voted for Roosevelt in a landslide victory over Republican incumbent Herbert Hoover. Upon taking office in March 1933, Roosevelt launched his plans to solve the Depression by in part modernizing America through his New Deal programs. Much needed to be done to accomplish this goal.

Home Modernization

For New Deal water and power projects to have any effect, however, America's homes had to be readied for the future cheap power. In promoting the National Housing Act in early 1934, Roosevelt identified electrical modernization as a key objective. The New Dealers had already taken action to help homeowners by continuing the Home Owner's Loan Corporation (HOLC) that refinanced home mortgages between 1932 and 1936. They also had established the Electric Home and Farm Authority (EHFA) in December 1933. The EHFA was initially designed to help private appliance manufacturers market electric appliances in the TVA service area. For this area manufacturers made special models to sell at lower prices than normal.

Roosevelt signed the act into law on June 27, 1934. The act created the Federal Housing Administration (FHA) that would promote private lending for modernizing homes and building new ones. The public, cash-strapped due to the Depression, could not afford to adequately upgrade houses on their own budgets. Because of the strong real estate industry the federal government, through the New Deal, could not establish national regulations set national standards guiding the construction of new houses. So the New Dealers, through this act, saw another route for influencing basic improvements in housing.

The National Housing Act made a major impact in modernizing homes simply through its program of guaranteeing the loans made by banks to prospective homeowners. The federally guaranteed loans took away much of the financial risk out of making loans by banks. Quickly banks became much more active in issuing consumer loans to homeowners. The requirement introduced by the New Dealers, however, was that for a new home to qualify for a loan it had to be modernized, meeting certain standards.

In this way the FHA established a national set of expectations regarding housing design. This standardization marked the biggest change in U.S. housing between the 1930s and 1920s. Electrical modernization was a key element of these new FHA standards. Before 1935 building contractors did not routinely design or build houses to support the use of electrical appliances. The houses were more like shells. The owner was responsible for making any changes necessary to accommodate different uses such as appliances and utilities. This manner of house construction unintentionally served to hold back electrical modernization through the 1920s.

For people to obtain loans for purchasing new homes, the homes had to be designed to receive electrical service. The standards required homes to have outlets for portable electric appliances as well as outlets for lights. No longer would such items have to be fixed in place. Homeowners would enjoy greater flexibility for living. To enforce this and other standards, the FHA issued a National Electrical Code. The code also required each house to have two circuits, one for lights and light appliances and another for appliances that required a greater amount of power. These standards were enforced simply by the availability of FHA loans only if such standards were met. Despite their revolutionary nature for the late 1930s, by 1945 these standards would be taken for granted as nearly every American wanted a house with these features. A national mass market for modernized homes was quickly created. By 1941 New Deal modernization policies had set the basis for a post-World War II (1939–1945) building boom. That boom lasted for many years within the New Deal policy framework of FHA loans and electrical codes.

Home modernization projects also qualified for loans. These projects involved installing wiring in homes and updating kitchens for the use of electric appliances. Nearly half of the loans for home modernization supported kitchen upgrades. In addition over 40 percent of those receiving loans purchased refrigerators.

By guaranteeing loans for purchasing new homes and modernizing existing ones, a major accomplishment of the New Deal was to expand consumer loans to low-income families by the federal government insuring the loans to customers. This meant appliance dealers could now provide long-term finance plans to customers, making appliances affordable to a much larger segment of the population. A long-term national boom in appliance sales resulted. With banks participating in many more consumer loans, the amount of credit for consumer durable goods such as appliances

and automobiles increased by 50 percent between 1934 and 1941. Households of a much broader income span were able to participate in the new mass consumption economy. This expansion of purchasing power was a key result the New Dealers were looking for in an effort to lead the nation's economy out of Depression.

Regulating Private Utilities

While dramatically changing the character of the average home in America based on modernization through electrification, the other major step was to get cheap and reliable power to the homes. This involved reducing the price of electricity already being produced by private utilities and expanding the availability of power.

A crucial step to reducing the cost of electricity supplied by private companies was to resolve the dilemma of multiple levels of holding companies owning private utilities. A holding company is a corporation that owns enough stock in another company to control its activities. In the early 1930s private utilities were the most distrusted by the American public of any industry in the nation. With strong public support, Congress passed the Public Utilities Holding Company Act (PUHCA) in 1935. The act required holding companies controlling private utilities to register with the Securities and Exchange Commission, an agency created by the New Deal in June 1934 primarily to regulate the stock market. The act also placed the interstate transmission of electricity under the authority of the Federal Power Commission, established in 1920 by the Federal Water Power Act, and the Federal Trade Commission, established in 1914. Roosevelt identified the act as key for lowering existing electricity rates and lessening the greed of holding companies.

PUHCA, however, was only a start. It did not necessarily reduce electrical costs though it did remove the high operating expenses posed by holding companies. Other means were needed to lower rates and to provide a much great supply of electricity to American homes and farms. Private utilities had long contended that rural electrification could not be profitable.

Tennessee River Valley

In the 1910s in support of the World War I (1914–1918) effort the government constructed two dams and two nitrate plants at the Muscle Shoals location of the Tennessee River in northwest Alabama. The rapids in the river at that location provided a good potential for hydropower. Not completed in time to aid the war effort, the facilities became the center of controversy between those wanting the government to pursue completion and operation and those, particularly the private utility companies in the region, opposed to further government involvement. U.S. Senator George Norris of Nebraska led the fight for government operation. The Tennessee River was well known for its periodic flooding and irregular water flows. Navigation was risky at best. A series of dams was envisioned for the watercourse to transform the region's economy by providing cheap power for industry, flood control, and reliable navigation of the river. Norris, however, was not able to get the support of Hoover's administration.

While campaigning in 1932 for the presidency Franklin Roosevelt was struck by the poverty he witnessed in Tupelo, Mississippi. The community had no electricity and other services such as sewers. This visit was one of several factors that spurred Roosevelt's interest in the potential of the Muscle Shoals facilities.

As a key part of the New Deal programs created during Roosevelt's first one hundred days of office, Congress passed legislation establishing the Tennessee Valley Authority (TVA) on May 18, 1933. The TVA was a massive experiment in regional economic planning. The TVA would enhance the region in various ways: provide flood control, improve navigability, assist agricultural and industrial development, operate nitrate plants for fertilizer, and even reforest nearby hills. Tupelo would become the first town to sign a contract with TVA to receive cheap electricity and would become a showcase for the project.

Regarding the goal of producing power, the TVA would build a series of dams and sell the resulting hydropower to rural cooperatives. A three-person board ran the independent agency. The three individuals who served through much of the Depression held very different views on how the program should be operated, particularly in relation to the region's private power companies. Nine dams would be built on the main stem of the river and others on tributaries. Navigation for ships was established from the confluence with the Ohio River 640 miles upstream to Knoxville, Tennessee. Though highly successful, the program was also highly controversial since it competed with already existing private power companies. These companies took the TVA to court claiming it was unconstitutional for the government to be in the power generation business. After years of court battles the TVA finally won with the Supreme Court decision in 1936 in *Ashwander v. Tennessee Valley Authority*. Competition from the TVA did force private power companies in the area to lower their rates for homeowners.

By 1941 the TVA was the largest producer of electrical power in the United States. It was also instrumental in World War II providing electricity for producing aluminum for aircraft production and other war materials and producing nitrates for munitions. It remained the largest utility in the United States through the remainder of the twentieth century.

Associated with the TVA was establishment by executive order of the Rural Electrification Administration (REA) in May 1935. The REA would provide loans to local electrical cooperatives to build electrical transmission systems and purchase electricity from power companies. Congress made the REA permanent in May 1936 with the Rural Electrification Act and it became part of the Department of Agriculture in 1939. Originally focused on the TVA region, its activity spread nationwide. By 1939 the REA had assisted over four hundred cooperatives and 268,000 households. Importantly both the TVA and REA promoted public cooperatives to purchase and distribute power to the rural homes and farms. This highly successful approach would be applied to other regions by the New Deal.

Developing the West

Until the 1930s the West was an underdeveloped region of the United States. The early years of the Depression had hit farming and mining, the two key industries historically important to the region, especially hard. There was little money available to bring change. The New Dealers, including Roosevelt and Ickes, believed the federal government should most appropriately fund and guide the course of economically development of the West so the benefit to all of society would best be realized. They both envisioned a more prosperous West built on agriculture, industry, and mining. The central element of this development would be massive multipurpose dams, patterned after TVA, located throughout the West. The electrical power would support new industries and new cities as well as small farmers and meet an increased demand for tourism given the recent advent of the automobile. Though President Hoover, an engineer from the West himself, also had such a vision of growth, he did not embrace the role of direct government involvement. He believed it was more the role of private enterprise to lead. As a result little occurred.

The New Dealers looked to the Bureau of Reclamation and the Corps of Engineers to guide the necessary development. Funding would come through the PWA and other relief agencies and through direct project appropriations from Congress. The Bureau of Reclamation was the primary agency concerned with

More About...

U.S. Bureau of Reclamation

The American West had long been noted for its vast expanses and low precipitation as settlement expanded westward in the nineteenth century. Irrigation was necessary for agricultural development of almost any sort. Streams were diverted into canals and runoff from rain and snowmelt stored in reservoirs. Individual ranchers and farmers, however, had limited capital for making such improvements on any sizable scale and lacked the necessary engineering skills. Even states had limited capabilities to undertake water projects of any large scale. Pressure increased for the federal government to provide assistance. The government had already been active in support of constructing railroads, harbors, roads, and other Western developments.

Spurred by President Theodore Roosevelt's interest in conservation on June 17, 1902, Congress passed the National Reclamation Act creating the U.S. Reclamation Service. The agency mission was to "reclaim" the West's arid lands for settlement. Charged with developing irrigation and hydropower projects in the 17 Western states, the agency would build dams, power plants, and canals creating water storage and irrigation networks. Thirty projects were begun between 1902 and 1907. In 1923 its name was changed

to the Bureau of Reclamation. Hoover Dam, authorized by Congress in 1928, would become the first large appropriation for the Bureau.

The Bureau's main period of dam construction began in the Great Depression and continued into the late 1960s. By 1970 the construction of large dams had largely come to an end and the Bureau shifted focus to operation and maintenance of its existing facilities. By 1992 the Bureau had invested $11 billion in reclamation projects. The water and power projects would serve to greatly stimulate settlement and economic development of the region. In its first one hundred years, the Bureau had constructed six hundred dams and reservoirs including Hoover Dam on the Colorado River and Grand Coulee Dam on the Columbia River. The agency's sale of water wholesale benefited over 30 million people and 140,000 farmers by 2001. Over 10 million acres of farmland were irrigated producing an estimated 60 percent of the nation's vegetables and 25 percent of its fruits and nuts. The Bureau's 58 power plants produce over 40 billion kilowatt hours of electricity making it the nation's second largest producer of hydroelectric power, second only to the TVA.

---

irrigation in the West under the Federal Reclamation Act of 1902. Through the 1910s and 1920s projects had become increasingly complex as the Bureau began looking at developing entire river systems and providing power as well as irrigation. For example in 1920 the Reclamation Service completed a hydroelectric dam and 630-mile canal system on the Snake River in Idaho. The project provided irrigation to 121,000 acres of desert. Idaho farmers formed local cooperatives to purchase power from the government facility. They installed almost three hundred miles of transmission lines to their homes and farms. This provided a good model for Roosevelt and the New Dealers. The private utilities, however, strongly opposed the direct purchases of power by farmers from the government and construction of the power lines.

At the start of the New Deal the Bureau of Reclamation had 26 construction projects underway involving over $335 million. It recommended to new Secretary of Interior Ickes that these projects be

completed. By the following year in 1934 the PWA would greatly increase the Bureau's construction budget amounting to half of what the Bureau had received the previous three decades in that one year. With the Army Corps of Engineers also planning river development, primarily for navigation and flood control as opposed to the Bureau's interest in irrigation and power, the two federal agencies often clashed over proposals. To better coordinate all of these agencies, Congress passed the Water Facilities Act in August 1937. The act established the PWA's National Resources Planning Board in charge of the coordination of the various agencies and projects.

To achieve the goals of cheap and plentiful power, the construction of large dams became an important part of President Roosevelt's New Deal work relief programs. The president would travel widely throughout the West between 1934 and 1938 promoting his New Deal programs including the massive water and power projects. Roosevelt inherited the ongoing con-

President Franklin D. Roosevelt tours Boulder Dam in 1935. The name of the dam was changed back to Hoover Dam in 1947. (© Bettmann/Corbis. Reproduced by permission.)

struction of Hoover Dam on the Colorado River between Arizona and Nevada. The Boulder Canyon Project Act of 1928 had been approved during the Calvin Coolidge (served 1923–1929) administration and construction actually began in 1930 during the Hoover administration. While initiating the Tennessee Valley Authority in 1933 in the Southeast, Roosevelt turned his gaze to other regions where water and power projects would be operated as public utilities. These water and power projects would not only provide more electricity than private companies were willing to provide, but the New Deal promoted the growth of these public utilities to use as a yardstick to evaluate the performance of private utilities, particularly the prices charged their customers. In 1934 cheap power was a major campaign issue used by Roosevelt in support of Democratic Party congressional candidates across the nation.

The most extensive water and power programs of the New Deal in the West involved the Colorado River in the Southwest, the Columbia River Basin of the Northwest, and the Central Valley of California. In addition to these regions other key water and power projects were also supported by the New Deal elsewhere in the West.

Colorado River

For many years a strong desire persisted by many to build a dam on the Colorado River to serve the water and power needs of Los Angeles and surrounding regions. In 1922 Secretary of Commerce Herbert Hoover helped negotiate the Colorado River Compact in which western states agreed to divide up the waters of the Colorado River. With the project gaining approval of Congress in 1928, in late 1930 President Herbert Hoover authorized the beginning of construction of the dam. An engineer himself, Hoover saw Hoover Dam as the key example of his administration trying to bring economic relief to those suffering from the Great Depression. The project would provide thousands of jobs through the construction firms contracted by the government to build the dam. The Bureau of Reclamation was the lead federal agency for the construction. He also saw the massive construction project as a way of affirming the public's faith in the existing economic system of private capitalism. The first major federal project with multipurpose goals, predating TVA by several years, Hoover Dam would indeed become a major engineering and construction feat.

At the peak of construction 5,200 men worked on the dam around the clock seven days a week. When the project office first opened it received 12,000 job applications given the dire employment conditions of the Great Depression. Because of the size of the undertaking, several large construction companies joined to form a giant business combination that would later tackle large New Deal projects. The companies included Morrison Knudsen Company of Idaho, Utah Construction Company, J.F. Shea Company and Pacific Bridge Company of Portland, Oregon, MacDonald and Kahn and W.A. Bechtel Company of San Francisco. The combination became known as Six Companies even though more than six companies were actually involved in the project. Morrison Knudsen company, leader of the business combination for Hoover Dam, would become one of the leading construction companies in the world.

At first workers on the Boulder Dam project lived in a number of tent settlements scattered around the construction area. Eventually a whole new town would be constructed for project employees and their families called Boulder City. The town would hold seven thousand residents at the height of construction in 1934. Following the decline in the number of workers on the project by 1935, two companies of another New Deal program employed the nation's young men in conservation projects, the Civilian Conservation Corps (CCC), used Boulder City as a camp.

As with many projects during the Great Depression, the dam project promoted racist policies. Those policies were in part resulting from the increased competition over jobs brought by the Depression. The original Boulder Canyon Project Act prohibited the hiring of "Mongolians" in reference to people of Asian descent. Scandinavians were favored with their reputation as skilled construction workers. The government did hire Apache Indians due to their acclimation to the desert conditions. Racist policies, however, were primarily aimed at black Americans. Few blacks worked on the project, and those who did were prohibited from living in Boulder City. They had to live in Las Vegas and commute from there to work. Boulder City restaurants even refused to serve black workers. The employment office opposed the hiring of blacks fearing their presence would create on-the-job tensions. These racial policies changed little as the Roosevelt administration took over the project.

The workers who were hired enjoyed the relative stability of employment on the project with it lasting four years. Work, however, was hard and dangerous. Fifty workers died during construction. In order to get started on the dam construction, the Colorado River

had to first be diverted. Four giant tunnels had to be dug through solid rock formations and five million tons of dirt would be removed from the proposed location of the concrete dam. By the spring of 1933 the forms to hold concrete for the dam began to be constructed. Twelve million tons of sand and gravel were needed for the concrete mix. Unskilled workers made 50 cents an hour and skilled workers such as carpenters made 75 cents an hour. Less than half of the five thousand workers had any prior construction experience.

The PWA provided $38 million in 1934, contributing to the total cost of $114 million. The resulting structure was 726 feet high—similar to a 50-story building—and 660 feet thick at its base. It was the world's largest dam at the time. The dam began storing water on February 1, 1935, and began producing electricity in September 1936. It remained one of the highest dams in the world into the twenty-first century. Though employing thousands of workers, the project in itself did little to ease the Great Depression as President Hoover had originally envisioned. Until the New Deal added many more water and power projects, it served more as a symbolic effort at economic recovery. The dam project would prove to be unique in being a rare thread of continuity between the Hoover and Roosevelt administrations. Near its completion, President Roosevelt traveled to the project in September 1935 to make a dedication address.

The 115-mile long reservoir behind the dam, the world's largest man-made lake, was named Lake Mead after Elwood Mead, director of the Bureau of Reclamation from 1926 to 1934. By 1939 waters from Lake Mead were irrigating over 2.5 million acres for agricultural production. Much of the acreage was in the Imperial Valley of Southeastern California. It also provided water to Los Angeles through a 260-mile long aqueduct. The hydroelectric power went to Los Angeles and Southern Arizona. Perhaps most importantly for the Great Depression, the Hoover Dam project set the precedent for more giant water and power projects through the 1930s.

The Hoover Dam project also set precedents in other ways, too. It was the first occasion in which multiple construction companies would work together and with the federal government. This strategy would become much more common in the future. Other Great Depression heavy construction projects would follow with various combinations of this group of companies including Bonneville and Grand Coulee dams on the Columbia River, foundations for the Golden Gate Bridge and Bay Bridge in San Francisco, and many other kinds of projects including tunnels, canals, pipelines, shipyards, subways, factories, and medical facilities. They all had a major affect on the economic development of the American West.

The large construction firms supported the New Deal's policy of large deficit spending to spur employment and the economy. Extensive public works projects were a key element of this policy. Marriner Eccles, who assumed the position of president of Utah Construction Company, was a leading industry spokesman in this regard and became a key figure in the New Deal. Eccles became the assistant secretary of the Treasury in January 1934 in the Roosevelt administration.

The continuity of the project between the two administrations did not lead to a continuity in the name of the dam. In 1930 the secretary of interior under President Hoover proposed the name Hoover Dam because Herbert Hoover had served as chairman of the Colorado River Commission in 1922 and then eight years later authorized construction of the dam. Public support for Hoover, however, plummeted over the next few years as the Great Depression worsened. With Roosevelt assuming office in March 1933, the new Secretary of Interior Harold Ickes proposed the name change to Boulder Dam in May. It remained Boulder Dam until 1947 when Congress restored the name Hoover Dam.

Hoover Dam was not the only New Deal water and power project on the lower Colorado River. In 1935 Ickes pressed Congress for authorization to build Parker Dam 150 miles downstream of Boulder Dam. Approved by Congress the dam was a Bureau of Reclamation project. Funds came from the Metropolitan Water District of Southern California with money from bonds sold to the Reconstruction Finance Corporation (RFC), a federal agency created by Hoover and adapted by the new Deal to help finance New Deal programs. The dam was for water storage for Los Angeles as well as flood control and irrigation water to much of central Arizona. Power was also sold to Central Arizona Light and Power Company.

Further diversion of Colorado River waters to the Imperial and Coachella valleys of California resulted from construction of the Imperial Diversion Dam and All-American Canal. The vast agriculturally rich region of interior Southern California had experienced $10 million in crop losses in 1934 due to a severe drought. The PWA provided initial funds amounting to $9 million to the Bureau of Reclamation for construction of an 80-mile main canal from the Colorado River to the Imperial Valley and a 103-mile long branch to Coachella Valley. Total cost of the project was $24 million and irrigation began in October 1940.

The headwaters of the Colorado River also received attention from the New Deal. Ickes proposed a massive project for the state of Colorado known as the Big Thompson Project. The proposal was to divert Colorado River water from its headwaters in southwest Colorado and transport it through the Rocky Mountains by canals and tunnels to the dry farming region of southeast Colorado. Congress authorized the project in 1937 under authority of the Bureau of Reclamation. The PWA provided funds in 1938 to begin construction. The project consisted of five power plants and complex tunnels including a 13-mile long tunnel through the mountains. The Big Thompson Project would become one of the largest Bureau projects providing irrigation water to 615,000 acres of farmland and power from five power plants for regions of Colorado. It would take 20 years to complete.

The Columbia Basin Project

A comprehensive study of the nation's potentials for dam construction by the Corps of Engineers, begun in 1925 and completed in 1931, included a plan for a system of 10 dams on the Columbia River. The Columbia River in the Pacific Northwest was recognized as a vast, unharnessed power source. It was estimated that the Columbia offered 40 percent of the nation's hydropower potential with a flow 10 times the Colorado River. The Grand Coulee Dam, to be located in northern Washington, was designated by the 1931 report as the primary project on the upper Columbia and the Bonneville Dam was the most downriver dam of the system. Spurred by the New Deal, this plan would ultimately guide development of the Columbia River for the next 40 years. At the time of completion of the report in 1931, however, the resulting response from the Hoover administration was to encourage private companies, states, or local governments to pursue the identified projects. The federal contribution would be limited to the U.S. Army Corps of Engineers providing funds for navigation locks and various stream channel improvements.

With the deepening of the Great Depression and the arrival of President Roosevelt to the White House, the proposed Columbia River projects were now looked upon as a great opportunity to provide work relief on public projects that would greatly benefit society for years. With Hoover Dam construction well underway, proposals for large dams on the Columbia River increased.

The Bonneville was the first project to begin. The site for the dam was about 40 miles east of Portland, Oregon. The Bonneville Dam would make the Columbia River available to navigation 48 miles further

A man stands dwarfed by the overflow of the Grand Coulee Dam, built by the BPA in the Columbia River gorge in Washington. (The Library of Congress.)

upstream for ocean-going vessels as well as abundant cheap power to the region. The Bonneville project presented a major engineering challenge. It would have to not only deal with a wide variation in stream flow through a year but also with a much more powerful volume of water than the Colorado River at Hoover Dam. Insurance consultants even advised that the project was too dangerous. While waiting for Congress to approve a dam project on the Columbia, the New Dealers decided in 1933 to help in the meantime given the high unemployment of the Pacific Northwest. They began issuing construction contracts through the PWA to start some preliminary preparation work. The PWA provided $20 million in 1933 to the Corps of Engineers. Representing the first federal project on the Columbia River, construction of the cofferdam began in October 1933. A flood in December, however, revealed problems with the original dam site location. The site was moved four miles upstream. In 1934 PWA provided another $11 million for contracts to construct the main spillway, the powerhouse, and the navigation lock. Excavation work started in February 1934 by the J.F. Shea Company on the powerhouse and in June 1934 by the Columbia Construction Company on the spillway dam. Work on the navigation

lock began in July by Shea. With construction well along in August 1935 Congress authorized use of regular federal appropriation funds for completion of the dam through passage of the River and Harbor Act. The project thus became funded outside the New Deal relief programs.

Construction of the Bonneville Dam provided much needed work relief to the Depression-weary Pacific Northwest. Total cost of the project was $80 million with the PWA contributing $42 million. The project employed three thousand workers. The resulting dam is 122 feet high and originally produced over 86,000 kilowatts. The spillway dam was closed to begin filling the reservoir in September 1937 as President Roosevelt arrived for dedication ceremonies of the project. After restating his policy of seeking the widest possible use of electricity, the president pushed a button lighting a string of lights. The first power from Bonneville's generators was produced by March 1938 and operation was well underway that summer.

With demand for more power to operate aluminum production plants and shipbuilding yards for World War II, work expanding the powerhouses was completed in December 1943. By the 1990s the power generation increased to over 518,000 kilowatts. As with TVA, critics of Bonneville claimed unfair competition between the federal government and private companies in providing electric power to the Northwest. The first powerhouse constructed would produce enough electricity to meet the needs of a city three times the size of Portland in 1935.

As the early difficult work on the Bonneville Dam began in 1934 talk increased regarding a proposed giant project—Grand Coulee Dam—upstream in northern Washington. A goal was to irrigate one million acres in the dry central Washington region to boost development of a major agricultural region. The State of Washington had committed $377,000 to begin the project in 1933. Federal funding for the Grand Coulee Dam project however was mired in controversy. Proponents for public power wanted a high dam that would generate a large amount of electricity. Private utility companies argued against government involvement in power generation and contended that a high dam would produce an oversupply of electricity for the region. At first Roosevelt chose a compromise keeping the dam low enough in height to keep power companies satisfied that power generation would be somewhat limited. Roosevelt would provide $14 million through the PWA in late 1933 for the project under the responsibility of the Bureau of Reclamation. Excavation at the dam site began in December.

More About...
Army Corps of Engineers

The U.S. Army Corps of Engineers was first organized on June 16, 1775, during the American Revolution (1775–1783). General George Washington ordered that breastworks (defensive structures) be built in the Boston area in preparation for the Battle of Bunker Hill. The Corps was permanently established in 1802 and became responsible for all military construction projects. With the Corps' focus at first primarily on coastal facilities, in 1838 Congress established the U.S. Corps of Topographical Engineers to address needs of the interior regions as the United States was rapidly expanding in size.

The Topographical Corps supported U.S. exploratory expeditions into the American West in the mid-nineteenth century exploring the new territories acquired by the United States. Their goal was to assess the potential for economic development and settlement. Lieutenant John C. Fremont of the Topographical Corps in 1842 journeyed to Oregon and California after having explored parts of the Southwest and Midwest stimulating settlement in the West that greatly grew in the 1840s. Fremont largely followed in the footsteps of earlier expeditions by Army person. Two Army officers, Captain Meriwether Lewis and Lieutenant William Clark led an expedition to the Columbia River region of the Pacific Northwest beginning in 1804. In 1832 Captain Benjamin Bonneville led an expedition to the Oregon Country to evaluate fur trade opportunities. Famed author Washington Irving published Bonneville's journals.

The Engineers also constructed military forts, built wagon roads and diversion dams in the Southwest, and improved West Coast harbors. With indus-trialization expanding in the East prior to the Civil War, new pressures mounted from business for access to the abundant natural resources and areas of settlement in the American West. State and local governments and entrepreneurs requested construction projects by the Topographic Engineers. In response the Engineers surveyed railroad routes, wagon roads, and other public projects though many projects were questionably more for the private profit of those benefiting most directly from the activities.

The Topographic Engineers would later merge with the main Corps during the Civil War in 1863. After the Civil War the Corps worked on many rivers nationwide, changing their course and deepening them for navigation. During the 1920s the Corps undertook large scale planning identifying potential projects around the nation. The River and Harbor Act of 1925 directed the Corps and the Federal Power Commission, created in 1920, to study and estimate the cost for potential power development projects. These were to be multipurpose dams involving navigation, flood control, irrigation, and power generation. In 1926 the Corps gave Congress a list of rivers worthy of further study and Congress authorized the Corps to pursue such a study beginning in 1927. The Corps undertook extensive fieldwork identifying potential dam sites, studying river flow characteristics, flood-prone areas, and surrounding topography. The study was coordinated with the Bureau of Reclamation and provided a strong basis for guiding New Deal water and power projects. The Corps' activities related to civilian hydropower development and navigation continued after World War II into the twenty-first century.

As initial work began the high dam proponents resumed a campaign for a larger dam. By 1935 Roosevelt changed the government design and adopted a high dam design. On August 30, 1935, in the River and Harbor Act, Congress approved funding for the high dam. With the expansion, Grand Coulee would become the largest dam in the world. Roosevelt regarded the Grand Coulee Dam as the model project of the New Deal's dam-building program further showcasing the potential of dams in regional economic development programs. He visited the construction site in 1937 to further stress his support. By 1941 a total of $69 million had been provided and construction of the dam was completed. Construction of the powerhouses and pumping plant was underway. The first power generated by Coulee Dam was transmitted on March 22, 1941. The project had employed six thousand workers laboring day and night.

At the end of the twentieth century Grand Coulee remained the largest concrete structure in the United States made of 12 million cubic yards of concrete. It was the third largest hydroelectric facility in the world.

Woody Guthrie composed songs for the Bonneville Power Administration, many of which became American folk classics. (The Library of Congress.)

The reservoir created by the dam, Lake Roosevelt, extended 150 miles upstream to the Canadian border. As initially envisioned in the 1931 Corps report, it was the major provider of electricity to the Pacific Northwest, producing 6.5 million kilowatts of power. The dam also irrigated over a half million acres of land in central Washington and provided flood control for the river and towns downstream.

Bonneville Power Administration

In June 1937 Roosevelt lobbied Congress to create "seven little TVAs" including: (1) the Great Lakes and Ohio River Valley region; (2) the Missouri and Red River region; (3) the Arkansas and Rio Grande River region; (4) the Colorado River; (5) the Columbia River Basin; (6) streams in Northwestern California; and, (7) the Tennessee and Cumberland region. Having seen such great success with the TVA, Roosevelt was eager to duplicate such broad planning programs elsewhere. The increasingly conservative Congress, however, was staunchly opposed. Seeing little chance for Congress to approve the projects on the same grand scale as TVA the New Dealers responded with somewhat scaled-down plans.

With power soon to be produced by Bonneville Dam, Roosevelt sought a means to market (sell) the electricity directly to the public. The Bonneville Power Act of August 1937 created the Bonneville Power Administration (BPA), patterned after parts of the TVA, to sell and distribute electricity generated by the Bonneville and later Columbia River public dams such as Grand Coulee Dam to the public. One key role of BPA was to avoid the monopolization of Columbia River power by private interests. Preference would be given to publicly owned distribution systems and systems operated by private cooperatives. The BPA revenues would repay the U.S. Treasury for the costs of construction, maintenance, and operation of the hydropower facilities. In 1935 only 31 percent of Oregon farms were electrified. The BPA, using PWA funds and in some cases WPA labor, constructed transmission lines and substations around the region. To promote the widest possible use of electricity in the region and attract manufacturers, BPA decided to charge a single rate for all users, regardless of how much power they used and how far they were located from the power facilities. BPA became the primary provider of electricity in the Pacific Northwest. Like TVA, the BPA marketing prices, which must be approved by the Federal Power Commission, provided a yardstick to measure the prices of private utilities operating in the Northwest. The demands for electricity brought by World War II led to rapid growth of BPA.

To spur public support of the New Deal dams of the Columbia River the BPA hired songwriter Woody Guthrie in May 1941 to travel the Columbia River region for 30 days and write a song a day about the New Deal efforts. Guthrie ended up writing 26 songs including "Grand Coulee Dam," "Roll on Columbia," "Jackhammer Blues," and "Pastures of Plenty."

With the New Deal spurring substantial water and power development in the Columbia River region, a problem of land speculation arose. Speculators were buying out small farmers in anticipation of receiving cheap federal electricity to run large farming operations. In addition there already existed some large dry-farming operations. The New Deal strongly favored assisting small farmers in the West. Therefore in 1937 Congress passed the Columbia River Basin Anti-Speculation Act on May 27. The act limited irrigated farms to 80 acres in size. Roosevelt and the New Dealers wanted the region to be one of small farms.

California Central Valley

In California the Bureau of Reclamation in cooperation with the State of California undertook a massive water and power project in the central part of the state involving flood control, irrigation, navigation, domestic water supplies, and hydroelectric generation.

Construction workers line up to be paid for their work on Shasta Dam. The dam irrigated two million acres of farmland, but contrary to the general goals of the New Deal, it benefited the large corporate farm operations more than the small farmer. (The Library of Congress.)

A key element was the transport of water from Northern California to the southern part in the San Joaquin Valley, a distance of over four hundred miles. A series of dams including the large Shasta Dam on the Sacramento River, the last of the giant dams proposed by the New Deal, were planned in addition to power plants, canals, and a large system of transmission lines. The state had been interested in the project for years and received some federal funds in 1935 to start. A final site was chosen in January 1937 for Shasta Dam on the northern end of the Sacramento Valley. Congress passed the Central Valley Project Act in August 1937 to provide full funding for the project.

Construction of Shasta Dam, a concrete dam second in size to Grand Coulee Dam, began in 1938. The first concrete was poured for the dam in July 1940. The Central Valley Project would also involve some PWA funds and CCC labor. Slowed by World War II, the project was not completed until 1947 at a total cost of $2.3 billion. Two million acres of farmland in the San Joaquin and Sacramento River Valleys were irrigated by the project. The project was one of the costliest of the Bureau's amounting to $2.3 billion. Contrary to the general goals of the New Deal, this project benefited the large corporate farm operations more than the small farmer.

Other Water and Power Projects

Though the Tennessee River Valley, the Colorado River, California Central Valley, and the Columbia River Basin were highlights of the New Deal water and power policies, many other projects were funded as well. Two notable projects were the Fort Peck Dam in Montana and the Pine View Dam in Utah.

The Corps of Engineers originally proposed the massive Fort Peck Dam project in 1933 to improve navigation of the upper Missouri River in Montana. Ickes accepted it for a public works project adding irrigation and flood control goals as well. The PWA provided $25 million to begin construction in spring of 1934. President Roosevelt paid a personal visit to the construction site on August 6 of that year. The Fort Peck Act of 1938 added hydroelectric production under the guidance of the Bureau of Reclamation. The Fort Peck Dam, one of the largest earthen dams in the world at 250 feet in height, was completed in 1939 at a total cost of $108 million. The resulting Fort Peck Reservoir behind the dam is the fifth largest man-made lake in the United States. The PWA had provided $49 million. The project employed seven thousand workers, irrigated 84,000 acres, and produced 182,000 kilowatts by the late 1990s.

More About...
Dams of the New Deal

Numerous dams of various size were constructed during the New Deal. Funding came from New Deal programs as well as from direct Congressional authorizations provide through various agencies such as the Bureau of Reclamation and the Corps of Engineers. The following is a selected list of dams built during or by the New Deal including those completed as late as 1943. Listed is the name, lead agency, date of completion, and height to give a rough estimate of relative size.

- Bonneville Dam, Corps of Engineers, 1938, 122 feet high
- Cherokee Dam, TVA, 1942, 175 feet
- Chickamauga, TVA, 1940, 129 feet
- Douglas, TVA, 1943, 202 feet
- Fort Loudon, TVA, 1943, 122 feet
- Fort Peck, Corps of Engineers, 1940, 250 feet
- Grand Coulee, Reclamation, 1942, 550 feet
- Guntersville, TVA, 1939, 94 feet
- Hoover, Reclamation, 1936, 726 feet
- Norris, TVA, 1936, 265 feet
- Pickwick Landing, TVA, 1938, 113 feet
- Watts Bar, TVA, 1942, 112 feet
- Wheeler, TVA, 1936, 72 feet

Pine View Dam was a Bureau of Reclamation project designed to provide irrigation water as well as storing water for the city of Ogden, Utah. Funded by the PWA, construction began in September 1934 using in part CCC labor. The dam and canals were completed in June 1937 with water channeled to 17,000 acres of farmland. Pine View was noted as one of the only single-purpose water and power projects of the New Deal era.

New Deal and Other Federal Agencies

A key New Deal program that funded construction of dams and hydroelectric facilities was the Public Works Administration (PWA). The PWA was cre-ated as part of the National Industrial Recovery Act to provide work relief programs for the jobless. Key supporters of the PWA were Secretary of Interior Harold Ickes and Secretary of Labor Frances Perkins. Ickes was appointed administrator of the PWA. The PWA provided loans to towns for building public electric systems. By 1935 the PWA had supported 274 public power systems that competed with private electric power companies. The PWA provided $6 billion for a wide range of projects in addition to water and power projects including public buildings, roads, bridges, sewage systems, and tunnels. As part of the $6 billion distributed, $1.8 billion was provided to federal agencies including the Bureau of Reclamation for water and power projects in the West between 1933 and 1941. Another $1.6 billion went to the six Great Plains states for a total of over $3 billion for water and power developments. Because of the slowness of the PWA to plan and construct large projects support wavered through the years with emphasis in work relief on more modest construction projects shifting to the newly formed Works Progress Administration (WPA) in 1935. Grand Coulee Dam would be one of the model projects tackled by the PWA that reflected high quality in design and construction. The WPA would also provide funds and work relief on public construction projects building such facilities as utility plants. The PWA, however, continued its course through the later 1930s completing its large projects.

Throughout the years of the New Deal the Bureau of Reclamation provided an average of $52 million a year to water and power projects. Previously it averaged less than $9 million a year. The National Reclamation Association, a private organization supporting Bureau of Reclamation projects, were active throughout the New Deal pushing projects through the administration and Congress. By the end of 1936 the Bureau had 19 dams under construction and employing thousands of workers. Economic benefits went beyond the immediate employment of construction workers with the large amounts of steel, cement, machinery, and other products used in the construction. The year 1937 was a particularly active year with 72 projects totaling almost $88 million. By 1940 near the end of the New Deal the Bureau had 23 power plants in operation throughout the West and 15 more still under construction. Aside from the large projects, the Bureau has constructed many small earthen dams to store water from smaller streams and provide more flood control.

By 1934 after the first year of New Deal programs, numerous federal agencies and programs had roles in public water and power projects, often with overlapping roles. For example the Farm Security Administration was mounting irrigation projects in the Great Plains for tracts purchased by the Resettlement Administration that was busy relocating farmers to better lands. To provide some coordination of activities by the PWA, TVA, Bureau of Reclamation, Federal Power Commission, and the Federal Trade Commission, Roosevelt created the National Power Policy Committee on July 5, 1934, under authority of the PWA. The committee helped coordinate electric utilities increasing generation capacities and standardizing generator equipment. Its work also led to the Public Utility Holding Company Act of 1935.

Meanwhile the efforts of New Deal agencies in upgrading existing homes continued. In August 1935 the Electric Home and Farm Authority (EHFA) was transferred to the REA. By 1938 the EHFA had provided over $15 million of loans in 33 states. The Farm Security Administration between 1937 and 1946 provided almost 900,000 rehabilitation loans. Homeowners were able to purchase refrigerators with loans from other New Deal agencies as well. Half of those receiving loans under the EHFA to purchase appliances purchased refrigerators. Almost half of those receiving funds from the REA purchased refrigerators. By 1940 over 44 percent of homes had refrigerators.

Flood Control Act of 1936

By the mid-1930s major damaging floods were still occurring throughout the United States. With industrial and residential development spreading increasingly out onto flood plains near rivers, a more comprehensive program of flood control was needed to protect property. Destruction was estimated to be amounting to millions of dollars a year from seasonal floods. The act represented another milestone federal policy over water resources. Navigation had been recognized a federal responsibility in 1824, reclamation of lands through irrigation in 1902, and now flood control in 1936. Declaring that flood control on navigable rivers was a federal responsibility, the Corps of Engineers was assigned responsibility for constructing flood control projects.

In addition to all the tangible benefits of the massive dam projects, a major intangible by-product was also realized. The dams offered a hope in the future for those demoralized by the Great Depression. The projects reestablished the public's faith in the U.S. capabilities and private business and were a great boost for modernization of the American home in the regions where they were built. The dams at least in part fulfilled Roosevelt's vision of cheap electricity for rural America.

Contributing Forces

Waterpower has been crucial to the U.S. economy since the early days of independence from Great Britain. The American colonists had previously used small streams to power sawmills and gristmills. By the early nineteenth century larger streams and rivers were powering factories. For example textile mills, powered by waterpower from waterwheels placed directly in a swift moving stream or waterfall, were a key part of the early U.S. industrial economy of the nineteenth century.

Early dams were primarily constructed for navigation purposes diverting water into canals to assist river traffic around rocky stretches in waterways. The U.S. Army Corps of Engineers began improving waterways for navigation by the mid-nineteenth century. The establishment of industrial centers in the United States following the Civil War (1861–1865) led to the construction of much larger dams to provide drinking water for the growing urban populations. San Francisco began receiving its water from a reservoir by 1887 and New York City by later in the 1890s.

In addition to navigation and water storage, dams assumed a new function in the 1890s providing hydroelectric power to the urban centers. Generators were situated along stream courses replacing the use of falling water to power mills. With less access to coal to generate power in the West, hydroelectric use grew quicker there. The Folsom River Dam in California was completed in 1895 to transmit electricity to Sacramento located 20 miles away. Orchards along the route became prosperous being able to tap into the electrical transmission lines to operate irrigation pumps. Electrical irrigation pumps began replacing steam and gas-driven pumps in limited areas. The electrical industry in the late nineteenth century was the most dynamic growth sector of the U.S. economy replacing the railroad industry as the lead industry. Stiff competition grew among companies to gain the upper hand in power generation and delivery. By 1892 only General Electric and Westinghouse survived to control the industry. The most noted early hydropower plant was built at Niagara Falls in the 1890s to drive industrial plants in Buffalo, New York. The amount of hydropower generated in the United States between 1902 and 1907 more than tripled with the focus primarily being the nation's population centers.

Yet there were signs of concern as hydropower development progressed. By the 1920s practically all of the electrical generating capacity was privately owned. It was reported that one-third of the waterpower in the United States was controlled by only 13 companies. Fears mounted that a monopoly over U.S. water resources was emerging that would control all future hydropower development as well as other uses of America's rivers.

Another national water issue arose. Flood control of rivers had become a bigger issue through the late nineteenth century as more and more industries were locating near water sources for power. In fact industrial cities were all located on rivers. Congress passed acts in 1917 and 1923 addressing the Mississippi River. Highly destructive floods hit the Mississippi River Valley in 1927. In 1928 the Congress adopted a Corps of Engineers' plan to construct levees and reservoirs, make channel improvements, and stabilize riverbanks along the Mississippi. The Sacramento River valley in California also received the attention of Congress in 1917. Various small flood control projects had been approved along the river. The New Deal would eventually fund more of these projects for the Mississippi, the Sacramento, and many other areas through work relief programs.

Rural America

Urban electrification would be a major driving force in the rapid industrialization of America. Electrification of factories was a primary factor behind development of assembly line production in the 1910s that transformed American industrial production. The growth of industry in turn led to the growth of cities and a demand for electric lighting and electric trolleys. Mass media industries grew as well including films, radio, and phonograph recordings. By 1920 the demand for electricity was escalating as more and more homes had electric stoves, radios, vacuum cleaners, and washing machines. The primary energy source of America particularly in the East was shifting from coal to electricity.

Though electrical power to urban industrial areas quickly developed, the agricultural industry was the last to see electrification. Attention began to shift to supplying rural areas in the United States during the 1910s. Some utilities that were interested included General Electric, the Samuel Insull utilities in the Chicago area, and several in the West such as the Mount Whitney Power and Electricity Company in southeastern California and the Northern Colorado Power Company. General Electric even promoted the all-electric farm. One of the earliest private water and power projects was Laguna Dam in Southern California, completed in 1907, to provide water and electricity to the California desert area near the Mexican border, an area that would become known as the Imperial Valley.

However the economic prosperity enjoyed by farmers during World War I actually stymied much interest in electricity. The farmer seemed to be doing just fine without regional electrical power supply systems. The prosperity did lead some forward-thinking individual farmers to install their own generating systems using waterpower from small dams on their property or any many cases, windmills. Tens of thousands of farmers used gasoline and kerosene-driven systems that included use of glass-jar batteries.

When President Theodore Roosevelt (served 1901–1909) was assessing the needs of rural America only two percent of farmers had electrical service. Gains over the next 20 years were modest. By the late 1920s 90 percent of farmers in the United States had no electrical service and those that did paid high rates, often double what urban homeowners paid because of their low density in rural areas. In actual numbers only 600,000 of the 6.5 million U.S. farms had electricity. Half of those were supplied by isolated generating systems and the other half by utilities and interurban lines. These electrically supplied farms were concentrated in the Northeast and Far West. Interurban power lines were lines transmitting power from one town to another. The farmers along the route could receive the electric current from these lines. Those receiving this service often enjoyed improved roads to city markets as well that greatly changed their manner of farming. They often would begin growing fruit and dairy products for city consumption.

By the 1930s the electrification gap between rural and urban areas was substantial. This gap would only grow more through the early 1930s. Urban residents enjoyed electric lights, washing machines, vacuum cleaners, irons, and running water driven by pumps, while farm families still had outhouses and kerosene lamps. Ice would be cut and hauled in the winter and stored in sawdust for use into the summer. Instead of farmers representing the Jeffersonian ideal of moral purity as they had always represented before, now they represented social backwardness.

Water and Power For the West

With the rise of industrialization in the East, the demand for raw materials of the West increased. With its small population and limited political influence, the West became like a colony to the East Coast with its resources being increasingly tapped to fuel East Coast industry. In 1900 only ten million people lived in the West, amounting to only 12 percent of the nation's population. Goods needed by Westerners were largely imported from the East Coast. To counter its loss of resources to Eastern companies, the West sought to

Workers remove dirt and rock from the construction site of Shasta Dam in 1942. Construction involved PWA funds as well as some CCC labor. (The Library of Congress.)

develop economically and industrialize. Vast amounts of money, however, were needed to construct much needed transportation networks and water projects. No single organization or state government had sufficient funds.

The federal government had already played a key role in the opening of the West. The government had subsidized construction of the railroads and provided land for agricultural settlement through homestead laws. The transcontinental railroad was built between 1869 and 1887 that opened up new markets and made the West potentially part of the nation's economy.

The American West had little coal to produce electricity and insufficient available capital to build hydroelectric dams. The demand for dams for agricultural purposes in the arid West began gaining momentum at the end of the nineteenth century. President Theodore Roosevelt promoted development of water resources as part of his Progressive political agenda. He pushed for a national policy to plan the development of water resources. This led to conflicts between private electrical companies and Roosevelt over the proper role of the federal government in constructing dams and developing power systems. Under the leadership of Roosevelt the federal government became involved in 1902 with the creation of the U.S. Reclamation Service. The

agency immediately began building small dams and canals in the west to irrigate the desert lands as well as provide power. By the 1920s small hydropower systems were operating throughout much of the West.

In response to push for increased hydroelectric development, Congress passed the Water Power Act in 1920. The act created the Federal Power Commission to guide further development of hydroelectric power. Little, however, would result from the act for much of the 1920s. The key development during the decade was increased standardization of existing electrical networks. Farmers and others who had electrical power found substantial incompatibility between various electrical systems. It was very difficult to install new motors or other devices into an existing system because of the lack of standardization. Often motors were too powerful for the existing electrical supply systems. By the late 1920s larger interconnected systems began evolving that could more efficiently make use of any new power generating plants.

The failure of private utility companies to deliver electricity to most American homes in the 1920s including much of the American West was very disappointing to the progressive reformers. Those pushing for widespread electrical modernization of America also strongly believed utility companies were charging too much for electricity. Influenced by big business wanting cheap electricity rates, utility companies sold electricity on graduated schedules that actually charged lower-income households higher electricity rates than larger users. With the initial block of electricity very expensive, households had to use a lot of electricity to qualify for lower rates. In essence the domestic electricity users were subsidizing industrial users who paid lower rates than households. The industrial users had economic clout to seek another power source if they could not get the rates they wanted from the utilities.

A movement for public power had little leadership until 1913 when controversy over the City of San Francisco's proposal to build the Hetch Hetchy Dam in Yosemite National Park stirred the national debate over public versus private power utilities. At that time the public power movement grew with Senator George W. Norris of Nebraska one of its leaders in Congress. They firmly believed power could be provided much cheaper. This would enable people to purchase the many new electrical appliances being produced and significantly reduce the amount of work needed to maintain a household. By the 1920s the manufacture of new electrical appliances made modernization of the home a real possibility.

Holding Companies

Another factor was also causing high electrical rates. The rise of holding companies in the utility industry during the 1920s was also another key economic factor standing in the way of cheap power. Before World War I electrical companies were local or regional businesses that could be more easily influenced by state commissions to keep prices reasonable. Holding companies were much more extensive in their operations, covering many states. These holding companies were able to raise, or pyramid, their stock values with each business combination they created. Samuel Insull of Chicago created one of the most noted holding company empires in the utility industry. After becoming president of Chicago Edison in 1892, Insull built a vast network of five corporate systems in the Midwest composed of 150 companies worth $2.5 billion and serving over four million customers. The two companies heading the holding company scheme were Insull Utility Investments and Corporation Securities Company of Chicago. Because of their interstate character, holding companies like Insull's were less susceptible to state regulation. They also substantially raised the operation expenses of the utilities by taking a good part of their profits for payment of the management services they provided to these holdings. This meant that the utilities had to

maintain high rates to its customers to pay what were increasingly multiple layers of holding companies. As the public became increasingly aware of these business combinations they became angry, demanding that something be done to control them and lower energy prices.

Demand For Dams Increases

The push for federal support of water projects was increasing in the late 1920s. One key proposal that was a part of the debate was the desire by Southern California to dam the Colorado River to provide drinking water, irrigation water, and hydropower. In 1928 Congress passed a bill authorizing $177 million to build a 726 foot-high dam, known at first as Boulder Dam.

The Columbia River had long been recognized as having vast potential for power generation. Prior to 1930 various state and local organizations in the Pacific Northwest advocated development of the Columbia River, often offering competing proposals. In addition the State of Washington lobbied for a major irrigation project for the central Washington area transected by the upper Columbia River. Advocates for a dam in the Grand Coulee area began organizing in 1917 leading to feasibility studies in the 1920s. The primary goal at that time was irrigation for the semiarid region. The project was supported by the 1931 Corps of Engineers study and a January 1932 Bureau of Reclamation report.

Perspectives

Public

The lack of modernization of U.S. farms persisting into the 1930s was in part philosophically justified by Jeffersonian agrarian ideals. These ideals were that farmers are self-sufficient and their lives are oriented around the natural cycles of the growing seasons. Many contended that electrical power would corrupt this relationship and undermine the independence of the farmer. Electric lights, heaters, freezers, incubators, fans, and pumps would disrupt the harmony and growing cycles. In reality sanitation, comfort, and increased productivity were sacrificed to maintain this antiquated ideal. In addition this argument ignored previous major improvements that had greatly changed farming through the nineteenth century into the early twentieth century. Fertilizers, steel plows, barbed wire, mechanical reapers, canals, hybrid seeds, windmills, new markets opened by railroads, and improved breeding of stock had already greatly altered farm production. In fact these improvements spawned chronic overproduction that lead to persistent low prices for farm products. In addition the perceived independence of farmers had already been shaken by greater reliance on banks and foreign markets because of the overproduction and falling prices. Farmer debt was mounting. In addition many of the rural houses were not technologically designed and built to consume much electricity. Farmers could not afford to upgrade their houses given the economic problems of agriculture. A bigger solution was needed to modernize the American home and farm.

In reaction to their being ignored by the power industry, farmers organized granges and cooperatives, and joined Populist political movements. The Ford Motor Company, owned by Henry Ford who grew up on a farm in Michigan, produced a series of films, Electricity for the Farm, which highlighted the benefits of electrification for farms. It demonstrated washing and ironing clothes, shelling corn, pumping water for irrigation, churning butter, and lighting for nighttime.

The electrical cooperatives were to provide their own electrical service. Such electrical distribution systems grew in Pennsylvania, Oregon, and Washington. The private utilities spent considerable time and energy fighting such developments. Their strategies included construction of zigzagging lines through the countryside tapping into more lucrative localities. Where this was done greatly undercut the ability for farmers to organize cooperatives in an economically effective way.

With lack of service by private utilities farmer support for nationalization of utilities was growing. Thomas Burton wrote the book *Bloodbird* that described the struggle of a group of farmers fighting to stop a utility company from taking their land and constructing a hydroelectric power complex. Not only were farmers fighting for their land, but control of the waterpower so that monopolies would not form.

The fight against public utilities extended into the 1930s as private utilities strongly lobbied Congress and tried to sway public opinion against the New Deal water and power projects. Not only did they argue it was wrong for a government financed utility to compete with private utilities, but they also claimed there was little need for the electricity that would be produced by the massive projects President Roosevelt was processing. They believed there was no market for that amount of electricity in the foreseeable future. Even during their construction, the federal dams were called "white elephants" and concrete monuments to the New Deal.

National

During the 1920s and first years of the New Deal private utilities argued that building power distribution lines to thinly populated rural areas was too costly. Besides, they argued the U.S. population was shifting to the cities anyway leaving fewer potential customers in the farmlands. Whereas each mile of distribution lines in cities could serve between 50 and two hundred customers, in rural areas it would serve only three. Even in Pennsylvania where waterpower was less abundant, a proposal to build a large coal-fired generating plant with distribution lines brought opposition from utility companies and was ultimately defeated in Congress.

The reformers seeking electrification saw two avenues available to them - through regulation of private utility companies or through public ownership. The controversy over public power became a national issue after 1913 when the city of San Francisco proposed to build a dam in the Hetch Hetchy Valley in Yosemite National Park. Private companies took strong opposition to the public involvement in such a project denouncing the prospect of competition between private and public utilities. Senator Robert M. LaFollette of Wisconsin who had fought for government regulation of railroads to reduce railroad rates also took up the fight to lower electrical rates. He, like others, argued that the more widespread use of electricity at lower rates would actually increase the profits of private utility companies.

Another spokesman for public ownership of utilities was New York newspaper owner William Randolph Hearst who broadly distributed his views through his newspapers. He argued utilities should serve a public need. In reaction New York governor Charles Evans Hughes claimed that such ownership was in opposition to the American spirit of individualism and would bring socialism to the United States.

Because individual electricity users and potential users had little influence over utility company practices, state governments established public commissions to provide some oversight. Their effectiveness, however, was primarily limited to safety issues. As a result policies of private power companies, including their rate schedules, acted against electrical modernization of American households, particularly those most in need. By the late 1920s the progressive reformers believed the utility companies were holding back a major social revolution in the United States that would be triggered by electrical modernization of homes. They wanted to raise the standard of living in small towns and farms, and wanted to disperse industry more out to these towns rather than concentrated in major urban centers. Governor Franklin D. Roosevelt of New York joined this "back to the land" crusade.

The main controversy focused on who should get water and electricity. Utilities did not oppose the dams themselves because of the large amount of funds needed to construct them. Utilities were primarily interested in the power generated by the dams. Besides hydropower the government was also interested in flood control, irrigation, navigation, and recreation that would be served by the dams. Therefore the private companies wanted the government to build dams, but let the private company operate the power generators. Many questioned whether it was appropriate for utilities to make money off of dams built with public funds. Utilities opposed such efforts as TVA building transmission lines directly to farms and communities. Roosevelt countered with his claim for a need for a yardstick to measure the performance of utilities. Roosevelt was accused by some newspaper editorials of promoting socialism. In addition they claimed the New Deal was producing electricity that nobody wanted or needed.

International

European governments adopted rural electrification as important national programs much earlier than the United States. The Electrical Exhibition of 1881 in Paris, France, highlighted the benefits of electricity for farming. By the late 1920s two-thirds of farms in Germany, France, Holland, and Scandinavia had inexpensive electrical service. In 1929 the United States remained well behind most other developed nations.

Roosevelt took the charge in advocating public water and power developments on behalf of rural America. Unlike Europe, the U.S. government primarily left electrification to private farmer cooperatives. By 1935 only 10 percent of the rural public in the United States had access to electricity. In contrast 90 percent of farms in France and Germany had electricity, 85 percent in Denmark, and 95 percent in Holland. Electrical service to American homes and farms would dramatically improved through the later 1930s due to the expansive New Deal water and power programs.

Back to the Land

A combination of movements and proponents encouraged electrification of rural America in the 1930s. Many had become disillusioned with the crowded, dirty industrialized cities. The glamour that cities did offer through the 1920s diminished even further as the Great Depression set in. The economic

boom turned into breadlines, shanty towns (referred to as Hoovervilles due to the President's lack of response), and sidewalk apple sellers. The population shift to the city that had been ongoing through the industrialization period, especially following the Civil War, had lost its appeal. Social critics began advocating getting "back to the land." Ralph Borsodi wrote two influential books on the subject, *This Ugly Civilization* and *Flight from the City.* The author himself had left the city in 1920 and become a successful subsistence farmer. Adding to this movement was a Southern Agrarian movement denouncing industrialization and calling for a return to rural life. A key part of the shift would be decentralization of industry that could be accomplished by rural electrification. Small scale factories and subsistence farming was considered the ideal goal for a new society. Other advocates for emphasizing a rural life was the National Catholic Rural Life Conference and architect Frank Lloyd Wright. A common theme of these various groups was that big business was morally bankrupt. Electrification was the key element to make the return shift to rural life possible.

In addition to the Back to the Land movement, another crusade to irrigate the West also took off between 1900 and 1918. Advocates envisioned millions of self-sufficient small farmers. Elwood P. Mead participated in the National Irrigation Congress to lobby for extensive federal aid. William Smythe authored *The Conquest of Arid America* in 1905 that raised public attention of the needs and potentials of the West. One proponent was President Theodore Roosevelt who supported passage of the National Reclamation Act in 1902 creating the Bureau of Reclamation. The act allowed money made by the United States through land sales to be used of irrigation projects in the West.

These inclinations toward rural life meshed well with president Franklin Roosevelt's personal thoughts. Roosevelt believed in the benefits of rural life over city life. He essentially embraced those trends through his New Deal water and power policies that transformed many rural regions of the United States.

Impact

Largely due to New Deal water and power programs, by 1945 most of the nation was electrified. The New Deal showed that even low-income Americans could enjoy electrical modernization and participate in the mass consumer economy. As a result what were considered luxury commodities of the 1920s, such as

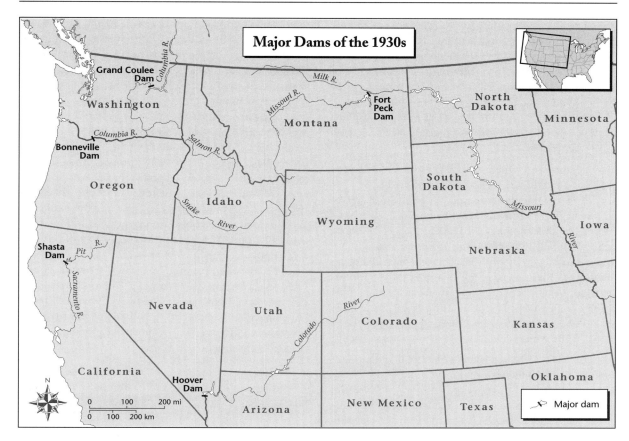

Map of major dams planned and constructed during the New Deal era.

(The Gale Group.)

refrigerators, became necessities of U.S. society by the late 1930s. Private utility companies also learned they could see increased profits with mass consumption of electricity. This was in contrast to their commonly held beliefs before the 1930s that focused only on high-density residential areas and industry. Through the New Deal's housing programs longer terms for loans through FHA made house payments as low as monthly rent payments and all but guaranteed the houses would be electrically modernized. Due to New Deal water and power policies, public power programs became accepted by industry and the public.

The New Deal played a major role in the modernization of the West's economy. No other source of such large capital was available to build the massive infrastructure necessary. The western states benefited the most from the New Deal spending on water and power.

World War II brought a huge demand for electrical power for the factories to produce war materials including aluminum production for aircraft and other

war materials. Boulder City at Hoover Dam enjoyed another boom period during the war. At TVA 12 dams were under construction at the same time in 1942 in another burst of construction. The TVA system of dams produced 2 billion kilowatt hours of electricity in 1939, 12 billion in 1945 following the war expansion, and 20 billion in 1973. In the late 1940s President Harry Truman tried to revive the multiple TVA idea of Roosevelt's with regional planning agencies. Like Roosevelt he was not successful in selling the concepts to Congress. Truman offered another need for cheap power. He firmly believed that cheap electricity was necessary for racial minorities to enjoy modern housing comforts. Still urban home ownership for non-whites increased from 20 percent in 1940 to 36 percent in 1960.

Another outcome of New Deal water and power projects was the growth of large construction companies that would become internationally known. In addition the federal government and large private business had formed a partnership partly focused around large construction projects. The giant construction company combinations spurred by New Deal water and power projects would continue through World War II and the post-war years. During the war they enjoyed huge profits through government guaranteed profit programs for defense related projects during the Depression. Following the war they operated steel mills, cement factories, and developed mines.

Federally funded construction of large dams continued as a major part of the U.S. economy in the post-war years and greatly increased the generating capacity. In fact several of the projects begun by the New Deal were not completed until late in the 1940s. Many local economies benefited first from the jobs created by the large construction projects and then from the benefits after completion. For example to the Columbia River system were added numerous dams including the Dalles Dam (1957) just upstream from Bonneville and John Day Dam (1968) and McNary Dam (1953) further upstream.

The New Deal's push for electrical modernization also contributed to a major building boom in the post-war period. The federal government insured the loans for over 50 percent of home loans. By the mid-1950s over three-fourths of American households lived in electrically modern homes in both urban and rural areas. The pre-1933 two-class system based on access to electrical modernization had been erased. This radical change in just 22 years represented a major redistribution in national wealth. Home ownership opened up availability to loan opportunities and an accumulation of wealth for the mass public. Refrigerators, washing machines, and other appliances offered greater leisure time. Electrification made recreational activities in the home much more feasible including televisions and later computers. In total electrical modernization spurred by the New Deal opened up new freedoms for the average American household.

The availability of inexpensive and a reliable supply of electricity continued into the 1990s when efforts to deregulate the power industry brought major changes including higher costs and less reliable supplies in the early twenty-first century.

Environmental Concerns

By the 1970s thousands of dams had been constructed and various concerns arose regarding their effects on migrating fish and other aspects of the environment. By the late 1970s the dam building era had drawn to a close. Some dams were even targeted for demolition. Hydroelectric power constituted 16 per-

cent of the nation's electric power by the late 1970s. The Columbia River dams were accused of being the primary factor of the major decline of fish in the Columbia River system, historically an important economic resource in itself. By the late twentieth century ten dams and thousands of miles of irrigation canals had made the Colorado River, like the Columbia, one of the most intensively managed rivers in the world. Cities and farms sprung up in what was once desert. The New Deal projects brought an end to the annual cycle of flooding, good from the farmer's perspective but the biological renewal of the river and its biological productivity of the region declined. Wildlife numbers dropped, as clam-rich tidal flats near its mouth in Mexico disappeared as did a lush river delta, due to by the dramatic decrease in the amount of water reaching the river's mouth at the Gulf of California. Decades later some were arguing that he New Deal's water and power projects may have provided abundant power that was cheap for its rate payers, but eventually expensive for its impacts on the environment.

Notable People

Maurice Cook (1872–1960). Born in Carlisle, Pennsylvania, Cook graduated from Lehigh University in 1895. He became a consulting engineer specializing in electric power and public works. After serving as director of the Philadelphia Department of Public Works in the 1910s, he worked with the War Industries Board and U.S. Shipping Board during the war. Afterwards he served as economic advisor to Pennsylvania Governor Gifford Pinchot. Impressed with his ideas, Governor Franklin Roosevelt of New York appointed Cook to the New York State Power Authority in 1929. With Roosevelt winning the presidential race in 1932, Cook became part of the New Deal in 1933 when Roosevelt appointed him to a position in the Public Works Administration (PWA). Cook was a key advocate for national economic planning. Cook was also appointed to the National Power Policy Committee. In 1935 Cooke became head of the Rural Electrification Administration (REA), a New Deal agency promoting cheap electricity to rural farm areas through partnership with private farm cooperatives. With the Great Plains suffering from a long-term drought he became chairman of the Great Plains Drought Area Committee established to restore the economy and environment of the Midwest. Cooke's influence continued through the 1940s as President Harry Truman appointed him in 1950 to chair the President's Water Resources Policy Committee.

Harold Ickes (1874–1952). Born in Franktown, Pennsylvania, Ickes graduated from the University of Chicago in 1897 and became a newspaper journalist. In the 1920s he practiced law in Chicago and fought the influence of the utilities empire built by Samuel Insull. He was also president of the Chicago chapter of the National Association for the Advancement of Colored People (NAACP). Ickes was politically progressive and disliked big business domination of local politics. In 1933 President Roosevelt appointed Ickes Secretary of Interior. With creation of the Public Works Administration (PWA), Roosevelt named Ickes head of that organization as well. Ickes campaigned for national planning, conservation of natural resources, and regulation of private power companies. Ickes was personally involved in the design and acceptance of all PWA projects. As both head of the PWA and Secretary of Interior, Ickes held much power in matters relating to unemployment relief and construction of public works projects. With his control of PWA funds for major projects, Ickes was the dominant figure and shaped a lasting influence on the economic development of the West.

Samuel Insull (1859–1938). Born in London, England, Insull attended private schools by the age of 20 began work for the European representative of the Thomas A. Edison electrical power industry in the United States. In 1881 after only two years Insull was transferred to the United States and soon became head of the Thomas A. Edison Construction Company. By 1892 Insull had become president of Chicago Edison. Over the course of the next three decades, Insull developed a vast system of holding companies controlling electrical service over a broad area of the Midwest. The stock market crash of October 1929 caused the collapse of the Insull empire. By 1932 Insull resigned and returned to Europe. Politicians including Franklin Roosevelt in 1932 used Insull as an example of corporate corruption that led to the Great Depression. Backlash against the holding company empires such as Insull's led to a number of New Deal reform legislation including the Banking Act of 1933, the Tennessee Valley Authority Act of 1933, the Securities Exchange Act of 1934, the Public Utility Holding Company Act of 1935, and the Rural Electrification Act of 1936 among others.

George Norris (1861–1944). Born in Sandusky Country, Ohio, Norris received a law degree in 1833 and began a law practice in Nebraska two years later. Norris became legal counsel to the Burlington and Missouri Railroad. With business down during the 1890s economic depression, Norris began public service as a prosecuting attorney and state judge. In 1902 he won nomination to Congress. In Washington Nor-

ris became a progressive Republican, supporting railroad reform. In 1913 he won election to the Senate where he served for the next 30 years. During the 1920s he opposed the Republican administrations' favoritism toward big business and fought hard for public ownership and operation of the hydroelectric facilities at Muscle Shoals, Alabama. He unsuccessfully presented a series of bills to have the government develop the region through a series of dams that would provide inexpensive hydroelectric power. Norris was also pro-agriculture and passed bills in favor of small farm operators. Though still a Republican, he endorsed Franklin Roosevelt for president in 1932 with whom he became close friends. Norris was the chief author of the bill creating the Tennessee Valley Authority in 1933 and he sponsored the Rural Electrification Act in 1936. Norris was a leading advocate of regional power projects around the nation, but had little success in getting their authorization through Congress. The first dam build by TVA was named after him as was a new community, Norris, Tennessee.

Primary Sources

On July 5, 1934, President Franklin Roosevelt established the National Power Policy Committee. Purpose of the Committee was to coordinate the New Deal's policy related to the production of electrical power. The following statement was provided in a letter to the Secretary of Interior Harold Ickes (from Roosevelt, pp. 339–340).

> I wish to establish in the Public Works Administration a Committee to be called the "National Power Policy Committee." Its duty will be to develop a plan for the closer cooperation of the several factors in our electrical power supply-both public and private-whereby national policy in power matters may be unified and electricity may be made more broadly available at cheaper rates to industry, to domestic and, particularly, to agricultural consumers.

> Several agencies of the Government, such as the Federal Power and Trade Commission, have in process surveys and reports useful in this connection. The Mississippi Valley Committee of Public Works is making studies of the feasibility of power in connection with water storage, flood control and navigation projects. The War Department and Bureau of Reclamation have under construction great hydro-electric plants. Representatives of these agencies have been asked to serve on the Committee. It is not to be merely a fact-finding body, but rather one for the development and unification of national power policy.

> As time goes on there undoubtedly will be legislation on the subject of holding companies and for the regulation

A boat and gasoline barge in the navigation locks of the Bonneville Dam in October 1941. Construction of the dam provided much needed jobs to three thousand workers in the Depression-weary Pacific Northwest.

(The Library of Congress.)

of electric current in interstate commerce. This Committee should consider what lines should be followed in shaping this legislation. Since a number of the States have commissions having jurisdiction over intrastate power matters ...

The Committee is to be advisory to the President. I hope that you will accept membership on this Committee and act as its Chairman.

Dedication of Bonneville Dam

President Roosevelt traveled to the Pacific Northwest in 1937 to promote several New Deal projects including construction of Bonneville Dam. The following remarks were delivered in a speech at the dam on September 28 (from Roosevelt, pp. 387–392).

"Today I have a feeling of real satisfaction in witnessing the completion of another great national project, and of pleasure in the fact that in its inception, four years ago, I had some part. My interest in the whole of the valley of the great Columbia River goes back to 1920 when I first studied its mighty possibilities. Again, in 1932, I visited Oregon and Washington and Idaho and took occasion in Portland to express views which have since, through the action of the Congress, become a recorded part of American national policy ...

The more we study the water resources of the Nation, the more we accept the fact that their use is a matter of

national concern, and that in our plans for their use our line of thinking must include great regions as well as narrower localities.

If, for example, we had known as much and acted as effectively twenty and thirty and forty years ago as we do today in the development of the use of land in that great semi-arid strip in the center of the country which runs from the Canadian border to Texas, we could have prevented in great part the abandonment of thousands and thousands of farms in portions of ten states (later referred to as the Dust Bowl) and thus prevented the migration of thousands of destitute families from those areas into the States of Washington and Oregon and California. We would have done this by avoiding the plowing up of vast areas, which should have been kept in grazing range, and by stricter regulations to prevent overgrazing. At the same time we would have checked soil erosion, stopped the denudation of our forests and controlled disastrous fires.

Some of my friends who talk glibly of the right of any individual to do anything he wants with any of his property take the point of view that it is not the concern of Federal or state or local government to interfere with what they miscall "the liberty of the individual." With them I do not agree and never have agreed because, unlike them, I am thinking of the future of the United States. My conception of liberty does not permit an individual citizen or group of citizens to commit acts of depredation against nature in such a way as to harm their neighbors, and especially to harm the future generations of Americans . . .

Coming back to the watershed of the Columbia River, which covers the greater part of the States of Oregon, Washington, Idaho and a part of Montana, it is increasingly important that we think of that region as a unit . . .

That is why in developing electricity from this Bonneville Dam, from the Grand Coulee Dam and from other dams to be built on the Columbia and its tributaries, the policy of the widest use ought to prevail. The transmission of electricity is making such scientific strides today that we can well visualize a date, not far distant, when every community in this great area will be wholly electrified . . .

Your situation in the Northwest is in this respect no different from the situation in the other great regions of the Nation. That is why it has been proposed in the Congress that regional planning boards be set up for the purpose of coordinating the planning for the future in seven or eight natural geographical regions . . .

To you who live thousands of miles away in other parts of the United States, I want to give two or three simple facts. This Bonneville Dam on the Columbia River, forty-two miles east of Portland, with Oregon on the south side of the river and Washington on the north, is one of the major power and navigation projects undertaken since 1933. It is 170 feet high and 1,250 feet long. It has been built by the Corps of Engineers of the War Department, and when fully completed, with part of its power installations, will cost $51,000,000. Its locks will enable shipping to sue this great waterway much further inland than at present, and give an outlet to the enormously valuable agricultural and mineral products of Oregon and Washington and Idaho. Its generators ultimately will produce 580,000 horsepower of electricity.

Truly, in the construction of this dam we have had our eyes on the future of the Nation. Its cost will be returned to the people of the United States many times over in the improvement of navigation and transportation, the cheapening of electric power, and the distribution of this power to hundreds of small communities within a great radius.

As I look upon Bonneville Dam today, I cannot help the thought that instead of spending, as some nations do, half their national income in piling up armaments and more armaments for purposes of war, we in America are wiser in using our wealth on projects like this which will give us more wealth, better living and greater happiness for our children.

Suggested Research Topics

- The movement to generate electrical power by publicly owned utilities met strong opposition from private power companies. Review the various arguments posed by the proponents of both public and private power generation.

- Explore the history of water and power projects in your region. Is the power to your power generated by hydroelectric, coal, nuclear, or some other source? Is it a publicly or privately owned power company? Did the New Deal influence the development of power sources for your community?

Bibliography

Sources

Hunter, Louis C. *A History of Industrial Power in the United States, 1780-1930.* Charlottesville: University Press of Virginia, 1979.

Lowitt, Richard. The New Deal and the West. Norman: University of Oklahoma Press, 1993.

Nash, Gerald D. *The Federal Landscape: An Economic History of the Twentieth-Century West.* Tucson: The University of Arizona Press, 1999.

Nye, David E. *Electrifying America: Social Meanings of a New Technology, 1880-1940.* Cambridge, MA: MIT Press, 1990.

Roosevelt, Franklin D. *The Public Papers and Addresses of Franklin D. Roosevelt.* New York: The Macmillan Company, 1941.

Tobey, Ronald C. *Technology as Freedom: The New Deal and the Electrical Modernization of the Home.* Berkeley: University of California Press, 1996.

Welsh, Michael E. *U.S. Army Corps of Engineers: Albuquerque District, 1935–1985.* Albuquerque, NM: University of New Mexico Press, 1987.

Further Reading

Cullen, Allan H. *Rivers in Harness: The Story of Dams.* New York: Chilton Books,1962.

Dunar, Andrew J., and Dennis McBride. *Building Hoover Dam: An Oral History of the Great Depression.* New York: Twayne Publishers, 1993.

Reisner, Marc. *Cadillac Desert: The American West and Its Disappearing Water.* New York: Penguin Books, 1993.

Stevens, Joseph E. *Hoover Dam: An American Adventure.* Norman: University of Oklahoma Press, 1988.

Wilkinson, Charles F. *Crossing the Next Meridian: Land, Water, and the Future of the West.* Washington, DC: Island Press, 1992.

Wolf, Donald E. *Big Dams and Other Dreams: The Six Companies Story.* Norman: University of Oklahoma Press, 1996.

See Also

New Deal (First, and Its Critics); Rural Electrification Administration; Tennessee Valley Authority

Women in Public Life

1933-1941

Introduction

On January 6, 1930, 12 national women's organizations appeared before the Senate Judiciary Committee. Their goal was to testify against the Equal Rights Amendment (ERA), a constitutional amendment that would grant women and men equal protection under the law. It had been only 10 years since the women's suffrage movement, a broad coalition of professional, social, and labor organizations, had succeeded in pressuring Congress to pass the Nineteenth Amendment giving women the right to vote.

The intervening decade had spawned an ever widening divide between women's organizations. The National Woman's Party (NWP), headed by Alice Paul, was the sole group lobbying for the ERA. To them, the ERA was a simple concrete objective that would become the new rallying cry for the women's movement that had splintered after suffrage was achieved. Representatives from the League of Women Voters, one of the 12 organizations that testified against the ERA, claimed that only legislation that recognized the real physical and social differences between men and women would achieve "true equality" for women. From the NWP viewpoint, this type of protective legislation would limit how, when, and where women and children worked. It would greatly interfere with a woman's right to earn an honest living. Such restricted financial opportunities would result in continued economic dependence.

This potential loss of job opportunities was especially critical as the Great Depression was taking shape and increasing numbers of workers, including husbands, were losing jobs or seeing their incomes reduced. Noted sociologist Sophonisba Breckinridge went one step further. She viewed protective legislation sought by most of the women's groups of the 1930s as one illustration of women's disillusionment with the voting process. Rather than voting for reform, women were pressuring government agencies and educational institutions to legislate reform.

But were women really disillusioned with voting so quickly? Eleanor Roosevelt later observed that women used their suffrage much in the same way that men did. Rather than voting as a bloc, a threat that many suffrage opponents believed would threaten the focus of the government, they voted as individuals. Although they could be swayed by group dynamics, their votes were more typically affected by their individual experiences and background. And women were indeed voting, and affecting change albeit slowly. By 1930 both Texas and Wyoming had elected women governors at least once. The League of Women Voters reported that six women were elected to the House of Representatives in 1930 and that there were more than 145 serving in 39 state legislatures. Women were poised to take on even greater responsibilities.

When President Franklin D. Roosevelt (served 1933–1945) was sworn into office in 1933, his New Deal programs brought a wealth of new opportunities for women. The New Deal was a wide range of federal social and economic relief, recovery, and reform programs designed to address the severe economic hardships brought by the Great Depression. By the end of the year 1935 women had been appointed to prominent positions in the federal government, many of them jobs never before held by a woman. Certainly there were women playing active roles in government before Roosevelt's election. Grace Abbott had been Chief of the Department of Labor's Children's Bureau since 1921 and Mary Anderson had led its Women's Bureau since 1920. Mary Norton had been elected to Congress in 1924 and was still serving. What was new and different was the growing assumption that women belonged in politics.

Although women made few advances in established agencies such as the Department of Commerce or the War Department and still had to contend with discriminatory legislation, they were well positioned to take advantage of the growth in government agencies brought about by the New Deal. From Frances Perkins's contributions to the Department of Labor to Ellen Sullivan Woodward's organization of the Works

Chronology:

1920: The Nineteenth Amendment to the U.S. Constitution gives women the vote and, as a result, a more active voice in American political issues.

June 30, 1932: Section 213 of the Economy Act mandates that spouses cannot be employed by the federal government at the same time. Although the statute does not dictate that wives should lose their jobs, the individuals who resign or who are fired are overwhelmingly female.

November 20, 1933: The Federal Emergency Relief Administration (FERA) sponsors the White House Conference on the Emergency Needs of Women.

April 30, 1934: The White House Conference on Camps for Unemployed Women attracts 75 people and recommends resident schools and camps for the female jobless.

1936: A broad coalition of women's organizations draft the Woman's Charter in an attempt to unify the women's movement.

May 1940: The Women's Division of the Democratic National Committee (DNC) holds a three-day National Institute of Government drawing five thousand women to register, far exceeding the one hundred women initially expected.

Progress Administration's (WPA) Women's Division their efforts and achievements were remarkable and their imprint on New Deal legislation very real.

Issue Summary

A few days before Franklin Roosevelt was sworn in as president, he called Frances Perkins, then Industrial Commissioner of the State of New York into his office and asked her to head up the Department of Labor. After a lengthy discussion during which Perkins outlined the conditions under which she would accept including his support for child labor laws, workmen's compensation, relief programs, and social security, she agreed to become the first woman to

Frances Perkins was the first woman to be appointed to a cabinet post. She served as FDR's secretary of labor from 1933 to 1945. (AP/Wide World Photos. Reproduced by permission.)

serve in the cabinet. Many thought his wife was behind the appointment. Eleanor denied contributing in any way to his decision. Others saw the influence of Molly Dewson, head of the Democratic National Campaign Committee's Women's Division. She also discounted her influence, saying that Roosevelt undoubtedly enjoyed breaking tradition. He would have appointed Perkins as secretary even if she had never taken the precaution to humorously claim that it was her price for the political work she did.

Six Million Rainbow Fliers

For Molly Dewson of the Women's Division, Perkin's appointment was payback. In early 1932 Dewson began her campaign on Roosevelt's behalf. Working with other top Democratic leaders including Sue Shelton White, Emily Newell Blair, Jo Coffin, Mary Chamberlain, and Lavinia Engle, Dewson's Women's Division devised a structure that exploited the strengths of an ever-growing network of local Democratic women. Each state would have a vice-chair and would be responsible for supplying county-wide contacts. These state and local correspondents would serve as the main vehicles for the distribution of campaign literature.

The literature of choice was the rainbow flier. A throwback to the state-by-state battle for suffrage, the rainbow flier was a single-sheet of campaign facts to be distributed door-to-door. The Women's Division delivered over six million during the 1932 campaign. Added to the rainbow fliers were incentives given to each state's vice-chair. They were invited to consult with Dewson and her staff in New York. Dewson also developed the Gas Money Plan which gave 10 dollars for gas to every vice-chair in a designated "fighting state." Her speakers' bureau used only the "best and most seasoned" women speakers, including Nellie Tayloe Ross of Wyoming, and representatives Ruth Bryan Owen and Mary Norton. It was an impressive grassroots effort that Roosevelt hoped would be the start of a long-term and highly effective women's organization.

The Women's Network

Even before Roosevelt's election was won in November 1932, Dewson was campaigning for Perkins as Secretary of Labor. She wrote Roosevelt in a note that Perkins's appointment would be all the "reward" she needed. After the election was over, she told her wide range of contacts—all of whom she encouraged to write Roosevelt in support of Perkins—that her appointment would prove that Roosevelt took women's contributions to politics and public life seriously and that he was willing to entrust women with unprecedented power and responsibility. Perkins was also not only the right woman for the job, she was the best individual available given her years of experience in New York and her well established relationship with Roosevelt.

For Dewson merely placing women in public office was not enough. They had to be the best available candidate. This was her brand of feminism. Perkins, who invited Dewson to attend her swearing-in, remained grateful to her friend for convincing her to accept the challenging appointment. In being offered the position she pronounced her pride in a sense representing all women in the nation.

Another appointment was Dewson herself, who, at the request of Eleanor Roosevelt, was named director of the newly created Women's Division of the Democratic National Committee (DNC). Her first task was to arrange a meeting with Eleanor and other top democratic women, including Nellie Tayloe Ross and Sue Shelton White, to compile a list of women they felt deserved appointments in Roosevelt's new administration. They kept the list to one hundred names and identified 15 women whom they felt were particularly deserving. Dewson went to work on Jim Farley, head of the DNC, believing it was essential for the success of the Democratic Party in the elections of 1934 and 1936. Progress was slow and frustrating. By May only seven women had been given jobs that Dewson considered routine appointments. By the fall of 1933 she was so annoyed by the lack of progress that she asked for a meeting with the president to speed up her requests.

Eventually some movement was made. Women active in the Democratic organization were rewarded first. Jo Coffin, head of the Labor Advisory Committee of the 1932 campaign, went to work for the Government Printing Office. Nellie Tayloe Ross became the first woman Director of the Mint. Another first for women was Ruth Bryan Owen, who was named minister to Denmark. Florence Allen, subject of another Dewson letter-writing campaign, held the highest position a woman ever had in the federal judiciary when she was named to the U.S. Circuit Court of Appeals.

Dewson's goal was to recognize at least one woman Democratic worker in every state. She also sought to place professionally trained social workers, many of whom she knew from her own years in the field. These were the people best trained to deal with the problems of the Great Depression. Reviewing her efforts at the White House Conference on the Emergency Needs of Women in November of 1933, she recognized that the women she helped place in the government could also serve as an informal policy making group. While Dewson did not claim personal responsibility for placing all of the women active in the New Deal in their jobs, her perseverance and her relationship with the Roosevelts were certainly strong contributing factors to getting most of them jobs.

Women in the New Deal

The New Deal created new opportunities for women for some very practical reasons. The federal response to the Depression was to take on a wealth of new responsibilities. In the 1930s the government provided work relief, social security, and unemployment compensation for the first time. The agencies created to provide these services were best staffed by social workers. They were the professionals best trained to fulfill these new government responsibilities and women made up the majority of trained social workers. By 1939 the percentage of women government employees had risen to almost 19 percent, increasing nearly five percent since 1929.

Women's rate of federal employment was increasing twice as fast as men's, but it was doing so in very specific areas of the government, namely the new federal agencies. While they made up only 15 percent of executive departments, their numbers were much higher in the recently established New Deal agencies. Women made up almost 45 percent of the WPA, and Ellen Sullivan Woodward's appointment, as WPA administrator, was one of Dewson's proudest achievements. In general women were more able to overcome traditional social prejudices when filling positions in newer agencies. Even though Frances Perkins was a member of the cabinet, she was secretary of the youngest department in the cabinet.

The influx of women into prominent and mid-level positions in the government was for many a natural progression of talent fulfilling need. Dewson believed it was women's energy and idealism that would bring out the humanitarian side of government. Eleanor Roosevelt agreed with Dewson's assessment, commenting that the growing concern for "welfare of human beings" that was demonstrated by the federal government in the 1930s was due to women.

What was most evident was the stamp of the social worker on New Deal legislation. Frances Perkins and Clara Beyer facilitated passage of labor standards and legislation with the Fair Labor Standards Act. The act contained many of the same provisions they had fought for in the state of New York including minimum wages and maximum hours. Among Perkins's many successes in the federal government were the creation of the Civilian Conservation Corps (CCC) and the Social Security Act. They contained many of the programs that were for her, conditions necessary for her continued employment in Roosevelt's cabinet.

Nicknamed derisively in the press as "Ma" Perkins, many factory workers and laborers adopted the name and soon called her, affectionately, Ma Perkins of the Poor People's Department. Perkins worked to ban child labor and to protect the right of workers to organize and bargain collectively. She fought for workmen's compensation, old age and unemployment insurance, and improvements in industrial health and safety. Although Perkins opposed many measures that discriminated against women in the National Recovery Act, she eventually agreed to them. She was once described as a "half-loaf girl," as she believed any legislation that improved the working conditions in factories was better than no legislation.

Her tenure was not without controversy. She was impeached (accused of misconduct) in the U.S. Senate along with the Commissioner of the Immigration and Naturalization Service, and then contained with the Department of Labor because she refused to deport

Biography:

Eleanor Roosevelt

1884–1962   Orphaned at a young age, Eleanor Roosevelt was raised by her mother's family in New York. In 1905 she married Franklin Roosevelt and they had six children together, one of whom died in infancy.

During World War I Eleanor became active in volunteer programs while her husband served as Assistant Secretary of the Navy. The couple's relationship changed significantly when Eleanor discovered Franklin's affair with Lucy Mercer, her friend and personal secretary. Although they remained married, the Roosevelts' relationship transitioned into a strong platonic partnership, focused on raising their children and advancing Franklin's burgeoning political career.

When Franklin Roosevelt was paralyzed by polio in 1921, Eleanor broadened her role in public life, partly to keep her husband's name in the public eye while he recovered. Her volunteerism expanded in the 1920s to include the Women's Division of the New York Democratic State Committee, the League of Women Voters, the Women's Trade Union League, and the National Consumers' League. These experiences gave her greater influence and knowledge to form her own ideas about social reform and the position of women.

Through her volunteer work Eleanor formed many personal and professional relationships that endured throughout her involvement with politics. It was at this time that Eleanor met Rose Schneiderman, then the president of the New York branch of the Women's Trade Union League, Molly Dewson of the National Consumers' League, and Nancy Cook and Marion Dickerman of the Democratic State Committee.

In 1928 Eleanor organized the women's Democratic national campaign for president, while her husband chose to run—successfully—for governor of New York. Eleanor was active in many programs, published articles, and became an accomplished public speaker.

When her husband ran for the U.S. presidency in 1932, Eleanor, with the help of Molly Dewson, organized Democratic women to help win the campaign. As First Lady, Roosevelt worked with Dewson to place many women in government posts. She also encouraged women journalists in Washington by holding press conferences for women only.

In 1936 Eleanor began to write a daily column, entitled "My Day," using it to publish her observations on her life in the White House and on her many trips. She also began a series of radio broadcasts to discuss policy issues and her views on human rights. Because of her extensive travel and use of the media, Eleanor soon acquired the nickname "Eleanor, everywhere."

While in the White House Eleanor used her position to advance a number of causes. She continued to champion the rights of women and often used her role as First Lady to improve their working conditions. She helped set up centers for unemployed women in New York City in 1932 and 1933, and offered to host conferences to bring attention to women's issues. As her public role expanded Eleanor became more vocal in her opposition to any form of discrimination and championed a variety of social causes.

Eleanor was a strong partner to the president and often presented issues to him. Gradually, however, she felt that the public no longer saw her as only a "mouthpiece" for the president and felt more at liberty to express her own views. She became more outspoken against racial discrimination and segregation, making clear statements through action when possible.

She continued her public works during World War II, working for the Office of Civilian Defense and touring England and the South Pacific. After her husband's death in 1945 she continued speaking and writing on behalf of causes she believed in. President Harry Truman appointed Eleanor as one of the five U.S. delegates to the United Nations (UN), where she was a representative to the UN Human Rights Commission and worked on the first international bill of rights.

Eleanor Roosevelt remained a major force in the Democratic Party throughout the 1950s, and in 1960 she again returned to the UN as President John Kennedy's appointed delegate to the Commission on the Status of Women. She remained an active champion of women's rights and civil rights until her death in 1962.

More About...

Photographing the Depression

Some of the most compelling images from the Depression were taken by two women photographers whose paths never crossed but whose pictures portrayed common themes of despair.

Dorothea Lange was working in San Francisco as a portrait photographer when the Depression began. One morning in 1931 she looked out the window to see an unemployed workman pausing to rest at her street corner. As she watched him decide which way to turn, she resolved to capture him on film. Soon she was photographing the unemployed waiting in bread lines, sleeping in the parks and in the streets, and loitering around the docks. These were what she called the historical moments of the Depression.

In 1934 she met Paul Schuster Taylor, an agricultural economist working for the state relief agency to study the flood of migrant workers into California. In 1935 he hired her to photograph his research subjects. Lange and Taylor married and traveled throughout the country on assignment for the New Deal's Farm Security Administration (FSA) studying and documenting the paths of migrant workers. Her photographs illustrated the transition in agriculture from its reliance on small family-owned farms to large agricultural corporations. Taylor later gave partial credit for the establishment of the FSA to Lange's compelling photographs of migrant workers.

In 1936 Lange took her most famous photograph of a migrant woman from Oklahoma. The "Migrant Mother," as the picture was later titled, was a widow in her thirties with seven children. She had sold the tires off her car for cash and was subsisting off what she and her children scrounged from the fields. The picture became the FSA symbol for the desperation and hopelessness caused by the Depression.

Across the country, Margaret Bourke-White lived in New York City, where she worked as a photojournalist for *Fortune,* the *New York Times Magazine, Vanity Fair,* and *Life Magazine.* Though she had an extensive and experienced career in photography, she later cited her work depicting Dust Bowl farmers as forming her true awareness of people. Sent out by *Fortune* to capture the great drought of 1934 on film, she spent a week touring from the Dakotas to Texas.

Shocked by the helpless people she encountered, Bourke-White was inspired to record in more depth the tragedy she saw being played out in America's agricultural center. When Southern novelist Erskine Caldwell approached her to collaborate on his project about southern sharecroppers, she eagerly accepted. In 1937 Caldwell and Bourke-White published *You Have Seen Their Faces.* Although criticized because the captions in the book were fictionalized quotes created by Caldwell and Bourke-White rather than being direct quotes, the book was for its creators a product that showed the effect of weather events and the Great Depression on everyday people.

Harry Bridges, a union president under investigation. Although later exonerated of any wrongdoing, the impeachment was later seen by the public as the real reason the Immigration and Naturalization Service was moved to the Department of Justice and the Social Security Board established as an independent agency. Despite such setbacks Perkins was remarkably successful at developing solutions that would protect the rights of workers while trying to foster an economic recovery from the Great Depression.

Working to provide women with work relief from the Great Depression, Ellen Woodward oversaw the work of 450,000 women through the Women's and Professional Projects of the WPA. The WPA programs had women actively pursuing domestic projects,

library work, public health programs, and research services. These were the programs that Molly Dewson and Eleanor Roosevelt described as the "human aspects of the New Deal."

Lorena Hickok, also known as "Hick," was one of the first women to work for the Associated Press. Used to reporting the hard news stories, she had covered everything from straight politics to murder trials when she was assigned to cover Eleanor Roosevelt on the campaign trail. The assignment was to profoundly change both her personal and professional life. Because her close relationship with Eleanor made it hard to maintain her professional standards of objectivity, Hickok left her groundbreaking post at AP and took a job working for Harry Hopkins of the New

Mary McLeod Bethune was appointed minority advisor to the National Youth Administration.

(UPI/Bettmann. Reproduced by permission.)

Deal's Federal Emergency Relief Administration (FERA).

Hopkins hired Hickok to be his chief investigator. She was to tour some of the worst afflicted areas of the country and to report frankly on conditions. Hopkins wanted the first-hand observations, her reactions rather than statistics or the view of social workers. Hickok's reports, beginning in the summer of 1933 and lasting until the end of 1936, were filled with stories of the people she met. She visited almost every part of the country and met nearly everyone involved with the relief programs from state and local officials, politicians, and civic leaders to the relief clients on New Deal's WPA projects.

Her reports allowed Hopkins to comprehend the human dimension of the problems facing the nation. They also gave Hopkins and FERA a dynamic and vital cross-section of American public opinion. Her reports demonstrated how significant a role was played by women administering programs under Hopkins' jurisdiction and pointed out the racial tensions caused by relief. She frequently was sent to investigate a community in crisis and was able to determine whether its root cause was a labor problem or natural disaster. Hopkins often passed her reports on to the president. Roosevelt wished they could be published

as they provided such a detailed picture of the urgent problems facing the country. Hickok's greatest talent was her ability to quickly assess a community. The intelligence she provided to Hopkins allowed him to better coordinate between Washington and local relief administrators.

Mary McLeod Bethune became the first black American woman to head a federal agency when she was appointed Negro Affairs Director for the National Youth Administration (NYA) in 1936. The agency was particularly successful in meeting the educational and employment needs of America's youth. Bethune successfully distributed NYA funds to black schools. She served as Roosevelt's Special Advisor on Minority Affairs from 1935 to 1944, in addition to serving as the Director of Negro Affairs of the National Youth Administration from 1936 to 1944.

She was the unofficial leader of Roosevelt's "Black Cabinet," a group of black American officials in federal agencies who advised Roosevelt informally. When Bethune opposed the exclusion of black American women from the Women's Interest Section of the War Department in 1941, Eleanor Roosevelt's influence eventually led to her participation in the advisory council. Because of Bethune, black American women became officers in the Women's Army Auxiliary Corps, established later that year.

Another prominent woman in the New Deal was Hallie Flanagan, who was appointed head of the Federal Theatre Project (FTP) in 1935. The FTP was part of the massive work relief program, the Works Progress Administration, which President Roosevelt launched as a key part of the Second New Deal. The FTP was controversial from the beginning as many argued against using public funds to employ actors and artists. Flanagan, however, through strong determination pushed the program forward employing over 12,000 actors, directors, stagehands, and others, and putting on productions in 105 theaters in 28 states. Finally, under intense pressure from Congress, the FTP ended in 1939.

The Reporter Plan

Nurturing grass-roots support for New Deal legislation was an essential component of Dewson's long-range plan to involve more women in the government at all levels. She achieved much of this through her Reporter Plan. The plan sought to educate women on the issues while also selling them on the benefits of New Deal. Although informing the female voting public was not a new concept—the League of Women Voters being one example of a group dedicated to educating women on political issues—Dewson's Reporter Plan took advantage of the existing network of Democratic women. It increased their numbers through a broad educational campaign carried out at the local level.

Each county Democratic organization would select a number of women reporters. These reporters would be responsible for monitoring the progress of a government agency. They would distribute their information to civic groups, clubs, and organizations throughout their communities. In effect they would form a grass-roots public information campaign. They would also be ready and educated on the issues when it came time to reelect Roosevelt. By the summer of 1934 five thousand women had signed up to be community reporters. By 1936 there were 15,000 reporters. By 1940 their number had doubled again. The Reporter Plan built on the belief that both women in official positions and women in the voting booths wanted the government to change society in new and positive ways. It capitalized on the prevailing wisdom in the 1930s that the support of women was crucial to the success of Roosevelt's New Deal.

In addition to the Reporter Plan the DNC's Women's Division sponsored regional conferences which combined politics, government, and education. Speakers from Frances Perkins to Ellen Woodward described women's relief programs and the role Social Security would play in providing a safety net for people at risk. For many women both in and outside of the administration, the changes put in place by the New Deal were the culmination of their careers spent pushing for social change. Perkins believed efforts by social workers led to successful legislation that helped address social inequalities. Such goals were key in the successes of the New Deal.

Dewson's work for the DNC's Women's Division reached its high point during the 1936 presidential campaign. Dewson wanted women on the platform committee, the group of Democrats who decided what promises would be made to the public during the campaign. Organizing a Women's Advisory Platform Committee in the spring of 1936, Dewson gathered 14 women she thought most appropriate. This group, headed by Congresswoman Caroline O'Day, identified the issues of greatest concern to women in public life including ratification of the Child Labor Amendment, consumers' rights, civil service, housing, education, and civil liberties.

When Dewson later suggested that alternates to the platform committee be of the opposite sex, her plan was accepted without comment. The women were given a very easy access to the platform committee since the mostly-male regular delegates frequently missed committee meetings. Unfortunately even though they were able to present and lobby for their suggestions and get many of their issues into the platform in general ways, the DNC did not endorse the Child Labor Amendment and was strangely silent on revising Section 213 of the Economy Act.

Spouses and Federal Employment

The "one black mark" against the Roosevelt record on women, which Dewson referred to as "that dumb clause," had actually been signed into law by President Herbert Hoover (served 1929–1933) in late 1932. Section 213 of the Economy Act stipulated that married persons could not be employed by the federal government at the same time. Although Hoover did not approve of the clause because he believed it was unfair to government employees, he signed the Economy Act believing that the next session of Congress, likely to be controlled by Democrats, would surely revise it. Instead of revising the bill, the Civil Service Commission added additional regulations barring spouses who lived apart from both being employed and requiring female government employees to take their husbands' names upon marriage. Although the original bill never stipulated that it should be the wives and not husbands to lose their jobs, the majority of the more than 1,600 government employees who resigned or were fired were women.

In May 1933 representatives from women's organizations asked for the dismissals of women to end and the bill be rescinded. Roosevelt responded by appealing to his attorney general to decide whether the Economy Act was temporary or permanent legislation. The attorney general ruled that it was permanent. Roosevelt claimed he was without the authority to modify Section 213. It was a politically convenient position to take as Section 213, while discriminatory, had a lot of public support from individuals who believed women working outside the home weakened the American family and took jobs away from men during the Depression when jobs were scarce.

The higher the unemployment figures the more criticism efforts to repeal the provision received. The only opposition to Section 213 from the White House came from Eleanor. It took five years to overturn Section 213, and in the end it was done by introducing the Cellar bill, which prohibited discrimination based on marital status. When the bill passed both House and Senate, Eleanor Roosevelt congratulated Congress in her daily column, remarking that determining when a man earns enough to support a family or whether a women should work outside the home should be left to the family to decide, not Congress or others.

Members of the "Women's Emergency Brigade," or "Red Berets," armed and ready to take on attacks against strikers at GM plants in Flint in 1937. The clubs they brandish were used to break the windows out of a plant that was gassed by police. (AP/Wide World Photos. Reproduced by permission.)

Section 213 of the Economy Act was opposed by virtually every women's organization in the country. From mainstream to radical, these groups lobbied Congress and the public until the law was repealed. It was the only issue they agreed on during the 1930s. After suffrage was achieved in 1920, the coalition of women's groups broke down and splintered into a variety of different causes. By the 1930s many women's organizations were strongly opposed to each other and unable to agree on how to better the lives

of women. Although the number of women in the labor force increased during the 1930s, most of the increases were seen in domestic service or seasonal employment. Women in professional employment actually lost ground during the 1930s because of the general public resentment of any woman holding down a job while a man was unemployed.

While there was generally widespread support for measures that provided mothers' pensions, banned child labor, and sought to eliminate restrictions against jury duty, little agreement could be reached on how best to achieve equal economic opportunity for women. Some of the most progressive legislation of the New Deal actually contained some of the most discriminatory measures. While the National Recovery Administration codes established minimum wages for both men and women—which benefited more women as they traditionally made less than men—the codes allowed for different, and in practice, lower wage levels for women workers. Even though many women's organizations filed protests, the lower wage provisions stayed in the codes. It was these types of laws that angered members of the National Women's Party and inspired their campaign for the Equal Rights Amendment.

Is Feminism Dead?

Alice Paul reorganized the National Women's Party (NWP), the successor to her militant suffrage organization the Congressional Union, in 1921. By 1923 they proposed the Equal Rights Amendment (ERA), for the first time simply asserting that men and woman should have equal rights throughout the United States. While the NWP promoted the ERA, other female activist promoted social reform legislation. The two movements clashed. The battle would carry forward through the 1920s and the 1930s.

In 1926 the NWP was one of the many women's groups participating in the Conference of Women in Industry called by Mary Anderson of the Women's Bureau. The NWP disrupted the conference with demands that the Bureau support the ERA. It urged the Bureau to consider the disadvantages, as well as the advantages of other so-called protective legislation that was being promoted at the time. Social reformers including Mary Anderson, Grace Abbott, and Frances Perkins believed such laws would protect women from economic exploitation. Laws restricting the number of hours a woman could work or from working at night or in their homes safeguarded women from companies that would take advantage of their subordinate status in American society. ERA supporters pointed to these very same laws as the reason women were not advancing economically. Social reformers countered that NWP members came from secure middle and upper class backgrounds and did not truly comprehend how disadvantaged lower-class women were.

Fundamentally divided on this issue, organizations such as the the General Federation of Women's Clubs, the League of Women Voters, the Consumers League, the American Association of University Women, and the Women's Bureau campaigned against the NWP and their proposed equal rights amendment. Although the NWP had prominent

Grace Abbott began her career in social work at Jane Addams's Hull House, and later became the director of the United States Children's Bureau.

(Hulton-Deutsch Collection/ Corbis-Bettmann. Reproduced by permission.)

women as their spokespersons, including aviator Amelia Earhart and businesswoman Helena Rubenstein, both of whom had struggled to achieve success in nontraditional roles, they lacked organizational support. Only the Business and Professional Women's Federation had endorsed the ERA by the end of the 1930s. It was the only women's organization beside the NWP to do so. Such conflicts had authors, such as Genevieve Pankhust, asking in exasperation in 1935 if feminism were dead because women had unduly suffered during the Depression. Feminists had failed in being their sisters' keepers and had done little to help them deal with gender discrimination when looking for a job or for relief.

The Women's Charter

In an attempt to answer such critics, Mary Anderson and the Women's Bureau gathered representatives from women's organizations active in social reform in 1936 to develop the Women's Charter. Her goal was to produce a document that would bring their groups and the NWP together. Presented as an alternative to the ERA, the Women's Charter sought to safeguard protective legislation for women. Perkins encouraged Anderson to continue working even though the committee was an unofficial group. It soon floundered in its attempts to include other women's organizations and to put something on paper that was agreeable to multiple groups.

When Anderson proposed incorporating the traditional view that domestic work should be just as valued as professional occupations, she was praised by women who opposed women working outside the home and condemned by organizations that believed women should be trained to work and should expect to work. Discussions broke down again over whether to include specific guarantees of the right of married women to work. Still more criticism came from representatives who viewed the charter solely as a defensive strategy to counter the NWP's ERA rather than offering something uniquely valuable. As the NWP was not invited to participate and did not view the Charter until it was released to the press, this particular criticism not without merit. NWP representatives dismissed the Women's Charter saying women couldn't have protection and ask for equal pay and opportunity. They responded with their own amended version that advocated labor legislation that protected the job rather than the sex of the worker. The committee rejected the NWP revisions. Calling the movement a total failure Anderson abandoned her efforts.

Margaret Sanger and the Birth Control Movement

In 1936 the U.S. Supreme Court ruled that doctors could distribute information on birth control. Margaret Sanger called the legal decision a momentous victory that marked the end of one era and beginning of another. The victory ended over 20 years of activism. For social historians the decision was the natural result of not only Sanger's long struggle but also the changes in society's attitude towards birth control brought about by World War I and the Great Depression.

Margaret Sanger began her campaign to legalize the distribution of birth control information in 1914. Indicted by a federal grand jury in New York City for violating the Comstock Law of 1873 through her publication of the *Woman Rebel,* Sanger arranged for her pamphlet on contraceptive techniques—*Family Limitation*—to be distributed and fled the country. Although the original charges were dropped, in part due to the court's reluctance to prosecute Sanger whose daughter had recently died, Sanger was arrested again in 1916. She served a short jail term for opening the first birth control clinic in Brooklyn, New York.

Sanger believed that the quickest way to change the law was to challenge its authority. Publicizing her cause through lectures, pamphlets, and several journals, she continued her strategy of antagonizing authorities. The strategy put the government on the defensive and in the position of prosecuting a woman who had devoted her life to humanitarian causes. She was especially pleased anytime her efforts were censored and saw many advantages to being "gagged." While it silenced her, it made millions of others talk about her and more importantly talk about the birth control movement. She established a wide variety of organizations to campaign for birth control, including the American Birth Control League in 1921, which aimed to cultivate mainstream respectability for birth control; the Birth Control Clinical Research Bureau in 1923, which studied and provided gynecological and contraceptive services; and the National Committee on Federal Legislation for Birth Control in 1929, which lobbied for legislation granting doctors the right to disseminate contraceptives. In 1942 the Birth Control Federation of America became the Planned Parenthood Federation of America.

Sanger was criticized on all fronts. The Catholic Church opposed her work and many doctors remained hostile to her efforts. It took the American Medical Association until 1937 to decide to endorse birth control as a viable medical treatment. Her methods were criticized as too disruptive by even many of the organizations she helped found. She resigned as president of the American Birth Control League in 1928 because the group viewed her exclusively feminist focus as a liability. When in 1939 the American Birth Control League and the Birth Control Clinical Research Bureau were merged into the Birth Control Federation of America, they hesitated to include the term "birth control" because it was considered too aggressive.

The idea of birth control steadily gained public acceptance. By 1936 more than 70 percent of individuals polled believed the distribution of birth control information should be legalized. The right of married women to plan their family was seen by sociologists as the natural result of the economic pressures facing society and the transformation of the United States from a largely agricultural nation, where large families were assets, to a largely industrial nation where large families were liabilities. Margaret Sanger's birth control movement was evolving during the Great Depression from radical social protest to mainstream medical advice.

The Changing Nature of the New Deal

The 1940 National Institute of Government gathered more than five thousand women in Washington. They were to meet with the government administrators in charge of solving the economic and social problems of the country. Graduates of Dewson's Reporter Program, these democratic women were knowledgeable, insightful, and interested in New Deal programs. When Dewson, who came out of retirement to attend the meeting, introduced the speakers at the celebratory dinner held the last night she felt much pride. She could look at the audience and see the success of her Reporter Plan and look at the speakers' table where the long line of highly qualified women was a vivid demonstration to the vital role played by women in Roosevelt's administration. What was less evident at the dinner and indeed during the three-day institute was how long these changes would last.

As the 1930s drew to a close, women's progress in the government also slowed. Dewson realized the changes made were just a start that had not stood the test of time. There were very pragmatic reasons for the slowdown. The New Deal was changing in the late 1930s. Spending for many New Deal programs was being reduced or eliminated outright. As new government agencies were the places of greatest opportunity for women, decreased funding meant decreased opportunities. The women themselves were also a factor. By 1940 Molly Dewson had retired. Eleanor Roosevelt's focus was shifting to international concerns and to broader civil rights issues.

It was Dewson's tenacity and Eleanor Roosevelt's attention that had formed the basis of the women's network. Through their efforts and because of the talent of the individuals placed in the government, the number of women placed in the administration during the New Deal grew from 12 to 35 during the first year of the New Deal. By 1940 there were 55 women holding prominent government positions. Women's politics went into a holding pattern as the emphasis switched from the New Deal to the growing conflict in Europe. The role they played in politics and in public life had lost its spotlight and its novelty.

Contributing Forces

Florence Kelley and the National Consumers' League

The women's network of the 1930s had its start in the Progressive era. Many organizations and movements, founded in the late 1890s and early 1900s, served as the training grounds for social workers. Social work was a profession still in its infancy but became the profession of choice for many women active in the New Deal. Grace Abbott, Mary Anderson, Molly Dewson, and Frances Perkins were all drawn to settlement houses in Chicago and New York. Settlement houses provided charitable services to its surrounding community while spurring social reform. These houses were modeled after Hull House, a female community founded by Jane Addams in 1889 in a poor section of Chicago.

One of Hull House's most notable graduates was Progressive reformer Florence Kelley, who lived there while studying the conditions of Chicago sweatshops. In 1899 Kelley moved to New York, where she joined the newly formed National Consumers' League (NCL) as its secretary. She was the driving force behind the NCL motto "investigate, agitate, legislate," and the leading promoter of protective labor legislation for women and children. Early activities of the NCL included the White Label program which awarded special labels to manufacturers that obeyed state factory laws, did not require overtime, and did not employ children under the age of 16. The NCL also campaigned to limit the number of hours a woman could work to 10 and provided research support to legislators seeking to restrict the woman's workday.

Although she supported laws that protected women and children, she also viewed this legislation as the necessary starting point towards achieving a safe workplace for both men and women. She used the same strategy when she began campaigning for a minimum wage for women in 1909. By 1919 fourteen states had passed minimum wage laws for women. These laws would later serve as the model for minimum wages for both men and women in the New Deal's Fair Labor Standards Law of 1938.

The NCL was also successful in its campaign for the U.S. Children's Bureau, which was founded in 1912. Kelley was particularly proud of the Children's Bureau's support for the Sheppard-Towner Act. The act had provided federal grants to health care programs for women and children.

In the 1920s the NCL employed many future government administrators including Frances Perkins, Clara Beyer, Josephine Roche, and Ellen Woodward. Its New York office was where Molly Dewson met Eleanor Roosevelt. NCL ties were so strong and its impact so great that Perkins later felt that the Consumers' League had been appointed as Secretary of Labor, not her. She was merely the figurehead who happened along.

The Women's Trade Union League

Founded four years after the National Consumers' League in 1903, the Women's Trade Union League (WTUL) sought to organize women workers into existing male-dominated trade unions. The

Jane Addams was a social worker who established a settlement house to help the needy in the impover-ished areas of Chicago. She won the Nobel Peace Prize in 1931. (AP/Wide World Photos. Reproduced by permission.)

strength of the WTUL was in its diverse membership. It included working class women, trade unionists, and female supporters from the middle and upper classes. Devoted to addressing the needs of women workers, the league advocated legislation that would limit hours and establish minimum wages for women. Emily Newell Blair, Jo Coffin, Caroline O'Day, Josephine Roche, Eleanor Roosevelt, Rose Schnei-derman, and Hilda Worthington Smith were involved with the WTUL.

In 1918 the U.S. Department of Labor created the Woman in Industry Service (WIIS) at the request of the WTUL to monitor women working in factories under U.S. defense contracts. The WIIS conducted nationwide studies to establish standard hours, wages, and condi-tions for women. At the end of the war President Woodrow Wilson (served 1913–1921) transitioned the WIIS into the Department of Labor's Women's Bureau and gave it the authority to enforce standards in facto-ries working on government contracts.

Suffrage

The most compelling experience for many of the women active in the New Deal was the fight to achieve suffrage. Dewson often fondly referred to her time spent campaigning for suffrage in Massachusetts. For women such as Hilda Worthington Smith, who was struggling to establish her career, the experience was revolutionary and led to many other advances as well. Many of the women who later worked in Roosevelt's administration during the New Deal held leadership positions in the suffrage movement. The only difference of opinion among them was related to the tactics used by various groups.

Calls for women's suffrage had been increasing steadily during the Progressive period. By 1910, however, only four states had given women the vote. The movement was revitalized when the women leaders realized that focusing on achieving suffrage would be the easiest way to eventually achieve social reform and that the best way to achieve suffrage would be through an amendment to the constitution rather than a state-by-state battle. The suffrage amendment became the common goal of groups as diverse as the General Federation of Women's Clubs and the Socialist Party of the United States.

The largest organization by far was the National American Woman Suffrage Association (NAWSA) which had more than two million members by 1914. NAWSA was led by Carrie Chapman Catt. Alice Paul and Lucy Burns joined NAWSA's Congressional Committee and encouraged Catt to adopt more flamboyant techniques. This included a suffrage parade down Pennsylvania Avenue on March 3, 1913, that was better attended than President-elect Woodrow Wilson's inauguration held the same day. Frustrated by NAWSA's more moderate approach, Paul and Burns split off from NAWSA to form the Congressional Union in 1914.

The Congressional Union, and its successor the National Woman's Party, concentrated on punishing the party in power be it Republican or Democrat. If the Democrats were in control of Congress, then the Congressional Union campaigned for Republicans regardless of any specific candidate's stand on the issue. By picketing the White House and organizing street marches and open-air meetings, the party's more dynamic methods appealed to a wide variety of women including working-class women, trade unionists, and wealthy socialites, including Alva Belmont whose millions provided the group's financial support.

NAWSA's tactics combined campaigns for state legislation with increasing support for the federal amendment in states where suffrage had already been

achieved. By 1918 the suffrage amendment was passed by the House of Representatives. The National Woman's Party laid down their picket signs at the White House. The victory was short-lived, as the Senate did not pass the amendment. It would take several more NAWSA state campaigns and continual picketing by NWP members before the amendment passed both houses. In August 1920 the thirty-sixth state ratified the amendment and suffrage was achieved.

Paul's Congressional Union, which had evolved into the Woman's Party in 1916 and the National Woman's Party in 1917, reorganized in the 1920s and began its new campaign for the Equal Rights Amendment. NAWSA shifted its focus to educating newly enfranchised women. In 1920 it renamed itself the League of Women Voters. The friendships formed during the suffrage movement set the foundation for pushing for greater roles of women in public life during the Great Depression.

Chivalry Between Women

During the decades preceding the Depression, the women who later worked in the New Deal established professional and personal relationships that would last the rest of their lives. Working for suffrage and for organizations promoting social change gave women the opportunity to develop a community dedicated to reforming local, and eventually national policy.

In 1929 Molly Dewson arranged a luncheon attended by 1,800 employees of the New York State Department of Labor. The guest of honor was Frances Perkins, a woman for whom Dewson had tremendous professional respect. During the lunch Perkins spoke of the growing cooperation that created the possibility of social justice. It was through the "wisdom of the women," that brought about social change. Later, when thanking Dewson for the luncheon and for the honor, Perkins wrote of the loyalty and fair mindedness growing among the nation's women. The strengths of their bonds formed through their volunteer and paid professional work were to sustain them through the 1930s and beyond.

Perspectives

The President

Franklin Roosevelt clearly respected women and was used to working with them. Dewson and Perkins both believed Roosevelt appreciated women's abilities more than other men of his generation did. He certainly had ample opportunity. As governor of New York he dealt with numerous women active in social

More About...
Working Women in Film

Women worked outside the home during the Great Depression, although rarely in the manner or with the morals portrayed in Hollywood films of the decade. While films about career women were very common in the 1930s and early 1940s, they seldom had anything good to say about the lives of their main characters. Barbara Stanwyck, Katherine Hepburn, Joan Crawford, and Bette Davis played writers, lawyers, doctors, artists, and nurses. Rosalind Russell alone played more than 20 different professional women. One of the more common roles in the Great Depression was the newspaper reporter with Bette Davis, Rosalind Russell, Jean Arthur, and Katherine Hepburn all taking on the job in film.

Typically career women fell into a few well-defined categories. The most consistent ending for a career woman in the Hollywood films of the 1930s and early 1940s is the happy renunciation of her job for the love of her man. In the 1932 film *Forbidden,* Barbara Stanwyck plays a librarian who's bored with her job and cashes out her bank account to take an ocean cruise where she naturally finds love. Bette Davis gives up the newspaper business in the 1935 *Front Page* for true love. Katherine Hepburn plays the *Woman of the Year* in the 1942 film loosely based on the life of journalist Dorothy Thompson. Marrying Spencer Tracey early in the film, she attempts to give up her career for full-time motherhood. While she is an abysmal failure in the kitchen and in the nursery, she is patted nicely on the head and consoled as the movie ends. Rosalind Russell walks away from a successful career as well in the 1941 *Take a Letter Darling* to follow her man At least in the movies women work until they find their husband, then they quit their not-so-satisfying job and go home happy contrary to real life with husbands losing jobs due to the Depression.

The ones who do not give up their job are rewarded according to how far they stray from society's chosen path. While Joan Crawford's character transitions from a bored socialite to a responsible family girl with a "man-sized job" until the stock market crashes and ruins her rich family in *Dance Fools Dance,* her character in *Grand Hotel,* a secretary who sleeps around on the side, has less moral integrity. Barbara Stanwyck plays a woman who sleeps her way to the top of a Wall Street firm in *Baby Face.* In the movies the woman who refuses to give up her career is eventually destroyed emotionally, or financially, or physically. According to Hollywood, clearly career women lacked morals and they get what they deserved.

---

reform and in politics. Working with women at the national level was a natural development of working with women at the state and local level. Through Eleanor, Franklin met numerous independent and intelligent women. Eleanor's business partners Nancy Cook and Marion Dickerman lived with them on the Hyde Park estate. He had known Frances Perkins since 1910 and was very familiar with her career long before he had ever thought of hiring her as Industrial Commissioner of New York or as Secretary of Labor.

Roosevelt also understood the importance of women to the Democratic Party, what Dewson referred to as other potential value. Women were a political force that was still waiting to be tapped. Critics have called Roosevelt a "ladies' man" partial to flattery and flirting. That even though he appointed women to positions never before held by women, they never made it to his inner circle. He was willing to give them the job and use the infor- mation they reported to him but their influence was limited. Women were never his primary advisors and he had his limits in how far he would go to court their vote.

The Nation

Roosevelt's predominantly high opinion of women was not necessarily held by the rest of the nation. American society during the Great Depression was often openly hostile to the almost 25 percent of women who worked outside their homes. While they continued to increase their numbers in the work force, progress during the Depression occurred despite severe economic dislocations and public opposition. Long hours and low wages were the norm, with the women's average yearly pay being $525, as compared to $1,027 for men. Married women who worked were particularly resented because the public believed their place was in the home, taking care of their children.

Those women that did work were taking jobs away from men during a time of job shortages.

It was rarely viewed as an economic necessity for women to work. Most believed women worked strictly for "pin money," a little bit of extra spending cash. Because of these stereotypes, discriminating against a married woman's right to work was perfectly acceptable. Teachers were affected the most. A 1930–1931 National Education Association survey reported that 77 percent of 1,500 school systems would not hire married women. Sixty-three percent dismissed women teachers if they married. By 1939 restrictions against hiring women existed in 84 percent of insurance companies, 65 percent of banks, and 63 percent of public utilities. Section 213 of the Economy Act was merely the federal stamp of approval on well-entrenched state and local traditions.

International Perspectives

Similar restrictions on women in public life were present in other countries. While England had preceded the United States in appointing a woman to their cabinet—Margaret G. Bondfield was their Minister of Labor—the rise in fascism and totalitarian regimes spawned back-to-the-home movements in both Italy and Germany. The NWP journal deplored the situation in Germany. They called on women to resist being kept out of the workforce and being regarded simply in terms of their childbearing functions. During the 1930s the NWP lobbied the League of Nations to approve the Equal Rights Treaty.

Although the United States was not a member of the League of Nations, NWP members used their own memberships in international women's groups to bring the treaty, the international version of the ERA, before the League. In 1935 the Juridical Commission of the League of Nations debated the Equal Rights Treaty for several days. After much discussion, the treaty was booted back for further study. Member governments were to decide the political status of women while the International Labour Office (ILO) was to study and make recommendations on protective legislation. Mary Anderson and the Women's Bureau staunchly opposed the Equal Rights Treaty telling ILO representatives that the NWP did not have the best interests of working women in mind. It was a much harder argument to make in Europe where women were far more afraid of their loss of economic opportunities if the ERA should be adopted.

In 1937 NWP representatives recommended four amendments to the League covenant then under revision. Women on both sides of the debate agreed with demands for suffrage, independent citizenship for married women, and full voting rights to all League bodies. They once again split over the Equal Rights Treaty and its rejection of protective legislation. Once again no progress was made. Alice Paul's newly founded World Woman's Party continued to support the Equal Rights Treaty and was successful in affiliating itself with several European feminist associations. Unfortunately most of them disappeared in the growing worldwide conflict leading to World War II (1939–1945). Alice Paul returned home as well.

Impact

During the 1940s, as the focus shifted from Depression to war, President Roosevelt placed social programs on hold. He began to appoint women as tokens only, in small departments without real opportunity to impact policy. While no woman put in place during the New Deal was removed from office, they were not necessarily replaced with women when they retired or moved on from political life. President Harry Truman (served 1945–1953) thanked Frances Perkins on the occasion of her retirement for the extraordinary achievements of her tenure. He promptly named as her successor Lewis B. Schwellenback, a former colleague of his from the Senate.

In 1953 the Women's Division of the DNC was abolished and its functions absorbed into the main branch of the organization. Presented as an advancement, the integration was seen by many women as a setback. Although many women active in the New Deal had retired, they still watched and commented. After John F. Kennedy (served 1961–1963) was elected president, Dewson wrote Clara Beyer that his only weakness was not being aware of what the solid support of women could mean for him politically. Eleanor Roosevelt was also watching. When Kennedy's first 240 appointments included only nine women, she paid him a visit bearing her own list of women qualified to help lead his administration.

Kennedy responded by asking her to chair his Commission on the Status of Women. The commission revitalized the women's movement. While it did not endorse the ERA it did agree that women needed to be considered equal under the law. This renewed interest in the rights of women resulted in the founding of the National Organization for Women (NOW) in 1966 to provide a means for women to pressure the government. Four years later, Martha Griffiths, a Democrat from Michigan reintroduced the ERA into the House of Representatives. The House approved the ERA and in 1972 the Senate followed suit.

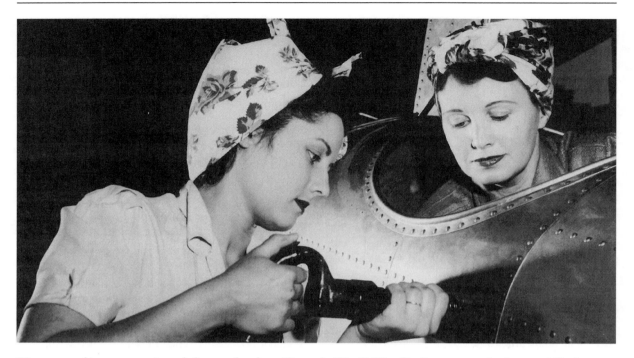

Women working on an aircraft for use by the military in World War II. One woman looks on while the other installs rivets. "Rosie the Riveter" became representative of all women who worked to support the war effort. (Archive Photos. Reproduced by permission.)

Although almost half the states immediately approved the Amendment, the ratification movement was hampered by a well-financed anti-ERA coalition. Even though the ERA was supported by a widespread coalition of groups, it once again failed to be ratified.

Notable People

Grace Abbott (1878–1939). Grace Abbott was best known for her years spent at the Department of Labor's Children's Bureau. She became Chief of the Bureau in 1921 and remained its head until 1934 when she turned the Bureau over to Katherine Lenroot.

Abbott was born in Nebraska to a family active in politics and in social welfare. Her father was a politician, her mother campaigned against slavery and for women's suffrage, and her sister Edith, with whom she maintained a life-long personal and professional relationship, was a scholar of economics, history, and social welfare. Abbott left Nebraska for Chicago where she lived at Hull House with Jane Addams. There she pursued work advocating for the rights of immigrants and for the rights of working class women. She joined the Department of Labor's newly formed

Children's Bureau in 1917 and worked two years for its founding chief Julia Lathrop whom she succeeded in 1921. As chief of the Children's Bureau, Abbott administered the Sheppard-Towner Act, the first legislation to provide federally matched grants to state for maternal and child health programs.

A life-long Republican, she and her sister campaigned heavily for the election of Herbert Hoover in 1928 whom they viewed as a tireless advocate for children's welfare. Their opinion of him soured when he supported efforts to transfer the health functions of the Children's Bureau over to the Department of Public Health and when he named William Doak as his Secretary of Labor even though Abbott was heavily favored. Unlike Abbott who spoke publicly of her concerns about the depth of the economic crisis during the early years of the Great Depression, Doak shared Hoover's optimistic conviction that federal involvement was dangerous.

Abbott believed strongly that without the support of organized labor and without legislation that guaranteed a certain level of pay and restricted the number of hours worked, women and children were easily exploited by industrial interests. She was actively involved during the 1920s and 1930s with National Consumers' League and the Women's Trade Union

League. Abbott wrote numerous articles and books on immigration and child welfare. She also served as president of the National Conference of Social Work.

Even though Abbott left the Children's Bureau in 1934 for an academic position at the University of Chicago School of Social Service Administration, she maintained her relationship with the organization as a dollar-a-year consultant. She contributed heavily during the New Deal to the provisions for mothers and children in the Social Security Act of 1935. Abbott suggested a broad and comprehensive children's program that included maternal and child health programs, child welfare services, neglected and delinquent child services, and aid to dependent children. She died in 1939 from tuberculosis.

Mary Anderson (1872–1964). Mary Anderson served as Chief of the Department of Labor's Women's Bureau from 1920 to 1944. A teenage immigrant, Anderson worked in the garment and shoe industries in Chicago. She became involved with the Women's Trade Union League (WTUL) in 1905 and maintained a lifelong affiliation and interest in their activities. She served as assistant director of the World War I (1914–1918) Women in Industry Service and was eventually named director of the Women's Bureau when Congress approved the bureau as a permanent addition to the Department of Labor.

Particularly concerned with educating women on their rights as workers, she organized a series of summer schools for women workers held at Bryn Mawr College. Although Anderson was a registered Republican, she often voted for Democratic candidates and considered the interests of women to be above partisan politics. She fervently believed in protective labor legislation that set hours and wages for women and actively campaigned against the Equal Rights Amendment proposed by Alice Paul and the National Women's Party and the League of Nation's Equal Rights Treaty. In 1936 she proposed the Woman's Charter, a treaty which attempted to unite women's social reform groups. Anderson later called the Charter, which promoted protective legislation for women a total failure.

Mary McLeod Bethune (1875–1955). Bethune was the daughter of former slaves who emphasized the importance of education. Bethune began her career as an educator. After teaching in several schools throughout the South, she married in 1898 and had one son. In 1899 Bethune moved to Florida where five years later she founded a school for black American girls. Starting with only five students she nurtured the school for over 20 years until 1925, when she merged the school with the Cookman Institute to form the co-

educational Bethune Cookman College. She was also active in the Florida Federation of Colored Women's Clubs from 1917 to 1925 and served as president of the Southeastern Federation of Colored Women's Clubs from 1920 to 1925.

Although Bethune campaigned for suffrage with the Equal Suffrage League, an offshoot of the National Association of Colored Women, and encouraged black American women to vote after suffrage was achieved, she always put the fight against racial discrimination before the fight for gender equality. She did, however, have a lifelong intense belief in the talents and abilities of women.

Bethune continued her public service career serving on the National Urban League's Executive Board. She founded the National Council Negro Women and served as president of the National Association of Colored Women's Clubs and as vice-president of the National Association for the Advancement of Colored People (NAACP). In 1932 Ida Tarbell named Bethune as one of the 50 greatest American women.

Her work in Washington started during President Calvin Coolidge's (served 1923–1929) presidency when she was invited to attend his Child Welfare Conference in 1928. President Herbert Hoover extended a similar invitation to his Conference on Child Health in 1930. Bethune developed close ties with both Eleanor and Franklin Roosevelt. She had known Eleanor since the early 1920s. As part of the Roosevelt administration Bethune was the Negro Affairs Director for the National Youth Administration (NYA) and was leader of a group of black American officials in federal agencies, known as the "Black Cabinet," who informally advised the president. Bethune died in 1955.

Clara Mortenson Beyer (1892–1990). Clara Beyer served in a number of positions in Roosevelt's administration rising to be Associate Director of the Division of Labor Standards within the Department of Labor from 1934 to 1957. Her career began in education. After she received a graduate degree from the University of California, she taught labor economics at Bryn Mawr. She moved on to government work holding positions with the War Labor Policies Board during World War I and the District of Columbia Minimum Wage Board.

In 1920 she married Otto Beyer, and in the following five years she gave birth to three sons. While her children were young, she worked part-time at the National Consumers League and was also active in the League of Women Voters. Molly Dewson, who worked with Clara Beyer at the Consumers League, kept after Clara to return to work full-time. She finally joined the Children's Bureau in 1928. Beyer, who believed women should return to work after their children were in school, later became director of the Children Bureau's Industrial Department. When the Department of Labor decided to establish a Division of Labor Standards in 1934, Beyer organized the department and was eventually named its associate director.

Emily Newell Blair (1877–1951). Even though Emily Blair called herself a "discouraged feminist" in 1931, she served the Roosevelt administration in the National Recovery Administration (NRA), a New Deal program aimed at recovery of industry and labor from the Great Depression. Born in Missouri, Blair attended college in Maryland and in Missouri without completing a degree. She married in 1900 and had two children. Her early career was spent campaigning for suffrage and writing numerous stories and articles. She founded and edited the *Missouri Woman* from 1914 to 1916 and was associate editor of *Good Housekeeping* from 1925 to 1933. Her writing credits also include a feminist novel published in 1931 that discussed the difficulties of combining career with marriage.

After World War I Blair helped organize the League of Women Voters and the Women's National Democratic Club. She spearheaded efforts to establish more than two thousand women's clubs and helped organized the "Schools of Democracy" which instructed women on party issues. By 1928 she was one of the most recognized Democratic women in the country and served as vice-chair of the DNC. Blair was very active in Roosevelt's 1932 campaign. She joined the Consumers' Advisory Board of the National Recovery Administration (NRA) in 1933 and chaired the board briefly in 1935 until it was declared unconstitutional. Blair's husband also served in the government as assistant attorney general. Blair's last public position was with the women's interest section of the War Department's bureau of public relations, which she ran until 1944. As was typical of many other Democratic women working in Roosevelt's administration, Blair believed that women's interests in politics were on par with men's. She disdained the title of feminist but believed that women would only achieve success if they supported each other until they achieved power.

Mary (Molly) Dewson (1874–1962). Although Dewson was widely acknowledged as the driving political force behind securing so many women prominent positions in the New Deal, she held relatively few political positions herself. The head of the Women's Division of the Democratic National Committee from 1932 to 1937, Dewson entered politics for the first

time at the age of 54 during Al Smith's 1928 presidential bid at the request of Eleanor Roosevelt who was coordinating the women's campaign.

Molly Dewson was born in Massachusetts. She graduated from Wellesley College in 1897 and began a career in social work. She was Superintendent of the Parole Department of the Massachusetts State Industrial School for Girls until 1912. It was during her tenure at the parole board that she met her partner of 52 years Polly Porter. In addition to helping draft Massachusetts' model minimum wage law, Dewson was also very active campaigning for women's suffrage with the National American Women's Suffrage Association.

As was typical of most of her career, she enjoyed the early stages of a project or a cause and would dedicate herself fully to it. Once the solution was figured out or the goal within sight, she moved on, usually giving herself a period to rest and reflect on what to do next. This was certainly the case with the national campaign for suffrage, which she left along with the dairy farm she and Porter had established, to travel together to France during World War I. There they worked for the Red Cross. After her return to the United States, Grace Abbott offered her a job at the Children's Bureau. Dewson chose to remain in New York and went to work for Florence Kelley at the National Consumers' League. Dewson also served as executive secretary of the Women's City Club of New York, a women's reform group. It was through these groups that she met and worked closely with Eleanor Roosevelt for the first time.

She served as floor manager for women at the 1932 National Democratic Convention and from 1932 to 1934 she was head of the women's division of the Democratic Party. She continued as Chairman of the Advisory Committee to the Women's Division and as Vice-Chairman of the Democratic National Committee. During these years she lobbied Franklin Roosevelt to place women in prominent political positions. Her most notable successes were Frances Perkins as Secretary of Labor, Ruth Owen as ambassador to Denmark, and Florence Allen to the U.S. Circuit Court of Appeals. Dewson believed her efforts were crucial not only for women's advancement in politics but also to show that women could handle the responsibilities. She toed a cautious line though, making sure never to appear too strident. She claimed not to be a feminist but a supporter of the Democratic Party and trying to increase its connection to women.

During Roosevelt's 1936 presidential campaign, Dewson's Women's Division organized 80,000 women to get out the vote for him. The success of the

Women's Division in the 1936 campaign was to be her last work for the Roosevelts. She told Eleanor that six years was enough. She worked briefly on the Social Security Board in 1937 at Roosevelt's request but retired after only nine months because of poor health. She spent the rest of her years in Maine at the home she shared with Porter.

In 1954 Eleanor Roosevelt and Lorena Hickok dedicated their book about women in politics, *Ladies of Courage,* to Dewson.

Jane Margueretta Hoey (1892–1968). Jane Hoey served as Director of the Bureau of Public Assistance from 1936 to 1953. After earning a graduate degree, Jane Hoey began her career in social work. Hired by Harry Hopkins, she worked in New York on the Board of Child Welfare from 1916 until 1917. She later spent 10 years as the Assistant Director of the Health Division of the Welfare Council of New York.

In 1936, after many attempts by Roosevelt and Hopkins to place her in a federal post, she finally accepted the job of organizing the Social Security Administration's Bureau of Public Assistance. It was a job that she felt would best utilize her talents as a social worker. She worked at the Bureau until 1953. From 1953 until 1957 she served as Director of Social Research for the National Tuberculosis Association.

Katharine Fredrica Lenroot (1891–1982). Katherine Lenroot succeeded Grace Abbott as Chief of the Children's Bureau in 1934. She held that position until 1949. She graduated from the University of Wisconsin in 1912 and her first professional job was with Wisconsin's Industrial Commission. She joined the Children's Bureau in 1914 as a special investigator. She also served as president of the National Conference of Social Work. She worked full-time for two years on the Social Security Act of 1935 and co-authored its section on aid to dependent children. She also suggested a legal strategy for enforcing child labor regulations. It was later backed by Frances Perkins and incorporated into the New Deal's 1938 Fair Labor Standards Act.

Alice Stokes Paul (1885–1977). Alice Paul, ERA supporter and founder of the National Woman's Party, earned her PhD in Sociology from the University of Pennsylvania. She also received law degrees from Washington College of Law and from American University. Paul was heavily influenced by British suffragist Emmaline Pankhurst who advocated violence, riots, arson, and hunger strikes in order to achieve women's suffrage in England. In 1913 Paul split off from the more mainstream National American Women Suffrage Association to form the Congressional

Union. The Union used picketing, hunger strikes, and parades to protest the lack of women's suffrage.

Once the Nineteenth Amendment was passed, Paul disbanded the Congressional Union and formed the National Woman's Party (NWP). In 1923 the NWP drafted the first version of the Equal Rights Amendment. Although publicly retired from the NWP, Paul served as a behind-the-scenes presence throughout the 1920s and 1930s as the NWP fought for adoption of the ERA. The NWP's goal was to achieve complete legal equality for women through the ERA in the United States and the Equal Rights Treaty and the Equal Nationality Treaty internationally. Paul and her party found themselves perpetually in conflict with social reformers such as Mary Anderson, Grace Abbott, and Frances Perkins because they believed that protective legislation restricted economic opportunities for women.

Paul spent most of the 1930s campaigning in Europe and in 1938 formed the World Woman's Party, which according to Paul would help defend the women of the world against unjust treaties. With the approach of World War II, the organization floundered. Paul returned to the United States in 1941.

Frances Perkins (1880–1965). Secretary of Labor from 1933 to 1945, Frances Perkins was the first woman to be appointed to a cabinet-level position. Perkins was raised in Massachusetts and graduated from Mount Holyoke College in 1902. She began her career as a social worker and spent time at both Hull House and the Chicago Commons. She moved to New York in 1910 to work on a study of Hell's Kitchen, a part of the city wrought with high unemployment and crime. There she completed her Master's degree in sociology and economics at Columbia.

Perkins began a long career advocating for labor legislation when she went to work for the National Consumers' League as a lobbyist for minimum wage legislation for women. She worked with Florence Kelley for the first time at the NCL and looked to her often for professional advice and mentoring. Perkins also served on the commission investigating the Triangle Fire, a factory fire in 1911 that killed 146 garment workers, most of them women who couldn't escape because the doors were locked. The experience profoundly impacted Perkins belief in the need for legislation that would protect working class women from dangerous working conditions.

Governor Al Smith of New York appointed Perkins to the State Industrial Commission in 1918 and later in 1926 appointed her chairman. When Franklin Roosevelt became governor in 1928, he promoted her to Industrial Commissioner of the State of

Ellen S. Woodward is sworn in as a member of the Social Security Board on December 30, 1938 as Eleanor Roosevelt looks on. (AP/Wide World Photos. Reproduced by permission.)

New York, the head of the state department of labor. Perkins was the first woman to run the largest state department of labor in the country.

When Roosevelt was elected president, he named Frances Perkins as the new Secretary of Labor, another first for Perkins, as no other woman had ever been appointed to the cabinet. With the exception of Secretary of Interior Harold Ickes, she was the Roosevelt's longest serving cabinet member retiring from the Department of Labor only after his death. She continued to work for the federal government on the Civil Service Commission until 1953. After her retirement from the government, she became a highly successful lecturer.

Josephine Roche (1886–1976). Josephine Roche held a variety of positions in Roosevelt's administration. She graduated from Vassar in 1908 and received a graduate degree from Columbia in 1910 where she met and became friends with Frances Perkins. She had a diverse career including director of a juvenile court's girls' department and editorial director of the of the Children's Bureau. In 1927 she returned to her home state of Colorado to run her father's coal mines. Her progressive approach to labor relations brought her to national attention. Roosevelt appointed her to be the first woman Assistant Secretary of the Treasury in 1934.

At the Treasury Roche was in charge of health service and welfare work and was responsible for the United States Public Health Service. In 1935 she became Chairman of the Executive Committee of the National Youth Administration. Although she resigned her Treasury position in 1937, she continued to chair the Interdepartmental Health Committee. Roche also became president of the National Consumers' League from 1938 to 1944. She ended her career at the United Mine Workers Union Welfare and Retirement Fund where she served as director from 1947 to 1971.

Nellie Tayloe Ross (1876–1977). Nellie Tayloe Ross served as the first woman Director of the Mint. She was also the first woman to be elected governor in the United States. Born in Missouri she was educated in Nebraska and married William Bradford Ross in 1902. For more than 20 years, Ross was a full-time wife and mother raising four sons, two of whom died. Her husband died before completing his second year as governor of Wyoming. Ross decided to run as the democratic candidate for governor in the special election to replace her husband. She told the voting public that she would be governed by her husband's goals and principles.

Elected governor in 1924, Ross felt the need to demonstrate the abilities of women to hold executive officer. In a speech to the National Women's Democratic Club dinner in 1925, Ross declared that women "must speak a new language in politics." In 1926 Ross was renominated as the democratic candidate for governor but lost the election. She lectured about her experiences as governor and became a vice-chair of the Democratic National Committee in 1928. A brief campaign to name her Al Smith's vice presidential candidate was defeated.

From 1929 to 1932 she was in charge of the national Democratic Party's women's activities. She campaigned for Franklin Roosevelt, and after Roosevelt's election he appointed her as director of the U.S. Mint. As director of the Mint, Ross administered eight institutions through the Great Depression and World War II into the postwar period. She retired from the Mint in 1952.

Rose Schneiderman (1882–1972). When Rose Schneiderman became the only woman member of the Labor Advisory Board of the National Recovery Administration (NRA), she was hailed in the national press as the leader of nine million American working women. A lifelong labor activist, Schneiderman emigrated from Russian Poland in 1890. Her education stopped in the eighth grade when she began work at the age of 13 as a cap-maker.

By 1905 she had taught herself the theory of trade unionism and joined the Women's Trade Union League. By 1910 she was a full-time organizer for its New York branch. She campaigned with the National American Woman Suffrage Association and in 1919 she traveled with Mary Anderson to represent women workers at the Paris Peace Conference. During the 1920s Schneideman served as president of both the New York and National Women's Trade Union Leagues. During these years she became a close friend of Eleanor Roosevelt's.

Schneiderman worked closely with Mary Anderson on the Bryn Mawr Summer School for Industrial Workers. After her job on the National Recovery Administration was finished, she returned to New York where she continued her WTUL work and served as New York Secretary of Labor from 1937 to 1943. She remained WTUL president until the National and New York Leagues disbanded in 1950 and 1955.

Sue Shelton White (1887–1943). Sue Shelton White is often portrayed as the bridge between mainstream and more radical suffrage groups. Born in Tennessee, she was very active in the Tennessee's suffrage fight setting up local suffrage groups from 1913 to 1920. In 1919 she was imprisoned for burning President Wilson in effigy. She worked as a teacher and a court reporter before receiving her law degree in

Washington in 1923. In 1930 she went to work for the Women's Division of the Democratic National Committee. She held a variety of positions during the 1930s including jobs with the Consumers' Division of the National Recovery Administration and the Social Security Board. By 1938 she was special assistant to the board's general counsel.

Ellen Sullivan Woodward (1887–1971). Woodward served as the administrator from 1933 to 1938 of the Works Progress Administration (WPA) and as a member of the Social Security Board from 1938 to 1946. Raised in Mississippi as the daughter of a politician and lawyer, Woodward graduated from college in 1905. She married at the age of 19 and had one son born in 1909. After being widowed in 1925, she pursued a career in state politics and social work culminating in her 1932 appointment to the Mississippi State Board of Public Welfare where her expertise in relief administration brought her to national attention.

Molly Dewson recommended Woodward to Harry Hopkins. Hopkins brought her to Washington in 1933 to set up the women's divisions of the Civil Works Administration and the Federal Emergency Relief Administration. In 1936 Woodward headed the Women's and Professional Projects division for the WPA. Dewson again recommended her to take over Dewson's position on the Social Security Board. Woodward later left the Social Security Board to work at the United Nations. She joined the Federal Security Agency in 1946 where she was director until her retirement in 1954.

Primary Sources

Women and the WPA

Working to provide women with work relief from the Great Depression, Ellen Woodward oversaw the work of 450,000 women through the Women's and Professional Projects of the WPA. The WPA programs had women actively pursuing domestic projects, library work, public health programs, and research services. Woodward delivered an overview of these programs to the Democratic Women's Regional Conference for Southeastern States on March 19, 1936 (from the WPA Papers, National Archives):

> There are two major functions of the Women's Division. The first is to develop and carry on in the various States work projects for eligible women on relief rolls—projects which are useful to the community and to the individual as well.
>
> If a woman has a profession or trade, we endeavor to place her on a project in her own field. If she is untrained

but must make her own living, we try to give her training which will prepare her for some useful work. The second function of the Women's Division is to see that employable women on relief rolls who are eligible for work receive equal consideration with men in this program.

I wonder whether the women in this country, and men too, realize just what the creation of the Women's Division in such a program signifies. It means the Administration is determined that women shall receive their fair share of work and that it has made special provision for the enforcement of that policy. When the President said that no able-bodied citizens were to be allowed to deteriorate on relief but must be given jobs, he meant women as well as men. Harry L. Hopkins, our Federal Administrator, has repeatedly stated that "needy women shall receive equal consideration with needy men." As evidence that this policy is being carried out, there was a study made about six or eight months ago, and it was found that at that time 53 percent of all the men who were eligible for work were working, and that 53 percent of all the women eligible for work were also working. At this particular time in the new program, approximately 65 percent of the employable women are now at work, and new projects are rapidly being put into operation to take care of the additional number who are eligible.

To fully appreciate the progress we are making, let's go back for a moment to the fall of 1933, when the Work Program for women started. There was no precedent to follow, for no program of the kind had ever been carried out in any country on a national basis.

We have come a long way since then and are no longer novices at this business of putting women to work. Under the past program we were able to give employment to some 350,000 women. Under the present program the number is more than 100,000. The knowledge we gained from the last two years' experience has been of immeasurable value to us in planning for the present Work Program. We know who these people are now, where they live and in general what they can ... be trained to do. We have learned that they represent some 250 different occupational classifications. We have learned to design projects which not only give women employment, but which increase their skill and keep them employable—so they will be ready to take advantage of the first opportunities for jobs in private industry.

Memories of Frances Perkins

Frances Perkins authored a book titled *The Roosevelt I Knew* in 1946, the year after Franklin Roosevelt's death. The volume presents an excellent first hand account of the first women to hold a cabinet position in U.S. history. The following excerpts, taken from the chapter describing the development of the Social Security Act, highlights the great deal of trust the president placed in Perkins (pp. 278–299).

> Before his Inauguration in 1933 Roosevelt had agreed that we should explore at once methods for setting up unemployment and old-age insurance in the United States . . . .

The President urged me to discuss the matter in as many groups as possible. . .

Hearings were held before Congress. Effective people were invited to testify. I myself made over a hundred speeches in different parts of the country that year, always stressing social insurance as one of the methods for assisting the unemployed in times of depression and in preventing depressions. . .

It was evident to us that any system of social insurance would not relieve the accumulated poverty. Nor would it relieve the sufferings of the presently old and needy. Nevertheless, it was also evident that this was the time, above all times, to be foresighted about future problems of unemployment and unprotected old age. . .

I asked him if he thought it best for me to be chairman, since the public knew I favored the general idea. Perhaps it would be better, from the point of view of Congress and the public, if the Attorney General were chairman. He was quick in his response. "No, no. You care about this thing. You believe in it. Therefore I know you will put your back to it more than anyone else, and you will drive it through. You will see that something comes out, and we must not delay. I am convinced. We must have a program by next winter and it must be in operation before many more months have passed. . ."

Finally, one day during Christmas week, 1934, I issued an ultimatum that the Committee would meet at eight o'clock at my house. . . and that we would sit all night, if necessary, until we had decided the thorny question once and for all. We sat until two in the morning, and at the end we agreed. . .to a recommend a federal-state system. . .

When the law was signed by the President, we made a little ceremony in his office. . .As he was signing the copies of the bills with pens that would be given to its sponsors, the President looked up at me. "Frances, where is your pen?" he asked.

"I haven't got one," I replied.

"All right," he said to McIntyre, his secretary, "give me a first class pen for Frances." And he insisted on holding me responsible and thanking me personally in very appreciative terms.

Suggested Research Topics

- Trace the educational and career paths of Molly Dewson, Frances Perkins, and Eleanor Roosevelt. What conclusions can be drawn by their similarities and their differences?

- The following questions were asked to the public by the American Institute of Public Opinion in 1938 and 1939. The results were published in the *Public Opinion Quarterly* (volume 3, number 4, pp. 594–596) in an article entitled "Surveys, 1938–1939." How would you answer them?: (1) Do you approve or disapprove of the way Mrs. Roosevelt has conducted herself as "First Lady"?

(2) Do you think the president's wife should engage in any business activity that interests her if she doesn't do it for profit? (3) The Daughters of the American Revolution organization would not let a well-known black American singer give a concert in one of their halls. As a protest against this, Mrs. Franklin D. Roosevelt resigned from the organization. Do you approve of her action?

Bibliography

Sources

Becker, Susan D. *The Origins of the Equal Rights Amendment: American Feminism Between the Wars.* Westport: Greenwood Press, 1981.

Black, Allida M., ed. *Courage in a Dangerous World: The Political Writings of Eleanor Roosevelt.* New York: Columbia University Press, 1999.

Costin, Lela B. *Two Sisters for Social Justice: A Biography of Grace and Edith Abbott.* Urbana: University of Illinois Press, 1983.

Evans, Sara M. *Born for Liberty: A History of Women in America.* New York: Free Press, 1989.

Lott, John R. and Lawrence W. Kenney. "Did Women's Suffrage Change the Size and Scope of Government?" *Journal of Political Economy,* 107 (6) [1999]: 1163–1198.

Lowitt, Richard and Maurine Beasley, eds. *One Third of a Nation: Lorena Hickok Reports on the Great Depression.* Urbana: University of Illinois Press, 2000.

Mcluskey, Audrey Thomas and Elaine M. Smith, eds. *Mary McLeod Bethune: Building a Better World, Essays and Selected Documents.* Bloomington: Indiana University Press, 1999.

Mohr, Lillian Holmen. *Frances Perkins: That Woman in FDR's Cabinet.* North River Press, 1979.

Orleck, Annelise. *Common Sense and a Little Fire: Women and Working-Class Politics in the United States, 1900–1965.* Chapel Hill: University of North Carolina Press, 1995.

Roosevelt, Eleanor. *The Autobiography of Eleanor Roosevelt.* New York: Harper and Borthers Publishers, 1958.

Scharf, Lois. *To Work and to Wed: Female Employment, Feminism, and the Great Depression.* Westport: Greenwood Press, 1980.

Sochen, June. "Mildred Pierce and Women in Film." *American Quarterly,* 30 (1) [1978]: 3–20.

Ware, Susan. *Beyond Suffrage: Women in the New Deal.* Cambridge: Harvard University Press, 1981.

———. *Partner and I: Molly Dewson, Feminism, and New Deal Politics.* New Haven: Yale University Press, 1987.

Woodward, Ellen. "Address before the Democratic Women's Regional Conference for Southeastern States." WPA Papers, National Archives, Record Group 69, Series 737, Box 8. [cited March 6, 2002] available from the World Wide Web at http://newdeal.feri.org/texts/501.htm.

Young, J. William T. and Oscar Handlin, ed. *Eleanor Roosevelt: A Personal and Public Life 2nd Edition.* New York: Longman, 1999.

Further Reading

Conway, Jill Ker, ed. *Written by Herself: Autobiographies of American Women: An Anthology.* New York: Vintage Books, 1992.

Franklin D. Roosevelt Library and Digital Archives Web Site, available from the World Wide Web at http://www.fdrlibrary.marist.edu/index.html

Internet Women's History Sourcebook, available from the World Wide Web at http://www.fordham.edu/halsall/women/womensbook.html

National Women's History Project, available from the World Wide Web at http://www.nwhp.org/index.html

Suffragists Oral History Project Web Site, available from the World Wide Web at http://bancroft.berkeley.edu/ROHO/ohonline/suffragists.html

Ware, Susan. *Holding Their Own: American Women in the 1930s.* Boston: Twayne Publishers, 1982.

Young, J. William T. and Oscar Handlin, eds. *Eleanor Roosevelt: A Personal and Public Life 2nd Edition.* New York: Longman, 1999.

See Also

Democratic Coalition; Everyday Life; Hollywood; Photography; Social Security

Works Progress Administration

1935-1943   Introduction

Following his inauguration as President of the United States in March 1933, Franklin Delano Roosevelt (served 1933–1945) initiated a series of work relief programs that culminated in the Works Progress Administration (WPA) in 1935. The Works Progress Administration was a unique program designed to get the unemployed off of the relief—welfare—rolls by providing work at minimal pay until they could find work for a private business. The Great Depression had been steadily worsening for over three years by Roosevelt's inauguration. By early 1933, 25 percent of the workforce was unemployed amounting to over 12 million people. In the first few months of his presidency Roosevelt introduced the New Deal, a vast array of federal social and economic programs to bring relief to the struggling nation. As part of the New Deal, the WPA program was developed in response to the horrible unemployment and destitution of the time, which affected almost every aspect of society.

In a radio address on October 12, 1933, Harry Hopkins, Roosevelt's friend, advisor, director of the Federal Relief Emergency Administration (FERA), and future head of the WPA, said (as quoted in June Hopkins, p. 163): "Who are these fellow-citizens? Are they tramps? Are they hoboes and ne'erdowells? Are they unemployables? Are they people who are no good and who are incompetent? Take a look at them, if you have not, and see who they are. There is hardly a person...who does not know of an intimate friend,

people whom you have known all your life, fine hardworking, upstanding men and women who have gone overboard and been caught up in this.... They are carpenters, bricklayers, artisans, architects, engineers, clerks, stenographers, doctors, dentists, farmers, ministers."

It was for these carpenters, bricklayers, and artisans that the WPA was developed, but one unique aspect of it went beyond traditional workers. The WPA offered projects targeted at unemployed artists, musicians, writers and actors. It was these programs that were most innovative, most controversial, and of most enduring interest in American history. The cultural work relief programs promoted an extraordinary growth in authentically American art.

The cultural work relief programs gave voice to the America of the time—angry, scared, defiant. The work was sometimes wonderful, often bad, and occasionally very critical of America, capitalism, and the government. It was this aspect of the work relief programs that provided fodder for critics and ultimately led to the program's demise.

Roosevelt and Hopkins supported the WPA and believed that work relief is what a society that aspires to be the best provides for its citizens during a time of great distress. At the same time, it was seen as a way to prevent political opportunists from realizing more radical responses to the Great Depression—more general relief or even a Communist revolution. In the trauma of the Great Depression, demonstrations and rebellions were increasingly common. Communists had taken over Russia, forming the Soviet Union. Involved in the organization of unions, socialists and Communist activity was on the rise in the United States. Some saw the move to provide relief and later work programs as a way of heading off a Communist revolution.

From 1935 to 1943 the WPA provided millions of people with work and money during a very difficult time, however, it was never able to reach more than about one third of those eligible to receive its benefits. Millions more were left to the care, and often neglect, of state and local organizations. Regardless, the WPA was immensely important to a great many people, putting money in their pockets and hope for the future. It was a bold experiment in a time of bold actions.

Chronology:

1932: The College Art Association begins a relief program for artists in New York City called the Emergency Work Bureau (EWB, later called the Emergency Relief Bureau). The EWB began the Works Division of the Emergency Relief Bureau, which later became part of the WPA in 1935.

1933: The New Deal arrives as Public Works of Art Project (PWAP) is established, as are the Civil Works Administration (CWA, a precursor to the WPA), the Federal Employment Relief Administration (FERA), and the Civilian Conservation Corps (CCC).

May 6, 1935: The Works Progress Administration is founded as an independent agency designed to provide meaningful work and minimal pay to the unemployed.

1935: The Women's Division of the WPA is combined with the Professional Projects Division at the urging of Ellen Woodward.

1938: The House Subcommittee on Un-American Activities begins hearings on the WPA, with particular scrutiny falling on the Federal Theatre Project and the Federal Writers' Project.

1939: The Reorganization Act of 1939 makes the WPA part of the Federal Works Agency. The Federal Theater Project, the most controversial of all the WPA programs, is disbanded. The Works Progress Administration alters its name to Work Projects Administration and the National Youth Administration is transferred to the Federal Security Agency.

1941: The Federal Writers' Project becomes part of the Writers' Unit of War Services Division of the WPA.

1942: The NYA is placed under the War Manpower Commission.

1943: The WPA is disbanded.

Issue Summary

The early 1930s were a tumultuous time. Following the stock market crash in 1929 the economic situation continued to get worse as the Great Depression lingered on. Businesses including banks closed. More and more people became unemployed and entire families became homeless. The country was increasingly poor and frightened.

Harry Hopkins addresses the U.S. Conference of Mayors in November of 1935. Hopkins was the director of the Works Progress Administration (WPA) from 1935 to 1938. (AP/Wide World Photos. Reproduced by permission.)

In early 1933 Franklin Delano Roosevelt became President of the United States. Only three months earlier an historical demonstration took place as the poor marched on Washington, DC, in the National Hunger March. Roosevelt had wrestled with poverty and joblessness as governor of New York, implementing a number of innovative programs that would become models for future federal programs.

A month after taking office, the Roosevelt Administration launched the Civilian Conservation Corps (CCC). The CCC was a work relief program designed to employ a quarter-million young men to build hiking trails, fight forest fires, lay telephone lines, and build dams. Work relief was a concept that Roosevelt had implemented successfully in New York. Instead of providing money to sustain someone without a job, work relief programs provided a job, allowing the participant to earn money.

President Roosevelt was a strong believer in work relief. He felt that relief—often called direct relief, or "the dole," as in "being on the dole"—was detrimental to morale and to self-respect. He characterized federal relief as addictive and a destroyer of the human spirit. Roosevelt wanted to do away with such forms of relief.

Despite his reluctance to continue direct relief, shortly after founding the CCC, Roosevelt established the Federal Emergency Relief Administration. FERA was designed after the Temporary Emergency Relief Administration that Roosevelt had set up in New York when he was governor. FERA provided direct financial aid to the unemployed. Harry Hopkins, who had headed the state organization under Roosevelt, now headed FERA.

With winter weather approaching and people needing money for shelter and food, in November 1933 Roosevelt established the Civil Works Administration (CWA) to provide temporary jobs to a few million of the unemployed. The men would be employed on projects requiring little investment, such as cleaning neighborhoods and digging drainage ditches. It was the first real federal program in work relief and a precursor to 1935's Works Progress Administration. The CWA became the largest employer in the nation's history. It put four million people to work within four weeks.

Also in 1933, the Roosevelt Administration created the Public Works Administration (PWA) under the direction of Secretary of Interior Harold L. Ickes. The PWA was an ambitious program that employed workers to construct thousands of new public facilities all across the country. Construction included more than five hundred municipal water systems, almost three hundred hospitals, and more than five hundred schools. With the introduction of the Works Progress Administration in 1935, the PWA and the WPA were constantly battling for funding until the PWA was disbanded in 1939.

When the Roosevelt Administration created the Works Progress Administration (WPA) in 1935 it was largely to take over some responsibilities of the FERA, the PWA, and the CWA. Roosevelt reportedly decided on the name "Works Progress Administration," and could not be dissuaded from it, even though it did not make sense to many. Like the others the WPA was created to provide work relief for the unemployed. It was a huge program—the largest public works program ever attempted—in the number of people employed, in money expended, and in volume of results.

An Innovative Program

Roosevelt appointed Harry Hopkins, his trusted advisor and head of the FERA and the CWA to lead the WPA. Hopkins was a social worker with years of experience directing relief and work relief programs, many of those years for Roosevelt in New York. Hopkins was a proponent of work relief and the potential of the government to improve people's lives.

Roosevelt and Hopkins wanted to be sure that the WPA did not compete with private enterprise. To that end, wages were intentionally kept significantly below positions in the private sector. This was done even though astronomical unemployment percentages (well into the double digits) indicated that private sector jobs were unavailable. Throughout its brief history, the WPA wrestled with how to make the jobs sufficiently attractive to boost the morale of the unemployed workers, without making them so attractive that the workers would prefer them to private employment. Low wages were one way that the WPA jobs were made less attractive.

The desire not to compete with private sector jobs showed itself in other ways than depressed wages. Projects were specifically chosen so as not to compete with a private company's ability to get the job. This sometimes caused the perception that the WPA workers were not doing useful work.

Roosevelt and Hopkins also believed that work relief should not be demeaning, especially in this time of high unemployment. To that end they were proponents of eliminating the means test for qualifying for work relief. A means test was given to possible aid recipients to measure their level of need in order to determine if they were eligible for relief. By choosing to apply for a position within the Works Progress Administration, applicants were indicating that their situation was such that they required the wages to survive. Demeaning visits by social workers to prove one was sufficiently poor were not necessary.

President Roosevelt's goal was to provide employment to individuals currently on direct relief. He believed direct relief to be debilitating and demor-

alizing. As such the WPA regulations required that 90 percent of those hired had to come from relief rolls. This requirement had the unanticipated outcome of discriminating against those who held out the longest against going on the dole. The proud people who did everything they could to avoid direct relief sometimes were not eligible to be hired by the WPA. The WPA also had a requirement that only one member of a family could be employed, which inadvertently discriminated against women.

Roosevelt's belief that direct relief was demoralizing was not without supporters. Researchers studied the effects of relief and unemployment on workers. Studies showed that beyond the meager income the WPA provided, many workers reaped significant psychological benefits from working compared to accepting relief. Studies showed that WPA workers were more socially adjusted with higher morale than those on direct relief were. Workers claimed that relief without work was okay to keep from starving, but it damaged self-respect.

Previous New Deal work relief programs had been left largely to the states to administer. In a change of direction Roosevelt and Hopkins designed the WPA to be completely administered by the federal government. This was in keeping with their view of the role (or potential role) of the federal government to directly support the needs of society. It was also in response to the clearly poor job that many states had done administering previous work relief programs. The WPA as a federally administered work relief program was a huge undertaking. When it was at its largest, the Works Progress Administration employed 30,000 administrators and an average of 2.3 million workers per year between 1935 and 1940.

The WPA was a large and comprehensive organization. The largest number of people in WPA was employed in engineering and construction projects where most of the money from the WPA was directed. In addition the WPA supervised the National Youth Administration, which provided education and training and employment to students and young people. But the WPA is best know for its cultural projects, collectively called Federal One, which provided work relief to artists, musicians, writers, and actors. The Federal Theatre Project, the Federal Art Project, the Federal Music Project, the Federal Writers' Project and the Historical Records Survey were, variously, praised and criticized, and always controversial.

Building America in the WPA

The largest contribution of the WPA was work relief in construction and engineering projects. Fully

The WPA Road Construction Project provided many jobs and was just one of many public works programs that was implemented to create jobs for the unemployed during the Depression. (Corbis Corporation. Reproduced by permission.)

75 percent of the WPA workforce worked on engineering and construction projects. The WPA workers completed projects in almost every county in the United States.

During the earliest days of the WPA there were problems effectively allocating workers and choosing projects. Workers were often assigned to jobs without considering their skills or their abilities. Projects were not carefully chosen or properly supervised. The administrators of the WPA were responsible for the inappropriate allocations. These highly-educated administrators tended to view blue-collar workers as an undifferentiated mass, and made little attempt to understand the subtleties of skills or job requirements.

This misunderstanding led to the lingering perception that work done by WPA workers was not necessary—it was invented to give them something to do. Workers were often portrayed as lazy or inept. The problems with effectively using workers' skills and identifying appropriate projects, however, were largely resolved in the first year or so.

Regardless of these administrative problems, the WPA workers were highly productive. WPA workers built or repaired 1.2 million miles of culverts and laid 24,000 miles of sidewalks. They built almost 600,000

miles in new roads and repaired 32,000 miles of existing roads. They built 75,000 bridges and repaired another 42,000. They installed 23,000 miles of storm and sanitary sewers and constructed 880 sewage disposal plants. They built 6,000 athletic fields and playgrounds, 770 new pools, 1,700 new parks, fairgrounds and rodeo grounds, 5,584 new school buildings, repaired 80 million library books, and served 900 million school lunches. They constructed or repaired 110,000 public libraries, schools, auditoriums, stadiums, and other public buildings.

The extraordinary contribution of the WPA workers significantly improved the infrastructure of the United States within a relatively short time. Almost every corner of the United States realized some improvement due to the WPA workers. Many of these buildings, roads, and parks were still in use at the beginning of the twenty-first century.

Federal One

The Works Progress Administration established a number of projects to provide work relief to artists, musicians, writers, and actors. These programs, collectively called Federal One, allowed the various types of artists to work in the areas of their profession. This alone was very controversial. Many people in the

United States had a hard time thinking of singing and dancing as work, much less work requiring work relief and federal support. Some Americans felt that these people were simply avoiding getting a "real job."

Roosevelt and Hopkins disagreed. In 1933 they had set up the Public Works Art Project (PWAP), under the administration of the Treasury Department. PWAP was not designed strictly as a work relief project. The artists it employed included some who were not on the relief rolls. PWAP was the forerunner to Federal One, however, and reflected the belief of Roosevelt and Hopkins that even singers and dancers deserved work relief appropriate to their occupation.

PWAP and later Federal One combined the economic desire to provide assistance, a renewed interest in democracy, and an interest in the development and exploration of American culture. Many of the projects completed under Federal One documented some aspect of American culture such as its folklore or its music. Federal One made a significant contribution to documenting a history that might otherwise have been lost.

Music From Coast to Coast

The Federal Music Project (FMP) was the least controversial of the Federal One projects. Under Nikolai Sokoloff, the FMP employed 15,000 out-of-work musicians. The Federal Music Project had a vision of starting regional orchestras all over the country and providing free or low-cost concerts and music lessons.

The Federal Music Project largely realized its vision, performing thousands of low-cost concerts in theaters and schools across the country, and introducing thousands of Americans to different kinds of music. Many of the newly established regional orchestras survived the cancellation of the FMP, and a few still existed at the end of the twentieth century.

In addition to concerts, the FMP made significant strides towards collecting and preserving folk music and other types of authentic, traditional American music. The music was documented, generally for the first time, so that it would not be lost forever as the traditional musicians died and communities disappeared. The Federal Music Project made a significant contribution to the scholarship of American music.

America's Voice

Somewhat more controversial was the Federal Writers' Project (FWP) led by Henry Alsberg. Employing almost seven thousand writers, researchers, and librarians in its peak year of 1936, the FWP sought to document many aspects of American life. The FWP writers prepared a complete set of

A poster for the Works Progress Administration encourages laborers to work for American prosperity. (The Library of Congress.)

tour guides, consisting of 51 large volumes, of major sites to visit in each state. Called the American Guide Series, many of the volumes are available in re-prints, and remained a valuable guide to important sites within the United States decades later.

The Federal Writers' Project also undertook a major effort in compiling oral histories. Oral histories are the memories of a time or event, told in the individual's voice. The FWP sent thousands of writers out to talk with American Indians, frontier women, Appalachian miners, and other individuals from various cultural groups around the United States. The collections are a powerful document of times that would soon be in the past. One of the most powerful collections compiled by the FWP writers is that of the *Slave Narratives* consisting of more than two thousand oral histories from black Americans who had formerly been slaves.

Many writers who were employed by the Federal Writers' Project would go on to become famous including Ralph Ellison, John Cheever, Conrad Aiken, Richard Wright, Saul Bellow, Studs Terkel, Dorothy West, and Zora Neale Hurston. Their writing from the FWP is still available and provides insightful portraits of life in the 1930s.

After the surprise attack by Japan on U.S. military installations at Pearl Harbor in December 1941, the Federal Writers' Project became part of the Writers' Unit of the War Services Division of the WPA. By the early 1940s, however, the Great Depression was waning as employment in war industries greatly increased. Many writers found other work. The guidebooks and the oral histories remained as their New Deal legacy.

Stories of Slavery

One of the lasting contributions of the Works Progress Administration was that of the Federal Writers' Project. The Federal Writers' Project (FWP) employed writers, teachers, and others to compile information on all aspects of American life. One of the most important oral histories collected by the FWP writers were the stories of former slaves.

The Slave Narratives include the transcripts of interviews with almost 2,300 Americans who were once slaves. The *Narratives* document their experiences as slaves, their recollections of the stories about their history as told to them by their ancestors, and their memories of newly won freedom. Transcribed as told to the FWP writers with dialect and slang included, the *Narratives* generally include just a brief observation by the writer. For example one *Narrative* profiles James Green, a half Native American, half black American who was born into slavery, freed, and then kidnapped and sold back into slavery in Texas.

In 1935 slavery had been illegal for 70 years. Most former slaves were old and most of their individual stories would not have been preserved if not for the efforts of the WPA writers. Rich in history, the Narratives provide an important record of a crucial part of American history.

Capturing History

The Historical Records Survey (HRS) was part of the Federal Writers' Project dedicated to cataloging national records. The smallest of the WPA projects, the HRS was directed by Luther Evans and supervised by noted bibliographer Douglas McMurtrie. It employed approximately six thousand writers, librarians, archivists, and teachers annually. The workers at HRS undertook a huge effort to compile and analyze the inventories of state and county records.

The HRS was extraordinarily prolific, preparing bibliographies of American history and literature, an atlas of congressional roll-call votes, an index to unnumbered executive orders, and a list of the collection of presidential papers. In addition they created surveys of portraits and manuscript collections in public buildings and church archives.

Art for the Millions

The Federal Art Project (FAP), led by director Holger Cahill, sought to employ artists and to make "art for the millions." Few Americans had seen a great work of art before. The FAP sought to make art more accessible. Artists painted thousands of pictures, and made thousands of posters and sculptures. By design the subjects many painted were subjects from everyday life: a fishery, or steel workers, or the poor.

By 1936 the Federal Art Project employed more than six thousand artists. About half of the workers were involved in the direct creation of art. They created more than 40,000 paintings and 1,100 murals. Others were involved in arts education and research. This included the compilation of the *Index of American Design* that documented American art, painting, sculpture, and folk art.

The best known and most lasting of the works of art created under FAP were the murals painted in public buildings across the nation. The FAP murals represented a renewed interest in American life. Victor Arnautoff's "City Life" in San Francisco's Coit Tower is one of the best examples. Many of the subjects were too pro-labor to suit members of the conservative Congress. As a result accusations of "communism" grew toward the end of the 1930s.

Many artists employed by the Federal Art Project would later become famous. These included Jackson Pollack, Willem De Kooning, Anton Refregier, and Yasuo Kuniyoshi. Critics, however, felt that much of the art was horribly bad and that anyone could claim to be an artist. There were no requirements for even the lowest standards of quality. Worse, many felt that the art was "leftist" portraying subjects that depicted the poverty and harsh conditions of the United States. They were meant to incite citizens to anger against the government. In response to this criticism of the FAP art, President Roosevelt responded that though some were good and others were not, it all reflected Americans' perceptions of their nation and the people in it.

Dangerous Theatre

The Federal Theatre Project (FTP) was the most controversial of the Federal One projects. The FTP was led by Hallie Flanagan, former head of the Vassar College Experimental Theatre and former classmate of Harry Hopkins at Grinnell College. Flanagan was described as having a spirit, dedication, and drive reminiscent of Eleanor Roosevelt. She was fully dedicated to building a truly national theater.

Flanagan, with the support of Hopkins, designed an incredibly ambitious program for the FTP. She started regional theatre groups all over the United

More About...

House Subcommittee on Un-American Activities

Toward the end of the 1930s the incredible support for New Deal programs enjoyed by the Roosevelt Administration from the U.S. Congress to combat the Great Depression was clearly waning. Republicans and conservative Democrats were challenging New Deal programs and Roosevelt himself. One form of the challenge was the House Subcommittee on Un-American Activities, later known as the House Un-American Activities Committee (HUAC).

In 1938 Representatives Martin Dies and J. Parnell Thomas began hearings on the projects of Federal One. The Federal Writers' Project and the Federal Theatre Project were of particular interest. Dies and Thomas believed that the projects were subversive. Dies accused the two projects of spreading communist propaganda more than the Communist Party itself. In April 1939 the Dies Committee ordered the investigation of all Federal One projects and placed Representative Clifton Woodrum in charge of the committee.

The Woodrum Committee heard several months of testimony, and, like the HUAC committee in the 1950s, was often more concerned with influencing public opinion against communism than finding the truth about Federal One. The Committee made much of the political messages in plays by the FTP and the art of the FAP. One painter had put a plea for Puerto Rican independence in a mural in a post office building. That the plea was written in Icelandic did not deter the horror at the inclusion of a political message in a work of art. The Committee charged that the Federal One projects were radicalizing America.

Toward the end of the hearings, Hallie Flanagan, director of the Federal Theatre Project was called to testify. In the course of a sometimes-eloquent defense of the program and the place of theatre in giving voice to ordinary people, she referenced renowned sixteenth century playwright Christopher Marlowe, author of *Doctor Faustus*. As she was quoting Marlowe, one of the congressmen interrupted her to ask who Marlowe was and whether he was a Communist. While the gallery laughed, the damage to the Federal Theatre Project from the hearings was done.

In the wake of the hearings, Congress passed the 1940 Emergency Relief Appropriations Act. The act significantly reduced funding for the WPA and put considerable constraints on remaining programs. The Federal Theatre Project was disbanded immediately. At the final production of the long-running *Pinocchio* in New York the cast and crew changed the ending: Pinocchio died and his casket read: "Born December 23, 1938; Killed by Act of Congress, June 30, 1939."

States, performing both classic productions and original plays for thousands of Americans. While the FTP had regional groups and tour groups that played widely, the center for theater was New York, and it was in New York that the FTP was most innovative. Flanagan wanted the theatre to be as broad and courageous as the American mind. As a result writers created plays on every possible subject and explored every possible idea.

The Federal Theatre in New York included the Living Newspapers, the Popular Price Theatre, an Experimental Theatre, a Negro Theatre, and a Try-out Theatre. Later it added the one-act play unit, dance theatre, the Theater for the Blind, marionette theatre, a Yiddish vaudeville unit, a German unit, an Anglo-Jewish theater, and the Radio Division, among other groups. The range of the productions was astounding.

Living Newspapers provided a strong example of the controversy found in the expression of ideas in theatre—those very ideas that ultimately led to the demise of the FTP. *Living Newspapers* were plays in the form of a documentary that provided information about and took a stand on the issues of the day. *Injunction Granted* dramatized the anti-union actions of the courts. *Created Equal* addressed the conflicts between property owners and citizens. *Triple-A Plowed Under* called for farmers and consumers to work together against greedy middlemen at a time when millions did not have enough to eat, and food rotted in warehouses because no one could afford to pay for it.

Like many other FTP productions, *Triple-A Plowed Under* was a great success, but was criticized as Communist propaganda because of its themes of hunger and starvation. *The Saturday Evening Post* claimed Flanagan was trying to "Russianize" the

Three young men receive training in mechanics through the National Youth Administration, a section of the WPA. (Corbis. Reproduced by permission.)

American stage. Many of the FTP productions were similarly criticized. A children's play about beavers fighting the human destroyer of their dam was considered to support workers rising up against business owners.

Even classic plays received a new treatment when produced by the Federal Theatre Project. One of the most popular productions was the Negro Unit's production of Shakespeare's *Macbeth,* directed by Orson Welles. Called *Voodoo Macbeth,* this all-black production was set in Haiti instead of Scotland and included voodoo priestesses as the three witches. It presented a true spectacle.

The Federal Theatre Project received the most virulent criticism for undermining traditionally held American values by the U.S. Congress. As the House Committee on Un-American Activities began hearings on Federal One, the FTP was singled out for particular criticism. Despite Flanagan's testimony the FTP didn't survive the attack and the Federal Theatre Project was disbanded in 1939.

Many actors, directors, and producers who were employed by the Federal Theatre Project would go on to become famous including, Orson Welles, Arthur Miller, John Huston, Joseph Cotton, E.G. Marshall, Will Geer, Burt Lancaster, and John Houseman. More

importantly, the Federal Theatre Project introduced thousands of Americans to theatre during a challenging time in America. It gave voice to the variety of views at the time. An estimated 30 million people attended productions of the Federal Theatre Project before it was disbanded in 1939.

Working Youth

The WPA supervised the activities of the National Youth Administration (NYA). The NYA provided part-time employment to people ages 18 to 25. Young people who were out of school could work 70 hours a month for no more than $25 a month. Most of the student workers worked out of their homes, but rural youth were moved to residential centers and trained in masonry, welding, baking, barbering, carpentry, and plumbing.

High school students were also eligible for part-time employment, since they often made a significant contribution to the family income. If high school students could not contribute while in school, they were likely to quit to try to find work. Under the NYA, high school students could work part-time for no more than $6 a month, and college students could make up to $20 a month.

NYA workers spruced up schools, landscaped parks, read to the blind, and worked as teacher's aides. They also constructed recreational facilities and parks, acted as nurse's aides and school cafeteria workers, and were museum guides. The work provided a way of making a meaningful contribution to a family's income while the students stayed in school.

The NYA had a better record than many federal agencies of the time in providing assistance to black American students. That success was largely due to Mary McLeod Bethune. Bethune led the NYA Division of Negro Affairs. She was an important advocate for black American rights and was the highest ranking black American in the Roosevelt Administration. Between 10 and 12 percent of those who participated in the NYA were black Americans, amounting to about 300,000 black men and women. Because of racial segregation and discrimination in the South, many more black Americans in the North were able to participate in NYA programs than those in the South.

Residential Centers for Depression-Era Youth

The National Youth Administration (NYA) was established in 1935 within the Works Progress Administration. Initially, the NYA provided part-time employment opportunities to youth who were still in school. As the administrators studied the situation of Depression-era youth, however, they determined that many had dropped out of school, often before completing the eighth grade. With the high unemployment of the 1930s, many youth were both not in school and not working. A significant number had become homeless and hoboes.

In response to the challenge to address the needs of these youth, the NYA developed a residential work program. The program provided homes for the youth in dormitory-type housing, education and training opportunities, and employment. The goal of the residential program was to provide a rich and fulfilling environment in order to create good citizens as well as good workers. The youth would clean, cook, and study and work. In addition, the residential centers provided cultural enrichment programs. Youth were strictly supervised and taught "how to live" as well as how to make a living.

Concerns regarding the unemployed youth were not unfounded, as young people on school campuses and elsewhere were joining the Young Communist League and other leftist organizations. Eleanor Roosevelt raised concerns regarding the message the country was sending to unemployed youth Mrs. Roosevelt became a strong advocate for the National Youth Administration.

The residential programs were less effective than the student work programs. Residential program participants would stay in the centers, learn a trade, and then return home only to discover again that there were no jobs. Many found the situation extremely disillusioning, though most participants found the centers themselves to be a good experience.

Women and the WPA

Women had a difficult time qualifying for and receiving work relief under the WPA. Many women on relief did not have a work history and were not, therefore, considered part of the labor force. In addition many women had children at home and were not available for full-time employment. These challenges were compounded by the fact that the male-dominated WPA administrators could not quite figure out what jobs women could do.

Ellen Woodward, who headed the Women's Division of the FERA and the CWA and later the Women's Division of the WPA, proposed 250 job categories appropriate for women. The administrators of the WPA disqualified almost all of them. Woodward was left with little but sewing. As a result most of the WPA women ended up in one of nine thousand sewing centers around the country.

A WPA supervisor instructs a woman in weaving a rag rug on a loom. Arts programs were the most controversial of all WPA programs. (The Library of Congress.)

Woodward also instituted training and employment programs in mattress making, bookbinding, domestic service, canning of relief foods, school lunch preparation, and supplemental childcare. Woodward petitioned to have the Women's Division become part of the Professional Division where there might be more seemingly appropriate jobs for women as stenographers and office workers. The WPA employed 600,000 women in 1938, its best year for involvement of women, but that did not begin to address the need.

Southern states did particularly poorly employing women in the WPA, especially black American women. Part of this had to do with segregation requirements. Black and white men could work on outdoor projects together. But the women's projects, which were indoors, had to be entirely segregated, making them more costly to run. In addition many Southerners objected to employment programs that would compete with domestic services for black American women. They wanted black American women to be available to work as maids and cooks in white people's homes for low wages.

More About...

The FTP's Cradle Will Rock

In the late 1930s, composer Virgil Thomson, director and producer John Houseman, and director and actor Orson Welles collaborated on a play. The play, to be a production of the Federal Theatre Project, was a celebration of the triumph of labor unions. Called *The Cradle Will Rock,* it became caught in the controversy regarding the FTP. The FTP came under increasing criticism for its reportedly "Communist-influenced" portrayals and was on the verge of being disbanded just as the production was about to premier.

On opening night the cast and crew arrived to a locked theater. The production had been cancelled and the unions had decreed that no actor could appear on stage. Houseman and Welles were determined that the show would go on, and searched for an alternative venue. With the audience beginning to line up outside the closed theater, an alternative theater 21 blocks away was found.

The cast, crew, and the audience (and the piano in a truck) began a parade to the new theater. Once inside, the piano was placed on stage, and Marc Blitzstein prepared to perform. He was going to sing—the play was a musical—all the roles since the cast had been ordered not to appear on stage. As he began to sing the opening song a voice joined his from the audience. It was Olive Stanton, the actress who was to sing the opening song. The actors performed their roles from the audience. *The Cradle Will Rock* became a triumph and played to acclaim all over the country.

In 1999 *Cradle Will Rock* was released as a Hollywood movie depicting the struggle around the production of a play. The movie starred Hank Azaria, John Cusack, Joan Cusack, Bill Murray, and Cherry Jones as Hallie Flanagan.

Un-American?

The WPA provided work relief for millions of people during a challenging time in American history of the Great Depression. It also took an innovative approach to including cultural expression into its employment program. In dong so the WPA quickly came under attack from conservatives in Congress.

U.S. Congressional Representatives Martin Dies and J. Parnell Thomas led the House Subcommittee on Un-American Activities in 1938. The committee searched for communist influence the WPA projects. They placed special emphasis on the Federal Writers' Project and the Federal Theatre Project.

Undeniably, a variety of opinions, including Communist views, were regularly being expressed in America in the 1930s. Those views were undoubtedly also expressed in the artistic communities of Federal One. Hearings were held and passionate defenses were offered. The Dies Committee placed Representative Clifton Woodrum in charge of the investigation. The Woodrum Committee ended up stripping $125 million from the WPA budget. In addition all WPA workers on the payroll for more than 18 months were to be dismissed and all future WPA workers had to sign a loyalty oath asserting support of the U.S. government. The Woodrum Committee also dictated that the Federal Theatre Project was to be discontinued immediately.

The other WPA projects continued for a few more years. In the early 1940s many of the WPA projects were transferred to various wartime agencies. The WPA was disbanded entirely in 1943.

Cultural Democracy

The New Deal's WPA was most importantly a work relief program. At a time when millions of Americans were without jobs because of the Great Depression, the WPA provided jobs and the wages that come with jobs. But the WPA was also something more than a work relief program, and that was also part of the design.

During the 1920s and 1930s, many Americans and, in fact, people all over the world had begun to advocate for more accessible culture. Cultural events should not be artificially divided between "high" culture for the wealthy and sophisticated and "low" culture for the masses. Everyone could enjoy opera and vaudeville; fiddle playing and contemporary art. Cultural events and their attendees should be determined by tastes, not by class. Many people were horrified that the majority of Americans had never heard a symphony or seen a "good" piece of art.

The cultural programs of Federal One were designed to address this gap. Hopkins, Flanagan, and Cahill in particular wanted to bring the "Arts to the Millions." They wanted everyone to be able to enjoy a good Shakespeare play or to see a Rembrandt. They also wanted the common art of the people to gain new respect. A play depicting the struggles of a family in a contemporary New York City tenement could be just as meaningful and just as much art as a play written three hundred years earlier.

In this goal of "democratizing culture," Federal One largely succeeded—at least for a time. Millions of Americans attended free concerts and plays, learned to paint, and saw "professional" art. Millions of Americans experienced what once was only art for the wealthy few, many for the first time.

Contributing Forces

The movement toward work relief programs that became the Works Progress Administration was most directly a result of the unemployment, poverty, and homelessness caused by the Great Depression. President Roosevelt had a strong belief in the possibilities afforded by appropriate exercise of the powers of the federal government, but without the arrival of the Great Depression his activism would likely have taken a different form. The specific characteristics of the WPA, however, particularly its specific inclusion of artists and actors, grew out of the 1920s.

During the 1920s, wealth in the United States became increasingly concentrated in a few individuals, following a trend begun during the early industrialization of the country. From 1922 to 1929 six million families—42 percent of the families in the United States—made less than $1,000 a year. At the same time, working conditions for many Americans were increasingly hazardous. Fewer Americans were self-employed and more worked in factories. Many worked long hours in terrible surroundings, where poor equipment, increased production requirements, and poor safety measures meant frequent injury and death. Most workers had no insurance. Injury or death often meant the entire family faced imminent poverty and homelessness.

Many Americans were horrified by these working and living conditions and the disparity in wealth. Even in the relatively prosperous 1920s, challenges to the existing economic system were growing. The idea of unionizing American workers was gaining acceptance in some areas. The unions were demanding better working conditions and better wages. Americans

were increasingly organizing to fight for improvements in their daily lives. The unemployed organized to fight for jobs, and tenants organized to fight for better housing. Even many among the more financially well off believed that both morality and practicality required a more equal approach to wealth and the benefits it accorded.

The 1920s also saw dramatic growth in the amount and diversity of art and music throughout the United States and the world. The relative prosperity allowed many Americans to explore music and plays. Increasingly many saw the enjoyment of art and music as a fundamental requirement of a civilized society. It was with this belief in the universal importance of art and music that programs such as the WPA's cultural programs for artists, musicians, writers, and actors would take root.

A certain arrogance of American ingenuity also gave rise to the WPA. There was a sense among many citizens that American minds can fix any problem, including economic problems. America had emerged from World War I (1914–1918) with strength and a world mission. It seemed that there was nothing Americans could not do. Given this new outlook many in the Roosevelt Administration felt that the United States could—and had a moral obligation to—provide relief for its citizenry. A civilized society provided for its people.

Perspectives

Criticism of the WPA came from all fronts. Conservatives felt that it would undermine the free enterprise system. Liberals felt that the low wages were unacceptable. Socialists and Communists felt that the WPA was a way of preventing a more basic change in U.S. society, and states-rights advocates felt that the federal government was taking away authority that rightly belonged to the states. The WPA did not escape criticism from almost every group in America.

The Right

Traditional conservatives included the Liberty League and many Republicans who saw the WPA as a means of undermining the capitalist system. While many of the conservatives were sympathetic to the poverty and hunger around them, they felt that the economy would eventually improve on its own leading to greater employment. The unemployment, while upsetting, was part of a "natural" cycle that would inevitably improve. They argued that by making the government the largest employer, even at depressed wages, the Roosevelt Administration was in fact delaying recovery.

In order to pay for the WPA, the U.S. Government had to levy taxes. In this time of massive unemployment, conservatives felt that taxes fell disproportionately upon the wealthy, including the owners of business. The conservatives believed that not only was this unfair, but by taxing the people we were depending on to expand their business though investment, new economic growth was being deterred.

Furthermore the conservatives criticized the WPA and other New Deal programs as being an inappropriate use of government. The conservatives saw the appropriate role of the government as being limited and carefully defined. They felt that a massive works program such as the WPA was outside the Constitutional scope of the U.S. government. The Roosevelt Administration saw the pervasiveness of the Great Depression and the depth of the problem as being too much for states to bear alone. Many of the states were too impoverished to address the poverty of their own people. Social welfare programs belonged most appropriately to the states, conservatives felt, and the Roosevelt Administration was fundamentally changing the balance of power between the states and the federal government.

Many conservatives also felt that the WPA, and in particular Federal One, was promoting liberal or even communist views. Much of the "Art for the Millions" was designed to show normal people in normal activities. Murals depicted workers and, sometimes, union organizers. The Federal Theatre Project's *Living Newspaper* criticized the issues of the day. The FTP came under the harshest scrutiny and, ultimately, was disbanded in the face of this criticism.

Others raised concerns about the employment by the federal government of such a large number of people. In comparison Adolph Hitler was Chancellor of Germany and beginning his rise in Europe. He had created military youth groups in support of him and his programs. Some feared that the WPA, Civilian Conservation Corps, and National Youth Administration could lead to militarized youth as in Germany. While this did not happen, the concern about the potential impact of organized youth was not unfounded.

The Left

On the other side of the political spectrum came criticism from liberals. Liberals deplored the low wages of the WPA. The Roosevelt Administration had intentionally kept wages below those in the private sector, and often below poverty level, in order to avoid making employment for the WPA preferable to employment in private industry. Many criticized the wages as insufficient and a punishment for being jobless.

Some radical critics, including *The New Republic's* Jonathan Mitchell, saw more devious causes behind the low wages. Mitchell believed that the low wages of the WPA represented a surrender of the U.S. Government to big business. He believed that the low wages were to be used as a tool to break up the unions.

On the further extreme, communists believed that work relief was a way to prevent more meaningful change. If the government kept the workers barely employed on barely sustainable wages they might be prevented from rebellion. Communists also believed that a fundamental change in the ownership of business and wealth was both desirable and inevitable. Small concessions, such as work relief, delayed the revolution.

General Public

Beyond the criticism of specific groups, many people raised concerns about the effectiveness of the program. Some felt that much of the work was make-work. Early in the program, some complained that WPA workers would dig a hole and other WPA workers would fill it in. In addition many people had a difficult time seeing singing and dancing as a real job. The idea that the government would pay people to do it seemed absurd.

Even people who supported the idea of the arts and saw work in the arts as real work raised concerns about government-sponsored art. Would all the art be propaganda? Would creativity be constrained? What if the government-sponsored art was bad art? This concern seemed to fizzle after the early days of the WPA as it became clear that much of the art was critical of the government. But as the House Subcommittee on Un-American Activities began to investigate the WPA and ultimately disband the FTP, the concern of government-sponsored art was raised anew.

While the Roosevelt Administration faced significant criticism and challenges regarding the WPA, and the program did not, in fact, last very long. The WPA had many supporters, particularly those personally helped by the program. Not only did many people credit the program with helping them to survive the Great Depression, but many people also highlighted that the United States was left with many buildings, art, and a richer history because of the workers of the WPA.

Impact

The Works Progress Administration helped many Americans to develop and cement their views about work relief. Franklin Roosevelt believed accepting relief without working for it undermines the self-esteem of the recipient. Many of the welfare-to-work programs implemented in the late twentieth century, often by conservative state governments, relied on this same belief. The concepts of work and welfare and the varying views of the appropriate (and inappropriate) role of the federal government were largely established during this time.

Perceptions about public workers that were predominately forged in the work relief programs of the 1930s remain today. Despite contrary evidence, public workers were often criticized for being overpaid and lazy. Highway workers are often deplored as wasting time and prolonging projects—not unlike the criticisms of the WPA workers digging a hole just to fill it. The American public is conflicted regarding its public employees. On the one hand the U.S. public needs them to deliver the mail and process the passports. But the public also suspects that government workers are being casual with the public's money.

Many of the buildings and highways and other projects built by the men of the WPA are still part of the American landscape. Much of the art, especially the many murals from the Federal Art Project, are still adorning public buildings around the United States. Many of the discussions about government-sponsored art are still held today, as controversial artists receive government grants, or have government grants repealed. The explosion in art during the Great Depression has been compared to a similar explosion during the Renaissance in Europe that coincidentally was also supported by government funds. The disagreements regarding the trade-offs involved in the public support of art, however, remained much the same in the 1990s as in the 1930s, with questions as to what federal agencies like the National Endowment for the Arts (NEA) and the National Endowment for the Humanities (NEH) should and should not be funding.

The convergence of the devastation of the Great Depression and the mastery and vision of President Roosevelt combined to create a situation where the federal government temporarily employed millions of workers as a form of relief. The New Deal, including the WPA, resonated throughout U.S. society ever since the Great Depression. Not only the tangible projects—the murals, the transcripts from history, the plays, and the buildings—remain, but also the ideas about the role of government in the lives of its citizens.

Notable People

Mary McLeod Bethune (1875–1955). A remarkable woman with many notable accomplishments, Bethune was born into a family of former slaves. Initially denied an education, Bethune became a proponent of the value of education in elevating black Americans. After several years of education and service, Bethune was appointed by a series of U.S. presidents to serve in various capacities. President Coolidge invited her to attend his Child Welfare Conference in 1928. President Herbert Hoover (served 1929–1933) appointed her to the White House Conference on Child Health in 1930. She was appointed President Roosevelt's Special Advisor on Minority Affairs from 1935 to 1944. From 1936 to 1944 she held the position of Director of the Division of Negro Affairs of the National Youth Administration, making her the first black American woman to become a federal agency head. As head of the NYA Division of Negro Affairs, Bethune was the highest-ranking black person in the New Deal. She was considered "Mother Superior" to the black American men and women working in Cabinet offices and federal agencies. This small group of men and women became known as the "Black Cabinet."

Holger Cahill (1893–1960). Cahill was born in St. Paul, Minnesota. Following a difficult childhood that led to him leave home at age of 13, Cahill moved to New York City to become a journalist. In New York he gained an education from Columbia University and the New School for Social Research. In the course of his journalism studies he became friends with artists in his Greenwich Village neighborhood. In 1932 he was appointed exhibitions director at the American Museum of Modern Art (MoMA) in New York City. In 1935 he was appointed National Director of the Federal Art Project (FAP) of the WPA. Cahill's political skills and love of popular and folk art made him effective in gaining public support for a federally funded arts program. Through his guidance the FAP employed 4,300 artists in 40 states.

Luther Evans (1902–1981). Director of the Historical Records Survey of the WPA, Evans, a Southerner from Alabama, was known for his efforts to promote racial equality within the program. Aside from his contributions to archiving and documenting America, Evans worked in opposition to censorship and made significant contribution to the world of libraries and librarianship. He was later to serve as librarian of Congress and director general of the United Nations Educational, Scientific, and Cultural Organization (UNESCO).

Hallie Flanagan (1889–1969). Flanagan, the director of Vassar College's Experimental Theatre, was recruited by Harry Hopkins to lead the Federal Theatre Project. It became the most controversial of all the WPA programs. Flanagan believed that theatre should both educate and entertain. The theatre programs she started included the Living Newspaper (a series of plays explaining and commenting on current events), regional theatre productions, and unusual interpretations of traditional plays. Flanagan asserted that for theatre to be good, it had to push accepted standards. The controversy surrounding the FTP's productions and the WPA in general resulted in questions of Communist influence. Flanagan defended her program before a Congressional Committee, but the FTP was disbanded in 1939.

Harry Hopkins (1890–1946). Hopkins was one of Franklin Delano Roosevelt's closest advisors. In 1931 New York Governor Roosevelt appointed the former social worker as the executive director of the New York State Temporary Emergency Relief Administration. Hopkins was an advocate of relief programs that provided work for the unemployed and trained the unskilled. When Roosevelt became president he recruited Hopkins to implement his various social welfare programs including from 1935 to 1938 the Works Progress Administration. Hopkins was charged by President Roosevelt with a program designed to move as many people as possible from the relief rolls to WPA jobs, and then on to private employment as quickly possible. Hopkins later served as Secretary of Commerce for Roosevelt from 1938 to 1940 and in various other roles throughout World War II.

Aubrey Williams (1890–1965). Born in Springville, Alabama, Williams was greatly disturbed by the poverty and racial injustice he witnessed as a youth. This experience led him to become a social worker. In 1922 Williams became executive secretary of the Wisconsin Conference of Social Work. There he sought to develop programs for poverty in the state. In the early years of the Great Depression Williams returned to the South where he coordinated activities of President Hoover's Reconstruction Finance Corporation in bringing economic relief to people of Texas and Mississippi. Soon after the inauguration of Franklin Roosevelt as president in March 1933, Harry Hopkins recruited Williams to be his assistant at the Federal Emergency Relief Administration. Impressed by Williams' dedication to New Deal work relief programs, Hopkins named Williams deputy director of the new Works Progress Administration (WPA) in 1933 and then also executive director of the National Youth Administration (NYA). Williams served as head of the NYA until 1943 when it stopped operation. Williams was well noted for his never-ending efforts of bringing youth and minorities into the New Deal work relief projects. Following World War II Williams continued working against racial discrimination in the South for the next 20 years.

Ellen Woodward (18??–1971). Born in Oxford, Mississippi, Woodward's father was a U.S. Senator from Mississippi from 1898 to 1901 and served in the U.S. House of Representatives briefly before that. Having grown up in Washington, DC, Woodward developed an interest in public affairs. In 1926 she became the second woman in history to serve in Mississippi's legislature. Woodward served as a top administrator of the Mississippi State Board of Development from 1926 to 1933. Through the board she directed economic development in the state. Having attracted the attention of Harry Hopkins in 1933 she was appointed to the Women's Division of the Federal Emergency Relief Administration (FERA). Woodward would serve similar functions for the Civil Works Administration (CWA), and the Women's Division of the Works Progress Administration (WPA). Having the strong support of First Lady Eleanor Roosevelt, Woodward established jobs programs for women in every state of the nation. By 1935 nearly 500,000 women were employed in work relief involving sewing, gardening and canning, and public healthcare among other activities. In 1936 Woodward became WPA director for writers, musicians, artists, and actors. These programs employed 250,000 workers. She was a staunch defender of the programs in the face of strong criticisms. Woodward left the WPA in December 1938 when President Roosevelt appointed her on the Social Security Board.

Primary Sources

A View From the President

On September 28, 1937, President Franklin Roosevelt described his perspective of WPA projects at Timberline Lodge on the upper slopes Mt. Hood east of Portland, Oregon. The lodge is a spectacular structure built at the upper tree line, a large building made of large stonework and heavy timbers (from Roosevelt, 1941, pp. 392–394).

Here I am on the slopes of Mount Hood where I have always wanted to come.

I am here to dedicate Timberline Lodge and I do so in the words of the bronze table directly in front of me on the coping of this wonderful building:

"Timberline Lodge, Mount Hood National Forest, dedicated September 28, 1937, by the President of the United

Timberline Lodge in Mount Hood National Forest, Oregon, was built by the WPA in 1937. The lodge is still in operation today as a resort and conference center. (National Archives-Pacific Alaska Region, Seattle)

States as a monument to the skill and faithful performance of workers on the rolls of the Works Progress Administration."

In the past few days I have inspected many great governmental activities—parks and soil protection sponsored by the Works Progress Administration; buildings erected with the assistance of the Public Works Administration; our oldest and best-known National Park, the Yellowstone, under the jurisdiction of the National Park Service; great irrigation areas fathered by the Reclamation Service; and a few hours ago a huge navigation and power dam built by the Army engineers . . .

This Timberline Lodge marks a venture that was made possible by W.P.A., emergency relief work, in order that we may test the workability of recreational facilities installed by the Government itself and operated under its complete control.

Here, to Mount Hood, will come thousands and thousands of visitors in the coming years . . .

I look forward to the day when many, many people from this region of the Nation are going to come here for skiing and tobogganing and various other forms of winter sports. Among them, all of those visitors, in winter and summer, spring and autumn, there will be many from the outermost parts of our Nation, travelers from the Middle Wet, the South and the East, Americans who are fulfilling a very desirable objective of citizenship—getting to know their country better.

So I take very great pleasure in dedicating this Lodge, not only as a new adjunct to our National Forests, but also as a place to play for generations of Americans in the days to come.

Governor Roosevelt on Work Relief

While governor of New York before becoming president, Franklin Roosevelt publicly expressed some of his earliest views on government relief programs in the summer of 1931. The message delivered to the New York state legislature asking for unemployment relief legislation was a signal of what would be coming to Congress two years later (as quoted in June Hopkins, p. 154).

This serious unemployment situation which has stunned the Nation for the past year and a half has brought to our attention in a most vivid fashion the need for some sort of relief to protect those men and women who are willing to work but who through no fault of their own cannot find employment. This form of relief should not, of course, take the shape of a dole in any respect. The dole method of relief for unemployment is not only repugnant to all sound principles of social economics, but is contrary to every principle of American citizenship and of sound government. American labor seeks no charity, but only a chance to work for its living. The relief to which the workers of the State should be able to anticipate, when engulfed in a period of industrial depression, should be one of insurance, to which they themselves have in a large part contributed. Each industry itself likewise should bear a part of the premium for this insurance, and the State, in the interest of its own citizens, and to prevent a recurrence of the widespread hardship of these days, should at least supervise its operation.

Harry Hopkins' View

Harry Hopkins, top administrator of the WPA, repeatedly defended work relief to the public, revealing the deep feelings he held for the work he was doing. The following quote is from a press conference in the summer of 1935 soon after the program had begun (as quoted in Charles, p. 131).

And some of us have the only chance we will ever again in our life have to do this job for all the people. Everyone one of us in this room is being paid for by the nation, they pay us, we work for all the people. This isn't our money. We are just agents of America, doing a job, and in a crisis like this—because when we have ten or eleven million people out of work don't let anybody tell you this isn't still a crisis—we have been given the greatest opportunity to serve not only the people but the nation, that we will every have again in our lives. I tell you, I have to pinch myself sometimes when I think how some of us have been catapulted into these positions and I will

tell you now of the faith and confidence that I have in you, the devotion which you have given to this thing for the past two years and I know I do not have to appeal to this crowd for support. What I need to do is to be sure that I can keep up with you in the kind of service you have been giving to this nation in the past two years. I am proud to do this job with you and I want you to be proud to do it with me.

A First Hand Overview of the WPA

In January 1937 Harry Hopkins provided testimony before a congressional committee. The testimony represented a fairly thorough assessment of the program after almost two years of operation by its top administrator (as quoted in Charles, pp. 170–171).

With a deficiency appropriation of $790,000,000, it is contemplated that $655,000,000 would be made available for the Works Progress Administration, including the National Youth Administration. With this amount it would be possible to employ 2,200,000 on Works Progress Administration projects in February; 2,150,000 in March; 2,000,000 in April; 1,800,000 in May; and 1,600,000 in June. In terms of dollars, the monthly obligations are estimated as follows: February, $151,700,000; March, $146,000,000; April, $134,500,000; May, $120,000,000; and June, $103,000,000.

The employment schedule, involving a reduction of 600,000 workers between February and June, anticipates a large and widespread increase in private employment over the period. Normally, there is a seasonal increase of about 800,000 private jobs during these 5 months; but an increase of from 1,200,000 to 1,500,000 private jobs will probably be necessary to remove 600,000 persons from the W.P.A.

Viewing the situation from another angle, our studies of the seasonal variation in relief show that the number usually declines about 15 per cent from February to June. This would mean that starting with 2,200,000 Works Progress Administration workers in February, we should ordinarily expect a decline of about 340,000 workers, leaving 1,860,000 on Works Progress Administration projects during June. To reduce Works Progress Administration employment to 1,600,000 workers, therefore, it will be necessary for 260,000 Works Progress Administration workers to find jobs over and above seasonal expectations.

These estimates are based on studies of our past experience during periods of reemployment, which indicate that the creation of two and one-half new jobs in private industry results in the removal of one family head from relief or from the W.P.A. On this basis, private employment will have to increase to the extent of 500,000 to 650,000 more than seasonal expectations if Works Progress Administration employment is to be reduced to 1,600,000 in June.

Debate Over the WPA

The debate over the worthiness of spending public funds on work relief was non-ending. As an example in defense of the WPA, the following excerpts are from an article by David Cushman Coyle published in the March 1939 issue of the journal *Forum* entitled "The WPA—Loafers or Workers?" (pp. 170–174).

Is it true, as you so often hear, that people on relief acquire the habit of living at ease and thenceforth refuse to go to work? Is it true that WPA workers cling to their soft snap and refuse to take jobs in private employment? Do Americans really like to work, or would they rather loaf? . . .

On the face of it and considering what has happened to some millions of helpless people, one would expect that the losses of morale would be stupendous. The astonishing thing is that so little trace of lost morale can be found in the records. Apparently the American people are tougher than anyone had a right to hope . . . What sort of people are "on" the WPA?

All sorts, of course. The most striking thing about them is how very American they are . . .

He represents the millions whose lives have been upset by the long depression but who are neither too sick nor too old to scramble for a toe-hold. He represents millions of employable men and women, white-collar workers and laborers, skilled mechanics, scientists, experienced and inexperienced workers, who, having lost their jobs and exhausted their private resources, have needed employment on WPA projects to tide them over a desperate period . . .

More than five thousand cases of alleged job refusals (of both WPA and private assignments), reported since 1935, have been investigated by agents of the federal government.

Only forty-two of these refusals, or less than 1 per cent, were found to be real cases of an individual's not wanting to work . . .

The experience of the depression has proved that the American people still want jobs. They learned in school that in America the boy who studies and works day and night will marry the boss's daughter and become president of the company. The vast majority still believe in work.

Fortune reported, as a result of a survey in 1937, that more than two thirds of the workers on relief had at some time held one job for more than five years. In each of the eleven localities covered in the Fortune survey, a board of local citizens was set up to rate the WPA workers and relief recipients as to employability. Only 25 per cent were rated unemployable, the principal reasons for this being old age and poor health. Even among those who were judged unemployable by these boards, one in eight was able to find work in the prosperous period of 1937 . . .

There can, of course, be a scarcity of labor and a surplus at the same time, because workers are not all alike. Most of our unemployed workers are unskilled, and most of the scarcity is in the skilled trades ...

It is generally agreed that there are from ten to twelve million unemployed in the country. The WPA had had from two to three million on its rolls. To blame the WPA for a shortage of labor is to charge that the tail is wagging the dog. What about those who are not on the WPA or on direct relief? Shortage of certain types of workers exist despite the millions who walk the streets.

It is significant that more than a million WPA workers have taken private jobs since the beginning of the program. The WPA is organized so that, with occasional local exceptions, it gears closely into private industry and serves as a reservoir of labor. It takes up some of the slack between private jobs and supplies workers, through the U.S. Employment Service, whenever they can be employed in industry or agriculture ...

As these reports show, the WPA has not been a large factor in the labor supply. There is a reserve of millions of unemployed, outside the WPA, to which industry can turn. Many labor shortages reported at the present time are recurring problems which first arose long before the WPA and have continued through the depression. When business is recovering, cases of local scarcity of certain kinds of labor are bound to occur from time to time.

The investigations of complaints turn up a surprisingly small number of actual cases of laziness or even of unwillingness to leave the WPA for the risks of private employment. Apparently the people who have borne the burnt of the long depression have kept the desire to work to get back on their feet. A pretty tough race of people, these Americans, and hard to kill. They'd better be, for it takes a long time to get America straightened out.

Suggested Research Topics

- The Works Progress Administration touched almost every county in the United States. Research what buildings, art projects, theatre productions or other WPA project impacted your community.

- A major concern regarding "the dole" in the 1930s was the impact on the self-esteem of the recipients. Work relief was heralded as a solution. In the late twentieth century many states implemented programs to require work from welfare recipients. Compare the arguments in the 1930s and in the 1990s regarding welfare and self-esteem.

- Discuss the pros and cons involved in government-sponsored art. How did debate over certain controversial art projects funded by the National Endowment for the Arts in the late twentieth century compare to debate of the WPA arts programs?

Bibliography

Sources

Bindas, Kenneth J. *All of This Music Belongs to the Nation: The WPA's Federal Music Project and American Society.* Knoxville, TN: University of Tennessee Press, 1996.

Bold, Christine. *The WPA Guides: Mapping America.* Jacksonville, MS: University Press of Mississippi, 1999.

Brinkley, Alan. "Legacies of the New Deal," in *The Chronicle of Higher Education.* May 19, 1995, p. B1.

Bustard, Bruce I. *A New Deal for the Arts.* Seattle, WA: University of Washington Press, 1997.

Charles, Searle F. *Minister of Relief: Harry Hopkins and the Depression.* Syracuse, NY: Syracuse University Press, 1963.

Coyle, David C. "The WPA—Loafers or Workers?" *Forum,* March 1939, pp. 170–174.

De Hart, Jane. "Democratizing Culture," in *The New Deal: Problems in American Civilization,* David E. Hamilton (ed.) Boston, MA: Houghton Mifflin Co., 1999.

Edsforth, Ronald. *The New Deal: America's Response to the Great Depression.* London and New York: Blackwell Publishers, 1999.

Folsom, Franklin. *Impatient Armies of the Poor: The Story of Collective Action of the Unemployed, 1808–1942.* Niwot, CO: University Press of Colorado, 1991.

Gustaitis, Joseph. "The Cradle that Rocked America," in *American History.* February 2000, v. 34:17.

Hopkins, June. *Harry Hopkins: Sudden Hero, Brash Performer.* New York: St. Marin's Press, 1999.

Housema, Lorraine Brown (Ed.). *Federal Theatre Project.* New York City: Routledge, Chapman & Hall, Inc., 1986.

Kazacoff, George. *Dangerous Theatre: The Federal Theatre Project as a Forum For New Plays.* New York City: Peter Lang Publishing, 1989.

Roosevelt, Franklin D. *The Public Papers and Addresses of Franklin D. Roosevelt.* New York: Random House, 1941.

Schlesinger, Jr., Arthur M. *The Coming of the New Deal.* New York: Houghton Mifflin Co., 1988.

U. S. Federal Works Agency Staff. *Final Report on the WPA Program, 1935–1943.* Westport, CT: Greenwood Publishing Group, Inc., 1976.

Watkins, T.H. *The Great Depression: America in the 1930s.* Boston, MA: Little, Brown & co., 1993.

———. *The Hungry Years: A Narrative History of the Great Depression in America.* New York City: Henry Holt and Company, 1999.

Further Reading

Baker, T. Lindsay and Julie P. Baker, eds. *The WPA Oklahoma Slave Narratives.* Oklahoma City, OK: University of Oklahoma Press, 1996.

Bascom, Lionel C. (ed.). *A Renaissance in Harlem: Lost Essays of the WPA, by Ralph Ellison, Dorothy West, and Other Voices of a Generation.* New York City: HarperCollins Publishers Inc., 1999.

Draden, Rena. *Blueprints for a Black Federal Theatre 1935–1939.* New York City: Cambridge University Press, 1994.

Hiller, Megan (Ed.). *An Ornery Bunch: Tales and Anecdotes Collected by the WPA Montana Writers' Project, 1935–1942.* Helena, MT: Falcon Publishing, Inc., 1999.

Ickes, Harold L. *The Secret Diary of Harold L. Ickes, Vols. 1–3.* New York City: De Capo Press, 1974.

La Vere, David. *Life among the Texas Indians: The WPA Narratives.* College Station, TX: Texas A&M University Press, 1998.

Mangione, Jerre. *The Dream and the Deal: The Federal Writers Project, 1935–1943.* Syracuse, NY: Syracuse University Press, 1996.

Melosh, Barbara. *Engendering Culture: Manhood and Womanhood in New Deal Public Art and Theater.* Washington, DC: Smithsonian Institution Press, 1991.

Parrish, Michael E. *Anxious Decades: America in Prosperity and Depression 1920–1941.* New York City: Norton, W. W. & Company, Inc., 1994.

Swain, Marsha H. *Ellen S. Woodward: New Deal Advocate for Women.* Minneapolis, MS: University Press of Mississippi, 1995.

See Also

New Deal (Second)

World War II Mobilization

Introduction

"If you are going to try to go to war, or to prepare for war, in a capitalist country, you have got to let business make money out of the process or business won't work." Secretary of War Henry Stimson made this comment in 1940 as preparations for World War II (1939–1945) gained momentum (quoted in Koistinen, p. 580). The global war would pit Allied forces, eventually composed primarily of the United States, Britain, China, and the Soviet Union, against the Axis powers consisting primarily of Germany, Japan, and Italy. U.S. businesses would play a key role in the mobilization efforts for war and the New Deal policies and programs would be largely curtailed. Funded by large military contracts, industry provided millions of new jobs and higher incomes than had been available through the Great Depression when millions of workers had lost their jobs or faced pay cuts. The mobilization effort focused on industry producing massive amounts of war goods including ships, tanks, arms, ammunition, and warplanes. Due to the strong U.S. public mood against international alliances, however, it took Roosevelt almost six years of lobbying with Congress, industry, and the public to begin earnest mobilization efforts.

The 1930s was clearly a troubled decade throughout much of the world. In the United States the stock market crash and Great Depression that followed brought rampant unemployment reaching up to 25 percent of the workforce by early 1933, or over 12 mil-

1939-1943

lion workers. President Herbert Hoover's (served 1929–1933) ineffective response through 1932 brought considerable social unrest with hunger marches and food riots. President Franklin Roosevelt's (served 1933–1945) arrival in early 1933 brought hope with his massive New Deal programs. But as the Depression lingered on, support for Roosevelt's programs slipped.

Meanwhile, in Europe dire economic problems in Germany following its defeat in World War I provided a fertile environment for the rise of radical politics. On to this stage stepped Adolf Hitler and the Nazi Party. Hitler preached a strong nationalistic way of life and a return to power for Germany built on military expansion. Similarly in Japan a weak government was replaced by its military, which also had strong desires to expand its control over China and other East Asian areas. Japan is poor in natural resources for its economy, and the expansion was in part designed to gain better access to these much-needed resources. The military leaders strongly glorified war and the training of its soldiers. As a result, the military route to gain access was considered most desirable by the Japanese leadership.

Due to the delay resulting from the strong isolationist mood of the nation, the United States faced a massive effort to prepare for war as German forces under Adolf Hitler stormed through Europe in 1939 and 1940. Many war materials were needed in addition to raising a large military force. As in World War I (1914–1918), the United States entered the war late. With the invasion of Poland by Germany in September 1939, Britain and France had declared war on Germany. President Franklin D. Roosevelt (served 1933–1945) was becoming more apprehensive about European developments and wanted to begin preparations. He faced, however, a public not wanting to be involved in another war across the Atlantic Ocean. But the situation in Europe continued to become more critical. With the fall of France to Germany in June 1940, the United States began providing shipments of arms and other provisions to Britain.

Converting industry to war production from production of civilian goods moved very slowly from 1939 through 1941. War mobilization would prove to be the event that would break a seeming deadlock between the New Dealers of President Roosevelt's administration and corporate leaders. The New Deal, a combination of economic relief and recovery programs first introduced by Roosevelt in early 1933, had taken a decided shift by 1935. The first two years had included efforts to work in partnership with business. By 1935, however, the focus

of those designing the programs, the New Dealers, had decidedly shifted to relief for the common worker and reform of business activities. Business leaders met reform measures with much opposition. Earlier in 1937, business and the increasingly conservative Congress were able to block any further New Deal programs from being created. They opposed such a strong role of government in the United States economic system. With war looming, the New Dealers had their own plans to mobilize the nation with close oversight provided by government. Business leaders feared greater government control of the economy and they resisted Roosevelt's early mobilization efforts. As a result, Roosevelt was hampered by several factors—a conservative Congress that had tired of New Deal programs, business hostility to New Deal programs, a public increasingly opposed to U.S. involvement in war overseas, and the lack of a specific crisis that could galvanize public opinion into unified action. The Japanese attack on Pearl Harbor on December 7, 1941, brought major changes including a full effort by the U.S. in 1942 and 1943.

The U.S. government was willing to spend as much money as needed to win the war. The federal budget increased from $8.9 billion in 1939 to over $95 billion in 1945. The gross national product, which is the total value of all goods and services produced by the nation's economy, increased from just over $90 billion to almost $212 billion. The total amount of war materials produced by 1945 was staggering. U.S. factories had made 296,000 warplanes, 86,000 tanks, 64,000 landing ships, six thousand navy vessels, millions of guns, billions of bullets, and hundreds of thousands of trucks and jeeps. U.S. production alone had exceeded the combined production of the Axis powers. The Axis was comprised of Germany, Italy, and Japan.

Increases in jobs and pay finally brought the Great Depression to a close. With increased military spending for war production, optimism over the national economy returned after the trying times of the Great Depression. Many Americans returned to work producing military weapons and supplies and many others went into the service. As with the New Deal, not all benefited from new economic opportunities. Black Americans and ethnic minorities still faced discrimination and inferior job opportunities. Women, though gaining more employment opportunities, still were faced with unequal pay. Some barriers were broken through, and each group played a major role in the home-front industrial production.

Issue Summary

A Series of War Mobilization Agencies

As Germany was beginning its expansion through Europe in 1938, U.S. business remained economically sluggish from the Great Depression, which had lowered production and left many Americans unemployed. Germany's invasion of Poland in September 1939 quickly led Britain and France to declare war on Germany. World War II had officially begun. Both countries had agreements with Poland to provide support in case of attack. The United States maintained its official neutrality, but President Roosevelt issued a proclamation of "limited" national emergency. It was time to begin looking at options toward planning for war. Roosevelt anticipated that if Europe and Britain fell to Germany, then the United States would be next to face the onslaught of Germany's well armed military. The U.S. government's first effort to begin preparations for war came with the creation of the War Resources Board (WRB). The board was to produce a plan identifying what would be needed to mobilize the nation's industries. Also in 1939, the military released its own Industrial Mobilization Plan. Despite these planning efforts, little translated into actual action and few new jobs resulted.

By May 1940 German troops were sweeping toward Paris and thousands of British troops began evacuating Europe at Dunkirk on the French coast. Increasingly alarmed President Roosevelt asked Congress to provide $1 billion for the production of 50,000 planes. Following the fall of France in June 1940 and the beginning of a German air assault on Britain later that summer, Roosevelt brought back the National Defense Advisory Commission (NDAC). The NDAC had previously existed during World War I (1914–1918). The commission was composed of members representing labor, agriculture, industry, and public consumers. Roosevelt was still facing an isolationist Congress and public, and an industry not eager to shift its focus from consumer goods to war materials. Roosevelt believed the NDAC could better overcome these hurdles than he could acting alone. Congress significantly boosted defense spending in 1940 and passed the first peacetime military draft for the United States. The commission, however, had little authority except to advise what action it thought was needed. Mobilization continued to progress slowly.

Following his 1940 reelection and with the air blitz, or attack, of Britain by German war planes well underway, President Roosevelt replaced the administratively weak NDAC with the Office of Production Management (OPM) in January 1941. The head of

Chronology:

1935: Germany begins a massive rearmament program that lasts for several years.

March 1938: Germany annexes Austria beginning an ambitious program of expansion in Europe.

September 28, 1938: The League of Nations labels Japan an aggressor nation for its military actions against China.

May 22, 1939: Germany and Italy under the dictator Benito Mussolini sign a pact of cooperation.

September 1, 1939: Germany invades Poland with massive forces; Britain and France proclaim war against Germany two days later.

October 4, 1939: Congress approves arms sales to European democracies.

April 9, 1940: Germany invades Denmark and Norway.

May 16, 1940: Roosevelt requests that Congress approve production of 50,000 planes per year.

June 22, 1940: France surrenders to Germany following Germany's invasion that began May 10.

August 8, 1940: The Battle of Britain begins with German bombing of selected targets in Britain; bombing would last into the following year.

March 11, 1941: President Roosevelt signs the Lend-Lease Act giving Britain access to America's "arsenal of democracy."

July 9, 1941: President Roosevelt announces extensive preparation for war.

December 7, 1941: The Japanese bomb U.S. military installations at Pearl Harbor in Hawaii leading the United States to enter the world war against both Germany and Japan.

January 16, 1942: The War Production Board (WPB) is established as the leading agency for war mobilization.

April 18, 1942: The War Manpower Commission (WMC) is created to help allocate manpower to industries and military services.

Map of German troop advances from 1939 to 1941.

(The Gale Group.)

OPM was William Knudsen, former chairman of General Motors. OPM was charged with getting industrial production going and distributing manpower and raw materials. As with the other planning organizations the OPM was largely controlled by corporate advisers who primarily acted to limit its authority over industry. Roosevelt was still having trouble convincing industry to replace their production of civilian goods with military production. Having little authority to require mobilization of industry, the OPM proved ineffective.

By May 1941, with Japan expanding southward toward the Philippines where the United States held direct interests, Roosevelt issued an "unlimited"

national emergency declaration. This declaration gave the president substantial powers to coordinate military and civilian activities. Gradually the preparation for World War II was considerably expanding the presidency. Roosevelt, however, still did not seek to use this power to challenge the well-organized corporate powers.

The Japanese bombing of Pearl Harbor, Hawaii, on December 7, 1941, finally triggered full mobilization. Japan had hoped the attack would demoralize the United States and prevent it from challenging Japan's expansion in the Far East, especially in the Philippines where the United States had held strong interest since 1898 when it was gained from Spain. The surprise

An anguished Frenchman sheds tears as German soldiers march into Paris on June 14, 1940. France surrendered to the Germans two days later. (National Archives and Records Administration. Reproduced by permission.)

attack by a massive air invasion consisting of 306 warplanes launched from Japanese ships situated some two hundred miles away struck hard at the main U.S. naval base and naval fleet in the Pacific region. The attack crippled the U.S. Pacific Fleet, sinking four battleships and almost two hundred planes. The United States also suffered 3,700 casualties. The United States public was shocked and enraged. War was declared on Japan the following day on December 8. Three days later Germany and Italy declared war on the United States.

In January 1942, while Germany was focused on capturing Russia, President Roosevelt established the War Production Board (WPB) to assume control over wartime mobilization. Corporate executives played a strong role on the board in addition to the military services. Industries were now required to convert to military production. The board sought to establish a system to distribute raw materials to industries based on priority needs. The manufacture of certain goods was limited, and in some cases was completely stopped so that raw materials such as steel and aluminum would be available for war projects. The actual procurement, or purchase, of war materials was left to the military services that worked closely with industries.

Still, the WPB did not have absolute power. The military and industry only loosely adopted board

decisions. Because of business pressure, the government applied little formal oversight and repercussions for not conforming to decisions. Contractors at times would still delay working on military contracts if conflicts occurred with their civilian production. Also, at this time, the remaining New Dealers who had not left the administration when foreign issues took over and domestic funding declined desired to have the flood of military contracts spread around. They particularly wanted them to go to areas still economically depressed. The corporate leaders, however, dictated to the military services how the contracts should be awarded. Between May and September 1942 as the war against Germany spread to Northern Africa, 80 percent of all contracts went to areas already experiencing labor shortages from earlier work increases while other areas still suffered from high unemployment. By 1943 the alliance between corporations and the military was in firm control of mobilization. In dropping his reform efforts Roosevelt had begun to informally refer to himself as "Dr. Win-the-War" rather than "Dr. New Deal" as some, including the press, had previously called him.

As the war efforts progressed conflicts still rose among industries over access to materials and labor. Continuing concern over the progress of mobilization

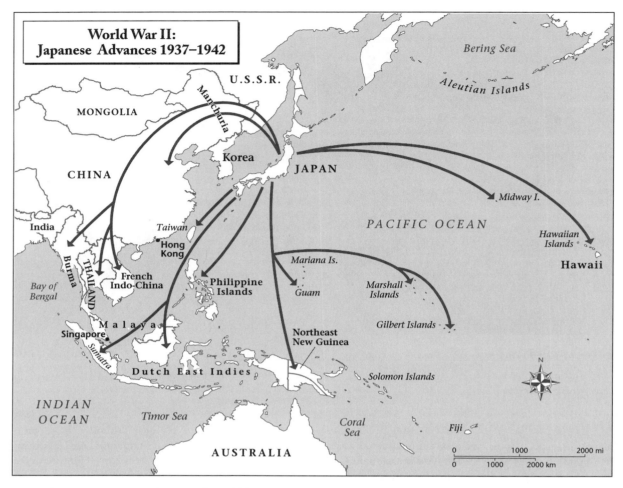

Map of Japanese troop advances from 1937 to 1942.

(The Gale Group.)

efforts once more led Roosevelt to create yet another small new temporary agency, the Office of War Mobilization (OWM), in May 1943. The German forces had surrendered in Northern Africa and the fight was about to move to Europe itself. Led by former U.S. Supreme Court justice James F. Byrnes, the organization was created to better coordinate activities among industries. OWM would resolve disputes that arose between industries over access to raw materials, labor, and other production issues. By July 1943, the wartime conversion of the U.S. economy was substantially completed. Allied forces invaded Italy that month leading to a surrender of Italy by September. Less than a year later a massive Allied force would land by sea on the west coast of Europe at Normandy. Through intensive fighting across Europe over most of the next year Germany would finally surrender in May 1945 ending the war in Europe.

Economic production in the United States more than doubled during the war years. After years of the Great Depression, the defense mobilization dramatically picked up the nation's economy. Seventeen million new jobs were created. More people were taking home paychecks, and those pay amounts were larger than ever. Average workers' hourly wages increased 22 percent through the war years. Debts incurred during the economic hardships of the Depression were paid, and savings began to grow once again.

The Home Front Economy

The war contracts awarded to industry produced a booming economy with eventual full employment reaching 98 percent employment of the workforce. Given its conversion to war materials, however, industry could only produce a limited amount of consumer goods needed at home. Therefore government had to establish some safeguards against inflation, which is when the cost of goods increase faster than income. This problem was solved in several ways. One approach was to take money out of circulation. This was accomplished through increased taxes and sales of war bonds. Another approach came in April 1941 with the establishment of the Office for Price Administration and Civilian Supply (OPACS). OPACS was created to stabilize prices and oversee the fragile civilian economy. With the rationing and shortage of domestic consumer goods, economic conditions were ripe for significant inflation that would weaken the war economy. OPACS set the maximum prices for most goods. New Dealers also saw OPACS as a way to challenge industry-controlled war mobilization agencies such as OPM and the numerous industry advisory committees that were forming to help guide individual industries. New Dealer economist Leon Henderson led OPACS. Henderson believed industry was slow in responding to the military needs of the nation while it still pursued a growing civilian economy that was improving as people gained increased income from wartime jobs.

To ensure the scarce civilian goods were distributed fairly among citizens, a rationing system was created. Reminiscent of the food stamp programs of the Great Depression, but for purposes of limiting consumption rather than expanding consumption, OPACS issued ration stamps that were used to purchase various items such as canned goods, meat, milk, cheese, and gasoline. Food was rationed according to family size. Gasoline was rationed according to individual needs. Most people got three gallons of gas a week.

An Employment Boost

Given the slow start, U.S. industry did not really begin feeling the effects of war mobilization until the summer of 1940, with the beginning of some war material production. Unemployment remained high into the middle of 1941, but shortages in certain types of skilled workers had already developed. The pace of mobilization picked up by the latter part of 1941 and more so after the attack on Pearl Harbor on December 7, when the nation firmly committed itself to a war on two fronts–in Europe against Germany and in Asia against Japan. The enlistment of men into the armed forces accelerated, and by early 1942 industry had to take more actions in attracting new people into the labor pool such as relaxing restrictions on minorities and women. Additionally, the need to shift workers from less-essential employment producing domestic goods to more-essential employment producing war materials became critical. Competition between industries over the available labor supply became more intense.

More About...

The Plight of Japanese Americans

When Japanese forces attacked U.S. military bases at Pearl Harbor on December 7, 1941 approximately 127,000 Japanese Americans lived in the United States. That amounted to only one-tenth of one percent of the nation's population. Most, however, lived on the West Coast where fears ran high that Japanese attacks on the mainland might occur with the aid of Japanese Americans or that acts of sabotage might occur. The racial prejudice against Asian Americans had been building up for years. Often the hatred was for economic reasons. Many claimed that the Asian Americans would willingly work for very low pay thus causing workers' pay overall to stay low. During the Depression they were accused of taking much needed jobs away from whites.

With this new fear of attack and sabotage, President Roosevelt came under pressure from the military and the public to evacuate Japanese Americans from the coast. In February 1942 Roosevelt signed an executive order to pursue such a course. The newly created War Relocation Authority (WRA) moved 112,000 Japanese Americans to ten internment camps located in seven states. Because of the prejudice of the U.S. population even in the interior states, the camps were forced to locate in desolate areas of the West away from established population centers. Bordered by barbed wire and armed guards, the camps consisted of wooden barracks covered by tarpaper and divided into one-room apartments. Japanese Americans were forced to live under these often unsanitary conditions until December 1944, well after the actual threat of attack had ended.

Labor shortages in certain areas, as a result of a shift in workers, led to the creation of the War Manpower Commission (WMC) in April 1942. The WMC was formed to help direct manpower into the more critical industries. Geared to get the most from the available U.S. workforce, the commission was to coordinate manpower needs of industry and the armed forces. It also facilitated the transfer of workers to industries considered more essential and which were facing shortages. In addition to more jobs available in private business and industry that received government contracts, the federal government, which had grown considerably during the Great Depression, grew substantially larger during the war. The number of federal civilian employees increased fourfold between 1941 and 1945 to oversee the war effort.

Mobilization was expensive. The federal government spent $290 billion on the war effort to mobilize and fight. To finance the war, several avenues were used to raise the money including taxes, the sale of war bonds, and obtaining loans. Taxes raised half the monies needed. The Revenue Act of 1942 increased taxes and established a national tax system that would continue into the twenty-first century. The system of withholding income taxes from paychecks began the following year, in 1943. Corporate taxes were also raised to 40 percent. The other half of the war expense was paid by selling liberty bonds and obtaining loans.

On February 9, 1943, President Roosevelt signed an executive order setting a minimum 48-hour workweek for workers in some industries and in certain areas of the nation where labor shortages existed. The War Manpower Commission would identify the industries and areas. Workers found that these changes in the workweek added greatly to their earnings, especially in industries subject to minimum wage requirements and for those in which unions had successfully obtained premium overtime payment. Industry also began working on an around the clock basis, using several shifts through the day. Large numbers of people worked in these industries and they received higher wages for the less desirable shifts, such as the midnight shift. Those working in industries producing aircraft, automobiles, ships, steel, and electrical machinery were particularly affected.

Workers also enjoyed wage increases reflected in hourly wage rates as well. By mid-1943 about 60 percent of factory wage earners, or over eight million workers, earned between 50¢ and $1 an hour. Three percent of the workers made over $1.50 an hour. Ten percent received less than 50 cents and two percent less than 40¢. These figures were well above hourly rates they received two years earlier reflecting Depression era rates. In January 1941, 17 percent of workers had made less than 40¢ an hour and 31 percent less than 50¢ an hour. With mobilization well underway in 1943, workers paid over $1 an hour were numerous in industries involving transportation equipment, rubber, machinery, and printing and publishing. Those workers earning less than 40¢ an hour were in food industries employing a relatively large percentage of women. The highest paid workers were almost all men. Those working in retail stores and non-war industries also saw improved wages, but at much lower rates than factory workers in war industries. Also wages of non-manufacturing workers were much lower than in the manufacturing industries. Wages in non-manufacturing rose considerably less than those in manufacturing following the beginning of war mobilization efforts. Nonetheless most were financially better off than they had been the previous decade.

Women in Mobilization

For women the war mobilization effort opened up many new job opportunities. Women had not had access to better employment positions up through the 1930s. Even with the improved job opportunities, however, gender discrimination remained a major factor. Through the 1920s women remained limited to domestic work and retail jobs. The Great Depression had only made conditions worse. Women were seen as competitors for jobs sought by unemployed men. As war mobilization began industrial jobs remained closed to women who were considered too physically inferior to perform industrial tasks. At first, plenty of unemployed men were available in the labor force. By 1942, however, with millions of men entering military service, industry began more aggressively recruiting women. The War Manpower Commission (WMC) focused on recruiting women where labor shortages were occurring.

Before long women were involved in almost all parts of the war industry. The number of women working increased from 14 million in 1941 to over 19 million in 1944 when 37 percent of adult women were working. In manufacturing, where women had been largely excluded earlier, the number of women working increased over 140 percent from 1940 to 1944. The percentage of women with jobs in the total labor force rose from 22 percent to almost 35 percent. By 1943 they even filled 10 percent of jobs in shipyards. New kinds of job opportunities opened including jobs in newspapers and radio stations. The number of women in labor unions quadrupled. Many government positions also became available for the first time. The percentage of government jobs held by women doubled from 19 percent to over 38 percent from 1940 to 1944. In addition several hundred thousand joined the military service.

Despite all of these job gains women were still largely excluded from management positions. Women faced discrimination both by employers and by unions. Though the National War Labor Board in 1942 called

Mary Josephine Farley, only twenty years old, was an expert airplane mechanic and one of many women that took jobs, previously performed by men, in industries that produced products used in World War II.
(FDR Library.)

for equal pay for women for equal work, many employers did not comply. Women were placed in lower paying positions and received less advancement. Women were also the first to be laid off when war industry work began to decline.

Changes in the Workforce

Major changes in the workforce resulted from mobilization. Between July 1940 and July 1943, 5.3 million male workers were no longer available to industry because they had joined the military services. That figure was offset by the addition of 3.9 million female workers to the labor force for the first time in the nation's history. By late 1943 the unemployment rate had dropped to a remarkably low 1.3 percent. Nine million workers had been jobless in 1939, as the nation struggled to make its way out of the Great Depression. By 1945, just six years later, that figure dropped to one million.

By 1943 the U.S. government was spending almost $90 billion annually on the war effort both in production of war goods and the actual combat expenses. The war effort was reflected in the nation's gross national product. By July 1943, 47 percent of the U.S. gross national product was taken for military purposes. This figure was compared to nine percent in mid-1941 and only two percent in 1939.

Most of the increase in manufacturing during mobilization occurred in the production of durable goods—goods not destroyed in use, such as machinery. Earlier, during the Depression, employment in non-durable goods, such as chemicals, paper, rubber, textile, apparels, and foods, actually exceeded employment in durable goods, as people cut back on new purchases and saved their money for those items, like food, that they needed to survive and demand for durable goods fell. That relationship switched as the nation mobilized for war. By July 1943 almost 60 percent of factory workers were employed producing durable goods. Aircraft and machinery production and shipbuilding were some of the larger growth industries in durable goods. Regarding non-durable goods, the chemical industry saw substantial increases as well.

Mexicans and Mexican Americans

World War II opened new job opportunities to Mexican Americans and Mexicans once again. With many Americans joining the military services or opting for higher paying industrial jobs in the cities, a sharp labor shortage in agriculture occurred. This shortage led to the United States to reverse its repatriation policies of the Great Depression. The United States began a program to recruit Mexican field laborers back to the United States. The government of Mexico, however, would not readily agree to such a program for its citizens after how they were treated during the Great Depression. The Mexican government insisted the U.S. government provide transportation, medical care, shelter, and food. With the United States needing to increase food production for the war effort, an agreement was soon reached.

Beginning in 1942, several hundred thousand Mexican immigrants, called "braceros," or "laborers," came into the United States to work for the next few years. In addition many Mexican Americans already living in the United States found work in the war industries. For example, no Mexican Americans worked in the Los Angeles shipyards in 1941. By 1944 some 17,000 were working in the shipyards. Another 400,000 Mexican Americans also joined the military services. Discrimination against Mexicans and Mexican Americans did continue as it did against other racial and ethnic groups in the United States. They often received lower wages for the same work as whites and were given jobs associated with miserable work conditions.

Labor Unions and Mobilization

Unions, though not playing a critical role in planning for mobilization, still saw major changes. Union membership increased by 1.5 million workers during the prewar mobilization period of 1939 to 1941. During the war labor union membership rose between 1941 and 1945 by over 50 percent. From 1941 the number of union members increased from 10.5 million to almost 15 million in 1945. By 1945, almost one-third of the U.S. labor force were union members. The CIO, representing the mass production industries, such as steel, rubber, and automobiles, became almost the same size as the older AFL.

With the government setting wage caps, the main labor issues focused on working conditions and fringe benefits. Unions pledged not to promote strikes. Many wildcat strikes, or strikes without union approval, however, did occur over issues of safety and employee relations. As available labor became more scarce, the labor unions began to be more successful in seeking increased wages.

Prosperity was not seen in every industry. One industry that saw wages decline during the war was coal mining—despite record levels of production. Safety was a major issue as almost two thousand miners died between 1940 and May 1943. Finally the United Mine Workers, led by union president John L. Lewis, went on strike. The striking workers and Lewis met strong public opposition and were accused of not being loyal to the war effort. In reaction Congress passed the Smith-Connally War Labor Disputes Act giving the government power to seize and operate industries in which workers were on strike.

Overall labor and employers began communicating much better during the busier war years than during the Great Depression. Job security increased as well as the stability of industry. Unions became more a part of the fabric of industry and less independent and militant.

Regulating Wartime Wages

The Fair Labor Standards Act of 1938 established minimum wage standards that directly affected the wage rates of certain war production industries, particularly the large number of workers in the lower paying industries. The minimum of 30 cents an hour that became effective in October 1939 rose to 40 cents by the spring of 1943. Opposition to the wage requirements

More About...

Black Americans

As America began preparing for World War II, black Americans were still facing a well-established, racially segregated society. The discriminatory Jim Crow laws of the South maintained a rigid separation of the races in all public aspects of life. With previous migration of thousands of blacks out of the South to escape the Jim Crow system, blacks became highly concentrated in Northern inner cities. They suffered high unemployment and unhealthy living conditions. President Roosevelt and the New Deal had offered little specifically for black Americans. Black citizens primarily benefited from New Deal programs designed to assist the poor in general.

Not surprisingly these longstanding social traditions of racial discrimination and segregation carried over into World War II mobilization efforts. Unemployment remained high among blacks as industries geared up and many whites found jobs. Employers were making requests to the U.S. Employment Service, an agency that assisted industry in finding workers, for whites only. The agency honored these requests. For example, the aircraft industry employed only 240 black Americans in 1940 out of one hundred thousand workers. The jobs that were given to blacks were commonly the low-paying positions of janitors and garage attendants.

Not only did barriers persist in industry, the military also remained rigidly segregated. Segregation was strong in the Army and Navy, and blacks were still not allowed in the Air Force or Marines. Secretary of War Henry Stimson, who oversaw mobilization, was a Republican with strong racist attitudes. Not only did he consider black Americans inferior, but he believed that desegregating the services would lower morale.

By early 1941 increased pressure was placed on the government to create more opportunities in industry and services for black Americans. To increase public awareness of the problems, A. Philip Randolph, head of the Brotherhood of Sleeping Car Porters, began organizing a massive march on Washington, D.C. for later in the year. President Roosevelt did not want to see such a march believing there was a pos-

sibility for violence. Randolph presented the president with demands that would have to be met before he would call off the march. These demands included an end to racial discrimination in private employment and an end to racial discrimination and segregation in the federal government and the armed forces. With Randolph not backing down, Roosevelt soon relented. He signed an executive order prohibiting racial discrimination in the federal government and in defense industries that received government contracts. The order also created the Fair Employment Practices Committee (FEPC) to investigate discrimination complaints. In response to the order Randolph called off the march. With little funding or legal authority to enforce actions, however, the FEPC proved ineffective in creating social change.

Following the attack on Pearl Harbor in December 1941 the need for manpower in the Army increased dramatically. The number of blacks in the Army rose from less than 98,000 in November 1941 to 468,000 in December 1942. Eventually almost one million would serve in the military. Segregation, however, remained rigid.

As during the New Deal era President Roosevelt did not promote racial equality during the mobilization period. He did become more involved in pushing for the hiring of black Americans by mid-1943 as labor shortages in critical industries began to appear. The U.S. Employment Service began rejecting requests for workers that specified race. Also the National Labor Relations Board that oversees labor union activity quit certifying unions that excluded minorities. Black employment increased from 4.4 million in 1940 to 5.3 million in 1944 with most of the increase occurring in 1943 and 1944. In 1942 only three percent of all war workers were black Americans. By 1945 the figure climbed to eight percent, closer to the percentage of black Americans represented in the U.S. population. The number of black Americans employed by the federal government rose from 60,000 to two hundred thousand during the war. Overall, during the war, some job barriers fell for black Americans, though racial discrimination remained pronounced.

had lessened by 1941 as the competition for workers increased. The act also had addressed overtime payment. It stated that workers covered by the act must be paid at least time and a half their regular pay rates for hours worked over 40 hours a week. It was this overtime provision that most affected incomes during the war mobilization period.

To keep control over the rise in wages and prices, a comprehensive program of wage-rate controls was begun in October 1942. The National War Labor Board had earlier been established in January 1942 to address wage disputes. The October executive order also charged the board with implementing price stabilization measures. The board was to keep prices, wages, and salaries close to September 1942 levels. The board had extensive powers to review proposed wage and price changes. Increases did continue, but more under the watchful eye of the board especially when large increases were proposed. As result of the stabilization efforts, the wage rates in manufacturing had increased almost 26 percent between January 1939 and October 1942, when the executive order was signed. Wage rates increased only just over five percent between October 1942 and July 1943. Most of these earlier increases occurred after January 1941.

A New Industry and Military Alliance

Despite sharp conflicts with business over New Deal policies through the later 1930s, early on President Roosevelt had to seek cooperation from business for mobilization efforts. Besides backing off from New Deal reform initiatives, particularly any more regulatory legislation aimed at industry, Roosevelt also offered financial incentives to businesses. The incentives included major tax breaks for building new manufacturing plants to produce war materials, suspending antitrust laws so companies could more freely cooperate, and issuing military contracts to purchase war goods that would guarantee good profits. In addition to war plants built by private business, the federal government also built plants and leased them to companies on very good terms. President Roosevelt essentially turned the war economy over to the country's business leaders. This both insured cooperation by industry and large profits for industry.

With business advisors brought in to help the Army and Navy prepare for war, the military began relying heavily on their main corporate contractors to make key decisions for them. A strong corporate-military association was forged. After years of economic stagnation through the Great Depression, business leaders were hungry to pursue profits from war mobilization. They favored the weaker oversight of mobilization by mili-

tary leadership, with business advisors formally included in the oversight process, rather than the potentially more restrictive civilian agencies led by the New Dealers. Through this industry-military alliance, much government authority would be transferred to major corporations and trade associations. Despite Roosevelt's consent for the arrangement, this transfer was in direct opposition to the New Dealers' desire to take the lead in the name of public interest. The New Dealers wanted to use this opportunity of a rising economy to promote social equality. They opposed the concentration of economic power in a limited number of businesses. They believed social inequality and concentrated corporate power were the basic causes of the Great Depression. Therefore debates over mobilization were a continuation of earlier debates that had run in government throughout the Great Depression. Out of necessity to lead a nation in war, however, Roosevelt held a decreasing commitment to social reform. Many disappointed New Dealers began leaving government as New Deal programs were terminated with no new programs to take their place.

Individuals involved in the debates included Leon Henderson and Robert Nathan for the New Dealers and Ferdinand Eberstadt, James Forrestal, and Robert Patterson for the military-industry alliance. Eberstadt, Forrestal, and Patterson were all corporate leaders recruited to lead military mobilization. The instability of organized labor did not help the cause of the New Dealers. Battles between the American Federation of Labor (AFL) and Congress of Industrial Organizations (CIO) continued and even increased with the influx of new workers during the mobilization. As a result organized labor played much less of a leading role during war mobilization than many expected. The combined hostility towards labor by the increasingly conservative Congress, the military, and business leaders proved effective in minimizing labor's influence.

Some New Deal Programs Close Their Doors

By 1940 a conservative Congress and numerous business leaders had gained increased power to develop government policy through the war mobilization program. Some New Deal programs did not fare well. Roosevelt himself understood the shifting nature of government and national priorities and realized his push for social and economic reform was largely over. The conservatives in government and business leaders strongly believed that New Deal programs were intrusive in private business and interfered with private initiatives. One of the more popular New Deal programs—and one of Roosevelt's personal

By 1945 U.S. factories produced 86,000 tanks for the war effort. WWII ushered in a new age of big business, with close ties forming between the military branch of the federal government and United States industry. (© Bettmann/Corbis. Reproduced by permission.)

favorites—the Civilian Conservation Corps (CCC) came to an end in 1942. Originally established to employ young men in projects conserving natural resources, the CCC began teaching its enrollees how to read blueprints and do other tasks that would be useful in the military as the U.S. role in World War II began. As more men joined the military services the number of CCC participants declined. Roosevelt had suggested that the CCC might still be useful for youth below the age required to enter the military, but Congress chose to close it out altogether.

Another New Deal program, the Works Progress Administration (WPA), lost two thirds of its workers to the war industry in 1942, where pay and jobs were better. As the year 1942 came to an end, the WPA was closed out as well. The National Youth Administration (NYA) lasted until 1943 because it began teaching vocational skills to youth that would be useful to the war industry. But as the available labor pool shrank, on-the-job training in industry became more common and the need for the NYA ended. Programs regarding farmers, the Farm Security Administration, designed to assist low-income farmers buy machinery and land, and the Rural Electrification Administration, which had long been opposed by private utility companies, were also subject to funding cutbacks.

The National Resources Planning Board (NRPB), created in 1933 by the National Industrial Recovery Act (NIRA), was originally charged to oversee industrial recovery during the Great Depression. By the early 1940s the NRPB, looking ahead, began planning for the nation's postwar economy. Its recommendations included expansion of social security for the needy and the poor and creation of public works projects. The projects would promote full employment once veterans returned from the war and the war industries scaled back to again provide just civilian production. Business leaders and the conservative Congress, however, were greatly alarmed by the proposals. They did not want to see a return to New Deal type programs fostering big government and growing influence over business. Congress reacted by cutting off funds to the agency, and it closed in 1943.

Despite loss of the NRPB and other New Deal programs, President Roosevelt did not entirely turn his back on social reform. To help maintain the wartime economic prosperity of workers, President Roosevelt, in the 1944 State of the Union address, proposed an Economic Bill of Rights. The proposal was a direct extension of New Deal ideals. He wanted to insure that everyone had a fair opportunity to have jobs, sufficient housing, education, and financial protection from old age, illness, and unemployment. The proposal, however, had no chance in the political climate. Roosevelt was able to extend generous benefits to war veterans. Congress passed the Servicemen's Readjustment Act, more commonly known as the GI Bill. The bill provided unemployment benefits, preference to veterans for hiring, and low-interest loans for purchasing homes, farms, and small businesses. The programs provided a major benefit to veterans through the rest of the twentieth century.

End of the Great Depression

By 1943 factory towns that had been stagnant since 1929 were suddenly prosperous. The New Deal through the 1930s had been successful in lessening the economic hardships brought on by the Great Depression, but it took full war mobilization to end the Depression and get the nation's economy moving again. The New Deal had attracted much antagonism, particularly from the business world and the South. As a result the corporate-military alliance, supported by Roosevelt, would guide the nation through World War II and beyond. The alliance's primary postwar goal was to establish financial prosperity through strong national security and by maximizing corporate profits. New Deal ideals of financial security for individuals, particularly the poor, largely fell to the wayside until they were revived again in the 1960s.

The New Deal also lost its leader. Well after many of the New Deal programs had been closed, mobilization had ended, and military victory in World War II was in sight, President Roosevelt died suddenly, leaving what was left of the New Deal movement without its star player. Roosevelt suffered a massive cerebral hemorrhage while relaxing at his Warm Springs, Georgia, retreat on April 12, 1945. He died within minutes. Vice-president Harry Truman (served 1945–1953) took over the presidency and immediately faced many difficult decisions. He inherited the immense task of following in the footsteps of a highly popular president. One of his early momentous decisions was how to use the newly developed atomic bomb to end the war. His fateful decision led to the death of almost a million Japanese citizens as two atomic bombs were dropped on Japanese soil, one on the city of Hiroshima and the other on Nagasaki, leading to Japan's surrender. On the domestic front, Truman did not discard all of Roosevelt's ideals. He adopted many of his predecessor's goals of providing economic security to citizens. Truman would later introduce the idea of the Fair Deal, a new postwar version of the New Deal. The Fair Deal proposals would include expanding federal government authority over industry as it transitioned back to peacetime produc-

tion, national health insurance program, protection of minority rights in employment, and establishing more public power projects.

Contributing Forces

World War I Mobilization and Inter-War Planning

World War II was not the first occasion for the United States to mobilize for war in the twentieth century. The spread of war in Europe after 1914 finally led to the United States joining in World War I (1914–1918) in 1916. With the United States having a small national government with very limited powers prior to World War I, the nation's corporate leaders had to step in and lead the mobilization effort for World War I. In particular Congress created the National Defense Advisory Commission (NDAC), which included corporate advisors to guide mobilization. Industry and financial leaders knew that government had to expand for war, but they wanted few permanent changes in the size of government. This same approach would be adopted for World War II in an effort to prevent growth of government aside from the military services. Therefore the NDAC promoted creation of industry groups to lead military purchasing programs. Businessmen were acting as government agents, often establishing contracts with their own industries. As war preparations progressed, public and congressional opposition grew to the heavy business role in governmental operations. As a result, the War Industries Board (WIB) was created in July 1917, to make the involvement of business advisors less obvious. Given the continued strong business influence, the WIB proved ineffective in decreasing corporate control of government activities.

Overall the U.S. military performed poorly in World War I. The military had greatly underestimated the size of the force that was needed to assist France and Britain in defeating Germany. As a result there were delays in getting an adequate forces, and once they did arrive they were poorly trained. Once there, the U.S. commander General John J. Pershing refused to use U.S. forces as reinforcements for the battle weary European forces, fighting separately. Much time was lost and inefficiency delayed ultimate victory. Embarrassed by the performance, Congress decided to continue military planning efforts after the war. This inter-war planning program continued the close cooperation between the military and business. In fact President Roosevelt and the New Dealers carried this model of military-industry cooperation into the New Deal government planning programs. The National Industrial Recovery Act (NIRA) was a primary example. Planning under the act was similar to the earlier WIB. Industry trade associations carried out government activities. This planning process, however, proved ineffective in economic recovery and Roosevelt abandoned this type of planning in 1935 for future New Deal programs.

Meanwhile the military, a major arm of the government outside New Deal activities of the 1930s, was gaining added experience in mobilization planning. Limited in size and extent of influence, the military suffered only limited affects of the Great Depression. The relationship between the military and major contracting industries strengthened due to interwar planning. At the same time Roosevelt was pursuing social and economic reforms under ever-expanding civilian government authority. The New Dealers, composed of lawyers, academics, and economists, opposed corporate roles in carrying out government activities. The reforms they proposed spurred conflicts between New Dealers who wanted the government to take a more active role in public life and business leaders who believed the expanding government was too intrusive in private business activities.

Late 1930s U.S. Political Developments

Strong Democratic majorities in Congress accompanied President Roosevelt's landslide reelection victory in the fall of 1936. Those political successes by the Democratic Party appeared to be a strong endorsement of further New Deal solutions to the nagging economic crisis of the Great Depression. A series of factors, however, would derail this seemingly inevitable development. Roosevelt's bold plan to reorganize the U.S. Supreme Court in early 1937 and a decline in the economy later that year caused many to question the effectiveness of Roosevelt and the New Dealers. Roosevelt's plan to restructure the Court especially caused alarm not only among New Deal adversaries, but some of Roosevelt's strongest supporters as well. Supporters wondered if Roosevelt's critics had not been right after all, that Roosevelt was making the presidency far more powerful than the U.S. Constitution allowed. In addition Roosevelt's support of labor unions and the increased occurrence of strikes in 1937 by unions seeking employer recognition, also alarmed conservative Democrats in Congress. Business continued to be very hostile toward New Deal programs. As a result of these events, a more conservative Congress was elected in the mid-term 1938 elections. The conservative Democrats joined Republicans in Congress to effectively stall further New Deal social reform programs.

Business leaders and the conservative Congress also feared a New Deal-like program to conduct the war. They wanted to block any further expansion of the civil part of the federal government. New Dealers saw the increasing war threat as another reason to expand governmental control over the economy. With no clear crisis pressing the U.S. into war in 1939, business leaders did not quickly respond to Roosevelt's urging for war mobilization. They feared business could become a war casualty with greater governmental regulation introduced by New Dealer control of wartime economic mobilization. The conservative Congress and the strong isolationist mood of the public also hampered Roosevelt's attempts to strongly push business.

Europe in Turmoil

Under the dictatorship of Adolf Hitler, Germany pursued a major mobilization or rearmament, or a build-up of weapons, program from 1935 to 1939. It applied lessons learned from the earlier war in its mobilization plans for World War II. Some of the last major battles of World War I showed that tanks and airplanes had become key weapons in waging war. As a result, massive offensive attacks became much more effective. Mechanization of the military, therefore, was the key to Germany's future war strategy. By 1939 the German air force, known as the *Luftwaffe,* was the most modern, efficient, and well equipped in the world. The mass-produced German armored tanks would become a key part of the World War II *blitzkriegs,* or rapid-hitting offensive attacks. The German tank divisions had no equal in Europe at that time.

During the inter-war years of the 1920s and 1930s, other European nations such as Britain and France did not produce new weapons nearly as quickly as Germany. In fact by 1939 Britain did not have any armored divisions in its military. Additionally, the technology of military airplanes had changed greatly during the inter-war period. They had become bigger, faster, and could fly much farther. Bomber planes were also becoming much larger and were capable of carrying more and larger bombs. Like the United States, many of Britain's and France's planes were becoming outdated in light of these technological advancements.

Germany's invasion of Poland in September 1939, spurred by Hitler's desire to conquer all of Europe and place it under German control, showcased the application of high-speed armored warfare. The Germany military used large numbers of armored tanks supported by swarms of aircraft to sweep with great force and speed across the border and deep into Poland. The German invasion force consisted of 1.5

The armed forces of Adolf Hitler, shown here with his mistress Eva Braun, overpowered many European nations during World War II. (*© Bettmann/Corbis. Reproduced by permission.*)

million troops, six armored divisions and four divisions of personnel carriers carrying troops swiftly to battlefronts. It was clear wars now would require considerable industrial production programs. Even though Germany had a far inferior navy to the Allied forces (composed of Britain, France, and their allies), they made use of submarine attacks, known as U-boats. During the first four months of war these attacks sank 110 vessels, including a British aircraft carrier and a battleship.

Germany was not the only aggressor in northern Europe. Russia, operating through a secret pact signed with Germany, also invaded Poland. Russia, like Germany, was intent on expanding its influence and control of the Eastern European region. Russia thundered in from the east on September 17, 1939. Russia also annexed, or took possession of, Estonia, Latvia, and Lithuania, and then invaded Finland on November 30. Though first repelled by Finnish troops, Russia made a renewed assault on February 1, 1940, and Finland surrendered on March 6, 1940.

After a lull of several months in the German ground offensive in Europe following the conquest of Poland, Hitler renewed his expansionist efforts. During this time the Allies did little, and many began calling this the "phony war." The lull, however, soon ended. On April 9, 1940, Germany attacked Norway

and occupied Denmark. Then, on May 10, Germany launched its attack on France and the Netherlands. At the time, France's army of 800,000 soldiers was considered the most powerful in Europe. With news of the new German assaults on Western Europe, British Prime Minister Neville Chamberlain (served 1937–1940), who had not supported a strong British involvement in the war, resigned. Prime Minister Winston Churchill (served 1940–1945), a much more aggressive leader, replaced him. The German forces swept through Western Europe with incredible speed, leading to an eventual massive evacuation by late May of British troops and others from Europe at the seaport of Dunkirk in northern France. The evacuation, though saving over 338,000 lives, left behind all of Britain's heavy military equipment. On June 14 German forces entered Paris and, two days later, France surrendered. The isolationist position of the U.S. public and Congress was beginning to weaken with this turn of events. Roosevelt boldly sent Britain a half million rifles and 80,000 machine guns to replace arms left at Dunkirk.

Roosevelt and others were concerned about Germany's military expansion through Europe. In particular they feared that the fall of Europe to Hitler would make the Western Hemisphere the next step in Nazi aggression. Clearly some Latin American countries,

German Calvary soldiers ride through Paris, France after occupying the city in 1940. The fall of France, Poland, and other western European countries directly fed the debate in the United States over war mobilization. (© Hulton-Deutsch Collection/Corbis. Reproduced by permission.)

with their political and economic instability, were vulnerable to the growing German influence. The United States could end up surrounded by a vastly superior armed aggressor. As a result, the fall of Poland, France, and other western European countries directly fed the debate in the United States over war mobilization. Isolationist feelings of the public and Congress were beginning to melt. War mobilization had become the top issue in Roosevelt's administration.

Following the collapse of France, Hitler looked next toward the conquest of Great Britain. With the English Channel, ranging in width from 21 to 100 miles, separating Britain from Europe, Germany was going to rely primarily on air warfare to defeat Britain. Germany had 1,300 bombers and 1,200 fighter planes compared to Britain's 600 fighters. But Britain also had a newly developed radar system. This new technology, used for the first time in defending against the

German assault, would prove crucial in alerting British forces of approaching German planes. The German air assaults began in the summer of 1940 and increased through the following winter. There were relentless bombings of London and other cities. Much anxiety existed in Washington, DC, Roosevelt and others believed Britain was the last stand of defense before the Western Hemisphere would become vulnerable to German expansion. British air defenses, however, proved superior, shooting down German planes faster than Germany could produce them. Germany would eventually lose 1,700 aircraft to Britain's 900. By May 1941 the German air assault declined. It was during this early period of war from 1939 to 1941, with the fall of France and attacks on Britain, that the U.S. began gradually mobilizing.

Japanese Expansion

The Great Depression hit the Japanese economy hard. As international trade declined many businesses in Japan failed. The democratic Japanese government was losing the confidence and support of its citizens. Through the early 1930s the Japanese military began assuming greater powers. Being a relatively small island, Japan did not have many of the natural resources such as oil and coal necessary for its industry to revive. The Japanese military leaders decided to establish a colonial empire much like Britain had done in India. In 1931 Japan seized Manchuria in northeastern China. Manchuria was rich in iron and coal. Though condemned by other nations of the world for its act of aggression, no action was taken against Japan. The peace and isolationist movements in the United States and elsewhere limited any forms of more aggressive reactions.

Following the invasion of Manchuria in 1931, in 1937 Japan attacked China leading toward war. Japanese planes bombed major cities, including that Chinese capital of Beijing. Killing thousands of Chinese citizens, Japanese troops gained control of central and northern China. Still the United States, determined to maintain its isolationism, did nothing in response to Japanese aggression, though concerns grew over threats to the U.S. territories of Guam and the Philippines. In July 1941 Japan began a southward push into Indochina, consisting of present-day Vietnam, Laos, and Cambodia. With this new expansion, the United States took action by cutting off trade with Japan, including much needed oil, in an attempt to diplomatically discourage further action by Japan. In early November 1941 Japan sent a special diplomat to Washington, DC, to discuss peace and an end to the trade embargo. With the talks not progressing well, the United States learned that Japan might attack U.S.

military bases somewhere in the Pacific and a special alert was sent to military commanders, including those at Pearl Harbor in Hawaii. Shortly after the alert, the devastating strike came at Pearl Harbor, killing 3,700 people including many U.S. servicemen. The United States could no longer maintain isolationism. Faced with an attack on its people, on its shores, the United States became an active participant in World War II and entered into a major wartime mobilization effort at home.

Perspectives

America's Workers

Though at great expense in human life and suffering, the wartime economy brought the American worker financial security once again. Many American factory workers saw a major boost in average weekly earnings between January 1939 and July 1943. During that period, hourly earnings increased an average of 52 percent while the weekly earnings increased over 84 percent, from $23.19 to $42.76 a week. The weekly earnings increased more when longer workweeks and overtime pay became more prevalent. In addition wage incentives offered to increase production also led to greater weekly earnings. Promotions and bonuses became more common as labor shortages increased. Given the rise in prices of goods during the war, the average purchasing power of factory workers increased by almost 50 percent. Workers enjoyed this increase primarily after the summer of 1940. Other salary increases also occurred in transportation, government service, and mining. Despite the increases in many sectors of the economy, some industries, such as construction, actually declined in employment.

A key part of the durable goods industry was manufacturing. Workers in manufacturing industries particularly enjoyed increases in prosperity, particularly because durable goods were in demand to aid the war effort. Employment in the manufacturing industries increased 70 percent between 1939 and July 1943, the most in any U.S. industry. With workweeks lengthening, the total number of hours worked in manufacturing in the United States increased by 100 percent. The average number of hours worked in a week increased from less than 38 hours in 1939 to more than 44 hours in 1943, an almost 18 percent increase for an individual worker. The average number of hours worked in a week by workers in manufacturing rose from 40.6 hours to 45.2 hours from 1941 to 1942 alone as mobilization escalated. Some workweeks were longer, such as machine-tool manufacture, which averaged 50 hours a week. Workers in manufacturing saw their average weekly earnings increase 65 percent from $32.18 to $47.12 from December 1941 to April 1945. Accounting for inflation during that period the increase in real earnings was still a strong 27 percent.

Farmers also played a large part in mobilization and enjoyed the financial gains. Although farm population declined by 17 percent during the war, farm production significantly increased. Many rural residents joined the military or moved to the city for factory work. Instead of the crop reduction policies of the New Deal under the Agricultural Adjustment Act, farmers were once again pressed to produce more. Advances in pesticides and fertilizers, machinery, and scientific advances contributed to this greater productivity. Correspondingly, farm income expanded as well. Farm prices more than doubled during the war and profits soared. After 20 years of economic difficulty since the end of World War I, farmers finally enjoyed prosperity again. Crop surpluses disappeared and produce prices rose. Net farm income increased from $5.3 billion in 1939 to $13.6 billion in 1944. The increase in income per person was actually greater for farmers than for industrial workers through the war years. Farm communities prospered and some became economic leaders in their regions. Farmers spent their profits on more land and improved farm machinery.

National Perspectives

On a national level private industry and the New Dealers in the civilian sector of government had very different ideas on how to mobilize the nation for war. Key decisions had to be made related to converting privately owned industries, expanding the mining and processing of raw materials, controlling how raw materials were distributed, and overseeing the military purchasing of war materials. The military had traditionally relied on the nation's largest corporations and their prime contractors. The New Dealers in Roosevelt's administration wanted to see this heavy reliance on big business end. They wanted to open up opportunities for military contracts to small businesses as well. New Dealers believed public needs and policies should take clear priority over private corporate interests of big business. Not only did New Dealers wish to get military contracts to smaller companies, but also to companies located in parts of the country still facing the Great Depression's effects. To accomplish these public goals, the New Dealers sought a central role in mobilization efforts.

Industry, on the other hand, wanted no interruption of their private civilian production or interference with civilian markets. Believing the war would be brief, they did not want to hamper production of civil-

ian goods. So industry wanted military production only in plants built with public funds or through special financial arrangements. They also wanted to be as free as possible of New Deal social reforms and labor laws, including limitations on profits. Business did not want to see increased wartime regulation. They clearly wanted no new permanent, large federal agencies to control mobilization and perhaps control the U.S. economy after the war.

The New Dealers were stymied by a conservative Congress and the strong anti-war mood of the nation's population. As he did during the Great Depression, Roosevelt had to make compromises to reach his goals of preparing the nation for war and build national unity. The nation's business leaders, hostile toward the New Deal programs of Roosevelt, played a strong role in shaping Roosevelt's wartime policies. Given the initial deadlock over how war mobilization should proceed, Roosevelt had to rely on a set of small temporary agencies heavily staffed with private business advisers. The War Resources Board (WRB), created in 1939, developed a decentralized plan based on voluntary industrial compliance.

The struggle over control over military mobilization between New Dealers and industrial leaders continued into 1940. Then, with the crisis of war becoming stronger and having to face a conservative Congress and the strong public mood of isolationism, Roosevelt chose to join forces with the corporate leaders and abandon any plans of developing a civilian government plan for mobilization. The corporate leaders and the military were called to take the lead while trying not to cause undue alarm to the isolationists. Though Roosevelt did not officially adopt the earlier WRB plan, the mobilization effort largely followed it. In addition to the later war planning agencies and a much stronger military involvement, was the creation of various industry advisory committees. War mobilization gave corporate leaders the opportunity to regain prestige and political power lost during the Great Depression. The New Dealers largely faded to the background in regards to war mobilization.

The corporate leaders opposed interference by New Dealers and organized labor. They did not want to see wartime authority placed into existing government agencies in which new permanent oversight of corporations would be established. Their desire was to rely on corporate volunteerism organized through temporary government agencies. Corporate leadership wanted a government role that could easily be dismantled following the war. Such was the War Resources Board dominated by corporate advisors. The board was the first mobilization agency. A series of such agencies evolved guided by business advisors as well as industry advisory committees and the military services. The corporate leaders supported expansion of military responsibilities. Industrial and financial leaders were united in this approach.

Conceding to the influence of industry in shaping U.S. mobilization policies and seeking to unify the nation as best as possible, President Roosevelt appointed Republican Henry L. Stimson as Secretary of War. A strong big business advocate, Stimson led the government in choosing to follow the guidance of industry leaders in preparing for war. This included providing industry with certain levels of support in various ways. As part of industry's demands, financial incentives and tax breaks were provided to support expansion of existing plants. Businesses wanted to minimize impact on their production of civilian goods and the profits that they were currently enjoying. Companies were also given some freedom from antitrust actions. They could cooperate with other companies if they could show their working relations were sufficiently important for war production. In addition, the government, trying to gain cooperation of industry, essentially guaranteed profits for contractors through a special finance system. Companies were guaranteed payments a certain percentage above their actual expenses in producing war goods.

Business advisers flooded into Washington, DC. Many business advisers stayed on their companies' payrolls while they served in federal agencies. They brought an entirely different perspective of the role of government than what the New Dealers had been promoting earlier. They believed in the limited role of government and the importance of big business. Under the advice of business leaders, contracts were primarily awarded to the largest corporations who had the largest pools of labor, research departments, and established assembly lines. Advisers contended these companies could be most readily converted to military production from civilian production. As a result, the 10 largest corporations of the early 1940s received one-third of all war contracts. The top 56 companies received three-fourths of the military contracts. Smaller companies were largely left to scramble for subcontracts from the bigger companies. Many small firms went out of business since the large companies were given priority access to raw materials by the federal government. In addition to small manufacturing firms going out of business, some three hundred thousand retail businesses also folded in 1942 not long after the war began. It was one of the sharpest drops in the number of businesses in U.S. history. In total over a half million businesses closed during the war.

International Perspectives

European allies had been thrust into war well before the United States. By late 1940 much of Europe had fallen to Germany, and Britain was enduring continual aerial assaults. Much to the dismay of European leaders and citizens, the United States had not been involved in supporting various European countries against Germany, due to its strong mood of isolationism. Even Great Britain had been only half-heartedly involved in the war effort until spring of 1940. That spring, Germany began its military offensive against Western European countries including France, and Prime Minister Chamberlain was replaced by Churchill. Great Britain and German-occupied parts of Europe, however, began looking increasingly to the United States for assistance.

Prime Minister Winston Churchill of Great Britain pressed harder for support from the United States, but public sentiment in America remained strong against entering the war. Following his reelection in November 1940 President Roosevelt addressed the nation in a fireside chat. Trying to drum up support and sway public perspective away from isolationism, he stressed that if Britain fell to Germany the United States would be in great peril. Roosevelt asserted that the United States would have to become "the great arsenal of democracy" to help defeat the Axis powers, represented primarily by Germany and Russia, as well as some smaller Eastern European states. The nation, however, could still officially claim neutrality while offering limited support to its allies.

Britain was largely out of cash by late 1940. Roosevelt offered a new plan of payment to Britain called lend-lease. This plan would replace the "cash and carry" plan established in late 1939. In the earlier plan America would sell arms to other nations as long as they paid cash and carried them home in their own ships. Under the new plan the United States would lend or lease arms and other supplies to any country whose defense was essential to the United States. U.S. isolationists strongly opposed the plan, but Congress passed the Lend-Lease Act in 1941, and Britain began receiving much needed supplies. The United States ultimately spent about $50 billion under the act. Not only was lend-lease aid sent to Britain, but to other nations as well, including Russia when it suddenly found itself under attack by Germany in June 1941. As British shipments of U.S. lend-lease supplies increasingly made their way across the Atlantic Ocean, Germany began launching hundreds of submarines to attack in an effort to hinder the receipt of arms from the United States. They operated in groups of 15 to 20, known as wolf packs. Between April and May 1941 Germany sank 1.2 million tons of British

Workers assemble an American light tank after it arrived in England as part of a lend-lease shipment.
(FDR Library.)

shipping. The U.S. supply of goods to Allied powers made on the home front proved invaluable in holding out against German onslaughts until the U.S. actively joined the war.

Impact

War mobilization revived the U.S. economy far more than the New Deal programs did. The unprece-dented industrial production of ships, tanks, planes, guns, and ammunition reshaped relationships between government and business. The character of the U.S. economic system actually changed through World War II. The war brought a new age of big business, this time closely tied to the military branch of the federal government. Following World War II corporate leaders and the military dominated national decision-making. National security interests would take prece-dence over domestic issues and the operation of the civilian branches of government. Leaders of industry and finance had gained a major position in guiding future U.S. political development.

Other social and economic changes occurred as well. Organized labor became a more established part of the U.S. economic system and society. No longer were unions primarily in the position of operating outside the establishment. Farmers saw prosperity once again, and major population shifts led to a growth of cities in the West and the South.

The political coalition of Southern Democrats and Republicans also grew stronger. Though progress still remained slow for inclusion of racial minorities and ethnic groups in U.S. society, some gains were made. Increased access to the military for blacks finally led President Harry Truman to sign an executive order in 1948 prohibiting racial segregation in the services. The presidency had also grown still more powerful.

Women also made gains outside the home. Not only were they filling the more traditional secretarial and clerical positions in greater numbers, but non-traditional physical labor and professional jobs also opened up. This expansion of women's role in the workplace was particularly significant by 1943, when labor shortages among the traditional workforce began appearing. Much of the gains, however, evaporated at the conclusion of the war as men returned home, and both men and women returned in large part to their more traditional pre-war roles in society. Women would again be faced with workplace discrimination for the remainder of the century, though more and more career opportunities would open up for women throughout the rest of the century.

Reconversion of Industry and the Postwar Economy

The alliance between business and the military wanted to ensure there was not a postwar revival of New Deal programs as production of civilian goods resumed. The continued hostility of business and the military to government civilian planning desires would block any efforts to stabilize prices and coordinate industrial reconversion following the war. As the war neared an end, however, the public was anxious over whether the U.S. economy would return to an economic depression.

The government had attempted postwar planning in a way New Dealers believed business would find acceptable. Reconversion planning by the War Production Board (WPB) began in early 1943 under the leadership of Donald Nelson, a former Sears-Roebuck executive. Even he ran into corporate opposition to the WPB plan announced in November 1943. The reconversion plan called for smaller businesses to resume

civilian production first as the larger corporations continued to complete their defense contracts. Business leaders, however, strongly opposed the plan. The large war contractors argued that small businesses would be given an unfair advantage in the postwar economy. They insisted that all U.S. businesses should reconvert simultaneously. The plan was killed. Meanwhile, the federal government established the Office of War Mobilization and Reconversion to assist industries in clearing manufacturing plants of war materials and to retool industrial facilities for the anticipated postwar economic boom.

In an effort to establish postwar economic stability on their own terms, business leaders formed the Committee for Economic Development (CED) in 1943. Congress began looking into the potential problem as well, but the CED largely won out favoring corporate oversight rather than government oversight. The CED sought a stabilized economy so as to avoid any need for further government intervention. The CED constituted a corporate brain trust.

Rise of the Military-Industrial Complex

The Cold War, in which the United States and Russia became two large superpowers, antagonistic with each other, provided the opportunity for the corporate-military alliance to continue through the next several decades. The military had gained substantial political strength at the expense of the civilian branches of government during World War II. This shift in power was largely due to business hostility to the New Deal that extended into the 1940s. As a result, national security replaced New Deal reform as the lead goal of the federal government.

Following the war business leaders realized they could neither go back to the *laissez-faire,* or minimum government regulation, policies of the 1920s that existed prior to the New Deal nor would they accept the Keynesian economic system—government big spending and oversight—practiced under the New Deal. They therefore sought to establish a new order to U.S. economics, a corporate internationalism built on international trade in conjunction with a strong military. The rise of the United States as both a world economic and military power corresponded with the collapse of European prestige. Business leaders would have a strong role in shaping U.S. domestic and foreign policy in the position of a new world superpower.

To maintain a strong economy following the end of the war, without relying on massive government assistance programs, international corporations sought to improve foreign markets for U.S. goods by rebuilding the European economies. Europe, they believed, would provide the outlet for the new U.S. surplus as full production continued following the war. The military also saw this business approach as beneficial because the foreign political systems would become stabilized. They would be less vulnerable to the rising Soviet communist influence. The resulting strategy for rebuilding Europe came in the 1947, European Recovery Program, better known as the Marshall Plan after Secretary of State George C. Marshall. The CED was one of the promoters of the Marshall Plan. In addition Congress passed the National Security Act of 1947, establishing national security as a key purpose for the postwar federal government. Industry leaders pressed President Truman to pursue a quick demobilization process so that companies would be as ready as possible for the expected economic boom.

The United States, through the Marshall Plan, provided $13 billion in economic aid to 17 European nations between 1948 and 1951. The plan proved a success as European economic productivity rose and various industries recovered rapidly.

Economic support also arrived with the emphasis to remobilize the military in response to the perceived growing Soviet threat. This military buildup increased with the onset of the Korean War (1950–1953). Following the Korean War the United States maintained military spending at unprecedented levels for peacetime. The business community knew that a strong military could keep access open to foreign markets.

The postwar economic boom did arrive as people bought consumer goods that were not available during the war using savings they had accumulated. The remobilization of the military to fight the spread of communism countered the usual major economic downturns that follow a boom. The government funded industry again for war materials. Through this process of integrating international trade with military strength, the national and economic security became interwoven. The Soviet threat provided the reason for keeping the new economic and military system together.

Notable People

James Forrestal (1892–1949). Born in Matteawan, New York, Forrestal attended Dartmouth College and Princeton University before joining a Wall Street investment firm. After serving in naval aviation in World War I, Forrestal returned to employment in a New York City investment firm, becoming its president by 1938. As war mobilization gained momentum in 1940, many business leaders were consulted on how it should best proceed. As part of this approach in June 1940 President Roosevelt named Forrestal an administrative assistant. Two months later he became undersecretary of the navy. In that post, Forrestal was responsible for preparing the navy for war on two oceans including encouraging major industrial expansion. As a key part of this effort, he guided a massive expansion of the navy and navy procurement programs. To do this Forrestal created the Office of Procurement and Material in January 1942 to oversee mobilization and coordinate with other military services. In May 1944 Forrestal became secretary of the navy replacing Frank Knox who died in office. Following World War II a new presidential cabinet position was established, the secretary of defense. This new position was created to prepare the military services to act as a post-war superpower. In September 1947 Forrestal became the first to fill that position and reorganize armed services. There he greatly influenced the developing character of the Cold War.

Leon Henderson (1895–1986). Born in Millville, New Jersey, Henderson would become a highly influential New Deal economist. After serving in the army in World War I, he graduated from Swarthmore College in 1920 with a degree in economics. Henderson then attended graduate school at the University of Pennsylvania between 1920 and 1922 where he was also an instructor in the Wharton business school at the university. From there he held various academic and government positions through the 1920s. Joining the New Deal in 1934 Henderson became director of the National Recovery Administration's (NRA) Research and Planning Division where he rose in prominence. Though intimately involved in the development of industrial codes under the NRA, he quickly became convinced that the codes were causing more problems than they were solving. Henderson clearly opposed trends in which the economy was becoming increasingly concentrated in the larger companies at the expense of small businesses. Henderson therefore argued for a basic shift in New Deal policy. Rather than pursuing a national planning approach by regulating businesses, he wanted to expand business competition and increase government spending to stimulate the economy.

During the presidential election year of 1936 Henderson became an economic advisor to the Democratic National Committee as well as economic advisor to Harry Hopkins, head of the Works Progress Administration (WPA). In 1938 Henderson became head of the Temporary National Economic Committee (TNEC) where he continued opposition to big business and favored competition. Congress established the committee to investigate anti-trust enforcement.

The committee lasted from late 1938 to early 1941. In 1939 he became a commissioner on the Securities and Exchange Commission (SEC) overseeing stock market activities.

With increasing needs to mobilize the nation's economy in preparation for war, Henderson played a key role for President Roosevelt. In May 1940 Roosevelt established the National Defense Advisory Commission (NDAC) with Henderson as a member. In 1941 Henderson became head of the Office of Price Administration and Civilian Supply (OPACS) and then a member of the War Production Board (WPB) in 1942. Henderson had been a major promoter of rapid mobilization, price controls on goods, and rationing. In pressing hard for these goals Henderson became highly unpopular among business leaders. He resigned later in 1942 to help relieve tensions between the administration and business. After leaving public service Henderson became president of the International Hudson Corporation and remained active in various political organizations.

Robert Patterson (1891–1952). Born in Glens Falls, New York, Patterson's father was a lawyer. Following his father's footsteps Patterson studied law at Harvard. Upon graduation he joined the prestigious law firm headed by Elihu Root. Root had been secretary of war and secretary of state in the President William McKinley (served 1897–1901) and Theodore Roosevelt (served 1901–1909) administrations. Influenced by Root, Patterson became a strong supporter for national defense. Enlisting in the New York National Guard Patterson was part of the U.S. expeditionary force sent to fight Pancho Villa on the Mexican border in 1916. Upon the U.S. entrance into World War I he joined the U.S. Army and became a second lieutenant serving in France. Following the war Patterson returned to New York where he established a successful new law firm through the economic boom years of the 1920s. Patterson's time for public service came in 1930 when President Herbert Hoover (served 1929–1933) appointed Patterson judge to the U.S. District Court of southern New York. In 1939 President Roosevelt appointed Patterson to the U.S. Court of Appeals.

With the onset of war mobilization Patterson resigned his appointment to the bench and joined the War Department as assistant secretary of war under Secretary Henry Stimson. With both he and Stimson being Harvard graduates and Republicans and both having served in World War I in the same Army division in France, they formed a close working relationship in opposing isolationism. Soon Patterson was elevated to undersecretary of war, a position he held the remainder of World War II. From that position Patterson with Stimson's support headed the army's multibillion-dollar procurement program, a highly important position during mobilization. Patterson believed, for the sake of efficiency, that military contracts should predominately go to major corporations. As a result Patterson was instrumental in forging a strong relationship between the military and industry that would last for the remainder of the twentieth century. Though Patterson staunchly opposed any New Dealer efforts toward seeking social reform through war mobilization programs, he also opposed racial segregation in the military services. Patterson also argued for the military services to be joined into one department. Such massive reorganization would eventually arrive with creation of the Department of Defense in 1947. In that year Patterson resigned from public service and returned to private law practice. He was killed in a commercial airliner crash only a few years later in 1952.

Henry Stimson (1867–1950). Stimson was born in New York City to a successful stockbroker. After graduating from Harvard Law School Stimson joined a New York law firm headed by Elihu Root who was to later become a U.S. secretary of war and secretary of state in the President William McKinley and Theodore Roosevelt administrations. In addition to his successful private law practice, Stimson became active in Republican Party politics. In 1906 President Theodore Roosevelt appointed Stimson U.S. attorney for the Southern District of New York where he tackled anti-trust cases. In 1911 President William H. Taft appointed him secretary of war. Then with the U.S. entrance into World War I, at 49 years of age, Stimson joined the Army and served as an artillery officer in France. Following the war Stimson returned to private law practice as a corporate lawyer on Wall Street. Then public service called again. President Calvin Coolidge (served 1923–1929) appointed him as diplomat to Nicaragua in 1927 and then to the Philippines in 1928. In 1929 President Herbert Hoover appointed Stimson as secretary of state.

With the Democrats returning to the White House in 1933, Stimson returned to private practice until 1940. In that year with another war looming, President Roosevelt appointed him to the crucial position of secretary of war. Roosevelt believed Stimson would be a great help in convincing the public to support war mobilization. Stimson also became a key supporter of Roosevelt's lend-lease aid to Britain. Stimson assembled a key team to guide the nation in mobilizing for war. Stimson, however, was also a key supporter of Japanese internment and maintaining strict racial segregation of the armed forces. Another one of Stimson's responsibilities was oversight of the top secret Manhattan Project charged with developing an atomic bomb. Stimson proved a major promoter of internationalist approaches to global issues that would greatly influence U.S. policies in future years.

Primary Sources

America Faces the Axis Powers

Following his unprecedented reelection to a third consecutive term of office, President Roosevelt delivered a crucial Fireside Chat to the American people on December 29, 1940. In this message he described more specifically than ever the dangers he saw developing in the world. Roosevelt described America's need to begin producing arms for Great Britain as that country fought against intense aerial attacks by Germany (from Roosevelt, Franklin D. *The Public Papers and Addresses of Franklin D. Roosevelt, 1938–1950*).

Tonight, in the presence of a world crisis, my mind goes back eight years to a night in the midst of a domestic crisis. It was a time when the wheels of American industry were grinding to a full stop, when the whole banking system of our country had ceased to function . . .

Tonight . . . this new crisis . . . faces America . . .

The Nazi masters of Germany have made it clear that they intend not only to dominate all life and thought in their own country, but also to enslave the whole of Europe, and then to use the resources of Europe to dominate the rest of the world . . .

Some of our people like to believe that wars in Europe and in Asia are of no concern to us. But it is a matter of most vial concern to us that European and Asiatic warmakers should not gain control of the oceans which lead to this hemisphere . . .

If Great Britain goes down, the Axis powers will control the continents of Europe, Asia, Africa, Australasia, and the high seas - and they will be in a position to bring enormous military and naval resources against this hemisphere. It is no exaggeration to say that all of us, in all the Americas, would be living at the point of a gun—a gun loaded with explosive bullets, economic as well as military . . .

Frankly and definitely there is danger ahead—danger against which we must prepare. But we will know that we cannot escape danger, or the fear of danger, by crawling into bed and pulling the covers over our heads . . .

The experience of the past two years has proven beyond doubt that no nation can appease the Nazis. No man can tame a tiger into a kitten by stroking it. There can be no appeasement with ruthlessness. There can be no reasoning with an incendiary bomb. We know now that a nation can have peace with the Nazis only at the price of total surrender.

The American appeasers ignore the warning to be found in the fate of Austria, Czechoslovakia, Poland, Norway, Belgium, the Netherlands, Denmark, and France. They tell you that the Axis powers are going to win anyway; that all this bloodshed in the world could be saved; that the United States might just as well throw its influence into the scale of a dictated peace, and get the best out of it that we can . . .

The British people and their allies today are conducting an active war against this unholy alliance. Our won future security is greatly dependent on the outcome of that fight. Our ability to "keep out of war" is going to be affected by that outcome.

Thinking in terms of today and tomorrow, I make the direct statement to the American people that there is far less chance of the United States getting into war, if we do all we can now to support the nations defending themselves against attack by the Axis than if we acquiesce in their defeat, submit tamely to an Axis victory, and wait our turn to be the object of attack in another war later on . . .

The people of Europe who are defending themselves do not ask us to do their fighting. They ask us for the implements of war, the planes, the tanks, the guns, and the freighters, which will enable them to fight for their liberty and for our security. Emphatically we must get these weapons to them in sufficient volume and quickly enough, so that we and our children will be saved the agony and suffering of war which others have had to endure . . .

In a military sense Great Britain and the British Empire are today the spearhead of resistance to world conquest. They are putting up a fight which will live forever in the story of human gallantry . . .

Our national policy is not directed toward war. Its sole purpose is to keep war away from our country and our people . . .

The worker possesses the same human dignity and is entitled to the same security of position as the engineer or the manager or the owner. For the workers provide the human power that turns out the destroyers, the airplanes, and the tanks . . .

Nine days ago I announced the setting up of a more effective organization to direct our gigantic efforts to increase the production of munitions. The appropriation of vast sums of money and a well-coordinated executive direction of our defense efforts are not in themselves enough. Guns, planes, ships, and many other things have to be built in the factories and arsenals of America . . .

American industrial genius, unmatched throughout the world in the solution of production problems, has been called upon to bring its resources and its talents into action. Manufacturers of watches, farm implements, linotypes, cash registers, automobiles, sewing machines, lawn mowers and locomotives are now making fuses, bomb packing crates, telescope mounts, shells, pistols, and tanks.

But all our present efforts are not enough. We must have more ships, more guns, more planes—more of

President Franklin D. Roosevelt signs the Declaration of War against Japan, December 8, 1941, the day after the attack on Pearl Harbor. (*National Archives and Records Administration. Reproduced by permission.*)

everything. This can only be accomplished if we discard the notion of "business as usual." This job cannot be done merely by superimposing on the existing productive facilities the added requirements of the nation for defense . . .

We must be the great arsenal of democracy.

I have the profound conviction that the American people are now determined to put forth a mightier effort than they have ever yet made to increase our production of all the implements of defense, to meet the threat to our democratic faith.

News of the Attack on Pearl Harbor Reaches FDR

Grace Tully, President Roosevelt's secretary, recounts the demeanor of the president as he dictates his speech to be given to Congress the next day (quoted in Colbert, *Eyewitness to America*, pp. 466–467).

Shortly before 5 o'clock the Boss called me to his study. He was alone, seated before his desk on which were two or three neat piles of notes containing the information of the past two hours. The telephone was close by his hand. He was wearing a gray sack jacket and was lighting a cigarette as I entered the room. He took a deep drag and addressed me calmly:

"Sit down, Grace. I'm going before Congress tomorrow. I'd like to dictate my message. It will be short."

I sat down without a word; it was no time for words other than those to become part of the war effort.

Once more he inhaled deeply, then he began in the same calm tone in which he dictated his mail. Only his diction was a little different as he spoke each word incisively and slowly, carefully specifying each punctuation mark and paragraph.

"Yesterday comma December 7 comma 1941 dash a day which will live in infamy dash the United States of America was suddenly and deliberately attacked by naval and air forces of the Empire of Japan period paragraph."

The entire message ran under 500 words, a cold-blooded indictment of Japanese treachery and aggression, delivered to me without hesitation, interruption or second thoughts.

Suggested Research Topics

- Identify the types of industries most affected by World War II mobilization including those that saw much more work and those that declined.

- Mobilization led to major geographic shifts in the population, even the creation of whole new communities where new industries were established. What were these shifts and which segments of society were most involved?

- Explore the problems that some segments of society experienced in attempting to enjoy the new economic benefits of expanded war production.

- Explore some of the stories written by women employed in the war industry. What were some their experiences in entering what was largely a male domain previously? What happened once the war ended?

Bibliography

Sources

Colbert, David, ed. *Eyewitness to America.* New York: Vintage Books, 1998.

Dallek, Robert. *Franklin D. Roosevelt and American Foreign Policy, 1932–1945.* New York: Oxford University Press, 1979.

Eiler, Keith E. *Mobilizing America: Robert P. Patterson and the War Effort, 1940–1945.* Ithaca, NY: Cornell University Press, 1997.

Heale, Michael. *Franklin D. Roosevelt: The New Deal and War.* New York: Routledge, 1999.

Hodgson, Godfrey. *The Colonel: The Life and Wars of Henry Stimson, 1867–1950.* New York: Knopf, 1990.

Hooks, Gregory M. *Forging the Military-Industrial Complex: World War II's Battle of the Potomac.* Urbana: University of Illinois Press, 1991.

Hoopes, Townsend, and Douglas Brinkley. *Driven Patriot: The Life and Times of James Forrestal.* New York: Vintage Books, 1993.

Koistenen, Paul. *Hammer and Sword.* New York: Arno Press, 1979.

Lichtenstein, Nelson. *Labor's War at Home: The CIO in World War II.* New York: Cambridge University Press, 1982.

Roosevelt, Franklin D. *The Public Papers and Addresses of Franklin D. Roosevelt.* New York: Random House, 1938–1950.

Smith, R. Elberton. *The Army and Economic Mobilization.* Washington, DC: Center of Military History, U.S. Army, 1991.

Waddell, Brian. *The War Against the New Deal: World War II and American Democracy.* DeKalb, IL: Northern Illinois University Press, 2001.

Further Reading

Cochran, Thomas C. *The Great Depression and World War II, 1929–1945.* Glenview, IL: Scott, Foresman, and Company, 1968.

Doenecke, Justus D., and Allan M. Winkler. *Home Front U.S.A.: America During World War II.* Wheeling, IL: Harlan Davidson, Inc., 2000.

Gilbert, Martin. *The Second World War: A Complete History.* New York: H. Holt, 1989.

Hartmann, Susan M. *The Home Front and Beyond: American Women in the 1940s.* Boston: Twayne Publishers, 1982.

Ketchum, Richard M. *The Borrowed Years, 1938–1941: America on the Way to War.* New York: Anchor Books, 1991.

O'Brien, Kenneth P., and Lynn Hudson Parsons, eds. *The Home-Front War: World War II and American Society.* Westport, CN: Greenwood Press, 1995.

Polenberg, Richard. *War and Society: The United States, 1941–1945.* Westport, CN: Greenwood Press, 1980.

Wilcox, Walter W. *The Farmer in the Second World War.* New York: DaCapo Press, 1973.

Wiltz, John E. *From Isolation to War, 1931–1941.* Arlington Heights, IL: Harlan Davidson, Inc., 1991.

See Also

Global Impact

World's Fairs

1933-1939

"I welcome the celebration you are now beginning. It is timely not only because it marks a century of accomplishment, but it comes at a time when the world needs nothing so much as a better mutual understanding of the peoples of the earth." The preceding quote is an excerpt from President Franklin D. Roosevelt's (served 1933–1945) message to the Chicago World's Fair on May 27, 1933.

World's Fairs are by design optimistic, celebrating what is and what may be ahead with modern technology. Beginning in London in 1851 world's fairs grew in international popularity. Their primary purpose is to showcase exhibits highlighting technological advances and advancing nationalism or, in some cases, corporate identity. They also frequently contain entertainment midways with amusement rides and other activities. Fairs represented a combination of efforts by governments, corporations, scientists, and engineers. They thus project hope and a vision of the future. This optimism was particularly critical during the Great Depression. More than ever before, many were questioning the effectiveness of the U.S. economic system driven by a free market economy and rampant industrialization.

The World's Fairs of the 1930s featured the current marvels of science, technology, and manufacturing. They sought to project or anticipate what life would be like in the future during rosier economic times. President Roosevelt, as part of his New Deal

programs created to provide economic relief and recovery to the nation held in the grips of the economic hard times of the Great Depression, also sought to demonstrate the government's concern for the economic and social welfare of Americans. With the high unemployment rates of the Depression, the fairs also provided thousands of much needed jobs around the country. Much of the architecture in the 1933 Chicago and 1939 New York fairs aspired to be "modern." Many buildings were of the Art Deco style of the 1930s with streamlined, flowing movement and minimal decoration. The Golden Gate International Exposition in San Francisco (1939), while constructed on a man-made island, drew upon historical architecture. Yet, in its exhibits the Golden Gate Exposition attempted to present a view, like the earlier Chicago exposition, of the "world of tomorrow."

World's Fairs were conceived, funded, developed, and offered by those with the political power and economic resources to try to celebrate and promote their vision of what a nation and the world should become. By their conception and development, each world's fair was thus a political and economic statement, a largely written editorial of special interests offering a vision of a world neither entirely realistic nor practical. For example in the early 1930s power companies displayed all electric homes, though most citizens had no access to electrical services and their homes were not even wired to receive electricity. World's Fairs displayed the visions of a selected few and enticed hundreds of thousands or millions of visitors to experience these visions.

By 1939 concerns over world conflicts were added to the economic concerns of the decade. In his remarks to 600,000 listeners at the New York World's Fair on April 30, 1939, President Roosevelt stressed the purposes of peace among nations. He said Americans had the desire to encourage peace and good will among all nations. Roosevelt's message was a common one in fairs that had participation by a number of nations. Many of the organizers of world's fairs of the twentieth century sought international cooperation and participation. They stressed themes of brotherhood, peace, trade, and common purpose.

Despite the affirmations of internationalism, however, the twentieth century was marked by two world wars and a major economic depression in between. The rise of communism and fascism tested the efforts to foster peace among nations. Increased trade barriers designed to improve national economies further divided nations. These barriers, mostly in the form of high taxes on imported goods, known as tariffs, greatly suppressed trade and international communication.

Chronology:

1876: The Centennial International Exhibition in Philadelphia, Pennsylvania, becomes the first world's fair in the United States.

1915: The Panama-Pacific Exposition is held in San Francisco, California, and the Panama-California Exposition is held in San Diego, California, to celebrate the opening of the Panama Canal.

1932: The Summer Olympic Games are held in a Roman-style coliseum in Los Angeles, California, providing another worldwide showcase.

May 27, 1933: The World's Fair, "Century of Progress," opens in Chicago, Illinois, and runs until November 12. It operated for a second season in 1934.

1936: The World's Fair, "Golden Gate International Exposition," opens in San Francisco in February under the theme, "A Pageant of the Pacific" and closes on October 29 with a debt of $4.1 million. The fair runs a second season in 1940.

April 30, 1939: President Franklin D. Roosevelt opens the World's fair, "World of Tomorrow," in New York. The Fair closes October 29, six weeks early and in debt, and runs for a second season in 1940.

The role of world's fairs in international politics and economics was uncharted territory. Would people be interest enough to attend? Would nations be interested in participating? Would the fairs inspire further technological progress and cooperation between nations? As time would show the fairs served, especially for the fairs in the United States in the 1930s, as important opportunities to bridge gaps between nations and raise people's hopes for the future during the hard times of the Great Depression.

Issue Summary

The economic disaster of the 1930s prompted America's top businessmen and politicians to promote capitalism, materialism, and national progress. They saw fairs as a means to affirm the values in which they

Eleanor Roosevelt visits the Chicago World's Fair, "Century of Progress," in 1933. *(FDR Library.)*

believed and created three world's fairs: Century of Progress Exposition, Chicago (1933), New York World's Fair (1939), and the Golden Gate International Exposition, San Francisco (1939). High hopes of regaining civic and national pride were pinned on these expositions. President Franklin Roosevelt's administration threw its support behind them, for the goals of the fairs coincided with the vision of the New Deal and the rebuilding of America. Besides the three World's Fairs of the 1930s another key opportunity came for the United States to promote itself. In 1932

California attracted, constructed facilities, and hosted the Summer Olympic Games in Los Angeles. Even though times were tough, Californians were interested in taking on big, civic projects.

In the 1930s corporations seized the opportunity to become exhibitors, especially in the three World's Fairs held in the United States. In their presentations, companies promoted the success of their research and manufacturing, with products visitors were told they needed. New foodstuffs, automobiles, chemical products, construction materials, and transportation were displayed and sold in the highly commercial pavilions.

Century of Progress Exposition, 1933, Chicago, Illinois

Held during the depths of the Great Depression, the Chicago Fair emphasized technology and progress, a utopia, or perfect world, founded on democracy and manufacturing. The Chicago Fair's official guidebook conveyed a basic slogan: "Science Finds—Industry Applies—Man Conforms." The message was that science and American life were wedded. The fair delivered the message that a prosperous, secure future for the United States rested on a foundation of scientific research and its close alliance with commerce and industry. Fair exhibits attempted to convey this message with working assembly lines, rocket-shaped cars on the Sky Ride, and windowless (but cheerfully lighted) buildings. Although planning for the fair began before the Depression, by the time it opened on May 27, 1933, Chicago's businessmen and politicians clearly hoped the tourists attracted to the fair would help jump start an economic recovery for their city.

Backers of the fair began laying plans in 1928, organizing as A Century of Progress Corporation. They acquired 424 acres of land, most of it submerged, along the shoreline of Lake Michigan. They unleashed architects to create a futuristic vision of America and how science and technology would shape that world. The link with science, in fact, helped open the Chicago fair. Astronomical observatories around the United States beamed light from Arcturus, a distant star, to photoelectrical cells that produced sufficient electricity to travel via Western Union lines to the fair. Reportedly, the light received from Arcturus had left the star 40 years before when the World's Columbian Exposition of 1893, which was also in Chicago, was closing. The underlying message delivered at the fair was that science, if properly funded and respected, would serve American civilization and catapult it into a better future.

This fair differed substantially from the Columbian Exposition held in the same city in 1893. Rather than buildings heavily drawn from ancient Greek architecture, the 1933 fair was dominated by two towers—1,850 feet apart—that supported the Skyride. Rising to 628 feet, the towers were the tallest structures in the city at that time. At two hundred feet above the ground, visitors could board a rocket car suspended from a cable and cross the lagoon to the other side of the fair. Most of the buildings of the fair were only facades. The *Official Guide* proudly stated: "These structures are for the most part unbroken

planes and surfaces of asbestos and gypsum board and plywood and other materials on light steel frames, rather than a parade of sculptured ornamentation." The guide further noted that "in construction as well as in architecture, it was intended that here should be a huge experimental laboratory, in which home builders and manufacturers can study, and from which they might borrow for their buildings of the future."

Fairgoers found themselves in a futuristic fantasyland that contrasted dramatically with the unemployment and economic misery of Chicago. Faith in progress, a faith severely shaken by the Depression, was reaffirmed for many attendees. Big business, which many Americans now blamed for the Depression, tried to improve its reputation. Businesses stressed scientific and industrial progress with exhibits of operating models of oil refineries, a radio-controlled tractor, and product-packaging demonstrations. It appeared that the Great Depression had not strongly affected American industry. Ford Motor Company built a nine hundred-foot long building for five million dollars. Inside Ford displayed an automobile assembly plant, a globe of Ford's international operations, and models of historic highways. The Ford exhibit proved to be the fair's most popular.

Although the Chicago Fair welcomed the world, the foreign exhibits were reduced to five: a Mayan Temple, an Old Heidelberg Inn, a Chinese village, a Belgian village, and a Moroccan village. Token commitments to international perspectives were made, however, with the reproduction of the "Golden Pavilion," a structure of 28,000 pieces that replicated the 1767 summer home of the Manchu emperors of China.

Some of the exhibits seemed contrived. The "Drama of Agriculture" building celebrated great advances in farming over the past 75 years. The "Dairy Building" and the "Color Organ" were bizarre. The *Official Guide* said:

> You enter into a large lobby. Beyond is a cyclorama on which streams of color play. At an organ console, a player's hands finger the keyboard, causing the variations of color. The instrument is the Clavilux, or color organ. With the 'color music' for accompaniment, a spectacle is presented showing the bringing of the first cows to the Plymouth colony, the trek of civilizations westward, and today's organized dairy industry.

Science exhibits touted the marvels of electricity, radio, communications, and lighting. The Indian Refining Company, makers of Havoline motor oil, constructed a 200-foot high tower. On its three faces visitors viewed ten-foot high numerals of the world's largest thermometer!

Chicago's businessmen and politicians hoped that the tourists attracted to the World's Fair would help jump start an economic recovery for their city.

(The Library of Congress.)

Similar to the 1893 event, however, developers of this fair called the carnival or pleasure area the "Midway," an echo of what attracted the attention of so many who came to the Columbian Exposition. Games, a roller coaster, and a "freak show" were promoted attractions. With little sensitivity, the fair organizers established a "Midget Village." The *Official Guide* strangely associated these people with other fair events: "Turn aside to visit the Midget Village, where sixty Lilliputians live in their tiny houses, serve you food, and entertain you with theatrical performances."

The fair also included token acknowledgments of history. Beyond the midway stood the log stockade and replica of Fort Dearborn, representing the early settlement of Chicago. Another exhibit area told the story of the life of Abraham Lincoln in Illinois. The black American community of Chicago lobbied hard and with ultimate success to secure mention of Jean Baptiste Pont De Saible, the first non-Indian resident of Chicago and founder of the city. Reconstruction of De Saible's cabin, after years of frustrating work by the De Saible Society, was funded by the city of Chicago.

Fair officials designated certain special days. November 8, dubbed Personal Responsibility Day,

celebrated the end of Prohibition. The fair provided free beer and sandwiches to 50,000 visitors. Attendees ate approximately 200,000 sandwiches and drank one thousand barrels of beer. Two days later fair officials admitted all people on government relief roles free if they produced their identity card.

The fair operated from May 27 to November 12, 1933. It returned for a second season from May 26 to October 31, 1934, to try to pay off its debts. At its close the fair managed a tiny profit. The fair had been popular, with 22.5 million tickets sold in 1933 and 16.4 million in 1934. Plans, however, to retain the structures as a permanent exhibition and amusement park failed. Chicago was in too much financial difficulty stemming from the Great Depression to be able to fund such a project. In the end, Chicago's Depression woes had not been alleviated by the fair as had been hoped.

Golden Gate International Exposition, 1939, Treasure Island, San Francisco, California

Residents of California remembered fondly and with nostalgia, two earlier fairs both held in 1915: the Panama-Pacific Exposition in San Francisco and the Panama-California Exposition in San Diego. Both events heralded the completion of the Panama Canal and the anticipated boom in trade and commerce for the West Coast of the United States. Architect Bertram Goodhue developed both temporary and permanent exposition buildings for San Diego's Balboa Park. He drew on Spanish Renaissance and Spanish colonial architecture for his designs. The San Francisco fair of 1915 was located on the edge of Golden Gate Park and included several grand buildings in the Beaux Arts Style, drawing from European designs. The success of these fairs and their association with prosperity encouraged Californians, in spite of the Great Depression, to embark on a major fair in San Francisco in the late 1930s.

Three completed major construction projects, the Golden Gate Bridge, the Bay Bridge, and Treasure Island enabled the undertaking of a fair in San Francisco. In large part, the Works Projects Administration (WPA) backed all the three construction projects. These were New Deal ventures designed to employ workers and rekindle the economy. The impressive construction projects connected Highway 101 across the harbor entrance, joined the east side of the bay to the west, and created an artificial island in San Francisco Bay. The Golden Gate Bridge, then the world's longest cable suspension bridge, took five years and the latest engineering skills to complete in 1937. The Bay Bridge—which was actually three bridges and a tunnel—connected both sides of the bay in 1936. The ferries, once common features of life on the harbor, diminished rapidly in importance.

The third huge project, undertaken with no regard to its environmental impacts, created an artificial island. Treasure Island was built in the middle of the bay between San Francisco and Oakland. Dumping millions of tons of boulders and pumping up dredged materials from the harbor, engineers constructed the 400-acre island. Reportedly, the mud used to build the island was laden with particles of gold that had washed out of the distant Sierra Nevada Mountains. The next great venture for the island was to construct a World's Fair on it and market its attractions to viewers. The purpose of the fair was not only to attract tourists to spark the San Francisco economy but to provide jobs for the unemployed. South from a sharp spire which rose 400 feet above the island called the Tower of the Sun was a rectangular pool, the Court of the Moon. East of the Tower was the Court of Reflection. North from the Tower was the Court of Seven Seas which ended in the Court of Pacifica. Dominating the court was an 80-foot statue, Pacifica, by Ralph Stackpole, representing peace. The island's anticipated future use was ultimately as both a military base and an airport.

The fair was conceived as "A Pageant of the Pacific," but was officially known as the Golden Gate International Exposition. The primary buildings were designed in a style invented by the architects. They called it "Pacific Basin" and used ancient building designs of the Mayan, Incan, Malayan, and Cambodian civilizations to inspire the structures they conceived for Treasure Island. The chief symbol of the fair was the Tower of the Sun, which worked as the graphic logo on much of the fair's literature and souvenirs. Architects involved in the designs included Arthur Brown, Jr., George Kelham, Timothy L. Pleuger, Bernard Maybeck, William Merchant, and Lewis Hobart. Arthur Brown, Jr., designer of the San Francisco City Hall, gained the commission for the fair's symbol, the Tower of the Sun, and the Court of Honor. The "Elephant Towers" flanking the Tower of the Sun were the work of Donald Macky. Ernest E. Weihe designed the Portals of the Pacific entryway.

The fair touted the United States's power and influence around the world. The grounds represented regions of the world where American military and economic control was most pronounced: a Latin American Court (featuring Mexico, Peru, El Salvador, Panama, Chile, Ecuador, but not Brazil or Argentina), and a Pacific Basin Area (spotlighting Hawaii and the Philippines).

More About...
William Gordon Huff, Sculptor

Sculpture often served to fix images or establish messages for World's Fairs. William Gordon Huff (1903–1993), a California sculptor, created some of the major artworks for the Golden Gate International Exposition of 1939–1940. Huff was born in Fresno, California, and studied at the California School of Arts and Crafts in Oakland, the California School of Fine Arts in San Francisco, the New York Art Student's League, and the Ecole Grande Chaumiere in Paris.

Huff created four massive sculptures surrounding the "Tower of the Sun," the central icon of the fair. The statues represented Science, Agriculture, Industry, and Art. These works towered over visitors and drew heavily from classical themes. The naked female figure for Art, for example, carried an ancient Greek theatrical mask. Huff's works for the fair included several large columns of carved human figures that flanked entrances of buildings. In addition to the public space sculptures, Huff crafted several relief panels and freestanding sculptures of prehistoric animals. These were used in the interpretive exhibits at the fair for the University of California's Museum of Paleontology. The animals included Pleistocene species recovered from the La Brea tar pits in Los Angeles.

Huff's commissions for these projects were representative of public commissions to artists during the Great Depression. In spite of economic hard times, world's fair commissions and city, state, and federal government officials sought to encourage the arts and public appreciation for sculpture, painting, etching, and other genres.

In keeping with New Deal programs of involving the public in art, the fair celebrated fine arts from the western tradition. Its borrowed exhibits exposed hundreds of thousands of visitors for the first time to the works of the "old masters" as well as American artists. The art show was borrowed from Italy, France, Britain, and the Netherlands.

Two important muralists associated with the fair were Diego Rivera and Miguel Covarrubias, both

Millions of visitors toured the Golden Gate International Exposition in 1939 and 1940. (© Lake County Museum/Corbis.
Reproduced by permission.)

Mexicans. Ironically at the time the United States, and California in particular, was sending thousands of Mexicans and Mexican Americans back to Mexico due to the bad economic conditions in the United States. Rivera designed and executed huge murals in the Palace of Fine Arts drawing on the peoples of the Western Hemisphere including American Indians, Mexicans, and Eskimoes.

The fair was assertive about the role of women in modern America. This statement fell largely under the control of a Women's Board with officials from the Girl Scouts and other organizations. The Women's Board played an important role in planning the expositions related to women, mostly in their roles as housewives. The features where women had a voice were related to serving as hostesses and in "beautifying" the city of San Francisco for the benefit of fair visitors.

Entertainment venues included the "Cavalcade of the Golden West," an outdoor pageant held on a stage nearly the size of a football field, which had a curtain of water from 2,500 jets spewing water into the air and lighted with color. The pageant introduced visitors to selected elements of western history: conquistadors, Indians on horseback, steam engines, and stage coaches. Other options included plane rides, puppet

shows, and a visit to a model gold mine. The fair had an almost carnival-like atmosphere in some respects, for visitors found vendors who guessed people's weight, sold caramel-corn and fried-potatoes, or offered to take them around the grounds in a rickshaw, on an "Elephant Train," or on chairs with rollers.

Many visitors to the fair traveled on the harbor ferries where the loudspeakers played "I Sailed Away to Treasure Island," a tune celebrating the fair. Richard Reinhardt, a visitor to the fair, recalled vividly a number of the special attractions: the fan dancer, Sally Rand; Botticelli's "Birth of Venus" (a painting on loan from the Uffizi Gallery in Florence, Italy); a B-314 Clipper floating on a lagoon; free samples of vegetable beef soup; and a crane that hoisted visitors some 200 feet into the sky. Reinhardt also remembered, "the Guatemalan marimba band, the Australian wallaroos, the giant cash register that showed the day's attendance, the electronic voice called Voder, the transparent car, [and] the mule-faced lady at Ripley's Odditorium" quoted in *American Heritage,* 53.

Light and lighting features, especially the use of color and nighttime events, shaped the impressions of many fair visitors. Arches of water crisscrossed over pools and at night; lights turned the arches, set against the indigo pool and rose-colored walls, golden. Jesse

Stanton and A. F. Dickerson were involved in the design of these theatrical-like effects. Lights were a major feature of the fair's landscape design.

The Golden Gate International Exposition had opened on February 18, 1939, and closed September 29, 1940 with a six-month closure in between. In spite of over 17 million visitors, the fair left a $559,423 debt, dashing the hopes of an economic watershed. The U.S. Navy took over the site. Structures were quickly torn down, the 80-foot symbol of peace, Pacifica, was pulled over and broken into pieces.

New York World's Fair, Flushing Meadows, New York City, 1939

Billed as the "World of Tomorrow," this world's fair opened on April 1, 1939, on top of the former Corona Garbage Dump in Queens, a sprawling site of 1,200 acres. Like the Chicago, fair, directors planned the fair as a direct attempt to improve New York City's Depression-laden economy. Promoters of the fair touted it as a city of visionary planning, a place to celebrate the wonders of streamlined design and the potentials of American capitalism. Major corporations exhibiting included RCA, American Telephone and Telegraph (AT&T), General Electric, Westinghouse, U.S. Steel, Kodak, Firestone, Heinz, General Motors, Chrysler, and Ford. International exhibits included an English pub, the Bendix Lama Temple, and Cuban and English villages; a Seminole village was also an attraction. "Democracity" was a diorama of the city of the future. The underlying theme of democracy ruled out participation by the fascist governments of Germany and Spain. National exhibits included those of Russia, Italy, and Great Britain.

Supposedly the New York World's Fair was held to celebrate the 150th anniversary of the inauguration of George Washington as the nation's first president. Larger icons and statues celebrating the "Four Freedoms," however, overshadowed the towering statue of Washington. The modernism of the fair, echoed in the Art Deco designs of the 1930s, was not that of the fine-lined European designs. Historian Paul Greenhalgh has, instead, referred to it in terms of the stage sets for "Flash Gordon," a science fiction character in movie serials of the 1930s, or for the film "Metropolis." The Trylon and Perisphere structures, symbolic logos of the fair, met this characterization well. The impractical but distinctive Trylon towered seven hundred feet above the grounds; its companion, the Perisphere, was 18 stories high and a block-wide.

Four industrial designers played major roles in shaping the appearance of the fair. Having embraced streamlined design—sleek, modern, and technologi-

This poster for the 1939 New York World's Fair, designed by Alice Mumford, set the theme for the futuristic displays found within. (The Library of Congress.)

cal—Norman Bel Geddes, Raymond Loewy, Walter Dorwin Teague, and Henry Dreyfus shared their vision of America of tomorrow with visitors. Accompanied by the music of the official theme song, "Dawn of a New Day" by Ira and George Gershwin, visitors walked through exhibits, buildings, and landscapes where they met "Mr. Peanut," "Moto-Man" (a robot), and viewed new consumer products.

Visitors to the "World of Tomorrow" had several encounters with America's imagined future. The most popular exhibit at the fair was Futurama, a model of the world in 1960, designed by Norman Bel Geddes. Strapped into moving armchairs, visitors were fascinated as they passed by an American city of the future with superhighways. In the Perisphere a conveyor to a vista lifted visitors 50 feet above a model of the Democracity. Democracity was a proposed community for a million Americans residing in a democratic garden city, free from the hold of European fascism or the limitations of a great economic depression. In contrast to Democracity, Italy constructed an exhibit gallery that featured a large statue of *Il Duce,* dictator Benito Mussolini, and a map of the Italian empire. The Russian exhibit included a statue of a worker, 79 feet tall, made of stainless steel and examples of daily life, transportation, and Russian arts and crafts.

A view of Constitution Mall at New York's Worlds Fair on May 13, 1939. In the foreground, at left, is the "Freedom of the Press" statue. The Trylon and Perisphere structures are in the background. (AP/Wide World Photos. Reproduced by permission.)

Democracy had to compete, to a degree, with Italian fascism and Russian communism in the international exhibit galleries.

The British used the World's Fair as a desperate gamble to try to lure Americans out of isolation and into support of their nation as a bulwark against European totalitarianism and fascism. To find a subject appealing to the U.S. audience, the British focused their exhibit on the Magna Carta, bringing a copy to

the United States and featuring it in "Magna Carta Hall." The Magna Carta was a charter of English personal liberties granted by King John in 1215 and became a symbol for the fight against government oppression. The exhibit literature celebrated the document as a statement for liberty and freedom. The designers conveniently placed it close to the genealogy of George Washington that affirmed his English ancestry. Through a twist of historical interpretation, the British linked the Magna Carta to the American Revolution. Without this important document, the British asserted, the American colonists' fight for independence would have been hopeless.

The New York Fair addressed the American housewife and, while it proposed to continue to confine her to domestic duties, suggested liberation of a sort through laborsaving devices. "Mrs. Modern" was to surpass "Mrs. Drudge" because she had a dishwasher. Other marvels included new types of vacuum cleaners, clothes washers, and appliances. The fair also featured new products such as Lucite, air conditioning, color film, and nylon stockings—products that had largely been out of reach for most families during the Great Depression.

Entertainment varied with the interests and tastes of visitors. The fair's entertainment guide identified more than one hundred shows and rides. These were variously named, suggesting either a locale or exotic experience. They included: "Auto Dodgem," "Skyride," "Living Magazine Covers," "Snapper," "Laff Land," "Admiral Byrd's Penguin Land," "Strange As It May Seem," "No-man's Land," "Arctic Girl's Tomb of Ice," and "Frank Buck's Jungleland." Among the events that were clearly shows were "Salvador Dali's Living Pictures," which included a tank filled with water inhabited by 'living liquid ladies' who swam among sculptures of Dali's artistic works. The fair also included Norman Bel Geddes "Mirror Show" in the "Crystal Gazing Palace," where a single dancer performed on a stage with so many mirrors that it gave the effect of viewing a chorus of dancers.

One of the most popular attractions of the fair was the introduction of synchronized swimming, a program orchestrated by Broadway musical producer Billy Rose. The success of this program, the "Aquacade," led to its relocation in 1940 to Treasure Island, the site of the Golden Gate International Exposition in San Francisco Bay. Viewers watched "Aquabelles" and "Aquabeux," wearing fluorescent bathing caps, perform to music. The stars of the show included Esther Williams, Johnny Weissmuller (who later played Tarzan in numerous movies), and Morton Downey. Admission to the show cost 40 cents.

The fair ultimately lost $18.7 million even after a second season in 1940. The New York fair failed to cure Depression economic ills, just as the Chicago and San Francisco fairs had failed in the past. The Great Depression not only frustrated efforts by promoters to make profits at the fairs that were realized, it also interrupted plans for at least one other world's fair in the United States. In 1925 an exposition company was formed to hold a fair in Portland, Oregon. The fair was

A cigarette-smoking, house-sweeping robot called Elektro was created by Westinghouse for the 1939 New York World's Fair in Flushing Meadows. The Fair featured futuristic technology and was called the "World of Tomorrow." (AP/Wide World Photos. Reproduced by permission.)

to be called the Pacific American International Exposition. The company, however, was unable to raise sufficient funds and planning was halted in 1930. The company was dissolved in 1945. Despite the problems of World's Fairs realized, and the problems of those that never were, such as the Pacific American International Exposition, the New York World's Fair is remembered as one of the most popular fairs of the century. It caught the imagination of the public and had them looking to the future. World War II would soon shatter the new optimism created by the fair.

Scientists Seek to Justify Their Labors and Funding

One of the most interesting stories of the World's Fairs of the 1930s was the close relationship between fair planners and scientists. Historian Robert Rydell has pointed out that the fairs, especially the Century of Progress Exposition in Chicago in 1933, were cooperative ventures where America's leading scientists joined with corporate sponsors out of self-interest. Rydell has argued that scientists consciously sought

At a Glance

Quick Facts on World's Fairs

On April 30, 1939, a crowd estimated at 600,000 people listened to President Franklin D. Roosevelt dedicate the New York World's Fair.

The Golden Gate International Exposition, San Francisco, closed on October 29, 1939, six weeks early and was $4.1 million in debt.

An estimated 28,000 visitors per day toured the General Motor's "Futurama" exhibit at the New York World's Fair, 1939.

An estimated 45 million visitors attended the New York World's Fair of 1939–1940.

---

to popularize science and to shape an American culture with scientific values. Their investment grew all the more important with the anti-scientific attitudes of the 1920s. In that decade the famous "Monkey Trial" in Dayton, Tennessee, led to the conviction of school teacher John Scopes for violating state law by teaching the theory of evolution. Fearing further rejection of science, a number of leading scientists jumped at the opportunity to celebrate the positive contributions of science to American life. World's Fairs became an opportunity for getting out their message.

The National Research Council (NRC) founded in 1916 by President Woodrow Wilson to encourage the use of science to strengthen the nation moved to the center of support for the Chicago World's Fair. Leaders of the NRC met regularly after 1927 with fair developers. In time a Science Advisory Committee (SAC), made up of 32 scientists and engineers, began advising on exhibits and fair content. By 1930 this SAC had 34 subcommittees and drew upon the ideas of more than 400 science advisers. Before the fair opened in 1933 these sub-committees had held more than 70 sessions to envision the contents of the Hall of Science and other science-related exhibits. In 1930–1931 the SAC scripted and narrated 30 nationwide radio broadcasts, each 15 minutes in length, to promote science and the science-related content of the fair. These were broadcast in schoolrooms and colleges nationally.

Scientists thus helped plan the Chicago Fair, more than any other group, hoping to turn opinion in favor of their labors and to illustrate how science could shape a better American future. Scientists generally found frustration in trying to upgrade science education and the role of science in American life in the New York and San Francisco Fairs of 1939.

Contributing Forces

The Social and Economic Roles of World's Fairs

World's Fairs became an international event following the successful mounting of the Crystal Palace Exposition in London in 1851. More and more nations became involved in putting together events to celebrate "progress," technology, and agendas of peace, capitalism, and visions of the future. These fairs had historical foundations in exhibitions held in numerous cities in Western Europe between 1818 and 1844.

The fairs evolved over time. The first exposition in London in 1851 was housed in a single building, a giant greenhouse or "crystal palace." Its construction and appearance was an architectural marvel. In a real sense, the building became the primary icon of the event. Subsequent fairs also sought distinctive architecture, symbols or icons, and themes, not always successfully. The Eiffel Tower, erected in 1889 for the exposition (another term for fair) in Paris, is one of the most famous fair symbols. Designers have experimented with new styles and have copied old ones. Over time the grounds of the fairs expanded from a few acres to hundreds. The landscapes of the fairs evoked gracious lifestyles and control of nature; they featured calculated placement of buildings, vegetation, plazas, and pedestrian walkways.

Philadelphia held the first World's Fair in the United States in 1876, the Centennial International Exhibition. The event celebrated the nation's one-hundredth birthday. In 1884 and 1885 residents of New Orleans showcased their vision of an industrialized America in the New Orleans World's Industrial Cotton Centennial Exposition. The one-hundred-year intervals played an important role in the rationale for fairs. Thus in 1893 residents of Chicago hosted the World's Columbian Exhibition, a celebration of achievements in the four hundred years since Christopher Columbus made his first voyage to the Americas.

Between 1895 and 1916 ten cities hosted world's fairs or expositions in the United States. Two fairs that had especially captured national pride were the Louisiana Purchase Exposition of 1904 in

St. Louis and the Panama Pacific International Exposition of 1915 in San Francisco. World's Fairs cost millions of dollars that were generally raised by private investors and governments. Planning took years. Unlike smaller state fairs, World's Fairs lasted for months, attracting millions of people from across the country.

A common goal was to try to firm up the image of the nation as cohesive, powerful, innovative, and industrial. Most of these fairs—ignoring the treatment of black Americans, Asian Americans, and American Indians—stressed the themes of unity and social harmony in the United States. The fairs placed considerable emphasis on the expansion of economic, political, and military might of the United States abroad. The Lewis & Clark Centennial Exposition in Portland, Oregon, in 1905, for example, had as its logo the two explorers on either side of "Liberty" (a female figure) marching toward the setting sun-presumably an American empire beyond the Pacific Ocean. Either consciously or without realization, these fairs celebrated American success founded on overseas conquest of new economic markets and the nation's economic subjugation of people of color. Subjugation means to bring a person or group of persons under control and governance.

By the latter part of the nineteenth century and early-twentieth century, fairs contained theme buildings that displayed objects of fine arts, food products, primitive cultures (often with "living exhibits" of native people in customary garb engaged in traditional activities), and manufactured goods. The "goods" were a statement of design, technological prowess, and manufacturing capability. Goods celebrated progress. In addition other nations were invited to construct their own buildings where they could display their products, cultures, and virtues. If the fair was more local, then counties or other states might construct and fill their own "national" buildings with wares or even photographs of people and places.

Perspectives

The Everyday American

Because of the Great Depression, millions of Americans could not afford to go to the World's Fairs. They did not have the income to travel or to stay in Chicago, San Francisco, or New York and to spend hours or days visiting exhibits, amusement parks, or pageants. For the millions that could go they generally marveled at the scientific and industrial advances. They came away with renewed hope and excitement about the future. On the other hand there was a disturbing aspect to all the progress. Many factory workers were keenly aware that the new machines were putting people out of work. There was a widely held fear that machines would take over the jobs of people.

Despite the promises of a better future, not all was bright for these large events held during a time of worldwide economic strife. Fair promoters hoped to advance the prospects of their cities and special industries. But immediate returns on their investments into the exhibits were limited due to the poor economy. Also, while the fairs drew millions of visitors, none of the fairs proved profitable. Each had to open for a second season to try to pay off debts.

Preaching Science

The 1920s and 1930s were decades when many Americans expressed doubts about science and teaching of science in the schools. A number of scientists decided that they needed to get out the message about the unity of science, technology, and American values. The vehicle they selected and promoted was to use world's fairs as great classrooms for instructing millions of viewers with the marvels they could tap and control. Light shows, new products—color film, television, cellophane, nylon—and industrial exhibits emphasizing the role of scientific research and its link to a healthy economy became consistent messages at the fairs.

Issues arose: Were the presentations honest? Were science and technology linked to America's future? Some leading scientists tried hard to make their cases. Benjamin Gruenberg, a prominent educator, wrote *Science and the Public Mind* (1935) to try to improve scientific competence in America. Unlike the close alliance between scientists and planners for the Chicago World's Fair, the promoters of the fairs in San Francisco and New York in 1939 were far less interested in science and cooperation. Gerald Wendt, director of the American Institute of New York City, tried but largely failed to interject good science into the New York Fair. Wendt published *Science for the World of Tomorrow* (1939) to try to integrate science into American life. He claimed science had far more value than just its inventions and products serving as useful commodities. Historian Peter J. Kuznick, in *American Quarterly,* has concluded, "Fair planners and corporate exhibitors implemented their own clearly defined agendas—which conflicted with, and superseded, those of scientists, who had long since lost any monopoly over the imagery, display, or uses of science" (1994, p. 365).

Media Depictions

Two videocassettes are available concerning the World's Fairs of the 1930s.

- *The World of Tomorrow,* videotape produced and directed by Tom Johnson and Lance Bird; narrated by Jason Robards, 1984. 83 minutes.
- *Wonderful Treasure Island: Golden Gate International Exposition (1939–1940)* Videocassette, color, 1988. 63 minutes. AV #82832.

Impact

The World's Fairs of the 1930s had several important impacts on the United States. Not all impacts were anticipated by the fair promoters who had hoped for profits and the conveying of messages they had carefully tried to develop.

World's Fairs offered Americans the view of a promising future. Given the long-lasting Great Depression, the world of tomorrow shown in these fairs appeared to have considerably more promise than the reality of the 1930s. The vision included planned cities, laborsaving gadgets, efficient transportation systems, and streamlined designs. Americans also saw the potentials of science and technology, mostly presented in science fiction-like "futuramas." Such wonders as color film, nylon, and television—popularized at the fairs—became important elements of life in the future.

Other exhibits existed at the fairs besides technology and science. The fairs introduced millions of Americans to fine arts: murals, paintings, sculptures, and landscape design. While the buildings of the fairs were temporary, the cultural experiences of those who attended the fairs were highly educational.

Besides the focus on science and technology there were social implications foreshadowing future race relations. In spite of their high objectives each fair reflected some of the narrow mindedness and racism of the 1930s. Minorities were often included only as "oddities" or were depicted as contrasts to the presumed "civilization" of those sponsoring and planning the fairs. This perspective was in keeping with the difficult times that seemed to accentuate racial hatred.

Unknowingly, it also anticipated the tumultuous civil rights era of the 1950s and 1960s in which these racial prejudices came to the forefront.

Following the interruption of world's fair events by World War II, they resumed in 1949. In the United States, world's fairs were held in Seattle (1962), New York (1964–1965), San Antonio (1968), Spokane, Washington (1974), Knoxville, Tennessee (1982), and New Orleans (1984). With several of the later American fairs losing money, no others were held in the United States following 1984. Eight fairs were held elsewhere since 1984 however including Japan (1985), Canada (1986), Australia (1988), Spain and Italy in 1992, South Korea (1993), Portugal (1998), and Germany (2000). The selection and organization of the fairs is provided by the Bureau of International Expositions, headquartered in Paris, France, and established in 1928. Fairs scheduled for the early twenty-first century included France (2004) and Japan (2005) with others being proposed through 2020.

Notable People

Norman Bel Geddes (1893–1958). Bel Geddes published *Horizons* (1932), a visionary concept of what he thought would be the future of America. An innovator in lighting, set and theater design, and industrial design, Bel Geddes designed more than 200 theatrical productions with innovation and quality. In 1926 he founded an industrial design company and sought to improve the appearance of mass-produced objects. He served as an architectural consultant for the 1933 World of Tomorrow World's Fair in Chicago. Because of the lack of funding support available due to the economic effects of the Great Depression, none of his designs and exhibits was actually built. General Motors, however, hired Bel Geddes to develop the "Futurama" exhibit for its pavilion at the 1939 New York World's Fair, one of the most popular attractions. Bel Geddes also designed a "Gnome Village" and a "South Sea Island" display—both reflective of his fascination with eugenics, which is the improvement of the human species through genetic selection. Neither of these projects was built due to limited funding. Later Bel Geddes' vision helped shape the commitment of the United States in the 1950s to construct an interstate freeway system.

Gordon W. Gilkey (1912–2000). Gilkey was a talented artist, teacher, and master of etching. Gilkey was employed to capture in sketches the construction sequences of the New York World's Fair. Educated at Albany College (later Lewis & Clark College), Gilkey took on his assignment with enthusiasm. The Board of the New York World's Fair was so pleased with his artwork that it enlisted Gilkey to write and illustrate *Etchings: New York World's Fair "Building the World of Tomorrow"* (1939). Gilkey went on to a distinguished career as an arts educator in Oregon and, during his long "retirement," was curator of the Gordon and Vivian Gilkey Center for the Graphic Arts of the Portland Art Museum.

Grover A. Whalen (1886–1962). Whalen served as president of the 1939 New York World's Fair. A businessman, promoter, and champion of the City of New York, Whalen had earlier worked at Wanamaker's Department Store for a decade before becoming private secretary to the mayor of New York in 1917. From 1919 to 1953 Whalen served as the city's official greeter. Between 1924 and 1934 Whalen was general manager of Wanamaker's, though, for a time, he also served as police commissioner. Between 1934 and 1937 Whalen was chairman of the board of the Schenley Distilling Corporation. Whalen fine-tuned the ticker-tape parades and massive gatherings of people who gathered to see Charles Lindbergh in 1927 and General Douglas MacArthur in 1951. Whalen had proposed the hosting of the New York World's Fair and then served as the head of the corporation that planned it. He helped raise $155 million to transform the Corona Dumps into the fairgrounds. In 1941 Whalen became chairman of Coty, a cosmetic manufacturer, and in 1956 became president of a Detroit hardware company. He died in 1962.

Primary Sources

The Progressiveness of Fairs

Norman Bel Geddes, visionary and exhibit designer including "Futurama" at the New York World's Fair in 1939, offered the following observations of the future of America in his 1932 book *Horizons*. The statement reflects the still progressive forces at work in America even at a time of great economic strife of the Great Depression.

> There is said to be a law that higher forms must, before maturity, pass through all the stages of evolution of their predecessors. This seems to hold true for the modern art of building. Mankind has had to re-experience the architectural development of the Egyptians, the Greeks, through the Gothic, the Renaissance and the Baroque, before it could express its own time in its own terms ... We are too much inclined to believe, because things have long been done a certain way, that *that* is the best way to do them. Following old grooves of thought is one method of playing safe. But it deprives one of initiative

and takes too long. It sacrifices the value of the element of surprise. At times, the only thing to do is to cut loose and *do the unexpected!* It takes more even than imagination to be progressive. It takes vision and courage.

Science in Chicago

The theme of the Century of Progress, Chicago World's Fair was "Science Finds, Industry Applies, Man Conforms." With ever-optimistic advertising for the fair being held at the depths of the Great Depression in 1933, the *Official Guide Book of the Fair 1933* offered the following invitation (cited June 9, 2001, available from the World Wide Web at http://members.aol.com/hta/chicfair/index.html).

> As two partners might clasp hands, Chicago's growth and the growth of science and industry have been united during this most amazing century. Chicago's corporate birth as a village, and the dawn of an unprecedented era of discovery, invention, and development of things to effect the comfort, convenience, and welfare of mankind, are strikingly associated.
>
> Chicago, therefore, asked the world to join her in celebrating a century of the growth of science, and the dependence of industry on scientific research.
>
> Other expositions have shown, most often in settings of splendor, the achievements of man as exemplified in the finished products of general use. But when the plans were in the making for the exposition of 1933, the thought came that Chicago's Centennial celebration should be used to help the American people to understand themselves, and to make clear to the coming generation the forces which have built this nation.
>
> The result is that A Century of Progress is not merely an exhibit of the products of industry. Exhibitors willingly have subordinated their showing of finished products to a dynamic presentation of actual processes. They are telling a story of the ways that they utilize the discoveries of the basic sciences.

Suggested Research Topics

- Identify, compare, and contrast the primary icons (popular images such as key structures) of the Chicago, New York and San Francisco World's Fairs of the 1930s and explain how these objects attempted to convey the messages of the fair sponsors.

- Examine the claims of the three world's fairs of the 1930s to speak to the future of America and assess the success of these events in anticipating the United States of the latter half of the twentieth century.

- Using books and websites for research, identify the types of souvenirs or promotional items associated with the World's Fairs of the 1930s and discuss what these objects suggest about the themes or content of the fairs.

- Examine the architecture of the principal buildings and public spaces of the World's Fairs of the 1930s and discuss the messages conveyed by the uses of materials, sculpture, open spaces, water, landscape plantings, and building styles.

Bibliography

Sources

Barrington, Thomas M. A Vision of a Modern Future: A Fantasy Theme and Rhetorical Vision Analysis of the New York World's Fair of 1939. Ph.D. Dissertation, 1992, Southwest Texas State University.

Bel Geddes, Norman. *Horizons.* Boston: Little, Brown, and Company, 1932.

Benedict, Burton, et al. *The Anthropology of the World's Fairs: San Francisco's Panama Pacific International Exposition of 1915.* Berkeley, CA: Lowie Museum of Anthropology and Scholar Press, 1983.

Cogdell, Christina. "The Futurama Recontextualized: Norman Bel Geddes's Eugenic 'World of Tomorrow.'" *American Quarterly* 52(2)[June, 2000]: 193–245.

Cull, Nicholas J. "Overture to an Alliance: British Propaganda at the New York World's Fair, 1939–1940." *Journal of British Studies* 36(1)[July, 1997): 325–354.

Harrison, Helen A. and Joseph P. Cusker, eds. *Dawn of a New Day: The New York World's Fair, 1939/40.* Flushing, NY: Queens Museum and New York University Press, 1980.

Kuznick, Peter J. "Losing the World of Tomorrow: The Battle Over the Presentation of Science at the 1939 New York World's Fair." *American Quarterly* 46(3)[September, 1994]: 341–373.

Neuhaus, E. *The Art of Treasure Island: First-hand Impressions of the Architecture, Sculpture, Landscape Design, Color Effects, Mural Decorations, Illumination, and other Artistic Aspects of the Golden Gate International Exposition of 1939.* Berkeley, CA: University of California Press, 1939.

Reed, Christopher R. "'In the Shadow of Fort Dearborn': Honoring De Saible at the Chicago World's Fair of 1933–1934." *Journal of Black Studies,* 21(4)[June, 1991]: 398–413.

Reinhardt, Richard. "The Other Fair," *American Heritage,* 40(4)[1989]: 42–53.

Rydell, Robert W. "The Fan Dance of Science: America's World Fairs in the Great Depression," *ISIS* 76(284)[December, 1985]: 525–541.

———. "Selling the World of Tomorrow: New York's 1939 World's Fair." *The Journal of American History* 77(3)[December, 1990]: 966–970.

The World of Tomorrow, Produced and directed by Tom Johnson and Lance Bird. 83 min. 1984. Videocassette.

Further Reading

Carpenter, P. F. and P. Totah. *The San Francisco Fair: Treasure Island 1939–1940.* San Francisco, CA: Scottwall Associates, 1989.

Cohen, Barbara, Steven Haller, and Seymour Chwast. *Trylon and Perisphere: The 1939 New York World's Fair.* New York: Abrams, 1989.

ExpoMuseum: World's Fair History, Architecture, and Memorabilia. Website: http://www.ExpoMuseum.com.

Findling, John, ed. *Historical Dictionary of World's Fairs and Expositions, 1851–1988.* New York: Greenwood Press, 1990.

Gelernter, David. *1939: The Lost World of the Fair.* New York: Avon Books, 1995.

Gilkey, Gordon W. *Etchings: New York World's Fair: 'Building the World of Tomorrow.* New York: Charles Scribner's Sons, 1939.

Greenhalgh, Paul. *Ephemeral Vistas: The Expositions Universalles, Great Exhibitions and World's Fairs, 1851–1939.* Manchester, England: Manchester University Press, 1988.

Hiton, Suzanne. *Here Today and Gone Tomorrow—The Story of World's Fairs and Expositions.* Philadelphia, PA: The Westminster Press, 1978.

Rydell, Robert W., John E. Findling, and Kimberly D. Pelle. *Fair America: World's Fairs in the United States.* Washington, DC: Smithsonian Institution Press, 2000.

"Voices from the 1933 Chicago World's Fair," available from the World Wide Web at http://park.org/Guests/WWWvoice/1933chi.html.

Glossary, Bibliography, & Master Index

Glossary

A

abstinence: a deliberate self denial of alcoholic beverages; an individual who does not drink any liquor is abstaining from liquor.

abstract expressionism: art that seeks to portray emotions, responses, and feelings rather than objects in their actual likeness.

absurd: something ridiculous or unreasonable.

academic freedom: freedom to teach without interference or unwanted influence by another group or government.

Academy Awards: annual awards granted by the Academy of Motion Pictures for outstanding acting, directing, script writing, musical scoring, service, and creative contributions to the film industry.

adaptation: something that is remade into a new form, as in a play being an adaptation of a short story.

administration: the art or science of managing public affairs. Public administration is the function of the executive branch of government and is the procedure by which laws are carried out and enforced. In the United States, the president is the head of the executive branch, which includes an advisory staff and many agencies and departments.

affiliate: a firm closely connected to another.

agribusiness: an industry involved in farming operations on a large scale. May include producing, processing, storing, and distributing crops as well as manufacturing and distributing farm equipment.

alien: foreign-born person who has not been naturalized to become a U.S. citizen. Federal immigration laws determine if a person is an alien.

Allies: nations or states that form an association to further their common interests. The United States' partners against Germany during World War II (1939–1945) are often known collectively as "The Allies" and include Great Britain and Russia. (*See also* Axis powers)

allottee: the legal owner of a specific parcel of land, held in trust by the federal government for a minimum of 25 years under the provisions of the General Allotment Act of 1887. An allottee has an allotment, a specific portion of a reservation that was held apart from other tribal lands for that person's use or the benefit of his or her descendents.

allotment: the parcel of land granted to an individual that was taken out of a tribe's communal land base known as a reservation. While allotments dated to colonial times, they became a major part of national Indian policy in the General Allotment Act of 1887.

AM: amplitude modulation, the first type of radio transmission, characterized by considerable static interference.

amendment: changes or additions to an official document. In the United States government, constitutional amendments refer to changes in the Constitution. Such amendments are rare and may be proposed only by a two-thirds vote of both houses of Congress or by a convention called by

Congress at the request of two-thirds of the state legislators.

American Federation of Labor (AFL): a national organization of craft unions that sought to give voice to the concerns primarily of skilled workers.

amortized: the payment of a loan by stable monthly payments which include both principle and interest over a period of time, resulting in a declining principle balance and repayment in full by the end of the loan period.

anarchism: a belief that no forms of government authority are necessary and that society should be based on the cooperative and free association of individuals and groups.

animated cartoon: a motion picture made from a series of drawings simulating motion by means of slight progressive changes in the drawings.

anti-Semitism: hateful sentiment or hostile activities towards Jews; racial or religious intolerance.

antitrust: opposing large combinations of businesses that may limit economic competition.

Anti-Trust Acts: federal and state laws to protect economic trade and combat discrimination between companies, price fixing, and monopolies.

appraisal: to set a value of a property by the estimate of an authorized person.

appropriations: Funds for specific government and public purposes as determined by legislation.

Aquacade: a program of lights, music, and synchronized swimming developed by Billy Rose for the 1939 New York World's Fair.

area coverage: a system of electrical service designed to serve all possible customers in a given area rather than only those customers pre-selected on the basis of their projected consumption or ability to pay.

assets: total value of everything owned by, and owed to, a business. A bank's assets include its physical building and equipment, the loans it has made on which interest is owed, stock owned in the Federal Reserve System, government bonds it owns, money in the bank's vaults, and money deposited in other banks.

assimilation: a minority group's adoption of the beliefs and ways of life of the dominant culture.

Axis powers: The countries aligned against the Allied nations in World War II (1939–1945). The term originally applied to Nazi Germany and Fas-cist Italy (Rome-Berlin Axis), and later extended to include Japan. (*See also* Allies)

B

B-Movie (B-Picture, B-Film): cheaply produced movies usually following a simple formula and intended to serve as the second film in a "double bill," the showing of two movies for one theater admission.

bank holiday: a day or series of days in which banks are legally closed to correct financial problems.

bank runs: occurred when worried depositors, fearing about the stability of a bank, rushed to the bank to withdraw their deposits.

benefits: financial aid in time of sickness, old age, or unemployment.

bill: a proposed law. In the United States bills may be drawn up by anyone, including the president or citizen groups, but they must be introduced in Congress by a senator or representative.

bipartisan: cooperation between the two major political parties; for example, Republican and Democratic.

bond: a type of loan, such as savings bonds, issued by the government to finance public needs that cost more than existing funds can pay for. The government agrees to pay lenders back the initial cost of the bond, plus interest.

budget deficit: occurs when money spent by the government or other organization is more than money coming in.

bureau: a working unit of a department or agency with specific functions.

bureaucracy: an administrative system, especially of government agencies, that handles day-to-day business and carries out policies.

Burlesque: a type of variety show that focuses on musical acts and skits with sexual overtones.

business cycle: an economic cycle usually comprised of recession, recovery, growth, and decline.

buying on margin: a fairly common practice in the 1920s when investors purchased stock on credit, speculating on its increase in value. They planned to pay their loans back with the money they anticipated making. Such risks sometimes proved disastrous.

bootlegger: a person who illegally transports liquor; an individual who produces or distributes liquor illegally; smuggler.

bootlegging: the illegal manufacture or distribution of alcoholic products.

boycott: refusal of a group of persons to buy goods or services from a business until the business meets their demands.

bribery: giving gifts of money or property in return for specific favors.

broker: a person who brings a buyer and a seller together and charges a fee for assisting in the exchange of goods or services. A stockbroker brings together sellers and buyers of stocks and bonds.

budget deficit: refers to a government spending more than it receives through revenues and other means; it must rely on borrowing of money thus creating a debt.

C

cabinet: a group of advisors. In the federal government the cabinet is made up of advisors who offer assistance to the president. Each president determines the make up and role of their cabinets, although most include the heads of major departments such as State, Treasury, and Justice, and the vice president.

capital: money invested in a business; capital in banking terms includes the bank's stockholders' investments; additional money invested by the bank owners; any earnings still in the bank that have not been divided up; funds for taxes, expansion, and interest on accounts. Capital is the amount banks owe its owners.

capitalism: an economic system where goods are owned by private businesses and price, production, and distribution is decided privately, based on competition in a free market.

cartel: a combination of producers of any product joined together to control its production, sale, and price so as to obtain monopoly and restrict competition in any particular industry or commodity.

CCC: the Civilian Conservation Corps, a make-work agency for men aged 18 to 25 which operated between 1933 and 1942 and worked on numerous projects on public lands across the U.S. and its territories.

CCC-LEM: the Civilian Conservation Corps, Local Experienced Men, consisting initially of older, local laborers with special skills in carpentry, blacksmithing, auto mechanics, and other trades who came in to teach CCC enrollees.

CCC-ID: units of the Civilian Conservation Corps-Indian Division, staffed with American Indian recruits working on reservation projects.

cells: transparent celluloid on which sketches of animation are traced, inked, and painted.

charter: legal authorization from a federal or state agency to carry out business. To be chartered, a bank must have sufficient capital, competent management, deposit insurance, and a commitment to the local community.

child-centered: hands-on learning with children actively participating in an activity such as counting with blocks or piecing together a puzzle of the United States. This type of learning is a departure from traditional highly structured learning where a teacher tells children information or children read information from a book and repeat it.

cinematographer: the person in charge of camera work during the production of a movie.

civil liberties: freedom of speech, freedom of the press, freedom from discrimination, and other right guaranteed by the U.S. Constitution that place limits on governmental powers.

civil rights: civil liberties that belong to an individual.

civil service: a term describing the system employing people in non-military government jobs. The system is based on merit classifications.

clause: a section or paragraph of a legal document, such as a specific part of the U.S. Constitution.

clergy: ordained as religious priests, pastors, or ministers.

coalition: an alliance between political or special interest groups forged to pursue shared interests and agendas.

collateral: something of value that a borrower agrees to hand over to the lender if the borrower fails to repay the loan. The pledged item protects the lender from loss.

collective bargaining: the negotiations between workers who are members of a union and their employer for the purpose of deciding upon such issues as fair wages and work-day hours.

collectivism: shared ownership of goods by all members of a group; a political or economic system where production and distribution are decided collectively.

colonialism: a foreign policy in which a nation exercises its control over residents of foreign countries.

commerce: exchanging, selling, or trading goods on a large scale involving transporting goods from one place to another.

Commerce Clause: a provision of the U.S. Constitution that gives Congress the exclusive power to regulate economic trade between states and with foreign countries.

commercial bank: national or state bank, owned by stockholders whose activities include demand deposits, savings deposits, and personal and business loans. Many commercial banks also provide trust services, foreign money exchange, and international banking.

commercialism: to manage a business for profit; sometimes used in referring to excessive emphasis on profit.

committee: a group of individuals charged by a higher authority with a specific purpose such as investigation, review, reporting, or determining action.

commodities: any moveable item of commerce subject to sale.

communism: a theory calling for the elimination of private property so that goods are owned in common and, in theory, available to all; a system of government where a single party controls all aspects of society such as the official ideology of United Soviet Social Republic (USSR) from 1917 until 1990.

Communist Party, U.S.A. (CPUSA): a U.S. political party promoting the political and economic teaching of German political philosopher Karl Marx that grew rapidly in membership during the 1930s.

company union: a worker organization formed by a company commonly requiring membership of all employees to prevent their joining a national labor union.

compulsory: something that is required.

"conchies": an abbreviation identifying conscientious objectors who declined to serve in the military when drafted but who took alternative duty at Public Service Camps (former CCC camps) from 1941 to 1947.

congregation: an assembly of persons gathered as a religious community.

Congress: the term used to describe the combined Senate and House of Representatives.

Congress of Industrial Organizations (CIO): a labor organization formed in 1935 initially as the Committee on Industrial Organization within the AFL. The CIO was founded on broad-based industrial unionization rather than specialized crafts or skills like the AFL.

conscientious objector: a person who refuses to serve in the military because of personal beliefs. In the United States a person cannot refuse to serve, but Congress has allowed conscientious objectors to participate in non-combat duty or complete an exemption process on religious grounds. This exemption does not include objection for political, sociological, philosophical, or personal reasons, although the Supreme Court has upheld some requests for exemption based on these grounds if they are held with the fervor of religious beliefs.

conservation: the planned management of natural resources, such as soil and forests.

conservative: politically referring to one who normally believes in a limited government role in social and economic matters and maintenance of long-standing social traditions; conservative thought in education often stresses traditional basic subject matter and methods of teaching.

consumer: a person who buys or uses economic goods.

contour plowing: to till a sloping hillside following the same elevation back and forth, rather than up and down the hill, to prevent water erosion from rains.

cooperative: a private, nonprofit enterprise, locally owned and managed by the members it serves, and incorporated (established as a legal entity that can hold property or be subject to law suits) under State law.

corporatism: a system in which companies are organized into a cooperative arrangement that is recognized by the government and granted exemptions from antitrust laws in exchange for observing certain controls.

correspondent: an individual who communicates news or commentary to a newspaper, magazine, radio, or television station for publication or broadcast.

counterculture: a culture with values that run counter to those of established society.

credit: loan; agreement by which something of value is given in exchange for a promise to repay something of equal value; an advance of cash or a product, such as a car, in exchange for a promise to pay a specific sum in the future.

cultural democracy: the concept of cultural democracy comprises a set of related commitments: protecting and promoting cultural diversity, and the right to culture for everyone in our society and around the world; encouraging active participation in community cultural life; enabling people to participate in policy decisions that affect the quality of our cultural lives; and assuring fair and equitable access to cultural resources and support.

curator: an individual in charge of the care and supervision of a museum.

curriculum: courses of study offered by educational institutions such as English, social studies, and mathematics.

D

dailies: newspapers published everyday.

débutante ball: extravagant parties thrown by the very wealthy to introduce their daughters to high society and advertise their eligibility for marriage.

default: failure to meet the payment terms of a legal contract such as failure to make loan payments in repayment of a home loan; the lender may then begin foreclosure proceedings to recoup his loses.

deficit: the amount by which spending exceeds income over a given period.

deficit spending: a government spending more money than it receives in through taxes and other sources by borrowing.

demand deposits: checking accounts.

democracy: a form of government in which the power lies in the hands of the people, who can govern directly, or indirectly by electing representatives.

democratic: relating to the broad masses of people and promoting social equality and rule by majority.

Democratic Party: one of the two major political parties in the United States that evolved from the Democratic-Republican group that supported Thomas Jefferson. In the twentieth century, the Democratic Party has generally stood for freer trade, more international commitments, greater government regulations, and social programs. Traditionally considered more liberal than the Republican Party.

denomination: a religious organization with local congregations united together under a name and set of specific beliefs under one legal and administrative body.

department: an administrative unit with responsibility for a broad area of an organization's operations. Federal departments include Labor, Interior, Health and Human Services, and Defense.

dependent: persons who must rely on another for their livelihood. Generally applied to children 18 years and younger. The term can also refer to a person 62 years old or older.

deportation: expulsion of an alien from the United States.

deposit insurance: government-regulated protection for interest-bearing deposits, such as savings accounts, to protect the depositor from failure of the banking institution.

depression: a period of economic decline usually marked by an increase in unemployment.

desegregation: to end the legally enforced separation of races.

devaluation: to reduce the value of a nation's currency relative to other nations' currencies; often by lowering its gold equivalency.

disarmament: to reduce the amount of military arms a nation controls that can be used to attack or for defense.

divest: something of value that a person must give up. For example, the Banking Act of 1933 required officers of banks to divest themselves of any loans granted to them by their own banks to avoid a conflict of interest. Bankers could no longer be accused of using their depositors' money for their own, sometimes risky, investments.

Dixiecrat: southern Democrats who bolted from the party during the 1948 presidential campaign because of President Harry Truman's support of civil rights issues, as well as their opposition to a growing federal government by supporting strong state governments.

doctrine: a principle of law established in past decisions.

documentary still photograph: a photographic image in black-and-white or color that is realistic, factual, and useful as a historic document.

dole: when a needy person or family receives a handout from the government in the form of money, food, or vouchers from the government for support, it is referred to as "going on the dole." Though rarely used in the United States anymore, it is still commonly used in Britain.

double bill: showing two movies for one admission to a theater, usually with a main feature and a B-Movie.

dramatization: acting out events that actually happened, as in the events surrounding the negotiations were dramatized for television.

drug trafficking: buying or selling illegal drugs, the drug racket.

drys: people who supported Prohibition.

dual banking: the system of banking in the United States that consists of national banks and state banks. National banks are chartered and supervised by the Office of Comptroller of the Currency in the Treasury Department. State banks are chartered and supervised by state banking authorities.

due process of law: a basic constitutional guarantee that laws are reasonable and not arbitrary and their affects are well considered when developed; also guarantees that all legal proceedings will be fair and that a person will be given notice and an opportunity to speak before government acts to take their life, liberties, or property.

durable goods: goods that are not consumed or destroyed when used, often repeatedly for a number of years. Examples include armored tanks, ships, airplanes, and machinery.

E

electric power grid: a system for distributing electricity, interconnecting electric power plants and end users and comprising such equipment as power lines, poles, transformers, and substations.

electrification: the process or event in which a house, farm, industry, or locality is connected to an electric power source.

embezzle: for a person legally entrusted with funds to steal some for his or her own benefit. Embezzlers typically work in banks or other business institutions where they have access to funds.

End Poverty In California (EPIC): Upton Sinclair's proposal to pay everyone over the age of 60 a pension of $50 a month. He also urged that unemployed be put to work to produce necessities of life.

entrepreneur: an individual willing to try new approaches, who takes the risks of organizing and managing new enterprises.

EPIC Tax: Upton Sinclair's proposal in 1934 in California to charge a tax on property assessed at greater than $100,000 in value and use the income to fund the Central Valley Project of irrigation and agriculture to combat the Great Depression.

epidemiology: the branch of medicine dealing with the incidence and prevalence of disease in large populations and with detection of the source and cause of epidemics.

equal protection: a constitutional guarantee that no person or class of persons will be denied the same protection of the laws in their lives, liberty, property, or pursuit of happiness as other people in similar circumstances.

ethnic group: a large number of people considered a group based on shared racial, tribal, national, linguistic, religious, or cultural background.

exchange rate: a key part of international trade in which a rate guides how much one kind of currency can purchase another currency; can be either set by free international market or fixed by governments.

executive order: a rule or regulation issued by the president or a governor that has the effect of law. Executive orders are limited to those that implement provisions of the Constitution, treaties, and regulations governing administrative agencies.

ex-officio: members of a committee determined solely because of the office they hold.

exports: goods shipped to another nation for trade.

extender: foodstuffs to be added to dishes to stretch the meal, make the meal portions seem bigger, and feed more people. Common depression extenders were potatoes, onions, macaroni and spaghetti, rice, breads, and garden vegetables.

extortion: gaining another's property, money, or favors by use of threats of violence, disruption, or disclosure. For example, a crime group visits a shopkeeper and demands protection money. If the shopkeeper does not pay, the group may strike at him or his property until the shopkeeper does pay or is forced out of business.

extras: people hired to act in a group scene in a motion picture; background actors.

F

fascism: an ideology that focuses on nationalism or race as a uniting factor. Fascism first arose in Italy and Germany in the 1920s and 1930s, where it was characterized by government dictatorship, militarism, and racism.

federal: relating to the central government of a nation rather than to individual states.

federal aid: funds collected by the federal government (generally through taxes) and distributed to states for a variety of reasons including education and disaster relief.

federal budget: The annual financial plan of the United States government including all sources and amounts of income and items and amounts of expenditure. The federal budget must be approved by Congress and the president.

federalist: one who supports a strong central government as opposed to those favoring most governmental powers residing with the states and a weak federal government. It was the name of an early political party in the United States.

Federal Reserve System: a system of 12 Federal Reserve banks, a board of governors appointed by the president and state banks that apply for membership that hold money reserves for the banks in their region.

feminism: organized activity seeking political, social, and economic equality of the sexes.

filibuster: a means of obstructing progress in a legislative assembly by a legislator or group of legislators holding the floor for a prolonged period of time to prevent action on a proposed bill.

FM: frequency modulation, a type of radio transmission discovered in the 1930s but not routinely used until later, characterized by a clear, precise transmission.

forced leisure: due to unemployment during the Great Depression a person had lots of time and little choice but to pursue activities traditionally considered as leisure pursuits.

foreclosure: the process in which a bank that loaned money to a customer to purchase property takes over the property when customer fails to make payments. For example, farmers who failed to keep up with payments would have their farm loan foreclosed, thereby losing their property.

Fourteenth Amendment: one of three amendments to the Constitution passed shortly after the Civil War; this amendment guarantees the same legal rights and privileges of the Constitution to all citizens by guaranteeing that state laws cannot deprive any person of life, liberty, or property without due process of law and equal protection of the laws.

fraud: illegal misrepresentation or hiding the truth to obtain property, money, business, or political advantage.

free silver: rallying cry of the People's Party in the 1890s and the Liberty Party in 1932, promoting the increase in silver coinage and the greater amount in circulation per capita.

G

genre: refers to a type or classification. For example, "thrillers" as a movie genre; science fiction as a literary genre.

gold standard: a monetary system in which a nation's unit of money is set as equal to a given weight of gold. For example, one ounce of gold equals $300.

Grange: a rural social and educational organization through which farmers combated the power of railroads and utility companies in the early twentieth century.

grant: money provided by a government or organization to an individual or group for a specific purpose. For example, the federal government makes education grants to students for college expenses and to states to improve schools.

grassroots: political organizing at the most fundamental level of society—among the people.

Grazing Service: a federal agency established after passage of the Taylor Grazing Act (June 28, 1934) to bring federal management to more than 150 million acres of public lands, located mostly in the West. This agency supervised CCC activities in many areas. The Grazing Service merged with the U.S. General Land Office (GLO) in 1946 to become the Bureau of Land Management (BLM).

Great Depression: period in U.S. history from 1929 until the early 1940s when the economy was so poor that many banks and businesses failed and millions of people lost their jobs and their homes. Business problems were combined with a severe drought that ruined many farms and contributed to the economic disaster.

Great Society: term used by Lyndon Johnson during his presidential administration (1963–1969) to describe his vision of the United States as a land without prejudice or poverty, that would be possible by implementing his series of social programs.

Gross Domestic Product (GDP): a measure of the market value of all goods and services produced within the boundaries of a nation, regardless of asset ownership. Unlike gross national product, GDP excludes receipts from that nation's business operations in foreign countries, as well as the share of reinvested earnings in foreign affiliates of domestic corporations.

Gross National Product: total value of all goods and services produced by the nation's economy.

grounds: there exist reasons sufficient to justify some form of legal relief.

H

hierarchy: leadership or ruling structure of clergy organized into rank.

hooch: alcoholic beverages that are made or acquired illegally and are frequently of inferior quality.

holding company: a company or corporation whose only purpose or function is to own another company or corporation.

Hollywood: a section of Los Angles, California, at the base of the Santa Monica Mountains where several film producers established studios to make movies in the first half of the twentieth century.

House of Representatives: one of the two bodies with specific functions that make up the legislative branch of the United States government. Each state is allocated representatives based on population. (*See also* Congress; Senate)

housing starts: the number of residential building construction projects begun during a specific period of time, usually a month.

humanitarian: a person who works for social reform and is concerned about the welfare of people.

hydroelectric power: to generate electricity from the energy of swift flowing streams or waterfalls.

I

icon: an image, picture, or logo that becomes closely associated with a particular event, belief, or organization.

immigration: the legal or illegal entry of foreigners into a country intending to remain permanently and become citizens.

income distribution: the portion of annual earnings or accumulated wealth held by members of a society. The poor have low incomes, while the wealthy usually have high incomes and a resultant growing accumulation of assets.

independent: a voter who does not belong to any political party and votes for individual candidates regardless of their party affiliation.

indoctrinate: to instruct so as to instill a particular point of view.

indolent: a person not working because of laziness.

industrialism: to change an area or economy from agricultural to industrial production.

infrastructure: permanent developments to support a community's economy such as roads, buildings, and bridges.

inflation: a sharp increase in prices for goods and services decreasing the value of currency.

injunction: a judicial order that requires someone to stop or avoid certain actions that might harm the legal rights of another.

inoculate: to inject or implant a vaccine, microorganism, antibody, or antigen into the body in order to protect against, treat, or study a disease.

installment buying: purchasing commodities on credit and, having taken possession of the item, paying for it with a fairly high rate of interest over months or even years. The system encouraged those without savings to buy unwisely.

integration: to unite different races together into equal participation in society.

internationalism: a government policy of cooperation with other nations.

interest: money paid to a lender for use of his money.

interest rate: a percentage of money borrowed that must be paid back in addition to the sum of the original loan for the privilege of being able to borrow.

interventionism: a governmental policy of becoming involved in political matters of another nation.

invalidate: to determine that a law does not have sufficient legal justification to be enforceable; therefore it is no longer valid.

isolationism: opposition to economic or political alliances with other nations.

J

Jim Crow laws: state laws and ordinances primarily created in the South, requiring the separation of races in almost every aspect of public life. Jim Crow laws lasted from the late nineteenth century to the middle of the twentieth century. The laws were powerful barriers to legal and social equality.

journalism: written description of newsworthy events or presentation of facts designed to be published in a newspaper, magazine, or delivered vocally over radio or television.

judicial restraint: for courts not to interfere with what would more properly be the role of a legislature or the executive branch to decide the wisdom of a particular law.

judiciary: relating to the courts and legal system.

jurisdiction: the geographic area over which legal authority extends, such as the legal jurisdiction of a city police force.

juvenile delinquency: criminal behavior of children or young teens.

K

Keynesian economics: the theory of economist John Keynes that advocates government spending and economic recovery programs to promote spending and increase employment.

L

labor market: the people available for employment.

labor racketeering: corrupt activities between labor unions and organized crime. Members of criminal groups position themselves in places of authority within a labor union. Once inside they use funds such as pension and health funds to their own advantage.

labor union: a group of organized workers who negotiate with management to secure or improve their rights, benefits, and working conditions as employees.

laissez faire: a political doctrine that opposed governmental interference in economic affairs except for the minimum necessary to protect property rights and for safety.

lard: hog fat obtained by rendering down the fat deposits that exist between the flesh and the skin and around internal organs of the pig.

laundered money: transferring huge sums of illegally obtained money through banks or businesses with large cash flows until the original source of the money is untraceable.

lay people: membership of a religious faith who are not clergy; the general membership; also referred to as laity.

League of Nations: the forerunner of the United Nations, envisioned by its originator, Woodrow Wilson, as a forum where countries could resolve their differences without resorting to war and promoted economic and social cooperation.

leftist: a term used to describe individuals whose beliefs are on the "left" side of the political spectrum, constituting more liberal views. Often used derogatorily.

legislation: measures that are intended to become law after approval by legislative bodies.

liabilities: what a person owes to others. A bank's liabilities include checking and savings account deposits, investment of stockholders, funds for taxes and expansion, interest to be paid to depositors on their accounts, and earnings not yet divided among the stock holders.

liberal: politically referring to one who commonly emphasizes government protection of individual liberties and supports government social and economic reforms and regulation of business to encourage competition; liberal thought in education is often associated with new methods of teaching or nontraditional subject matter.

liquidate: to convert property into cash by selling it.

liquidity: being able to meet the demands of depositors to withdraw funds and to meet the needs of borrowers for credit (loans) or cash. Liquid assets include cash on hand and securities that can be sold quickly for cash.

loan sharking: loaning money at exorbitantly high interest rates and using threats to receive repayment.

lump-sum payment: one time only payment.

lumpenproletariat: those on the very bottom of the social scale described in the *Communist Manifesto* as "social scum."

M

Mafia: organized crime syndicate concerned with power and profit. The term originated in Italy some six centuries ago from the slogan: *Morte Alla Francia Italia anela!* ("Death to the French is Italy's cry.")

mafioso: member or members of the Mafia. Plural form is mafiosi.

"making do": creating filling and tasty meals with limited ingredients, with foods at hand or those readily available. Typical "making do" foods were flour, cornmeal, lard, eggs, potatoes, and onions.

maldistribution: a substantially uneven distribution of income or wealth to such an extent that it can cause general economic problems.

mandate: an authorization to act given by a political electorate to its representative.

margin call: when a creditor, who has loaned money, calls for immediate payment of the amount due.

Marxism: the theories—political, economic, and social—of Karl Marx, calling for class struggle to establish the proletariat (work class) as the ruling class, with the goal of eventually establishing a classless society.

means test: a battery of questions about a person's financial, employment, and residential history used to determine eligibility for charity or financial assistance.

mechanization: the increasing use of gas or diesel powered machinery such as tractors, harvesters, and combines; often replacing human or animal labor and introducing greater efficiency in growing and harvesting farm crops.

mediation: the intervention of an unbiased party to settle differences between two other disputing parties; any attempt to act as a go-between in order to reconcile a problem.

Mobilization: to assemble war materials and manpower and make ready for war.

melodrama: movies, sometimes referred to as "weepies," focused on characters living through a series of adverse and tragic circumstances. A character with a terminal illness is a frequently used plot.

Memorial Day Massacre: a 1937 Steel Workers' Organizing Committee strike in Chicago at the Republic steel mill of U.S. Steel that led to the deaths of ten workers and 30 others wounded by police.

minimum wage: the wage established by law as the lowest amount to be paid to workers in particular jobs.

minstrel shows: stage performances of black American traditional melodies and jokes performed by white actors impersonating blacks, including having their faces blacked.

moderation: acting in a responsible, restrained manner, avoiding excessive behaviors.

modernism: the cultural expression of Western society including the United States since the late nineteenth century, primarily as expressed in literature and visual designs.

modernist art: modernist art may be defined by its self-conscious interest in experimentation with the materials and creative processes of each individual art medium. Freed from representing objects as they actually exist, Modernist artists have tended to stress the subjective uniqueness of their own particular visions.

monopoly: when only one seller of a product, or a combination of sellers, exists who can set his own price.

moonshiner: maker or seller of illegal liquor.

moratorium: a legally authorized period of delay in performing some legal obligation; a waiting period set by an authority; a suspension of activity.

mortgage: normally involves a long-term real estate loan; the borrower gives the bank a mortgage in return for the right to use the property. The borrower agrees to make regular payments to the lender until the mortgage is paid up.

movie star: an actor or actress groomed for celebrity status by a movie production studio.

muckraking: a type of journalism that exposes the misdeeds and corruption in American business and politics of a prominent individual.

munitions: war supplies, particularly ammunition and weapons.

mutual fund: an investment company that invests the money of its shareholders in a diversified group of securities.

N

National Labor Relations Board: a board created in 1935 by the National Labor Relations Act to assist employees in the free selection of representative organizations (unions) to deal with employers, to prevent unfair labor practices, and to see that employers bargained in good faith.

National Union for Social Justice (NUSJ): an organization founded in 1935 by Father Charles Coughlin, the "Radio Priest" of Royal Oak, Michigan, who began a strong lobbying effort to influence Congress on the course of the New Deal.

nationalism: a strong loyalty to one's own nation above all others.

naturalization: the process in which an alien can apply to become a U.S. citizen. Requirements include five years of legal residence, literacy in English, and a record of good behavior.

Nazism: a political philosophy based on extreme nationalism, racism, and military expansion; dominated Germany from 1933 to 1945.

neutrality: policy of not becoming involved in war between two other nations.

New Deal: the name given to Franklin Roosevelt's plan to save the nation from the devastating effects of the Great Depression. His programs included direct aid to citizens and a variety of employment and public works opportunities sponsored by the federal government.

nickelodeon: an early movie theater, usually charging a nickel for admission.

non-durable goods: goods that are consumed or destroyed when used. Examples include chemicals, paper, rubber, textile, apparels, and foods.

O

old-age insurance: assurance of cash payments, generally made monthly, to retired workers' pensions.

oral history: the memories of an event or time, captured in the words of the person who lived it.

organized crime: a specialized form of crime with two major characteristics: organized into loosely or rigidly structured networks of gangs with certain territorial boundaries; the networks with rigid structures have bosses and a centralized management; and devoted to producing, protecting, and distributing illegal goods and services.

P

pacifism: opposed to armed conflict or war to settle disputes.

papal encyclical: an official letter from the Pope stating the Catholic Church's position on timely social issues and offering guidance for Catholic living.

parish: a local area or community of the members of a church.

partisan: adhering to a particular political party.

patron: a wealthy or influential supporter of an artist.

patronage: the power of public officials to make appointments to government jobs or grant other favors to their supporters, or the distribution of such jobs or favors.

pension(s): money given to an employee when they retire from a company. Pensions can be funded by the government, an employer, or through employee contributions.

philanthropy: humanitarian gifts to be distributed for the welfare of the fellow man.

photojournalism: emerged in the 1930s as a special filed of print communications. Magazines, newspapers, and movie newsreels tapped talented photographers to document labor, rural and urban settings, nature, warfare, and other subjects.

Photo-Secession: an informal society and a movement among photographers in the United States founded in 1903 by Alfred Stieglitz. The movement pursued pictorial photography and high aesthetic standards.

pictorial photography: using the camera to create artwork and moving photography outside of the studio. The techniques included soft-focus, manipulation of the negative and print in the dark room, and production of photographs to mimic paintings, watercolors, and other works of art.

pluralism: a situation in a nation when diverse ethnic, racial, or social groups participate in a common political and economic system.

pogrom: planned massacres of groups of people as the massacres experienced by the Jewish people.

pope: the bishop of Rome and head of the worldwide Roman Catholic Church.

pocket veto: a means by which the president of the United States can prevent a bill passed by Congress from becoming law by delaying the signing of the bill within the 10-day time limit required by the Constitution while the Congress is not in session. In contrast should the president fail to sign the bill while the Congress is in session, it would automatically become law.

Ponzi scheme: a fraud racket in which innocent profit-seeking investors pay their money only to discover the company has few assets and no potential to make a profit. Most such schemes collapsed with a few investors running off with the money of many unhappy people.

popular culture: popular culture consists of expressive forms widely available in society. Such forms include, but are not limited to, theater, television, festivals, architecture, furniture, film, the Internet, books, magazines, toys, clothing, travel souvenirs, music, dance, and body customization. Popular culture can also include folk culture and most of what is thought of as elite culture (i.e. the fine arts).

Popular Front: at the direction of the communist leadership in the Soviet Union, the Communist Party, USA, waged strong opposition from 1935 to 1939 against fascism. Part of its strategy was to support the New Deal and President Roosevelt.

populist: to represent the concerns of common people in political matters.

preference hiring: to legally favor members of a particular racial or ethnic group over other people in hiring for work.

protectionism: adoption of policies that protect a nation's economy from foreign competition.

price supports: a government financial aid program for farmers in which commodity prices are set at a certain level at or above current market values. If the market value is less than the set value, the government will pay the farmer the difference. Usually price supports are combined with limitations on production and with the storing of surpluses.

principal: the actual amount of money loaned that must be repaid.

private sector: business not subsidized or directed by the government.

progressive: one who believes in political change, especially social improvement through government programs.

progressive education: educational approach based on child-centered activities that involve hands-on learning in contrast to the highly structured traditional classroom setting focused on memorization.

prohibition: legal prevention of the manufacture, sale, or distribution of alcoholic beverages. The goal of Prohibition is partial or total abstinence from alcoholic drinks. Prohibition officially began on January 16, 1920, when the Eighteenth Amendment took effect, and ended December 5, 1933, when the amendment was repealed.

proletariat: a low social or economic group of society generally referring to the working class who must sell their labor to earn a living.

protestant work ethic: a code of morals based on the principles of thrift, discipline, hard work, and individualism.

public utility: a business that provides an essential public service, such as electricity, and is government regulated.

public works: government funded projects that are intended to benefit the public such as libraries, government buildings, public roads, and hydropower dams.

pump priming: an economic theory as applied by the New Dealers that if enough people received paychecks once again, that they would once again buy goods and services, and the economy would eventually come back into balance.

Q

quotas: the number of people of a certain kind, such as a race or nation, allowed to legally immigrate into a country.

R

racketeering: engaging in a pattern of criminal offenses. Examples of racketeering include gambling, robbery, loan sharking, drug trafficking, pornography, murder, prostitution, money laundering, kidnapping, extortion, fraud, counterfeiting, obstruction of justice, and many more.

ratify: approve.

reactionary: a strongly conservative response or a strong resistance to change.

receiver: a device, such as part of a radio, that receives incoming signals and translates them into something perceptible, such as sound.

recession: an economic slowdown of relatively short duration. During a recession, unemployment rises and purchasing power drops temporarily.

reconversion: to change something, such as industry production, back to what it was before its more recent changes.

refinance: arrange new loan terms so that regular payments can be more affordable. This usually involves adjustment of the interest rate and the length of the repayment period.

regionalism: an artistic movement primarily associated with the 1920s and 1930s in which artists chose to represent facets of American rural and urban life.

relief: when a needy person or family receives money, food, or vouchers from the government for support. This term is not commonly used in the United States anymore, it is currently called welfare.

render: to cook and thereby melt out fat from fatty animal tissue. The cooked fat is then put into a press and the lard squeezed out The remaining product is called crackling.

reorganization: refers to the Indian Reorganization Act of 1934 and a major shift in federal policy toward American Indians during the New Deal. Under Reorganization, the federal government encouraged native arts and crafts, tribalism, and protection of native lands and resources.

repatriation: return to the country of origin.

republic: a government in which political power is primarily held by the citizens who vote for elected officials to represent them.

Republican Party: one of the two major political parties in the United States. The Republican Party emerged in the 1850s as an antislavery party. In the twentieth century, the Republican Party represents conservative fiscal and social policies and advocates a more limited role for federal government.

retrenchment: cutting of expenses from budgets; school retrenchment of the 1930s also included cutbacks in instruction, teacher salaries, number of teachers, and resulted in larger class size.

rhetoric: the use of language effectively toward influencing the conduct of others.

rumrunner: an individual bringing illegal liquor across a border; rumrunners often use boats and sometimes airplanes for the illegal transportation.

S

scabs: non-union laborers brought in to replace striking laborers.

screwball comedy: comedies with sophisticated plots and characters.

scrip: coupons or certificates, usually paper, issued as substitutes for cash in retail establishments to be used for goods and services. The coupons are assigned a specific value and are used as temporary money.

securities: stocks and bonds.

securities loan: a bank loan that uses stocks or bonds as collateral; or a bank's loan to a stockbroker.

segregation: maintaining a separation of the races, normally in public facilities such as restaurants, hotels, theaters, and other public places.

seminary: an institution of higher learning for the religious training for ministers, priests, or rabbis.

Senate: one of the two bodies with specific functions that make up the legislative branch of the United States government. Each state is allocated two senators. (*See also* Congress; House of Representatives)

sensationalism: arousing interest or emotions with shocking, exaggerated treatments and presentation of the news.

separate but equal: an early Supreme Court doctrine established in 1897 held that racial segregation in public facilities did not violate equal protection of the law if equal facilities are available.

separation of powers: the constitutional division of responsibilities between the three independent branches of government—executive, judicial, and legislative.

serial drama: a drama that takes place over a series of episodes, such as a soap opera.

Share-Our-Wealth Plan: Huey Long, senator from Louisiana, promoted the idea of wealth distribution by heavy government taxation of the rich and guaranteeing every family an average wage of $2,000 to $3,000 per year. This concept was carried starting in 1935 by the Share-Our-Wealth Society.

sharecroppers: farm workers who worked the land of a landowner and often could keep half the value of their crops; for the other half they received from the landowner land to farm, housing, fuel, seed, tools, and other necessities in return for part of the crops raised.

shyster: a slick, smart movie character, usually portraying a lawyer, politician, or newspaperman, who was professionally unscrupulous in their dealings.

silver screen: nickname for motion pictures based on the color of the projection screen in a theater where images of adventure and romance entertained viewers.

sit-down strike: a strike where workers remain in the workplace but decline to work. This action effectively blocked the employer from replacing them with other workers. The Supreme Court outlawed this practice in 1939.

slapstick: films employing comedy and farce to entertain viewers.

slums: severely overcrowded urban areas characterized by the most extreme conditions of poverty, dilapidated housing, and crime-ridden neighborhoods.

soap opera: a drama that takes place over a series of episodes. Takes its name from the early sponsorship of radio serial dramas by soap manufacturers.

social insurance: a broad term referring to government sponsored social welfare programs of old age assistance and old age pensions, unemployment supports, worker's compensation, and healthcare programs. The term has two elements: (1) the social element meaning its programs applied to groups not just individual self-interests;

and, (2) the insurance principle under which people are protected in some way against a risk.

social legislation: a bill or legislative proposal sent to Congress which addresses social issues such as old age assistance, pensions, unemployment supports, worker's compensation, and healthcare programs.

social reconstructionism: a more radical form of progressive education; calls for the establishment of a new, more equitable social order accomplished through instruction by teachers in the schools.

Social Security: a public program that provides economic aid and social welfare for individuals and their families through social insurance or assistance. In the United States, Social Security was passed into law in 1935, as a life and disability insurance and old age pension for workers. It is paid for by employers, employees, and the government.

socialism: various political and economic theories calling for collective ownership and administration either by the people or government of the means of production and distribution of goods; sometimes thought of an in-between step between capitalism and communism.

speakeasy: a place where alcoholic beverages were sold illegally during Prohibition; patrons gained admission by giving a simple password, thus the name "speakeasy."

speculation: high risk investments such as buying stocks and/or bonds in hopes of realizing a large profit.

stalemate: a situation in which the two sides in a contest are evenly matched and neither is able to win.

standard of living: basic necessities of food, clothing, and shelter, plus any other conveniences or luxuries the family is unwilling to do without.

stock: certificate of ownership in a company also known as shares.

stock market: a market where shares of stock, or certificates of ownership in a company, are bought and sold.

strike: a labor stoppage where workers, usually through the action of their union, refuse to work until management addresses their complaints or requests about wages, hours, working conditions, and benefits.

strip plowing or strip cropping: to till an agricultural field in strips leaving untilled areas between the tilled strips.

studio system: operating between 1930 and 1945 to produce over 7,500 feature films, eight "studios" or major companies dominated film production, distribution, and exhibition. Studios not only made films, they owned theaters that projected their products. They also secured exclusive contracts with actors and actresses.

substantive due process of law: pertaining to the purpose of the act such as limitations put on someone.

suburb: a community on the outskirts, but within commuting distance, of a city.

suburbanization: to create suburbs around a central city.

suffrage: the right to vote especially in a political election.

survivors' insurance: monthly cash benefits paid to the surviving family members of a worker who has died. Survivors may include the wife, dependent children under eighteen years of age, and a dependent parent age 62 or older.

swashbuckler: movies generally set among pirates and knights with melodrama, sword play, and cannon fire.

swing: a type of rhythm driven jazz that became very popular during the depression era. Like other forms of jazz, swing incorporates improvisation. Swing is also associated with "big bands" of sixteen musicians or more. Vocalists were also associated with swing and big bands. The term swing is often credited to Duke Ellington and the 1932 song "It Don't Mean a Thing (if it ain't got that swing);" the dance craze of the mid- to late 1930s.

syndicate: an association or network of groups of individuals who cooperate to carry out activities of an enterprise. The groups may be formal or informal and may carry out legal or illegal activities.

syndicated: to sell a piece or column written by one journalist to many newspapers across the country for publication at the same time. The column is generally signed by the author.

synthetic: something made by artificially combining components, unlike a process which occurs naturally.

T

talkie: a motion picture with sound accompaniment.

tariff: a tax on items imported, often in the form of duties or customs. It is intended to make foreign-made goods more expensive than goods made in the United States.

tenant farming: an agricultural system in which farmers rented farmland and provided their own tools. They received two-thirds to three-fourths of the value of their crops. Often they purchased tools, clothing, and food with loans against crops they expected to grow the following season. The landlord kept records and computed earnings.

tenement: large housing structures containing apartment dwellings that barely meet or do not meet minimum standards of sanitation and comfort.

tenure: an assurance of job stability.

temperance: the use of alcoholic beverages in moderation or abstinence from their use.

terracing: changing a sloped hillside into a series of flat planting areas.

totalitarianism: a political system in which the government exercises complete control over its citizens.

Townsend Plan: proposal of Dr. Francis E. Townsend of Long Beach, CA., in 1933, calling for the federal government to give a pension of $200 a month to every U.S. citizen on the condition that the money be spent within 30 days.

Townsendites: advocates of the Townsend Plan who pressed hard for their version of old-age pension benefits between 1933 and 1940.

Townsend Weekly: a publication of the supporters of the Townsend Plan which articulated their views and discontent with the Social Security Act.

transcription show: in early radio, a show that was recorded on disc for distribution to radio stations for later transmission.

transients: a person traveling around, usually in search of work.

transmitter: a device that generates a carrier wave encapsulating a signal derived from speech or music or other sources, and radiates the results from an antenna.

trespass: to unlawfully enter the land of another person.

tribalism: maintaining the social integrity of a traditional Indian tribe through support of its customs and beliefs.

trilogy: a series of three artistic works such as three musical pieces or books.

trust: the fiduciary (legal and monetary) responsibility of the federal government is known as trust or "trust responsibility." This concept was guaran-

teed by treaties and supported by the findings of the U.S. Supreme Court in the case of *Cherokee Nation v. Georgia* (1831). The trust responsibility compels the federal government to act in the best interest of tribes when setting policy or passing laws.

trustee: one to whom property is entrusted to be administered for the benefit of another, or one of a number of persons appointed to manage the affairs of an institution.

U

unconstitutional: to determine that a federal or state law is not in agreement with the Constitution.

underworld: the world of organized crime.

underwrite: to guarantee financial support of a company or program, assuming financial responsibility.

unemployment insurance: cash payments made for a certain period of time to a worker who involuntarily loses their job. The worker must be able and willing to work when a new job is available.

unionism: a belief in the right of workers to organize and bargain collectively with employers over work conditions.

urban: relating to a city.

urbanization: people moving from farms and small rural communities to large cities.

V

vaccine: any preparation introduced into the body to prevent a disease by stimulating antibodies against it.

vagrant: a person wandering about with no permanent address and no visible or permanent means of financial support.

variety show: a form of entertainment, usually consisting of a series of acts, such as songs, comedy, and dances.

Vaudeville: emerged out of burlesque in the early twentieth century for family audiences. Vaudeville consists of musical acts, short plays, comedy acts, and skits. Vaudeville, unable to compete with the movies, virtually disappeared in the early 1930s with many vaudeville theaters converted to movie houses.

venereal disease: contagious disease acquired through sexual intercourse.

ventriloquist: the art of projecting one's voice, often into a wooden dummy. A form of entertainment that includes a dialogue between the dummy and the ventriloquist.

vivisection: the action of cutting into or dissecting a living body; the practice of subjecting living animals to cutting operations in order to advance physiological and pathological knowledge.

volunteer: carrying out a service out of one's own free will and without payment for the action.

W

Wall Street: the location in New York City of the New York Stock Exchange.

welfare: when a needy person or family receives money, food, or vouchers from the government for support. Traditionally called "going on the dole," or relief.

welfare-to-work: term used in the late twentieth century in the United States to describe programs that seek to move welfare recipients from welfare to private employment.

western: a film genre which became popular in the 1930s and despite some criticism remained popular through the years.

wets: those who opposed Prohibition.

wildcat strike: a locally organized work stoppage, not necessarily endorsed by a labor union, to try to achieve worker goals.

workers' compensation: programs designed to provide cash benefits and medical care to workers who sustain a work-related illness or injury.

work relief: when the government provides a needy person with a paying job instead of simply giving them money for support. Different from the current term, welfare-to-work, in that the "work" in work relief is on a government-sponsored project; the "work" in welfare-to-work is in the private sector. The term is not commonly used anymore in the United States.

Y

yardstick: in a sense like a real yardstick, a standard by which to measure. As used by Franklin D. Roosevelt, the term refers to a government program or agency set up to perform a task normally done by private industry in order to assess whether that private industry is charging a fair price for its services.

yellow dog contract: a signed agreement in which an employee promises not to join a labor union.

yellow journalism: an extreme form of sensationalism taking real life events and twisting and turning stories to catch the public's attention. Stories are not only exaggerated but misrepresented.

Young Communist League: An organization focused on teenagers and Americans in their twenties promoting the philosophy and politics of the Communist Party, USA; active in the 1920s and 1930s.

Z

Zionism: the movement to established a national homeland for the Jewish people in Palestine.

General Bibliography

This bibliography contains a list of sources, including books, periodicals, novels, and websites, that will assist the reader in pursuing additional information about the topics contained in this volume.

Books

Adams, Henry H. *Harry Hopkins: A Biography.* New York: G.P. Putnam's Sons, 1977.

Agee, James, and Walker Evans. *Let Us Now Praise Famous Men: Three Tenant Families.* Boston: Houghton Mifflin Co., 2000.

Altmeyer, Arthur J. *The Formative Years of Social Security.* Madison: The University of Wisconsin Press, 1968.

Andersen, Kristi. *The Creation of a Democratic Majority, 1928–1936.* Chicago: University of Chicago Press, 1979.

Anderson, James D. *The Education of Blacks in the South, 1860–1935.* Chapel Hill: University of North Carolina Press, 1988.

Appel, Benjamin. *The People Talk: American Voices from the Great Depression.* New York: Simon & Schuster, 1982.

Balderrama, Francisco E., and Raymond Rodríguez. *Decade of Betrayal: Mexican Repatriation in the 1930s.* Albuquerque: University of New Mexico Press, 1995.

Barber, William J. *Designs within Disorder: Franklin D. Roosevelt, the Economists, and the Shaping of American Economic Policy, 1933–1945.* New York: Cambridge University Press, 1996.

———. *From New Era to New Deal: Herbert Hoover, the Economists, and American Economic Policy, 1921–1933.* New York: Cambridge University Press, 1985.

Bauman, John F., and Thomas H. Goode. *In the Eye of the Great Depression: New Deal Reporters and the Agony of the American People.* DeKalb: Northern Illinois University Press, 1988.

Bentley, Joanne. *Hallie Flanagan: A Life in the American Theatre.* New York: Alfred A. Knopf, 1988.

Bergman, Andrew. *We're in the Money: Depression America and Its Films.* New York: New York University Press, 1971.

Bernstein, Irving. *A Caring Society: The New Deal, the Worker, and the Great Depression.* Boston: Houghton Mifflin Co., 1985.

———. *Turbulent Years: A History of the American Worker, 1933–1941.* Boston: Houghton Mifflin Co., 1970.

Best, Gary D. *The Critical Press and the New Deal: The Press Versus Presidential Power, 1933–1938.* Westport: Praeger, 1993.

Bindas, Kenneth J. *All of This Music Belongs to the Nation: The WPA's Federal Music Project and American Society.* Knoxville: University of Tennessee Press, 1995.

Black, Gregory D. *Hollywood Censored: Morality Codes, Catholics, and the Movies.* New York: Cambridge University Press, 1994.

Bloomfield, Maxwell H. *Peaceful Revolution: Constitutional Change and American Culture from Progressivism to the New Deal.* Cambridge, MA: Harvard University Press, 2000.

Brinkley, Alan. *Culture and Politics in the Great Depression.* Waco, TX: Markham Press Fund, 1999.

———. *The End of Reform: New Deal Liberalism in Recession and War.* New York: Alfred A. Knopf, 1995.

———. *Voices of Protest: Huey Long, Father Coughlin, and the Great Depression.* New York: Knopf, 1982.

Brown, Lorraine, and John O'Connor. *Free, Adult, Uncensored: The Living History of the Federal Theatre Project.* Washington, DC: New Republic Books, 1978.

Brown, Robert J. *Manipulating the Ether: The Power of Broadcast Radio in Thirties America.* Jefferson, NC: McFarland & Co., 1998.

Buhite, Russell D., and David W. Levy, eds. *FDR's Fireside Chats.* Norman: University of Oklahoma Press, 1992.

Burns, Helen M. *The American Banking Community and New Deal Banking Reforms.* Westport: Greenwood Press, 1974.

Bustard, Bruce I. *A New Deal for the Arts.* Seattle: University of Washington Press, 1997.

Caldwell, Erskine, and Margaret Bourke-White. *You Have Seen Their Faces (1937).* New York: Derbibooks, 1975.

Ciment, James. *Encyclopedia of the Great Depression and New Deal.* Armonk: M.E. Sharpe, Inc., 2001.

Clarke, Jeanne N. *Roosevelt's Warriors: Harold L. Ickes and the New Deal.* Baltimore: Johns Hopkins University Press, 1996.

Clavin, Patricia. *The Failure of Economic Diplomacy: Britain, Germany, France and the United States, 1931–36.* New York: St. Martin's Press, 1996.

Cole, Olen, R., Jr. *The African American Experience in the Civilian Conservation Corps.* Gainesville: University Press of Florida, 1999.

Cole, Wayne S. *Roosevelt and the Isolationists, 1932–1945.* Lincoln: University of Nebraska Press, 1983.

Conkin, Paul Keith *The New Deal.* Arlington Heights: Harlan Davidson, 1992.

Cook, Blanche W. *Eleanor Roosevelt: Vol. 2, The Defining Years, 1933–1938.* New York: Penguin, 2000.

Crouse, Joan M. *The Homeless Transient in the Great Depression: New York State, 1929–1941.* Albany: State University of New York Press, 1986.

Cushman, Barry. *Rethinking the New Deal Court: The Structure of a Constitutional Revolution.* New York: Oxford University Press, 1998.

Davis, Kenneth S. *FDR: The New Deal Years, 1933–1937.* New York: Random House, 1986.

DeNoon, Christopher. *Posters of the WPA.* Los Angeles: Wheatley Press, 1987.

Dickinson, Matthew J. *Bitter Harvest: FDR, Presidential Power, and the Growth of the Presidential Branch.* New York: Cambridge University Press, 1997.

Dubofsky, Melvyn. *Hard Work: The Making of Labor History.* Urbana: University of Illinois Press, 2000.

Dubofsky, Melvin, and Stephen Burnwood, eds. *Women and Minorities During the Great Depression.* New York: Garland Publishing, 1990.

Edsforth, Ronald. *The New Deal: America's Response to the Great Depression.* Malden, MA: Blackwell Publishers, 2000.

Eliot, Thomas H. *Recollections of the New Deal: When the People Mattered.* Boston: Northeastern University Press, 1992.

Fausold, Martin L. *The Presidency of Herbert C. Hoover.* Lawrence: University Press of Kansas, 1985.

Federal Writers Project. *These Are Our Lives.* New York: W.W. Norton & Company, Inc., 1939.

Fine, Sidney. *Sit-Down: The General Motors Strike of 1936–1937.* Ann Arbor: University of Michigan Press, 1969.

Flanagan, Hallie. *Arena: The Story of the Federal Theatre.* New York: Duell, Sloan and Pearce, 1940.

Flynn, George Q. *American Catholics and the Roosevelt Presidency, 1932–1936.* Lexington: University Press of Kentucky, 1968.

Fraser, Steve, and Gary Gerstle, eds. *The Rise and Fall of the New Deal Order, 1930–1980.* Princeton: Princeton University Press, 1989.

Freidel, Frank. *Franklin D. Roosevelt: Launching the New Deal.* Boston: Little, Brown, 1973.

———. *Franklin D. Roosevelt: A Rendezvous with Destiny.* New York: Little, Brown & Co., 1990.

French, Warren, Ed. *A Companion to the "The Grapes of Wrath."* New York: Penguin Books, 1989.

Fried, Albert. *FDR and His Enemies.* New York: Palgrave, 1999.

Galbraith, John Kenneth. *The Great Crash, 1929.* Boston: Houghton Mifflin Company, 1997.

Gall, Gilbert J. *Pursuing Justice: Lee Pressman, the New Deal, and the CIO.* Albany: State University of New York Press, 1999.

Graham, Maury, and Robert J. Hemming. *Tales of the Iron Road: My Life as King of the Hobos.* New York: Paragon House, 1990.

Greenberg, Cheryl Lynn. *"Or Does It Explode?": Harlem in the Great Depression.* New York: Oxford University Press, 1991.

Gregory, James N. *American Exodus: The Dust Bowl Migration and Okie Culture in California.* New York: Oxford University Press, 1989.

Guerin-Gonzales, Camille. *Mexican Workers and American Dreams: Immigration, Repatriation, and California Farm Labor, 1900–1939.* New Brunswick: Rutgers University Press, 1994.

Hall, Thomas E., and J. David Ferguson. *The Great Depression: An International Disaster of Perverse Economic Policies.* Ann Arbor: University of Michigan Press, 1998.

Hamilton, David E. *From New Day to New Deal: American Farm Policy from Hoover to Roosevelt, 1928–1933.* Chapel Hill: University of North Carolina Press, 1991.

Harris, Jonathan. *Federal Art and National Culture: The Politics of Identity in New Deal America.* New York: Cambridge University Press, 1995.

Hastings, Robert J. *A Nickel's Worth of Skim Milk: A Boy's View of the Great Depression.* Carbondale: Southern Illinois University Press, 1986.

Healey, Dorothy, and Maurice Isserman. *Dorothy Healy Remembers: A Life in the Communist Party.* New York: Oxford University Press, 1990.

Hill, Edwin G. *In the Shadow of the Mountain: The Spirit of the CCC.* Pullman, WA: Washington State University Press, 1990.

Himmelberg, Robert F. *The Origins of the National Recovery Administration.* New York: Fordham University Press, 1976.

Hockett, Jeffrey D. *New Deal Justice: The Constitutional Jurisprudence of Hugo L. Black, Felix Frankfurter, and Robert H. Jackson.* Lanham: Rowman & Littlefield Publishers, 1996.

Horan, James D. *The Desperate Years: A Pictorial History of the Thirties.* New York: Bonanza Books, 1962.

Hurt, Douglas. *American Agriculture: A Brief History.* Ames: Iowa State University Press, 1994.

Hurt, R. Douglas. *The Dust Bowl: An Agricultural and Social History.* Chicago: Nelson-Hall, 1981.

Ickes, Harold L. *The Secret Diary of Harold L. Ickes: The First Thousand Days, 1933–1936; The Inside Struggle, 1936–1939; The Lowering Clouds, 1939–1941.* 3 vols. New York: Simon & Schuster, 1952–54.

Jeansonne, Glen. *Messiah of the Masses: Huey P. Long and the Great Depression.* New York: HarperCollins College Publishers, 1993.

Jellison, Charles A. *Tomatoes Were Cheaper: Tales from the Thirties.* Syracuse, NY: Syracuse University Press, 1977.

Jonas, Manfred. *Isolationism in America, 1935–1941.* Ithaca: Cornell University Press, 1966.

Kalfatovic, Martin R. *The New Deal Fine Arts Projects: A Bibliography, 1933–1992.* Metuchen: Scarecrow Press, 1994.

Kennedy, David M. *Freedom From Fear: The American People in Depression and War, 1929–1945.* New York: Oxford University Press, 1999.

Kindleberger, Charles P. *The World in Depression, 1929–1939.* Berkeley: University of California Press, 1986.

Kirby, John B. *Black Americans in the Roosevelt Era: Liberalism and Race.* Knoxville: University of Tennessee Press, 1980.

Klein, Maury. *Rainbow's End, The Crash of 1929.* New York: Oxford University Press, 2001.

Kornbluh, Joyce L. *A New Deal for Workers' Education: The Workers' Service Program, 1933–1942.* Urbana: University of Illinois Press, 1987.

Lacy, Leslie A. *The Soil Soldiers: The Civilian Conservation Corps in the Great Depression.* Radnor: Chilton Book Company, 1976.

Leuchtenberg, William E. *The FDR Years: On Roosevelt and His Legacy.* New York: Columbia University Press, 1995.

———. *Franklin D. Roosevelt and the New Deal, 1932–1940.* New York: Harper & Row, 1963.

———. *New Deal and Global War.* New York: Time-Life Books, 1964.

Lindley, Betty, and Ernest K. Lindley. *A New Deal for Youth: The Story of the National Youth Administration.* New York: Viking, 1938.

Long, Huey P. *Every Man a King: The Autobiography of Huey P. Long.* New Orleans: National Book Company, Inc., 1933.

Low, Ann Marie. *Dust Bowl Diary.* Lincoln: University of Nebraska Press, 1984.

Lowitt, Richard. *The New Deal and the West.* Bloomington: Indiana University Press, 1984.

Lubov, Roy. *The Struggle for Social Security, 1900–1935.* 2nd ed. Pittsburgh: University of Pittsburgh Press, 1986.

Maidment, Richard A. *The Judicial Response to the New Deal.* New York: Manchester University Press, 1991.

Martin, George. *Madam Secretary: Frances Perkins.* Boston: Houghton Mifflin, 1976.

McElvaine, Robert S. *The Great Depression: America, 1929–1941.* New York: Times Books, 1993.

McJimsey, George. *Harry Hopkins: Ally of the Poor and Defender of Democracy.* Cambridge: Harvard University Press, 1983.

———. *The Presidency of Franklin Delano Roosevelt.* Lawrence: University of Kansas Press, 2000.

Meltzer, Milton. *Brother, Can You Spare a Dime? The Great Depression, 1929–1933.* New York: New American Library, 1977.

———. *Driven From the Land: The Story of the Dust Bowl.* New York: Benchmark Books, 2000.

Melzer, Richard. *Coming of Age in the Great Depression: The Civilian Conservation Corps in New Mexico.* Las Cruces: Yucca Tree Press, 2000.

Mettler, Suzanne. *Dividing Citizens: Gender and Federalism in New Deal Public Policy.* Ithaca: Cornell University Press, 1998.

Milner, E.R. *The Lives and Times of Bonnie and Clyde.* Carbondale, IL: Southern Illinois University Press, 1996.

Moley, Raymond, and Eliot A. Rosen. *The First New Deal.* New York: Harcourt, Brace & World, Inc., 1966.

Nye, David E. *Electrifying America: Social Meanings of a New Technology.* Cambridge: The MIT Press, 1990.

Ohl, John K. *Hugh S. Johnson and the New Deal.* De Kally: Northern Illinois University Press, 1985.

Olson, James S., ed. *Historical Dictionary of the 1920s: From World War I to the New Deal, 1919–1933.* Westport: Greenwood, 1988.

———, ed. *Historical Dictionary of the New Deal: From Inauguration to Preparation for War.* Westport: Greenwood, 1985.

———. *Saving Capitalism: The Reconstruction Finance Corporation and the New Deal, 1933–1940.* Princeton: Princeton University Press, 1988.

Parker, Stamford. *FDR: The Words That Reshaped America.* New York: Quill, 2000.

Parrish, Michael E. *Anxious Decades: America in Prosperity and Depression, 1920–1941.* New York: W.W. Norton, 1992.

———. *Securities Regulation and the New Deal.* New Haven: Yale University Press, 1970.

Perkins, Frances. *The Roosevelt I Knew.* New York: The Viking Press, 1946.

Perkins, Van L. *Crisis in Agriculture: The Agricultural Adjustment Administration and the New Deal, 1933.* Berkeley: University of California Press, 1969.

Philip, Kenneth R. *John Collier's Crusade for Indian Reform, 1920–1954.* Tucson: University of Arizona Press, 1977.

Phillips, Cabell. *From the Crash to the Blitz, 1929–1939.* New York: Macmillan, 1969.

Potter, Claire Bond. *War on Crime: Bandits, G-Men, and the Politics of Mass Culture.* New Brunswick, NJ: Rutgers University Press, 1998.

Powers, Richard Gid. *G-Men, Hoover's FBI in American Popular Culture.* Carbondale: Southern Illinois University Press, 1983.

Radford, Gail. *Modern Housing for America: Policy Struggles in the New Deal Era.* Chicago: University of Chicago Press, 1996.

Reagan, Patrick D. *Designing a New America: The Origins of New Deal Planning, 1890–1943.* Amherst: University of Massachusetts Press, 1999.

Reiman, Richard A. *The New Deal and American Youth: Ideas and Ideals in a Depression Decade.* Athens: University of Georgia Press, 1992.

Reisler, Mark. *By the Sweat of Their Brow: Mexican Immigrant Labor in the United States, 1900–1940.* Westport, CN: Greenwood Press, 1976.

Rogers, Agnes. *I Remember Distinctly: A Family Album of the American People, 1918–1941.* New York: Harper & Brothers Publishers, 1947.

Roosevelt, Eleanor. *The Autobiography of Eleanor Roosevelt.* New York: Da Capo Press, 2000.

———. *The Autobiography of Eleanor Roosevelt.* New York: Harper and Brothers Publishers, 1958.

Roosevelt, Franklin D. *The Public Papers and Addresses of Franklin D. Roosevelt.* 5 vols. New York: Random House, 1938-1950.

Rose, Nancy E. *Put to Work: Relief Programs in the Great Depression.* New York: Monthly Review Press, 1994.

Rothermund, Dietmar. *The Global Impact of the Great Depression, 1929–1939.* New York: Routledge, 1996.

Rozell, Mark J., and William D. Pederson. *FDR and the Modern Presidency: Leadership and Legacy.* Westport, CN: Praeger, 1997.

Ruth, David E. *Inventing the Public Enemy: The Gangster in American Culture, 1918–1934.* Chicago: University of Chicago Press, 1996.

Rutland, Richard A. *A Boyhood in the Dust Bowl, 1926–1934.* Boulder: University Press of Colorado, 1997.

———. *The Democrats: From Jefferson to Clinton.* Columbia: University of Missouri Press, 1995.

Salmond, John A. *The Civilian Conservation Corps, 1933–1942: A New Deal Case Study.* Durham: Duke University Press, 1967.

Schieber, Sylvester J., and John B. Shoven. *The Real Deal: The History and Future of Social Security.* New Haven: Yale University Press, 1999.

Schlesinger, Arthur M., Jr. *The Coming of the New Deal: The Age of Roosevelt.* Boston: Houghton Mifflin Company, 1988.

Schwartz, Jordan A. *The New Dealers: Power Politics in the Age of Roosevelt.* New York: Alfred A. Knopf, 1993.

Sennett, Ted. *This Fabulous Century: The Thirties.* New York: Time-Life Books, 1967.

Shindo, Charles J. *Dust Bowl Migrants in the American Imagination.* Lawrence: University Press of Kansas, 1997.

Sitkoff, Harvard. *A New Deal for Blacks: The Emergence of Civil Rights as a National Issue, the Depression Years.* New York: Oxford University Press, 1978.

Skidelsky, Robert. *John Maynard Keynes: The Economist as Saviour, 1920–1937.* New York: Viking Penguin, 1994.

Smith, Page. *Redeeming the Time: A People's History of the 1920s and the New Deal.* 8 vols. New York: Penguin, 1987.

Smith, Wendy. *Real Life: The Group Theatre and America, 1931–1940.* New York: Knopf, 1990.

Sobel, Robert. *The Great Bull Market: Wall Street in the 1920s.* New York: Norton, 1968.

Sternsher, Bernard. *Rexford Tugwell and the New Deal.* New Brunswick Rutgers University Press, 1964.

Stevens, J .E. *Hoover Dam: An American Adventure.* Norman: University of Oklahoma Press, 1988.

Storrs, Landon R.Y. *Civilizing Capitalism: The National Consumers' League, Women's Activism, and Labor Standards in the New Deal Era.* Chapel Hill: University of North Carolina Press, 2000.

Svobida, Lawrence. *Farming in the Dust Bowl.* University Press of Kansas, 1986.

Swados, Harvey, ed. *The American Writers and the Great Depression.* New York: Bobbs-Merrill Company, Inc., 1966.

Swain, Martha H. *Ellen S. Woodward: New Deal Advocate for Women.* Jackson: University Press of Mississippi, 1995.

Szostak, Rick. *Technological Innovation and the Great Depression.* Boulder: Westview Press, 1995.

Terkel, Studs. *Hard Times: An Oral History of the Great Depression.* New York: Pantheon Books, 1986.

Thompson, Kathleen, and Hilary MacAustin, eds. *Children of the Depression.* Bloomington: Indiana University Press, 2001.

Tobey, Ronald C. *Technology as Freedom: The New Deal and the Electrical Modernization of the American Home.* Berkeley: University of California Press, 1996.

Toland, John. *The Dillinger Days.* New York: Da Capo Press, 1995.

Tugwell, R. G. *The Brain Trust.* New York: Viking Press, 1968.

Tyack, David, Robert Lowe, and Elisabeth Hansot. *Public Schools in Hard Times: The Great Depression and Recent Years.* Cambridge: Harvard University Press, 1984.

Uys, Errol Lincoln. *Riding the Rails: Teenagers on the Move During the Great Depression.* New York: TV Books, 2000.

Ware, Susan. *Beyond Suffrage: Women and the New Deal.* Cambridge: Harvard University Press, 1981.

———. *Partner and I: Molly Deson, Feminism, and New Deal Politics.* New Haven: Yale University Press, 1987.

Watkins, T. H. *The Hungry Years: A Narrative History of the Great Depression in America.* New York: Henry Holt and Company, 1999.

———. *Righteous Pilgrim: The Life and Times of Harold L. Ickes, 1874–1952.* New York: Henry Holt & Co., 1990.

Wicker, Elmus. *The Banking Panics of the Great Depression.* New York: Cambridge University Press, 1996.

Wigginton, Eliot, ed. *Refuse to Stand Silently By: An Oral History of Grass Roots Social Activism in America, 1921–1964.* New York: Doubleday, 1992.

Winfield, Betty H. *FDR and the News Media.* New York: Columbia University Press, 1994.

Winslow, Susan. *Brother, Can You Spare a Dime? America From the Wall Street Crash to Pearl Harbor: An Illustrated Documentary.* New York: Paddington Press, 1979.

Worster, Donald. *Dust Bowl: The Southern Plaines in the 1930s.* New York: Oxford University Press ,1982.

Zieger, Robert H. *The CIO, 1930–1935.* Chapel Hill: University of North Carolina Press, 1995.

Periodicals

Adamic, Louis. "John L. Lewis's Push to Power," *Forum,* March 1937.

Amberson, W.R. "The New Deal for Share-Croppers," *Nation,* February 13, 1935.

Ballantine, A.A. "When All the Banks Closed," *Harvard Business Review,* March 1948.

Berle, A.A., Jr. "What's Behind the Recovery Laws," *Scribner's,* September 1933.

Broun, Heywood. "Labor and the Liberals," *Nation,* May 1, 1935.

Cannon, Brian Q. "Power Relations: Western Rural Electric Cooperatives and the New Deal," *Western Historical Quarterly,* vol. 31, Number 2 (2000).

Childs, M.W. "The President's Best Friend," *Saturday Evening Post,* April 26, 1941.

Cole, Olen, Jr. "The African-American Experience in the Civilian Conservation Corps," *Western Historical Quarterly,* vol. 31, no. 4 (2000).

Daniels, Jonathan. "Three Men in a Valley," *New Republic,* August 17, 1938.

Don Passos, John. "Washington: The Big Tent," *New Republic,* March 14, 1934.

Epstein, Abraham. "Social Security Under the New Deal," *Nation,* September 4, 1935.

Fleck, Robert K. "Population, Land, Economic Conditions, and the Allocation of New Deal Spending," *Explorations in Economic History,* Volume 38, Number 2 (2001).

Flynn, J.T. "The New Capitalism," *Collier's,* March 18, 1933.

Fogel, Jared A., and Robert L. Stevens. "The Cavas Mirror: Painting as Politics in the New Deal," *Magazine of History,* vol. 16, no. 1 (2001).

Garraty, John A. "Unemployment During the Great Depression," *Labor History,* Spring 1976.

Hirsch, Arnold R. "'Containment' on the Homefront: Race and Federal Housing Policy From the New Deal to the Cold War," *Journal of Urban History,* vol. 26, no. 2 (2000).

Hopkins, Harry L. "Beyond Relief," *New York Times Magazine,* August 19, 1934.

Ickes, Harold L. "My Twelve Years with F.D.R.," *Saturday Evening Post,* June 12, 1948.

Lord, Russell. "Madame Secretary," *The New Yorker,* September 2 and 9, 1933.

McCormick, Anne O'Hare. "The Great Dam of Controversy," *New York Times Magazine,* April 20, 1930.

McWilliams, Carey. "A Man, a Place, and a Time: John Steinbeck and the Long Agony of the Great Valley in an Age of Depression, Oppression, and Hope," *The American West,* May 1970.

Metzer, Richard. "Coming of Age in the Great Depression: The Civilian Conservation Corps Experience in New Mexico, 1933–1942," *Western Historical Quarterly,* vol. 32, no. 3 (2001).

Morgenthau, Henry, Jr. "The Paradox of Poverty and Plenty," *Collier's,* October 25, 1947.

Naison, Mark D. "Communism and Black Nationalism in the Depression: The Case of Harlem," *Journal of Ethnic Studies,* Summer 1974.

Nelson, Daniel. "Origins of the Sit-Down Era: Worker Militancy and Innovation in the Rubber Industry, 1934–1938," *Labor History,* Spring 1982.

Ohanian, Lee E. "Why Did Productivity Fall So Much During the Great Depression?," *American Economic Review,* vol. 91, no. 2 (2001).

Perkins, Frances. "Eight Years as Madame Secretary," *Fortune,* September 1941.

Poe, J.C. "The Morgan-Lilienthal Feud," *Nation,* October 3, 1936.

Pringle, H.F. "The President," *The New Yorker,* June 16–23, 1934.

Richberg, Donald. "The Future of the NRA," *Fortune,* October 1934.

Sherwood, Robert E. "Harry Hopkins," *Fortune,* July 1935.

Shover, John L., ed. "Depression Letters From American Farmers," *Agricultural History,* July 1962.

Stevens, Robert L., and Jared A. Fogel. "Images of the Great Depression: A Photogrpahic Essay," *Magazine of History,* vol. 16, no. 1 (2001).

Summers, Mary. "The New Deal Farm Programs: Looking for Reconstruction in American Agriculture," *Agricultural History,* vol. 74, no. 2 (2000).

Swing, R.G. "Father Coughlin," *Nation,* January 2, 1935.

Swing, R.G. "The Purge at the AAA," *Nation,* February 20, 1935.

Tugwell, Rexford. "The Price Also Rises," *Fortune,* January 1934.

Tugwell, Rexford. "America Takes Hold of Its Destiny," *Today,* April 28, 1934.

Webbink, Paul. "Unemployment in the United States, 1930–40," *American Economic Review,* February 1941.

White, Edward G. "The Constitution and the New Deal," *Journal of Interdisciplinary History,* vol. 32, no. 2 (2001).

Novels

Adamic, Louis. *My America (1938).* New York: Da Capo Press, 1976.

Caldwell, Erskine. *Tobacco Road.* Thorndike, ME: G.K. Hall, 1995.

Cantwell, Robert. *The Land of Plenty.* Carbondale: Southern Illinois University Press, 1971.

Dos Passos, John. *U.S.A.* New York: Penguin Books, 1996.

Farrell, James T. *Studs Lonigan: A Trilogy.* New York: The Modern Library, 1938.

Hurston, Zora Neale. *Their Eyes Were Watching God (1937).* New York: Harper & Row, 1990.

Lee, Harper *To Kill a Mockingbird.* Philadelphia: Chelsea House Publishers, 1998.

Steinbeck, John. *The Grapes of Wrath.* New York: The Viking Press, 1939.

Wright, Richard. *Uncle Tom's Children.* New York: The World Publishing Company, 1938.

———. *Native Son.* New York: Harper & Row, 1940.

Websites

Bonneville Power Administration. http://www.bpa.gov

Civilian Conservation Corps Alumni. http://www.cccalumni.org

Franklin D. Roosevelt Library and Museum. http://www.fdrlibrary.marist.edu

Roosevelt University. Center for New Deal Studies. http://www.roosevelt.edu/newdeal.htm

Library of Congress. American Memory. http://memory.loc.gov/ammem/fsowhome.html

New Deal Network. http://newdeal.feri.org

Riding the Rails. The American Experience. Public Broadcast System. Website: http://www.pbs.org/wgbh/amex/rails/

Social Security Administration. http://www.ssa.gov

Tennessee Valley Authority. http://www.tva.gov

Index

Bold page numbers indicate a primary article about a topic. Italic page numbers indicate illustrations. Tables and charts are indicated by a t following the page number. The index is sorted in word-by-word order.

A

AAA. *See* Agricultural Adjustment Administration (AAA)

AALL (American Association for Labor Legislation), 3:47–48, 181, 191

AAPA (Association Against the Prohibition Amendment), 3:6–7, 31

Abbott, Edith, 3:89

Abbott, Grace, 3:53, 291, 298–99

Abbott, Robert, 2:181

Abstract expressionism, 1:36

ACLU (American Civil Liberties Union), 1:140, 178–79

ACTU (Association of Catholic Trade Unionists), 3:132–33

Adamic, Louis, 2:211, 213, 225

Adams, Ansel, 2:123

ADC (Aid to Dependent Children), 3:187

Addams, Jane, 1:209, 2:130, 150, *294*, 3:293

Adjustable rate mortgages (ARM), 1:61

Adventist, 3:128

Advertising
    agriculture and, 1:95

anti-Sinclairism advertisement, 2:331–32

electric appliances, 3:259

growth of, 2:127, 131–32

newspaper, 2:159, 164, 175, 180

radio, 1:266, 3:59–60, 70

regulation of, 2:130

Spam advertisement, 2:*32*

AFC (America First Committee), 2:144–45, 149

Affirmative action, 1:218, 225

AFI (American Film Institute), 1:268, 2:85

AFL. *See* American Federation of Labor (AFL)

AFT (American Federation of Teachers), 1:193, 194, 205

Agee, James, 2:15, 170, 213, 300

Agricultural Adjustment Act, 2:279

Agricultural Adjustment Administration (AAA)
    benefits of, 2:9–10
    black Americans and, 1:81
    creation of, 2:6–7, 258
    farmer relief, 2:258–59
    food processing tax, 2:6, 9, 14, 279
    hunger relief and, 2:25
    isolationists support of, 2:141
    Mexican Americans and, 1:293
    Supreme Court ruling, 1:174, 2:9, 279, 3:210–11
    See also Agricultural relief programs

Agricultural Marketing Act, 1:95

Agricultural relief programs, 2:**1–20**
    benefits checks for, 1:*246*
    CCC and, 1:9, 115, 2:7

Commodity Credit Corporation loans, 2:8, 261, 3:109

Emergency Farm Mortgage Act, 1:172–73, 2:6, 101, 258

Farm Credit Administration, 1:173, 2:6, 257, 260, 3:108–9

Farm Mortgage Moratorium Act, 1:173, 183, 184, 2:263

Farm Mortgage Refinancing Act, 2:101, 261

Federal Farm Bankruptcy Act, 2:262

FSA loans, 2:301

grazing regulations, 1:182, 2:7

impact of, 2:15–16

land laws, 2:3

New Deal and, 1:172–74, 2:277–79, 3:108–9

perspectives on, 2:13–15

price-control issues, 2:4, 8, 9, 11–12, 279

Resettlement Administration loans, 1:76, 83, 174, 2:297

See also Agricultural Adjustment Administration (AAA); Conservation

Agriculture
    agricultural colleges, 2:3
    bank failures and, 2:11
    crop surplus, 1:95, 98, 99, 2:11, 25, 26, 279
    drought, 1:168–69, 177, 178, *182*, 2:7
    economic decline, 1:56, 95, 99, 2:3–4
    economic prosperity, 1:98–99, 2:1, 2–3

Fifteenth Amendment, 1:79, 80
Fifth Amendment, 3:207–8
Fight for Freedom Committee, 2:145
Filburn, Wickard v. (1941), 2:9
Filipino Americans, 1:291
Films, 1:268–72, 2:**70–96**
  American Film Institute list, 2:85
  animated, 1:270, 2:72–73
  attendance, 1:129, 2:70, 71, 72, 79*t*, 89, 3:59
  attracting audiences, 2:73–74
  black Americans in, 2:83–84
  box office receipts, 2:87*t*
  comedies, 1:269–70, 2:76–77, 80
  contributing forces, 2:84
  costume dramas, 1:271
  crime, 1:129–30, 131, 133
  Depression era films, 2:307
  development of, 2:84
  documentary, 2:167, 186, 307, 310, 327
  environmental, 1:173
  as escapism, 2:84
  in Europe, 1:278, 2:88
  everyday life and, 1:310–12
  G-men, 2:79–80
  home films, 1:266
  horror, 1:271, 2:82
  impact of, 2:88–90
  juvenile delinquents, 1:131
  law enforcement in, 2:80, 95
  literary adaptations, 1:272, 2:82
  on the medical profession, 3:47
  melodrama, 1:271
  messages of, 1:277
  Movie Palaces, 2:87, 88–89
  musicals, 1:270–71, 2:78–79
  newsreels, 1:309, 2:186
  notable people, 2:90–94
  overview, 1:311–12, 2:70–71
  perspectives on, 2:86–88
  on the Political "Left," 2:327
  popularity of, 2:123
  post-depression era, 2:89–90
  power of, 2:88
  production codes, 2:78, 87, 88, 3:140
  race films, 2:83–84
  Shirley Temple films, 1:270, 311, 313–14, 2:79
  shyster films, 2:75–76
  social conscious films, 2:81–82
  sound and color techniques, 2:73
  swashbuckler, 1:271, 2:82
  "talkies," 1:129, 321, 2:71, 73, 76, 86
  television series, 2:90
  themes for, 1:268
  thrillers, 1:271–72, 2:82
  by TVA, 3:241
  Westerns, 1:271, 2:80
  women in, 2:77–78, 3:296
  World War I and, 2:89, 96

  See also Gangster films; Hollywood; Movie theaters
Filne, Edward, 1:250
Financial Institutions Reform, Recovery and Enforcement Act (FIRREA), 1:61
Finland, 2:57, 3:27, 340
Finn, Evelyn, 1:85
Fireside chats, 1:*153*, 3:*72*
  author of, 2:270
  on the banking crisis, 1:50, *58*, 64, 2:256, 3:108
  fighting German expansion, 2:156–57
  instilling public confidence, 1:326, 3:57, 65
  popularity of, 1:121, 2:267, 3:65
  reorganizing the Supreme Court, 2:74, 3:226–27
  on U.S. involvement in World War II, 3:344, 349–50
  warmth and charm in, 2:163
Firestone, 2:235–36
FIRREA (Financial Institutions Reform, Recovery and Enforcement Act), 1:61
First Amendment, 3:213
First hundred days, 2:25, 255–56, 257, 268–69, 272–73
Fisher, Boyd, 3:160
Fitzgerald, Ella, 1:280
Fitzgerald, Scott F., 2:131, 214, 219
Five-Power Treaty, 2:149
Flammable Fabrics Act, 1:224
Flanagan, Hallie
  about, 1:36
  Arena, 1:37, 38
  as Federal Theater Project director, 3:288, 312–14, 320
  Hopkins, Harry and, 1:37
  House Un-American Activities Committee and, 1:38
Flanigan, Fan, 1:327
Flash Gordon, 1:313, 3:359
Fletcher, Duncan, 1:51, 62
Flight from the City (Borsodi), 3:276
Flood control, 3:271, 272
Florida League for Better Schools, 1:196
Florida real estate speculation, 1:92
Floyd, Charles "Pretty Boy," 1:132, 134
Flynn, John, 2:145, 154–55
FMP. *See* Federal Music Project (FMP)
Folk and domestic art, 1:33–34, 2:123
Folk music, 1:31, 273–74, 279
Folk schools, 1:197, 208
Folsom, Marion, 3:193
Folsom River Dam, 3:271
Fonda, Henry, 2:15
Food, 2:**21–49**
  basics, 2:26–28, 29, 31, 34, 40
  canned food, 2:31, 34, 40, 41, 42

chain stores, 1:321, 2:36–37
  cost of, 1:307–8, 2:40*t*
  desserts, 2:29–33, 34, 35, 36, 48
  during World War II, 2:40–41
  food distribution, 2:25, 37–38, 42
  food entrepreneurs, 2:23, 31–33, 47
  food riots, 1:126, 2:24, 37
  frozen food, 2:33, 42
  from gardens, 2:29, 30–31, 36, 47
  genetically modified, 2:42
  making do, 1:307–8, 2:22, 26–27, 39, 47
  malnutrition and, 1:205, 239, 319, 321, 2:23, 24
  new foods, 2:40
  nutrition, 2:36, 40
  organic, 2:42
  overview, 2:21–22
  packaging and labeling standards, 3:46, 49
  preserving, 2:31
  processed food, 2:34–35, 42
  rationing, 2:40, 3:331
  safety issues, 1:223, 224, 2:43–44, 284
  starvation, 2:24, 40
  stealing, 2:24
  storage, 3:167
  vitamins A and B, 2:36
  WPA student lunches, 1:200
  See also Consumer protection; Cookbooks; Crops; Hunger relief; Recipes
Food Administration, 2:36
Food and Drink in America: A History (Hooker), 2:46–47
Food and Drug Administration (FDA), 1:223, 2:44, 3:35, 46
Food coupons, 1:244
Food riots, 1:126, 2:24, 37
Food Stamp Act, 1:224, 2:43
Food stamps, 1:224, 2:25–26, 42–43
Food store chains, 1:321, 2:36–37
Football, 1:274
Footlight Parade (film), 2:78
For Whom the Bell Tolls (Hemingway), 2:212, 214
Forbidden (film), 3:296
Ford, Gerald, on Social Security, 3:200
Ford, Henry
  about, 2:204
  anti-Semitism of, 3:136, 246
  Muscle Shoals bid of, 3:246, 248
  outdoor museum of, 2:124
Ford, John, 2:15, 82, 92, 307
Ford Motor Company
  anti-union tactics, 2:205
  assembly line of, 2:120, 199
  banking crisis and, 3:104–5
  Chicago World's Fair exhibit, 3:355
  electricity film series, 3:275
  labor unions opposed by, 2:234
  Model T's, 2:106, 119, 204

Index

International News Service (INS), 2:175, 180

Internationalism *vs.* isolationism, 1:161, 2:139

Interpretations: 1933-1935 (Lippmann), 2:186–87

Interstate Commerce Commission (ICC), 3:100

Interstate Freeway system, 2:328

Interstate Liquor Act, 3:17

Interstate Migration report, 1:179

Interwar era, 2:**117–37**
 architecture, 2:121–22
 contributing forces, 2:126–29
 golden age of sports, 2:124–25
 impact of, 2:132
 media, 2:122–23
 notable people, 2:132–35
 overview, 2:117–18
 perspectives on, 2:64, 129–32
 preserving the past, 2:123–24
 science, business and technology, 2:119
 transportation, 2:119–21
 See also World War II; World War II mobilization

Investment banks, 1:45, 53, 62

The Invisible Man (film), 1:272

The Invisible Scar (Bird), 1:318–19

IRA. *See* Indian Reorganization Act (IRA)

IRCA (Immigration Reform and Control Act), 1:302

Irrigation, 3:262, 264, 266, 271

Irrigation pumps, 3:271

Islam, 3:138

Isolationism, 2:**138–58**
 American economic concerns and, 2:149
 contributing forces, 2:146–49
 Hawley-Smoot Tariff Act and, 2:15
 Hoover, Herbert and, 2:151
 impact of, 2:152–53
 international perspectives on, 2:151–52
 internationalism *vs.,* 1:159–61, 2:139
 national perspectives on, 2:149–51
 Neutrality Acts, 2:143–44, 150, 156
 New Deal and, 2:138–39, 140–42, 143
 notable people, 2:153–56
 Nye Committee investigations, 2:142–43, 150–51
 overview, 1:96, 2:138–40
 peace movement and, 2:149
 political and cultural, 1:34
 responses against, 2:145–46
 shifting away from, 2:150
 support for, 2:138–39, 140–41, 144–45, 149
 World War I and, 1:96, 101–2, 2:15

Israel, Edward, 3:129–30, 149, 150

Isserman, Maurice, 2:321, 332

It Can't Happen Here (Lewis), 2:212, 214, 219, 222

It Happened One Night (film), 2:80

Italy, 2:145

IWW (Industrial Workers of the World), 2:322, 324

J

Jacks, 1:279

Jackson, Andrew, 1:17, 154

Jackson, Kenneth, 2:103, 116

Jackson, Robert, 3:221

Japan
 Great Depression and, 2:56, 59
 Pearl Harbor bombed, 2:145, 146, 3:67, 328–29
 U.S. bombing of, 3:338
 World War II expansion, 3:328, 342

Japanese American Citizens League (JACL), 1:292

Japanese Americans
 immigration to U.S., 1:298
 overview, 1:290–91
 relocation during World War II, 1:117, 294, 300, 3:331
 support organizations, 1:292

Jazz, 1:79, 266, 278, 312, 2:84, 3:67–68. *See also* Swing

The Jazz Singer (film), 2:73, 86

Jefferson, Thomas, 1:17, 154, 3:259, 274

Jell-O, 2:34–35

Jewish Americans
 American culture and, 2:126, 132
 anti-Semitism, 2:318, 3:135, 136–37, 142, 246
 charities of, 3:134
 concerns about European Jews, 3:118–19
 education and, 3:134–35
 Great Depression and, 3:134–35
 immigration of Jewish refugees, 3:136, 137, 145
 New Deal and, 3:145
 perspectives on, 3:145
 prominence of, 2:126
 in sports, 2:125
 on Supreme Court, 1:156
 Zionist movement, 3:137, 142

Jews, Movies, Hollywoodism and the American Dream (film), 2:94

Jews Without Money (Gold), 2:210

J.F. Shea Company, 3:266

Jigsaw puzzles, 1:264, 265, *324,* 325

Jim Crow Concert Hall, 1:85

Jim Crow laws, 1:77–78, 83, 3:335

Jive talk, 1:312, 313

Job Corps, 1:119, 219

Johnny cakes, 2:28

Johnson, Hiram, 1:7, 2:144

Johnson, Hugh
 about, 2:248–49, 271
 "Buy Now" program, 2:237
 Ford, Henry and, 2:234
 Ickes, Harold and, 2:238
 "Memorandum 228" and, 2:241
 NRA conflicts and, 2:233, 237–39, 246, 248–49
 NRA production controls and, 2:236

Johnson, James, 1:79

Johnson, Lady Bird, 1:234

Johnson, Lyndon B.
 about, 1:222
 affirmative action and, 1:217–18
 centralizing governmental powers, 1:218
 civil rights and, 1:217
 Economic Opportunity Act, 1:119
 education and, 1:221
 environmentalism of, 1:223
 on the Great Society, 1:215
 Great Society programs, 1:11, 162
 Great Society speech, 1:237
 New Deal and, 1:218, 222
 program of social reform, 1:215
 Public Law, 1:36
 Roosevelt, Franklin and, 1:*220*
 segregation and, 1:217
 social reform and, 1:229
 special task force groups, 1:218–19
 State of the Union address, 1:216
 unemployment program, 1:256–57
 Vietnam War and, 1:163, 231
 voting rights speech, 1:237–38

Johnson, Lyndon B, *See also* Great Society

Johnson, William, 1:36, 3:16–17

Johnson Act, 2:56–57, 142

Johnson-O'Malley Act (JOM), 1:6–7, 9, 20–21

Joint Commission of the Emergency in Education, 1:196

Jolson, Al, 2:73, 86

Jones, Jesse, 1:46, 63, 3:105–6, 108, 111, 114–15

Jones, Mary Harris "Mother," 2:322

Jones & Laughlin Steel Corp., NLRB v. (1937), 1:159, 3:213–15, 220

Jones & Laughlin Steel Corporation, 3:213–14

Journal of Education, 1:191

Journal of the American Medical Association, 3:47

Journalism, 2:**159–88**
 1920s, 2:176–77
 business and, 2:178
 conservatism of, 2:163
 criticisms of, 2:163
 documentary journalism, 2:207
 everyday reporters, 2:164
 impact of, 2:179–81

Office of War Mobilization (OWM), 3:330

Office of War Mobilization and Reconversion, 3:346

Official Guide Book of the Fair 1933, 3:365

Oglethorpe, James, 3:12

Ohio Emergency Relief Administration, 1:244

Ohio unemployment insurance plan, 3:180

Ohlin, Lloyd, 1:229

Oil discoveries on Indian land, 1:19

Oil prices, 1:61

O'Keefe, Georgia, 2:123

Old-Age Insurance (OAI), 3:186–87, 188–89

Olds, Ransom, 2:106

Oldsmobile automobile, 2:106

Olson, Floyd, 2:317

Olympic Games, Los Angeles, 1:275, 3:354

O'Malley, Thomas, 1:7

One Flew Over the Cuckoo's Nest (film), 1:38

One Hour With You (film), 2:77

100,000,000 Million Guinea Pigs, 3:46

One Third of a Nation: Lorena Hickock Reports on the Great Depression, 1:247

Oral histories, 3:311, 312

Oregon, Muller v. (1908), 3:218

An Organic Architecture (Wright), 2:135

Organized crime
  business ventures of, 1:128
  drug trafficking, 1:128, 142, 3:25
  end of gangster period, 1:128–29
  FBI and, 1:135
  gambling operations, 1:137
  growth of, 1:135, 138
  labor racketeering, 1:128, 131
  mafia, 1:130–31, 135, 136, 138
  overview, 1:137–38, 140–42
  racketeering, 1:141
  See also Bootlegging; Capone, Alphonse "Al"

Organized Crime Control Act, 1:140

Origins of the TVA: The Muscle Shoals Controversy, 1920-1932, (Hubbard), 3:232, 254

Orphanages, 1:321

The Other America (Harrington), 1:229

Otis, Harrison Gray, 2:173

OTS (Office of Thrift Supervision), 1:61

Out of the Dust (Hesse), 1:175

The Outline of History (Wells), 2:216

Owen, Ruth Bryan, 3:285

Owens, Jesse, 1:82, 275, 2:125

Oxley, Lawrence, 1:73

"Ozzie and Harriet" show, 3:63

P

Pacifica statue, 3:357

Pacifism, 3:145–46

Page, Kirby, 3:125

Paige, Leroy "Satchel," 2:125

Paley, William, 3:73

Palmer, A. Mitchell, 1:143

"Palmer raids," 1:143

Panama-California Exposition, 3:356

Panama-Pacific International Exposition, 3:356, 363

Panama Refining Company v. Ryan (1935), 3:205–7, 226

Pankhust, Emmaline, 3:301

Pankhust, Genevieve, 3:291

Papal encyclicals, 3:118, 129

Paper dolls, 1:279

Paramount Studios, 2:72, 76

Parker, Bonnie, 1:132, 134–35

Parker Dam, 3:265

Parks, Rosa, 1:83

Parran, Thomas, 3:43–44, 52, 54

Parrish, West Coast Hotel v. (1937), 3:214

Parsons, Louella, 3:64

Partisan, 3:202

Partisan Review, 2:216

Pastime. *See* Leisure time

Pastures of Heaven (Steinbeck), 2:224

Patterson, Eleanor, 2:185

Patterson, Robert, 3:348

Paul, Alice, 3:301

Paul, Nancy, 3:291, 295

Peace advocates, 2:142, 145, 149, 150

Peace Corps, 1:217

Pearl Harbor bombed, 2:145, 146, 3:67, 328–29

Pearson, Drew, 2:163

Pecora, Ferdinand, 1:51, 63, 104

Pecora hearings, 1:51, 104

Peek, George, 2:17

Pegler, Westbrook, 2:161, 185

Penicillin, 3:42, 44

Pentecostal churches, 3:128, 138

The People, Yes (Sandburg), 2:218

People's Party, 2:316, 323–24

Pepperidge Farm, 2:32

Perisphere structure, 3:359, *360*

Perkins, Edwin, 2:32

Perkins, Frances
  about, 2:204–5, 3:179, 301–2
  child labor and, 3:285
  Dewson, Molly and, 3:284
  as first women cabinet member, 3:302
  Kelley, Florence and, 3:301
  on the National Consumers' League, 3:293
  protective labor legislation and, 3:291
  Roosevelt, Franklin and, 3:*180,* 183, 193, 295, 296

as Secretary of Labor, 3:283–84, 285–87

social insurance speeches, 3:181–82

Social Security and, 3:183, 187, 199

Pershing, John, 3:338

Personal Responsibility and Work Opportunity Reconciliation Act, 3:88

Pesotta, Rosa, 1:289–90

Petroleum Administration Board, 3:205, 226

Philadelphia Electric Company, 3:168, 170

Philippines, 2:151, 3:328

Phillips, Cabell, 1:326

Phonographic record player, 3:59

Photo-Secession Movement, 2:304

Photography, 2:**295–314**
  as art form, 2:308
  color, 2:307
  commercial photography, 2:308
  contributing forces, 2:304–6
  documentary, 1:31, 174, 2:295, 296–301, 303, 304, 307–8
  First International Photographic Exposition, 2:302
  historic photographs, 2:302
  impact of, 2:301, 307–8
  New Deal agencies use of, 2:303
  notable people, 2:309–12
  overview, 2:295–96
  as pastime, 1:265–66
  perspectives on, 2:306–7
  photojournalism, 2:170, 184, 303–4, 308
  small cameras, 2:301
  for TVA, 3:241
  web sites, 2:302, 307
  WPA photography projects, 2:302–3
  See also Farm Security Administration (FSA); Resettlement Administration (RA)

Photojournalism, 2:170, 184, 303–4, 308

Phylon journal, 2:182

Physicians, 1:319*t*, 3:48, 51, 52

Pickling foods, 2:31

Pie Town photographs (Lee), 2:300

Pierce v. Society of Sisters (1925), 3:141

Piggly Wiggly, 2:36

Pinchot, Gillford, 3:168, 169, 174, 175, 242, 249

Pine View Dam, 3:269, 270

Pinocchio (film), 2:73

Pittsburgh Courier, 2:174

Pius XI (Pope), 3:118, 129, 140

"A Place to Lie Down" (Algren), 2:211

Places in the Heart, (film), 1:175, 2:90

Redcaps union, 2:194
Reed, Stanley, 3:214, 220
Reed College, 1:197, 198
Refrigerators, 2:37, 3:172, 239, 271
Reid, Robert, 2:313
Religion, 3:**118–52**
    Adventist, 3:128
    of American Indians, 1:5, 17, 19
    Baptists, 3:124
    black churches, 3:119, 137–38
    civil rights movement and, 3:146
    contributing forces, 3:139–42
    Disciples of Christ, 3:124
    election of 1932 and, 3:127
    election of 1936 and, 3:128, 133–34
    Episcopalian, 3:124
    film censorship, 3:140
    Great Depression and, 3:121
    Holiness movement, 3:138
    inter-faith cooperation, 3:143
    leftist views, 3:124–26
    local church efforts, 3:122–23
    New Deal and, 3:123–24, 127
    notable people, 3:146
    organized labor and, 3:127
    Pacifism, 3:145–46
    Pentecostal churches, 3:128, 138
    perspectives on, 3:142–46
    post World War I, 3:139
    post World War II, 3:146
    Presbyterians, 3:124, 140, 141
    Social Gospel movement, 3:139
    social services of, 3:121–23
    Unitarians, 3:124
    See also Catholicism; Jewish
        Americans; Protestants
Reno, Milo, 2:17
Repatriation, 1:286, 288, 300
Report of the Commissioner of Indian
    Affairs (Collier), 1:22–23
Report on the Survey of Hopi Crafts
    (Whiting), 1:8
Reporter Plan, 3:288–389
Republic Steel, 1:*127*, 128, 2:197,
    3:213
Republican Party
    anti-slavery viewpoint, 1:149, 154
    big business and, 1:155, 157
    black voters and, 1:80
    Bonus Army and, 1:148
    business ideas, 1:147–48
    conservative movement, 1:227, 228
    decline of, 1:148, 155
    election of 1938 and, 1:152
    government role limited by, 1:155,
        2:253
    laissez-faire approach, 1:148, 157
    as minority party, 1:148, 150, 155
    Muscle Shoals project and, 3:246
    nationalism of, 1:156
    New Deal programs and, 1:150
    origins of, 1:149
    policies of, 1:162

    progressive Republicans, 2:138–39,
        140–41, 3:194
    push for tax cuts, 1:233
    radio used by, 3:67
    return of, 1:156–57, 163
    Roosevelt, Franklin and, 1:151
    Social Security and, 3:185, 194
    supply-side economics, 1:164
    TVA and, 3:246
    values of, 1:149
Rerum Novarum (Pope Leo XIII),
    3:129
Reserve banks, 1:55
Resettlement Administration (RA)
    agricultural relief programs, 1:31
    American Indians and, 1:9
    creation of, 1:174, 2:8
    documentary photos, 2:296–97, 303
    FSA and, 1:174, 2:8
    Historical Section, 1:31, 174, 2:297,
        303
    loans to farmers, 1:76, 83, 174,
        2:297
    medical
    plans, 3:51
    purpose of, 1:174, 2:297
    relocating farmers, 1:176, 2:275,
        297
    Special Skills Division, 1:31
    See also Farm Security
        Administration (FSA)
Resolution Thrift Corporation (RTC),
    1:61
Resources. *See* Natural resources
Retirement pensions, 1:43
Retrenchment, 1:*189*, 190–96
Reuther, Walter, 2:*198*, 205
Revenue Act of 1942, 3:332
Reynolds, George, 3:96
RFC. *See* Reconstruction Finance
    Corporation (RFC)
Rhoads, Charles, 1:251
Richard Wright—Black Boy (film),
    2:327
Richberg, Donald, 2:241, 242, 249,
    3:212
Riding the rails, 3:**76–91**
    dangers of, 3:79–81
    Davis, Kingsley on, 3:89–90
    everyday life of, 2:225–26, 3:87
    film on, 2:82, 3:81
    language of, 3:84
    public perspectives on, 3:85–87
    reasons for, 3:76
    web sites on, 1:111
    women, 3:81
    youth on, 1:111, 116–17, 275,
        3:*78, 86, 90*
    See also Homelessness; Transients
Riding the Rails: Teenagers on the
    Move During the Great
    Depression (Uys), 3:91
Rigby, Cora, 2:174–75

Right wing. *See* Conservatives
Riis, Jacob, 2:108, 305–6
Riots
    food riots, 1:126, 2:24, 37
    race riots, 1:72, 78, 83, 227
    Watts riot, 1:326
The Rise of American Civilization
    (Beard), 1:209, 2:216
Ritz Crackers, 2:30, 34
The River (film), 1:173
River and Harbor Act, 3:266, 267
Rivera, Diego, 1:32–33, 3:357–58
The Road to War: America, 1914-1917
    (Millis), 2:143
Roadside Americana, 2:120
Roberts, Owen, 3:204, 205, 207, 208
Robeson, Paul, 2:83–84
Robinson, Bill, 2:84, 93
Robinson, Edward G., 1:129, 2:75, 80,
    95
Robinson, Joseph, 3:212, 215–16
Roche, Josephine, 3:302
Rockefeller, John D., 3:30–31
Rockefeller Center, 1:32–33, 2:122
Rockefeller Foundation, 1:15, 22, 198,
    3:35, 36
Rocky Mountain spotted fever, 3:41
Rodriguez, Raymond, 1:303
Rogers, Ginger, 1:270, 2:79
Rogers, Jimmie, 1:274
Rogers, Will, 1:64, 2:165
Rombauer, Irma, 2:22, 33–34, 44, 45
Rooney, Mickey, 2:82, 93
Roosevelt, Eleanor
    about, 1:85, 326, 3:286
    Antioch College and, 3:252
    "Chambers of Horrors" exhibit and,
        3:46
    at Chicago World's Fair, 3:*354*
    coal-mine workers and, 2:*283*
    Dewson, Molly and, 3:284
    Hickock, Lorena and, 3:287
    Kennedy, John F. and, 3:297
    marriage of, 1:121, 3:286
    "My Day" newspaper column,
        2:183, 3:286
    NRA supported by, 2:*168*
    press conferences, 2:168
    public attitude toward, 2:39
    radio broadcasts, 1:268, 3:286
    serving food, 2:*42*
    victory garden of, 2:41
    Woodward, Ellen and, 3:*302*
Roosevelt, Franklin, Jr., 3:46
Roosevelt, Franklin Delano, 3:*211*
    about, 1:120–21, 326, 2:18, 252
    belief in work relief, 3:308
    Bonneville Dam dedication speech,
        1:257, 3:280–81
    at Boulder Dam, 3:*263*
    campaign speech, 1932, 3:259
    Chicago World's Fair address,
        3:352